Legal Materials for Social Workers

Legal materials for social workers

First edition

Hugh Brayne
Graeme Broadbent

OXFORD
UNIVERSITY PRESS

OXFORD
UNIVERSITY PRESS

Great Clarendon Street, Oxford OX2 6DP

Oxford University Press is a department of the University of Oxford.
It furthers the University's objective of excellence in research, scholarship,
and education by publishing worldwide in

Oxford New York

Auckland Bangkok Buenos Aires Cape Town Chennai
Dar es Salaam Delhi Hong Kong Istanbul Karachi Kolkata
Kuala Lumpur Madrid Melbourne Mexico City Mumbai Nairobi
São Paulo Shanghai Taipei Tokyo Toronto

Oxford is a registered trade mark of Oxford University Press
in the UK and in certain other countries

Published in the United States
by Oxford University Press Inc., New York

A Blackstone Press Book

British Library Cataloguing in Publication Data

Data available

Library of Congress Cataloging in Publication Data

ISBN 1-84-174191-4

Typeset by Newgen Imaging Systems (P) Ltd., Chennai, India
Printed in Great Britain by
Ashford Colour Press Limited, Gosport, Hampshire

OUTLINE CONTENTS

PART I **Introduction and Context**   **1**

1   Social work and the legal framework   3
2   Human rights law   68
3   Anti-discrimination law   83

PART II **Community Care**   **117**

4   Community care   119
5   Mental health   170

PART III **Children**   **273**

6   Children   275

PART IV **Criminal Justice**   **385**

7   Social workers in the justice system   387
8   Children as victims of crime   471

DETAILED CONTENTS

Preface ix
Acknowledgements xi
Table of Cases xiii
Table of Statutes xvi

PART I **Introduction and Context**   1

1   Social work and the legal framework   3

1.1   The statutory duties of social workers *3*
1.2   The social services committee within the local authority *15*
1.3   Administrative law — court scrutiny of local authority exercise of
        statutory functions *19*
1.4   Suing the local authority for failing to carry out statutory duties *48*
1.5   Critical reflections on social work law as a discipline *60*

2   Human rights law   68

2.1   The post-1945 human rights framework *68*
2.2   UN Human Rights documents *69*
2.3   The Human Rights Act 1998 *72*

3   Anti-discrimination law   83

3.1   The concept of discrimination *83*
3.2   Discrimination on grounds of race *83*
3.3   Sex discrimination *93*
3.4   Disability discrimination *100*

PART II **Community Care**   117

4   Community care   119

4.1   Introduction *119*
4.2   Community care *123*
4.3   Residential care *148*

5	**Mental health**	**170**

5.1   Mental health *170*
5.2   Court of Protection *241*
5.3   Powers of Attorney *250*
5.4   Reform *261*

PART III	**Children**	**273**

6	**Children**	**275**

6.1   Introduction *275*
6.2   The Children Act 1989 *300*

PART IV	**Criminal Justice**	**385**

7	**Social workers in the justice system**	**387**

7.1   Philosophy, statutory framework, issues, and role of the social worker *387*
7.2   Investigation of crime and procedures before charge *406*
7.3   What happens after charge — remand, bail, and appearance in court *434*
7.4   Trial and sentencing options for child offenders *440*

8	**Children as victims of crime**	**471**

8.1   Offences against children *471*
8.2   Children as witnesses in criminal cases *474*

Index 511

PREFACE

Collections of materials are designed to meet a number of needs. We have compiled this particular volume to fulfil a number of functions.

First, it is designed to complement Brayne, Martin, and Carr's *Law for Social Workers* (Oxford University Press, 7th ed., 2001). A textbook will provide you with an overview of the law, and will make reference to primary sources. This book gives you access to many of the materials discussed in the textbook. We have not exactly replicated the content of that book, but, rather, have sought to complement it.

Secondly, we have tried to collect together the law in various areas relevant to social work in one place. English law, notoriously, develops in a piecemeal fashion. Statutes are amended by other statutes and cases superseded by other cases. It is often difficult and time consuming to piece together the changes to the law, particularly with regard to legislation. We have done some of that work for you in collecting together legal materials by subject area.

Thirdly, many social work students have limited access to a law library, or lack the time to consult the reference materials available there — if they are indeed available. Although, in an ideal world, students would have ready access to the primary materials they need, in practice this ideal is not always realised. Having a collection of materials goes some way to meeting this need, and also provides a portable library which should help to give flexibility in study time.

Fourthly, in addition to providing primary materials we have included some commentaries on those materials which provide a range of perspectives not possible in a textbook. The articles and reports included are designed to help you to reflect on the issues raised by the primary materials and to form your own judgements about the law in theory and practice. Although in compiling this collection of materials we have social work students primarily in mind, we hope that it will also be of use and interest to social work practitioners.

This collection thus provides two types of material. The first — the cases, statutes, regulations, and guidance — not only illustrate the law but *are* the law. The second type of material — the extracts from articles, commentaries, and the like — are designed to contribute to an understanding of the law and how it operates.

In compiling this collection, we have not attempted to provide a complete picture of all the law you will need as a social work student or practitioner. That would require a book of immense proportions. We have, instead, included materials under three headings. First, we introduce the legal framework within which social work operates by considering statutory duties, human rights, and anti-discrimination legislation. Secondly, we focus on the law relating to three key client groups — adults in need of community care; those suffering from mental incapacity or disorder; and children. The third part looks at issues relating to the role of the social worker in the criminal justice system. We have excluded, for reasons of space, areas such as family law and housing law. These are covered in *Law for Social Workers*.

This book is not designed to be read from cover to cover, but used selectively as part of your legal studies. It might, however, be helpful to look at Chapters 1, 2, and 3 before embarking on the rest of the book.

We would like to express our gratitude to the library staff at the University of Sunderland, Jane Kavanagh and Katy Plowright at Oxford University Press, and Andrew Beetham at Sunderland University for various forms of assistance in relation to the production of this volume. We have included materials available to us to the end of April 2002.

Hugh Brayne
Graeme Broadbent
May 2002

ACKNOWLEDGEMENTS

The authors and publishers are grateful to the following for permission to reproduce copyright material:

Ashgate Publishing Co., Helen Westcott, and Jocelyn Jones: Sarah Nelson 'The Memorandum: Quest for the Impossible' chapter 12 in Helen Westcott and Jocelyn Jones (eds.) *Perspectives on the Memorandum: policy, practice, and research in investigative interviewing* (1997).

Blackwell Publishing: Ellie Palmer and Maurice Sunkin 'Needs: Resources and Abhorrent Choices' 61 *Modern Law Review* [1998] 401.

Bloomsbury Publishing and the British Academy of Forensic Science: Herschel Prins 'Can the Law Serve as the Solution to Social Ills? The case of the Mental Health (Patients in the Community) Act 1995' *Medicine, Science and the Law* vol. 36 no. 3 [1996] 217.

BMJ Publishing Group: J A Muir Gray 'Section 47' *Journal of Medical Ethics* vol. 7 [1981] 146.

Butterworths: All England Law Reports (*see* Reed Elsevier (UK) Ltd); Family Court Reports.

Children's Legal Centre, University of Essex: Sue Bandalli, 'Juvenile Justice — a new government but the same direction?' *Childright* vol. 141 [1997] 2.

Council of Europe: judgments of the European Court of Human Rights; Convention for the Protection of Human Rights and Fundamental Freedoms.

Commission for Racial Equality: *Guide To The Race Relations 1976 Act*.

HMSO: all statutes, statutory instruments, parliamentary debates, government publications.

Incorporated Council of Law Reporting for England and Wales: the Law Reports; Weekly Law Reports.

Jordans: Family Law Reports; Ken Oliphant 'W v Essex County Council: Local authority liability for acts of children in foster care' *Child and Family Law Quarterly* [1998] 303; Loraine Gelsthorpe and Allison Morris 'Much ado about nothing — a critical comment on key provisions relating to children in the Crime and Disorder Act 1998' *Child and Family Law Quarterly* [1999] 209; Julia Fionda 'R v Secretary of State for the Home Department ex parte Venables and Thompson: The age of innocence? — the concept of childhood in the punishment of young offenders' *Child and Family Law Quarterly* [1998] 77; Phil Bates 'The Youth Justice and Criminal Evidence Act — the Evidence of children and vulnerable adults' *Child and Family Law Quarterly* [1999] 289.

Legal Action Group: Community Care Law Reports.

Kluwer Law International: Luke Clements 'Community Care — Towards a Workable Statute' *The Liverpool Law Review* vol. XIX(2) [1997].

Oxford University Press and Philip Fennell: Philip Fennell 'Doctor knows best? Therapeutic detention under common law, the Mental Health Act, and the European Convention' *Medical Law Review* vol. 6 no. 3 [1998] 322.

Reed Elsevier (UK) Ltd: *All rights reserved. No part of this publication may be reproduced in any material form (including photocopying or storing it in any medium by electronic means) and whether or not transiently or incidentally to some other use of this publication without the written permission of the copyright owner except in accordance with the provisions of the Copyright, Designs and Patents Act 1998 or under the terms of a licence issued by the Copyright Licensing Agency Ltd, 90 Tottenham Court Road, London, England W1P 0LP. Application for the copyright owner's permission to reproduce any part of this publication should be addressed to the publisher.*

Warning: The doing of an unauthorised act in relation to a copyright work may result in both a civil claim for damages and criminal prosecution. © *Reed Elsevier (UK) Ltd 1998.*

Routledge/Taylor & Francis: Michael Preston-Shoot, Gwyneth Roberts, and Stuart Vernon 'Social Work law: from interaction to integration' *Journal of Social Welfare and Family Law* [1998] 20(1) 65; Michael Preston-Shoot, Gwyneth Roberts, and Stuart Vernon 'Working together in social work law' *Journal of Social Welfare and Family Law* [1998] 20(2) 137.

Staffordshire County Council: Allan Levy and Barbara Kahan *The Pindown Experience and the Protection of Children* (1991).

Sweet and Maxwell: Housing Law Reports.

United Nations: UN Convention on Human Rights; Declaration on the Elimination of All Forms of Racial Discrimination; Convention on the Elimination of All Forms of Discrimination against Women; Declaration on the Rights of Disabled Persons; Standard Rules on the Equalization of Opportunities for Persons with Disabilities.

TABLE OF CASES

A v *UK* [1998] 2 FLR 959 77, 474

Agar-Ellis, Re 24 ChD 317 322, 323

Airedale NHS Trust v *Bland* [1993] 1 All ER 821; [1993] AC 789 211

Anns v *Merton London Borough Council* [1978] AC 728 51

Associated Provincial Picture Houses Limited v *Wednesbury Corporation* 20, 43, 133,
 [1948] 1 KB 223 141, 213, 502

Avon CC v *Hooper* [1997] 1 WLR 1605 23

B v *Croydon Health Authority* [1995] 1 All ER 683, [1995] Fam 133 212

Beaney dcd, Re [1978] 1 WLR 770 251

C (A Minor), Re (Residence Order: Lesbian Co-parents) [1994] 67
 Family Law, 468

C and B, Re (children) (Care Order: Future Harm) [2000] 2 FCR 614 310

Costello-Roberts v *UK* (1993) 19 EHRR112 77

D, Re (Child Abuse Interviews) [1998] 2 FLR 10 504

Dellow's Will Trusts, Re [1964] 1 WLR 451 358

DPP v *M* [1997] 2 FLR 804 478

Entick v *Carrington* (1765) 19 St Tr. 1029 219

Ex parte Moyle [2000] Lloyd's Rep Med 143 230

F v *Lambeth LBC* [2002] 1 F.L.R. 217; [2001] 3 F.C.R. 738; 307
 [2002] Fam. Law 8

F v *West Berkshire Health Authority (Mental Health Act* 210
 Commission Intervening) [1989] 2 AH ER 545; [1990] 2 AC 1

F, Re (Mental Patient: Sterilisation) [1990] 2 AC 1 245

G v *DPP* [1997] 2 FLR 810 501

Gibbons v *Wright* (1954) 91 CLR 423 251

Gillick v *West Norfolk and Wisbech Area Health Authority* 314, 321
 [1986] A.C. 112

Groves v *Wimborne (Lord)* [1998] 2 QB 402 51

H (Minors) (Sexual Abuse: Standard of Proof), sub nom. H (Minors) 61, 62, 355
 (Child Abuse: Threshold Conditions), Re; H and R (Child Sexual Abuse:
 Standard of Proof), Re [1996] A.C. 563; [1996] 2 W.L.R. 8; [1996]
 1 All E.R. 1; [1996] 1 F.L.R. 80

Hewer v *Bryant* [1970] 1QB 357 322

Home Office v *Dorset Yacht Co Ltd* [1970] A.C. 1004; [1970] 2 W.L.R. 1140 51

Johnson v *UK* (1997) 27 EHRR 296 221, 229

Johnston v *Wellesley Hospital* (1970) 17 DLR (3d) 139 324

K, Re [1988] 1 All ER 358; [1988] Ch 310   251, 253, 254

Luberti v *Italy* February 23, 1984, unreported   222

M, Re (a minor) (Care Orders: Threshold Conditions) [1994] 2 AC 424   358
Meering v *Grahame-White Aviation Co. Ltd* (1919) 122 L.T. 44   193
Murray v *Ministry of Defence* [1988] 1 WLR 692   193

Newham LBC v *AG* [1993] 1 FLR 281   356
Nottinghamshire CC v *P* [1994] Fam. 18   328

Osman v *OK* (1999) Crim LR82   77, 78

P, Re (A Minor) (Care: Evidence) [1994] 2 FLR 751   358

R, Re [1990] 2 All ER 893   254
R v *Avon County Council, ex parte M* [1994] 2 FLR 1006   30
R v *Birmingham City Council, ex parte O* [1982] 1 WLR 679   15
R v *Brent LBC, ex parte S* [1994] 1 FLR 203   43
R v *Bristol City Council, ex parte Penfold* (1998) 1 CCLR 315   37
R v *Community and Mental Health NHS Trust, ex parte L* [1999] 1 AC 458   186
R v *D* [1984] AC 778   322, 323
R v *Davies and others*, November 3, 1995, unreported   503
R v *East Sussex C, ex parte Tandy* [1998] AC 714 inv   47, 48
R v *Epsom Rural District Council* [1922] 1 KB 383   19
R v *Gloucester CC, ex parte Barry* [1997] A.C. 584   44, 47, 48, 61, 62,
                                                                                                                           132, 139, 140, 143
R v *Gloucestershire CCl, ex parte Mahfood* [1997] 1 CCLR 7   33, 63, 67, 148
R v *Hallstrom, ex parte W (No. 2), R* v *Gardner, ex parte L* [1986]   212
   2 All ER 306 at 314; [1986] QB1090
R v *Hammersmith and Fulham LBC, ex parte M The Times*   139
   February 19, 1997
R v *Howard* [1966] 1 WLR 13   322
R v *Howes* (1860) 3 E. & E. 332   322
R v *Islington LBC, ex parte Rixon* [1998] 1 CCLR 119   17, 27, 64
R v *Kirklees MBC, ex parte Good* [1998] 1 CCLR 506   25
R v *Lewisham LBC, ex p Pinzon and Patino* [1998] 2 CCLR 152   34
R (H) v *London North and last Region Mental Health Review*   75, 227
   Tribunal (Secretary of State for Health intervening) [2001]
   EWCA Civ 415, [2001] 3 WLR 512
R v *N* (1992) 95 CrAppR 256   480
R v *North Yorkshire County Council, ex parte Hargreaves* (1997)   30, 64
   1 CCLR 104
R. (on the application of Mellor) v *Secretary of State for the Home*   80
   Department; sub nom. R. v *Secretary of State for the Home Department,*
   ex parte Mellor [2001] EWCA Civ 472; [2002] Q.B. 13; [2001] 3 W.L.R. 533;
   [2001] 2 F.L.R. 1158

R v *Secretary of State for the Home Department, ex parte Venables; joined*   394–7
    cases R v *Secretary of State for the Home Department, ex parte Thompson*
    [1998] A.C. 407; [1997] 3 W.L.R. 23
R v *South Western Hospital Managers, ex parte M* [1994] 1 All ER 161;   213
    [1993] QB 683
R v *Tower Hamlets LBC, ex parte Bradford* (1997) 29 HLR 756 I   40
R v *Wallwork* [1958] 42 Cr AppR 153   479
R v *Wandsworth LBC, ex parte Beckwith* [1996] 1 WLR 60   153
R v *Wilson, ex parte Williamson* [1996] COD 42   213
R v *Wright; joined case R* v *Ormerod* [1987] 90 Cr App R 91   479

S, Re (Minors) (Care Order: Implementation of Care Plan) [2002]   305
    UKHL 10; 2 WLR 720, CA
S, Re (Parental Responsibility) [1995] 3 FCR 225   318
S-C, Re (Mental Patient: Habeas Corpus) [1996] 1 All ER 532;   212
    [1996] QB 599
S v *S* [1970] 3 All ER107; [1972] AC 24   211
St George's Healthcare NHS Trust v *S* [1998] 3 All ER 673   209
Short v *Poole Corporation* [1926] Ch. 66   21
Sutton LBC v *Davis* [1994] 1 FLR 737   64

T, Re (Adult: Refusal of Medical Treatment) [1992] 4 All ER 649;   212
    [1993] Fam 95
Thompson and another, Re (Tariff Recommendations) [2001] 1 All ER 737   401–02

W, Re (Minors) (Sexual Abuse Standard of Proof) [1994] 1 FLR 419   361
W v *Essex CC* [2000] 1 FLR 657   55
W v *Official Solicitor* [1970] 3 All ER107; [1972] AC 24   211
Wassink v *Netherlands*, September 27, 1990, unreported   222
Winterwerp v *The Netherlands* (1979) 2 EHRR 387   173, 221, 229

X (Minors) v *Bedfordshire CC* [1995] 2 A.C. 634   49, 60
X and Y v *Switzerland* (1979) 13 DR 242   80

Z v *United Kingdom* [2001] 2 FLR 612   57

TABLE OF STATUTES

Page references in **bold** indicate that the section is set out in full.

Abduction Acts 1557 *et seq.*		323
Adoption Act 1976		13, 325
	s. 9(2)	163
	s. 16	317
	s. 18	327, 362
	s. 55	362
	s. 56	349
Adoption (Intercountry Aspects) Act 1999	s. 1(3)	163
	s. 2(4)	15
Audit Commission Act 1998		18
Bail Act 1976	s. 3(6)	436
Bradford Corporation Act 1925	s. 56	168
Care Standards Act 2000		155, 384
	Pt II	156, 157, 340
	Pt III	165
	s. 2	157
	s. 3	**156**
	s. 5	**156**
	s. 6	**156**
	s. 7	**156**
	s. 8	157
	s. 9	157
	s. 11	**158**
	s. 12	**158**
	s. 13	**158**
	s. 14	**161**
	s. 15	**159**
	s. 17(4)(a)	159
	s. 20	**161–2**
	s. 21	**162**
	s. 22	158, **159–61**
	s. 23	157, **161**
	s. 31	**162–3**, 164
	s. 32	**163–4**
	s. 56(1)	159, 160
Carers and Disabled Children Act 2000		15
	s. 1	26
	s. 2	145
	s. 2(1)	144

Carers (Recognition and Services) Act 1995		62, 63, 122
	s. 1	15, 26, **131**
Child Abduction and Custody Act 1985	s. 25(1)	369
Child Care Act 1980		319
	s. 1	335
Children Act 1908		394
Children Act 1948	s. 1	3
Children Act 1989		14, 49, 52, 78, 79, 161, 191, 250, 292, 299, 301, 305, 306, 308, 392, 403, 429, 469
	Pt I	325
	Pt II	324, 325, 329, 471
	Pt III	131, 331, 333, 343, 344, 353
	Pt IV	303, 325, 353, 456, 471
	Pt V	303, 338, 353, 359, 372
	Pt VI	384
	Pt VII	384
	Pt VIII	384
	Pt XI	311
	s. 1	**312**, 431, 433
	s. 1(3)	321
	s. 1(5)	431
	s. 2	**312–13**
	s. 2(6)	315
	s. 2(8)	315
	s. 2(9)	315
	s. 2(11)	315
	s. 3	307, **313**, 318
	s. 3(1)	307, 314
	s. 3(2)(b)	307
	s. 3(4)	314
	s. 4	307, **313–14**, 315
	s. 4(1)	314
	s. 4(2)	315
	s. 4(3)	315
	s. 4(4)	315

s. 5	313, **315–16**
s. 5(10)	318
s. 5(3)	317
s. 5(4)	317
s. 5(5)	317
s. 5(6)	317
s. 5(7)	317
s. 5(8)	317
s. 5(9)	317
s. 5(5)	318
s. 6	**316–17**
s. 6(1)	318
s. 6(3)	318
s. 6(4)	318
s. 6(7)	318
s. 8	319, 324, **325**, 326, 328
s. 8(1)	329
s. 8(3)	**357**, 431
s. 8(4)	431
s. 9	**325**
s. 9(1)	305
s. 9(2)	329
s. 9(5)	328
ss. 9–13	328
s. 10	**326**
s. 11	**327**
s. 12	**327–8**
s. 12(1)	315
s. 12(4)	314
s. 13	**329**
s. 17	41, 42, 54, 61, 63, **331–2**, 335, 343, 425
s. 17(1)	335
s. 17(1)(a)	302
s. 17(1)(b)	302
s. 17(3)	334
s. 17(5)	320, 335
s. 17(6)	336
s. 17(7)–(9)	341, 342, 344
s. 17(10)	42, 302
s. 17A	**332–3**
s. 17B	**333**

s. 18	332, 335, **336**
s. 19	**336**, 343
s. 20	41, 42, 332, 335, **337–8**, 343
s. 21	**338**, 343, 350
s. 22	309, **338–9**
s. 22(4)	341
s. 22(5)	62, 341
s. 23	43, 332, 335, **339–40**, 343
s. 23(2)(a)	163, 346
s. 23(4)	346
s. 23(5)	346
s. 23(2)(f)	346
s. 23(8)	43
s. 23A	**340–1**, 342
s. 23B	339, **341**, 343
ss. 23B–D	332
s. 23C	**342**
s. 23D	**342**
s. 23E	**343**
s. 24	343
s. 24(14)	**18**
s. 24A	332
s. 24B	332, 339
s. 24B(1)	18, 342
s. 24B(2)	18, 342
s. 24B(3)	342
s. 25	435, 436
s. 26	64, 309, 349
s. 27	302, 320
s. 27(4)	320
s. 28	320
s. 28(1)	320
s. 30	320
s. 31	329, 330, 355, 374, 430
s. 31(1)(a)	433
s. 31(2)	310, 355, 356, 357, 360, 365, 430, 433
s. 31(2)(a)	356, 357, 358, 359, 360

s. 32	**362**
s. 33	**362–3**
s. 34	**363–4**, 373, 375
s. 35	**364**
s. 36	**364–5**
s. 37	**330–1**
s. 37(1)	365
s. 37(4)	365
s. 38	**365–6**
s. 38(6)	63
s. 38A	**366**
s. 38B	**366–7**
s. 39	**367**
s. 41	**432**
s. 43	**373–4**
s. 43(8)	63
s. 44	**374–6**
s. 44(1)(a)(ii)	376
s. 44A	**376–7**
s. 44B	**377–8**
s. 45	**377–8**
s. 46	353, 377, **378–9**
s. 46(7)	63, 380
s. 46(3)(f)	338
s. 47	61, **380–1**, 431
s. 47(1)(a)(iii)	432
s. 47(1)(b)	374
s. 48	**381–2**
s. 59(2)	163
s. 82(5)	340, 467
s. 84	310
s. 90	**467**
s. 91	369, **467–8**
s. 92	**468**
s. 93	**468**
s. 100(2)	325, 329
s. 100(2)(c)	305
s. 100(2)(d)	305
s. 105	357
Sch. 2	53, 302, 331, 335, 340, 341,

		342, **343–54,** 403, 406
	Sch. 2, para. 3	334
	Sch. 2, para. 7	389, 431
	Sch. 2, para. 19	363
	Sch. 3	**367–72**
	Sch. 9A, para. 1	337
	Sch. 9A, para. 2	337
	Sch. 14, para. 4	315
Children (Leaving Care) Act 2000		18, 353
Children and Young Person's Act 1933		391, 428
	Pt III	12, 425
	Pt IV	12
	s. 1	315, **473–4**
	s. 8(1)	**443**
	s. 16(2)	**443**
	s. 31(1)	**391**
	s. 34(2)	**391**
	s. 34A	**425**
	s. 34A(1)	**391**
	s. 38(1)	476
	s. 39	**402,** 403
	s. 39(1)	**392**
	s. 44	396, 402, 439
	s. 44(1)	389
	s. 46	**443**
	s. 46(1)	392, 393
	s. 47(2)	**392**
	s. 49(1)	**392**
	s. 50	390
	s. 53(1)	395
	s. 56	442
	s.150	443
Children and Young Persons Act 1963		6, 10, 13
Children and Young Persons Act 1969		392
	s. 15	392
	s. 16	392
	s. 18	**393**
	s. 23	404, 435, 436, 437
	s. 23(1)	338, 436
	s. 23(2)	436, 438, 439
	s. 23(4)	438
	s. 23(4A)	439, 440

	s. 23(5)	436, 437, 439
	s. 23(6)	438, 440
	s. 23(8)	437
	s. 23(9)(b)	437
	s. 23(9A)	439, 440
	s. 23(10)	436
	s. 24(1)	**394**
	s. 24(1A)	**394**
Chronically Sick and Disabled Persons Act 1970		61, 142, 334
	s. 1	123, 132, 139
	s. 2	26, 41, 45, 62, **130**, 131, 132, 133, 137, 139, 146
	s. 2(1)	28, 35, 44, 46, 47, 130, 133, 134, 135, 136, 137, 141, 142, 143
	s. 8	130
Civil Evidence Act 1995	ss. 1–4	425
Community Care (Direct Payments) Act 1996		15, 63, 143
Community Care (Residential Accommodation) Act 1992	s. 1	155
	s. 1(1)	153
Crime and Disorder Act 1998		403, 423
	Pt III	404
	s. 8	**426**
	s. 8(4)(b)	429
	s. 9	426, **427**
	s. 11	325, 380, 384, 390, **429**
	s. 12	325, 384., 429, **430**
	s. 37	389, 404
	s. 38	**404–05**, 406
	s. 38(2)	406
	s. 39	**405**
	s. 40	**405–06**
	s. 42	387
	s. 51	443
	s. 65	406
	s. 65(1)	**417–18**
	s. 66	418
	s. 66(1)	**418**

	s. 75	405
	s. 97	437, 438
	s. 98	438
Crime (Sentences) Act 1997	s. 31	404
Criminal Justice Act 1982		388
Criminal Justice Act 1988		501
	s. 2A	478
	s. 32(2)	476, 487
	s. 32A	480, 487
	s. 33A(2A)	478, 479
	s. 33A(3C)	479, 502
	s. 34(2)	476
Criminal Justice Act 1991		63, 476, 477, 489, 499
	s. 37(4A)	404
	s. 54	479
	s. 59	413
	s. 61	438
	s. 65	404
	s. 95	62
Criminal Justice and Public Order Act 1994		63
	Pt III	412
	s. 4(3)(b)	469
	s. 24	413
Criminal Law Act 1977	s. 54	**473**
Disability Discrimination Act 1995	Pt IV	115
	Pt V	115
	s. 1	**105**
	s. 3	107
	s. 4	**109**
	s. 5	**107–08**
	s. 6	**108–09**, 113
	s. 7	109, 113
	s. 8	113
	s. 15	113
	s. 19	**113–14**, 114
	s. 20	113, **114**
	s. 21	113, **114–15**
	Sch. 1, para. 1	**105**
	Sch. 1, para. 2	**105**
	Sch. 1, para. 3	**105–06**
	Sch. 1, para. 4	**106**
	Sch. 1, para. 5	**106**
	Sch. 1, para. 6	**106**

	Sch. 1, para. 7	**106–07**
	Sch. 1, para. 8	**107**
Disabled Persons (Employment) Act 1944	s. 6	106
Disabled Persons (Employment) Act 1958	s. 3	12
Disabled Persons (Services, Consultation and Representation) Act 1986		142, 334, 344
	ss. 1–5	14
	s. 3	129
	s. 4	28, 35, 129, 130, 136, 137
	s. 7	14
	s. 8	14, 28, **130**, **131**
Domestic Proceedings and Magistrates' Courts Act 1978		325
Education Act 1944		7
	s. 8	28
Education Act 1981		320, 334
Education Act 1986	s. 47	474
Education Act 1993		48, 343
	Pt III	14
	s. 166	14
Education Act 1994	s. 1	114
Education Act 1996		88, 372
	Part IV	344
	s. 7	370
	s. 9	371
	s. 19	47
	s. 437	364, 371
	s. 411	371
	s. 423	371
	s. 443	426
	s. 444	364, 370, 426
	s. 532	405, 426
	s. 548	474
Employment and Training Act 1973	s. 2	113
Enduring Powers of Attorney Act 1985	s. 1	**254–5**, 256, 257
	s. 3	**255**
	s. 13	**255**
Family Law Act 1996		63, 325
	s. 47(6)	366, 376
	s. 47(7)	366, 376
	s. 47(11)	366, 376
	s. 47(12)	366, 376

	s. 48	366, 376
	Sch. 5	366
Family Law Reform Act 1969	s. 7(4)	13
Family Law Reform Act 1987	s. 1	312, 314
	s. 4	315
Guardianship Act 1973	s. 1(2)	314
Health and Safety at Work etc. Act 1974		100
Health Service and Public Health Act 1968		10, 26
	s. 5(1)(c)	13
	s. 45	13, 125
	s. 45(1)	23, 145
	s. 45(9)	13
	s. 65	13
Health and Social Care Act 2001		143
	s. 50(1)	**150**
	s. 57(3)–(5)	332, 333
	s. 57(7)	332
	s. 57	**144–5**
Health and Social Services and Social Security Adjudications Act 1983	s. 17	14, 23
	s. 17(1)	**145**
	Sch. 9, para. 1	145
Health Visiting and Social Work (Training) Act 1962		12
	s. 5(1)(b)	13
Housing Act 1996	s. 167	35, 39
	s. 167(1)	36
	s. 167(2)	36
Housing Grants Construction and Regeneration Act 1996	s. 22	48
	s. 23	48
	s. 23(1)	48
	s. 24(3)	48
Human Rights Act 1998		68, 72, 169, 172, 227, 305, 307, 310, 372, 396
	s. 2(1)	**75**
	s. 3	308
	s. 3(1)	**75**
	s. 4(1)	**75**
	s. 6	75, 308
	s. 6(1)	**76**
	s. 7	308
	s. 8	308

Indecency with Children Act 1960	s. 1	**473**
Local Authority Social Services Act 1970		3, 22, 52, 339, 392, 469
	s. 1	11
	s. 2	45, 138, 140
	s. 2(1)	28, 30
	s. 2(3)	11
	s. 3(3)	15
	s. 7	17, 18, 25, 27, 34, 119, 130, 155, 300
	s. 7(1)	27, 29
	s. 7A	17, 27, 63
	ss. 7B–D	27
	s. 7B	**64**, 147
	s. 7B(1)	**17**
	s. 7C	18
	s. 7C(1)	**17**
	s. 7D	18, 19, 147
	s. 7D(1)	**17**
	s. 17	24
	s. 29	29
	Sch. 1	11, 12, 49, 387, 403
	Sch. 1, para. 5	**403–04**
Local Government Act 1972	s. 195(6)	139
	Sch. 23	139
Local Government Act 1974	Pt III	147
Lunacy Act 1890	s. 4	184, 185
Magistrates Court Act 1980		486
	s. 24	393
	s. 65	429
	s. 128	439
	s. 128A	439
	s. 144	456
Maternity and Child Welfare Act 1918		6
Matrimonial Causes Act 1973		325
Matrimonial and Family Proceedings Act 1984	Pt III	325
Mental Deficiency Acts 1913–1938		6
Mental Health Act 1959		6, 26, 184
	s. 2	226
	s. 5	185, 186
	s. 5(1)	190, 194
	s. 5(2)	191
	s. 8	12

Mental Health Act 1983

		79, 179, 180, 184, 192, 195, 201, 211, 212, 221, 247, 255, 257, 262, 263, 264, 266, 268, 425, 481
Pt I		183
Pt II		13, 126, 209
Pt III		13, 126, 369
Pt IV		170, 172, 194, 217
Pt VI		13
Pt VII		175, 183, 241, 245
s. 1(2)		222
s. 2		189, **197–8**, 203, 206, 207, 209, 210, 213
s. 2(2)		213, 214
s. s(a)		214
s. 2(2)(b)		202, 214
s. 2(3)		213
s. 3		189, **198**, 203, 206, 209, 213, 230, 231, 256
s. 3(2)		**228**
s. 3(2)(c)		202
s. 3(4)		256
s. 3(5)		256
s. 4		189, **198–9**, 206, 207, 209
s. 5		189, **215**, 220
s. 5(2)		217
s. 5(4)		217
s. 6(5)(a)		252
s. 7		**215–16**
s. 8		208, **216**, 256
s. 8(2)(a)		256
s. 11		**199–200**
s. 11(4)		203
s. 12		**200**, 205, 369, 460
s. 12(2)		**175**
s. 13(1)		213

s. 13(2)	62, 63, 213
s. 13(4)	205
s. 19	209
s. 23	203, **225**
s. 25	**225**, 232
s. 25A	207, **232**
s. 25A(4)	233
s. 25B	232, **233–4**
s. 25B(6)	234, 235
s. 25C	232, **234–5**
s. 25D	233, **235–6**, 237
s. 25E	**236–7**
s. 25F	**237**
s. 25G	**238–9**
s. 25H	**239–40**
s. 25I	238
s. 26	**175–6**
s. 29	**176–7**, 204, 206
s. 29(4)	198
s. 34	**175**
s. 35	217
s. 37	209, 227, 228, 231, 240
s. 37(4)	217
s. 41	227, 228, 240
s. 42(2)	217
s. 47	231
s. 48	231
s. 56	**217**
s. 57	**217–18**
s. 57(2)	192
s. 58	217, **218**
s. 59	217
s. 60	217
s. 62	217
s. 63	181
s. 66	13, 176
s. 66(1)	226
s. 67	13
s. 69	176
s. 69(1)	13
s. 72	**226–7**, 229, 230

s. 72(1)	228, **230–1**
s. 72(1)(b)	228
s. 73	217, **227**, 228, 229, 230
s. 73(1)	228, **231**
s. 73(2)	222
s. 73(7)	222
s. 74	217
ss. 93–113	245
s. 93	**241**
s. 94	**241–2**
s. 94(2)	**175**
s. 95	**242**, 243
s. 95(1)(a)	245
s. 96	**242–3**
s. 96(1)(k)	245
s. 114	13, 65, **177–8**
s. 115	13, **219**
s. 116	13
s. 117	13, 125, 135, 232, 233, 235, 236, 237, 238, 239, 240
s. 121(4)	189
s. 129	208
s. 130	13
s. 131	184, **185–6**
s. 131(1)	187, 188, 190, 191, 194
s. 131(2)	191
s. 132	208
s. 135	202, 217, **219**
s. 136	217, **220**
s. 145	175, 177
Mental Health (Patients in the Community) Act 1995	232, 240
Mental Health (Scotland) Act 1984 s. 83	219
Mental Treatment Act 1930	184
National Assistance Act 1948	3, 6, 10, 26, 319
Pt III	45, 125, 155
s. 2(1)	30
ss. 21–27	12
s. 21	**149**, 151, 153, 154, 155

	s. 21(1)	139, 153
	s. 21(1)(a)	152, 154
	s. 22	145, **149**, 151
	s. 26	**149**, 151, 153, 154, 155
	s. 26(1)	154
	s. 26A	150
	s. 28	145
	ss. 29–30	12, 139
	s. 29	23, 26, 28, 30, 35, 45, 123, 124, 130, 131, 132, 135, 139, 145
	s. 29(1)	124, 135, 139
	s. 29(2)	135
	s. 29(4)(g)	124
	s. 31	139
	s. 42	151
	ss. 43–45	12
	s. 47	**164**, 166, 167, 168, 169
	s. 47(11)	12
	s. 48	12
	s. 49	12
	s. 56	151
	s. 56(3)	12
National Assistance (Amendment) Act 1951	s. 1	**165–6**
National Health Act 1997		23
National Health Service Act 1946		6
National Health Service Act 1977		35, 129, 165
	s. 21	125, **126**
	Sch. 8	13, 23, 125, **126–7**, 145, 319
National Health Service and Community Care Act 1990		17, 29, 61, 119, 320, 343, 425
	Pt III	148
	s. 42(1)	153
	s. 46	14, 27, 28, **125**, 129
	s. 46(2)	26
	s. 46(3)	28, 125, 131, 132

	s. 47	34, 35, 37, 38, 39, 41, 53, **129–30**, 136, 140, 142, 144
	s. 47(1)	28, 137, 146
	s. 47(1)(a)	26, 150
	s. 47(2)	137, 142
	s. 47(3)	150
	s. 50	64
	s. 66	153
	Sch. 9, para. 5	153
National Health Service (Scotland) Act 1978		165
Offences Against the Person Act 1861	s. 27	**473**
Police and Criminal Evidence Act 1984		78, 220
	s. 34(1)	**406–07**
	s. 37(1)	**407**
	s. 38	338, 407, 434
	s. 38(1A)	**407**
	s. 38(6)	338, **408**, 413
	s. 38(6B)	**408**
	s. 41(7)	**407**
	s. 46	**414**
	s. 46(1)	**434–5**
	s. 78	498, 503
	s. 78(1)	502
Powers of Attorney Act 1971	s. 1435	**250**
	s. 10	**251**
	Sch. 1	251
Powers of Criminal Courts (Sentencing) Act 2000		443
	s. 1	444
	s. 12	444
	s. 19(5)	426, 427
	s. 6(2)	394
	s. 16	**444–5**, 449
	s. 17	**445**
	s. 18	**445**
	s. 19(5)	469
	s. 20	**445–6**
	s. 21	**446**
	s. 22	**446–7**
	s. 23	445, **447**, 450
	s. 23(5)	448
	s. 24(6)	440

s. 25	**447–8**
s. 26	**448–9**
s. 27	**499**
s. 27(4)	450
s. 35	**453**
s.36	**453–4**
s. 37	**462–3**
ss. 37–40	462
s. 38	**463**
s. 52(4)	464
s. 63	**456–7**
s. 63(1)	371
s. 63(6)(b)	461
s. 64	**457**
s. 69	**454–5**
s. 69(5)	**453**
s. 70	454, **455–6**
s. 71	455, **456**
s. 73	**451**
s. 74	**451–2**
ss. 90–92	444, 463, 464
s. 90	468
s. 91	468
s. 91(1)	394
s. 91(2)	394
s. 91(3)	394
s. 92	350, 468
s. 93	463, 464, 468
s. 100	**464**
ss. 100–107	463, 464
s. 101	**464–5**
s. 102	**465–6**
s. 103	**466**
s. 103(1)	465
s. 104	**466**
s. 104(3)(b)	468
s. 105	**466–7**
s. 107	**467**
ss. 130–134	469
s. 135	**468**
s. 136	**468, 468**
s. 137	**468–9**
s. 138	468

	s. 150	**469–70**
	Sch. 1	426, 427,
		449–50
	Sch. 1, para. 13	469
	Sch. 2	453
	Sch. 3	462, 463, 468
	Sch. 6	453, **457–62,**
		461
	Sch. 6, para. 5	338
	Sch. 7	461
	Sch. 7, para. 7	338, 371
	Sch. 8	451, **452–3,**
		455, 456, 468
Protection of Children Act 1999		384
Public Health Act 1875	s. 53	19, 20, 477, 478
Public Health Act 1936		6, 167
Public Health Act 1961		167
Public Health (Control of Disease) Act 1984	s. 46(2)	14
	s. 46(5)	14
Public Order Act 1986		92
Race Relations Act 1976		85, 94
	Pts II–IV	91
	Pt II	88
	Pt VII	92
	Pt VIII	92
	s. 1	**86**
	s. 2	**86**
	s. 3	**86–7,** 88
	s. 4	**87**
	s. 4(1)	91
	s. 4(2)	91
	s. 5	**87–8**
	s. 17	**88**
	s. 19B	**85**
	ss. 20–26	88
	s. 20	89
	s. 21	89
	s. 22	**89**
	s. 22(2)	89
	s. 25	**89–90**
	s. 26	88, 90
	s. 26(1)	**90**
	s. 26(2)	90

	s. 28	**90**
	s. 29	**90**
	s. 30	**90**
	s. 31	**90–1**
	s. 35	**91**
	s. 36	**91**
	s. 37	**91**
	s. 38	**92**
Race Relations (Amendment) Act 2000		85
	s. 71	85
	s. 71(1)	**85**
Registered Homes Act 1984		12, 155, 161
Residential Homes Act 1980	s. 8	23, 145
	s. 76	54
	Sch. 9	23
School Standards and Framework Act 1998	s. 131	474
Sex Discrimination Act	s. 1	**94**
	s. 2	**95**
	s. 2A	**95**
	s. 3	**95**
	s. 4	95
	s. 6	**96**
	s. 7	**96**
	s. 14	97
	s. 22	98
	s. 26	97, **98**
	s. 47	**98–9**
	s. 48	**99**
	s. 49	**99**
	s. 63	100
	s. 65	100
	s. 66	100
Sex Offenders Act 1997		419
Sexual Offences Act 1956	s. 1	**471**
	s. 5	**471**
	s. 6	**471**
	s. 10	**472**
	s. 12	**472**
	s. 13	**472**
	s. 14	467, **472**
	s. 15	467, **472**
	s. 16(1)	**472**
	s. 17	**472**

	s. 19	**472**
	s. 46	**473**
	Sch. 2	473
Sexual Offences Act 1993	s. 1	**471**
Social Security Contributions and Benefits Act 1992	Pt VII	332, 350
Sunday Entertainments Act 1932		20
Supplementary Benefits Act 1976	Sch. 5	13
Supreme Court Act 1981	s. 89	241
Wills Act 1837	s. 9	316
Youth Justice and Criminal Evidence Act 1999		392, 474, 475, 480, 498, 501
	s. 16	**480-1**, 483
	s. 16(1)(a)	482
	s. 17	**481**, 482
	s. 18	481, 483
	s. 18(2)	482
	s. 19	**481-2**
	s. 19(2)	482
	s. 20	482, 483
	s. 21	**482-3**, 484
	s. 22	**483-4**
	s. 23	**484**
	s. 24	482, **484**, 486
	s. 25	**484-5**
	s. 26	**485**
	s. 27	482, **485-6**, 483
	s. 28	**486**, 483
	s. 29	**486-7**
	s. 30	**487**
	s. 31	**487**
	s. 32	**487**
	s. 35	482, 483
	s. 45	402, 403

TABLE OF STATUTORY INSTRUMENTS

Page references in **bold** indicate that the section is set out in full.

SI 1990/2244 Local Authority Social Services   18
(Complaints Procedure) Order

SI 1991/893 Placement of Children with   329
Parents etc. Regulations

SI 1991/895 Review of Children's   309
Cases Regulations

SI 1992/2071 Magistrates' Courts   440
(Children and Young Persons) Rules

	r.4	440
	r.5	**440**
	r.7	**440**
	r.8	**440**
	r.9	**441**
	r.10	**441, 442**
	r.11	**442**
	r.17	**442**
	r.18	**442**
	r.19	**442**
	r.20	**442**
	r.22	**442, 443**
	r.24	**487, 488**

SI 2001/3965 Care Homes Regulations   155

SI 2001/3969 National Care Standards   155
Commission (Registration) Regulations

SI 2001/3980 National Care Standards   155
Commission (Fees and Frequency of
Inspections) Regulations

TABLE OF EUROPEAN LEGISLATION

Page references in **bold** indicate that the section is set out in full.

Dir.76/207	art.2	**93**
Dir. 79/7	art.4	**93**

TABLE OF FOREIGN LEGISLATION

Netherlands Mentally Ill Persons Act   174

TABLE OF CONVENTIONS, TREATIES AND DECLARATIONS

Page references in **bold** indicate that the section is set out in full.

Convention on the Elimination of All Forms of Discrimination against Women 1979	Art.1	**93**
	Art.2	**93**, **94**
	Art.3	**94**
	Art.4	**94**
	Art.5	**94**
European Convention on Human Rights		172
	Protocol 1	82
	Art.1	**76**
	Art.2	**76**, **77**
	Art.3	57, **77**, 397
	Art.4	**77**
	Art.5	**77**, **78**
	Art.6	57, **78**, 305
	Art.6(1)	**400**, 401
	Art.7	**79**
	Art.8	57, **79**, 305
	Art.9	**79**
	Art.10	**79**, **80**
	Art.11	**80**
	Art.12	**80**
	Art.13	57, **80**
	Art.14	**81**
	Art.15	**81**
	Art.16	**81**
	Art.17	**81**, **82**
	Art.18	**82**
United Nations Convention on the Rights of the Child	Art.37(a)	**397**
	Art.37(b)	**398**
	Art.40	**398**

United Nations Treaty on Human Rights	Art.1	69
	Art.2	69
	Art.3	69
	Art.4	69
	Art.5	69
	Art.6	69
	Art.7	69
	Art.8	69
	Art.9	69
	Art.10	69
	Art.11	69
	Art.12	70
	Art.13	70
	Art.14	70
	Art.15	70
	Art.16	70
	Art.17	70
	Art.18	70
	Art.19	70
	Art.20	70
	Art.21	70
	Art.22	71
	Art.23	71
	Art.24	71
	Art.25	71
	Art.26	71
	Art.27	71
	Art.28	71
	Art.29	71
	Art.30	72
Treaty of Rome	Art.141	93
	formerly 119	
United Nations Declaration on the Elimination of All Forms of Racial Discrimination	Art.1	83
	Art.2	83, 84
	Art.3	84
	Art.4	84
	Art.5	84
	Art.6	84
	Art.7	84
	Art.8	84
	Art.9	84

PART I

Introduction and context

1

Social work and the legal framework

1.1 The statutory duties of social workers

What is social work law? Our perspective, in this book, defines social work as a statutory service. But there can be other perspectives, so to help you reflect on this, this chapter ends with two extracts from articles which grapple with the question of what social work law really is.

Social work is like other welfare services, such as health work, education, access to justice or the provision of welfare benefits. Who should provide society with these services? How should they be regulated? Although society's answers to these questions start as political decisions, the decisions are turned into action through legislation, which is then interpreted by practitioners and the courts. The starting point for social work is the Local Authorities Social Services Act 1970 (LASSA).

1.1.1 The birth of a profession — the Local Authority Social Services Act 1970 (LASSA)

Statutory duties for local authorities in relation to children and adult services existed before LASSA. For example the National Assistance Act 1948 had already created a range of duties for local authorities in the field we would now call community care. Much of this legislation still applies (see Chapter 4). The Children Act 1948 (now replaced) similarly set out the duties of local authorities with regard to children, which were principally, according to s 1, to 'provide for orphans, deserted children etc'. But LASSA provided a new framework, a framework which, after much patching up, still defines law for social workers.

The Seebohm Report

Why was a new organizing framework needed by 1970 for these existing statutory duties? To make sense of legislation it helps to read the reports commissioned by the government, and to read the parliamentary debates. In 1968 Parliament received the *Report of the Committee on Local Authority and Allied Personal Social Services* (Cmnd 3703), chaired by Frederic Seebohm. This Report led directly to the passing of the Local Authority Social Services Act 1970.

What was the thinking of this Committee?

1.   We were appointed on 20th December, 1965
'to review the organisation and responsibilities of the local authority personal social services in England and Wales, and to consider what changes are desirable to secure an effective family service'.

2.   We now have the honour to submit our Report. We recommend a new local authority department, providing a community based and family oriented service, which will be available to all. This new department will, we believe, reach far beyond the discovery and rescue of social casualties; it will enable the greatest possible number of individuals to act reciprocally, giving and receiving service for the well-being of the whole community.

3.   The new department will have responsibilities going beyond those of existing local authority departments, but they will include the present services provided by children's departments, the welfare services provided under the National Assistance Act 1948, educational welfare and child guidance services, the home help service, mental health social work services, other social work services provided by health departments, day nurseries, and certain social welfare work currently undertaken by some housing departments.

4.   In our opinion, local authorities should immediately review needs and services in their own areas in order to determine current priorities. As a committee we have not attempted this task, for it can be performed only in relation to the needs and circumstances of specific areas, including their previous investment in particular services.

5.   However, we foresee that most local authorities are likely to feel that today children under 5 and very old people call for special attention and some local authorities will have clear 'priority areas' within their boundaries. For the nation as a whole we consider that the community approach and the training of staff for the social service department, including the field staff of the area teams and the staff for residential accommodation, will be crucial to the success of the new service.

But why, you might wonder, should certain services be handled by a local authority, and others, such as health, be left to a national health service? As you will see later (in the case of *Avon County Council* v *Hooper* [1997] 1 WLR 1605, see pp. 23–5) this issue has continued to be problematic. You might equally wonder why certain services concerning children were given to social services departments, but others to education departments. Why is housing for the vulnerable (whether adult or children) not a social service function? These were among the issues which Seebohm considered:

14.   We do not recommend any radical change in the pattern of responsibility for local authority housing, but in chapter XIII (not reproduced) we emphasise the fundamental importance of adequate housing for the provision of an effective family service and, in particular, the need to pay special attention to the housing problems of elderly and physically handicapped people, large families, and one-parent families. We urge that housing departments should take a wider view of their responsibilities and be specifically and directly concerned, not only with building houses and managing those they own, but also with the whole range of housing problems of the area in question. We are against any division of the responsibility for housing — by, for example, giving the social service department responsibility for letting and managing specific groups of houses for groups of people in special need. In particular, we recommend that the responsibility for accommodating homeless families, as distinct from providing limited overnight accommodation, should be placed squarely on housing departments. We suggest that social workers from the social service department might be attached for all or part of their time to housing departments in order

to help deal with the more difficult social problems among council tenants or people in need of housing.

51.　The local authority personal social services have varied points of origin both in this century and the last. Some owe much to the endeavour of voluntary bodies both as initiators and as agents of the local authorities. Indeed, legislation has given local authorities considerable scope to support and use voluntary organisations on an agency basis, in order to fulfil all or part of their statutory responsibilities.

52.　The roots of other local authority personal social services are, to varying degrees, located in the Poor Law. At one time the general Poor Law dealt with orphaned and deprived children, the mentally ill and the mentally subnormal, as well as many of the elderly poor. It housed the homeless and offered a roof to the unmarried mother and her child. Different categories of need were gradually separated off from the Poor Law system but this process was not completed until 1948. The duties of the local authority public assistance committees were then divided between two new local authority departments (children and welfare) and the National Assistance Board took over the functions of financial assistance. However, throughout the break-up of the Poor Law a key factor was the conviction that certain groups had special needs, which demanded special treatment surpassing what was or could be offered by an all purpose Poor Law system.

53.　Some of the present personal social services also developed primarily as offshoots of other major local services like health, education and housing. Each of these encountered families in distress as well as the individual or family unable to benefit fully from the service offered either because of reluctance or through physical, mental or social handicap. The early school attendance officers, certain workers in the school health service, and housing welfare officers were variously concerned with non-users, difficult or handicapped users, or with others who would not (or could not) use the normal service in a correct or responsible manner. The home help service grew as a result of concern about the health of mothers confined at home, and day nurseries received their greatest stimulus during the last war when the labour of married women was urgently needed as part of the national effort.

54.　The erratic course which the development of the personal social services has taken is attributable to other factors as well as these different points of origin. Many of them dealt and still deal with people or families whose problems or behaviour mark them as deviant and enlist little if any public sympathy and understanding. This, inevitably, has affected the public willingness to support, and eventually to finance, certain services. Deprived children have, for instance, been regarded more benevolently in this respect than the delinquent adolescent or the unmarried mother. However, some services which deal with those who are socially disapproved have developed none the less, partly because of the assumption that they would achieve a measure of social control.

55.　Since the last war in particular, the rate at which different local authority personal social services have developed and the direction in which they have moved have been partly the result of the extent to which they have been able to recruit trained staff. Not only has this meant that different services have developed somewhat differently but that the same services in different authorities have varied. In general, those services containing the larger proportions of trained staff appear to have been influenced by a growing sense of professionalism amongst social workers.

56.　Thus the services with which we are mainly concerned have developed from different points, some reflecting and building upon the work done by voluntary organisations; some gradually being separated out from the Poor Law, whilst others grew as a response to the difficulties encountered in providing other local authority services. The local authority personal social services have, therefore, not only emerged at different times but also for somewhat different reasons and to meet certain specially defined needs. They have been influenced in their orientation by their antecedents and by the staff they have recruited. Hence today we have a variety of services which are not only fragmented in terms of departmental responsibility and objectives but are also at different stages of development. They have not been reviewed and examined in a comprehensive fashion since the existing structure was set up in the period immediately after the war.

...

Seebohm clearly recognized social work as rooted in both social welfare and social control. The following paragraphs review the range of powers and responsibilities vested, at the time of writing, in different organizations, including local authorities:

57.   The present children's service is based upon the Children Act 1948. Before this, responsibility for the care of deprived children was divided at the local authority level between three main committees: public assistance, health, and education. The main organisational effect of the 1948 Act was to concentrate this responsibility in the children's committee and oblige local authorities to appoint children's officers, as a general rule without other responsibilities. Children's authorities had a duty under the Act to aim at the restoration to their families of children who had been received into care, and in some areas this responsibility came to form the basis of work to prevent the breakdown of families. Following the recommendations of the Ingleby Committee, the Children and Young Persons Act 1963 extended the duties of local authorities considerably. It required them to make available 'such advice, guidance and assistance as may promote the welfare of children by diminishing the need to receive children into or keep them in care ... or to bring children before a juvenile court' (section 1). This provided the legal basis upon which preventive work which was already being undertaken by some authorities with children and their families in their own homes could be developed.

58.   The framework of the local authority welfare services was established by the National Assistance Act 1948 which completed the dissolution of the Poor Law by separating the responsibility for financial assistance to needy people (which was placed upon the National Assistance Board) from the responsibility for providing accommodation and other services for the elderly, the physically handicapped and homeless families (which was placed upon county councils and county boroughs).

59.   The personal social services provided by local authority health departments are mostly specified in the National Health Service Act 1946, though many of them have a much longer history. For instance, the Maternity and Child Welfare Act 1918 empowered local authorities to employ home helps to assist during a mother's lying-in period; the powers were continued in the Public Health Act 1936 and extended by Defence Regulations during the war to include the provision of domestic help to sick and infirm people and to families where the mother was absent or where several members were ill.

60.   Before the National Health Service Act 1946, institutional care and a limited amount of community care for the mentally ill and the mentally sub-normal were provided mainly by county councils and county borough councils under the Lunacy and Mental Treatment Acts 1890–1913 and the Mental Deficiency Acts 1913–1938, partly under public assistance legislation, and partly by voluntary hospitals and voluntary organisations. The Act of 1946 divided the services between the hospital boards and the local health authorities whose powers under that Act were extended by the Mental Health Act 1959. This not only reformed the classification of mental disorder but placed a more comprehensive responsibility upon local authorities to assist the mentally ill and mentally sub-normal in their areas.

61.   Other services of a social work nature have been developed by local health departments, particularly under their duties to prevent illness, to care for people suffering from illness and to provide aftercare for them. These services were originally mainly concerned with people suffering

from infectious or chronic disease and their families but in some areas now cover general work with 'problem families'.

62.   Education welfare services have been developed in conjunction with the main educational service under the 1944 Education Act. Machinery for enforcing school attendance is as old as compulsory education though it has changed radically over the years. Other aspects, such as the provision of free meals, clothing and grants for maintenance have also developed within education departments mainly in response to needs which have become apparent in the schools and which must be met if a child is to benefit fully from education. The school health service meets a variety of other needs and prevents problems of ill-health arising. The child guidance service is of particular interest to us in these contexts.

63.   Local authority housing departments have also developed their housing welfare functions, partly as they have increasingly become involved in slum clearance, redevelopment and the consequent rehousing of large numbers of families, but also as they have accommodated more old people. There is indeed a long tradition of 'welfare' in housing management which can be traced back to the work of Octavia Hill and others.

Seebohm then goes on to consider how this fragmented approach leads to problems of coordination. The Report, in paragraphs not reproduced here, describes how different departments and outside agencies can cooperate in case conferences or coordinating committees. But the Committee still identified shortcomings in the way services were organised. Some of what you read may sound familiar and you may wish to consider as you read this book to what extent the present legal framework has improved the situation:

74.   Local authority personal social services are not fully meeting needs for which, on the basis of the duties placed on them by statutes, they are clearly responsible. Obvious examples can be derived from the waiting lists for different kinds of day and residential care for the mentally ill, the mentally sub-normal, the handicapped and the aged. There is no doubt also that in many areas domiciliary services like home helps or meals on wheels are falling short of meeting obvious needs which those in the services think they ought to be meeting.

...

76.   There are some needs (or certain groups of people with needs) for which no service has a clearly defined responsibility. This is particularly true of newly recognised or newly emergent problems and ones which do not fit neatly into the conventional categories. The fragmented nature of the existing services tends to produce separate spheres of responsibility with neglected areas between. The evidence of the County Councils' Association was very clear on this point. 'The present division of responsibility at field work level means that each of the services is responsible for limited groups of persons in need of social work support, often over only a limited period of time. This results in a lack of continuity in the help and support provided and some groups, such as the socially inadequate and alcoholics, tend to be regarded as outside the responsibilities of any of the present agencies.'

...

79.   ... The present structure of the personal social services and the division of responsibilities between them is based upon the definition of certain kinds of problems (mental illness, homelessness, or physical handicap, for instance); upon age groupings (the old or school children), and upon legal and administrative classifications (delinquency or deemed maladjustment). Such divisions do not reflect the fact that families comprise members falling into a variety of

these categories or that individuals may face a combination of inter-related problems for which different services (or none) are responsible. Under these circumstances the growing desire to treat both the individual and the family as a whole and to see them in their wider social contexts creates accentuated difficulties of co-ordination both at policy and field levels.

80.   Other closely allied developments have also exacerbated this problem. Greater emphasis has been laid upon community rather than institutional care and there has been more movement between the two. Good co-ordination is required to support such policies for, of necessity, a person living in the community needs the services of more departments and organisations than someone with similar problems accommodated residentially. Likewise the family which supports a handicapped or disturbed member at home often requires a variety of forms of help.

81.   There has also been a growing interest in undertaking preventive work. This involves a broader view of social and individual problems than the present structure of services easily permits and often demands considerable collaboration between several organisations and professions.

82.   Thus co-ordination between the various social agencies working in an area is becoming more difficult and is, for this reason more likely to be deficient, with the result that families and individuals receive less than adequate service and scarce resources are used inefficiently.

Seebohm considered a range of models to remedy these perceived defects, such as having a separate department for children and families and another for old people and handicapped adults, or having a casework department acting on an agency basis for other departments. They considered absorbing social work into the health or the education departments, and even taking social care away from local government altogether:

137.   This is a proposal which could have profound implications for the whole local government system and we did not consider it in detail because we understood our terms of reference as implying that the services in question should remain the responsibility of local government. In any event we see a high level of citizen participation as vital to the successful development of services which are sensitive to local needs, and we do not see how, at present, this participation can be achieved outside the local government system. It will be clear elsewhere in the report, however, that we see a close partnership between central and local government as crucial to the success of any reorganisation.

But finally the recommendation was for each county council to have one unified social services department:

138.   Finally there are the proposals to set up a new department to meet the social needs of individuals, families, and communities, which would incorporate the present functions of children's and welfare departments, together with elements from the education, health and housing departments, with important additional responsibilities designed to ensure an effective family service.

Before we go on to see how Parliament viewed these recommendations in the Bill which followed, you might like to ponder on whether any of the proposed solutions would have been as good — why do you think social services are better provided as a uniform service for the adults and children? Why is health provided by an elected central government, but community care by elected local government? Have the underlying assumptions about the benefits of a unified approach to meeting needs proved appropriate or is it time for further reorganization? What is the role for local authorities (district councils) in county areas where they do not have a social services function?

The Parliamentary debates

The Bill was introduced by Richard Crossman, Secretary of State for Social Services. In Hansard 26 February 1970 column 1406, he defended the proposed new framework:

The services concerned are organised today on the basis of legislation of 1945 to 1948, and looking back on that legislation now we can see that it did four main things. First, it established a National Health Service in a tripartite form, one of the three parts being a local authority responsibility. Secondly, it established an interlocking system of family allowances, national and industrial insurance and national assistance the combined effect of which was to make the central Government responsible for cash benefits generally. Thirdly, it established on a new footing the local authority social services, known as the 'welfare' group; that is, the accommodation of elderly people who cannot live alone or with their families, the accommodation and welfare of the physically handicapped and temporary accommodation of the homeless. Fourthly, and lastly, it concentrated in a local authority children's service the various forms of care for children deprived for whatever reasons of a normal home life with parents or relatives.

This great body of legislation, taken as a whole, finally broke up the old Poor Law and established for the first time a body of national minimum standards for welfare in the widest sense and thereby created what we now call the Welfare State.

The Minister stated that the three pillars of the post-war welfare state were intended to be a health service, social security and national insurance provision, and personal social services. His speech continues at column 1407:

The primary objective of the personal social services we can best describe as strengthening the capacity of the family to care for its members and to supply, as it were, the family's place where necessary; that is, to provide as far as may be social support or if necessary a home for people who cannot look after themselves or be adequately looked after in their family.

One of the objections which followed in the debates on the Bill, as you will see, was the argument that the legislation amounts to nothing more than a framework: it has nothing to say about the service itself. The minister hinted strongly that this would be temporary; a reorganization of the law could be expected to follow in the wake of local government and NHS reorganisation:

We have not sought *on this occasion* to rewrite the whole of the law on personal social services (column 1411, emphasis added).

Seebohm wanted personal social services to be a local authority service for reasons of local accountability. Why, though, does this argument not apply equally to the delivery of health services? Mr Crossman's justification for the boundaries between health and social services could be described as superficial: the fact that social workers had one set of skills and health professionals another. In other words a national health service and a local personal social service structure was set up for the convenience of the suppliers rather than the needs of the customers.

Lord Balniel, for the opposition, at column 1443 expressed his concerns on this issue. (Despite being a Lord he was actually an MP):

I believe that our task in Committee will very largely be concerned with seeing that this dividing line does not become an 'iron curtain' between the services. We must see that it does not become a new source of division between the health services and the welfare services.

At column 1428 Lord Balniel dealt with the principles — or as he implies, lack of principles — underlying the Bill:

The Bill gathers together in Schedule 1 a series of local authority responsibilities which are today spread among the children's department, the welfare committee and the health committee, and puts them, I believe rightly, into the new social services department. I would make it more dramatic. It should not be just a shuffling around of existing functions. It should be more forward-looking. It should not just be machinery. There should be a declaratory clause of this committee's new general duty to promote social welfare in the community.

Shirley Williams responded to this point for the government in a later debate, at volume 801, 11 May 1970, column 952, when she pointed out that there were already declarations of duties and powers which set out the actual principles of social service: the Children and Young Persons Act 1963 provided a duty to promote welfare of children; the National Assistance Act 1948 set out the duty to provide accommodation for elderly infirm, disabled or homeless, and power to provide it for others, and the Health Service and Public Health Act 1968 established a general power to promote the welfare of the elderly. The new act would not need to repeat these.

Although this list of Acts cited by Mrs Williams is no longer accurate, that remains the position today. LASSA is the Act which tells social services what their functions are, but it does so by referring to the actual powers and duties and procedures set out in other Acts.

So the Act which unifies social work is merely a listing Act. Lord Sanford, who we quote below, predicted that this would be a recipe for confusion. If the law of social work practice is hard to understand, is this in part the cause? Do you think a general duty would make social services more effective? The task of a social worker clearer? Allocation of resources more generous? The rights of the client more enforceable?

When the Bill reached the House of Lords Baroness Serota, for the government, at HL 14 May 1970 column 726, gave the following glowing account of the proposals for a unified local authority social work profession:

For the first time our local authority personal social services will be recognised in law and practice as an entity. Many have said for years that they should be, and some indeed that this reform is now overdue. It will now be possible for the local authorities to plan comprehensively the social services of their area. It will be their responsibility to consider together the provision of social services, social care and social support for children and young persons; for mothers, including unmarried mothers and babies; the elderly, the handicapped and the mentally handicapped: in fact, to provide the comprehensive community based, family orientated service recommended by the Seebohm Committee.

For the opposition Lord Sandford stated with similar euphoria (HL 14 May 1970 column 729):

[S]ince the introduction of this Bill to Parliament we have seen the birth, or maybe it would be better to say the coming of age, of a new profession of British social workers; a new comprehensive unified social work profession now needing to establish itself beside the lawyers, doctors, clergy, soldiers, sailors, airmen and so on.

But he tempered this with the reservation that (HL 14 May 1970 column 731):

[T]here has been a failure to include anywhere in the Bill ... any comprehensive duty to promote social welfare in broad and general terms over the whole area for which each local authority is responsible.

...

Those aspirations are now, I submit, deflated and dragged down to the level of a Schedule at the back of the Bill. It is only by reference to pieces out of this Schedule — such as the Health Services and Public Health Act 1968, Section 12, Section 13, Section 45, and so on; and then by reference back to Section 2, subsection (2), Section 2, subsection (3)(*b*), subsection (4) and so on — that we get any view of what the new department is going to have as its main role. It is clear that we need precision of that kind in legislation such as this, particularly if it involves, as it does, the imposition of mandatory obligations on all county councils, all county boroughs and all the London boroughs. But is it really asking too much to have set out alongside those sections and subsections, 'notwithstandings' and 'without prejudices', *et cetera*, a clause or two describing comprehensively, clearly and accurately the main object of this whole exercise, the whole scope of the Bill, the full role of the new department and the broad duties of those who work in it?

The Local Authority Social Services Act 1970 (LASSA)

LASSA enacts the aspirations of Seebohm and the rhetoric of the legislators. It creates a unified local authority service. It provides the starting point for local authority social workers' duties and powers. Since 1970 it has been heavily amended, and the extracts we provide include those amendments.

Section 1 of the Act defines which local authorities have social service functions:

Councils of non-metropolitan counties, metropolitan districts and London boroughs and the Common Council of the City of London but in Wales shall be the councils of the counties and county boroughs.

Section 2 — which cross refers to Sch. 1 of the Act — defines the duties of the social services committee. The duties are those of the committee and not of the individual social worker. In fact LASSA does not mention social workers at all:

(1)   Every local authority shall establish a social services committee and, subject to subsection (3) below, there shall stand referred to that committee all matters relating to the discharge by the authority of —
  (a)   their functions under the enactments specified in the first column of Schedule 1 to this Act (being the functions which are described in general terms in the second column of that Schedule); and
  (b)   such other of their functions as, by virtue of the following subsection, fall within the responsibility of the committee.
(2)   The Secretary of State may by order designate functions of local authorities under any other enactment for the time being in force as being appropriate for discharge through a local authority's social services committee other than functions which by virtue of that or any other enactment are required to be discharged through some other committee of a local authority; and any functions designated by an order under this section which is for the time being in force shall accordingly fall within the responsibility of the social services committee.

Schedule 1, then, is the definitive list of the different parts of a range of statutes spanning over 70 years which prescribe the functions of the social services committees. You then need to refer to the relevant sections of the various Acts to find the functions themselves. The most important of these will be set out in the relevant statutes on Mental Health, Community Care and Children.

The list of functions is presented in chronological order in sch. 1, starting with the Children and Young Person's Act 1933. Schedule 1 is amended frequently to take out and add in social service functions, so do not be surprised that most of the functions derive from Acts passed after LASSA itself was passed.

Children and Young Persons Act 1933	
Part III	Protection of the young in relation to criminal and summary proceedings; children appearing before court as in need of care, protection or control; committal of children to approved school or care of fit person, etc.
Part IV	Remand homes, approved schools and children in care of fit persons.
National Assistance Act 1948	
Sections 21 to 27	Provision of residential accommodation for the aged, infirm, needy, etc.
Sections 29 and 30	Welfare of persons who are blind, deaf, dumb or otherwise handicapped or are suffering from mental disorder; use of voluntary organisations for administration of welfare schemes.
Sections 43 to 45	Recovery of costs of providing certain services.
Section 48	Temporary protection of property belonging to persons in hospital or accommodation provided under Part III of the Act, etc.
Section 49	Defraying expenses of local authority officer applying for appointment as receiver for certain patients.
Section 56(3) except so far as it relates to an offence under section 47(11)	Prosecution of offences.
Disabled Persons (Employment) Act 1958 section 3	Provision of facilities for enabling disabled persons to be employed or work under special conditions.
Mental Health Act 1959 section 8 and the Registered Homes Act 1984 so far as its provisions relate to mental nursing homes	Welfare and accommodation of mentally disordered persons.
Health Visiting and Social Work (Training) Act 1962	Research into matters relating to local authority welfare services.

section 5(1)(b), and as
extended by section 45(9) of the
Health Services and Public
Health Act 1968

Section 5(1)(c) — Research into matters relating to functions of local authorities.

Children and Young Persons Act 1963 — Powers relating to young persons in need of care, protection or control; further provisions for protection of the young in relation to criminal proceedings.

Health Services and Public
Health Act 1968

Section 45 — Promotion of welfare of old people.

Section 65 — Financial and other assistance to voluntary organisations.

Family Law Reform Act 1969
section 7(4) — Supervision of ward of court.

Adoption Act 1976 — Maintenance of Adoption Service; functions of local authority as adoption agency; applications for orders freeing children for adoption; inquiries carried out by local authorities in adoption cases; care possession, and supervision of children awaiting adoption.

Supplementary Benefits Act
1976 Schedule 5 — Provision and maintenance of resettlement units for persons without a settled way of living.

National Health Service Act
1977 Schedule 8 — Care of Mothers and young children; prevention, care and after-care; home help and laundry facilities.

Mental Health Act 1983 Parts II,
III and VI — Welfare of the mentally disordered; guardianship of persons suffering from mental disorders, including such persons removed to England and Wales from Scotland or Northern Ireland; exercise of functions of nearest relative or persons so suffering.

Sections 66, 67, 69(1) — Exercise of functions of nearest relative in relation to applications and references to Mental Health Review Tribunals.

Section 114 — Appointment of approved social workers.

Section 115 — Entry and inspection.

Section 116 — Welfare of certain hospital patients.

Section 117 — After-care of detained patients.

Section 130 — Prosecutions.

Health and Social Services and
Social Security Adjudications — Charges for local authority welfare services provided under the services

Act 1983 (c 41) Section 17, so far as relating to
Public Health (Control of Disease) Act 1984 Section 46(2) and (5)

enactments mentioned in subsection (2)(a) to (c).
Burial or cremation of person dying in accommodation provided under Part III of the National Assistance Act 1948, and recovery of expenses from his estate.

Disabled Persons (Services, Consultation and Representation) Act 1986 sections 1 to 5, 7 and 8 except in so far as they assign functions to a local authority in their capacity as a local education authority

Representation and assessment of disabled persons.

Children Act 1989
The whole Act, in so far as it confers functions on a local authority within the meaning of that Act.

Welfare reports.
Consent to application for Residence Order in respect of child in care.
Family Assistance Orders.
Functions under Part III of the Act (local authority support for children and families).
Care and supervision.
Protection of children.
Functions in relation to community homes, voluntary homes and voluntary organisations, registered private children's homes, private arrangements for fostering children, child minding and day care for young children.
Research and returns of information.
Functions in relation to children accommodated by health authorities, National Health Service trusts and local education authorities or in residential care, nursing or mental nursing homes or in independent schools, care homes, independent hospitals or schools.

National Health Service and Community Care Act 1990 (c 19)
Section 46

Preparation of plans for community care services.

Section 47

Assessment of needs for community care services.

Education Act 1993 section 166

Help for local education authority in exercising functions under Part III of the Act.

Carers (Recognition and Services) Act 1995 section 1	Assessment of ability of carers to provide care.
Community Care (Direct Payments) Act 1996	Functions in connection with the making of payments to persons in respect of their securing the provision of community care services or services under the Carers and Disabled Carers Act 2000.
Housing Act 1996 section 213(1)(b)	Co-operation in relation to homeless persons and persons threatened with homelessness.
Adoption (Intercountry Aspects) Act 1999 section 2(4)	Functions under Article 9(a) to (c) of the Convention on Protection of Children and Co-operation in respect of Intercountry Adoption, concluded at the Hague on 29th May 1993
Carers and Disabled Children Act 2000 The whole Act, in so far as it confers functions on a local authority within the meaning of that Act	Assessment of carers' needs. Provision of services to carers. Provision of vouchers.

1.2 The social services committee within the local authority

LASSA does not legislate for the creation of social workers, but it does require a social services committee and director, and inevitably these need staff. Our first question is: what is the relationship between the social services committee, its staff, and the rest of the authority? The case which follows, *R v Birmingham City Council, ex parte O* [1982] 1 WLR 679, establishes, to some extent, autonomy for the committee and the social services department. It also raises the issue of confidentiality.

In this case, a pair of foster parents had been approved by the local authority as adoptive parents. But a councillor, not herself a member of the social services committeee, had learned through membership of the housing committee that one of the prospective adopters had a prison record. (We note in passing that this is less likely to happen today, as those coming into contact with children are rigorously vetted.) The councillor felt she had a duty to have this adoption approval re-opened. To succeed in this campaign she would need more information, including access to the social services department records. The social services department had refused the access. The council's lawyer, however, advised the full council to resolve to allow the files to be seen. The adoptive parents applied for a court order to prevent the council allowing the files to be seen by anyone not involved with the social services function.

The key question for the court relates to s 3(3) of LASSA, which states:

A local authority may delegate to their social services committee any of their functions matters relating to which stand referred to the committee by virtue of section 2 of the Act...

This is how Lord Denning and the majority of the judges approached the issue in the Court of Appeal. The name of the councillor who wanted to see the social services records is Mrs Willetts.

On the one hand there is the public interest in maintaining the confidence in the files — so as to ensure that the contents are not communicated any more widely than is necessary. On the other hand, there is the public interest in the members of the council being sufficiently well informed to carry out their duties.

Holding the balance between these two public interests, I am quite clear that the files should be available only to the members of the social services committee and the officers of the social services department. The duties and the responsibilities of the council have been specially delegated to them. There is no need whatever for the files to be shown to other members, like Mrs Willetts, who are not members of the committee and have no particular duty or responsibility in the matter. I think that Mrs Willetts did all that was required of her when she communicated her discoveries to the social services department. They took them all into account and, nevertheless, thought that the foster parents should be recommended as suitable to be adoptive parents. If Mrs Willetts still felt uneasy, she could raise the matter at a full meeting of the council. If they thought it right, they could appoint her to be a member of the social services committee. Then she would be able to see all the files.

Lord Justice Donaldson disagreed with the majority. Although his conclusion was rejected his consideration of the statutory role of social services committees is in itself accurate:

The work done by social workers is not new, but until modern times was undertaken by voluntary organisations, family doctors, the clergy and neighbours. The change to paid and trained workers and the growth of their professionalism are of recent origin. In many ways this is all to the good, particularly the professionalism. Every profession has to develop its own ethics and those ethics must take full account of the circumstances in which the member is working and his or her relationship with those with whom they are working. In the case of the social work professions, this development is taking place, but in some respects it is going astray. Their work necessarily involves acquiring highly confidential and sensitive information from and about those whom they seek to help. Indeed, it would be impossible to obtain such information without an express or implied promise of confidentiality. The social workers' recognition of their own professionalism has led them to speak and think of those whom they seek to help as their 'clients.' This in turn has led some of them to equate their relationship with their 'clients' to that of a doctor, lawyer or accountant with their patients or clients. From this it has been a short step to the belief that professional ethics should and do prevent them revealing the full details of confidential information to anyone other than professional colleagues under seal of professional secrecy, and further prevent them passing on even the substance of this information to anyone other than one who has the immediate responsibility for decision making.

I do not criticise this. Indeed, I applaud the professional instinct which engenders it. But I think that it is to some extent misguided. The fundamental fallacy is to regard a local authority social worker as being in the same position as a general practitioner operating under the

National Health Service. One is not more professional than the other. It is just that they are different. It is no part of the duties of the National Health Service to treat patients. Its function is to provide doctors who will do so. The resulting relationships are (a) employer and employed doctor, and (b) doctor and patient. By contrast, it is the duty of a local authority to care for children and to play a part in the process of their adoption. For this purpose local authorities employ social workers. The resulting relationships are (a) local authority and employed social workers, and (b) local authority, social workers and the 'clients/patients' of both.

Once this is understood, it disposes of the professional objection to revealing confidential information to members of the local authority, on the basis that to do so would be a breach of a professional relationship. In fact, such a dissemination of confidential information still keeps it within the bounds of the professional relationship, since this exists not only between the social worker and the 'client' but also embraces the local authority itself.

The decision of the majority in the Court of Appeal means that, although the social services committee is a part of an elected authority, funded and appointed by it, it has some operational independence, and its duties to its clients can therefore override the wishes of the authority.

The most important of the remaining parts of LASSA are to be found in s 7. These sections set out who the social services committee answers to. (Sections 7 and 7A are cited in *R v Islington LBC, ex parte Rixon* (below) and not reproduced at this stage.)

The Social Services committee may be subject to inquiry or even direct interference by the Secretary of State in relation to failure to carry out their duties properly. The Secretary of State will be informed by the reports of the Social Services Inspectorate, an arm of the Department of Health.

The following sections were inserted into LASSA by the 1990 National Health Service and Community Care Act:

7B(1) The Secretary of State may by order require local authorities to establish a procedure for considering any representations (including any complaints) which are made to them by a qualifying individual, or anyone acting on his behalf, in relation to the discharge of, or any failure to discharge, any of their social services functions in respect of that individual.

(2) In relation to a particular local authority, an individual is a qualifying individual for the purposes of subsection (1) above if —

(a) the authority have a power or a duty to provide, or to secure the provision of, a service for him; and

(b) his need or possible need for such a service has (by whatever means) come to the attention of the authority;

or if he is in receipt of payment from the authority under the Community Care (Direct Payments) Act 1996.

(3) A local authority shall comply with any directions given by the Secretary of State as to the procedure to be adopted in considering representations made as mentioned in subsection (1) above as to the taking of such action as may be necessary in consequence of such representations.

(4) Local authorities shall give such publicity to any procedure established pursuant to this section as they consider appropriate.

7C(1) The Secretary of State may cause an inquiry to be held in any case where, whether on representations made to him or otherwise, he considers it advisable to do so in connection with the exercise by any local authority of any of their social services functions (except in so far as those functions relate to persons under the age of eighteen).

7D(1) If the Secretary of State is satisfied that any local authority have failed, without reasonable excuse, to comply with any of their duties which are social services functions (other than a duty imposed by or under the Children Act 1989), he may make an order declaring that authority to be in default with respect to the duty in question.

(2) An order under subsection (1) may contain such directions for the purpose of ensuring that the duty is complied with within such period as may be specified in the order as appear to the Secretary of State to be necessary.

(3) Any such direction shall, on the application of the Secretary of State, be enforceable by mandamus.

Note that ss. 7C and 7D above seem to omit powers of the Secretary of State to hold an inquiry or make orders where the local authority is alleged to have failed in its duties towards children. This is not the case. Equivalent procedures exist under the Children Act 1989.

24(14) Every local authority shall establish a procedure for considering any representations (including any complaint) made to them by a person qualifying for advice and assistance about the discharge of their functions under this Part in relation to him.

(15) In carrying out any consideration of representations under subsection (14), a local authority shall comply with any regulations made by the Secretary of State for the purposes of this subsection.

24B(1) Every local authority shall establish a procedure for considering representations (including complaints) made to them by —

(a) a relevant child for the purposes of section 23A or a young person falling within section 23C;

(b) a person qualifying for advice and assistance; or

(c) a person falling within section 24B(2),

about the discharge of their functions under this Part in relation to him.

(Section 24B(2) refers to new local authority duties to care leavers under Children (Leaving Care) Act 2000.)

Section 7 of LASSA is not in itself complete. It gives a power to the Secretary of State to compel local authorities to establish a complaints procedure. Has that power been exercised? This question gives an opportunity to examine a piece of delegated legislation. The answer is to be found in the Local Authority Social Services (Complaints Procedure) Order 1990 (SI 2244/1990). This specifies that:

Every local authority shall establish a procedure for considering any representations (including any complaints) which are made to them by a qualifying individual, or anyone acting on his behalf, in relation to the discharge of, or any failure to discharge, any of their social services functions in respect of that individual.

Although perhaps none the wiser as to what the complaints procedure should look like — time limits for answering complaints etc — you now know that such a procedure must exist.

There is another means by which the performance of its duties by the social services committee is to be kept in check. The Audit Commission Act 1998 opens the committee and individual social workers to the following:

37(1) At the request of the Secretary of State, the Commission may assist the Secretary of State in any study designed to improve economy, efficiency, effectiveness and quality of performance in the discharge of social services functions by local authorities.

(4)   If the Commission requires —
    (a)   a local authority included in a study, or
    (b)   an officer or member of such an authority, to supply the Commission or an authorised person with such information as is needed for the purposes of the study, the authority or officer or member shall supply the information.

(5)   If the Commission requires a local authority included in a study to make available for inspection by the Commission or an authorised person documents which relate to the authority and are needed for the purposes of the study, the authority shall make the documents available.

The statutory provisions we have cited make clear that the exercise of social services functions is subject to scrutiny, and if necessary control, by government. If you look again at all of them you will see only one reference to the powers of the courts in all of this, although you probably did not recognise it as such. Section 7D ended with a reference to the word *mandamus*, a Latin term used by the courts to describe a power to compel a public body to take a particular course of action. (In the new court rules it is called a *mandatory order*.) But even where no court procedure is specified, and notwithstanding the clear procedures for complaints, direction, inquiry and intervention set out in s 7, courts can, and do, get involved in supervising local authorities' exercise of their statutory powers. That, in fact, is what most of the remainder of the chapter is about.

1.3 Administrative law — court scrutiny of local authority exercise of statutory functions

1.3.1 A requirement to act reasonably and lawfully

Courts have the power to scrutinise the way public bodies exercise their statutory powers. Lawyers call this type of case administrative law. This scrutiny power affects social services departments but is by no means confined to them, since all public bodies must act in compliance with the law. The next two cases, although old, illustrate the principles. The first relates to a local authority's statutory duty to drain septic tanks and the second to its statutory powers to grant licences to cinemas.

In *Leek* v *Epsom Rural District Council* [1922] 1 KB 383 the court was asked to review the way the authority was, or was not, complying with its duty under s 43 of the Public Health Act 1875. This Act, now superseded, required the local authority to empty a resident's cesspool unless — and here we can see that the law cannot always be drafted with precision — they had a 'reasonable excuse' for not doing so. So what is meant by reasonable and can the authority be compelled to act if their view of a reasonable excuse is different from that of the householder with the overflowing pool?

Under the Act, as is common still in public health cases, the householder could first complain to the magistrates. The case was appealed from there to the King's Bench. The facts are conveniently summarized in the publishers' headnote:

The respondents, the local authority, after having for a considerable time cleansed the cesspools in their district whenever requested so to do by the occupiers of houses, decided that for the future, in view of the expense and the frequency with which emptying of cesspools had to be performed, they would only do this work once every three months, but that if the occupier of any house desired his cesspool to be emptied more frequently they would do so if he bore the cost. The respondents having been required by the appellant, the occupier of a house in the district, to empty his cesspool free of cost before the expiration of three months since it was last emptied, and they having failed to comply with his requirement, the appellant took proceedings against them under s. 43 of the Public Health Act, 1875, in respect of their failure. The justices dismissed the complaint, finding that the respondents' decision to cleanse the cesspools in the district every three months was in the circumstances reasonable and sufficient and that the respondents had a 'reasonable excuse' within s. 43 for not complying with the appellant's requirement:

Lord Trevithin dismissed the householder's appeal:

The justices in finding that the respondents had a 'reasonable excuse' for not complying with the appellant's request had evidence before them upon which they could so find. The respondents had already emptied nearly 30,000 gallons from this cesspool during the year and they were willing to empty it whenever requested, upon payment. The respondents had, in those circumstances, a 'reasonable excuse' for not complying with the appellant's notice. Whether the undertaking to empty cesspools at certain intervals is reasonable must be judged by reference to the needs of the community as a whole, and not to the case of a particular individual who wants an excessive amount of user of his cesspool. If the justices thought, as they did, that, upon the facts before them, an undertaking by the respondents to empty the cesspools in the district every three months was reasonable, they were entitled to come to that conclusion. The appeal must therefore be dismissed.

The case appears to make the analysis of what is reasonable easy. The next case might reinforce your view that this area of law is not rocket science. The defining case is *Associated Provincial Picture Houses Limited* v *Wednesbury Corporation* [1948] 1 KB 223. The 1932 Sunday Entertainments Act had loosened up restrictions on cinemas opening on a Sunday, by delegating to the local authority the decision on what should be permitted. Wednesbury Corporation — remember this is 1948 — declared that it would be bad for the welfare of children and so Sunday showings should exclude anyone under 15. The court was asked by the cinema owners to declare that this decision was *ultra vires* (Latin for outside its legal powers) since the moral welfare of children had not been referred to in the legislation. Lord Greene MR stated the law to be as follows:

The courts must always, I think, remember this: first, we are dealing with not a judicial act, but an executive act; secondly, the conditions which, under the exercise of that executive act, may be imposed are in terms, so far as language goes, put within the discretion of the local authority without limitation. Thirdly, the statute provides no appeal from the decision of the local authority.

What, then, is the power of the courts? They can only interfere with an act of executive authority if it be shown that the authority has contravened the law. It is for those who assert that the local authority has contravened the law to establish that proposition. On the face of it, a condition of the kind imposed in this case is perfectly lawful. It is not to be assumed prima facie that responsible bodies like the local authority in this case will exceed their powers; but the court, whenever it is alleged that the local authority have contravened the law, must not substitute itself for that authority. It is only concerned with seeing whether or not the proposition is made good. When an executive discretion is entrusted by Parliament to a body such as the local authority in this case, what appears to be an exercise of that discretion can only be challenged in the courts in a strictly limited class of case. As I have said, it must always be remembered that the court is not a court of appeal. When discretion of this kind is granted the law recognizes certain principles upon which that discretion must be exercised, but within the four corners of those principles the discretion, in my opinion, is an absolute one and cannot be questioned in any court of law. What then are those principles? They are well understood. They are principles which the court looks to in considering any question of discretion of this kind. The exercise of such a discretion must be a real exercise of the discretion. If, in the statute conferring the discretion, there is to be found expressly or by implication matters which the authority exercising the discretion ought to have regard to, then in exercising the discretion it must have regard to those matters. Conversely, if the nature of the subject-matter and the general interpretation of the Act make it clear that certain matters would not be germane to the matter in question, the authority must disregard those irrelevant collateral matters. There have been in the cases expressions used relating to the sort of things that authorities must not do, not merely in cases under the Cinematograph Act but, generally speaking, under other cases where the powers of local authorities came to be considered. I am not sure myself whether the permissible grounds of attack cannot be defined under a single head. It has been perhaps a little bit confusing to find a series of grounds set out. Bad faith, dishonesty — those of course, stand by themselves — unreasonableness, attention given to extraneous circumstances, disregard of public policy and things like that have all been referred to, according to the facts of individual cases, as being matters which are relevant to the question. If they cannot all be confined under one head, they at any rate, I think, overlap to a very great extent. For instance, we have heard in this case a great deal about the meaning of the word 'unreasonable.'

It is true the discretion must be exercised reasonably. Now what does that mean? Lawyers familiar with the phraseology commonly used in relation to exercise of statutory discretions often use the word 'unreasonable' in a rather comprehensive sense. It has frequently been used and is frequently used as a general description of the things that must not be done. For instance, a person entrusted with a discretion must, so to speak, direct himself properly in law. He must call his own attention to the matters which he is bound to consider. He must exclude from his consideration matters which are irrelevant to what he has to consider. If he does not obey those rules, he may truly be said, and often is said, to be acting 'unreasonably.' Similarly, there may be something so absurd that no sensible person could ever dream that it lay within the powers of the authority. Warrington LJ in *Short* v *Poole Corporation* [1926] Ch. 66, 90, 91 gave the example of the red-haired teacher, dismissed because she had red hair. That is unreasonable in one sense. In another sense it is taking into consideration extraneous matters. It is so unreasonable that it might almost be described as being done in bad faith; and, in fact, all these things run into one another.

...

It is clear that the local authority are entrusted by Parliament with the decision on a matter which the knowledge and experience of that authority can best be trusted to deal with. The subject-matter with which the condition deals is one relevant for its consideration. They have considered it and come to a decision upon it. It is true to say that, if a decision on a competent matter is so unreasonable that no reasonable authority could ever have come to it, then the courts can interfere. That, I think, is quite right; but to prove a case of that kind would require something overwhelming, and, in this case, the facts do not come anywhere near anything of that kind. ... The effect of the legislation is not to set up the court as an arbiter of the correctness of one view over another. It is the local authority that are set in that position and, provided they act, as they have acted, within the four corners of their jurisdiction, this court, in my opinion, cannot interfere.

...

In the result, this appeal must be dismissed. I do not wish to repeat myself but I will summarize once again the principle applicable. The court is entitled to investigate the action of the local authority with a view to seeing whether they have taken into account matters which they ought not to take into account, or, conversely, have refused to take into account or neglected to take into account matters which they ought to take into account. Once that question is answered in favour of the local authority, it may be still possible to say that, although the local authority have kept within the four corners of the matters which they ought to consider, they have nevertheless come to a conclusion so unreasonable that no reasonable authority could ever have come to it. In such a case, again, I think the court can interfere. The power of the court to interfere in each case is not as an appellate authority to override a decision of the local authority, but as a judicial authority which is concerned, and concerned only, to see whether the local authority have contravened the law by acting in excess of the powers which Parliament has confided in them. The appeal must be dismissed with costs.

Lord Greene's statement represents, over half a century later, the legal principles involved where courts are asked to declare that a social services department has behaved unlawfully in the exercise, or refusal to exercise, its statutory duties and powers. Local authorities must act within their legal powers, which come from statutes, or not act at all. If the statute grants them discretion, they must exercise it in a 'Wednesbury reasonable' way.

1.3.2 Court review of community care services

We will take you through a sample of cases which show how a person can challenge the social services department in court in a claim that the local authority has acted illegally. Court action is a measure of last resort: few clients will obtain the funding, and the normal challenge is by way of complaint to the department, the ombudsman or to a councillor. Courts will generally not consider a legal challenge if the complainant could have used the complaints procedure set out in LASSA (above). A court will only intervene if the authority has acted illegally. That means it has not carried out its statutory duties in a legal manner.

But these statutory duties, particularly in relation to community care services, are often confusing. We suggested above that deciding if statutory duties have been undertaken lawfully or unlawfully might not be rocket science. Let's change the metaphor. If urban growth can be an analogy, these social services statutory duties have grown up like a shantytown and they could now do with demolition and rebuilding. But they are the law. The courts' judgments have to relate to that complexity, and judges will have to find a pathway through that confusion. You will, in the extracts reproduced, encounter some microscopic examination of the exact wording of the statutory duties, of government guidance and of what the judges said. It is not easy to predict the right answer.

In the case extracts which follow you will be introduced to some of the legislation relating to community care services for adults, where the worst confusion arises, and to services for children in need and child protection. This is only a taster: the legislation will be introduced to you more systematically in the relevant chapters later. You only need at this stage to be aware that there is a wide range of statutory duties, contained in a number of different Acts, and to follow the gist of the various judges' reasoning as they grapple with the question of whether they have the power to review the way the various departments have carried out their duties or exercised their powers, and to overturn their decisions.

The case of *Avon County Council* v *Hooper* [1997] 1 WLR 1605 nicely illustrates the difficulties predicted in the parliamentary debates above, preceding LASSA. It concerns confusion over the overlap between health care (provided, as you may recall from the debates, by national government) and social care (provided by local government). The factual background is that a child, Daniel Hooper, had been seriously brain damaged at birth and had died at age 13. Daniel had lived from age three, when he left hospital, in a residential home at the expense of the local authority. As you will see in Chapter 4, the local authority was supporting Daniel under statutory duties set out in the 1948 National Assistance Act, s 29 and the 1997 National Health Act. The legislation, set out below, allowed the department to make a charge for the residential care. Up to now it had not seen fit to do so. But then they learned that the Health Authority had admitted it was responsible for the brain damage caused by its negligence during Daniel's birth. This meant they were liable to Daniel's estate for substantial financial damages. The local authority at this point recognized that part of the damages would be the extra costs incurred by the family in providing care for Daniel, so they sued to recover these costs from the estate, knowing that the cost would be passed to the Health Authority. For this reason the argument becomes a dispute about liability between the Health Authority saying the charges should not be imposed retrospectively and social services saying they are entitled to charge in the circumstances.

Set out below is the statutory power to make charges, set out in the Health and Social Security Adjudications Act 1983, s 17. We have emphasized *in italics* the important words.

(1)   Subject to subsection (3) below, an authority providing a service to which this section applies *may recover such charge (if any) for it as they consider reasonable.*
(2)   This section applies to services provided under the following enactments — (a) section 29 of the National Assistance Act 1948 (welfare arrangements for blind, deaf, dumb and crippled persons etc.); (b) section 45(1) of the Health Services and Public Health Act 1968 (welfare of old people); (c) Schedule 8 to the National Health Service Act 1977 (care of mothers and young children, prevention of illness and care and after-care and home help and laundry facilities); (d) section 8 of the Residential Homes Act 1980 (meals and recreation for old people); and (e) paragraph one of Part II of Schedule 9 to this Act.
(3)   If a person — (a) avails himself of a service to which this section applies, and (b) satisfies the authority providing the service that his means are insufficient for it to be reasonably practicable for him to pay for the service the amount which he would otherwise be obliged to pay for it, *the authority shall not require him to pay more for it than it appears to them that it is reasonably practicable for him to pay.*

The question of law in the case was whether it was *reasonable* to impose charges so long after they had been incurred? Note how important the question of 'reasonableness' is in the Court of Appeal's judgment. (You will see a barrister referred to in the judgment called Mr Grace; he was arguing the case for the Health Authority, that the imposition of charges was unreasonable.)

Hobhouse LJ: It is implicit both in the language of the section and in the general law governing the activities of local authorities that the power must be exercised reasonably, that is to say, that the local authority must have relevant and reasonable grounds for choosing to exercise the power. Nothing turns upon how one construes the final words of the subsection 'such charge (if any) for it as they consider reasonable.' As a matter of language, these words carry the implication that the charge may be waived and that the local authority need only make any charge if it considers it reasonable to do so. Thus, there is an overriding criterion of reasonableness which governs the local authority's exercise of the power which is given by subsection (1).

This criterion of reasonableness provides the primary answer to the arguments of Mr Grace. If the right to charge has been waived, clearly no charge can be recovered. If the service was provided in circumstances under which it would be unreasonable for the authority subsequently to charge for it, then the authority is not entitled later to seek to recover a charge. Similarly, if, having provided a service, the local authority seeks to recover a charge, it must be prepared to justify the reasonableness of doing so. The reasonableness of any conduct falls to be assessed at the time of the relevant conduct and having regard to all the relevant circumstances then existing. If the claim is first made some time after the provision of the services, the local authority must be prepared to justify the reasonableness of making the claim notwithstanding the delay. If the local authority is acting unreasonably, its claim will fail. If the local authority is acting reasonably, there is no basis in subsection (1) [of s. 17 of the Act] for the person availing himself of the service to say that the local authority should not recover.

If the local authority decides to charge and is acting reasonably in doing so, the person availing himself of the service has, in those circumstances, to satisfy the authority under subsection (3) that his means are insufficient for it to be reasonably practicable for him to pay the amount which he would otherwise be obliged to pay. It is for the recipient of the service to discharge this burden of persuasion. He must show that he has insufficient means. The time at which he has to do this is the time when the local authority is seeking to charge him for the services. If his means have been reduced, as might be the case with a businessman whose business had run into difficulties after his being injured, the reduction in his means is something upon which he would be entitled to rely as making it impracticable for him to pay, even though at an earlier date he might have been better off. The consideration under subsection (3)(b) is the practical one: are his means such that it is not reasonably practicable for him to pay?

This also bears on the alternative argument of Mr Grace that only cash should be taken into account. This is too narrow a reading of subsection (3). As a matter of the ordinary use of English, the word 'means' refers to the financial resources of a person: his assets, his sources of income, his liabilities and expenses. If he has a realisable asset, that is part of his means; he has the means to pay. The subject matter of paragraph (b) is the practicability of his paying. If he has an asset which he can reasonably be expected to realise and which will (after taking into account any other relevant factor) enable him to pay, his means make it practicable for him to pay.

Where the person has a right to be indemnified by another against the cost of the service, he has the means to pay. He can enforce his right and make the payment. There is nothing in any part of section 17 which suggests that it intended that subsection (3) should have the effect of relieving those liable to indemnify the recipient of the service for the cost of the service from their liability. On the contrary, it is clear that the intention of the section is to enable the local authority to recover the cost, save when it is unreasonable that it should do so or impracticable for the recipient to pay. The argument of the health authority would, if accepted, frustrate the clear intention of the section.

...

The primary duty of the local authority is to provide the services to those in need of them. The power to charge is consequential upon the provision of the service. Whether it is reasonable to charge has to be considered at an appropriate time which will not necessarily be before the time the services are rendered and will most probably be later when the local authority has put itself in possession of the relevant information. Similarly, the question of means and the practicability of paying will very often have to be the subject of later inquiry and consideration. Once it is recognised that the local authority must act reasonably, the section can be seen to have a sensible and practicable scheme which is not subject to the artificial restraint for which Mr Grace argues.

As regards the reasonableness of taking into account after-acquired means under subsection (3), no problem arises in the present case. Daniel's cause of action against the health authority was something of which he was possessed from before the time that the county council first provided him with any services. The reasonableness of the county council's conduct in demanding that the charges be paid once it learnt of his right of recovery was considered at the trial. The county council manifestly acted reasonably and no argument to the contrary has been advanced before us.

Reasonableness is a key criterion for the courts reviewing decisions of the social services department. But sometimes the courts will refuse to hear arguments at all, on the basis that the law provides other ways of resolving disputes about the department's decisions. Judicial review by the court is a last resort when no other means exists to test the legality of the department's decision.

The case of *R v Kirklees MBC, ex p Good* [1998] 1 CCLR 506 illustrates the reluctance of the courts to get involved. The justification for ducking out is that LASSA s 7 establishes the way of handling a dispute between the individual and the authority. The case also illustrates the problems over the lack of a unifying set of statutory duties which, you may recall, were criticised in the parliamentary debates. The complexity of the legislation and confusion of duties will be apparent not just in this case but again and again. The facts of the case are set out in Mr Justice Popplewell's judgment. The case turns on the question of whether the community care legislation requires social services departments to assess and provide for carers in their own right as well as for the clients (in this case the disabled elderly clients Mr and Mrs Good) themselves.

The first part of the argument of the Goods' carers is reproduced to show two things: firstly, the complexity of the range of legislation involved in making a simple decision about whether to provide financial assistance to the carers; secondly how judges will generally read the legislation quite restrictively — they will generally read it literally, without adding words which would allow them to arrive at a more compassionate result:

Mr Justice Popplewell: The facts of this case are sad. The applicants, Mr and Mrs Good senior, are an elderly married couple who have disabling medical conditions. It is not necessary to set them out and they have been getting very much worse.

They live in a house on the ground floor where the conditions are such that it is quite inappropriate that they should go on living there in those conditions, unless some steps are taken to provide them, among other things, with a bath and other facilities.

Living on the floor above them are Mr and Mrs Good junior, as they have been described. They have four children. It is a small three-bedroomed house and they are living in a degree of considerable discomfort. Mr and Mrs Good junior are full-time carers for Mr and Mrs Good senior and Mr Good has given up his job in order to act as a full-time carer and they are much to be commended for their loyalty and devotion to the Good seniors.

The issues which now arise in this case are really twofold: there has been an application under the Housing Act for a grant to improve the condition of this house. The dispute between the parties now, although this dispute had been going on for a long time, is not as to the ground floor, where it is now agreed that a grant should be given for the benefit of Mr and Mrs Good senior and to some extent that will alleviate their position, the argument is whether the Council should not provide a grant so that Mr and Mrs Good junior and their children can have improved conditions so that, as it is put, Mr and Mrs Good can more tenderly care for Mr and Mrs Good senior and, therefore, that they should provide a grant to Mr Good so that he can obtain a mortgage, because he is not able to work, he is unable to keep the premises.

...

The question of the liability of the Council to assist the Good juniors is said to arise under the Carers Act which is a recent piece of legislation. It is called the Carers (Recognition and Services) Act 1995. It is an Act that provides for the assessment and ability of carers to provide care and for connecting purposes. Section 1 is headed 'Assessment of ability of carers to provide care: England and Wales':

'(1)   Subject to subsection (3) below, in any case where —
    (a) a local authority carry out an assessment under section 47(1)(a) of the National Health
          Service and Community Care Act 1990 of the needs of a person ("the relevant person")
          for community care services, and
    (b) an individual ("the carer") provides or intends to provide a substantial amount of care
          on a regular basis for the relevant person,
the carer may request the local authority, before they make their decision as to whether the needs of the relevant person call for the provision of any services, to carry out an assessment of his ability to provide and continue to provide care for the relevant person; and if he makes such a request, the local authority shall carry out such an assessment and shall take into account the results of that assessment in making that decision.'

It is submitted on behalf of the Council that that is only designed to have regard to the actual ability of a carer, that is to say to make sure they are fit enough, intelligent enough and so on, to carry out the job of caring.

Looking at the basis upon which the Act was brought, it seems to me to have somewhat wider purpose and that is to say to ensure that for instance a carer who is not living in such a condition that he or she is not able to carry out the duty of carer properly.

However, it is clear that simply making an assessment does not get anyone anywhere. Unless there is power under this Act to make the sort of provision which it is suggested should be made for the Good juniors, there is nothing in the Act which appears to me to require the local authority to give a grant in respect of the premises upstairs.

The request, it is clear, has been made under the Carers Act. It is clear from s 1 of the Carers Act that the provisions relate to community care services which have the meaning given by s 46(2) of the National Health Service and Community Care Act 1990. It is equally clear that those provisions mean services which may be made under the National Assistance Act, the Health Services and Public Health Act, National Health Service Act and the Mental Health Act. None of those are relevant to the instant application.

The application for the grant is under the Local Government and Housing Act. In my judgment, the argument which the local authority have put forward, namely, that the Carers Act is not relevant to the present exercise is a correct one.

It is sought to be said that s 2 of the Chronically Sick and Disabled Persons Act 1970 had an application in the instant case. Section 2 reads as follows:

'(1)   Where a local authority having functions under section 29 of the National Assistance
    Act 1948 are satisfied in the case of any person to whom that section applies who is ordinarily

resident in their area that it is necessary in order to meet the needs of that person for that authority to make arrangements for all or any of the following matters, namely —

    (a) the provision of practical assistance for that person in his home;

…

    (e) the provision of assistance for that person in arranging for carrying out of any works of adaptation in his home or the provision of any additional facilities designed to secure his greater safety, comfort or convenience; …'

I do not read s 2 as putting or casting any duty on the local authority to provide the Good juniors with an adaptation for their premises, which no doubt, will provide greater safety, comfort and convenience to them as obligating the local authority to provide that circumstance to the Goods themselves, that is to say, that while they are under an obligation to secure the adaptation for the benefit of the Good seniors they are not under any obligation to secure the adaptation of the premises which the Good juniors presently occupy.

Accordingly, it seems to me that although there is an interesting academic argument that the local authority are under a duty if requested to carry out an assessment of Mr and Mrs Good junior, in the instant case such an assessment would be no practical use whatsoever.

The other line of argument of the court also went against the Goods:

Finally, there is a further point taken by the local authority, namely, that by the Local Authority Social Services Act 1970, ss 7B to 7D, there is provision made whereby if the local authority fail to carry out their statutory duties the Secretary of State may cause an enquiry to be held and if he is satisfied that a local authority has failed to comply with any of their duties they may make an order declaring the authority being at fault which is the same power that this court has.

It is submitted on behalf of the local authority that in compliance with the well known cases that if there is an alternative remedy judicial review should not lie, that this application in any case is doomed to failure.

That last point seems also to me to be decisive of this case in addition to the points that I have already made. I fear I have not done full justice to all the arguments that have been put before me, but in the end the points come down to very simple ones and whatever sympathies one may have with the young Goods in their situation, I am sorry to say that these applications must be dismissed.

R v Islington LBC, ex p Rixon [1998] 1 CCLR 119 is another sad case. It throws up an issue under LASSA s 7, which is the legal effect of guidance and directions issued by the Secretary of State under s 7(1) and 7A. Mr Justice Sedley's opening remarks sum up the limited role the law can play:

This application for judicial review concerns alleged failures of the London Borough of Islington to make provision according to law for the social, recreational and educational needs of the applicant, Jonathan Rixon, who is now 25 and suffers from Seckels syndrome. He is blind, microcephalic, practically immobile, doubly incontinent and largely unable to communicate. He suffers from severe deformities of the chest and spine, a hiatus hernia and a permanent digestive disorder. His size and weight are those of a small child, but his helplessness and dependency are those of a baby. He is reliant on the devoted care of his mother and of others who assist her.

With the support of concerned organisations the applicant's mother has for some time now been in dispute with her local authority, the London Borough of Islington, about the provision of statutory services suitable to Jonathan's needs and condition. The dispute has now reached this court, and although it has been conducted on both sides with moderation and with a shared concern for Jonathan's welfare, it has presented the court with problems some of which are beyond the competence of courts of law. This judgment is confined to those issues which I consider to be justiciable and on which the evidence is sufficiently clear to enable me to reach a conclusion. It deliberately avoids incursion into difficult and sensitive areas of specialised decision-making, some of them within the local authority's province and some within that of Jonathan's carers.

Sedley J (the J afterwards is shorthand for saying Mr/Ms/Mrs Justice) goes on to discuss the relevant law:

Some of the relevant legislation contains what are known as 'target duties'. This is a phrase coined by Woolf LJ in *R v Inner London Education Authority, ex parte Ali* (1990) 2 Admin LR 822, 828, in relation to the duty created by section 8 of the Education Act 1944 for every local education authority to secure that there are in their area schools sufficient in number, character and equipment to afford education to pupils of all ages, abilities and aptitudes. The metaphor recognises that the statute requires the relevant public authority to aim to make the prescribed provision but does not regard failure to achieve it without more as a breach.

By section 46 of the National Health Service and Community Care Act 1990 local authorities are required to publish and keep under review a plan for the provision of community care services in their area. By section 47(1) it is provided that, subject to exceptions which are not presently material:

'...where it appears to a local authority that any person for whom they may provide or arrange for the provision of community care services may be in need of any such services, the authority —

(a) shall carry out an assessment of his needs for those services; and

(b) having regard to the results of that assessment, shall then decide whether his needs call for the provision by them of any such services.'

By subsection (2) this duty is extended, in the case of a disabled person, to deciding under section 4 of the Disabled Persons (Services, Consultation and Representation) Act 1986, whether the disabled person's needs call for the provision by the authority of welfare services under section 2(1) of the Chronically Sick and Disabled Persons Act 1970 — exercise in which, by section 8 of the Act of 1986, regard is to be had to the carer's ability to provide continuing regular care.

So far, therefore, the legislation creates a duty to assess the needs of a disabled person and to decide what local authority provision they call for, but not to implement the decision.

It is section 2(1) of the Chronically Sick and Disabled Persons Act 1970 which creates the principal duty to respond to assessed need. Because it is predicated upon section 29 of the National Assistance Act 1948, it is first necessary to set out the latter provision in its amended form:

'(1) A local authority may, with the approval of the Secretary of State, and to such extent as he may direct in relation to persons ordinarily resident in the area the local authority shall make arrangements for promoting the welfare of persons to whom this section applies, that is to say persons aged 18 or over who are blind ... or who suffer from mental disorder of any description, and other persons aged 18 or over who are substantially and permanently handicapped by ... congenital deformity ...'

Subsection (4) gives examples of arrangements which may be made under subsection (1), including instruction and recreation. All provision under this section comes within the definition of community care services for the purposes of the National Health Service and Community Care Act 1990: see section 46(3) of that Act.

In relation to such persons, section 2(1) of the Act 1970 provides:

'Where a local authority having functions under section 29 of the National Assistance Act 1948 are satisfied in the case of any person to whom that section applies who is ordinarily resident in their area that it is necessary in order to meet the needs of that person for that authority to make arrangements for all or any of the following matters, namely ...

(c) the provision for that person of lectures, games, outings or other recreational facilities outside his home or assistance to that person in taking advantage of educational facilities available to him;

then, subject to the provisions of section 7(1) of the Local Authority Social Services Act 1970 (which requires local authorities in the exercise of certain functions, including functions under the said section 29, to act under the general guidance of the Secretary of State) ... it shall be the duty of that authority to make those arrangements in the exercise of their functions under the said section 29.'

This section, therefore, creates a positive duty to arrange for recreational and 'gateway' educational facilities for disabled persons. It is, counsel agree, a duty owed to the individual and not simply a target duty. I will come later to the question of its legal ambit and content. It introduces in turn section 7(1) of the Local Authority Social Services Act 1970:

'Local authorities shall, in the exercise of their social services functions, including the exercise of any discretion conferred by any relevant enactment, act under the general guidance of the Secretary of State.'

He then turns to the issue of the guidance issued by the Secretary of State. Reading this — it may take some careful study to understand — will reveal that the authority cannot ignore the guidance altogether, but that it can act with considerable latitude so long as it pays attention to the guidance:

What is the meaning and effect of the obligation to 'act under the general guidance of the Secretary of State'? Clearly guidance is less than direction, and the word 'general' emphasises the non-prescriptive nature of what is envisaged.

...

The Secretary of State between the passage and the coming into force of the National Health Service and Community Care Act 1990 issued guidance under section 7 of the 1970 Act which remains in force, 'Caring for People: Community care in the next decade and beyond'. It describes itself as 'policy guidance', setting out what government expects of statutory authorities and the framework within which community care should be planned and implemented, distinguishing this from how, by good practice, to give effect to the policy guidance. It allocates the latter to three processes: assessment, design of a care package, and implementation and monitoring of the package. Under the heading 'Care Plans' the guidance says:

'3.24 Once needs have been assessed, the services to be provided or arranged and the objectives of any intervention should be agreed in the form of a care plan.'

It then sets out a broad order of priorities, starting with 'Support for the user in his or her own home' and moving through alternative forms of accommodation. In particular it says:

'3.25 The aim should be to secure the most cost-effective package of services that meets the user's care needs, taking into account the user's and carer's own preferences. Where supporting the user in a home of their own would provide a better quality of life, this is to be preferred to admission to residential or nursing home care. However, local authorities also have a responsibility to meet needs within the resources available and this will sometimes involve difficult decisions where it will be necessary to strike a balance between meeting the needs identified within available resources and meeting the care preferences of the individual.

Where agreement between all parties is not possible, the points of difference should be recorded.

3.26 Decisions on service provision should include clear agreement about what is going to be done, by whom and by when, with clearly identified points of access to each of the relevant agencies for the service user, carers and for the care manager.'

Returning, then, to section 29 of the National Assistance Act 1948, this section operates in tandem with section 2(1) of the Act of 1970. Not only does the latter trigger a duty to exercise the functions spelt out in the former; the former contains its own trigger provision in the form of any direction given by the Secretary of State, the effect of which is to make mandatory what is otherwise discretionary under the section. The Secretary of State has given such directions, initially in 1974 and now in a consolidating measure captioned 'Secretary of State's Approvals and Directions under Section 29(1) of the National Assistance Act 1948', published as an appendix to departmental circular LAC(93)10 and coming into force on 1st April 1993. Paragraph 2 of the Approvals and Directions provides:

'(1) The Secretary of State hereby approves the making by local authorities of arrangements under section 29(1) of the Act [of 1948] for all persons to whom that subsection applies and directs local authorities to make arrangements under section 29(1) of the Act in relation to persons who are ordinarily resident in their area for all or any of the following purposes —

    (b) to provide, whether at centres or elsewhere, facilities for social rehabilitation and adjustment to disability including assistance in overcoming limitations of mobility or communication;

    (c) to provide, whether at centres or elsewhere facilities for occupational, social, cultural and recreational activities ...'

...

The pattern, in broad terms, is therefore this. For people with such disabilities and needs as Jonathan's, the local authority is to assess the individual's needs and to decide accordingly which community care and welfare services those needs call for. The local authority is then required to make arrangements for the provision for that individual of recreational and gateway educational facilities and 'in relation to' such persons, for rehabilitative and adjustment facilities and for social and cultural activities.

...

A failure to comply with the statutory policy guidance is unlawful and can be corrected by means of judicial review: *R v North Yorkshire County Council, ex parte Hargreaves* (1997) 1 CCLR 104 (Dyson J, 30th September 1994). Beyond this, there will always be a variety of factors which the local authority is required on basic public law principles to take into account. Prominent among these will be any recommendations made in the particular case by a review panel: *R v Avon County Council, ex parte M* [1994] 2 FLR 1006 (Henry J). In contradistinction to statutory policy guidance, a failure to comply with a review panel's recommendations is not by itself a breach of the law; but the greater the departure, the greater the need for cogent articulated reasons if the court is not to infer that the panel's recommendations have been overlooked.

The Court finally considered whether the authority had acted illegally in their response to Jonathan's assessed needs in the light of the government guidance. The Court concluded that a decision which is based entirely on lack of resources, taken separately from the assessment of Jonathan's needs, is illegal. (The reference to Miss Richards is to Jonathan's barrister.)

Until July 1990 Jonathan went to a special needs school where, it appears, he enjoyed the company and learnt some elementary skills such as holding a cup and using a spoon. Since leaving school, such intermittent care provision as has been made for him has not preserved these skills. SCOPE (formerly the Spastics Society) believes that Jonathan has more potential than has been appreciated. But in attempting to make provision for him the respondent local authority, recognising a shortfall (though not one as great as Mrs Rixon contends), has been forced to plead a lack of the necessary resources. It is not necessary for me to recount the unhappy history in any detail. It included, however, a complaint by Mrs Rixon that the assessment of Jonathan's needs completed in August 1993 was deficient. In July 1994 a panel of the local authority concluded that:

'... there should be an immediate thorough review of the care plan — and continuing reviews thereafter — to ensure that Jonathan's care package was in response to and maintains a balance between, his recreational, therapeutic, educational and rehabilitative needs and his mother's concerns that he remains close to home. The Panel would expect the revised care plan to demonstrate in detail how the individual activities in the care plan will try to meet Jonathan's identified needs, and will reverse the deterioration in Jonathan's skills since he left school.

The Panel expressed the clear view that the current care plan is not a satisfactory document as it does not make clear how the specific services being provided are intended to meet Jonathan's needs.'

The panel was also critical of the want of communication with Mrs Rixon and of delay in decision-making. In consequence of the report the local authority carried out a reassessment of Jonathan's community care needs, formulating its reassessment in the new care plan of February 1995 which has been the immediate focus of the present challenge.

It is Miss Richards' first submission that in order to comply with the statutory duties, both personal and 'target', and to demonstrate that regard has been had to other relevant matters, the local authority must prepare a care plan which addresses the issues required by law and, where it deviates from the target, explains in legally acceptable terms why it is doing so. Mr McCarthy responds by pointing out first of all that nowhere in the legislation is a care plan, by that or any other name, required. This Miss Richards accepts, but she contends, in my judgment rightly, that she is entitled to look to the care plan (which is commended in the statutory policy guidance) as the best available evidence of whether and how the local authority has addressed Jonathan's case in the light of its statutory obligations. If, of course, further evidential material bears on this question, it too is admissible in relation to the challenge before the court. In other words, as I think Mr McCarthy accepts, his submission that a care plan is nothing more than a clerical record of what has been decided and what is planned, far from marginalising the care plan, places it at the centre of any scrutiny of the local authority's due discharge of its functions. As paragraph 3.24 of the policy guidance indicates, a care plan is the means by which the local authority assembles the relevant information and applies it to the statutory ends, and hence affords good evidence to any inquirer of the due discharge of its statutory duties. It cannot, however, be quashed as if it were a self-implementing document.

The 1995 care plan tabulates Jonathan's needs, beginning with all the things that he cannot do for himself and continuing:

'(12) Jonathan needs opportunities for social contact and to meet people and be with people on a regular basis, particularly people of his own age.

(13) Jonathan needs access to recreational activities, including opportunities to use and explore different equipment. He needs opportunities to exercise his choice and show his preferences.

(14) Jonathan needs regular exercise and his carers need ongoing advice on the management of his physiotherapy needs.

(15) Jonathan needs companionship and physical contact.

(16) Jonathan needs help in breaking habits stemming from boredom, i.e. grinding his teeth, bashing and pawing his face.

(17) Jonathan needs daytime activities which will stimulate and promote his sensory, physical, intellectual and emotional capabilities.

(18) Jonathan needs suitable transport when travelling outdoors and an escort at all times.

(19) Jonathan needs someone to wheel his buggy for him.

(20) Jonathan needs his personal and daycare needs to be provided within a warm and safe environment.

(21) Jonathan needs his care needs to be met by people who have time to get to know him well in order that they can understand his verbal and non-verbal communication and that he can recognise them.'

The challenges

First Miss Richards points to the current timetable of provision for Jonathan. It includes some provision on every day of the week from a variety of sources including the Independent Living Fund. There is respite care on two days. But the only positive provision made by Islington is through its Shape Project from 1.30 p.m. to 5.00 p.m. on Friday afternoons for massage and from 2.00 p.m. to 5.00 p.m. on Wednesdays for swimming with the Flexiteam service. The latter, however, is subject to a fallback plan of attendance at home from 3.30 p.m. to 5.00 p.m. if swimming is not available; and the evidence indicates that this has been the more usual situation, often because of the want of specially trained lifesavers at the swimming bath. The massage session on Fridays is funded by the local authority but is actually provided by a Crossroads worker. It is Miss Richards' submission that this care plan is so deficient as to amount to a non-compliance with the statutory and related duties of the local authority.

The practice guidance to which I have referred counsels against trimming the assessment of need to fit the available provision. For reasons I have given, this properly reflects the law. The guidance then counsels the inclusion of specific objectives for each relevant service provider and an agreement with each service provider as to how each service is to be delivered and measured. It also counsels:

'Having completed the care plan, the practitioner shall identify any assessed need which it has not been possible to address and for what reason. This information should be fed back for service planning and quality assurance. It needs to be recorded and collated in a systematic way.'

Its model outline of a care plan proposes the following headings:

The overall objectives

The specific objectives of

– users

– carers

– service providers

The criteria for measuring the achievement of these objectives

The services to be provided by which personnel/agency

The cost to the user and the contributing agencies

The other options considered

Any point of difference between the user, carer, care planning practitioner or other agency

Any unmet needs with reasons — to be separately notified to the service planning system

The named person(s) responsible for implementing, monitoring and reviewing the care plan

The date of the first planned review.

The present care plan, Miss Richards submits, is deficient in the following respects: it fails to indicate how the proposed services will reverse the deterioration in Jonathan's skills; it fails to show in detail how the proposed activities will meet Jonathan's needs; it fails to identify his unmet needs and the reasons why they are not being met; it fails to set out the objectives of social services intervention; and it omits any criteria for measuring the achievement of the objectives. Such linkage between needs and services as it contains, she submits, is so inadequate as to represent a non-compliance with the statutory duty. Thus the proposal that Jonathan's recreational needs should be supplied by the Flexiteam and by the Shape Project does little or nothing to meet the complaint panel's recommendations as reflected in paragraphs 13 and 17 of the care plan's own assessment of Jonathan's needs, and does little more than recycle the previous, flawed care plan. Miss Richards submits accordingly that the implicit view that the plan meets the needs which it identifies is simply untenable and so irrational; and that if, instead, it represents a decision to depart from the complaint panel's recommendations it does so without any visible reasons and indeed without recognising that it is doing so. Further, she submits, it fails to follow the mandatory policy guidance and departs from the advisory guidance without any or adequate reason.

Mr McCarthy accepts that there has been to date a shortfall in comprehensively addressing Jonathan's needs. In addition to unplanned lacunae there continue to be gaps dictated by a lack of available resources. It is accepted, moreover, that the current care plan does not fully match up to, at least, the relevant practice guidance. Beyond this, however, there is a difference between Islington on the one hand and Mrs Rixon's advisers on the other as to the full extent of Jonathan's needs. For all these reasons the respondent local authority accepts that the care plan needs to be reviewed — as, currently, it is being.

Moreover, although Islington has day centre provision for both the physically disabled and the learning disabled, it has no centre for adults with difficulties of the same order as Jonathan's. For a good 3 years it has recognised this unmet need in the borough, and for the last 2 years has been planning to meet it. The plans have now reached the point at which daycare provision for the severely physically and learning disabled is imminently to be made at the St John's Centre. It is to be run by an independent organisation, Real Life Options.

In these circumstances, although Miss Richards understandably urges me to decide, to the extent which the evidence makes possible, the issues of law which she has canvassed in relation to the current care plan and provision for Jonathan, there are two major objections to my doing this. One is that the material upon which I am asked to decide is obsolescent. The other is that the legal issues shade at many points into specialist judgments which this court is unequipped to evaluate, much less to undertake on its own. But there remains, I accept, a live interest for both parties in approaching the new care plan and its implementation on a correct basis of law, and it is to this end that such findings as I consider can usefully be made are directed.

There are two points at which, in my judgment, the respondent local authority has fallen below the requirements of the law. The first concerns the relationship of need to availability. The duty owed to the applicant personally by virtue of section 2(1) of the Chronically Sick and Disabled Persons Act 1970 includes the provision of recreational facilities outside the home to an extent which Islington accepts is greater than the care plan provides for. But the local authority has, it appears, simply taken the existing unavailability of further facilities as an insuperable obstacle to any further attempt to make provision. The lack of a day care centre has been treated, however reluctantly, as a complete answer to the question of provision for Jonathan's recreational needs. As McCowan LJ explained in the *Gloucestershire* case [*R v Gloucestershire County Council, ex p Mahfood* [1997] 1 CCLR 7, cited earlier in this judgment] the section 2(1) exercise is needs-led and not resources-led. To say this is not to ignore the existing resources either in terms of regular voluntary care in the home or in budgetary terms. These, however, are balancing and not blocking factors. In the considerable volume of evidence which the local authority has provided, there is no indication that in reaching its decision on provision for Jonathan the local authority undertook anything resembling the exercise described in the *Gloucestershire* case of adjusting provision to need.

The care plan, as Mr McCarthy readily admits, does not comply either with the policy guidance or the practice guidance issued by central government. There has been a failure to comply with the guidance contained in paragraph 3.24 of the policy document to the effect that following assessment of need, the objectives of social services intervention as well as the services to be provided or arranged should be agreed in the form of a care plan. For the reasons which I have given, if this statutory guidance is to be departed from it must be with good reason, articulated in the course of some identifiable decision-making process even if not in the care plan itself. In the absence of any such considered decision, the deviation from the statutory guidance is in my judgment a breach of the law; and so *a fortiori* is the reduction of the Flexiteam service from 3 hours as originally agreed, whatever the activity, to 3 hours swimming or $1\frac{1}{2}$ hours at home. I cannot accept Mr McCarthy's submission that the universal knowledge that no day centre care was available for Jonathan was so plainly the backdrop of the section 2 decision that there was no need to say so. It is one thing for it to have been a backdrop in the sense of a relevant factor, but another for it to have been treated as an immoveable object. The want of any visible consideration of it disables the respondent from showing that it was taken into account in the way spelt out in the *Gloucestershire* case.

...

The care plan also fails at a number of points to comply with the practice guidance on, for example, the contents of a care plan, the specification of its objectives, the achievement of agreement on implementation on all those involved, leeway for contingencies and the identification and feeding back of assessed but still unmet need. While such guidance lacks the status accorded by section 7 of [Local Authority Social Services Act 1970], it is, as I have said, something to which regard must be had in carrying out the statutory functions. While the occasional lacuna would not furnish evidence of such a disregard, the series of lacunae which I have mentioned does, in my view, suggest that the statutory guidance has been overlooked.

The case of *R* v *Lewisham LBC, ex p Pinzon and Patino* [1998] 2 CCLR 152 rounds off our extracts from challenges to social services decisions relating to adult services. It illustrates again how difficult it is for an aggrieved client to get the courts to direct the social services department towards a particular outcome. The difficulty is compounded when client needs are not only for personal social services but also for housing, which, you may now appreciate, is provided by a different department, often part of a different level of authority. It also illustrates the difficulty highlighted in the parliamentary debates (see above) of providing a 'joined up' approach to social welfare. You will see in this case, as with the case shown earlier of *R* v *Kirklees*, that though there is just one family under consideration there is a bewildering range of statutory duties and agencies concerned with meeting these needs. While the law may be clear on each aspect, the overall result leads perhaps to a feeling of disappointment at the inadequacies of the statutory framework:

Mr Justice Laws: This application for judicial review is brought with leave of Sullivan J, granted on 17 October 1997. It concerns the statutory obligations of the London Borough of Lewisham, primarily arising under Section 47 of the National Health Service and Community Care Act 1990. There are two applicants, Mrs Pinzon and her elderly mother Mrs Patino.

Mrs Pinzon lives with her husband, her two daughters and her mother (the second applicant) at council premises rented from Lewisham. The daughters are aged 15 and two-and-a-half respectively. The property has three bedrooms. There is a double bedroom, which is occupied by Mrs Pinzon and her husband, and two single rooms, one of which is shared by the two girls and the other is occupied by the second applicant, Mrs Patino.

Unhappily, Mrs Patino is a disabled lady. She suffers from osteoarthritis and osteoporosis. Her handicaps are said to be quite severe and her condition has deteriorated over time. The family have made known their desire to move to a larger property, in particular a four-bedroom property. The council have declined to accommodate that desire.

The application for judicial review specifically complains of the way in which the local authority have approached their duties owed under Section 47 of the 1990 Act, and there is also a complaint concerning the council's housing allocation scheme which is made under what is now Section 167 of the Housing Act 1996. In order to explain the issues in the case I must travel a little further into the statutory provisions.

Section 47 of the 1990 Act provides in part as follows:

'(1)   Subject to subsections (5) and (6) below, where it appears to a local authority that any person for whom they may provide or arrange for the provision of community care services may be in need of any such services, the authority —

(a)   shall carry out an assessment of his needs for those services and

(b)   having regard to the result of that assessment, shall then decide whether his needs call for the provision by them of any such services.

(2)   If at any time during the assessment of the needs of any person under subsection (1) (a) above it appears to a local authority that he is a disabled person, the authority —

(a)   shall proceed to make such a decision as to the services he requires as is mentioned in section 4 of the Disabled Persons (Services, Consultation and Representation) Act 1986 without his requesting them to do so under that section; and

(b)   shall inform him that they will be doing so and of his rights under that Act.

(3)   If at any time during the assessment of the needs of any person under subsection (1) (a) above, it appears to a local authority —

(a)   that there may be a need for the provision to that person by such [Health Authority] as may be determined in accordance with regulations of any services under the National Health Service Act 1977, or

(b)   that there may be a need for the provision to him of any services which fall within the functions of a local housing authority (within the meaning of the Housing Act 1985 [now 1996], which is not the local authority carrying out the assessment,

the local authority shall notify that [Health Authority] or local housing authority and invite them to assist, to such extent as is reasonable in the circumstances, in the making of the assessment; and, in making their decision as to the provision of the services needed for the person in question the local authority shall take into account any services which are likely to be made available for him by that [Health Authority] or local housing authority.'

The reference in subsection (2) (a) to the 1986 Act is more closely understood when one turns to that statute. Section 4 of the Disabled Persons (Services, Consultation and Representation) Act 1986 provides:

'When requested to do so by —

(a)   a disabled person,

(b)   his authorised representative, or

(c)   any person who provides care for him in the circumstances mentioned in section 8,

a local authority shall decide whether the needs of the disabled person call for the provision by the authority of any services in accordance with section 2(1) of the 1970 Act (provision of welfare services).'

The 1970 Act is a reference to the Chronically Sick and Disabled Persons Act of 1970. Miss Belgrave, for the applicant, referred to part of Section 2(1) which reads:

'Where a local authority having functions under section 29 of the National Assistance Act 1948 are satisfied in the case of any person to whom that section applies who is ordinarily resident in their area that it is necessary in order to meet the needs of that person for that authority to make arrangements for all or any of the following matters, namely — [...and I may go to...]

(e) the provision of assistance for that person in arranging for the carrying out of any works of adaptation in his home or the provision of any additional facilities designed to secure his greater safety, comfort or convenience ...'

The Secretary of State has issued Policy Guidance relating to the administration by local authorities of their community care responsibilities. I was shown a document published in 1990. I read only paragraph 3.24 which is headed 'Care Plans'. That passage is in these terms:

'Once needs have been assessed, the services to be provided or arranged and the objectives of any intervention should be agreed in the form of a care plan. The objective of ensuring that service provisions should, as far as possible, preserve or restore normal living implies the following order of preference in constructing care packages which may include health provision, both primary and specialist, housing provision and social services provision ...'

There are then what are nowadays called bullet points as follows:

'• support for the user in his or her own home including day and domiciliary care, respite care, the provision of disability equipment and adaptations to accommodation as necessary;
• a move to more suitable accommodation, which might be sheltered or very sheltered housing, together with the provision of social services support;
• a move to another private household ...
• residential care;
• nursing home care;
• long stay care in hospital.'

There is also a circular, LAC circular 10 of 92, which refers, amongst other things, to the 1990 Act. Paragraph 9 states:

'The Act also requires a more systematic assessment of the needs of those who may require care. From April 1993 social services authorities will have a statutory duty to assess individuals' need for community care services, with the aim of ensuring that all support needs are identified, not only needs for which the social services authority is responsible. Section 47 of the Act requires social services authorities to notify the local housing authority if there appears to be a housing need and invite them to assist in the assessment.'

In Paragraph 10:

'Both housing and social services authorities should adopt joint arrangements to deal with assessments and should consider the need to nominate particular officers to be responsible for liaising and agreeing the possible housing options.'

11:

'Housing authorities and social services authorities are asked to co-operate fully in the planning and assessment processes, bringing in other housing providers in both the public and voluntary sectors, especially housing associations where they may be able to help.'

Miss Belgrave submits on behalf of the applicants that there has here been a failure of proper co-operation between the social services department and the housing department of the Lewisham Council which is a unitary authority.

Section 167(1) of the Housing Act 1996 provides:

'Every local housing authority shall have a scheme (their "allocation scheme") for determining priorities, and as to the procedure to be followed, in allocating housing accommodation.'

Then subsection 2:

'As regards priorities, the scheme shall be framed so as to secure that reasonable preference is given to —
(a) people occupying insanitary or overcrowded housing or otherwise living in unsatisfactory housing conditions ...'

and then

'(e) households consisting of or including someone with a particular need for settled accommodation on medical or welfare grounds.'

In relation also to this statute there is guidance given by the minister in the shape of a minister-ial circular [Code of Guidance on Housing Act 1996 Parts VI and VII], paragraph 2.15 of which states in part:

'A joint approach should be agreed between local housing and social services and health authorities, to include: [... then the second indent ...]

co-ordination between housing and social services assessments.

2.16: Local authority housing, social services and health authorities should liaise over the best solution for each client, recognising, for example, that the provision of more appropriate housing may assist in the delivery of social services; ...'

Before returning to the facts, I should notice the decision of Scott-Baker J in *R v Bristol City Council ex p Penfold* (1998) 1 CCLR 315, to which Miss Belgrave referred. In that case the learned judge pointed out that Section 47 of the 1990 Act imposed a mandatory duty upon authorities to carry out assessments envisaged by the section and that, accordingly, the state of the authority's resources were not a relevant consideration in deciding whether to undertake an assessment. I mention it out of respect to Miss Belgrave because, as I understand the facts of the matter, there is nothing here to suggest that the council have declined to carry out a Section 47 assessment on financial or any other such grounds.

I return to the facts. In February 1996 an assessment was carried out in relation to Mrs Patino, the second applicant, by the community occupational therapist. The document is headed Community Occupational Therapy Service Assessment of Housing Needs. The name of the sec-ond applicant is given. It is not necessary to take time with this document save to notice the statement on the second page:

'Stairlift would benefit client but house too small for family.'

Under the heading: Recommendations of Community Occupational Therapy Service.

'Bed size required — four.'

The housing department of the local authority considered that document. They wrote to the applicant's solicitors on 28 July 1997 after, I apprehend, a certain amount of intervening corres-pondence. There is a heading in the letter 'Type and Size and Allocation of Property' under which is written:

'The Pinzon family remains a three bedroom need.'

Whilst I agree that two of the rooms in the property at which they reside would be too small to accommodate two persons in a single bedroom, events seem to have progressed and the family have made a request for Mrs Patino to be rehoused separately.

The report from the occupational therapist for a four-bedroom property, to which I have just referred, made a recommendation on the grounds of family make-up and not on the grounds of Mrs Patino's disability. Nevertheless, Lewisham's housing's policy requires that Mr and Mrs Pinzon can make use of one room, the female children and Mrs Patino can use the second and third.

The family clearly need to be moved to a property capable of adaptation for Mrs Patino's needs unless she wishes to be rehoused in her own right. I continue:

'I would reiterate that I do not have access to the medical advisers records in respect of Mrs Patino's medical assessment, this assessment was made in respect of her medical condi-tion and not her needs in respect of her disability. This issue of disability was considered within the report of the occupational therapist. Rehousing in respect of disability is facili-tated through the occupational health section of social services who have a priority listing. When properties become available, the priority list is used to allocate properties based on need, mention is made within the Lewisham housing policy.'

In February 1998 there was a medical assessment relating to Mrs Patino. The doctor, Dr Barbara Stones, who carried it out stated as follows:

'I have carried out a reassessment based on the following information.'

There follows reference to an occupational therapy report, two medical assessment reports and a medical form completed by Mrs Patino. The doctor continued:

'Taking into account the information from the above reports I have made the following recommendations: an ordinarily adapted property suitable for a chairlift, wheelchair access, central heating, category B, 80 points.'

That latter reference is a reference to the point system within the housing allocation policy. There is a document showing that 'category B, 80 points', refers to:

'Any household which includes a person with a chronic illness or disability of a severe nature, which is affected by their living conditions, a move is recommended to improve the health and quality of life of the individual.'

The doctor reporting in February 1998 also wrote in manuscript at the front of the medical assessment form the words:

'Ordinarily adapted property suitable for a stairlift, wheelchair access.'

That is repeated in that part of the document I have already read.

The second applicant has been the subject of a further assessment much more recently on 10 September 1998. That again was carried out by the occupational therapist. Upon this occasion she stated under recommendations:

'Please could this client be reviewed and given a category A.'

If that was done she would qualify for 100 points under the allocation scheme. The assessment continues:

'Family require three bedrooms, client's bedroom needs to be large enough to give circulation space for zimmerframe and allow carer to assist her getting in and out of bed and dressing. If house straight, stairs for stairlift.'

I imagine that latter reference is pointing to the fact that a stairlift might be installed if the staircase in the house, as it were, had no corners.

That, as I say, was a document prepared on 10 September 1998. Presumably it is still under consideration within the local authority. There is no material, at present, to show whether any new executive decision has yet been made in relation to this family's housing on the strength of that assessment.

Against the whole of that background, Miss Belgrave first submits that the local authority have failed properly to assess Mrs Patino under Section 47 of the 1990 Act. When she developed her submissions it appeared that one of her primary arguments was that there was here some failure of co-operation between social services and the housing department, a point to which I have already adverted. I do not see the basis for this on the facts before me, nor indeed in relation to the applicable legal provision. It is entirely right that the Secretary of State, both in the context of the 1990 Act and the context of the Housing Legislation, recommends or requests such co-operation is not itself a legal duty imposed by statute.

It is clear here that the documents prepared by the occupational therapist go to the housing authority which then consider them as they consider also material put before them by the medical assessor, as in this case by the medical assessor such as Dr Stones, who made the report in February 1998.

Even if there were some argument as to want of co-operation between the relevant departments of this council, I cannot see that it would avail the applicant in this case. Her application for judicial review seeks relief in the form of an order of certiorari to quash the decision that the applicants are only entitled to a three-bedroom property, next mandamus requiring the authorities to determine the applicant's needs according to law and then a declaration that the council is under a duty to assess the applicant pursuant to Section 47.

As regards the first of these, it is entirely plain to me that these applicants, as of today's date, have no legal entitlement, enforceable by judicial review proceedings, to a four-bedroom property, certainly not on the basis of Mrs Patino's unfortunate serious disabilities. I have already demonstrated that the recommendation for a four-bedroom property was made, not by virtue of those disabilities but because the occupational therapist, perhaps exceeding her brief thought that the house was too small for the family as a whole. In particular, I imagine, it was considered that it would be desirable if the two girls, one of whom is 15, could have separate bedrooms. This has nothing to do with Mrs Patino's disabilities.

There is nothing in the refusal of four-bedroom accommodation that discloses any breach of the council's obligations under Section 47 as regards the application for a mandamus requiring the respondent to determine the applicant's needs, according to law, so far as that relates to Mrs Patino's needs and Mrs Pinzon, her daughter, who is also an applicant, why there has been a further Section 47 assessment done only last month. There is no reason to suppose that the authority will not respond to that assessment in one way or another.

I cannot think, and I am asked to infer, that they will respond unlawfully. As regards the application for a declaration that the respondent is under a duty to make a Section 47 assessment, why such an assessment has been made.

There is, in my judgment, nothing in the complaint that Section 47 has not been fulfilled in this case. It is said that the council's decisions, both presumably in relation to Section 47 and otherwise as regards their housing responsibilities, are unreasonable in the *Wednesbury* sense. There is nothing in that.

All that remains in this case is the allegation that the housing policy of the Lewisham Council is, itself, unlawful. In relation to that, as I understand it, really only one point is taken: that when one looks at the policy, and the relevant document is before me, one sees that the points system which it includes, does not allow for any points to be given specifically for disability. The points, it will be obvious, are a means of rating applicants for housing on the waiting list. The scheme includes and I state this merely by way of example:

'Category 3, homelessness and insecurity. One homeless, 150 points and no points to be awarded for existing property factors.'

Then there are other matters under that category. 150 points, as it happens, are also awarded in racial harassment and sexual harassment cases where a transfer of accommodation has been requested. There are other matters relating to personal attacks, neighbour disputes and breakdowns of relationships. Then, more pertinently, category 5 is headed: 'Health Needs' and under that numbered (1) 'Health Priority' there are four subcategories A, B, C and D which respectively attract 100, 80, 60 and 40 points. The applicant Mrs Patino was, I think, put up to subcategory B and thus obtained 80 points and a current recommendation is to award 100 points under category A.

It is true that the document does not, on its face, refer to disability but Section 167 of the 1996 Act cannot be read as requiring specific provision of that kind to be made. In fact, I apprehend, that at any rate in most cases persons suffering from disabling conditions such as that unhappily suffered by this lady, would fail to have such conditions recognised under the health priority category. It would appear, moreover, from the decision letter of July 1997 which I have read, that this authority does indeed contemplate rehousing in respect of disability. It will be recalled that the letter says:

'Rehousing in respect of disability is facilitated through the occupational health section of social services who have a priority listing. When properties become available the priority list is used to allocate properties based on need.'

Miss Belgrave, however, developed her argument relating to the absence of any points score for disability by indicating that since disability, as such, scored no points, a person in Mrs Patino's position would be unlikely ever to be rehoused since there would be no basis on which she would attract the necessary number of points. As I have already indicated, she has 80 points by virtue of her case being allotted to subcategory B under health needs.

Miss Belgrave further submitted that the affidavit evidence shows that a four-bedroom property will only be allocated to a person who is able to claim between 500 and 900 points and that is far and away above any points score that might be obtained in Mrs Patino's case by virtue of her health needs.

It seems to me that these arguments are misconceived. First, Mrs Patino has no legal complaint on any basis that she should be awarded a four-bedroom property. Her disabilities do not require any allocation of a house with a greater number of bedrooms and I do not intend to diminish their gravity. She has her own bedroom in the present house. It is recognised by the council that she ought to have a bigger one so as to accommodate such matters as the need for her zimmerframe.

It remains for the future whether, following the September 1998 assessment, a larger three-bedroom house will be offered to the family. It follows that any argument based on the council's refusal to place this family in a four-bedroom house cannot possibly succeed so far as it is alleged to arise from the council's duties to Mrs Patino. Anything else, it seems to me, is academic. Whether there might be a case in which a person, or a family, should be rehoused by virtue of a mandatory statutory duty owed by the council yet is not rehoused because the points system in question does not allow, it is a matter with which I am not concerned today, at least in relation to Mrs Patino's claim.

It is true that Mrs Pinzon is also before the court as an applicant and it is really in her case rather than Mrs Patino's that the points system is inadequate or unlawful, but so far as her application is concerned she, of course, cannot complain of any absence in the points scheme of allowances to be made for disability for she is not the disabled person. Nor can she complain that the points scheme ought to be such as now allow her to a four-bedroom property, for that would be a complaint on the merits of the matter with which, of course, I am not concerned.

It is obvious and elementary that many local authorities, and I am sure they include Lewisham, have many pressing and difficult claims upon their housing department in the city areas. It is well-known that the housing stock is sometimes run down and often not sufficiently large to accommodate all those with claims upon it. Authorities must, of course, obey the law but when they elaborate allocation schemes under the 1996 Act their duty is to do their honest and reasonable best to measure and weigh the competing claims which they know will be made upon them. I have no reason to think that Lewisham has not done that in this case. This application will be refused.

1.3.3 Court review of decisions on services for children

R v *Tower Hamlets LBC, ex p Bradford* [1997] 29 HLR 756 is similar to the cases we have already considered concerning adult services. Though the case is concerned with the Children Act 1989, you will see that the family needed assessment for adult services as well, and brought proceedings for judicial review to force the department to carry out an assessment of the needs of both parent and child:

Kay J: Simon Bradford is 11 years old. He lives in a two bedroomed flat in the London Borough of Tower Hamlets with his parents Raymond and Anita Bradford. The family have lived in this home since November 1993.

Mrs Bradford is severely disabled suffering from epilepsy and arthritis. Her epilepsy results in her suffering four or five epileptic fits a day and two or three grand mal fits a week resulting in double incontinence. Her arthritis is severe and frequently she is unable to wear boots or shoes. The care of Mrs Bradford is undertaken by Mr Bradford assisted by Simon. Simon, himself, has special educational needs and experiences difficulty in interacting with other children.

As a family they are the subject of very considerable harassment in the area in which they live. Mrs Bradford has been mugged on three occasions. Simon has been bullied and taunted, particularly on his way to and from school. The family has been harassed within the home by abusive and hoax telephone calls. This campaign of hatred has culminated in attempted arson on their home and the daubing of phlegm and faeces over the door of their flat and their car.

In the summer of 1995, Mr and Mrs Bradford applied to be rehoused and Mr Bradford orally requested assessments for community care services. On December 11, 1995, their solicitors wrote to the respondent requesting comprehensive assessment of the family's needs under the National Health Service and Community Care Act 1990, the Chronically Sick and Disabled Persons' Act 1970 and the Children Act 1989.

On December 21, 1995, an application was made to this court on behalf of each of the three members of the family for leave to apply for Judicial Review of the failure and/or refusal of the respondent authority to make a service provision decision in 'respect of each of the applicants under (as appropriate) the National Health Service and Community Care Act 1990, section 47 and/or the Chronically Sick and Disabled Persons' Act 1970, section 2 and/or the Children Act 1989, section 17 and to provide such services pursuant to such decision or by way of emergency provision'.

On January 8, 1995, the matter came before Morrison J, *ex parte* on notice. The respondent was present and opposed the grant of leave. Having heard argument, Morrison J granted leave and indicated that in his view urgent relief was required, particularly expressing his concern as to Simon.

At a preliminary hearing the local authority undertook to the court that they would carry out a Children Act assessment for Simon and the adult members of the family. By the time the case reached the court, the local authority had assessed the mother's needs, and also Simon's educational needs. But the case continued on the basis that, as a child in need, Simon's needs had to be fully and separately assessed under the Children Act 1989. The dispute centred on s. 17(a), which defines a child as being in need if:

he is unlikely to achieve or maintain, or have the opportunity of achieving or maintaining, a reasonable standard of health or development without the provision for him of services by a local authority ...

and s. 20, which obliges the social services authority to provide accommodation for a child in need where the person caring for the child cannot meet that need. This is how the authority, in their affidavit to the court, viewed the requirements of the Children Act:

(14)   It has been suggested by the applicants' legal advisers that the Authority could exercise its powers under the Children Act to, if necessary, provide temporary accommodation to the family. (15)   I am fully aware of the Authority's powers under section 20 of the Children Act to accommodate a child in need. If the factual criteria of s. 20 were satisfied the Authority would accept that it was under a duty to Simon to provide him with accommodation. However, it is not a realistic view of the present situation to maintain that the criteria are met. The relevant duty under section 20 would arise if the person caring for him is being prevented temporarily from providing suitable accommodation. In the present circumstances Simon is housed with his parents. The family's housing needs are being addressed through the housing allocations policy and as I have already indicated no complaint is made about the number of points allocated under that policy. The family are placing restrictions (on the choice of accommodation they will accept under the housing allocations policy) that will have the effect of restricting the possibility of an early offer of a transfer being made. ...

(16)   I am also aware of the Authority' s wide duty and discretion to provide services under section 17 of the Children Act 1989. Section 17 allows the Authority to assess and meet the needs of Simon, including those of accommodation. In this instance my view is that his needs for accommodation can be met by the housing authority and therefore it is not necessary to safeguard the welfare of Simon by providing alternative accommodation for him and his family under section 17.

...

Mr Drew concluded:

> 'The family's need for suitable accommodation will be met by the Housing Authority. Once the family is rehoused it appears likely that there will be no ongoing need for care and attention. Their accommodation may not be ideal but they are not without the basic necessities of life. In the interim their circumstances are not such that they are unable to remain resident at their current flat. I will however ensure that his welfare continues to be monitored by social workers and educational staff and I will consider the provision of further services as the need arises.'

This then is the factual basis and history upon which this matter falls to be considered. In summary form, Mr Gordon argues that the only conclusion that can be reached in the circumstances is that Simon's needs for rehousing have never been assessed under section 17 of the Children Act 1989. The respondents, he argues, have limited such assessment as has been made by a fundamental misapprehension of its statutory powers under section 17. The resulting assessment is, therefore, not one that is in accordance with the law.

The Bradfords' case was that the Council were legally required to assess Simon's needs for accommodation under section 20, and could not avoid this through referring to any other work the authority was doing on behalf of the family. The court agreed. Kay J cited s 17(10) of the Children Act, which imposes the duty to provide a range and level of services appropriate to the needs of a child in need, and continued:

The assessment specifically made upon Simon's needs as a Child in Need was that made by [the case worker] dated January 30, 1996. As already recorded that focused exclusively on the need to improve his attendance at school. The only reasonable view at that time was that there was another important factor that was likely to affect his development in the sense defined by section 17(11) and that was his housing. The events of the summer of 1996 only served to underline how acute a problem it was. An assessment of these needs was clearly called for.

It is said that the needs have been considered along with the needs of the whole family, but different considerations may well apply. It may be reasonable for the family as a whole to stay where they are for some time particularly if the parents are taking an unreasonably restrictive view of the area to which they will move. However, looked at from Simon's point of view as a Child in Need, it is necessary to consider what affect a prolonged stay in that flat will have on his development even if it results from the unreasonable attitude of his parents. All these are matters that need assessment, and I can detect nowhere any evidence that such an assessment has been made.

I believe that the reason for this failure is [...] that those responsible for the assessment approached it with a fundamental misunderstanding of their powers in relation to rehousing under the Children Act 1989.

...

I, therefore, conclude that the assessment that was made was fundamentally flawed and that whilst I accept it was done without any deliberate or improper intent, the undertaking given to the court to assess Simon's needs under section 17 has not been fully and properly complied with.

Law reports are sometimes frustrating to read. They tell a fascinating story of people's personal lives, but the facts are restricted to what you need to know to understand the court's decision. How did things turn out for the Bradfords after the court ordered a proper assessment? The legal requirement is that the authority had to reassess him. So long as they then took the relevant factors into account, followed the correct procedures and were not influenced by irrelevant factors they could still lawfully decide that the family did not need rehousing.

So far none of our cases have dealt with cost of services. But any social worker will know that the welfare needs of its clients can only be met to the extent that the social services department can produce the resources to pay for the services. What do the courts have to say where a department is alleged to have failed to carry out its statutory duties not because of failing to carry out a proper assessment of the client's needs but because they took available resources into account? Does the Law expect the assessed needs to be met, or is it legitimate to provide services according to resource limits?

The answer is not completely clear. We have already made clear our view on the complexity and piecemeal nature of the legislation. In conformity with this legislative confusion you will see that resources will play different roles in making decisions on provision of services, depending on the particular statutory duty or power being considered. We start with a piece of drafting from the Children Act 1989, which states in s 23(8):

Where a local authority provide accommodation for a child whom they are looking after and who is disabled, they should, *so far as is reasonably practicable*, secure that the accommodation is *not unsuitable* to his particular needs [our emphasis].

Is it mere semantics, or can 'not unsuitable' accommodation be of a lower standard than 'suitable' accommodation? In any event 'reasonably practicable' will allow the authority to argue that in a given case this provision is the best they can do. So long as they have not made the decision in a way the courts would describe as '*Wednesbury* unreasonable' (see above) it will be hard to challenge the adequacy of accommodation provided on behalf of a child with disability. This is illustrated in the case of *R v London Borough of Brent, ex p S* [1994] 1 FLR 203.

D was a child looked after by Brent social services, and fostered with his grandparents. He was autistic and hyperactive, and required round-the-clock supervision. The grandparents wanted to be rehoused. The department agreed that they needed a garden and also a bedroom on the same level as D's bedroom. But social services could not itself provide housing; they secured many offers from the housing department which were all considered by the grandparents as unsuitable. The Council said they had done what was reasonably practicable under s 23.

On an application for judicial review, which reached the Court of Appeal, Lord Justice Peter Gibson concluded as follows:

All that the court is required to do in a case such as the present is to determine whether the decision to offer 85 Chaplin Road, in fulfilment of its statutory duty to secure so far as is reasonably practicable that the accommodation offered is not unsuitable to D's particular needs, is '*Wednesbury* unreasonable' (see *Associated Provincial Picture House Ltd* v *Wednesbury Corporation*

[1948] 1 QB 223) or otherwise impugnable on the other familiar grounds for judicial review. In so holding I reject Miss Lawson's submission that the court must determine as a fact whether or not the test of reasonable practicability was satisfied.

In a case such as this I would expect a respondent local authority to be anxious to demonstrate by its evidence that it had done and is doing its best so far as is and has been reasonably practicable. I have to say that the evidence of the council leaves a good deal to be desired. It is clear that the council has not sought to look outside its own housing stock to rehouse D and a suggestion by his solicitors in correspondence that the council might rent property in the private sector is not expressly dealt with in the council's evidence. Nor does it appear from the evidence how many houses owned by the council would fall within D's special needs were they to become available, so as to give D and the court some indication of how realistic it is for the council to go on waiting for an available house rather than go to the private sector. However it also has to be said that D's advisers have not sought further information from the council in these proceedings. Further, the financial constraints on the council when faced with excessive housing demands on limited resources do appear from the evidence.

The wording of the duty in s 23(8) seems to me designed to avoid placing an unrealistically heavy burden on local authorities. The accommodation to be secured is not required to be suitable to the particular needs of the child, but only to be not unsuitable, and the duty to secure even that is qualified by what is reasonably practicable. Accordingly, it may not be reasonably practicable to secure accommodation which is not unsuitable, but so long as the council is doing the best it can, within the bounds of what is reasonably practicable, to secure not unsuitable accommodation, I do not think that it is in breach of its statutory duty. In my judgment it has not been shown that the decision to offer 85 Chaplin Road to D was *Wednesbury* unreasonable or that otherwise it can be impugned. True it is that the house failed to meet all of the special requirements of D in that the internal space was less than the present accommodation, but it did meet the other requirements specified in Esther Block's letter and I have no reason to doubt that it was the best available that the council could offer from its housing stock. It has not been shown to my satisfaction that it was irrational of the council to seek to meet its duty to rehouse D without recourse to the private sector.

...

I reach this conclusion with regret, as I have considerable sympathy with D and Mr and Mrs S. The judge said that there seems to have been unreasonable delay and an apparent failure to ensure co-operation between the council's social services department and its housing department. It appears to me essential for D's welfare that the council should procure that he is rehoused as soon as possible. If Mr S remains dissatisfied with the way the council is discharging its functions, he now knows that the representations procedure is available to him.

Perhaps the landmark case where resources and need have had to be balanced by courts was *R v Gloucester County Council, ex p Barry* [1997] A.C. 584. (This important case is considered again in Chapter 4.) The facts and Court of Appeal judgment from which Mr Barry appealed are set out in the Law Report's headnote:

The applicant was elderly and infirm. In September 1992 his needs were assessed by the respondent council, pursuant to section 2(1) of the Chronically Sick and Disabled Persons Act 1970, as 'home care ... for shopping, pension, laundry, cleaning. Meals on wheels.' In August 1993 his needs were assessed as being the same. In September 1994 the council informed him that, because the money allocated to it by central government had been reduced and there was not enough to meet demand, his cleaning and laundry services would be withdrawn. He, with others, brought proceedings against the council for judicial review, claiming that his needs were the same, that Parliament had imposed a duty on the council to do what was necessary to meet them and that it was no answer that it was short of money. Its case was that in assessing his needs it was entitled to have regard to its overall financial resources. The Divisional Court of the Queen's Bench Division held that a local authority under section 2(1) of the Act of 1970 was entitled to take account of its resources in assessing needs and in deciding whether it was necessary to make arrangements to meet those needs, but granted the applicant a declaration that the council had acted unlawfully in withdrawing services previously provided to him without a reassessment of his needs. The Court of Appeal by a majority allowed an appeal by the applicant, holding that a local authority was not entitled to take account of its resources when assessing or reassessing whether it was necessary to make arrangements to meet an applicant's needs.

The House of Lords were unanimous in stating that no reduction in service could lawfully take place without a reassessment of the client's needs. The issue remaining was whether such a reassessment was allowed to take into account the Council's reduced resources. By a majority of three to two, the Lords ruled that an authority were entitled to take into account resources when assessing and meeting needs.

The legislation under which the duty arose to meet Mr Barry's needs was the Chronically Sick and Disabled Persons Act 1970, s 2 and the National Assistance Act 1948, s 29. You will encounter these in Chapter 4. The 1948 Act merely *empowers* the department to make specified arrangements for welfare services, such as support in the home, to meet the needs of people with disability. But the 1970 Act had turned the power into a *duty* to make those arrangements, once the department was satisfied that such arrangements were necessary. Mr Barry's *actual* personal needs did not suddenly reduce when the Council's resources were cut, although the Council's case was that his *assessed* needs could be reduced.

Lord Lloyd was one of the pair of Law Lords who thought the duty existed independently of the Council's resources:

Simply looking at the language of section 2 of the Act of 1970, against the background of Part III of the Act of 1948, it is clear enough that Parliament did not intend that provision for the needs of the disabled should depend on the availability of resources. The intention was to treat disability as a special case. That is why the Act of 1970 has always been regarded as such an important landmark in the care of the disabled.

...

Parliament cannot have intended that the standards and expectations for measuring the needs of the disabled in Bermondsey should differ from those in Belgrave Square.

This brings me, last of all, to the wretched position in which the council now find themselves, through no fault of their own. I have read the affidavits of Mr Deryk Mead, the Director of Social Services, and Mr Honey, Chief Executive, with something approaching despair. Equally depressing is the evidence of Margaret Newland, chair of Age Concern, Gloucestershire, and the numerous letters written by the council to the Secretary of State. Most depressing of all are the minutes of the community care sub-committee of the social services committee, especially those of the meeting held on 14 October 1994, in which members expressed their abhorrence at the choices which the Social Services Department was being required to make. The chairman commented:

'It was deplorable that there was no other way forward apart from the exclusion of certain people from access to community care through the device of rationing services.'

By your Lordships' decision today the council has escaped from the impossible position in which they, and other local authorities, have been placed. Nevertheless, I cannot help wondering whether they will not be regretting today's decision as much as Mr Barry. The solution lies with the Government. The passing of the Act of 1970 was a noble aspiration. Having willed the end, Parliament must be asked to provide the means.

I would dismiss the appeal.

Lord Nicholls in contrast spoke for the majority view:

My Lords, this appeal raises an important point of interpretation of section 2(1) of the Chronically Sick and Disabled Persons Act 1970. Can a local authority properly take into account its own financial resources when assessing the needs of a disabled person under section 2(1)? The Gloucestershire County Council and the Secretary of State for Health say 'Yes,' the applicant, Mr Barry, says 'No.' The question has given rise to a considerable difference of judicial opinion, so I shall give my conclusion in my own words.

At first sight the contentions advanced on behalf of Mr Barry are compelling. A person's needs, it was submitted, depend upon the nature and extent of his disability. They cannot be affected by, or depend upon, the local authority's ability to meet them. They cannot vary according to whether the authority has more or less money currently available. Take the case of an authority which assesses a person's needs as twice weekly help at home with laundry and cleaning. In the following year nothing changes except that the authority has less money available. If the authority's financial resources can be properly taken into account, it would be open to the authority to reassess that person's needs in the later year as nil. That cannot be right: the person's needs have not changed.

This is an alluring argument but I am unable to accept it. It is flawed by a failure to recognise that needs for services cannot sensibly be assessed without having some regard to the cost of providing them. A person's need for a particular type or level of service cannot be decided in a vacuum from which all considerations of cost have been expelled.

I turn to the statute. Under section 2(1) 'needs' are to be assessed in the context of, and by reference to, the provision of certain types of assistance for promoting the welfare of disabled persons: home help, meals on wheels, holidays, home adaptation, and so forth. In deciding whether the disability of a particular person dictates a need for assistance and, if so, at what level, a social worker or anyone else must use some criteria. This is inevitably so. He will judge the needs for assistance against some standard, some criteria, whether spoken or unspoken. One important factor he will take into account will be what constitutes an acceptable standard of living today.

Standards of living, however, vary widely. So do different people's ideas on the requirements of an acceptable standard of living. Thus something more concrete, capable of being applied uniformly, is called for when assessing the needs of a given disabled person under the statute. Some more precisely defined standard is required, a more readily identifiable yardstick, than individual notions of current standards of living.

Who is to set the standard? To this there can be only one answer: the relevant local authority, acting by its social services committee. The local authority sets the standards to be applied within its area. In setting the standards, or 'eligibility criteria' as they have been called, the local authority must take into account current standards of living, with all the latitude inherent in this concept. The authority must also take into account the nature and extent of the disability. The authority will further take into account the manner in which, and the extent to which, quality of life would be improved by the provision of this or that service or assistance, at this or that level: for example, by home care, once a week or more frequently. The authority should also have regard to the cost of providing this or that service, at this or that level. The cost of daily home care, or of installing a ground floor lavatory for a disabled person in his home and widening the doors to take a wheelchair, may be substantial. The relative cost will be balanced against the relative benefit and the relative need for that benefit.

Thus far the position is straightforward. The next step is the crucial step. In the same way as the importance to be attached to cost varies according to the benefit to be derived from the suggested expenditure, so also must the importance of cost vary according to the means of the person called upon to pay. An amount of money may be a large sum to one person, or to one person at a particular time, but of less consequence to another person, or to the same person at a different time. Once it is accepted, as surely must be right, that cost is a relevant factor in assessing a person's needs for the services listed in section 2(1), then in deciding how much weight is to be attached to cost some evaluation or assumption has to be made about the impact which the cost will have upon the authority. Cost is of more or less significance depending upon whether the authority currently has more or less money. Thus, depending upon the authority's financial position, so the eligibility criteria, setting out the degree of disability which must exist before help will be provided with laundry or cleaning or whatever, may properly be more or less stringent.

...

In the course of the argument some emphasis was placed upon a submission that if a local authority may properly take its resources into account in the way I have described, the section 2(1) duty would in effect be limited to making arrangements to the extent only that the authority should decide to allocate money for this purpose. The duty, it was said, would collapse into a power. I do not agree. A local authority must carry out its functions under section 2(1) in a responsible fashion. In the event of a local authority acting with *Wednesbury* unreasonableness, a disabled person would have a remedy.

This interpretation does not emasculate section 2(1). The section was intended to confer rights upon disabled persons. It does so by giving them a valuable personal right to see that the authority acts reasonably in assessing their needs for certain types of assistance, and a right to have their assessed needs met so far as it is necessary for the authority (as distinct from others) to do so. I can see no basis for reading into the section an implication that in assessing the needs of disabled persons for the prescribed services, cost is to be ignored. I do not believe Parliament intended that to be the position.

The House of Lords has ruled. An optimist would now assume that the law has been settled, and that the general principle would be that resources can be overtly taken into account in making an assessment and meeting a need. But the problem is that social services departments perform a range of statutory duties, and they all derive from different language and, in relation to community care, are set out in statutes dating from 1948. The position becomes further complicated by the fact that other agencies including education departments and housing departments also have to face similar questions arising from different legislation. How far does case law in education or housing affect obligations in social services? It did not take long for the *Barry* judgment to be picked apart.

R v East Sussex County Council, ex p Tandy [1998] AC 714 involved a reduction in home tuition for a girl suffering from ME. Education is not a duty falling on social services departments and we do not have the space to cite the judgment. But the key point is that the Lords, in the judgment of Lord Browne-Wilkinson, were able to distinguish the Barry decision. Talking of Barry he says:

The statutory duty was to arrange certain benefits to meet the 'needs' of the disabled persons but the lack of certain benefits enumerated in the section could not possible give rise to 'need' in the stringent sense of the word. Thus it is difficult to speak of the lack of a radio or a holiday or a recreational activity as giving rise to a need.

He compares this with the council's clear statutory duty to provide education under what is now s 19 of the Education Act 1996. In the *Barry* case the council can juggle its priorities and make assessments based on what it can afford. In the *Tandy* case education is to be provided and there is no scope for debate about it:

The argument is not one of insufficient resources to discharge the duty but of a preference for using the money for other purposes.

This reasoning, rather than the *Barry* decision, was followed in *R* v *Birmingham City Council, ex p Mohammed* [1998] 3 All ER 788, which concerned an application to a housing department for a disabled facilities grant (DFG) under the Housing Grants Construction and Regeneration Act 1996 section 24(3) which states:

(3) A local housing authority shall not approve an application for a disabled facilities grant unless they are satisfied —

    (a) that the relevant works are necessary and appropriate to meet the needs of the disabled occupant ...

The applicant thought that once the needs were proved, the grant must follow. The housing authority, by contrast, thought that *Barry* let them off the hook as they were short of resources. The court in fact chose to follow *Tandy*. Dyson J thought that the type of facilities to be provided for disabled people, as in *Barry* (such as radio and holidays), could not so easily be shown to be objectively needed as facilities in the home of a disabled person under s 22 of the 1996 Act, (such as access, safety, ability to get to a lavatory):

I do not consider that *Ex p Barry* provides the answer to the question that I have to decide. The important differences between the two statutes include the following. First, the needs mentioned in s 23(1) of the 1996 Act are real needs for disabled occupants as defined. The observation by Lord Browne-Wilkinson that the lack of certain of the enumerated facilities could not possibly give rise to 'need' in any stringent sense of the word is not applicable to the facilities enumerated in s 23 of the 1996 Act.

    ...

The concluding words of Lord Browne-Wilkinson's speech in *Ex p Tandy* are entirely apt to the statutory provisions with which this case is concerned. Parliament has chosen to impose a statutory duty in relation to DFGs within s 23(1) purposes. The court should be slow to downgrade such a duty into a mere discretion over which the court would have very little control. If Parliament wishes to redirect public expenditure on meeting the needs of disabled occupants of buildings, then it is for Parliament so to provide. In the 1996 Act, it seems to me that, for the reasons I have given, Parliament has made it even clearer than it did in the provisions of the Education Act 1993 that were considered in *Ex p Tandy* that, subject to certain express limitations, local housing authorities are obliged to approve DFGs within s 23(1) purposes whatever the resource implications of doing so may be.

1.4 Suing the local authority for failing to carry out statutory duties

Social work protects the vulnerable. Failure to protect can lead to harm. If there is a statutory duty and the department fails to properly carry it out, can the victim sue? In the cases we will look at the challenge to the local authority arose through the law of tort. Tort is a branch of law enabling a person to claim financial compensation for breach of a legal duty. An example of tort is where, say, a blind person trips on a badly maintained pavement and sues the highway authority for not keeping it to the standard necessary to avoid foreseeable injuries.

Our chosen examples involve claims for breach of the statutory duties under LASSA to protect or safeguard the welfare of children. Later in the chapter we will show how one of these cases was then appealed from the House of Lords, which took the stance traditional in English law of not wanting to open the floodgates by creating new areas of tort, to the European Court of Human Rights, which thought victims of negligence should have a right to sue. (To understand the role of the European Court of Human Rights see next chapter.)

A few words to explain tort are needed to help understand what follows. A person or body can be sued for compensation if three things are proved:

(a) that the person/authority owed a duty of care to the claimant. This itself requires two decisions:

- as a matter of law, is this the type of situation where courts recognise such a duty to exist?
- if it is, and only if it is, could a defendant in this position reasonably be expected to foresee that their actions or failure to act could harm someone in the defendant's position?

(b) the defendant fell below standards reasonably expected of someone acting in their position, such as the standards of a careful social work department;

(c) any harm suffered is shown to be a result of that breach of duty.

The cases we look at focus on the first part of the first of these questions: do social services departments owe a duty of care in tort to their clients? You might think that the existence of the duty is beyond doubt. After all, it is stated in LASSA and it is stated in the Acts listed in Schedule 1. But LASSA duties are public law duties — obligations created to classes of people for the good of society. Tort claims, by contrast, are private law — matters of interest only to the individuals in dispute.

The question of whether that private law duty and the potential right to compensation exists is answered by looking at common law, which means the law evolved by judges and found in case reports. There is a fiction that in the common law the judges do not make law but discover it. In fact, because the common law in this area is still evolving, and there are no clear precedents, the judges have had to make policy decisions. Their answer is that on policy grounds there is and should be no duty of care in tort towards the clients of social services departments; but this answer has been found wanting by the European Court of Human Rights.

The first case is X *(Minors)* v *Bedfordshire CC* [1995] 2 A.C. 634. The judgment dealt with a number of different cases against many local authorities, but for our purposes the parts relating to the alleged failures of the Bedfordshire Social Services Department are sufficient. The Children Act 1989, and its predecessors, imposed a statutory duty on social service departments to identify children in need and take the necessary measures to protect them from harm. The appeal concerned only one issue: did the council owe the children a duty of care which could lead to compensation if the necessary facts were proved? This is a purely legal question, and the facts alleged by the claimants would only need to be heard in evidence if the duty itself exists. But a quick view of the complaints by the former clients of Befordshire social services show that this was a very serious case.

Lord Browne Wilkinson: The plaintiffs are five children of the same parents who sue by the Official Solicitor as their next friend. The eldest child was born in October 1982 and the youngest in May 1990. The only defendant is the county council which is sued as the local authority responsible for social services in the area where the children lived. The facts pleaded fall into various periods. The first runs from November 1987 to December 1989. During this period reports about these children were made to the county council by relatives, neighbours, the police, the family's general practitioner, the head teacher of the school which the two older children attended, the National Society for the Prevention of Cruelty to Children ('NSPCC'), a social worker and a health visitor. The reports were to the effect that the children were at risk, including the risk of sexual abuse; the children were locked out of the house for long periods of time with the oldest child (aged five) supervising the next two (aged three and two); the third child was observed to have an abrasion which could have been caused by cigarette burns with the oldest child being found to be pale, depressed, pathetic and possibly hungry; the children's bedroom had been found to be squalid and to have faeces smeared on the walls; their home was in a disgusting state, with the second and third children's beds sodden with urine; the two older children attended school looking dishevelled and smelly; there was concern for the children's emotional wellbeing. In December 1989 the county council rejected a health visitor's recommendation that the first four children be placed on the child protection register. No case conference was held.

The second period runs from March 1990 to January 1991. During this period reports of a similar kind were made to the county council. A case conference was held in January 1991. It was decided not to place any of the children on the child protection register and not to apply for any court orders.

The third period began in July 1991 when the children's father asked the county council to take the children into care for adoption, a suggestion he made again in May 1992. The county council took no action. For nine days in August 1991 the three older children were placed on their mother's application with foster parents who found them dirty, underfed and with poor personal hygiene. In September 1991 the county council was told the condition of the second and third children's bedroom had deteriorated further; that the children were said to have been locked outside the family home and to have screamed constantly; that the children were left in their bedrooms for long periods and smeared faeces on the windows; and that the second, third and fourth of the children had been seen stealing food. No action was taken save that respite care was recommended to assist the mother. In November 1991 the mother asked the county council to accommodate the three older children: the county council offered her short term respite care. On their mother's application, the three older children spent much of the early months of 1992 with foster parents with whom they gained in weight. In March 1992 the county council considered the results of this foster placement and respite care and monitoring were recommended. In April 1992 the mother asked the county council to remove the second and third children from her care and place them for adoption. In June 1992 the mother told the county council that if the children were not removed from her care she would batter them. As a result the county council placed the children with foster parents. On 22 June 1992 the children were placed on the child protection register but the county council took no steps to seek care orders. The county council did accept that the children should not return to live with their parents. In October 1992 the county council decided to seek care orders and took steps to that end. As a result interim care orders were made in December 1992 and final orders in April 1993. It is fair to add that the children's plight was not being ignored. The statement of claim refers to no less than 13 meetings held to discuss their position.

In June 1993 the five children launched these proceedings. The county council applied to strike out the proceedings and, on 12 November 1993, Turner J struck them out.

Lord Browne-Wilkinson sums up the law's attitude to providing private law remedies for public law duties:

The question is whether, if Parliament has imposed a statutory duty on an authority to carry out a particular function, a plaintiff who has suffered damage in consequence of the authority's performance or non-performance of that function has a right of action in damages against the authority. It is important to distinguish such actions to recover damages, based on a private law cause of action, from actions in public law to enforce the due performance of statutory duties, now brought by way of judicial review. The breach of a public law right by itself gives rise to no claim for damages.

...

The principles applicable in determining whether such statutory cause of action exists are now well established, although the application of those principles in any particular case remains difficult. The basic proposition is that in the ordinary case a breach of statutory duly does not, by itself, give rise to any private law cause of action. However a private law cause of action will arise if it can be shown, as a matter of construction of the statute, that the statutory duty was imposed for the protection of a limited class of the public and that Parliament intended to confer on members of that class a private right of action for breach of the duty. There is no general rule by reference to which it can be decided whether a statute does create such a right of action but there are a number of indicators. If the statute provides no other remedy for its breach and the Parliamentary intention to protect a limited class is shown, that indicates that there may be a private right of action since otherwise there is no method of securing the protection the statute was intended to confer. If the statute does provide some other means of enforcing the duty that will normally indicate that the statutory right was intended to be enforceable by those means and not by private right of action: *Cutler* v *Wandsworth Stadium Ltd* [1949] AC 398; *Lonrho Ltd* v *Shell Petroleum Co. Ltd (No. 2)* [1982] AC 173. However, the mere existence of some other statutory remedy is not necessarily decisive. It is still possible to show that on the true construction of the statute the protected class was intended by Parliament to have a private remedy. Thus the specific duties imposed on employers in relation to factory premises are enforceable by an action for damages, notwithstanding the imposition by the statutes of criminal penalties for any breach: see *Groves* v *Wimborne (Lord)* [1898] 2 QB 402.

...

Most statutes which impose a statutory duty on local authorities confer on the authority a discretion as to the extent to which, and the methods by which, such statutory duty is to be performed. It is clear both in principle and from the decided cases that the local authority cannot be liable in damages for doing that which Parliament has authorised. Therefore if the decisions complained of fall within the ambit of such statutory discretion they cannot be actionable in common law. However if the decision complained of is so unreasonable that it falls outside the ambit of the discretion conferred upon the local authority, there is no a priori reason for excluding all common law liability.

That this is the law is established by the decision in the *Dorset Yacht* case [1970] AC 1004 and by that part of the decision in *Anns* v *Merton London Borough Council* [1978] AC 728 which, so far as I am aware, has largely escaped criticism in later decisions. In the *Dorset Yacht* case Lord Reid said [1970] A.C. 1004, 1031:

'Where Parliament confers a discretion the position is not the same. Then there may, and almost certainly will, be errors of judgment in exercising such a discretion and Parliament cannot have intended that members of the public should be entitled to sue in respect of such errors. But there must come a stage when the discretion is exercised so carelessly or unreasonably that there has been no real exercise of the discretion which Parliament has conferred. The person purporting to exercise his discretion has acted in abuse or excess of his power. Parliament cannot be supposed to have granted immunity to persons who do that.'

...

It follows that in seeking to establish that a local authority is liable at common law for negligence in the exercise of a discretion conferred by statute, the first requirement is to show that the decision was outside the ambit of the discretion altogether: if it was not, a local authority cannot itself be in breach of any duty of care owed to the plaintiff.

In deciding whether or not this requirement is satisfied, the court has to assess the relevant factors taken into account by the authority in exercising the discretion. Since what are under consideration are discretionary powers conferred on public bodies for public purposes the relevant factors will often include policy matters, for example social policy, the allocation of finite financial resources between the different calls made upon them or (as in *Dorset Yacht*) the balance between pursuing desirable social aims as against the risk to the public inherent in so doing. It is established that the courts cannot enter upon the assessment of such 'policy' matters. The difficulty is to identify in any particular case whether or not the decision in question is a 'policy' decision.

Lord Browne-Wilkinson then considered a number of previous decisions and continued:

From these authorities I understand the applicable principles to be as follows. Where Parliament has conferred a statutory discretion on a public authority, it is for that authority, not for the courts, to exercise the discretion: nothing which the authority does within the ambit of the discretion can be actionable at common law. If the decision complained of falls outside the statutory discretion, it *can* (but not necessarily will) give rise to common law liability. However, if the factors relevant to the exercise of the discretion include matters of policy, the court cannot adjudicate on such policy matters and therefore cannot reach the conclusion that the decision was outside the ambit of the statutory discretion. Therefore a common law duty of care in relation to the taking of decisions involving policy matters cannot exist.

What this means is that no case can be brought in tort on the basis that the local authority had exercised any statutory discretion wrongly, only that it could be brought if the discretion had been, effectively, abused. But these remarks were only introductory: the biggest hurdle for the children's case was to show a duty of care can exist at all.

Lord Browne-Wilkinson recited the public law duties set out in the Children Act, which you will find later in Chapter 5 and which, in summary, require an authority to make enquiries where child welfare is at risk, to safeguard and promote the welfare of children in need, and provide them where necessary with accommodation. He also referred to the complaints procedure which exists under the Children Act and LASSA. This is how the judgment then resumes:

The Court of Appeal were unanimous in striking out these claims in both actions. I agree. My starting point is that the Acts in question are all concerned to establish an administrative system designed to promote the social welfare of the community. The welfare sector involved is one of peculiar sensitivity, involving very difficult decisions how to strike the balance between protecting the child from immediate feared harm and disrupting the relationship between the child and its parents. Decisions often have to be taken on the basis of inadequate and disputed facts. In my judgment in such a context it would require exceptionally clear statutory language to show a parliamentary intention that those responsible for carrying out these difficult functions should be liable in damages if, on subsequent investigation with the benefit of hindsight, it was shown that they had reached an erroneous conclusion and therefore failed to discharge their statutory duties.

It is true that the legislation was introduced primarily for the protection of a limited class, namely children at risk, and that until April 1991 the legislation itself contained only limited machinery for enforcing the statutory duties imposed. But in my view those are the only pointers in favour of imputing to Parliament an intention to create a private law cause of action. When one turns to the actual words used in the primary legislation to create the statutory duties relied upon in my judgment they are inconsistent with any intention to create a private law cause of action.

...

So far as the Act of 1989 is concerned, the duty relied on in section 17 is described as 'a general duty' which has two parts: (a) to safeguard the children and (b) 'so far as is consistent' with (a) to promote the upbringing of the children by their families. Thus not only is the duty not a specific one but the section itself points out the basic tension which lies at the root of so much child protection work: the decision whether to split the family in order to protect the child. I find it impossible to construe such a statutory provision as demonstrating an intention that even where there is no carelessness by the authority it should be liable in damages if a court subsequently decided with hindsight that the removal, or failure to remove, the child from the family either was or was not 'consistent with' the duty to safeguard the child.

All the duties imported by Schedule 2 to the Act of 1989 are to 'take reasonable steps' to do certain things. The duty to make inquiries under section 47 is limited to 'such inquiries as they consider necessary.' Thus all the statutory provisions relied upon in the *Bedfordshire* case are, as one would expect, made dependent upon the subjective judgment of the local authority. To treat such duties as being more than public law duties is impossible.

...

Is it, then, just and reasonable to superimpose a common law duty of care on the local authority in relation to the performance of its statutory duties to protect children? In my judgment it is not. Sir Thomas Bingham MR took the view, with which I agree, that the public policy consideration which has first claim on the loyalty of the law is that wrongs should be remedied and that very potent counter considerations are required to override that policy [...]. However, in my judgment there are such considerations in this case.

First, in my judgment a common law duty of care would cut across the whole statutory system set up for the protection of children at risk. As a result of the ministerial directions contained in 'Working Together' the protection of such children is not the exclusive territory of the local authority's social services. The system is inter-disciplinary, involving the participation of the police, educational bodies, doctors and others. At all stages the system involves joint discussions, joint recommendations and joint decisions. The key organisation is the Child Protection Conference, a multi-disciplinary body which decides whether to place the child on the Child Protection Register. This procedure by way of joint action takes place, not merely because it is good practice, but because it is required by guidance having statutory force binding on the local authority. The guidance is extremely detailed and extensive: the current edition of 'Working Together' runs to 126 pages. To introduce into such a system a common law duty of care enforceable against only one of the participant bodies would be manifestly unfair. To impose such liability on all the participant bodies would lead to almost impossible problems of disentangling as between the respective bodies the liability, both primary and by way of contribution, of each for reaching a decision found to be negligent.

Second, the task of the local authority and its servants in dealing with children at risk is extraordinarily delicate. Legislation requires the local authority to have regard not only to the physical wellbeing of the child but also to the advantages of not disrupting the child's family environment: see, for example, section 17 of the Act of 1989. In one of the child abuse cases, the local authority is blamed for removing the child precipitately: in the other, for failing to remove the children from their mother. As the Report of the Inquiry into Child Abuse in Cleveland 1987 (Cm. 412) said, at p. 244:

'It is a delicate and difficult line to tread between taking action too soon and not taking it soon enough. Social services whilst putting the needs of the child first must respect the rights of the parents; they also must work if possible with the parents for the benefit of the children. These parents themselves are often in need of help. Inevitably a degree of conflict develops between those objectives.'

Next, if a liability in damages were to be imposed, it might well be that local authorities would adopt a more cautious and defensive approach to their duties. For example, as the Cleveland Report makes clear, on occasions the speedy decision to remove the child is sometimes vital. If the authority is to be made liable in damages for a negligent decision to remove a child (such negligence lying in the failure properly first to investigate the allegations) there would be a substantial temptation to postpone making such a decision until further inquiries have been made in the hope of getting more concrete facts. Not only would the child in fact being abused be prejudiced by such delay: the increased workload inherent in making such investigations would reduce the time available to deal with other cases and other children.

The relationship between the social worker and the child's parents is frequently one of conflict, the parent wishing to retain care of the child, the social worker having to consider whether to remove it. This is fertile ground in which to breed ill feeling and litigation, often hopeless, the cost of which both in terms of money and human resources will be diverted from the performance of the social service for which they were provided. The spectre of vexatious and costly litigation is often urged as a reason for not imposing a legal duty. But the circumstances surrounding cases of child abuse make the risk a very high one which cannot be ignored.

If there were no other remedy for maladministration of the statutory system for the protection of children, it would provide substantial argument for imposing a duty of care. But the statutory complaints procedures contained in section 76 of the Act of 1980 and the much fuller procedures now available under the Act of 1989 provide a means to have grievances investigated, though not to recover compensation. Further, it was submitted (and not controverted) that the local authorities Ombudsman would have power to investigate cases such as these.

But what of the claims against the individual social workers and psychiatrists, whose alleged failures led to the council's alleged failure to protect the children?

The social workers and the psychiatrist were retained by the local authority to advise the local authority, not the plaintiffs. The subject matter of the advice and activities of the professionals is the child. Moreover the tendering of any advice will in many cases involve interviewing and, in the case of doctors, examining the child. But the fact that the carrying out of the retainer involves contact with and relationship with the child cannot alter the extent of the duty owed by the professionals under the retainer from the local authority. The Court of Appeal drew a correct analogy with the doctor instructed by an insurance company to examine an applicant for life insurance. The doctor does not, by examining the applicant, come under any general duty of medical care to the applicant. He is under a duty not to damage the applicant in the course of the examination: but beyond that his duties are owed to the insurance company and not to the applicant.

...

In my judgment in the present cases, the social workers and the psychiatrist did not, by accepting the instructions of the local authority, assume any general professional duty of care to the plaintiff children. The professionals were employed or retained to advise the local authority in relation to the well being of the plaintiffs but not to advise or treat the plaintiffs.

So the result is, in his Lordship's view:

Although anyone would have great sympathy for the plaintiffs in both these cases (if the allegations which they make are true), for these reasons I agree with the Court of Appeal that they have no private law claim in damages. I would dismiss both appeals.

The House of Lords' policy decision is that the ability of social services departments to perform their public law duties under the various statutes would be compromised if their clients had a right to sue when this duty was breached. But this decision is not the end of the story. Just as we saw with the *Barry* case above, that an important statement of legal principle can be distinguished on its particular facts or the particular statute under scrutiny, we have a further House of Lords case and a decision of the European Court of Human Rights to make things, perhaps, less clear cut.

W v *Essex County Council* [2000] 1 FLR 657 sets out an alternative analysis. You will see that Lord Slynn has no great difficulty in finding potential for a duty of care owed not only to the children who allegedly suffered sexual abuse — which the local authority had conceded by this stage — as a result of the department's actions but also to their parents.

The parents contend that the defendants were negligent in placing a known sexual abuser in their home when the defendants knew of G's history and of the parents' anxiety not to have a known sex abuser in their home with four young children aged between 8 and 12 at the relevant time. When they discovered the serious acts of sexual abuse including anal and vaginal penetration and oral sex on 7 May the plaintiffs suffered psychiatric illness and damage including severe depression and post-traumatic stress disorder as described in the medical reports they relied on.

Lord Slynn then considers the argument put forward by the authority that there is no basis for a duty of care to exist:

It seems to me that it cannot be said here that the claim that there was a duty of care owed to the parents and a breach of that duty by the defendants is unarguable, that it is clear and obvious that it cannot succeed. On the contrary whether it is right or wrong on the facts found at the end of the day, it is on the facts alleged plainly a claim which is arguable. In their case the parents made it clear that they were anxious not to put their children at risk by having a known sex abuser in their home. The council and the social worker knew this and also knew that the boy placed had already committed an act or acts of sex abuse. The risk was obvious and the abuse happened. Whether the nature of the council's task is such that the court should not recognise an actionable duty of care, in other words that the claim is not justiciable, and whether there was a breach of the duty depend, in the first place, on an investigation of the full facts known to, and the factors influencing the decision of, the defendants.

On the question of primary and secondary victims (an issue arising in tort as to where to draw the boundaries — for example where nervous shock is suffered by relatives, the secondary victims, who learn of a horrific accident to the primary victims) Lord Slynn went on:

[I]t seems to me impossible to say that the psychiatric injury they claim is outside the range of psychiatric injury which the law recognises. Prima facie pleaded it is more than 'acute grief.' Thus in the case of the parents it is said:

'The mother has suffered reactive depression, sleep disturbance, nightmares, tearfulness, exacerbation of her condition of diabetes and from hypertension. She is no longer able to work as a foster parent. The father has suffered reactive depression and post-traumatic stress disorder with sleep disturbance, nightmares and he was unable to continue work as a foster parent or a youth worker. The parents' marriage, which had previously been a happy one, was placed under extreme stress and they have subsequently separated. Their sexual relationship was affected and they suffered guilt characterised by feelings of helplessness and powerlessness. Dr Bawden, in the report dated 11 September 1994 describes how: "The effect on the family as a whole has been devastating... From a previously well-functioning family since they were assessed as being able to foster disturbed adolescents, their functioning has deteriorated markedly. They have lost employment. Their marital relationship has deteriorated and both parents have had increased ill-health since the disclosure of these events".'

Nor do I find it possible to say that a person of reasonable fortitude would be bound to take in his or her stride being told of the sexual abuse of his or her young children when that person had even innocently brought together the abuser and the abused. A judge might find on a full investigation of the circumstances that they might. I do not feel sufficiently informed on the detailed facts at this stage to rule it out.

The decision reached is not at this stage that damages should be awarded, merely that the issues may proceed to trial. Here is how one commentator views such a result (though the article was commenting not on the parents' claim, but on the decision of the Court of Appeal not to strike out the children's claim). Ken Oliphant, in a case commentary in *Child and Family Law Quarterly* vol. 10 no. 3 1998 writes:

For what it is worth, *my* gut instinct is that the policy considerations which justified Lord Browne-Wilkinson's decision not to impose a duty of care on the local authorities in *X* v *Bedfordshire* ought also to be regarded as decisive here. Of the two principal justifications for his conclusion, I would rely less on overkill and deterrence — considerations which, as the present case clearly demonstrates, are difficult to assess and can pull both ways — and more on the fear of opening the floodgates of liability. It is well known that local authority social services departments have to struggle with tightly limited resources, which are already threatened by documented increases in the number and quantum of claims made against them and, consequently, in their public liability insurance premiums. Weir, writing in 1989, was able to estimate the extent of this trend by referring to the files of Municipal Mutual Insurance, which at that time insured the vast majority (about 90 per cent) of local authorities against liability. He discovered in the most recent six-year period for which figures were available an increase in excess of 50 per cent in the number of claims received annually, and an increase in excess of 150 per cent in the total amount paid out annually on third-party policies (excluding motor vehicle and employers' liability policies). He predicted that these would be quickly reflected in increased public liability premiums for local authorities. Inevitably, the increases must be accommodated either by raising the level of council tax, or local authority income from other sources, or by reducing the level of council services. Neither option is very palatable, given especially the alternative remedies that are available in cases such as *W* v *Essex County Council* to ensure compensation and accountability. The victim of physical or sexual abuse has a claim to a substantial award under the Criminal Injuries Compensation Scheme, as was noted in the present case by Stuart-Smith LJ. His Lordship added, with convincing logic: 'Since the source of the compensation is in any event public funds I do not see any particular merit in making the local authority who have failed to protect the children from G liable in preference to the statutory scheme set up for the very purpose of compensating the victims of the criminal violence such as that perpetrated by G'. Additionally, we should note that, in cases falling short of physical or sexual abuse, payment of small sums of compensation by the local authority may be recommended by the Local Government Ombudsman. The Ombudsman's investigation of allegations of maladministration also ensures that local authorities are publicly accountable in respect of the performance of their statutory functions. Mechanisms already exist, then, to ensure the compensation of the victims of child abuse and the accountability of local authority social services departments. If Parliament feels that these mechanisms are inadequate, then it is for Parliament to do something about it. It should not be for the courts to intervene by holding local authorities liable at common law for tortious acts committed by third parties ...

The *Bedfordshire* case saw the House of Lords finally dismiss the right for children to proceed to trial with their claim that social services failed to rescue them from harm. The claimants subsequently took the striking out of their claim further, to the European Court of Human Rights. (Please see the following chapter for more discussion on human rights.) *In Z and others* v *United Kingdom* [2001] 2 FLR 612 (which is the same case under a different name) the Court first of all looked at the allegation that Article 3 of the European Convention had been breached.

3.   The applicants alleged that the local authority had failed to take adequate protective measures in respect of the severe neglect and abuse which they were known to be suffering due to their ill-treatment by their parents and that they had no access to court or effective remedy in respect of this. They invoked Articles 3, 6, 8 and 13 of the Convention.

I. Alleged violation of Article 3 of the Convention

69.   The applicants alleged that the local authority had failed to protect them from inhuman and degrading treatment contrary to Article 3 of the Convention which provides:
    'No one shall be subjected to torture or to inhuman or degrading treatment or punishment.'
74.   There is no dispute in the present case that the neglect and abuse suffered by the four child applicants reached the threshold of inhuman and degrading. ... This treatment was brought to the local authority's attention, at the earliest in October 1987. It was under a statutory duty to protect the children and had a range of powers available to them, including removal from their home. ... The Court acknowledges the difficult and sensitive decisions facing social services and the important countervailing principle of respecting and preserving family life. The present case however leaves no doubt as to the failure of the system to protect these child applicants from serious, long-term neglect and abuse.
75.   Accordingly, there has been a violation of Article 3 of the Convention.

Alleged violation of Article 6 of the Convention

78.   The applicants complained that they had been denied access to court to determine their claims against the local authority in negligence, invoking Article 6 of the Convention.
79.   Article 6 para. 1 provides in its first sentence:
    'In the determination of his civil rights and obligations or of any criminal charge against him, everyone is entitled to a fair and public hearing within a reasonable time by an independent and impartial tribunal established by law.'

Referring to the lack of any remedy under the English law the Court continued:

102.   It is ... the case that the interpretation of domestic law by the House of Lords resulted in the applicants' case being struck out. The tort of negligence was held not to impose a duty of care

on the local authority in the exercise of its statutory powers. Their experiences were described as 'horrific' by a psychiatrist ... and the Court has found that they were victims of a violation of Article 3 (see paragraph 74 above). Yet the outcome of the domestic proceedings they brought is that they, and any children with complaints such as theirs, cannot sue the local authority in negligence for compensation, however foreseeable — and severe — the harm suffered and however unreasonable the conduct of the local authority in failing to take steps to prevent that harm. The applicants are correct in their assertions that the gap they have identified in domestic law is one that gives rise to an issue under the Convention, but in the Court's view it is an issue under Article 13, not Article 6, para. 1.

IV. Alleged violation of Article 13 of the Convention

105. The applicants submitted that they had not been afforded any remedy for the damage which they had suffered as a result of the failure of the local authority to protect them, invoking Article 13 of the Convention which provides:

'Everyone whose rights and freedoms as set forth in the Convention are violated shall have an effective remedy before a national authority notwithstanding that the violation has been committed by persons acting in an official capacity.'

106. The applicants argued that the exclusionary rule established by the House of Lords in their case deprived them of any effective remedy within the national legal system for the violation of Article 3 which they suffered. While the remedy required by Article 13 need not always be judicial in character, in their case a judicial determination was required. This was because the tort of negligence was the only remedy in national law capable of determining the substance of their complaint and which (but for the alleged immunity) would closely match the requirements of the Convention. Also the accountability of public officials, central to both Articles 3 and 13, required a right of access to court whereby the individual could hold the responsible officials to account in adversarial proceedings and obtain an enforceable order for compensation if the claim was substantiated. The wording of Article 13 also prohibited the creation of immunities for public officials and any such immunity must be regarded as contrary to the object and purpose of the Convention.

109. ... Where alleged failure by the authorities to protect persons from the acts of others is concerned, Article 13 may not always require that the authorities undertake the responsibility for investigating the allegations. There should however be available to the victim or the victim's family a mechanism for establishing any liability of State officials or bodies for acts or omissions involving the breach of their rights under the Convention. Furthermore, in the case of a breach of Articles 2 and 3 of the Convention, which rank as the most fundamental provisions of the Convention, compensation for the non-pecuniary damage flowing from the breach should in principle be available as part of the range of redress.

111. The Court finds that in this case the applicants did not have available to them an appropriate means of obtaining a determination of their allegations that the local authority failed to protect them from inhuman and degrading treatment and the possibility of obtaining an enforceable award of compensation for the damage suffered thereby. Consequently, they were not afforded an effective remedy in respect of the breach of Article 3 and there has, accordingly, been a violation of Article 13 of the Convention.

121. ... The breach of Article 3 concerned the failure of the local authority to take reasonable steps available to them to protect them from that damage. There is a direct causal link therefore between the breach and the damage suffered by the children. While it is correct, as asserted by the Government, that there is no finding that the children should have immediately been taken into care and that they might have suffered damage even if effective steps had been taken at an earlier stage, the Court notes that the severity of the damage suffered by the children is inextricably linked to the long period of time over which the abuse persisted, which factor is also at the heart of the violation of Article 3 in this case.

The court then assessed the prognosis for each claimant. Paragraph 127 assesses the losses that can be quantified and paragraph 130 assesses those that cannot be.

127. Bearing in mind the uncertainties of the applicants' situations, and making an assessment on an equitable basis, the Court awards Z the sum of GBP 8,000 for future medical costs; A the sum of GBP 50,000 for future medical costs and GBP 50,000 for loss of employment opportunities; B the sum of GBP 50,000 for future medical costs and GBP 30,000 for loss of employment opportunities; and C the sum of GBP 4,000 for future medical costs.

130. The children in this case suffered very serious abuse and neglect over a period of more than four years. Z, A and B suffered, and in the case of the two boys, still suffer, psychiatric illness as a result. A and B also suffered physical injury and C neglect in respect of an eye condition. The description of the conditions which they endured and the traumatic effects which this had on the children leave the Court with no doubt that a substantial award to reflect their pain and suffering is appropriate.

131. In making this assessment, the Court recalls that the rates applied in domestic cases, though relevant, are not decisive. It does not consider it appropriate or desirable to attempt to distinguish between the children in this context. Making an assessment on an equitable basis, the Court awards each child the sum of GBP 32,000.

The influence of *Z* v *UK* has already been felt in subsequent cases. In *S* v *Gloucestershire County Council* [2000] 2 FCR 345, the claimant alleged that the council had been negligent within the law of tort, in that they had placed him as a child with foster parents who abused him sexually. The case reached the Court of Appeal on the same legal question: did the council owe him a duty of care. The council applied to have the claim struck out without the facts being considered. They succeeded at first instance and the claimant appealed. May LJ set out the principles:

In my view, a number of strands of the relevant law ... may be summarised as follows: (a) depending on the particular facts of the case, a claim in common law negligence may be available to a person who claims to have been damaged by failings of a local authority who were responsible under statutory powers for his care and upbringing. In each of the cases before this court, the claims were sensibly limited to common law negligence claims; (b) the claim will not succeed if the failings alleged comprise actions or decisions by the local authority of a kind which are not justiciable. These may include, but will not necessarily be limited to, policy decisions and decisions about allocating public funds; (c) the border line between what is justiciable and what is not may in a particular case be unclear. Its demarcation may require a more extensive investigation than is capable of being made from material in traditional pleadings alone; (d) there may be circumstances in which it will not be just and reasonable to impose a duty of care of the kind contended for. Here again, it may often be necessary to conduct a detailed investigation of the facts to determine this question; (e) in considering whether a discretionary decision was negligent, the court will not substitute its view for that of the local authority upon whom the statute has placed the power to exercise the discretion, unless the discretionary decision was plainly wrong. But decisions of, for example, social workers are capable of being held to have been negligent by analogy with decisions of other professional people. Here again, it may well be necessary to conduct a detailed factual inquiry.

It is clear from these principles that in an ordinary case a local authority defendant are unlikely to establish a defence which relies on a blanket immunity. There would be a blanket immunity for this purpose if it were decided without reference to particular facts that all cases which have certain basic characteristics were not justiciable; or that in every case with certain characteristics it was not just or reasonable to impose a duty of care. Thus it seems to me that it would be incorrect to say, as counsel for the local authorities were inclined to submit in appeals before this court, that cases which may be labelled as child abuse cases are bound to fail as a class.

Unfortunately, beyond saying that there should be a proper trial rather than a decision that cases of this sort always fail, the judgment does not set out a clear legal principle. The impression might be a grudging recognition that the claimant has won on procedural grounds — striking out is a breach of his right to a proper hearing — but that the action is doomed when the detail is considered.

The allegations of negligence concern the whole course of S's care by the defendants after he was placed for fostering with Mr and Mrs M. The relevant decisions and actions of the defendants do not, as in the *Bedfordshire* cases, centrally concern the question whether S should be taken into care. Once a child is taken into care, the local authority have assumed responsibility for the child and a duty of care will more readily be found. The facts (which for present purposes are assumed) that Mr M gravely and repeatedly abused S sexually during the six-week-period of his fostering and that he abused at least one other boy during that same period call in question the defendants' selection of him as a foster parent. There has been no disclosure by the defendants on this topic and it cannot be said without investigation that this element of the claim is bound to fail. Accepting that S is recorded as having said on two occasions in February 1990 that he had not himself been assaulted, Miss Gumbel [the claimant's barrister] nevertheless submits that this alone should not be seen at this stage as determinative. It is not certain that a full consideration of the facts would not show want of care by the defendants. It could be that a full consideration of the facts relating to Mr and Mrs M as foster parents, the abuse of the other boy and the facts about S's fostering would show that more extensive and more sensitive inquiries should have been made. These could have then revealed the fact and extent of the abuse. The subsequent history of S's case of care by the defendants shows a failure to deal effectively with emerging emotional and psychological problems. A negligence case arising from this history is one which properly merits investigation at trial. Miss Gumbel accepts that there was mention of multi-disciplinary consideration for S. But the main decisions which are questioned were not inter-disciplinary nor were they delicate or confrontational in the way that those in the *Bedfordshire* cases were.

1.5 Critical reflections on social work law as a discipline

You have now been exposed to materials dealing with the statutory framework for the practice of social work; and you will shortly encounter more detail in a range of areas. Putting all of this together, how would we — how would you — define the field of social work law. Brayne Martin and Carr take as their starting point the statutory framework, and you can see the influence of this thinking on this volume. But there can be other approaches to this discipline, and the chapter ends with some material which encourages you to reflect on this.

The list extract is from 'Social work law: from interaction to integration', *Journal of Social Welfare and Family Law* 20(1) [1998] 65, an article by Michael Preston-Shoot, Gwyneth Roberts, and Stuart Vernon.

From interaction towards integration
For Blom-Cooper, social work practice was to be understood and conceptualized simply in terms of the statutory responsibilities placed upon social work agencies:

'We are strongly of the view that social work can in fact be defined *only* in terms of the functions required of its practitioners by their employing agency operating within a statutory framework.' [Blom-Cooper, 1985: 12]

The approach to social work practice prescribed by Blom-Cooper carries several dangers. For Blom-Cooper, the statutory mandate is the single prescriber of social work action, an approach that obscures the uncertainties inherent in everyday practice. It avoids the dilemma of which duties to prioritize, particularly in a context where resources are increasingly limited (for instance, the duty to promote the welfare of children (section 17 of the Children Act 1989), as against the duty to investigate suspicions of significant harm (section 47)). Social work is a far more complex process than simply executing the relevant legislation. Such complexity may be glimpsed in recent case-law where the courts have had to grapple with particular aspects of the statutory base of child care and community care social work. In the judgments in *Re H and R (Child Sexual Abuse: Standard of Proof)* [1996] 1 FLR 80, the Law Lords discussed the issue of child sexual abuse, and whether in order to be satisfied that a child is 'likely to suffer significant harm' (a threshold criterion for a care order) on the sole grounds of *alleged* sexual abuse in the past, a finding of *actual* abuse was necessary: in other words, must 'likelihood' of significant harm be based on proven fact? In *R v Gloucestershire County Council and Another, ex parte Barry* [1997] *The Times*, 21 March, the House of Lords considered the definition of need for services for disabled people and the extent to which legislation (here the Chronically Sick and Disabled Persons Act 1970 and the NHS and Community Care Act 1990) may be defined as imposing an absolute duty on local authorities to assess such need and provide services to meet it. Both cases are examples of judges wrestling with the relationship between the law and social issues, and with the extent to which the boundaries of what is relevant to decision-making may be opened out beyond narrow legal interpretation. The complexity also derives from the law attempting to balance apparently conflicting principles and practices. Thus, the welfare of a child is not always the paramount consideration (Children Act 1989 — secure accommodation orders), and the community care mandate is confused on what controls questions of service provision [...].

Furthermore, Blom-Cooper's approach creates an impression that social workers have greater powers than they have. It obscures the legal checks and balances under which they operate and, in so far as the law is expressed through agency policies, conflates procedurally correct practice with good practice. These dangers have been illustrated in community care litigation, where local authorities have been deemed to have acted unlawfully, unreasonably or irrationally.

It also promotes a simplistic linear view that the law alone can correct an action which has inspired its use. Neither child abuse nor delinquency can simply be legislated away (Braye and Preston-Shoot, 1990). Moreover, reliance on the law to resolve questions of welfare may be misplaced because of the adversarial nature of legal dispute resolution, and its narrow emphasis on questions of evidence and procedure can produce over-simplified responses to real practice dilemmas (King and Trowell, 1992; Pietroni, 1995).

If Blom-Cooper's view of social work was an over-simplification, so too was Stevenson's response (1988) to *The Law Report* (Ball *et al.*, 1988). She perceived social work as primarily grounded in an ethical duty of care, but she appeared not to recognize social workers' accountability to the law and to their employers, and the tensions which arise when these conflict. However superficially appealing, this response also obscures the reality of practitioners feeling unsupported and under-valued; economics rather than effectiveness or needs determining agency provision; and draconian resource constraints which leave practitioners and managers struggling with irreconcilable demands or conceding to the erosion of social work values as the only means of survival practice dilemmas which are derived from conflicting imperatives and from ambiguities within the legal mandate. Social work law is such a subject discipline.

...

1. Legal powers and duties
Legal powers and duties, set out in a number of statutory provisions and further defined by various judicial decisions, provide social workers with their basic mandate to practise. These are

ntained within a series of statutory provisions, including the Children Act 1989, Health Act 1983, and the NHS and Community Care Act 1990. These statutes set out ns social work functions:

for instance providing supportive services in relation to children in need (section 17, Children Act 1989) or community care services (section 47, NHS and Community Care Act 1990);
- *protection*, for instance applying for a Care Order to prevent significant harm to a child, or an application for compulsory admission to hospital under the Mental Health Act 1983.

These powers and duties also define the service user groups towards whom such statutory duties and powers should be directed, including *children in need*; people with *mental disorder*, including mental illness and learning disability; people with *chronic illness*; people with *sensory impairment* or *physical disability*; *vulnerable older people*; and *offenders*.

The statutory mandate, therefore, can promote and encourage good social work practice. It does this by emphasizing the importance of prevention and rehabilitation. It sets out the conditions under which compulsory intervention is permissible, and provides legal safeguards to ensure that it takes place in accordance with due process of law and adherence to the principles of natural justice. Some of these statutory provisions have been the subject of judicial interpretation — for example, the nature, burden and proof required to establish the likelihood of significant harm (*Re H and R (Child Sexual Abuse: Standard of Proof)* [1996]); and the meaning of assessment of need (*R v Gloucestershire County Council and Another, ex parte Barry* [1997]).

However, the legal mandate alone cannot accurately reflect the complexity of many people's lives, locating problems and solutions, as it predominantly does, within individuals and families, without acknowledging structural inequality, disadvantage and exclusion. The question, then, is whether the legal system can ever challenge these features of people's lives. It also offers insufficient safeguards for service users. Thus, if one argument is that the law itself is problematic, another is that statute and guidance are being misused. Judicial review and ombudsman decisions, together with research evidence (for example, Rickford, 1992; Colton et al., 1995) have found agencies failing to assess in a structured way, or to interpret guidance accurately. Duties are being interpreted by local authorities more narrowly than envisaged by guidance, whilst written plans are not always provided nor reviews regularly held. Complaints procedures are not always managed fairly (for a review of cases, see Preston-Shoot, 1996).

2. Social work values and knowledge
Social workers practise also on the basis of certain ethical and professional values. These include a commitment to:
- equal opportunities and anti-discriminatory practice
- partnership
- the right of individuals to receive care, treatment and control in the context of
  - the least restrictive alternative
  - normalization/non-stigmatization
  - ethnic, cultural and language needs
- social order: for example, the right of society to protection from significant risk, danger or harm; the recognition of the rights of significant others, for instance victims and carers
- self-determination.

Social work law, as expressed in statute and guidance, codifies and legitimates practice founded on these values, as the following examples illustrate:
- *equal opportunities*: Criminal Justice Act 1991 (s. 95); Children Act 1989 (ss. 1(3) and 22(5));
- *partnership*: Carers (Recognition and Services) Act 1995; Mental Health Act 1983 (s. 13(2)) and Code of Practice (DoH. 1993); child care and child protection (DoH. 1989a);
- *normalization*: Chronically Sick and Disabled Persons Act 1970 (s. 2);
- *cultural needs*: Children Act 1989 (ss. 1(3) and 22(5));

- *balancing care and control*: Mental Health Act 1983 (s. 13(2)); Children Act 1989 (s. 17); principles of residential care for adults (DoH, 1989b);
- *social order*: Criminal Justice Act 1991 and Criminal Justice and Public Order Act 1994 (child witnesses); Family Law Act 1996 (provision to add exclusion orders to Emergency Protection and Interim Care Orders);
- *self-determination*: Community Care (Direct Payments) Act 1996; LAC(92)27 — choice of accommodation; young people and consent to medical treatment (Children Act 1989, ss. 38(6), 43(8) and 44(7)).

There are occasions, however, where the legal provisions are more restrictive than social work's professional values. The exclusion of some service user groups from the scope of the Community Care (Direct Payments) Act 1996 would be one example; another lies in a court's ability to dispense in certain circumstances with the necessity of commissioning a pre-sentence report (Criminal Justice and Public Order Act 1994) prior to sentencing an offender. Thus, there are occasions where social work values are endorsed: others where they are undermined (such as the protection of the rights of the accused at the expense of the welfare of a child in criminal proceedings where the child is a witness and therapeutic intervention is therefore delayed).

...

3. Aspects of administrative law

Most social work practice in Britain today is located within corporate organizations which are subject, ultimately, to the jurisdiction and control of the courts as well as to scrutiny by non-judicial authorities such as the Commissioner for Local Administration. It is here, in fact, that conflict between social work values and social work practice is most likely to occur. This is because organizational directives which follow from political decision-making, particularly in the context of severe resource pressures, do not necessarily equate with judicial decisions, guidance or social work principles. Accordingly, a third essential strand in social work law is the influence upon social work practice of certain aspects of administrative law, such as judicial review which sometimes acts as a check upon local authority processes and which specifies a code of practice encapsulated in rules of natural justice. However, judicial review is a discretionary procedure providing discretionary remedies, and is dependent on an individual or organization making an application and establishing their standing (*locus standi*) to do so. This renders independent monitoring organizations, such as the Mental Health Act Commission, all the more important, to ensure that services are properly and appropriately provided within the law.

It is upon the local authority itself, as a consequence of its status as an incorporated body, that most statutory powers and duties are placed. As public bodies, they must then translate these powers and duties into services for individual users, their families and carers, by means of *delegation* and *designation* of authority to employees to act (see Ball et al., 1995: 18). For example, it is only *Approved Social Workers* (that is, designated social workers who have been 'approved' by the authority in accordance with section 145, Mental Health Act 1983) who are assigned the necessary legal authority to carry out certain functions under the Act, such as applying for the compulsory admission of a mentally disordered patient to hospital.

In addition, a social worker's activities are shaped to a considerable degree by Directions and policy guidance issued under section 7A of the Local Authority Social Services Act 1970. Although Directions must be strictly adhered to, guidance can prove more problematic. Sometimes it does not add much clarity to statute, as in the case of policy guidance issued under the Carers (Recognition and Services) Act 1995 in relation to the meaning of 'substantial and regular' care (LAC(96)7). Sometimes it does not prioritize objectives, as in community care where the proper assessment of need sits alongside taking account of what is affordable and available (DoH, 1990). None the less, local authorities must not ignore guidance which is issued under section 7A (*R v Gloucestershire County Council, ex parte Mahfood and others* [1995]

CO 3507–94), nor must they give disproportionate weight to one component of guidance at the expense of the overall context (*Sutton LBC* v *Davis* [1994] 1 FLR 737). Moreover, the courts have also stressed that local authorities should take account of general advice set out in practice guidance (*R* v *Islington LBC, ex parte Rixon* [1996], *The Times*, 17 April).

A social worker's activities are also shaped by local policy whose validity must be measured by reference to what the courts regard as reasonable, rational and lawful, and as falling within the terms of the statutory duties and powers placed upon it, and as using powers and duties in the right and proper way which Parliament, when conferring them, is presumed to have intended.

Accountability within this structure is provided not only through an individual social worker's contract with his/her employing agency, but also through mechanisms such as complaints procedures (set out in section 26, Children Act 1989 and in section 7B, Local Authority Social Services Act 1970 (as inserted by section 50 of the NHS and Community Care Act 1990)), and by means of particular tribunals (such as the Mental Health Review Tribunal). Other more general means of scrutinizing the decisions of bodies such as local authorities lie with ministerial default powers, the Local Government Ombudsman and judicial review.

Redress is, however, limited. Judicial review is entirely discretionary, and the focus is not on the facts or merits of a decision, but on the decision-making process and whether the authority has approached its decisions legally, rationally and with procedural propriety. The Ombudsman may enquire more widely into discrimination, incompetence, delay or other maladministration, but this process too is lengthy, and he/she has no power to require a local authority to alter its decision. The findings of complaints procedures are not binding on the local authority, the test being whether departures from a complaints panel's recommendations are reasonable (*R* v *North Yorkshire County Council, ex parte Hargreaves* [1994] CO/878/94).

...

Conclusion

The relationship between social workers and the law is unique. Not only is the law a defining mandate in a sense not applicable to, say, doctors and police officers, but it is an insufficient mandate to reflect the complexity both of practice and of service users' lives. Three final points can be made. First, to negotiate the dilemmas which social work law involves, a shared language must be created between social workers and lawyers, making accessible the constituent elements of this discipline. That will be the subject of another article.

Secondly, the curriculum needs to prepare students for the content of practice — law, and social work knowledge, values and skills: and for the context of practice — managing the organizational location. Academic tutors and practice teachers need to model an integrated approach by teasing out from scenarios and cases all the constituent elements of social work law as identified in this article, and by developing students' skills in decision-making concerning the content of practice — what is to be done, why and how — and the context of practice — how to secure the most from an organization for and with service users. Models for the academic curriculum have been developed (for example, Braye and Preston-Shoot, 1991: Eadie and Ward, 1995). Less is known on how practice teachers are responding to their increased responsibilities concerning CCETSW's requirements (1995) in respect of law teaching and assessment. The authors of this article are currently researching that question (Preston-Shoot et al., 1997).

References

Ball, C., Preston-Shoot, M., Roberts, G. and Vernon, S. (1995) *Law for Social Workers in England and Wales*, London: CCETSW.

Blom-Cooper, L. (1985) *A Child in Trust. The Beckford Report*. London: Borough of Brent.

King, M. and Trowell, J. (1992) *Children's Welfare and the Law. The Limits of Legal Intervention*. London: Sage.

Pietroni. M. (1995) 'The nature and aims of professional education for social workers: a post-modern perspective', in M. Yelloly and M. Henkel (eds) *Learning and Teaching in Social Work*, London: Jessica Kingsley.

Stevenson, O. (1988) 'Law and social work education: a commentary on the "Law Report"', *Issues in Social Work Education* 8(1): 37–45.

In a follow up article the same authors continue this exploration: 'Working together in Social Work Law', *Journal of Social Welfare and Family Law* 20(2) [1998], 137.

Lawyers and social workers — the legacy of professional status

In understanding the interactions between lawyers and social workers it is important to recognize the differences in status and loyalties between the two professions, reflected in the different relationship they have with their respective service users. The statutory mandate of social work law establishes the social work practitioner in a delegated and/or a designated position. The delegated position of social work arises from the imposition of social services responsibilities upon the authority itself, as a corporate body, which, in turn, employs social workers to operationalize those statutory responsibilities. A designated position exists where an individual social worker, employed by a local authority, is also designated to carry out a particular statutory function, for example where a social worker is appointed by a local authority to act as an approved social worker under section 114 of the Mental Health Act 1983. The statute then imposes duties and powers upon them directly. Consequently a social worker may owe responsibilities concurrently to the statutory mandate, to their employers, to the service user (their client) and to the values of their profession.

The tensions inherent within this multiplicity of accountability are intensified by ambiguities in the form which social work law takes, that is a mix of statute, case-law and official guidance. The child protection mandate is now being modified by calls for a lighter touch through a renewed emphasis on prevention (DoH, 1995), but with limited clarification on how, in the context of resource constraints, these dual and competing responsibilities are to be met. The community care mandate remains confused over the degree to which needs, rights and resources control questions of service provision. The different meanings which may be attributed to partnership, consumerism, empowerment, choice and quality are further examples of the ambiguity which surrounds what balance should be struck between autonomy, protection and empowerment. The very complexity of social work practice, suffused with dilemmas and choices, means that when and how to intervene, and to what degree, is not always obvious.

Contrast the complexity of these relationships between social work practitioners and their service users, with that between lawyers and their clients. For private practitioners the central relationship is with the client and is instructional by nature, though the nature of the relationship will determine that instructions from the client are subject to objective testing against established rules of law and procedure, the availability of evidence and other essentially legalistic concerns which give power within the relationship to the lawyer. However, the client has the ultimate power to dispense with the services of their lawyer. For the local authority lawyer the situation is not so clear-cut since their position is made more ambiguous by their employment by a statutory body. However, their status within the legal profession permits them a degree of independence which is generally not available to the employed social worker.

A further important element of the relationship between lawyers and social workers is provided by the fact that the practice of social work is more and more frequently subject to accountability through the law. Increasing legalism is a feature of contemporary social work practice, reflected through, among other things, national standards, court involvement in decisions which were previously the province of professionals alone, and a burgeoning amount of guidance and regulations. Indeed, social work practice has itself been judged by lawyers in public enquiries and by legal processes such as judicial review. Inquiries into the abuse of children have implied a direct challenge to social work practice (Cochrane, 1993) and were based on the norms of the legal system, with its stress on rules and procedures, rather than evaluating the complex components of a child's welfare, as well as the social, economic and organizational factors which may impinge upon families and social work practice.

The increasingly legalistic context of social work reflects the prominence accorded to legalism and 'the rule of law', and therefore to lawyers, in contemporary society. One consequence of this is the increasing number of circumstances in which lawyers and social workers are likely to work together. Another consequence is the identification of professional status and values as issues of potential conflict or tension.

Bell and Daly (1992:257) argue that the professions of law and social work are at different stages in their historical development.

'Social work is a profession in adolescence, with a wide field of relevance and application, but lacking a coherent identity and beset by changes in role and social expectation. Law, by comparison, has a long history and tradition, carrying a relatively narrow focus on task and relevance and a dislike of risk-taking. Law was one of the three original professions, and the status of lawyers as professionals is not in doubt. By contrast, there are difficulties for social workers in attaining professional status. These are attributable to a number of factors, such as the multi-faceted nature of their work and an unclear conceptual base.'

Since lawyers and social workers have unequal professional status, one might expect to see this reflected in their professional relationship, compounded by the fact that professional work which involves both lawyers and social workers frequently takes place in a location, such as a court of law, or at earlier stages of litigation, where the values, judgements and interests of social work and the social worker are secondary to those of the law and the lawyer. This argument holds for lawyers employed by local authorities, for whom questions of evidence and legal procedures will have primacy over social workers' judgements about whether a child is the likely victim of significant harm.

Tensions imposed by the law and the legal system

Lawyers and social workers work with a knowledge base and value system which are inculcated by means of education, training and practice, and which are distinct to the two professions. There are, therefore, inevitable tensions between social work values and practice, and legal values and practice. The difficulty of achieving shared understanding and common goals is amply demonstrated by the following examples:

- The adversarial and partisan tradition and culture of the legal process and profession may seem at odds with the values and practice of social work.
- The individualization of legal decision-making which cannot reconcile or embrace the interests of a single litigant with the interests of an unknown number of other possible claimants for services whose needs may be known to social workers and considered in their determinations. These difficulties are amply demonstrated by judicial review cases concerning the distribution of finite community care services.
- The inappropriateness of law to determine questions of welfare, and to balance conflicting but legitimate claims to justice and rights. These are essentially social policy questions.
- The concern of social work to empower service users and the ability and suitability of the law for this purpose, given the limitations of the remedies available in terms of their discretionary nature and their individualized effect.
- The use of largely inquisitorial processes (complaints, procedures, tribunals) to determine disputes between service users and authorities responsible for the provision of social work services. Lawyers are more accustomed to the adversarial procedures of the courts. It should, though, be recognized that some court-based hearings concerning social work, such as family proceedings hearing child care cases, adopt a hybrid procedure which encompasses both adversarial and inquisitorial characteristics.

• The legal or quasi-legal enforcement of service user rights against social work authorities committed to the principles of partnership and cooperation with service users.

There will be times when these 'structural' differences will tend toward misunderstandings between social workers and lawyers and even to professional tensions, frustration, resentment and distrust. These circumstances are more likely when the social work profession has 'lost control' of an issue or case to the legal or quasi-legal system. Examples would include complaints to the local government Ombudsman, judicial review applications and inquiries headed by lawyers. Of course, lawyers may see the same circumstances in a different light, as examples of situations where the discretionary power of the social work profession is being properly subjected to the accountability of the law or quasi-law. It should be acknowledged that the growth of legalism within and around social work, and the development of good practice, should make the use of arbitrary and unaccountable power much less likely than previously, although courts have had to remind social work practitioners and managers that the duty to act lawfully transcends any duty to act according to an employer's instructions (*R* v *Gloucestershire County Council, ex parte Mahfood and others* [1995] CO 3507–94). It should also be acknowledged that some, though not all, judicial decisions (for example, *Re C (A Minor) (Residence Order: Lesbian Co-parents)* [1994] Family Law, 468; *Re C (a minor)* [1996]) have upheld social work values and judgements of good practice. Lawyers are able to call social workers as expert witnesses in circumstances where the values of social work are part of the expertise that is being called as evidence in a legal context so that its status is recognized and valued outside social work. Equally, social workers may need to call upon the use of compulsory powers; such powers are situated within the law, and sanctioned by it, and this status allows the practitioner to identify their objective and legal status as an element of their power without having to compromise the essentially non-compulsive nature of social work practice. The lawyer offers objective legal advice and a rigorous testing of the case put forward by reference to evidence, statutory criteria and case-law. The social worker offers not only the details of *this* case but also accompanying research evidence, a value position, and knowledge derived from theory and practice, and looks to the law for endorsement.

References
Bell, M. and Daly, R. (1992) 'Social workers and solicitors: working together?' *Family Law* (June): 257–61.

Cochrane, A. (1993) 'Challenges from the centre', in J. Clarke (ed.) *A Crisis in Care? Challenges to Social Work*, Milton Keynes: Open University Press.

DoH (1995) *Child Protection — Messages from Research*, London: HMSO.

2

Human rights law

A power struggle between monarch and subjects, going back to Magna Carta, is a running theme of British history. The constitutional result is the rule of law, which means no-one is above the law, and the supremacy of an elected parliament able to make any law and accountable only to its electorate. It could be claimed that this provides the finest safeguard of individual rights, better than giving powers, under a bill of rights, to unelected judges to strike down the legislation and decisions of elected politicians.

But the incorporation of a statement of enduring principles into the law, indeed into a position in law where they are superior to other laws, can provide a check on the exercise of arbitrary power by government, public authorities and even by Parliament.

2.1 The post-1945 human rights framework

Human rights are often expressed as if they have always existed, waiting to be discovered — the US declaration of independence uses the terms 'inalienable' and 'self-evident' — but it is more accurate to see them as representing the expression of the political, economic, and social developments over the past three centuries. In particular the European Convention on Human Rights, which has been brought into English law, is a reaction to the horrors of World War II.

Declarations of rights do not assure rights just by being written on paper. The writers of the US Declaration of Independence would have been amazed to discover that the rights they set out for 'all men' extended to their wives, daughters and slaves. Victims of ethnic massacres in Rwanda in the 1990s had a right to life under the country's constitution. Rights work only if there is a mechanism for enforcing them. There are rights set out in a range of UN covenants — rights which we will shortly extract — which are not incorporated into English law and cannot be used as the basis for a claim. Although they bind governments at a rhetorical level, and many states have incorporated the principles directly into their law, in the UK these covenants are at best persuasive and at worst irrelevant to the aggrieved individual. By contrast, the Human Rights Act 1998 changed the law which the courts observe.

2.2 **UN Human Rights documents**

The UN Convention on Human Rights was approved by the UN General Assembly in 1948 and has been ratified by the UK government.

Article 1
All human beings are born free and equal in dignity and rights. They are endowed with reason and conscience and should act towards one another in a spirit of brotherhood.

Article 2
Everyone is entitled to all the rights and freedoms set forth in this Declaration, without distinction of any kind, such as race, colour, sex, language, religion, political or other opinion, national or social origin, property, birth or other status.

...

Article 3
Everyone has the right to life, liberty and the security of person.

Article 4
No one shall be held in slavery or servitude; slavery and the slave trade shall be prohibited in all their forms.

Article 5
No one shall be subjected to torture or to cruel, inhuman or degrading treatment or punishment.

Article 6
Everyone has the right to recognition everywhere as a person before the law.

Article 7
All are equal before the law and are entitled without any discrimination to equal protection against any discrimination in violation of this Declaration and against any incitement to such discrimination.

Article 8
Everyone has the right to an effective remedy by the competent national tribunals for acts violating the fundamental rights granted him by the constitution or by law.

Article 9
No one shall be subjected to arbitrary arrest, detention or exile.

Article 10
Everyone is entitled in full equality to a fair, and public hearing by an independent and impartial tribunal, in the determination of his rights and obligations and of any criminal charge against him.

Article 11
Everyone charged with a penal offence has the right to be presumed innocent until proven guilty according to law in a public trial at which he has had all the guarantees necessary for his defence.
    No one shall be held guilty of any penal offence on account of any act or omission which did not constitute a penal offence, under national or international law, at the time when it was committed. Nor shall a heavier penalty be imposed than the one that was applicable at the time the penal offence was committed.

Article 12
No one shall be subjected to arbitrary interference with his privacy, family, home or correspondence, nor to attacks upon his honour and reputation. Everyone has the right to the protection of the law against such interference or attacks.

Article 13
Everyone has the right to freedom of movement and residence within the borders of each State.
  Everyone has the right to leave any country, including his own, and to return to his country.

Article 14
(1)   Everyone has the right to seek and to enjoy in other countries asylum from persecution.
(2)   This right may not be invoked in the case of prosecutions genuinely arising from non-political crimes or from acts contrary to the purposes and principles of the United Nations.

Article 15
(1)   Everyone has the right to a nationality.
(2)   No one shall be arbitrarily deprived of his nationality nor denied the right to change his nationality.

Article 16
(1)   Men and women of full age, without any limitation due to race, nationality or religion, have the right to marry and to found a family. They are entitled to equal rights as to marriage, during marriage and at its dissolution.
(2)   Marriage shall be entered into only with the free and full consent of the intending spouses.
(3)   The family is the natural and fundamental group unit of society and is entitled to protection by society and the State.

Article 17
(1)   Everyone has the right to own property alone as well as in association with others.
(2)   No one shall be arbitrarily deprived of his property.

Article 18
Everyone has the right to freedom of thought, conscience and religion; this right includes freedom to change his religion or belief, and freedom, either alone or in community with others and in public or private, to manifest his religion or belief in teaching, practice, worship and observance.

Article 19
Everyone has the right to freedom of opinion and expression; this right includes freedom to hold opinions without interference and to seek, receive and impart information and ideas through any media and regardless of frontiers.

Article 20
(1)   Everyone has the right to freedom of peaceful assembly and association.
(2)   No one may be compelled to belong to an association.

Article 21
(1)   Everyone has the right to take part in the government of his country, directly or through freely chosen representatives.
(2)   Everyone has the right of equal access to public service in his country.
(3)   The will of the people shall be the basis of the authority of government; this will shall be expressed in periodic and genuine elections which shall be by universal and equal suffrage and shall be held by secret vote or by equivalent free voting procedures.

Article 22
Everyone, as a member of society, has the right to social security and is entitled to realization, through national effort and international cooperation and in accordance with the organization and resources of each State, of the economic, social and cultural rights indispensable for his dignity and the free development of his personality.

Article 23
(1) Everyone has the right to work, to free choice of employment, to just and favourable conditions of work and to protection against unemployment.
(2) Everyone, without any discrimination, has the right to equal pay for equal work.
(3) Everyone who works has the right to just and favourable remuneration ensuring for himself and his family an existence worthy of human dignity, and supplemented, if necessary, by other means of social protection.
(4) Everyone has the right to form and to join trade unions for the protection of his interests.

Article 24
Everyone has the right to rest and leisure, including reasonable limitation of working hours and periodic holidays with pay.

Article 25
(1) Everyone has the right to a standard of living adequate for the health and well-being of himself and of his family, including food, clothing, housing and medical care and necessary social services, and the right to security in the event of unemployment, sickness, disability, widowhood, old age or other lack of livelihood in circumstances beyond his control.
(2) Motherhood and childhood are entitled to special care and assistance. All children, whether born in or out of wedlock, shall enjoy the same social protection.

Article 26
(1) Everyone has the right to education. Education shall be free, at least in the elementary and fundamental stages. Elementary education shall be compulsory. Technical and professional education shall be made generally available and higher education shall be equally accessible to all on the basis of merit.
(2) Education shall be directed to the full development of the human personality and to the strengthening of respect for human rights and fundamental freedoms. It shall promote understanding, tolerance and friendship among all nations, racial or religious groups, and shall further the activities of the United Nations for the maintenance of peace.
(3) Parents have a prior right to choose the kind of education that shall be given to their children.

Article 27
(1) Everyone has the right freely to participate in the cultural life of the community, to enjoy the arts and to share in scientific advancement and its benefits.
(2) Everyone has the right to the protection of the moral and material interests resulting from any scientific, literary or artistic production of which he is the author.

Article 28
Everyone is entitled to a social and international order in which the rights and freedoms set forth in this Declaration can be fully realized.

Article 29
(1) Everyone has duties to the community in which alone the free and full development of his personality is possible.

(2)   In the exercise of his rights and freedoms, everyone shall be subject only to such limitations as are determined by law solely for the purpose of securing due recognition and respect for the rights and freedoms of others and of meeting the just requirements of morality, public order and the general welfare in a democratic society.

(3)   These rights and freedoms may in no case be exercised contrary to the purposes and principles of the United Nations.

Article 30
Nothing in this Declaration may be interpreted as implying for any State, group or person any right to engage in any activity or to perform any act aimed at the destruction of any of the rights and freedoms set forth herein.

This declaration is the parent of numerous subsequent human rights covenants. Some of these are considered in the next chapter. Additionally, there is a Covenant on Economic Social and Cultural Rights setting out important rights to welfare, health, development, employment etc. These documents are not incorporated into English law, but can be quoted in an English court, since if there is any doubt the judges are prepared to presume that our law will be compliant with our internationally agreed obligations. Government compliance with UN covenants is monitored, and on occasion the UK has been criticized by UN committees, for example in respect of its juvenile trial procedures.

2.3 The Human Rights Act 1998

The Government published a white paper Rights Brought Home (Cm 3782) setting out how the new Act should work. The Convention referred to is the European Convention on Human Rights.

A new requirement on public authorities
2.2   Although the United Kingdom has an international obligation to comply with the Convention, there at present is no requirement in our domestic law on central and local government, or others exercising similar executive powers, to exercise those powers in a way which is compatible with the Convention. This Bill will change that by making it unlawful for public authorities to act in a way which is incompatible with the Convention rights. The definition of what constitutes a public authority is in wide terms. Examples of persons or organisations whose acts or omissions it is intended should be able to be challenged include central government (including executive agencies); local government; the police; immigration officers; prisons; courts and tribunals themselves; and, to the extent that they are exercising public functions, companies responsible for areas of activity which were previously within the public sector, such as the privatized utilities. The actions of Parliament, however, are excluded.
2.3   A person who is aggrieved by an act or omission on the part of a public authority which is incompatible with the Convention rights will be able to challenge the act or omission in the courts. The effects will be wide-ranging. They will extend both to legal actions which a public authority pursues against individuals (for example, where a criminal prosecution is brought or where an administrative decision is being enforced through legal proceedings) and to cases which individuals pursue against a public authority (for example, for judicial review of an executive

decision). Convention points will normally be taken in the context of proceedings instituted against individuals or already open to them, but, if none is available, it will be possible for people to bring cases on Convention grounds alone. Individuals or organisations seeking judicial review of decisions by public authorities on Convention grounds will need to show that they have been directly affected, as they must if they take a case to Strasbourg.

2.4   It is our intention that people or organisations should be able to argue that their Convention rights have been infringed by a public authority in our courts at any level. This will enable the Convention rights to be applied from the outset against the facts and background of a particular case, and the people concerned to obtain their remedy at the earliest possible moment. We think this is preferable to allowing cases to run their ordinary course but then referring them to some kind of separate constitutional court which, like the European Court of Human Rights, would simply review cases which had already passed through the regular legal machinery. In considering Convention points, our courts will be required to take account of relevant decisions of the European Commission and Court of Human Rights (although these will not be binding).

2.5   The Convention is often described as a 'living instrument' because it is interpreted by the European Court in the light of present day conditions and therefore reflects changing social attitudes and the changes in the circumstances of society. In future our judges will be able to contribute to this dynamic and evolving interpretation of the Convention. In particular, our courts will be required to balance the protection of individuals' fundamental rights against the demands of the general interest of the community, particularly in relation to Articles 8–11 where a State may restrict the protected right to the extent that this is 'necessary in a democratic society'.

Remedies for a failure to comply with the Convention

2.6   A public authority which is found to have acted unlawfully by failing to comply with the Convention will not be exposed to criminal penalties. But the court or tribunal will be able to grant the injured person any remedy which is within its normal powers to grant and which it considers appropriate and just in the circumstances. What remedy is appropriate will of course depend both on the facts of the case and on a proper balance between the rights of the individual and the public interest. In some cases, the right course may be for the decision of the public authority in the particular case to be quashed. In other cases, the only appropriate remedy may be an award of damages. The Bill provides that, in considering an award of damages on Convention grounds, the courts are to take into account the principles applied by the European Court of Human Rights in awarding compensation, so that people will be able to receive compensation from a domestic court equivalent to what they would have received in Strasbourg.

Interpretation of legislation

2.7   The Bill provides for legislation — both Acts of Parliament and secondary legislation — to be interpreted so far as possible so as to be compatible with the Convention. This goes far beyond the present rule which enables the courts to take the Convention into account in resolving any ambiguity in a legislative provision. The courts will be required to interpret legislation so as to uphold the Convention rights unless the legislation itself is so clearly incompatible with the Convention that it is impossible to do so.

2.8   This 'rule of construction' is to apply to past as well as to future legislation. To the extent that it affects the meaning of a legislative provision, the courts will not be bound by previous interpretations. They will be able to build a new body of case law, taking into account the Convention rights.

A declaration of incompatibility with the Convention rights

2.9   If the courts decide in any case that it is impossible to interpret an Act of Parliament in a way which is compatible with the Convention, the Bill enables a formal declaration to be made that its provisions are incompatible with the Convention. A declaration of incompatibility will be an important statement to make, and the power to make it will be reserved to the higher courts. They will be able to make a declaration in any proceedings before them, whether the case originated with them (as, in the High Court, on judicial review of an executive act) or in considering an appeal from a lower court or tribunal. The Government will have the right to intervene in any proceedings where such a declaration is a possible outcome. A decision by the High Court or Court of Appeal, determining whether or not such a declaration should be made, will itself be appealable.

Effect of court decisions on legislation

2.10   A declaration that legislation is incompatible with the Convention rights will not of itself have the effect of changing the law, which will continue to apply. But it will almost certainly prompt the Government and Parliament to change the law.

2.11   The Government has considered very carefully whether it would be right for the Bill to go further, and give to courts in the United Kingdom the power to set aside an Act of Parliament which they believe is incompatible with the Convention rights. In considering this question, we have looked at a number of models. The Canadian Charter of Rights and Freedoms 1982 enables the courts to strike down any legislation which is inconsistent with the Charter, unless the legislation contains an explicit statement that it is to apply 'notwithstanding' the provisions of the Charter. But legislation which has been struck down may be re-enacted with a 'notwithstanding' clause. In New Zealand, on the other hand, although there was an earlier proposal for legislation on lines similar to the Canadian Charter, the human rights legislation which was eventually enacted after wide consultation took a different form. The New Zealand Bill of Rights Act 1990 is an 'interpretative' statute which requires past and future legislation to be interpreted consistently with the rights contained in the Act as far as possible but provides that legislation stands if that is impossible. In Hong Kong, a middle course was adopted. The Hong Kong Bill of Rights Ordinance 1991 distinguishes between legislation enacted before and after the Ordinance took effect: previous legislation is subordinated to the provisions of the Ordinance, but subsequent legislation takes precedence over it.

2.12   The Government has also considered the European Communities Act 1972 which provides for European law, in cases where that law has 'direct effect', to take precedence over domestic law. There is, however, an essential difference between European Community law and the European Convention on Human Rights, because it is a *requirement* of membership of the European Union that member States give priority to directly effective EC law in their own legal systems. There is no such requirement in the Convention.

2.13   The Government has reached the conclusion that courts should not have the power to set aside primary legislation, past or future, on the ground of incompatibility with the Convention. This conclusion arises from the importance which the Government attaches to Parliamentary sovereignty. In this context, Parliamentary sovereignty means that Parliament is competent to make any law on any matter of its choosing and no court may question the validity of any Act that it passes. In enacting legislation, Parliament is making decisions about important matters of public policy. The authority to make those decisions derives from a democratic mandate. Members of Parliament in the House of Commons possess such a mandate because they are elected, accountable and representative. To make provision in the Bill for the courts to set aside Acts of Parliament would confer on the judiciary a general power over the decisions of Parliament which under our present constitutional arrangements they do not possess, and would be likely on occasions to draw the judiciary into serious conflict with Parliament. There is no evidence to suggest that they desire this power, nor that the public wish them to have it. Certainly, this Government has no mandate for any such change.

The Bill became the Human Rights Act 1998 (HRA). We now look at the key sections. Sections 2 and 3 state that ECHR articles and judgments must be applied as law by English and Welsh courts, unless they are clearly incompatible with the English statute. Section 4 allows a court to declare the home legislation incompatible with the Convention, which enables the Government to fast-track amendments to the legislation to make it compatible.

2.(1)　A court or tribunal determining a question which has arisen in connection with a Convention right must take into account any —

　(a)　judgment, decision, declaration or advisory opinion of the European Court of Human Rights ... whenever made or given, so far as, in the opinion of the court or tribunal, it is relevant to the proceedings in which that question has arisen.

3.(1)　So far as it is possible to do so, primary legislation and subordinate legislation must be read and given effect in a way which is compatible with the Convention rights.

　(2)　This section —

　(a)　applies to primary legislation and subordinate legislation whenever enacted;

　(b)　does not affect the validity, continuing operation or enforcement of any incompatible primary legislation; and

　(c)　does not affect the validity, continuing operation or enforcement of any incompatible subordinate legislation if (disregarding any possibility of revocation) primary legislation prevents removal of the incompatibility.

4.(1)　Subsection (2) applies in any proceedings in which a court determines whether a provision of primary legislation is compatible with a Convention right.

　(2)　If the court is satisfied that the provision is incompatible with a Convention right, it may make a declaration of that incompatibility.

　(3)　Subsection (4) applies in any proceedings in which a court determines whether a provision of subordinate legislation, made in the exercise of a power conferred by primary legislation, is compatible with a Convention right.

　(4)　If the court is satisfied —

　(a)　that the provision is incompatible with a Convention right, and

　(b)　that (disregarding any possibility of revocation) the primary legislation concerned prevents removal of the incompatibility,

it may make a declaration of that incompatibility.

An early example of a declaration of incompatibility was: *R (H)* v *London North and East Region Mental Health Review Tribunal (Secretary of State for Health intervening)* [2001] EWCA Civ 415, [2001] 3 WLR 512. Sections 72 and 73 Mental Health Act 1983 were declared incompatible with Arts 5(1) and 5(4) (the right to liberty). These sections place onto the detained patient the burden of proving to the Mental Health Review Tribunal that the grounds for detention no longer exist. The right to liberty means it should be for the state to prove there is a ground for detention. So the legislation is incompatible with the Convention, but the detention of H nevertheless remained lawful. See further Chapter 5 pp. 227–30.

Section 6 is perhaps the most crucial section. It is very far-reaching, since a public authority includes not only obvious ones such as a social services department; it also means a court or tribunal. The effect of s 6 is that the courts must apply Convention law even where it overrides English case law. At a stroke the entire common law (the system of law built up case by case since the thirteenth century) has been amended. (But s 6 does not permit a court to overrule an English statute, as we saw above.)

6.(1)   It is unlawful for a public authority to act in a way which is incompatible with a Convention right.
   (2)   Subsection (1) does not apply to an act if —
      (a)   as the result of one or more provisions of primary legislation, the authority could not have acted differently; or
      (b)   in the case of one or more provisions of, or made under, primary legislation which cannot be read or given effect in a way which is compatible with the Convention rights, the authority was acting so as to give effect to or enforce those provisions.
   (3)   In this section 'public authority' includes —
      (a)   a court or tribunal, and
      (b)   any person certain of whose functions are functions of a public nature.

The Act is the vehicle by which the European Convention rights were introduced. Let us turn to the rights themselves. They are set out in the European Convention of Human Rights and Fundamental Freedoms, which apart from Art. 1 (requiring the Member States to put the rights into effect) and Art. 13 (the reasons for it not being incorporated are set out below) are also found in the Human Rights Act, Sch. 1. We set these out with, where relevant, a short commentary beside each article.

Convention for the Protection of Human Rights and Fundamental Freedoms Rome, 4.XI.1950

The governments signatory hereto, being members of the Council of Europe,

Considering the Universal Declaration of Human Rights proclaimed by the General Assembly of the United Nations on 10th December 1948;

Considering that this Declaration aims at securing the universal and effective recognition and observance of the Rights therein declared;

Considering that the aim of the Council of Europe is the achievement of greater unity between its members and that one of the methods by which that aim is to be pursued is the maintenance and further realisation of human rights and fundamental freedoms;

Reaffirming their profound belief in those fundamental freedoms which are the foundation of justice and peace in the world and are best maintained on the one hand by an effective political democracy and on the other by a common understanding and observance of the human rights upon which they depend;

Being resolved, as the governments of European countries which are like-minded and have a common heritage of political traditions, ideals, freedom and the rule of law, to take the first steps for the collective enforcement of certain of the rights stated in the Universal Declaration,

Have agreed as follows:

Article 1 — Obligation to respect human rights
The High Contracting Parties shall secure to everyone within their jurisdiction the rights and freedoms defined in Section I of this Convention.

[The HRA does not include this since the Act itself purports to achieve this result.]

Article 2 — Right to life
1.   Everyone's right to life shall be protected by law. No one shall be deprived of his life intentionally save in the execution of a sentence of a court following his conviction of a crime for which this penalty is provided by law.

2. Deprivation of life shall not be regarded as inflicted in contravention of this article when it results from the use of force which is no more than absolutely necessary:

    a.   in defence of any person from unlawful violence;

    b.   in order to effect a lawful arrest or to prevent the escape of a person lawfully detained;

    c.   in action lawfully taken for the purpose of quelling a riot or insurrection.

While there has been much litigation in Strasbourg over this right, such as the right of IRA terrorists not to be killed without considering whether at the time they posed a danger, little of relevance to a social worker has appeared in the case reports. A parent whose child died because of the failure of social services to protect his life from an abuser might have an action under this article. (See the *Osman* case referred to in relation to Art. 6 below.)

Article 3 — Prohibition of torture
No one shall be subjected to torture or to inhuman or degrading treatment or punishment.

Under this article the court in Strasbourg has declared corporal punishment of children in school to be illegal: *Costello-Roberts* v *UK* (1993) 19 EHRR 112. The failure of the English law to protect a child from a vicious beating by his step-father, who was acquitted by a jury under the law which permitted 'reasonable chastisement', was in breach of the convention in *A* v *UK* [1998] 2 FLR 959, requiring a change to the law which has not yet been achieved. As we saw in Chapter 1, the failure of Bedfordshire Social Services to protect children from serious abuse could — if proved — amount to breach.

Article 4 — Prohibition of slavery and forced labour
1. No one shall be held in slavery or servitude.
2. No one shall be required to perform forced or compulsory labour.
3. For the purpose of this article the term 'forced or compulsory labour' shall not include:

    a.   any work required to be done in the ordinary course of detention imposed according to the provisions of Article 5 of this Convention or during conditional release from such detention;

    b.   any service of a military character or, in case of conscientious objectors in countries where they are recognised, service exacted instead of compulsory military service;

    c.   any service exacted in case of an emergency or calamity threatening the life or well-being of the community;

    d.   any work or service which forms part of normal civic obligations.

Article 5 — Right to liberty and security
1. Everyone has the right to liberty and security of person. No one shall be deprived of his liberty save in the following cases and in accordance with a procedure prescribed by law:

    a.   the lawful detention of a person after conviction by a competent court;

    b.   the lawful arrest or detention of a person for non-compliance with the lawful order of a court or in order to secure the fulfilment of any obligation prescribed by law;

    c.   the lawful arrest or detention of a person effected for the purpose of bringing him before the competent legal authority on reasonable suspicion of having committed an offence or when it is reasonably considered necessary to prevent his committing an offence or fleeing after having done so;

    d.   the detention of a minor by lawful order for the purpose of educational supervision or his lawful detention for the purpose of bringing him before the competent legal authority;

e. the lawful detention of persons for the prevention of the spreading of infectious diseases, of persons of unsound mind, alcoholics or drug addicts or vagrants;

f. the lawful arrest or detention of a person to prevent his effecting an unauthorised entry into the country or of a person against whom action is being taken with a view to deportation or extradition.

2. Everyone who is arrested shall be informed promptly, in a language which he understands, of the reasons for his arrest and of any charge against him.

3. Everyone arrested or detained in accordance with the provisions of paragraph 1.c of this article shall be brought promptly before a judge or other officer authorised by law to exercise judicial power and shall be entitled to trial within a reasonable time or to release pending trial. Release may be conditioned by guarantees to appear for trial.

4. Everyone who is deprived of his liberty by arrest or detention shall be entitled to take proceedings by which the lawfulness of his detention shall be decided speedily by a court and his release ordered if the detention is not lawful.

5. Everyone who has been the victim of arrest or detention in contravention of the provisions of this article shall have an enforceable right to compensation.

This article is of clear relevance to social workers who have to control sometimes violent children in local authority accommodation. But as a juvenile cannot be locked up without using powers under the Children Act 1989 or the Police and Criminal Evidence Act 1984, it is unlikely that this article creates further rights. The UK was found in breach of this article in the appeal by the killers of Jamie Bulger (see Chapter 7 for a case extract). The UK was also in breach for failing to provide protection to a schoolboy and his father when the latter was killed by an obsessed teacher of the former and the police had known of the danger: the case arose under this article because English law prevented the police being sued, so the family had no recourse to law (*Osman* v *UK* (1999) Crim LR 82).

Article 6 — Right to a fair trial
1. In the determination of his civil rights and obligations or of any criminal charge against him, everyone is entitled to a fair and public hearing within a reasonable time by an independent and impartial tribunal established by law. Judgment shall be pronounced publicly but the press and public may be excluded from all or part of the trial in the interests of morals, public order or national security in a democratic society, where the interests of juveniles or the protection of the private life of the parties so require, or to the extent strictly necessary in the opinion of the court in special circumstances where publicity would prejudice the interests of justice.

2. Everyone charged with a criminal offence shall be presumed innocent until proved guilty according to law.

3. Everyone charged with a criminal offence has the following minimum rights:

a. to be informed promptly, in a language which he understands and in detail, of the nature and cause of the accusation against him;

b. to have adequate time and facilities for the preparation of his defence;

c. to defend himself in person or through legal assistance of his own choosing or, if he has not sufficient means to pay for legal assistance, to be given it free when the interests of justice so require;

d. to examine or have examined witnesses against him and to obtain the attendance and examination of witnesses on his behalf under the same conditions as witnesses against him;

e. to have the free assistance of an interpreter if he cannot understand or speak the language used in court.

This is one of the most important of the articles. The UK was found in breach both in relation to the way in which 11-year-old boys charged with the murder of Jamie Bulger had been tried in an inappropriate court, the Crown Court, and the fact that the length of the detention was determined in a political rather than judicial manner (because this case illustrates the relationship between public mood, politics and criminal law, it is discussed in some detail in Chapter 7). Any unfairness, in a civil or criminal trial, is open to challenge using this Article. Any procedure whereby a person's rights are determined can be scrutinized under this Article, such as the detention of a mental patient under the Mental Health Act.

Article 7 — No punishment without law
1.   No one shall be held guilty of any criminal offence on account of any act or omission which did not constitute a criminal offence under national or international law at the time when it was committed. Nor shall a heavier penalty be imposed than the one that was applicable at the time the criminal offence was committed.
2.   This article shall not prejudice the trial and punishment of any person for any act or omission which, at the time when it was committed, was criminal according to the general principles of law recognised by civilised nations.

Article 8 — Right to respect for private and family life
1.   Everyone has the right to respect for his private and family life, his home and his correspondence.
2.   There shall be no interference by a public authority with the exercise of this right except such as is in accordance with the law and is necessary in a democratic society in the interests of national security, public safety or the economic well-being of the country, for the prevention of disorder or crime, for the protection of health or morals, or for the protection of the rights and freedoms of others.

Child protection involves a careful balance between the rights of individuals to their family life, particularly parents, and the obligation of the state to protect its most vulnerable members. Although the law before the Children Act 1989 permitted interference which breached this right (in that it failed to lay down procedures for contact arrangements between a boy in care and his uncle for example: *Boyle* v *UK* (1994) 19 EHRR 179), the Children Act is likely now to comply with this article.

Article 9 — Freedom of thought, conscience and religion
1.   Everyone has the right to freedom of thought, conscience and religion; this right includes freedom to change his religion or belief and freedom, either alone or in community with others and in public or private, to manifest his religion or belief, in worship, teaching, practice and observance.
2.   Freedom to manifest one's religion or beliefs shall be subject only to such limitations as are prescribed by law and are necessary in a democratic society in the interests of public safety, for the protection of public order, health or morals, or for the protection of the rights and freedoms of others.

Article 10 — Freedom of expression
1.   Everyone has the right to freedom of expression. This right shall include freedom to hold opinions and to receive and impart information and ideas without interference by public authority and regardless of frontiers. This article shall not prevent States from requiring the licensing of broadcasting, television or cinema enterprises.

2. The exercise of these freedoms, since it carries with it duties and responsibilities, may be subject to such formalities, conditions, restrictions or penalties as are prescribed by law and are necessary in a democratic society, in the interests of national security, territorial integrity or public safety, for the prevention of disorder or crime, for the protection of health or morals, for the protection of the reputation or rights of others, for preventing the disclosure of information received in confidence, or for maintaining the authority and impartiality of the judiciary.

Interestingly this includes the right to receive information, but not a duty to provide it. The UK was not in breach for failing to provide a person with his adoption records — *Gaskin* v *UK* (1986) 12 EHRR 36.

Article 11 — Freedom of assembly and association
1. Everyone has the right to freedom of peaceful assembly and to freedom of association with others, including the right to form and to join trade unions for the protection of his interests.
2. No restrictions shall be placed on the exercise of these rights other than such as are prescribed by law and are necessary in a democratic society in the interests of national security or public safety, for the prevention of disorder or crime, for the protection of health or morals or for the protection of the rights and freedoms of others. This article shall not prevent the imposition of lawful restrictions on the exercise of these rights by members of the armed forces, of the police or of the administration of the State.

Article 12 — Right to marry
Men and women of marriageable age have the right to marry and to found a family, according to the national laws governing the exercise of this right.

Prisoners and mental patients can marry already under English law. The article does not allow the person to insist on cohabitation if lawfully detained (*X and Y* v *Switzerland* (1979) 13 DR 242). *In R v Secretary of State for the Home Department, ex p Mellor* (4 April 2001, Court of Appeal unreported) a prisoner challenged the Home Office to permit him to provide sperm in order for his wife to conceive, but it was held that this was not a breach of his right to found a family, which he was not entitled to exercise at any moment of his choosing, and which right he had deprived himself of through his own criminal actions. The question of whether prisoners or mental patients can insist on being permitted sexual relations with each other remains to be tested.

Article 13 — Right to an effective remedy
Everyone whose rights and freedoms as set forth in this Convention are violated shall have an effective remedy before a national authority notwithstanding that the violation has been committed by persons acting in an official capacity.

This article has not been incorporated under the Human Rights Act. In theory, and in most instances in practice, English law will provide a remedy. There can still be a case where a right is alleged to have been breached and the English law does not provide a remedy. This could arise in two circumstances. First it can happen if a court acknowledges that a piece of legislation is incompatible with the Convention rights (see s 5 HRA above); the legislation will then prevail as far as the decision of that court goes. Secondly it can arise where a court claims to be applying the Convention but a party believes the court is applying the Convention law wrongly. In both situations, even though the ECHR has been incorporated into English law, the only recourse for the aggrieved person will be to petition the European Court of Human Rights.

There are also many relevant judgments of the Strasbourg Court made before the advent of the Human Rights Act. For example one of the grounds of the decision in the *Bedfordshire* case (*Z v UK* — see Chapter 1) was that English case law prevented the children taking legal action against the local authority. They had no effective remedy under Article 13 and no way of getting a decision on the alleged breach of their Article 3 right not to suffer inhumane treatment. The Strasbourg Court held they must have the right to sue.

Article 14 — Prohibition of discrimination
The enjoyment of the rights and freedoms set forth in this Convention shall be secured without discrimination on any ground such as sex, race, colour, language, religion, political or other opinion, national or social origin, association with a national minority, property, birth or other status.

It is important to be aware of the limits to this Article. At first sight it is very wide ranging. For example it appears to forbid discrimination on grounds of poverty. However the Article only applies if there has been discrimination in relation to one of the Convention rights, and not to any other form of discrimination. The next chapter will examine anti-discrimination legislation in relation to race, gender and disability.

Article 15 — Derogation in time of emergency
1.   In time of war or other public emergency threatening the life of the nation any High Contracting Party may take measures derogating from its obligations under this Convention to the extent strictly required by the exigencies of the situation, provided that such measures are not inconsistent with its other obligations under international law.
2.   No derogation from Article 2, except in respect of deaths resulting from lawful acts of war, or from Articles 3, 4 (paragraph 1) and 7 shall be made under this provision.
3.   Any High Contracting Party availing itself of this right of derogation shall keep the Secretary General of the Council of Europe fully informed of the measures which it has taken and the reasons therefor. It shall also inform the Secretary General of the Council of Europe when such measures have ceased to operate and the provisions of the Convention are again being fully executed.

In acquiring legislative powers to detain without trial terrorist suspects of foreign nationality following the attacks on 11 September 2001 on the US, the UK government formally derogated from its obligations under Art. 6. However, in July 2002 the Special Immigration Appeals Commission declared the detention of foreign—as apposed to all—terror suspects unlawful under Article 14, from which no derogation had been declared (*Guardian* 31.7.02).

Article 16 — Restrictions on political activity of aliens
Nothing in Articles 10, 11 and 14 shall be regarded as preventing the High Contracting Parties from imposing restrictions on the political activity of aliens.

Article 17 — Prohibition of abuse of rights
Nothing in this Convention may be interpreted as implying for any State, group or person any right to engage in any activity or perform any act aimed at the destruction of any of the rights

and freedoms set forth herein or at their limitation to a greater extent than is provided for in the Convention.

Article 18 — Limitation on use of restrictions on rights
The restrictions permitted under this Convention to the said rights and freedoms shall not be applied for any purpose other than those for which they have been prescribed.

The first ECHR protocol, which includes the right to enjoy possession of property is not reproduced, but is also incorporated within the HRA.

3

Anti-discrimination law

3.1 The concept of discrimination

Discriminating is a necessary part of the social worker's professional role. You discriminate when you assess one person as being in need of community care services, another as a child in need who should be placed on an at-risk register, but a third person as not entitled to any service or intervention. However where discrimination arises from assumptions and prejudice, rather than individual circumstance and need, the law can play a role.

This chapter provides a framework for the law relating to three aspects: race, sex and disability discrimination. We do not have the space to cite cases or discursive articles, nor to include all of the legislation or guidance. The law is currently silent on other areas of discrimination, notably sexual orientation, religion and age discrimination. Age discrimination will be outlawed under European directive 2000/78, coming into effect in 2006, and is subject to a voluntary code of practice (not reproduced — see **www.agepositive.gov.uk/**). The same directive requires the government to legislate against workplace discrimination on grounds of religion and sexual orientation by December 2003.

3.2 Discrimination on grounds of race

3.2.1 United Nations Declaration on the Elimination of All Forms of Racial Discrimination 1963

Article 1
Discrimination between human beings on the ground of race, colour or ethnic origin is an offence to human dignity and shall be condemned as a denial of the principles of the Charter of the United Nations, as a violation of the human rights and fundamental freedoms proclaimed in the Universal Declaration of Human Rights, as an obstacle to friendly and peaceful relations among nations and as a fact capable of disturbing peace and security among peoples.

Article 2
1. No State, institution, group or individual shall make any discrimination whatsoever in matters of human rights and fundamental freedoms in the treatment of persons, groups of persons or institutions on the ground of race, colour or ethnic origin.

2.   No State shall encourage, advocate or lend its support, through police action or otherwise, to any discrimination based on race, colour or ethnic origin by any group, institution or individual.

3.   Special concrete measures shall be taken in appropriate circumstances in order to secure adequate development or protection of individuals belonging to certain racial groups with the object of ensuring the full enjoyment by such individuals of human rights and fundamental freedoms. These measures shall in no circumstances have as a consequence the maintenance of unequal or separate rights for different racial groups.

Article 3
1.   Particular efforts shall be made to prevent discrimination based on race, colour or ethnic origin, especially in the fields of civil rights, access to citizenship, education, religion, employment, occupation and housing.

2.   Everyone shall have equal access to any place or facility intended for use by the general public, without distinction as to race, colour or ethnic origin.

Article 7
1.   Everyone has the right to equality before the law and to equal justice under the law. Everyone, without distinction as to race, colour or ethnic origin, has the right to security of person and protection by the State against violence or bodily harm, whether inflicted by government officials or by any individual, group or institution.

2.   Everyone shall have the right to an effective remedy and protection against any discrimination he may suffer on the ground of race, colour or ethnic origin with respect to his fundamental rights and freedoms through independent national tribunals competent to deal with such matters.

Article 8
All effective steps shall be taken immediately in the fields of teaching, education and information, with a view to eliminating racial discrimination and prejudice and promoting understanding, tolerance and friendship among nations and racial groups, as well as to propagating the purposes and principles of the Charter of the United Nations, of the Universal Declaration of Human Rights, and of the Declaration on the Granting of Independence to Colonial Countries and Peoples.

Article 9
1.   All propaganda and organizations based on ideas or theories of the superiority of one race or group of persons of one colour or ethnic origin with a view to justifying or promoting racial discrimination in any form shall be severely condemned.

2.   All incitement to or acts of violence, whether by individuals or organizations against any race or group of persons of another colour or ethnic origin shall be considered an offence against society and punishable under law.

3.   In order to put into effect the purposes and principles of the present Declaration, all States shall take immediate and positive measures, including legislative and other measures, to prosecute and/or outlaw organizations which promote or incite to racial discrimination, or incite to or use violence for purposes of discrimination based on race, colour or ethnic origin.

3.2.2 Guidance on English race discrimination law

We start with an extract from the website of the Commission for Racial Equality (**www.cre.gov.uk**) explaining the workings of the English legislation. A more detailed guide to the Act, not reproduced, can be found at the Home Office website: **www.homeoffice.gov.uk/raceact/guide.htm**.

What is discrimination?

The Race Relations Act is concerned with people's actions and the effects of their actions, not their opinions or beliefs. Racial discrimination is not the same as racial prejudice or 'racism'.

Prejudice literally means 'pre-judging' someone — knowing next to nothing about them but jumping to conclusions because of some characteristic, like their appearance.

Racism is the belief that some 'races' are superior to others — based on the false idea that different physical characteristics (like skin colour) or ethnic background make some people better than others.

Discrimination occurs when someone is treated less favourably on grounds of their colour, race, nationality or national or ethnic origin. It is not necessary to prove that someone intended to discriminate against you: it is sufficient only to show that the outcome of their action was that you received less favourable treatment.

The Race Relations Act identifies three main types of racial discrimination:

Direct racial discrimination

This occurs when you are able to show that you have been treated less favourably on racial grounds than others in similar circumstances. To prove this, it will help if you can give an example of someone from a different racial group who, in similar circumstances, has been treated more favourably than you. Racist abuse and harassment are forms of direct discrimination.

Indirect racial discrimination

This occurs when you or people from your racial group are less likely to be able to comply with a requirement or condition, and the requirement cannot be justified other than on racial grounds.

For example, a requirement that employees or pupils must not wear headgear could exclude Sikh men and boys who wear a turban, Jewish men or boys who wear a yarmulka or Pakistani women and girls who wear a hijaab (headscarf), in accordance with cultural and religious practice.

Victimisation

This has a special legal meaning in the Race Relations Act. It occurs if you are treated less favourably because you have complained about racial discrimination or supported someone else who has.

3.2.3 **The Race Relations Act 1976**

We start with the section governing the duties of public authorities. It was inserted into the 1976 Act by the Race Relations (Amendment) Act 2000 to toughen up the anti-discrimination practices of public authorities in the wake of the Stephen Lawrence Inquiry. We do not reproduce the schedule to the Act, is mentioned in s 71, which establishes which public bodies are covered, including a local authority.

71.(1)   Every body or other person specified in Schedule 1A or of a description falling within that Schedule shall, in carrying out its functions, have due regard to the need —

   (a)   to eliminate unlawful racial discrimination; and
   (b)   to promote equality of opportunity and good relations between persons of different racial groups.

Section 19B of the Act declares that:

19B.(1)   It is unlawful for a public authority in carrying out any functions of the authority to do any act which constitutes discrimination.

(2)   In this section 'public authority' —

(a)   includes any person certain of whose functions are functions of a public nature;

What, in law, counts as discrimination? S 1 defines direct and indirect discrimination, and s 2 defines discrimination by way of victimisation:

1.(1)   A person discriminates against another in any circumstances relevant for the purposes of any provision of this Act if —

(a)   on racial grounds he treats that other less favourably than he treats or would treat other persons; or

(b)   he applies to that other a requirement or condition which he applies or would apply equally to persons not of the same racial group as that other but —

(i)   which is such that the proportion of persons of the same racial group as that other who can comply with it is considerably smaller than the proportion of persons not of that racial group who can comply with it; and

(ii)   which he cannot show to be justifiable irrespective of the colour, race, nationality or ethnic or national origins of the person to whom it is applied; and

(iii)   which is to the detriment of that other because he cannot comply with it.

(2)   It is hereby declared that, for the purposes of this Act, segregating a person from other persons on racial grounds is treating him less favourably than they are treated.

2.(1)   A person ('the discriminator') discriminates against another person ('the person victimised') in any circumstances relevant for the purposes of any provision of this Act if he treats the person victimised less favourably than in those circumstances he treats or would treat other persons, and does so by reason that the person victimised has —

(a)   brought proceedings against the discriminator or any other person under this Act; or

(b)   given evidence or information in connection with proceedings brought by any person against the discriminator or any other person under this Act; or

(c)   otherwise done anything under or by reference to this Act in relation to the discriminator or any other person; or

(d)   alleged that the discriminator or any other person has committed an act which (whether or not the allegation so states) would amount to a contravention of this Act,

or by reason that the discriminator knows that the person victimised intends to do any of those things, or suspects that the person victimised has done, or intends to do, any of them.

(2)   Subsection (1) does not apply to treatment of a person by reason of any allegation made by him if the allegation was false and not made in good faith.

Section 3 defines a racial group:

3.(1)   In this Act, unless the context otherwise requires —

'racial grounds' means any of the following grounds, namely colour, race nationality or ethnic or national origins;

'racial group' means a group of persons defined by reference to colour, race, nationality or ethnic or national origins, and references to a person's racial group refer to any racial group into which he falls.

(2)   The fact that a racial group comprises two or more distinct racial groups does not prevent it from constituting a particular racial group for the purposes of this Act.

(3)   In this Act —

(a)   references to discrimination refer to any discrimination falling within section 1 or 2; and

(b)   references to racial discrimination refer to any discrimination falling within section 1,

and related expressions shall be construed accordingly.

(4)   A comparison of the case of a person of a particular racial group with that of a person not of that group under section 1(1) must be such that the relevant circumstances in the one case are the same, or not materially different, in the other.

Discrimination on grounds of religion is not included (so long as it is based on religion alone, and not also colour, race etc). To this extent the legislation fails to live up to the UN Declaration. However a denial of any of the specific human rights set out in the European Convention (see Chapter 2) on grounds of religion would constitute unlawful discrimination in breach of the Human Rights Act 1998. Under the European Directive workplace discrimination on religious grounds must be made unlawful by December 2003.

The extent to which discrimination is unlawful is the subject matter of Part II of the Act, which deals with employment, and Part III, which deals with other fields, including education and goods and services. We will now look at some of these.

Discrimination in employment

4.(1)   It is unlawful for a person, in relation to employment by him at an establishment in Great Britain, to discriminate against another —

(a)   in the arrangements he makes for the purpose of determining who should be offered that employment; or

(b)   in the terms on which he offers him that employment; or

(c)   by refusing or deliberately omitting to offer him that employment.

(2)   It is unlawful for a person, in the case of a person employed by him at an establishment in Great Britain, to discriminate against that employee —

(a)   in the terms of employment which he affords him; or

(b)   in the way he affords him access to opportunities for promotion, transfer or training, or to any other benefits, facilities or services, or by refusing or deliberately omitting to afford him access to them; or

(c)   by dismissing him, or subjecting him to any other detriment.

(3)   Except in relation to discrimination falling within section 2, subsections (1) and (2) do not apply to employment for the purposes of a private household.

Section 5 deals with occasions where the Act permits discrimination if the reason is genuinely related to the job:

5.(1)   In relation to racial discrimination —

(a)   section 4(1)(a) or (c) does not apply to any employment where being of a particular racial group is a genuine occupational qualification for the job; and

(b)   section 4(2)(b) does not apply to opportunities for promotion or transfer to, or training for, such employment.

(2)   Being of a particular racial group is a genuine occupational qualification for a job only where —

(a)   the job involves participation in a dramatic performance or other entertainment in a capacity for which a person of that racial group is required for reasons of authenticity; or

(b)   the job involves participation as an artist's or photographic model in the production of a work of art, visual image or sequence of visual images for which a person of that racial group is required for reasons of authenticity; or

    (c) the job involves working in a place where food or drink is (for payment or not) provided to and consumed by members of the public or a section of the public in a particular setting for which, in that job, a person of that racial group is required for reasons of authenticity; or

    (d) the holder of the job provides persons of that racial group with personal services promoting their welfare, and those services can most effectively be provided by a person of that racial group.

  (3)   Subsection (2) applies where some only of the duties of the job fall within paragraph (a), (b), (c) or (d) as well as where all of them do.

  (4)   Paragraph (a), (b), (c) or (d) of subsection (2) does not apply in relation to the filling of a vacancy at a time when the employer already has employees of the racial group in question —

    (a) who are capable of carrying out the duties falling within that paragraph; and

    (b) whom it would be reasonable to employ on those duties; and

    (c) whose numbers are sufficient to meet the employer's likely requirements in respect of those duties without undue inconvenience.

The remaining sections in Part II deal with partnerships, contract workers, seamen, overseas employment, employment agencies, bodies conferring qualifications, and discrimination in the police service, and are not reproduced.

Discrimination in education

Discrimination in provision of educational facilities is unlawful if the reason for discrimination can be shown to be based on race, as defined in s. 3:

17.   It is unlawful, in relation to an educational establishment falling within column 1 of the following table, for a person indicated in relation to the establishment in column 2 (the 'responsible body') to discriminate against a person —

    (a) in the terms on which it offers to admit him to the establishment as a pupil; or

    (b) by refusing or deliberately omitting to accept an application for his admission to the establishment as a pupil; or

    (c) where he is a pupil of the establishment —

        (i)   in the way it affords him access to any benefits, facilities or services, or by refusing or deliberately omitting to afford him access to them; or

        (ii) by excluding him from the establishment or subjecting him to any other detriment.

The table is not reproduced. It covers local education authority schools, independent schools, special schools, further and higher education, and the governing bodies, authorities or proprietors of these.

    The legislation does not outlaw faith schools, even though these indirectly discriminate. Indeed there are requirements in the Education Act 1996 which promote the involvement of religious institutions, in particular, of the Church of England and the Roman Catholic Church, in educational management.

Discrimination in relation to goods services and premises

Sections 20 to 26 deal with discrimination in housing, goods and services. Notice in what follows that the law seems to fight shy of outlawing discrimination in private affairs. There is an exemption (s. 26) below for people to be allowed to form exclusive associations for their own racial cultural or ethnic groups.

20.(1) It is unlawful for any person concerned with the provision (for payment or not) of goods, facilities or services to the public or a section of the public to discriminate against a person who seeks to obtain or use those goods, facilities or services —

    (a) by refusing or deliberately omitting to provide him with any of them; or

    (b) by refusing or deliberately omitting to provide him with goods, facilities or services of the like quality, in the like manner and on the like terms as are normal in the first-mentioned person's case in relation to other members of the public or (where the person so seeking belongs to a section of the public) to other members of that section.

    (2) The following are examples of the facilities and services mentioned in subsection (1) —

    (a) access to and use of any place which members of the public are permitted to enter;

    (b) accommodation in a hotel, boarding house or other similar establishment;

    (c) facilities by way of banking or insurance or for grants, loans, credit or finance;

    (d) facilities for education;

    (e) facilities for entertainment, recreation or refreshment;

    (f) facilities for transport or travel;

    (g) the services of any profession or trade, or any local or other public authority.

21.(1) It is unlawful for a person, in relation to premises in Great Britain of which he has power to dispose, to discriminate against another —

    (a) in the terms on which he offers him those premises; or

    (b) by refusing his application for those premises; or

    (c) in his treatment of him in relation to any list of persons in need of premises of that description.

    (2) It is unlawful for a person, in relation to premises managed by him, to discriminate against a person occupying the premises —

    (a) in the way he affords him access to any benefits or facilities, or by refusing or deliberately omitting to afford him access to them; or

    (b) by evicting him, or subjecting him to any other detriment.

    (3) Subsection (1) does not apply to a person who owns an estate or interest in the premises and wholly occupies them unless he uses the services of an estate agent for the purposes of the disposal of the premises, or publishes or causes to be published an advertisement in connection with the disposal.

22.(1) Sections 20(1) and 21 do not apply to the provision by a person of accommodation in any premises, or the disposal of premises by him, if —

    (a) that person or a near relative of his ('the relevant occupier') resides, and intends to continue to reside, on the premises; and

    (b) there is on the premises, in addition to the accommodation occupied by the relevant occupier, accommodation (not being storage accommodation or means of access) shared by the relevant occupier with other persons residing on the premises who are not members of his household; and

    (c) the premises are small premises.

Small premises are defined in s 22(2) as covering no more than two households in addition to the landlord.

25.(1) This section applies to any association of persons (however described, whether corporate or unincorporate, and whether or not its activities are carried on for profit) if —

    (a) it has twenty-five or more members; and

    (b) admission to membership is regulated by its constitution and is so conducted that the members do not constitute a section of the public within the meaning of section 20(1); and

    (c) it is not an organisation to which section 11 applies [trades unions, employers', or trade associations].

(2) It is unlawful for an association to which this section applies, in the case of a person who is not a member of the association, to discriminate against him —

(a) in the terms on which it is prepared to admit him to membership; or

(b) by refusing or deliberately omitting to accept his application for membership.

(3) It is unlawful for an association to which this section applies, in the case of a person who is a member or associate of the association, to discriminate against him —

(a) in the way it affords him access to any benefits, facilities or services, or by refusing or deliberately omitting to afford him access to them; or

(b) in the case of a member, by depriving him of membership, or varying the terms on which he is a member; or

(c) in the case of an associate, by depriving him of his rights as an associate, or varying those rights; or

(d) in either case, by subjecting him to any other detriment.

(4) For the purposes of this section —

(a) a person is a member of an association if he belongs to it by virtue of his admission to any sort of membership provided for by its constitution (and is not merely a person with certain rights under its constitution by virtue of his membership of some other association), and references to membership of an association shall be construed accordingly;

(b) a person is an associate of an association to which this section applies if, not being a member of it, he has under its constitution some or all of the rights enjoyed by members (or would have apart from any provision in its constitution authorising the refusal of those rights in particular cases).

26.(1) An association to which section 25 applies is within this subsection if the main object of the association is to enable the benefits of membership (whatever they may be) to be enjoyed by persons of a particular racial group defined otherwise than by reference to colour; and in determining whether that is the main object of an association regard shall be had to the essential character of the association and to all relevant circumstances including, in particular, the extent to which the affairs of the association are so conducted that the persons primarily enjoying the benefits of membership are of the racial group in question.

(2) In the case of an association within subsection (1), nothing in section 25 shall render unlawful any act not involving discrimination on the ground of colour.

[The triple negative in 26(2) means no small association may discriminate on grounds of colour.]

Responsibility for allowing or encouraging other people to discriminate

Sections 28 and 29 (not reproduced) define as discrimination acts which encourage others to discriminate or advertisements indicating intention to discriminate. Liability for the actions of others is covered in sections 30 to 32.

30. It is unlawful for a person —

(a) who has authority over another person; or

(b) in accordance with whose wishes that other person is accustomed to act,

to instruct him to do any act which is unlawful by virtue of Part II or III, or procure or attempt to procure the doing by him of any such act.

31.(1) It is unlawful to induce, or attempt to induce, a person to do any act which contravenes Part II or III.

(2) An attempted inducement is not prevented from falling within subsection (1) because it is not made directly to the person in question, if it is made in such a way that he is likely to hear of it.

32.(1)   Anything done by a person in the course of his employment shall be treated for the purposes of this Act (except as regards offences thereunder) as done by his employer as well as by him, whether or not it was done with the employer's knowledge or approval.

(2)   Anything done by a person as agent for another person with the authority (whether express or implied, and whether precedent or subsequent) of that other person shall be treated for the purposes of this Act (except as regards offences thereunder) as done by that other person as well as by him.

(3)   In proceedings brought under this Act against any person in respect of an act alleged to have been done by an employee of his it shall be a defence for that person to prove that he took such steps as were reasonably practicable to prevent the employee from doing that act, or from doing in the course of his employment acts of that description.

Positive discrimination

Preventing discrimination is one goal of equal opportunities legislation. Promoting opportunity is another goal, requiring some discrimination to be excluded from the requirement not to discriminate:

35.   Nothing in Parts II to IV shall render unlawful any act done in affording persons of a particular racial group access to facilities or services to meet the special needs of persons of that group in regard to their education, training or welfare, or any ancillary benefits.

36.   Nothing in Parts II to IV shall render unlawful any act done by a person for the benefit of persons not ordinarily resident in Great Britain in affording them access to facilities for education or training or any ancillary benefits, where it appears to him that the persons in question do not intend to remain in Great Britain after their period of education or training there.

37.(1)   Nothing in Parts II to IV shall render unlawful any act done in relation to particular work by any person in or in connection with —

(a)   affording only persons of a particular racial group access to facilities for training which would help to fit them for that work; or

(b)   encouraging only persons of a particular racial group to take advantage of opportunities for doing that work,

where it reasonably appears to that person that at any time within the twelve months immediately preceding the doing of the act —

(i)   there were no persons of that group among those doing that work in Great Britain; or

(ii)   the proportion of persons of that group among those doing that work in Great Britain was small in comparison with the proportion of persons of that group among the population of Great Britain.

(2)   Where in relation to particular work it reasonably appears to any person that although the condition for the operation of subsection (1) is not met for the whole of Great Britain it is met for an area within Great Britain, nothing in Parts II to IV shall render unlawful any act done by that person in or in connection with —

(a)   affording persons who are of the racial group in question, and who appear likely to take up that work in that area, access to facilities for training which would help to fit them for that work; or

(b)   encouraging persons of that group to take advantage of opportunities in the area for doing that work.

(3)   The preceding provisions of this section shall not apply to any discrimination which is rendered unlawful by section 4(1) or (2).

38.(1) Nothing in Parts II to IV shall render unlawful any act done by an employer in relation to particular work in his employment at a particular establishment in Great Britain being an act done in or in connection with —

(a) affording only those of his employees working at that establishment who are of a particular racial group access to facilities for training which would help to fit them for that work; or

(b) encouraging only persons of a particular racial group to take advantage of opportunities for doing that work at that establishment,

where any of the conditions in subsection (2) was satisfied at any time within the twelve months immediately preceding the doing of the act.

(2) Those conditions are —

(a) that there are no persons of the racial group in question among those doing that work at that establishment; or

(b) that the proportion of persons of that group among those doing that work at that establishment is small in comparison with the proportion of persons of that group —

(i) among all those employed by that employer there; or

(ii) among the population of the area from which that employer normally recruits persons for work in his employment at that establishment.

(3) Nothing in section 11 [which deals with trades unions, employers', and trade associations] shall render unlawful any act done by an organisation to which that section applies in or in connection with —

(a) affording only members of the organisation who are of a particular racial group access to facilities for training which would help to fit them for holding a post of any kind in the organisation; or

(b) encouraging only members of the organisation who are of a particular racial group to take advantage of opportunities for holding such posts in the organisation,

where either of the conditions in subsection (4) was satisfied at any time within the twelve months immediately preceding the doing of the act.

(4) Those conditions are —

(a) that there are no persons of the racial group in question among persons holding such posts in that organisation; or

(b) that the proportion of persons of that group among those holding such posts in that organisation is small in comparison with the proportion of persons of that group among the members of the organisation.

(5) Nothing in Parts II to IV shall render unlawful any act done by an organisation to which section 11 [trades unions, etc.] applies in or in connection with encouraging only persons of a particular racial group to become members of the organisation where at any time within the twelve months immediately preceding the doing of the act —

(a) no persons of that group were members of the organisation; or

(b) the proportion of persons of that group among members of the organisation was small in comparison with the proportion of persons of that group among those eligible for membership of the organisation.

Enforcement

The enforcement sections of the Act can be found in Parts VII (establishment of the Commission for Racial Equality) and Part VIII (right to take employment cases to a tribunal and other cases to the county court), and are not reproduced. Criminal offences such as incitement to racial hatred are set out in the Public Order Act 1986 (not reproduced).

3.3 **Sex discrimination**

3.3.1 **International treaties and European Community Law**

The pace of English law in relation to sex discrimination has been forced by the law of the European Union, with which UK laws must comply as a result of our accession in 1973 to the Treaty of Rome.

Article 141 (formerly 119) Treaty of Rome mandates equal pay legislation:

Each Member State shall … maintain the application of the principle that men and women should receive equal pay for equal work.

Directive 76/207 states in Art. 2:

… the principle of equal treatment shall mean that there shall be no discrimination whatsoever on grounds of sex either directly or indirectly by reference in particular to marital or family status.

Directive 79/7 Art. 4 takes this further:

The principle of equal treatment means that there shall be no discrimination whatsoever on ground of sex either directly, or indirectly by reference to marital or family status … .

The ideals of laws to end discrimination against women are clearly expressed in the UN declaration of 1979, from which the following extracts are taken.

Convention on the Elimination of All Forms of Discrimination against Women 1979

Part I
Article 1
For the purposes of the present Convention, the term 'discrimination against women' shall mean any distinction, exclusion or restriction made on the basis of sex which has the effect or purpose of impairing or nullifying the recognition, enjoyment or exercise by women, irrespective of their marital status, on a basis of equality of men and women, of human rights and fundamental freedoms in the political, economic, social, cultural, civil or any other field.

Article 2
States Parties condemn discrimination against women in all its forms, agree to pursue by all appropriate means and without delay a policy of eliminating discrimination against women and, to this end, undertake:
(a) To embody the principle of the equality of men and women in their national constitutions or other appropriate legislation if not yet incorporated therein and to ensure, through law and other appropriate means, the practical realization of this principle;
(b) To adopt appropriate legislative and other measures, including sanctions where appropriate, prohibiting all discrimination against women;
(c) To establish legal protection of the rights of women on an equal basis with men and to ensure through competent national tribunals and other public institutions the effective protection of women against any act of discrimination;
(d) To refrain from engaging in any act or practice of discrimination against women and to ensure that public authorities and institutions shall act in conformity with this obligation;

(e) To take all appropriate measures to eliminate discrimination against women by any person, organization or enterprise;

(f) To take all appropriate measures, including legislation, to modify or abolish existing laws, regulations, customs and practices which constitute discrimination against women;

(g) To repeal all national penal provisions which constitute discrimination against women.

Article 3
States Parties shall take in all fields, in particular in the political, social, economic and cultural fields, all appropriate measures, including legislation, to ensure the full development and advancement of women, for the purpose of guaranteeing them the exercise and enjoyment of human rights and fundamental freedoms on a basis of equality with men.

Article 4
1. Adoption by States Parties of temporary special measures aimed at accelerating de facto equality between men and women shall not be considered discrimination as defined in the present Convention, but shall in no way entail as a consequence the maintenance of unequal or separate standards; these measures shall be discontinued when the objectives of equality of opportunity and treatment have been achieved.
2. Adoption by States Parties of special measures, including those measures contained in the present Convention, aimed at protecting maternity shall not be considered discriminatory.

Article 5
States Parties shall take all appropriate measures:
(a) To modify the social and cultural patterns of conduct of men and women, with a view to achieving the elimination of prejudices and customary and all other practices which are based on the idea of the inferiority or the superiority of either of the sexes or on stereotyped roles for men and women;
(b) To ensure that family education includes a proper understanding of maternity as a social function and the recognition of the common responsibility of men and women in the upbringing and development of their children, it being understood that the interest of the children is the primordial consideration in all cases.

3.3.2 **The legislation**

As with the Race Relations Act, the Sex Discrimination Act first defines the three types of discrimination: direct, indirect and victimisation.

1.(1) In any circumstances relevant for the purposes of any provision of this Act, other than a provision to which subsection (2) applies, a person discriminates against a woman if —
(a) on the ground of her sex he treats her less favourably than he treats or would treat a man, or
(b) he applies to her a requirement or condition which he applies or would apply equally to a man but —
　　(i) which is such that the proportion of women who can comply with it is considerably smaller than the proportion of men who can comply with it, and
　　(ii) which he cannot show to be justifiable irrespective of the sex of the person to whom it is applied, and
　　(iii) which is to her detriment because she cannot comply with it.

(2)   In any circumstances relevant for the purposes of a provision to which this subsection applies, a person discriminates against a woman if —

  (a)   on the ground of her sex, he treats her less favourably than he treats or would treat a man, or

  (b)   he applies to her a provision, criterion or practice which he applies or would apply equally to a man, but —

    (i)   which is such that it would be to the detriment of a considerably larger proportion of women than of men, and

    (ii)   which he cannot show to be justifiable irrespective of the sex of the person to whom it is applied, and

    (iii) which is to her detriment.

(4)   If a person treats or would treat a man differently according to the man's marital status, his treatment of a woman is for the purposes of subsection (1)(a) or (2)(a) to be compared to his treatment of a man having the like marital status.

2.(1)   Section 1, and the provisions of Parts II and III relating to sex discrimination against women, are to be read as applying equally to the treatment of men, and for that purpose shall have effect with such modifications as are requisite.

(2)   In the application of subsection (1) no account shall be taken of special treatment afforded to women in connection with pregnancy or childbirth.

2A.(1)   A person ('A') discriminates against another person ('B') if A treats B less favourably than he treats or would treat other persons, and does so on the ground that B intends to undergo, is undergoing or has undergone gender reassignment.

(2)   Subsection (3) applies to arrangements made by any person in relation to another's absence from work or from vocational training.

(3)   For the purposes of subsection (1), B is treated less favourably than others under such arrangements if, in the application of the arrangements to any absence due to B undergoing gender reassignment —

  (a)   he is treated less favourably than he would be if the absence was due to sickness or injury, or

  (b)   he is treated less favourably than he would be if the absence was due to some other cause and, having regard to the circumstances of the case, it is reasonable for him to be treated no less favourably.

(4)   In subsections (2) and (3) 'arrangements' includes terms, conditions or arrangements on which employment, a pupillage or tenancy or vocational training is offered.

3.(1)   In any circumstances relevant for the purposes of any provision of Part 2, a person discriminates against a married person of either sex if —

  (a)   on the ground of his or her marital status he treats that person less favourably than he treats or would treat an unmarried person of the same sex, or

  (b)   he applies to that person a provision, criterion or practice which he applies or would apply equally to an unmarried person, but —

    (i)   which is such that it would be to the detriment of a considerably larger proportion of married persons than of unmarried persons of the same sex, and

    (ii)   which he cannot show to be justifiable irrespective of the marital status of the person to whom it is applied, and

    (iii) which is to that person's detriment.

Section 4 provides that victimisation is a form of discrimination. The wording is similar to the equivalent part of the Race Relations Act (see page 86) and is not reproduced.

Discrimination in employment

6.(1)   It is unlawful for a person, in relation to employment by him at an establishment in Great Britain, to discriminate against a woman —

    (a) in the arrangements he makes for the purpose of determining who should be offered that employment, or

    (b) in the terms on which he offers her that employment, or

    (c) by refusing or deliberately omitting to offer her that employment.

  (2)   It is unlawful for a person, in the case of a woman employed by him at an establishment in Great Britain, to discriminate against her —

    (a) in the way he affords her access to opportunities for promotion, transfer or training, or to any other benefits, facilities or services, or by refusing or deliberately omitting to afford her access to them, or

    (b) by dismissing her, or subjecting her to any other detriment.

  (7)   Subsection (2) does not apply to benefits, facilities or services of any description if the employer is concerned with the provision (for payment or not) of benefits, facilities or services of that description to the public, or to a section of the public comprising the woman in question, unless —

    (a) that provision differs in a material respect from the provision of the benefits, facilities or services by the employer to his employees, or

    (b) the provision of the benefits, facilities or services to the woman in question is regulated by her contract of employment, or

    (c) the benefits, facilities or services relate to training.

7.(1)   In relation to sex discrimination —

    (a) section 6(1)(a) or (c) does not apply to any employment where being a man is a genuine occupational qualification for the job, and

    (b) section 6(2)(a) does not apply to opportunities for promotion or transfer to, or training for, such employment.

  (2)   Being a man is a genuine occupational qualification for a job only where —

    (a) the essential nature of the job calls for a man for reasons of physiology (excluding physical strength or stamina) or, in dramatic performances or other entertainment, for reasons of authenticity, so that the essential nature of the job would be materially different if carried out by a woman; or

    (b) the job needs to be held by a man to preserve decency or privacy because —

      (i)   it is likely to involve physical contact with men in circumstances where they might reasonably object to its being carried out by a woman, or

      (ii) the holder of the job is likely to do his work in circumstances where men might reasonably object to the presence of a woman because they are in a state of undress or are using sanitary facilities; or

   (ba) the job is likely to involve the holder of the job doing his work, or living, in a private home and needs to be held by a man because objection might reasonably be taken to allowing to a woman —

      (i)   the degree of physical or social contact with a person living in the home, or

      (ii) the knowledge of intimate details of such a person's life,

which is likely, because of the nature or circumstances of the job or of the home, to be allowed to, or available to, the holder of the job; or

    (c) the nature or location of the establishment makes it impracticable for the holder of the job to live elsewhere than in premises provided by the employer, and —

      (i)   the only such premises which are available for persons holding that kind of job are lived in, or normally lived in, by men and are not equipped with separate sleeping accommodation for women and sanitary facilities which could be used by women in privacy from men, and

   (ii) it is not reasonable to expect the employer either to equip those premises with such accommodation and facilities or to provide other premises for women; or

(d) the nature of the establishment, or of the part of it within which the work is done, requires the job to be held by a man because —

   (i) it is, or is part of, a hospital, prison or other establishment for persons requiring special care, supervision or attention, and

   (ii) those persons are all men (disregarding any woman whose presence is exceptional), and

   (iii) it is reasonable, having regard to the essential character of the establishment or that part, that the job should not be held by a woman; or

(e) the holder of the job provides individuals with personal services promoting their welfare or education, or similar personal services, and those services can most effectively be provided by a man, or

(g) the job needs to be held by a man because it is likely to involve the performance of duties outside the United Kingdom in a country whose laws or customs are such that the duties could not, or could not effectively, be performed by a woman, or

(h) the job is one of two to be held by a married couple.

(3)　Subsection (2) applies where some only of the duties of the job fall within paragraphs (a) to (g) as well as where all of them do.

(4)　Paragraph (a), (b), (c), (d), (e) or (g) of subsection (2) does not apply in relation to the filling of a vacancy at a time when the employer already has male employees —

(a) who are capable of carrying out the duties falling within that paragraph, and

(b) whom it would be reasonable to employ on those duties and

(c) whose numbers are sufficient to meet the employer's likely requirements in respect of those duties without undue inconvenience.

Discrimination in training

Sections of the Act relating to discrimination in partnerships, trades unions, establishments conferring qualifications, employment agencies, police, prisons and religious employment are not reproduced here. However s 14 is worth noting:

14.(1)　It is unlawful, in the case of a woman seeking or undergoing training which would help fit her for any employment, for any person who provides, or makes arrangements for the provision of, facilities for such training to discriminate against her —

(a) in the terms on which that person affords her access to any training course or other facilities concerned with such training, or

(b) by refusing or deliberately omitting to afford her such access, or

(c) by terminating her training, or

(d) by subjecting her to any detriment during the course of her training.

Discrimination in education

Sex discrimination in education is unlawful in the provision of education, though you will see under s 26 below that this does not extend to banning single sex schools.

22.   It is unlawful, in relation to an educational establishment falling within column 1 of the following table, for a person indicated in relation to the establishment in column 2 (the 'responsible body') to discriminate against a woman —

   (a) in the terms on which it offers to admit her to the establishment as a pupil, or
   (b) by refusing or deliberately omitting to accept an application for her admission to the establishment as a pupil, or
   (c) where she is a pupil of the establishment —
      (i)   in the way it affords her access to any benefits, facilities or services, or by refusing or deliberately omitting to afford her access to them, or
      (ii) by excluding her from the establishment or subjecting her to any other detriment.

We have not reproduced the table of establishments.

26.(1)   Section 22(a) and (b) and 25 [not reproduced — covers education authorities] do not apply to the admission of pupils to any establishment (a 'single-sex establishment') which admits pupils of one sex only, or which would be taken to admit pupils of one sex only if there were disregarded pupils of the opposite sex —

   (a) whose admission is exceptional, or
   (b) whose numbers are comparatively small and whose admission is confined to particular courses of instruction or teaching classes.

   (2)   Where a school which is not a single-sex establishment has some pupils as boarders and others as non-boarders, and admits as boarders pupils of one sex only (or would be taken to admit as boarders pupils of one sex only if there were disregarded boarders of the opposite sex whose numbers are comparatively small), and sections 22(a) and (b) and 25 do not apply to the admission of boarders and sections 22(c)(i) and 25 do not apply to boarding facilities.

   (3)   Where an establishment is a single-sex establishment by reason of its inclusion in subsection (1)(b), the fact that pupils of one sex are confined to particular courses of instruction or teaching classes shall not be taken to contravene section 22(c)(i) or the duty in section 25.

Discrimination in goods, facilities and services — responsibilities for the actions of other people

No discrimination is permitted in the provision of goods, facilities or services, with exceptions where people are permitted to choose who to live with. Space does not permit us to reproduce these sections, but there is similarity with the race legislation. Similar provisions also exist in relation to responsibility for the discriminatory acts of others.

Positive discrimination training

Discrimination in the provision of training is unlawful, save where positive discrimination is required to redress past imbalances within the workforce. Discrimination is also permissible in circumstances where women are entitled to protection under health and safety laws.

47.(1)   Nothing in Parts II to IV shall render unlawful any act done in relation to particular work by any person in, or in connection with —

   (a) affording women only, or men only, access to facilities for training which would help to fit them for that work, or
   (b) encouraging women only, or men only, to take advantage of opportunities for doing that work,

where it reasonably appears to that person that at any time within the 12 months immediately preceding the doing of the act there were no persons of the sex in question doing that work in

Great Britain, or the number of persons of that sex doing the work in Great Britain was comparatively small.

(2)   Where in relation to particular work it reasonably appears to any person that although the condition for the operation of subsection (1) is not met for the whole of Great Britain it is met for an area within Great Britain, nothing in Parts II to IV shall render unlawful any act done by that person in, or in connection with —

(a)   affording persons who are of the sex in question, and who appear likely to take up that work in that area, access to facilities for training which would help to fit them for that work, or

(b)   encouraging persons of that sex to take advantage of opportunities in the area for doing that work.

(3)   Nothing in Parts II to IV shall render unlawful any act done by any person in, or in connection with, affording persons access to facilities for training which would help to fit them for employment, where it reasonably appears to that person that those persons are in special need of training by reason of the period for which they have been discharging domestic or family responsibilities to the exclusion of regular full time employment.

The discrimination in relation to which this subsection applies may result from confining the training to persons who have been discharging domestic or family responsibilities, or from the way persons are selected for training, or both.

(4)   The preceding provisions of this section shall not apply in relation to any discrimination which is rendered unlawful by section 6.

48.(1)   Nothing in Parts II to IV shall render unlawful any act done by an employer in relation to particular work in his employment, being an act done in, or in connection with —

(a)   affording his female employees only, or his male employees only, access to facilities for training which would help to fit them for that work, or

(b)   encouraging women only, or men only, to take advantage of opportunities for doing that work,

where at any time within the twelve months immediately preceding the doing of the act there were no persons of the sex in question among those doing that work or the number of persons of that sex doing the work was comparatively small.

(2)   Nothing in section 12 shall render unlawful any act done by an organisation to which that section applies in, or in connection with —

(a)   affording female members of the organisation only, or male members of the organisation only, access to facilities for training which would help to fit them for holding a post of any kind in the organisation, or

(b)   encouraging female members only, or male members only, to take advantage of opportunities for holding such posts in the organisation,

where at any time within the twelve months immediately preceding the doing of the act there were no persons of the sex in question among persons holding such posts in the organisation or the number of persons of that sex holding such posts was comparatively small.

49.(1)   Nothing in the following provisions, namely —

(a)   Part II,

(b)   Part III so far as it applies to vocational training, or

(c)   Part IV so far as it has effect in relation to the provisions mentioned in paragraphs (a) and (b),

shall render unlawful any act done by a person in relation to a woman if —

(i)   it was necessary for that person to do it in order to comply with a requirement of an existing statutory provision concerning the protection of women, or

(ii)   it was necessary for that person to do it in order to comply with a requirement of a relevant statutory provision (within the meaning of Part I of the Health and Safety at Work etc. Act 1974) and it was done by that person for the purpose of the protection of the woman in question (or of any class of women that included that woman).

(2) In subsection (1) —

(a) the reference in paragraph (i) of that subsection to an existing statutory provision concerning the protection of women is a reference to any such provision having effect for the purpose of protecting women as regards —

(i) pregnancy or maternity, or

(ii) other circumstances giving rise to risks specifically affecting women,

whether the provision relates only to such protection or to the protection of any other class of persons as well; and

(b) the reference in paragraph (ii) of that subsection to the protection of a particular woman or class of women is a reference to the protection of that woman or those women as regards any circumstances falling within paragraph (a)(i) or (ii) above.

Remedies

Remedies for a person alleging she, or he, was a victim of discrimination are similar to those available in cases of race discrimination. Sections 63, 65 and 66 (not reproduced) establish these. The remaining sections of the Act establish the Equal Opportunities Commission. This body has the function of keeping the legislation under review, assisting individuals with claims, and assisting (if necessary using enforcement notices) employers to eliminate discriminatory practices. Its website contains a list of relevant publications and the full text of many guidance notes and a detailed code of practice. The address is **http://www.eoc.org.uk/**.

3.4 Disability discrimination

The sections addressing employment rights for people with disability was implemented earlier than the parts relating to services, but all parts will be in place by 2004. The philosophy behind the Disability Discrimination Act 1995 (DDA) is slightly different from Acts to combat sex and race discrimination. In order to obtain the dignity, respect and enjoyment of political and economic rights set out in the Universal Declaration, people of different genders and racial backgrounds, in the long run, do not need to be treated very differently, they need discriminatory behaviour to be removed. For people with disabilities there are additional obstacles to overcome.

3.4.1 The UK's international obligations to combat disability discrimination

1. The term 'disabled person' means any person unable to ensure by himself or herself, wholly or partly, the necessities of a normal individual and/or social life, as a result of deficiency, either congenital or not, in his or her physical or mental capabilities.

2.   Disabled persons shall enjoy all the rights set forth in this Declaration. These rights shall be granted to all disabled persons without any exception whatsoever and without distinction or discrimination on the basis of race, colour, sex, language, religion, political or other opinions, national or social origin, state of wealth, birth or any other situation applying either to the disabled person himself or herself or to his or her family.

3.   Disabled persons have the inherent right to respect for their human dignity. Disabled persons, whatever the origin, nature and seriousness of their handicaps and disabilities, have the same fundamental rights as their fellow-citizens of the same age, which implies first and foremost the right to enjoy a decent life, as normal and full as possible.

4.   Disabled persons have the same civil and political rights as other human beings; paragraph 7 of the Declaration on the Rights of Mentally Retarded Persons applies to any possible limitation or suppression of those rights for mentally disabled persons.

5.   Disabled persons are entitled to the measures designed to enable them to become as self-reliant as possible.

6.   Disabled persons have the right to medical, psychological and functional treatment, including prosthetic and orthetic appliances, to medical and social rehabilitation, education, vocational training and rehabilitation, aid, counselling, placement services and other services which will enable them to develop their capabilities and skills to the maximum and will hasten the processes of their social integration or reintegration.

7.   Disabled persons have the right to economic and social security and to a decent level of living. They have the right, according to their capabilities, to secure and retain employment or to engage in a useful, productive and remunerative occupation and to join trade unions.

8.   Disabled persons are entitled to have their special needs taken into consideration at all stages of economic and social planning.

9.   Disabled persons have the right to live with their families or with foster parents and to participate in all social, creative or recreational activities. No disabled person shall be subjected, as far as his or her residence is concerned, to differential treatment other than that required by his or her condition or by the improvement which he or she may derive therefrom. If the stay of a disabled person in a specialized establishment is indispensable, the environment and living conditions therein shall be as close as possible to those of the normal life of a person of his or her age.

10.   Disabled persons shall be protected against all exploitation, all regulations and all treatment of a discriminatory, abusive or degrading nature.

11.   Disabled persons shall be able to avail themselves of qualified legal aid when such aid proves indispensable for the protection of their persons and property. If judicial proceedings are instituted against them, the legal procedure applied shall take their physical and mental condition fully into account.

12.   Organizations of disabled persons may be usefully consulted in all matters regarding the rights of disabled persons.

13.   Disabled persons, their families and communities shall be fully informed, by all appropriate means, of the rights contained in this Declaration.

The UN also adopted a set of Standard Rules on the Equalization of Opportunities for Persons with Disabilities in 1993. Some of these are now reproduced:

II. Target areas for equal participation

Rule 5. Accessibility
States should recognize the overall importance of accessibility in the process of the equalization of opportunities in all spheres of society. For persons with disabilities of any kind, States should (a) introduce programmes of action to make the physical environment accessible; and (b) undertake measures to provide access to information and communication.

(a) Access to the physical environment
1.   States should initiate measures to remove the obstacles to participation in the physical environment. Such measures should be to develop standards and guidelines and to consider enacting legislation to ensure accessibility to various areas in society, such as housing, buildings, public transport services and other means of transportation, streets and other outdoor environments.
2.   States should ensure that architects, construction engineers and others who are professionally involved in the design and construction of the physical environment have access to adequate information on disability policy and measures to achieve accessibility.
3.   Accessibility requirements should be included in the design and construction of the physical environment from the beginning of the designing process.
4.   Organizations of persons with disabilities should be consulted when standards and norms for accessibility are being developed. They should also be involved locally from the initial planning stage when public construction projects are being designed, thus ensuring maximum accessibility.

(b) Access to information and communication
5.   Persons with disabilities and, where appropriate, their families and advocates should have access to full information on diagnosis, rights and available services and programmes, at all stages. Such information should be presented in forms accessible to persons with disabilities.
6.   States should develop strategies to make information services and documentation accessible for different groups of persons with disabilities. Braille, tape services, large print and other appropriate technologies should be used to provide access to written information and documentation for persons with visual impairments. Similarly, appropriate technologies should be used to provide access to spoken information for persons with auditory impairments or comprehension difficulties.
7.   Consideration should be given to the use of sign language in the education of deaf children, in their families and communities. Sign language interpretation services should also be provided to facilitate the communication between deaf persons and others.
8.   Consideration should also be given to the needs of people with other communication disabilities.
9.   States should encourage the media, especially television, radio and newspapers, to make their services accessible.
10.   States should ensure that new computerized information and service systems offered to the general public are either made initially accessible or are adapted to be made accessible to persons with disabilities.
11.   Organizations of persons with disabilities should be consulted when measures to make information services accessible are being developed.

Rule 6. Education
States should recognize the principle of equal primary, secondary and tertiary educational opportunities for children, youth and adults with disabilities, in integrated settings. They should ensure that the education of persons with disabilities is an integral part of the educational system.
1.   General educational authorities are responsible for the education of persons with disabilities in integrated settings. Education for persons with disabilities should form an integral part of national educational planning, curriculum development and school organization.
2.   Education in mainstream schools presupposes the provision of interpreter and other appropriate support services. Adequate accessibility and support services, designed to meet the needs of persons with different disabilities, should be provided.
3.   Parent groups and organizations of persons with disabilities should be involved in the education process at all levels.

4. In States where education is compulsory it should be provided to girls and boys with all kinds and all levels of disabilities, including the most severe.

5. Special attention should be given in the following areas:
   (a) Very young children with disabilities;
   (b) Pre-school children with disabilities;
   (c) Adults with disabilities, particularly women.

6. To accommodate educational provisions for persons with disabilities in the mainstream, States should:
   (a) Have a clearly stated policy, understood and accepted at the school level and by the wider community;
   (b) Allow for curriculum flexibility, addition and adaptation;
   (c) Provide for quality materials, ongoing teacher training and support teachers.

7. Integrated education and community-based programmes should be seen as complementary approaches in providing cost-effective education and training for persons with disabilities. National community-based programmes should encourage communities to use and develop their resources to provide local education to persons with disabilities.

8. In situations where the general school system does not yet adequately meet the needs of all persons with disabilities, special education may be considered. It should be aimed at preparing students for education in the general school system. The quality of such education should reflect the same standards and ambitions as general education and should be closely linked to it. At a minimum, students with disabilities should be afforded the same portion of educational resources as students without disabilities. States should aim for the gradual integration of special education services into mainstream education. It is acknowledged that in some instances special education may currently be considered to be the most appropriate form of education for some students with disabilities.

9. Owing to the particular communication needs of deaf and deaf/blind persons, their education may be more suitably provided in schools for such persons or special classes and units in mainstream schools. At the initial stage, in particular, special attention needs to be focused on culturally sensitive instruction that will result in effective communication skills and maximum independence for people who are deaf or deaf/blind.

Rule 7. *Employment*

States should recognize the principle that persons with disabilities must be empowered to exercise their human rights, particularly in the field of employment. In both rural and urban areas they must have equal opportunities for productive and gainful employment in the labour market.

1. Laws and regulations in the employment field must not discriminate against persons with disabilities and must not raise obstacles to their employment.

2. States should actively support the integration of persons with disabilities into open employment. This active support could occur through a variety of measures, such as vocational training, incentive-oriented quota schemes, reserved or designated employment, loans or grants for small business, exclusive contracts or priority production rights, tax concessions, contract compliance or other technical or financial assistance to enterprises employing workers with disabilities. States should also encourage employers to make reasonable adjustments to accommodate persons with disabilities.

3. States' action programmes should include:
   (a) Measures to design and adapt workplaces and work premises in such a way that they become accessible to persons with different disabilities;
   (b) Support for the use of new technologies and the development and production of assistive devices, tools and equipment and measures to facilitate access to such devices and equipment for persons with disabilities to enable them to gain and maintain employment;

(c) Provision of appropriate training and placement and ongoing support such as personal assistance and interpreter services.

4.   States should initiate and support public awareness-raising campaigns designed to overcome negative attitudes and prejudices concerning workers with disabilities.

5.   In their capacity as employers, States should create favourable conditions for the employment of persons with disabilities in the public sector.

6.   States, workers' organizations and employers should cooperate to ensure equitable recruitment and promotion policies, employment conditions, rates of pay, measures to improve the work environment in order to prevent injuries and impairments and measures for the rehabilitation of employees who have sustained employment-related injuries.

7.   The aim should always be for persons with disabilities to obtain employment in the open labour market. For persons with disabilities whose needs cannot be met in open employment, small units of sheltered or supported employment may be an alternative. It is important that the quality of such programmes be assessed in terms of their relevance and sufficiency in providing opportunities for persons with disabilities to gain employment in the labour market.

8.   Measures should be taken to include persons with disabilities in training and employment programmes in the private and informal sectors.

9.   States, workers' organizations and employers should cooperate with organizations of persons with disabilities concerning all measures to create training and employment opportunities, including flexible hours, part-time work, job-sharing, self-employment and attendant care for persons with disabilities.

Rule 8. Income maintenance and social security

States are responsible for the provision of social security and income maintenance for persons with disabilities. [Detailed provisions not reproduced]

Rule 9. Family life and personal integrity

States should promote the full participation of persons with disabilities in family life. They should promote their right to personal integrity and ensure that laws do not discriminate against persons with disabilities with respect to sexual relationships, marriage and parenthood.

1.   Persons with disabilities should be enabled to live with their families. States should encourage the inclusion in family counselling of appropriate modules regarding disability and its effects on family life. Respite-care and attendant-care services should be made available to families which include a person with disabilities. States should remove all unnecessary obstacles to persons who want to foster or adopt a child or adult with disabilities.

2.   Persons with disabilities must not be denied the opportunity to experience their sexuality, have sexual relationships and experience parenthood. Taking into account that persons with disabilities may experience difficulties in getting married and setting up a family, States should encourage the availability of appropriate counselling. Persons with disabilities must have the same access as others to family-planning methods, as well as to information in accessible form on the sexual functioning of their bodies.

3.   States should promote measures to change negative attitudes towards marriage, sexuality and parenthood of persons with disabilities, especially of girls and women with disabilities, which still prevail in society. The media should be encouraged to play an important role in removing such negative attitudes.

4. Persons with disabilities and their families need to be fully informed about taking precautions against sexual and other forms of abuse. Persons with disabilities are particularly vulnerable to abuse in the family, community or institutions and need to be educated on how to avoid the occurrence of abuse, recognize when abuse has occurred and report on such acts.

Rules on culture, sport and religion, not reproduced, are also set out.

3.4.2 The Disability Discrimination Act 1995 (DDA)

Meaning of "disability" and "disabled person"
1.(1)   Subject to the provisions of Schedule 1, a person has a disability for the purposes of this Act if he has a physical or mental impairment which has a substantial and long-term adverse effect on his ability to carry out normal day-to-day activities.

(2)   In this Act 'disabled person' means a person who has a disability.
Schedule 1 defines more precisely what is a disability.

Impairment
1.(1)   'Mental impairment' includes an impairment resulting from or consisting of a mental illness only if the illness is a clinically well-recognised illness.
(2)   Regulations may make provision, for the purposes of this Act —
   (a)   for conditions of a prescribed description to be treated as amounting to impairments;
   (b)   for conditions of a prescribed description to be treated as not amounting to impairments.
(3)   Regulations made under sub-paragraph (2) may make provision as to the meaning of 'condition' for the purposes of those regulations.

Long-term effects
2.(1)   The effect of an impairment is a long-term effect if —
   (a)   it has lasted at least 12 months;
   (b)   the period for which it lasts is likely to be at least 12 months; or
   (c)   it is likely to last for the rest of the life of the person affected.
(2)   Where an impairment ceases to have a substantial adverse effect on a person's ability to carry out normal day-to-day activities, it is to be treated as continuing to have that effect if that effect is likely to recur.
(3)   For the purposes of sub-paragraph (2), the likelihood of an effect recurring shall be disregarded in prescribed circumstances.
(4)   Regulations may prescribe circumstances in which, for the purposes of this Act —
   (a)   an effect which would not otherwise be a long-term effect is to be treated as such an effect; or
   (b)   an effect which would otherwise be a long-term effect is to be treated as not being such an effect.

Severe disfigurement
3.(1)   An impairment which consists of a severe disfigurement is to be treated as having a substantial adverse effect on the ability of the person concerned to carry out normal day-to-day activities.
(2)   Regulations may provide that in prescribed circumstances a severe disfigurement is not to be treated as having that effect.

(3) Regulations under sub-paragraph (2) may, in particular, make provision with respect to deliberately acquired disfigurements.

Normal day-to-day activities

4.(1) An impairment is to be taken to affect the ability of the person concerned to carry out normal day-to-day activities only if it affects one of the following —

- (a) mobility;
- (b) manual dexterity;
- (c) physical co-ordination;
- (d) continence;
- (e) ability to lift, carry or otherwise move everyday objects;
- (f) speech, hearing or eyesight;
- (g) memory or ability to concentrate, learn or understand; or
- (h) perception of the risk of physical danger.

(2) Regulations may prescribe —

- (a) circumstances in which an impairment which does not have an effect falling within sub-paragraph (1) is to be taken to affect the ability of the person concerned to carry out normal day-to-day activities;
- (b) circumstances in which an impairment which has an effect falling within sub-paragraph (1) is to be taken not to affect the ability of the person concerned to carry out normal day-to-day activities.

Substantial adverse effects

(5) Regulations may make provision for the purposes of this Act —

- (a) for an effect of a prescribed kind on the ability of a person to carry out normal day-to-day activities to be treated as a substantial adverse effect;
- (b) for an effect of a prescribed kind on the ability of a person to carry out normal day-to-day activities to be treated as not being a substantial adverse effect.

Effect of medical treatment

6.(1) An impairment which would be likely to have a substantial adverse effect on the ability of the person concerned to carry out normal day-to-day activities, but for the fact that measures are being taken to treat or correct it, is to be treated as having that effect.

(2) In sub-paragraph (1) 'measures' includes, in particular, medical treatment and the use of a prosthesis or other aid.

(3) Sub-paragraph (1) does not apply —

- (a) in relation to the impairment of a person's sight, to the extent that the impairment is, in his case, correctable by spectacles or contact lenses or in such other ways as may be prescribed; or
- (b) in relation to such other impairments as may be prescribed, in such circumstances as may be prescribed.

Persons deemed to be disabled

7.(1) Sub-paragraph (2) applies to any person whose name is, both on 12th January 1995 and on the date when this paragraph comes into force, in the register of disabled persons maintained under section 6 of the Disabled Persons (Employment) Act 1944.

(2) That person is to be deemed —

- (a) during the initial period, to have a disability, and hence to be a disabled person; and
- (b) afterwards, to have had a disability and hence to have been a disabled person during that period.

(3) A certificate of registration shall be conclusive evidence, in relation to the person with respect to whom it was issued, of the matters certified.

(4)   Unless the contrary is shown, any document purporting to be a certificate of registration shall be taken to be such a certificate and to have been validly issued.

(5)   Regulations may provide for prescribed descriptions of person to be deemed to have disabilities, and hence to be disabled persons, for the purposes of this Act.

(6)   Regulations may prescribe circumstances in which a person who has been deemed to be a disabled person by the provisions of sub-paragraph (1) or regulations made under sub-paragraph (5) is to be treated as no longer being deemed to be such a person.

Progressive conditions

8.(1)   Where —

(a)   a person has a progressive condition (such as cancer, multiple sclerosis or muscular dystrophy or infection by the human immunodeficiency virus),

(b)   as a result of that condition, he has an impairment which has (or had) an effect on his ability to carry out normal day-to-day activities, but

(c)   that-effect is not (or was not) a substantial adverse effect,

he shall be taken to have an impairment which has such a substantial adverse effect if the condition is likely to result in his having such an impairment.

(2)   Regulations may make provision, for the purposes of this paragraph —

(a)   for conditions of a prescribed description to be treated as being progressive;

(b)   for conditions of a prescribed description to be treated as not being progressive.

Section 3 (not reproduced) allows the government to issue codes of practice, which help to explain the Act and may be taken into account by a court or tribunal. Annex 1 to the Code of Practice for the elimination of discrimination in the field of employment against disabled persons or persons who have had a disability, issued in 1996, helps to explain what is, in the legislation, a disability. This is reproduced in part below. It can be accessed at **http://www.disability.gov.uk/dda/dle/cop-elim.html**.

Disability and employment

Discrimination is defined in terms initially similar to those used in RRA and SDA, but with a general requirement on employers to make reasonable adjustments to accommodate the needs of disabled persons.

5.(1)   For the purposes of this Part, an employer discriminates against a disabled person if —

(a)   for a reason which relates to the disabled person's disability, he treats him less favourably than he treats or would treat others to whom that reason does not or would not apply; and

(b)   he cannot show that the treatment in question is justified.

(2)   For the purposes of this Part, an employer also discriminates against a disabled person if —

(a)   he fails to comply with a section 6 duty imposed on him in relation to the disabled person; and

(b)   he cannot show that his failure to comply with that duty is justified.

(3)   Subject to subsection (5), for the purposes of subsection (1) treatment is justified if, but only if, the reason for it is both material to the circumstances of the particular case and substantial.

(4)   For the purposes of subsection (2), failure to comply with a section 6 duty is justified if, but only if, the reason for the failure is both material to the circumstances of the particular case and substantial.

(5)   If, in a case falling within subsection (1), the employer is under a section 6 duty in relation to the disabled person but fails without justification to comply with that duty, his

treatment of that person cannot be justified under subsection (3) unless it would have been justified even if he had complied with the section 6 duty.

6.(1)   Where —

    (a)   any arrangements made by or on behalf of an employer, or

    (b)   any physical feature of premises occupied by the employer,

place the disabled person concerned at a substantial disadvantage in comparison with persons who are not disabled, it is the duty of the employer to take such steps as it is reasonable, in all the circumstances of the case, for him to have to take in order to prevent the arrangements or feature having that effect.

  (2)   Subsection (1)(a) applies only in relation to —

    (a)   arrangements for determining to whom employment should be offered;

    (b)   any term, condition or arrangements on which employment, promotion, a transfer, training or any other benefit is offered or afforded.

  (3)   The following are examples of steps which an employer may have to take in relation to a disabled person in order to comply with subsection (1) —

    (a)   making adjustments to premises;

    (b)   allocating some of the disabled person's duties to another person;

    (c)   transferring him to fill an existing vacancy;

    (d)   altering his working hours;

    (e)   assigning him to a different place of work;

    (f)   allowing him to be absent during working hours for rehabilitation, assessment or treatment;

    (g)   giving him, or arranging for him to be given, training;

    (h)   acquiring or modifying equipment;

    (i)   modifying instructions or reference manuals;

    (j)   modifying procedures for testing or assessment;

    (k)   providing a reader or interpreter;

    (l)   providing supervision.

  (4)   In determining whether it is reasonable for an employer to have to take a particular step in order to comply with subsection (1), regard shall be had, in particular, to —

    (a)   the extent to which taking the step would prevent the effect in question;

    (b)   the extent to which it is practicable for the employer to take the step;

    (c)   the financial and other costs which would be incurred by the employer in taking the step and the extent to which taking it would disrupt any of his activities;

    (d)   the extent of the employer's financial and other resources;

    (e)   the availability to the employer of financial or other assistance with respect to taking the step.

This subsection is subject to any provision of regulations made under subsection (8).

  (5)   In this section, 'the disabled person concerned' means —

    (a)   in the case of arrangements for determining to whom employment should be offered, any disabled person who is, or has notified the employer that he may be, an applicant for that employment;

    (b)   in any other case, a disabled person who is —

      (i)   an applicant for the employment concerned; or

      (ii)   an employee of the employer concerned.

  (6)   Nothing in this section imposes any duty on an employer in relation to a disabled person if the employer does not know, and could not reasonably be expected to know —

    (a)   in the case of an applicant or potential applicant, that the disabled person concerned is, or may be, an applicant for the employment; or

    (b)   in any case, that that person has a disability and is likely to be affected in the way mentioned in subsection (1).

(7)   Subject to the provisions of this section, nothing in this Part is to be taken to require an employer to treat a disabled person more favourably than he treats or would treat others.

Employers with less than 15 staff (this figure, reduced from the original 25, is set out in s 7 of the Act, not reproduced) must not discriminate against a disabled person in the ways set out in s 4. (There is no unlawfulness — unlike sex or race cases — in discriminating in favour of a disabled person, but no requirement to do so either.)

4.(1)   It is unlawful for an employer to discriminate against a disabled person —
    (a)   in the arrangements which he makes for the purpose of determining to whom he should offer employment;
    (b)   in the terms on which he offers that person employment; or
    (c)   by refusing to offer, or deliberately not offering, him employment.
  (2)   It is unlawful for an employer to discriminate against a disabled person whom he employs —
    (a)   in the terms of employment which he affords him;
    (b)   in the opportunities which he affords him for promotion, a transfer, training or receiving any other benefit;
    (c)   by refusing to afford him, or deliberately not affording him, any such opportunity; or
    (d)   by dismissing him, or subjecting him to any other detriment.

The Code of Practice provides examples of these provisions:

For example, a woman with a disability which requires use of a wheelchair applies for a job. She can do the job but the employer thinks the wheelchair will get in the way in the office. He gives the job to a person who is no more suitable for the job but who does not use a wheelchair. The employer has therefore treated the woman less favourably than the other person because he did not give her the job. The treatment was for a reason related to the disability — the fact that she used a wheelchair. And the reason for treating her less favourably did not apply to the other person because that person did not use a wheelchair.
If the employer could not justify his treatment of the disabled woman then he would have unlawfully discriminated against her.
For example, an employer decides to close down a factory and makes all the employees redundant, including a disabled person who works there. This is not discrimination as the disabled employee is not being dismissed for a reason which relates to the disability.
4.3   A disabled person may not be able to point to other people who were actually treated more favourably. However, it is still 'less favourable treatment' if the employer would give better treatment to someone else to whom the reason for the treatment of the disabled person did not apply. This comparison can also be made with other disabled people, not just non-disabled people. For example, an employer might be discriminating by treating a person with a mental illness less favourably than he treats or would treat a physically disabled person.
4.6   … For example, someone who is blind is not shortlisted for a job involving computers because the employer thinks blind people cannot use them. The employer makes no effort to look at the individual circumstances. A general assumption that blind people cannot use computers would not in itself be a material reason — it is not related to the particular circumstances.
For example, a factory worker with a mental illness is sometimes away from work due to his disability. Because of that he is dismissed. However, the amount of time off is very little more than the employer accepts as sick leave for other employees and so is very unlikely to be a substantial reason.
For example, a clerical worker with a learning disability cannot sort papers quite as quickly as some of his colleagues. There is very little difference in productivity but he is dismissed. That is very unlikely to be a substantial reason.

For example, an employer seeking a clerical worker turns down an applicant with a severe facial disfigurement solely on the ground that other employees would be uncomfortable working alongside him. This will be unlawful because such a reaction by other employees will not in itself justify less favourable treatment of this sort — it is not substantial. The same would apply if it were thought that a customer would feel uncomfortable.

For example, an employer moves someone with a mental illness to a different workplace solely because he mutters to himself while he works. If the employer accepts similar levels of noise from other people, the treatment of the disabled person would probably be unjustified — that level of noise is unlikely to be a substantial reason.

For example, someone who has psoriasis (a skin condition) is rejected for a job involving modelling cosmetics on a part of the body which in his case is severely disfigured by the condition. That would be lawful if his appearance would be incompatible with the purpose of the work. This is a substantial reason which is clearly related — material — to the individual circumstance.

4.7 ... For example, an employee who uses a wheelchair is not promoted, solely because the work station for the higher post is inaccessible to wheelchairs — though it could readily be made so by rearrangement of the furniture. If the furniture had been re-arranged, the reason for refusing promotion would not have applied. The refusal of promotion would therefore not be justified.

For example, an applicant for a typing job is not the best person on the face of it, but only because her typing speed is too slow due to arthritis in her hands. If a reasonable adjustment — perhaps an adapted keyboard — would overcome this, her typing speed would not in itself be a substantial reason for not employing her. Therefore the employer would be unlawfully discriminating if on account of her typing speed he did not employ her and provide the adjustment.

For example, an employer refuses a training course for an employee with an illness which is very likely to be terminal within a year because, even with a reasonable adjustment to help in the job after the course, the benefits of the course could not be adequately realised. This is very likely to be a substantial reason. It is clearly material to the circumstances. The refusal of training would therefore very likely be justified.

For example, someone who is blind applies for a job which requires a significant amount of driving. If it is not reasonable for the employer to adjust the job so that the driving duties are given to someone else, the employer's need for a driver might well be a substantial reason for not employing the blind person. It is clearly material to the particular circumstances. The non-appointment could therefore be justified.

The Code also gives guidance on reasonable adjustments

4.12 ... For example, a man who is disabled by dyslexia applies for a job which involves writing letters within fairly long deadlines. The employer gives all applicants a test of their letter-writing ability. The man can generally write letters very well but finds it difficult to do so in stressful situations. The employer's arrangements would mean he had to begin his test immediately on arrival and to do it in a short time. He would be substantially disadvantaged compared to non-disabled people who would not find such arrangements stressful or, if they did, would not be so affected by them. The employer therefore gives him a little time to settle in and longer to write the letter. These new arrangements do not inconvenience the employer very much and only briefly delay the decision on an appointment. These are steps that it is reasonable for the employer to have to take in the circumstances to prevent the disadvantage — a 'reasonable adjustment'.

4.13 If a disabled person cannot point to an existing non-disabled person compared with whom he is at a substantial disadvantage, then the comparison should be made with how the employer would have treated a non-disabled person.

4.14 How to comply with this duty in recruitment and during employment is explained in paragraphs 5.1–5.29 and 6.1–6.21. The following paragraphs explain how to satisfy this duty more generally.

What 'physical features' and 'arrangements' are covered by the duty?
4.15   Regulations define the term 'physical features' to include anything on the premises arising from a building's design or construction or from an approach to, exit from or access to such a building; fixtures, fittings, furnishings, furniture, equipment or materials; and any other physical element or quality of land in the premises. All of these are covered whether temporary or permanent (under Employment Regulations — see paragraph 1.6).

4.16   The Act says that the duty applies to 'arrangements' for determining to whom employment should be offered and any term, condition or arrangement on which employment, promotion, transfer, training or any other benefit is offered or afforded (s. 6(2)). The duty applies in recruitment and during employment; for example, selection and interview procedures and the arrangements for using premises for such procedures as well as job offers, contractual arrangements, and working conditions.

For example, the design of a particular workplace makes it difficult for someone with a hearing impairment to hear. That is a disadvantage caused by the physical features. There may be nothing that can reasonably be done in the circumstances to change these features. However, requiring someone to work in such a workplace is an arrangement made by the employer and it might be reasonable to overcome the disadvantage by a transfer to another workplace or by ensuring that the supervisor gives instructions in an office rather than in the working area.

What 'disadvantages' give rise to the duty?
4.17   The Act says that only substantial disadvantages give rise to the duty (s. 6(1)). Substantial disadvantages are those which are not minor or trivial.

For example, an employer is unlikely to be required to widen a particular doorway to enable passage by an employee using a wheelchair if there is an easy alternative route to the same destination.

What adjustments might an employer have to make?
4.20   The Act gives a number of examples of 'steps' which employers may have to take, if it is reasonable for them to have to do so in all the circumstances of the case (s. 6(3)). Steps other than those listed here, or a combination of steps, will sometimes have to be taken. The steps in the Act are:

- making adjustments to premises
  For example, an employer might have to make structural or other physical changes such as: widening a doorway, providing a ramp or moving furniture for a wheelchair user; relocating light switches, door handles or shelves for someone who has difficulty in reaching; providing appropriate contrast in decor to help the safe mobility of a visually impaired person.
- allocating some of the disabled person's duties to another person
  For example, minor or subsidiary duties might be reallocated to another employee if the disabled person has difficulty in doing them because of the disability. For example, if a job occasionally involves going onto the open roof of a building an employer might have to transfer this work away from an employee whose disability involves severe vertigo.
- transferring the person to fill an existing vacancy
  For example, if an employee becomes disabled, or has a disability which worsens so she cannot work in the same place or under the same arrangements and there is no reasonable adjustment which would enable the employee to continue doing the current job, then she might have to be considered for any suitable alternative posts which are available. (Such a case might also involve reasonable retraining.)
- altering the person's working hours
  For example, this could include allowing the disabled person to work flexible hours to enable additional breaks to overcome fatigue arising from the disability, or changing the disabled person's hours to fit with the availability of a carer.

- assigning the person to a different place of work
  For example, this could mean transferring a wheelchair user's work station from an inaccessible third floor office to an accessible one on the ground floor. It could mean moving the person to other premises of the same employer if the first building is inaccessible.
- allowing the person to be absent during working hours for rehabilitation, assessment or treatment
  For example, if a person were to become disabled, the employer might have to allow the person more time off during work, than would be allowed to non-disabled employees, to receive physiotherapy or psychoanalysis or undertake employment rehabilitation. A similar adjustment might be appropriate if a disability worsens or if a disabled person needs occasional treatment anyway.
- giving the person, or arranging for him to be given, training
  For example, this could be training in the use of particular pieces of equipment unique to the disabled person, or training appropriate for all employees but which needs altering for the disabled person because of the disability. For example, all employees might need to be trained in the use of a particular machine but an employer might have to provide slightly different or longer training for an employee with restricted hand or arm movements, or training in additional software for a visually impaired person so that he can use a computer with speech output.
- acquiring or modifying equipment
  For example, an employer might have to provide special equipment (such as an adapted keyboard for a visually impaired person or someone with arthritis), or an adapted telephone for someone with a hearing impairment or modified equipment (such as longer handles on a machine). There is no requirement to provide or modify equipment for personal purposes unconnected with work, such as providing a wheelchair if a person needs one in any event but does not have one: the disadvantage in such a case does not flow from the employer's arrangements or premises.
- modifying instructions or reference manuals
  For example, the way instruction is normally given to employees might need to be revised when telling a disabled person how to do a task. The format of instructions or manuals may need to be modified (e.g. produced in braille or on audio tape) and instructions for people with learning disabilities may need to be conveyed orally with individual demonstration.
- modifying procedures for testing or assessment
  For example, this could involve ensuring that particular tests do not adversely affect people with particular types of disability. For example, a person with restricted manual dexterity might be disadvantaged by a written test, so an employer might have to give that person an oral test.
- providing a reader or interpreter
  For example, this could involve a colleague reading mail to a person with a visual impairment at particular times during the working day or, in appropriate circumstances, the hiring of a reader or sign language interpreter.
- providing supervision
  For example, this could involve the provision of a support worker, or help from a colleague, in appropriate circumstances, for someone whose disability leads to uncertainty or lack of confidence.

The Code then discusses how to determine what is reasonable for the employer: for example the relative cost and availability of grants will be taken into account.

Sections 7 and 8 provide for complaints to be taken to an employment tribunal and are not reproduced. The next section is cited to illustrate that employers cannot hide behind obstacles such as landords' refusal to allow alterations to premises.

16.(1)   This section applies where —
  (a)   an employer or trade organisation ('the occupier') occupies premises under a lease;
  (b)   but for this section, the occupier would not be entitled to make a particular alteration to the premises; and
  (c)   the alteration is one which the occupier proposes to make in order to comply with a section 6 duty or section 15 duty. [s. 15 requires trade organizations to address discriminatory arrangements or physical features.]
  (2)   Except to the extent to which it expressly so provides, the lease shall have effect by virtue of this subsection as if it provided —
  (a)   for the occupier to be entitled to make the alteration with the written consent of the lessor;
  (b)   for the occupier to have to make a written application to the lessor for consent if he wishes to make the alteration;
  (c)   if such an application is made, for the lessor not to withhold his consent unreasonably; and
  (d)   for the lessor to be entitled to make his consent subject to reasonable conditions.

3.4.3 Discrimination in relation to goods and services

19.(1)   It is unlawful for a provider of services to discriminate against a disabled person —
  (a)   in refusing to provide, or deliberately not providing, to the disabled person any service which he provides, or is prepared to provide, to members of the public;
  (b)   in failing to comply with any duty imposed on him by section 21 in circumstances in which the effect of that failure is to make it impossible or unreasonably difficult for the disabled person to make use of any such service;
  (c)   in the standard of service which he provides to the disabled person or the manner in which he provides it to him; or
  (d)   in the terms on which he provides a service to the disabled person.
  (2)   For the purposes of this section and sections 20 and 21 —
  (a)   the provision of services includes the provision of any goods or facilities;
  (b)   a person is 'a provider of services' if he is concerned with the provision, in the United Kingdom, of services to the public or to a section of the public; and
  (c)   it is irrelevant whether a service is provided on payment or without payment.
  (3)   The following are examples of services to which this section and sections 20 and 21 apply —
  (a)   access to and use of any place which members of the public are permitted to enter;
  (b)   access to and use of means of communication;
  (c)   access to and use of information services;
  (d)   accommodation in a hotel, boarding house or other similar establishment;
  (e)   facilities by way of banking or insurance or for grants, loans, credit or finance;
  (f)   facilities for entertainment, recreation or refreshment;
  (g)   facilities provided by employment agencies or under section 2 of the Employment and Training Act 1973;
  (h)   the services of any profession or trade, or any local or other public authority.

(4)   In the case of an act which constitutes discrimination by virtue of section 55, this section also applies to discrimination against a person who is not disabled.

Subsection (5) (not reproduced) exempts educational bodies from this requirement. However provisions against discrimination can be found in a range of legislation relating to education — for example the Education Act 1994, s 1.

20.(1)   For the purposes of section 19, a provider of services discriminates against a disabled person if —
  (a)   for a reason which relates to the disabled person's disability, he treats him less favourably than he treats or would treat others to whom that reason does not or would not apply; and
  (b)   he cannot show that the treatment in question is justified.
  (2)   For the purposes of section 19, a provider of services also discriminates against a disabled person if —
  (a)   he fails to comply with a section 21 duty imposed on him in relation to the disabled person; and
  (b)   he cannot show that his failure to comply with that duty is justified.
  (3)   For the purposes of this section, treatment is justified only if —
  (a)   in the opinion of the provider of services, one or more of the conditions mentioned in subsection (4) are satisfied; and
  (b)   it is reasonable, in all the circumstances of the case, for him to hold that opinion.
  (4)   The conditions are that —
  (a)   in any case, the treatment is necessary in order not to endanger the health or safety of any person (which may include that of the disabled person);
  (b)   in any case, the disabled person is incapable of entering into an enforceable agreement, or of giving an informed consent, and for that reason the treatment is reasonable in that case;
  (c)   in a case falling within section 19(1)(a), the treatment is necessary because the provider of services would otherwise be unable to provide the service to members of the public;
  (d)   in a case falling within section 19(1)(c) or (d), the treatment is necessary in order for the provider of services to be able to provide the service to the disabled person or to other members of the public;
  (e)   in a case falling within section 19(1)(d), the difference in the terms on which the service is provided to the disabled person and those on which it is provided to other members of the public reflects the greater cost to the provider of services in providing the service to the disabled person.
  (5)   Any increase in the cost of providing a service to a disabled person which results from compliance by a provider of services with a section 21 duty shall be disregarded for the purposes of subsection (4)(e).
21.(1)   Where a provider of services has a practice, policy or procedure which makes it impossible or unreasonably difficult for disabled persons to make use of a service which he provides, or is prepared to provide, to other members of the public, it is his duty to take such steps as it is reasonable, in all the circumstances of the case, for him to have to take in order to change that practice, policy or procedure so that it no longer has that effect.
  (2)   Where a physical feature (for example, one arising from the design or construction of a building or the approach or access to premises) makes it impossible or unreasonably difficult for disabled persons to make use of such a service, it is the duty of the provider of that service to take

such steps as it is reasonable, in all the circumstances of the case, for him to have to take in order to —

    (a) remove the feature;

    (b) alter it so that it no longer has that effect;

    (c) provide a reasonable means of avoiding the feature; or

    (d) provide a reasonable alternative method of making the service in question available to disabled persons.

    (4)   Where an auxiliary aid or service (for example, the provision of information on audio tape or of a sign language interpreter) would —

    (a) enable disabled persons to make use of a service which a provider of services provides, or is prepared to provide, to members of the public, or

    (b) facilitate the use by disabled persons of such a service,

it is the duty of the provider of that service to take such steps as it is reasonable, in all the circumstances of the case, for him to have to take in order to provide that auxiliary aid or service.

    (6)   Nothing in this section requires a provider of services to take any steps which would fundamentally alter the nature of the service in question or the nature of his trade, profession or business.

    (7)   Nothing in this section requires a provider of services to take any steps which would cause him to incur expenditure exceeding the prescribed maximum.

No maximum has yet been prescribed under subsection (7).

For reasons of space we do not reproduce Part V, which deals with accessibility to public transport, or the parts of Part IV dealing with access to premises. However, a Code of Practice on Rights of Access, Goods, Facilities, Services and Premises was issued in 1995. This contains extensive guidance and can be accessed at **http://www.disability.gov.uk/dda/codedda.html**.

PART II

Community care

4

Community care

4.1 Introduction

Community care admits of a number of definitions and descriptions. In his article 'Community Care — Towards a Workable Statute' ([1997] vol. XIX(2) Liverpool Law Review 181; see below), Luke Clements argues that it is easier to say what it is not than to say what it is. He says that it 'is not the provision of medical or housing services nor the duplication of functions discharged by DSS (now DWP). Put loosely, it is about the public provision of practical assistance (which may take the form of direct payments) to enable a person to live with basic comfort and better cope with our social and built environment' (p. 184). In the white paper, *Caring for People* (Cm 849 (1989)), which preceded the National Health Service and Community Care Act 1990, the Government said: 'Community care means providing the services and support which people who are affected by problems of ageing, mental illness, mental handicap or physical or sensory disability need to be able to live as independently as possible in their own homes or in "homely" settings in the community' (para. 1.1). The 1990 Act, however, defines community care in terms of services by reference to provisions authorising such services: see below.

As it stands, the law on community care creates a framework which identifies criteria to be applied to the assessment of need and the provision of services to those assessed as having needs for community care services. It establishes the concepts to be applied and the procedural framework within which decisions may be made. The key concept is need. The local authority is under a duty to assess need, both generally and in respect of individuals, within its area. It is under a duty to publish information, and to make decisions in respect of individuals who may have a need for community care services. In assessing need, it must follow any statutory criteria and guidance from the Secretary of State issued under s. 7 of the Local Authority Social Services Act 1970 (LASSA). Subject to this, the social services authority has the power to decide what criteria to apply in assessing need. It also has the power to decide whether, on the application of any criteria adopted or required, a person has a need for services and, if so, what services that person needs. A further issue relates to the question of payment for such services, a matter of keen interest to local authority and service user alike.

It is thus quite clear from the various pieces of legislation that decision making in this area ultimately rests with the professional judgment of the local authority (or, in practical terms, with those acting on its behalf) and not with the potential service user. In this respect the law is contentious: some would argue that it should be for the service user to determine needs. Nor are the concepts clear: the whole idea of 'need' is a relative concept with no fixed standards, leading to variations in provision. This is, in part, due to the fact that the legislation governing community care assessments is not found in one place but in several. The legal framework has to be pieced together from several statutes, as interpreted by the courts, a difficult enough task for the lawyer trained in such things, but even more so for social worker and service user alike.

In the White Paper *Caring for People*, the Government expressed the following aspirations for the development of the law:

Helping people to lead, as far as is possible, full and independent lives is at the heart of the Government's approach to community care. Improving the services that enable them to do that is a continuing commitment shared by all concerned.

...

Community care means providing the services and support which people who are affected by problems of ageing, mental illness, mental handicap or physical or sensory disability need to be able to live as independently as possible in their own homes, or in 'homely' settings in the community. The Government is firmly committed to a policy of community care which enables such people to achieve their full potential.

...

The Government believes that for most people community care offers the best form of care available — certainly with better quality and choice than they might have expected in the past. The changes outlined in this White Paper are intended to:

- enable people to live as normal a life as possible in their own homes or in a homely environment in the local community;
- provide the right amount of care and support to help people achieve maximum possible independence and, by acquiring or reacquiring basic living skills, help them to achieve their full potential;
- give people a greater individual say in how they live their lives and the services they need to help them to do so.

Promoting choice and independence underlies all the Government's proposals.

The Government acknowledges that the great bulk of community care is provided by friends, family and neighbours. The decision to take on a caring role is never an easy one. However, many people make that choice and it is right that they should be able to play their part in looking after those close to them. But it must be recognised that carers need help and support if they are to continue to carry out their role; and many people will not have carers readily available who can meet all their needs.

The Government therefore believes that the key components of community care should be:

- services that respond flexibly and sensitively to the needs of individuals and their carers;
- services that allow a range of options for consumers;
- services that intervene no more than is necessary to foster independence;
- services that concentrate on those with the greatest needs.

The Government's proposals have six key objectives for service delivery:

- *to promote the development of domiciliary, day and respite services to enable people to live in their own homes wherever feasible and sensible.* Existing funding structures have worked against the development of such services. In future, the Government will encourage the targeting of home-based services on those people whose need for them is greatest.

- *to ensure that service providers make practical support for carers a high priority.* Assessment of care needs should always take account of the needs of caring family, friends and neighbours;
- *to make proper assessment of need and good case management the cornerstone of high quality care.* Packages of care should then be designed in line with individual needs and preferences;
- *to promote the development of flourishing independent sector alongside good quality public services.* The Government has endorsed Sir Roy Griffiths' recommendation that social services authorities should be 'enabling' agencies. It will be their responsibility to make maximum possible use of private and voluntary providers, and so increase the available range of options and widen consumer choice;
- *to clarify the responsibilities of agencies and so make it easier to hold them to account for their performance.* The Government recognises that the present confusion has contributed to poor overall performance;
- *to secure better value for taxpayers' money by introducing a new funding structure for social care.* The Government's aim is that social security provisions should not, as they do now, provide any incentive in favour of residential and nursing home care.

...

Enabling people to live as independently as possible in the community is at the heart of community care. To do so, people frequently need both social care and health care. The Government's primary focus in this White Paper is on the reform of the organisation and funding of social care. The responsibilities of the health service are essentially unaltered, and the health care contribution to community care remains of fundamental importance. The emphasis in the NHS will continue to be to support people in the community, through the general practitioner and community health services, wherever and whenever that is practical. Improved social care should make it possible in a greater number of cases.

Community care means providing the right level of intervention and support to enable people to achieve maximum independence and control over their own lives. For this aim to become a reality, the development of a wide range of services provided in a variety of settings is essential. These services form part of a spectrum of care, ranging from domiciliary support provided to people in their own homes, strengthened by the availability of respite care and day care for those with more intensive care needs, through sheltered housing, group homes and hostels where increasing levels of care are available, to residential care and nursing homes and long-stay hospital care for those for whom other forms of care are no longer enough.

The contribution of carers

While this White Paper focuses largely on the role of statutory and independent bodies in the provision of community care services, the reality is that most care is provided by family, friends and neighbours. The majority of carers take on these responsibilities willingly, but the Government recognises that many need help to be able to manage what can become a heavy burden. Their lives can be made much easier if the right support is there at the right time, and a key responsibility of statutory service providers should be to do all they can to assist and support carers. Helping carers to maintain their valuable contribution to the spectrum of care is both right and a sound investment. Help may take the form of providing advice and support as well as practical services such as day, domiciliary and respite care.

Social care

Social care and practical assistance with daily living are key components of good quality community care. The services and facilities, at present largely the responsibility of social services authorities, which will be essential to enable people to live in the community include help with personal and domestic tasks such as cleaning, washing and preparing meals, with disablement equipment and home adaptations, transport, budgeting and other aspects of daily living. Suitable good quality housing is essential and the availability of day care, respite care, leisure facilities and employment and educational opportunities will all improve the quality of life enjoyed by a person with care needs.

The Government recognises that some people will continue to need residential or nursing home care. For such people, this form of care should be a positive choice. And there will be others, in particular elderly and seriously mentally ill people and some people with serious mental handicaps together with other illnesses or disabilities, whose combination of health and social care needs is best met by care in a hospital setting. There will be a continuing need for this form of care.

Nearly a decade later, in the White Paper *Modernising Social Services* (Cm 4169 (1998)), a government of a different political complexion said:

We believe that the guiding principle of adult social services should be that they provide the support needed by someone to make most use of their own capacity and potential. All too often, the reverse is true, and they are regarded as services which do things for and to dependent people.

Because of resource pressures, councils are tending to focus more and more on those most dependent people living in their community. For example, although there has been an increase in the overall level of domiciliary care supporting people in their own homes, that increase has been concentrated on those getting more intensive support, and the number of people receiving lower levels of support has actually dropped ... This means that some people who would benefit from purposeful interventions at a lower level of service, such as the occasional visit from a home help, or over a shorter period, such as training in mobility and daily living skills to help them cope with visual impairment, are not receiving any support. This increases the risk that they in turn become more likely to need much more complicated levels of support as their independence is compromised. That is good neither for the individual nor, ultimately, for the social services, the NHS and the taxpayer.

People generally want to live in their own homes if they can, and admission to institutional care (whether in hospital or in residential care or nursing homes) can lead to lower self-confidence and a decline in activity. Yet the evidence is that many authorities are setting a financial ceiling on their domiciliary care packages, particularly in services for older people, which can lead to premature admissions to care homes when care at home would have been more suitable.

The number of emergency admissions to hospital of people over 75 has been rising steadily. These admissions, which may well lead to permanent institutionalisation, are avoidable in many cases. People are also being admitted directly to permanent residential or nursing home care on discharge from hospital, even though in a sizeable minority of cases, better rehabilitation or recuperation services could have helped them return to their own homes.

Once services are being provided, they are often not reviewed. This again contributes to a culture of dependency rather than one of enablement. A great deal of effort is put into initial assessment of care needs, but after that there may be very little review of progress (particularly in residential and nursing home placements) to see whether the user's needs have changed or whether the services are providing the best outcomes. Joint Reviews and SSI inspections of various aspects of adult services in recent years have consistently shown this.

And finally, the care system does not adequately recognise the enormous contribution that informal carers make to maintaining the independence of people with care needs. Carers are the most important providers of social care: according to the 1995 General Household Survey of Great Britain, they number 5.7 million, with 1.7 million of them providing care for 20 hours or more each week. The Carers (Recognition and Services) Act 1995 provided greater rights for carers, but implementation of it remains patchy. Greater efforts need to be made to recognise and cater for carers' needs.

...

The Government will take action to reverse these trends, and to put greater independence at the heart of social services for adults. Our programme of action includes:
- better preventive services and a stronger focus on rehabilitation
- extension of direct payments schemes
- better support for service users who are able to work
- improved review and follow-up to take account of people's changing needs
- improved support for people with mental health problems
- more support for carers.

...

This third way for social care is based on key principles which should underlie high quality effective services. These principles are at the heart of our modernisation programme set out in this White Paper:
- care should be provided to people in a way that supports their independence and respects their dignity. People should be able to receive the care they need without their life having to be taken over by the social services system
- services should meet each individual's specific needs, pulling together social services, health, housing, education or any others needed. And people should have a say in what services they get and how they are delivered
- care services should be organised, accessed, provided and financed in a fair, open and consistent way in every part of the country
- children who for whatever reason need to be looked after by local authorities should get a decent start in life, with the same opportunities to make a success of their lives as any child. In particular they should be assured of a decent education
- every person — child or adult — should be safeguarded against abuse, neglect or poor treatment whilst receiving care. Where abuse does take place, the system should take firm action to put a stop to it
- people who receive social services should have an assurance that the staff they deal with are sufficiently trained and skilled for the work they are doing. And staff themselves should feel included within a framework which recognises their commitment, assures high quality training standards and oversees standards of practice
- and people should be able to have confidence in their local social services, knowing that they work to clear and acceptable standards, and that if those standards are not met, action can be taken to improve things.

How far these aspirations have been realised and are reflected in the law is a matter of legitimate debate.

4.2 Community care

Local authorities are involved with the assessment of need for community care services at a number of levels. First, a local authority is under a duty to appraise itself of the characteristics of the population in its area. In particular, it must find out about persons falling under s. 29 National Assistance Act 1948.

Section 1 of the Chronically Sick and Disabled Persons Act 1970 (as amended) states:

1.(1)   It shall be the duty of every local authority having functions under section 29 of the National Assistance Act 1948 to inform themselves of the number of persons to whom that section applies within their area and of the need for the making by the authority of arrangements under that section for such persons.

(2) Every such local authority —

    (a) shall cause to be published from time to time at such times and in such manner as they consider appropriate general information as to the services provided under arrangements made by the authority under the said section 29 which are for the time being available in their area; and

    (b) shall ensure that any such person as aforesaid who uses any of those services is informed of any other service provided by the authority (whether under any such arrangement or not) which in the opinion of the authority is relevant to his needs and of any service provided by any other authority or organisation which in the opinion of the authority is so relevant and of which particulars are in the authority's possession.

Section 29 of the National Assistance Act 1948 (as amended) states:

29.(1) A local authority may, with the approval of the Secretary of State, and to such extent as he may direct in relation to persons ordinarily resident in the area of the local authority shall, make arrangements for promoting the welfare of persons to whom this section applies, that is to say persons aged eighteen or over who are blind, deaf or dumb or who suffer from mental disorder of any description and other persons aged eighteen or over who are substantially and permanently handicapped by illness, injury or congenital deformity or such other disabilities as may be prescribed by the Minister.

The Department of Health circular LAC (93) 10 contains approvals and directions from the Secretary of State in relation to s. 29:

2.(1) The Secretary of State hereby approves the making by local authorities of arrangements under section 29(1) of the Act for all persons to whom that subsection applies and directs local authorities to make arrangements under section 29(1) of the Act in relation to persons who are ordinarily resident in their area for all or any of the following purposes —

    (a) to provide a social work service and such advice and support as may be needed for people in their own homes or elsewhere;

    (b) to provide, whether at centres or elsewhere, facilities for social rehabilitation and adjustment to disability including assistance in overcoming limitations of mobility or communication;

    (c) to provide, whether at centres or elsewhere, facilities for occupational, social, cultural and recreational activities and, where appropriate, the making of payments to persons for work undertaken by them (a);

  (2) The Secretary of State hereby directs local authorities to make the arrangements referred to in section 29(4)(g) of the Act (compiling and maintaining registers) in relation to persons who are ordinarily resident in their area.

  (3) The Secretary of State hereby approves the making by local authorities of arrangements under section 29(1) of the Act for all persons to whom that subsection applies for the following purposes —

    (a) to provide holiday homes;

    (b) to provide free or subsidised travel for all or any persons who do not otherwise qualify for travel concessions, but only in respect of travel arrangements for which concessions are available;

    (c) to assist a person in finding accommodation which will enable him to take advantage of any arrangements made under section 29(1) of the Act;

    (d) to contribute to the cost of employing a warden on welfare functions in warden assisted housing schemes;

(e) to provide warden services for occupiers of private housing.

(4) Save as is otherwise provided for under this paragraph, the Secretary of State hereby approves the making by local authorities of all or any of the arrangements referred to in section 29(4) of the Act(a) (welfare arrangements etc.) for all persons to whom section 29(1) applies.

Under the National Health Service and Community Care Act 1990, the local authority must prepare a plan for the provision of community care services in its area.

Section 46 National Health Service and Community Care Act 1990 (as amended) states:

46.(1) Each local authority —
   (a) shall, within such period after the day appointed for the coming into force of this section as the Secretary of State may direct, prepare and publish a plan for the provision of community care services in their area;
   (b) shall keep the plan prepared by them under paragraph (a) above and any further plans prepared by them under this section under review; and
   (c) shall, at such intervals as the Secretary of State may direct, prepare and publish modifications to the current plan, or if the case requires, a new plan.

(2) In carrying out any of their functions under paragraphs (a) to (c) of subsection (1) above, a local authority shall consult —
   (a) any Health Authority the whole or any part of whose district lies within the area of the local authority;

...

   (c) in so far as any proposed plan, review or modifications of a plan may affect or be affected by the provision or availability of housing and the local authority is not itself a local housing authority, within the meaning of the Housing Act 1985, every such local housing authority whose area is within the area of the local authority;
   (d) such voluntary organisations as appear to the authority to represent the interests of persons who use or are likely to use any community care services within the area of the authority or the interests of private carers who, within that area, provide care to persons for whom, in the exercise of their social services functions, the local authority have a power or a duty to provide a service.
   (e) such voluntary housing agencies and other bodies as appear to the local authority to provide housing or community care services in their area; and
   (f) such other persons as the Secretary of State may direct.

Section 46(3) defines 'community care services':

(3) 'community care services' means services which a local authority may provide or arrange to be provided under any of the following provisions —
   (a) Part III of the National Assistance Act 1948;
   (b) section 45 of the Health Services and Public Health Act 1968;
   (c) section 21 of and Schedule 8 to the National Health Service Act 1977; and
   (d) section 117 of the Mental Health Act 1983.

The provisions mentioned in s. 46(3) are:

   (a) Part III National Assistance Act 1948 (see below)

   (b) Section 45 Health Services and Public Health Act 1968 which (as amended) states:

45(1) A local authority may with the approval of the Secretary of State and to such extent as he may direct shall, make arrangements for promoting the welfare of old people.

(c) Section 21 and Schedule 8 National Health Service Act 1977 which (as amended) state:

21(1)   ... the services described in Schedule 8 to this Act in relation to —
  (a)   care of mothers,
  (b)   prevention, care and after care,
  (c)   home help and laundry facilities,
are functions exercisable by local social services authorities, and that Schedule has effect accordingly.

Schedule 8
1.(1)   A local social services authority may, with the Secretary of State's approval, and to such extent as he may direct shall, make arrangements for the care of expectant and nursing mothers other than for the provision of residential accommodation for them ...
2.(1)   A local social services authority may, with the Secretary of State's approval, and to such extent as he may direct shall, make arrangements for the purpose of the prevention of illness and for the care of persons suffering from illness and for the after-care of persons who have been suffering and in particular for —

...

  (b)   the provision, for persons whose care is undertaken with a view to preventing them from becoming ill, persons suffering from illness and persons who have been so suffering, of centres and other facilities for training them or keeping them suitably occupied and the equipment and maintenance of such centres;
  (c)   the provision, for the benefit of such persons as are mentioned in paragraph (b) above, of ancillary or supplemental services; and
  (d)   for the exercise of the functions of the authority in respect of persons suffering from mental disorder who are received into guardianship under Part II or III of the Mental Health Act 1983 ...
3.(1)   It is the duty of every local social services authority to provide on such a scale as is adequate for the needs of their area, or to arrange for the provision on such a scale as is so adequate, of home help for households where such help is required owing to the presence of a person who is suffering from illness, lying-in, an expectant mother, aged, handicapped as a result of having suffered from illness or by congenital deformity...and every such authority has power to provide or arrange for the provision of laundry facilities for households for which help is being, or can be, provided under this sub-paragraph.
(4A)   This paragraph does not apply in relation to persons under the age of 18.
(4AA)   No authority is authorised or may be required under this paragraph to provide residential accommodation for any person.

The circular LAC (93) 10 provides further guidance:

Services for expectant and nursing mothers
2.   The Secretary of State hereby approves the making of arrangements under paragraph 1(1) of Schedule 8 to the Act for the care of expectant and nursing mothers (of any age) other than the provision of residential accommodation for them.

Services for the purpose of the prevention of illness etc.
3.(1)   The Secretary of State hereby approves the making by local authorities of arrangements under paragraph 2(1) of Schedule 8 to the Act for the purpose of the prevention of illness, and the care of persons suffering from illness and for the aftercare of persons who have been so suffering and in particular for —
  (a)   the provision, for persons whose care is undertaken with a view to preventing them becoming ill, persons suffering from illness and persons who have been so suffering, of

centres or other facilities for training them or keeping them suitably occupied and the equipment and maintenance of such centres;

(b) the provision, for the benefit of such persons as are mentioned in paragraph (a) above, of ancillary or supplemental services.

(2)   The Secretary of State hereby directs local authorities to make arrangements under paragraph 2(1) of Schedule 8 to the Act for the purposes of the prevention of mental disorder, or in relation to persons who are or who have been suffering from mental disorder —

(a) for the provision of centres (including training centres and day centres) or other facilities (including domiciliary facilities), whether in premises managed by the local authority or otherwise, for training or occupation of such persons;

(b) for the appointment of sufficient social workers in their area to act as approved social workers for the purposes of the Mental Health Act 1983(a);

(c) for the exercise of the functions of the authority in respect of persons suffering from mental disorder who are received into guardianship under Part II or III of the Mental Health Act 1983 (whether the guardianship of the local social services authority or of other persons);

(d) for the provision of social work and related services to help in the identification, diagnosis, assessment and social treatment of mental disorder and to provide social work support and other domiciliary and care services to people living in their homes and elsewhere.

(3)   Without prejudice to the generality of sub-paragraph (1), the Secretary of State hereby approves the making by local authorities of arrangements under paragraph 2(1) of Schedule 8 to the Act for the provision of —

(a) meals to be served at the centres or other facilities referred to in sub-paragraphs (1)(a) and (2)(a) above and meals-on-wheels for house-bound people not provided for —
  (i)   under section 45(1) of the Health Services and Public Health Act 1968(a), or
  (ii) by a district council under paragraph 1 of Part II of Schedule 9 to the Health and Social Services and Social Security Adjudications Act 1983(b);

(b) remuneration for persons engaged in suitable work at the centres or other facilities referred to in sub-paragraphs (1)(a) and (2)(a) above, subject to paragraph 2(2)(a) of Schedule 8 to the Act(c);

(c) social services (including advice and support) for the purposes of preventing the impairment of physical or mental health of adults in families where such impairment is likely, and for the purposes of preventing the break-up of such families, or for assisting in their rehabilitation;

(d) night-sitter services;

(e) recuperative holidays;

(f) facilities for social and recreational activities;

(g) services specifically for persons who are alcoholic or drug-dependent.

(d) Section 117 of the Mental Health Act 1983 (see Chapter 6)

Section 49 of the Health and Social Care Act 2001 specifically excludes nursing care from the scope of community care services:

49.(1) Nothing in the enactments relating to the provision of community care services shall authorise or require a local authority, in or in connection with the provision of any such services, to —

(a) provide for any person, or

(b) arrange for any person to be provided with,

nursing care by a registered nurse.

(2)   In this section 'nursing care by a registered nurse' means any services provided by a registered nurse and involving —
(a)   the provision of care, or
(b)   the planning, supervision or delegation of the provision of care,
other than any services which, having regard to their nature and the circumstances in which they are provided, do not need to be provided by a registered nurse.

The local authority is also under a duty to make assessments of individual needs, which must follow any statutory criteria and guidance issued by the Secretary of State under s. 7 of the Local Authority Social Services Act 1970. So, for example, the circular states that assessment should be carried out in collaboration with the applicant and should take account of any preferences expressed by her/him. The policy guidance *Community Care in the next decade and beyond* states:

Although assessment is a service in its own right it can be distinguished from the services that are arranged as a consequence. The needs-led approach pre-supposes a progressive separation of assessment from service provision. Assessment does not take place in a vacuum: account needs to be taken of the local authority's criteria for determining when services should be provided, the types of service they have decided to make available and the overall range of services provided by other agencies, including health authorities.

The individual service user and normally, with his or her agreement, any carers should be involved throughout the assessment and care management process. They should feel that the process is aimed at meeting their wishes. Where a user is unable to participate actively it is even more important that he or she should be helped to understand what is involved and the intended outcome.

It may be possible for some service users to play a more active part in their own care management, for example assuming responsibility for the day to day management of their carers may help to meet the aspirations of severely physically disabled people to be as independent as possible. In these circumstances systems of accountability will have to be clearly defined. Authorities are reminded that Section 29 of the 1948 Act and Schedule 8 to the 1977 Act, as well as Section 45 of the 1968 Act prohibit the making of cash payments in place of arranging services.

To enable users and carers to exercise genuine choice and participate in the assessment of their care needs and in the making of arrangements for meeting these needs, local authorities should publish readily accessible information about their care services. This should be compiled in consultation with health and housing authorities and other service providers. The information should cover residential care homes, nursing homes and other community care facilities available in all sectors. It should include the authority's criteria for determining when services should be provided and the assessment procedures, showing how and where to apply for an assessment and giving information about how to make representations and complaints.

The assessment and care management process should take into account particular risk factors for service users, carers and the community generally; abilities and attitudes; health (especially remediable conditions or chronic conditions requiring continuing health care) and accommodation and social support needs.

Assessment arrangements should normally include an initial screening process to determine the appropriate form of assessment. Some people may need advice and assistance which do not call for a formal assessment, others may require only a limited or specialist assessment of specific needs, others may have urgent needs which require an immediate response. Procedures should be sufficiently comprehensive and flexible to cope with all levels and types of need presented by different client groups.

The legislation provides for two types of assessment, depending on whether the person is a disabled person or not, as s. 47 of the National Health Service and Community Care Act (as amended) 1990 indicates:

47.(1) Subject to subsections (5) and (6) below, where it appears to a local authority that any person for whom they may provide or arrange for the provision of community care services may be in need of any such services, the authority —
- (a) shall carry out an assessment of his needs for those services; and
- (b) having regard to the results of that assessment, shall then decide whether his needs call for the provision by them of any such services.

(2) If at any time during the assessment of the needs of any person under subsection (1)(a) above it appears to a local authority that he is a disabled person, the authority —
- (a) shall proceed to make such a decision as to the services he requires as is mentioned in section 4 of the Disabled Persons (Services, Consultation and Representation) Act 1986 without his requesting them to do so under that section; and
- (b) shall inform him that they will be doing so and of his rights under that Act.

(3) If at any time during the assessment of the needs of any person under subsection (1)(a) above, it appears to a local authority —
- (a) that there may be a need for the provision to that person by such Health Authority as may be determined in accordance with regulations of any services under the National Health Service Act 1977, or
- (b) that there may be a need for the provision to him of any services which fall within the functions of a local housing authority (within the meaning of the Housing Act 1985) which is not the local authority carrying out the assessment,

the local authority shall notify that Health Authority or local housing authority and invite them to assist, to such extent as is reasonable in the circumstances, in the making of the assessment; and, in making their decision as to the provision of the services needed for the person in question, the local authority shall take into account any services which are likely to be made available for him by that Health Authority or local housing authority.

(4) The Secretary of State may give directions as to the manner in which an assessment under this section is to be carried out or the form it is to take but, subject to any such directions and to subsection (7) below, it shall be carried out in such manner and take such form as the local authority consider appropriate.

(5) Nothing in this section shall prevent a local authority from temporarily providing or arranging for the provision of community care services for any person without carrying out a prior assessment of his needs in accordance with the preceding provisions of this section if, in the opinion of the authority, the condition of that person is such that he requires those services as a matter of urgency.

(6) If, by virtue of subsection (5) above, community care services have been provided temporarily for any person as a matter of urgency, then, as soon as practicable thereafter, an assessment of his needs shall be made in accordance with the preceding provisions of this section.

(7) This section is without prejudice to section 3 of the Disabled Persons (Services, Consultation and Representation) Act 1986.

(8) In this section —

'disabled person' has the same meaning as in that Act; and

'local authority' and 'community care services' have the same meanings as in section 46 above.

Section 4 of the Disabled Persons (Services, Consultation and Representation) Act 1986 states:

When requested to do so by —
(a)   a disabled person
(b)   his authorised representative
(c)   any person who provides care for him in the circumstances mentioned in section 8, a local authority shall decide whether the needs of the disabled person call for the provision by the authority of any services in accordance with section 2(1) of the Chronically Sick and Disabled Persons Act 1970.

Section 2 of the Chronically Sick and Disabled Persons Act 1970 states:

Where a local authority having functions under section 29 of the National Assistance Act 1948 are satisfied in the case of any person to whom that section applies who is ordinarily resident in their area that it is necessary in order to meet the needs of that person for that authority to make arrangements for all or any of the following matters, namely —
(a)   the provision of practical assistance for that person in his home;
(b)   the provision for that person of, or assistance to that person in obtaining, wireless, television, library or similar recreational facilities;
(c)   the provision for that person of lectures, games, outings or other recreational facilities outside his home or assistance to that person in taking advantage of educational facilities available to him;
(d)   the provision for that person of facilities for, or assistance in, travelling to and from his home for the purpose of participating in any services provided under arrangements made by the authority under the said section 29 or, with the approval of the authority, in any services provided otherwise than as aforesaid which are similar to services which could be provided under such arrangements;
(e)   the provision of assistance for that person in arranging for the carrying out of any works of adaptation in his home or the provision of any additional facilities designed to secure his greater safety comfort or convenience;
(f)   facilitating the taking of holidays by that person, whether at holiday homes or otherwise and whether provided under arrangements made by the authority or otherwise;
(g)   the provision of meals for that person whether in his home or elsewhere;
(h)   the provision for that person of, or assistance to that person in obtaining, a telephone and any special equipment necessary to enable him to use a telephone, then, subject to.... [guidance and directions under s. 7 Local Authority Social Services Act 1970] ... it shall be the duty of that authority to make those arrangements in exercise of their functions under the said section 29.

An assessment must take into account the position of any carer. Section 8 of the Disabled Persons (Services, Consultation and Representation) Act 1986 states:

8.(1)   Where —
(a)   a disabled person is living at home and receiving a substantial amount of care on a regular basis from another person (who is not a person employed to provide such care by any body in the exercise of its functions under any enactment), and
(b)   it falls to a local authority to decide whether the disabled person's needs call for the provision by them of any services for him under any of the welfare enactments, the local authority shall, in deciding that question, have regard to the ability of that other person to continue to provide such care on a regular basis.

Section 1 of the Carers (Recognition and Services) Act 1995 states:

1.(1) Subject to subsection (3) below, in any case where —

(a) a local authority carry out an assessment under section 47(1)(a) of the National Health Service and Community Care Act 1990 of the needs of a person ('the relevant person') for community care services, and

(b) an individual ('the carer') provides or intends to provide a substantial amount of care on a regular basis for the relevant person,

the carer may request the local authority, before they make their decision as to whether the needs of the relevant person call for the provision of any services, to carry out an assessment of his ability to provide and to continue to provide care for the relevant person; and if he makes such a request, the local authority shall carry out such an assessment and shall take into account the results of that assessment in making that decision.

(2) Subject to subsection (3) below, in any case where —

(a) a local authority assess the needs of a disabled child for the purposes of Part III of the Children Act 1989 or section 2 of the Chronically Sick and Disabled Persons Act 1970, and

(b) an individual ('the carer') provides or intends to provide a substantial amount of care on a regular basis for the disabled child,

the carer may request the local authority, before they make their decision as to whether the needs of the disabled child call for the provision of any services, to carry out an assessment of his ability to provide and to continue to provide care for the disabled child; and if he makes such a request, the local authority shall carry out such an assessment and shall take into account the results of that assessment in making that decision.

(3) No request may be made under subsection (1) or (2) above by an individual who provides or will provide the care in question —

(a) by virtue of a contract of employment or other contract with any person; or

(b) as a volunteer for a voluntary organisation.

(4) The Secretary of State may give directions as to the manner in which an assessment under subsection (1) or (2) above is to be carried out or the form it is to take but, subject to any such directions, it shall be carried out in such manner and take such form as the local authority consider appropriate.

(5) Section 8 of the Disabled Persons (Services, Consultation and Representation) Act 1986 (duty of local authority to take into account ability of carers) shall not apply in any case where —

(a) an assessment is made under subsection (1) above in respect of an individual who provides the care in question for a disabled person; or

(b) an assessment is made under subsection (2) above.

(6) In this section —

'community care services' has the meaning given by section 46(3) of the National Health Service and Community Care Act 1990;

'child' means a person under the age of eighteen;

'disabled child' means a child who is disabled within the meaning of Part III of the Children Act 1989;

'disabled person' means a person to whom section 29 of the National Assistance Act 1948 applies;

'local authority' has the meaning given by section 46(3) of the National Health Service and Community Care Act 1990; and

'voluntary organisation' has the same meaning as in the National Assistance Act 1948.

Where a local authority makes an assessment in respect of a disabled person, and is satisfied that it is necessary to meet the needs of that person, it is then under a duty to make arrangements for any or all of the matters in s. 2 of the Chronically Sick and Disabled Persons Act 1970 (see above). However, it has a power to decide, for example, how much or how often a person needs services for which a need has been assessed.

Where the person is not a disabled person, then the local authority having carried out an assessment and having regard to the results of that assessment shall then decide whether her/his needs call for the provision of community care services, within the meaning given by s. 46(3) National Health Service and Community Care Act 1990 (see above).

The question of whether an authority making an assessment of needs in relation to s. 2 of the Chronically Sick and Disabled Persons Act 1970 is entitled to balance the severity of the applicant's condition against the cost of arrangements necessary to meet that need and the availability of resources was considered in the leading and well-known case of *R v Gloucestershire County Council ex p Barry* [1997] AC 584 to which reference has also been made in Chapter 1. The facts are set out by Lord Lloyd of Berwick:

My Lords, under section 29 of the National Assistance Act 1948 as originally enacted local authorities had the *power* to make arrangements for promoting the welfare of disabled persons. Under section 1 of the Chronically Sick and Disabled Persons Act 1970 local authorities were, for the first time, placed under a *duty* to inform themselves of the need for making arrangements for disabled persons within their area. Section 2 of the Act of 1970, on which the present appeal turns, provides that where a local authority is satisfied in the case of a disabled person within their area that it is necessary to make arrangements in order to meet the needs of that person, then the local authority is under a further *duty* to make those arrangements. It was common ground that the duty imposed on the local authority under section 2 of the Act of 1970 is a duty owed to the disabled person individually. In that respect section 2 is almost unique in the field of community care, the only other example of such a duty (so it was said) being section 117 of the Mental Health Act 1983.

Mr Michael Barry lives in Gloucestershire. He was born in 1915, so he is coming up for his eighty-second birthday. In the summer of 1992 he spent a short spell in Gloucestershire Royal Hospital suffering from dizzy spells and nausea. He was told that he had suffered a slight stroke. He has also had several heart attacks, and cannot see well. After discharge from hospital, he returned home, where he lives alone. He gets around by using a Zimmer frame, as a result of having fractured his hip several years ago. He has no contact with any of his family. But two friends call from time to time to do things for him. On 8 September 1992 he was referred to the Social Services Department of Gloucestershire County Council. On 15 September his needs were assessed as: 'Home care to call twice a week for shopping, pension, laundry, cleaning. Meals on wheels four days a week.' The council arranged to provide these services. Nearly a year later, on 3 August 1993 Mr Barry received a routine visit from the Social Services Department. His needs were assessed as being the same.

Then on 29 September 1994 Mr Barry received a letter from the council regretting that they would no longer be able to provide Mr Barry with his full needs as assessed. Cleaning and laundry services would be withdrawn. The reason given was that the money allocated to the council by central government had been reduced by £2.5 m. and there was 'nowhere near enough to meet demand.' It is only fair to add that the letter was sympathetic in tone.

Mr Barry, and other residents, commenced proceedings for judicial review. His case is that his needs are the same as they always were. Parliament has imposed a duty on the council to do what is necessary to meet those needs, and it is no answer that they are short of money, as no doubt they are. The council's case is that in assessing Mr Barry's *needs* they are entitled to have regard to their overall financial resources.

The case came before the Divisional Court on 6 June 1995. In the meantime the council had, very properly, continued to provide Mr Barry with the same services as before, pending the outcome of the proceedings. Mr Gordon, who appeared for Mr Barry, did not press his claim for an order of mandamus to compel the council to perform their statutory duty. But he was granted a declaration in the terms:

'That the [council] has acted unlawfully in that it has, on the sole basis of having exhausted available resources, withdrawn services previously provided or offered to the applicant pursuant to section 2 of the Chronically Sick and Disabled Persons Act 1970, without a lawful reassessment of the applicant.'

On the broader question of whether the council is entitled to take resources into account in assessing an individual's needs, McCowan LJ (1995) 30 BMLR 20, 30 said that a local authority would face an impossible task unless it could have regard to the size of the cake before deciding how to cut it:

'For these reasons I for my part have concluded that a local authority is right to take account of resources both when assessing needs and when deciding when it is necessary to make arrangements to meet those needs.'

The test proposed by the Divisional Court was:

'A balancing exercise must be carried out assessing the particular needs of that person in the context of the needs of others and the resources available, but if no reasonable authority could conclude other than that *some* practical help was necessary, that would have to be its decision.'

This seems to reduce the minimum obligation under section 2 of the Act of 1970 to the level of *Wednesbury* unreasonableness (*Associated Provincial Picture Houses Ltd* v *Wednesbury Corporation* [1948] 1 KB 223).

Following the decision of the Divisional Court on the narrow question, the council reassessed some 1,500 people in receipt of services under section 2 of the Act of 1970. As a result of the reassessment the number was reduced to 1,060. But meanwhile Mr Barry had launched an appeal on the broader question. On 27 June 1996 the Court of Appeal [1996] 4 All ER 421 allowed his appeal by a majority, with Hirst LJ dissenting. The Court of Appeal granted declarations:

'(i) that by withdrawing the said services without the council being satisfied that the applicant's previously assessed needs had diminished, the [council] is in breach of its continuing duty under section 2 of the Chronically Sick and Disabled Persons Act 1970; (ii) that in assessing or reassessing whether it is necessary to make arrangements to meet them, a local authority is not entitled to take account of the resources available to such local authority.'

The first of these declarations is no longer of practical effect, since the reassessment has been carried out, and the services reduced as a consequence.

The House of Lords decided, by a majority of 3-2 (Lords Nicholls of Birkenhead, Hoffmann and Clyde; Lords Lloyd of Berwick and Steyn dissenting), that resources available to the authority were a proper factor to take into account when assessing the needs of a person in relation to the Chronically Sick and Disabled Persons Act 1970, though, as the extracts below make clear, for different reasons. The result in this case was by no means inevitable, as the differing opinions of the judges indicate:

Lord Nicholls of Birkenhead. My Lords, this appeal raises an important point of interpretation of section 2(1) of the Chronically Sick and Disabled Persons Act 1970. Can a local authority properly take into account its own financial resources when assessing the needs of a disabled person under section 2(1)? The Gloucestershire County Council and the Secretary of State for Health say 'Yes,' the applicant, Mr Barry, says 'No.' The question has given rise to a considerable difference of judicial opinion, so I shall give my conclusion in my own words.

At first sight the contentions advanced on behalf of Mr Barry are compelling. A person's needs, it was submitted, depend upon the nature and extent of his disability. They cannot be affected by, or depend upon, the local authority's ability to meet them. They cannot vary according to whether the authority has more or less money currently available. Take the case of an authority which assesses a person's needs as twice weekly help at home with laundry and cleaning. In the following year nothing changes except that the authority has less money available. If the authority's financial resources can be properly be taken into account, it would be open to the authority to reassess that person's needs in the later year as nil. That cannot be right: the person's needs have not changed.

This is an alluring argument but I am unable to accept it. It is flawed by a failure to recognise that needs for services cannot sensibly be assessed without having some regard to the cost of providing them. A person's need for a particular type or level of service cannot be decided in a vacuum from which all considerations of cost have been expelled.

I turn to the statute. Under section 2(1) 'needs' are to be assessed in the context of, and by reference to, the provision of certain types of assistance for promoting the welfare of disabled persons: home help, meals on wheels, holidays, home adaptation, and so forth. In deciding whether the disability of a particular person dictates a need for assistance and, if so, at what level, a social worker or anyone else must use some criteria. This is inevitably so. He will judge the needs for assistance against some standard, some criteria, whether spoken or unspoken. One important factor he will take into account will be what constitutes an acceptable standard of living today.

Standards of living, however, vary widely. So do different people's ideas on the requirements of an acceptable standard of living. Thus something more concrete, capable of being applied uniformly, is called for when assessing the needs of a given disabled person under the statute. Some more precisely defined standard is required, a more readily identifiable yardstick, than individual notions of current standards of living.

Who is to set the standard? To this there can be only one answer: the relevant local authority, acting by its social services committee. The local authority sets the standards to be applied within its area. In setting the standards, or 'eligibility criteria' as they have been called, the local authority must take into account current standards of living, with all the latitude inherent in this concept. The authority must also take into account the nature and extent of the disability. The authority will further take into account the manner in which, and the extent to which, quality of life would be improved by the provision of this or that service or assistance, at this or that level: for example, by home care, once a week or more frequently. The authority should also have regard to the cost of providing this or that service, at this or that level. The cost of daily home care, or of installing a ground floor lavatory for a disabled person in his home and widening the doors to take a wheelchair, may be substantial. The relative cost will be balanced against the relative benefit and the relative need for that benefit.

Thus far the position is straightforward. The next step is the crucial step. In the same way as the importance to be attached to cost varies according to the benefit to be derived from the suggested expenditure, so also must the importance of cost vary according to the means of the person called upon to pay. An amount of money may be a large sum to one person, or to one person at a particular time, but of less consequence to another person, or to the same person at a different time. Once it is accepted, as surely must be right, that cost is a relevant factor in assessing a person's needs for the services listed in section 2(1), then in deciding how much weight is to be attached to cost some evaluation or assumption has to be made about the impact which the cost will have upon the authority. Cost is of more or less significance depending upon whether the authority currently has more or less money. Thus, depending upon the authority's financial position, so the eligibility criteria, setting out the degree of disability which must exist before help will be provided with laundry or cleaning or whatever, may properly be more or less stringent.

I have considered whether, instead of taking into account the actual resources of the paying authority, the significance of cost could be evaluated by some more general criterion, for instance, that there should be attached to cost the weight which would be attributed to the amount in question by any reasonable authority. This could not work. This would be meaningless as a yardstick. What are the resources to be attributed to the hypothetical reasonable authority at any particular time?

In the course of the argument some emphasis was placed upon a submission that if a local authority may properly take its resources into account in the way I have described, the section 2(1) duly would in effect be limited to making arrangements to the extent only that the authority should decide to allocate money for this purpose. The duty, it was said, would collapse into a power. I do not agree. A local authority must carry out its functions under section 2(1) in a responsible fashion. In the event of a local authority acting with *Wednesbury* unreasonableness, a disabled person would have a remedy.

This interpretation does not emasculate section 2(1). The section was intended to confer rights upon disabled persons. It does so by giving them a valuable personal right to see that the authority acts reasonably in assessing their needs for certain types of assistance, and a right to have their assessed needs met so far as it is necessary for the authority (as distinct from others) to do so. I can see no basis for reading into the section an implication that in assessing the needs of disabled persons for the prescribed services, cost is to be ignored. I do not believe Parliament intended that to be the position.

...

[Lord Clyde]   Now there is no doubt that in the exercise of its powers under section 29 of the Act of 1948 it was proper for a local authority to take into account the extent of the resources which were available to it. So in approaching section 2(1) of the Act of 1970, set as it is in the context of section 29, one would expect that the extent of available resources would remain a proper consideration, or at least that if for some reason at any stage of the operation of the provisions of section 2(1) no regard was to be paid to considerations of available resources that would be made very clear in the terms of the section. But the section is silent on the matter.

The Act of 1970 came in as a private member's Bill. Section 2(1) was in its day an important innovation. While section 29(1) of the Act of 1948 gave the local authority a power to make welfare arrangements for the persons there described, a power which they might have a duty to perform by virtue of an appropriate direction under section 29(2), section 2(1) imposed a duty on the local authority to make welfare arrangements for an individual where they were satisfied that in the case of that individual it was necessary in order to meet his needs to make the arrangements. This was not a general but a particular duty and it gave a correlative right to the individual which he could enforce in the event of a failure in its performance. Such a provision in this area of the legislation is not common. We were referred only to one other example of it, in section 117 of the Mental Health Act 1983.

The right given to the person by section 2(1) of the Act of 1970 was a right to have the arrangements made which the local authority was satisfied were necessary to meet his needs. The duty only arises if or when the local authority is so satisfied. But when it does arise then it is clear that a shortage of resources will not excuse a failure in the performance of the duty. However neither the fact that the section imposes the duty towards the individual, with the corresponding right in the individual to the enforcement of the duty, nor the fact that consideration of resources is not relevant to the question whether the duty is to be performed or not, means that a consideration of resources may not be relevant to the earlier stages of the implementation of the section which lead up to the stage when the satisfaction is achieved. The earlier stages envisaged by the section require to be distinguished from the emergence of the duty. And if that distinction is kept in mind, the risk of which counsel for Mr Barry warned, namely the risk of the duty becoming devalued into a power, should not arise.

The words 'necessary' and 'needs' are both relative expressions, admitting in each case a considerable range of meaning. They are not defined in the Act and reference to dictionary definitions does not seem to me to advance the construction of the subsection. In deciding whether there is a necessity to meet the needs of the individual some criteria have to be provided. Such criteria are required both to determine whether there is a necessity at all or only, for example, a desirability, and also to assess the degree of necessity. Counsel for Mr Barry suggested that a criterion could be found in the values of a civilised society. But I am not persuaded that that is sufficiently precise to be of any real assistance. It is possible to draw up categories of disabilities, reflecting the variations in the gravity of such disabilities which could be experienced. Such a classification might enable comparisons to be made between persons with differing kinds and degrees of disability. But in determining the question whether in a given case the making of particular arrangements is necessary in order to meet the needs of a given individual it seems to me that a mere list of disabling conditions graded in order of severity will still leave unanswered the question at what level of disability is the stage of necessity reached. The determination of eligibility for the purposes of the statutory provision requires guidance not only on the assessment of the severity of the condition or the seriousness of the need but also on the level at which there is to be satisfaction of the necessity to make arrangements. In the framing of the criteria to be applied it seems to me that the severity of a condition may have to be to be matched against the availability of resources. Such an exercise indeed accords with everyday domestic experience in relation to things which we do not have. If my resources are limited I have to need the thing very much before I am satisfied that it is necessary to purchase it. It may also be observed that the range of the facilities which are listed as being the subject of possible arrangements, 'the service list,' is so extensive as to make it unlikely that Parliament intended that they might all be provided regardless of the cost involved. It is not necessary to hold that cost and resources are always an element in determining the necessity. It is enough for the purposes of the present case to recognise that they may be a proper consideration. I have not been persuaded that they must always and necessarily be excluded from consideration. Counsel for Mr Barry founded part of his submission on the claim that on the appellants' approach there would be an unmet need. However once it is recognised that criteria have to be devised for assessing the necessity required by the statutory provision it will be possible to allege that in one sense there will be an unmet need; but such an unmet need will be lawfully within what is contemplated by the statute. On a more exact analysis, whereby the necessity is measured by the appropriate criteria, what is necessary to be met will in fact be met and in the strict sense of the words no unmet need will exist.

Section 2(1) has now to be implemented in the context of section 47 of the Act of 1990. The first two subsections of that section provide:

'(1) ... where it appears to a local authority that any person for whom they may provide or arrange for the provision of community care services may be in need of any such services, the authority (a) shall carry out an assessment of his needs for those services, and (b) having regard to the results of that assessment, shall then decide whether his needs call for the provision by them of any such services. (2) If at any time during the assessment of the needs of any person under subsection (1)(a) above it appears to such a local authority that he is a disabled person, the authority — (a) shall proceed to make such a decision as to the services he requires as is mentioned in section 4 of the Disabled Persons (Services, Consultation and Representation) Act 1986 without his requesting them to do so under that section; and (b) shall inform him that they are doing so and of his rights under that Act.'

Section 4 of the Disabled Persons (Services, Consultation and Representation) Act 1986 provides:

'When requested to do so by — (a) a disabled person ... a local authority shall decide whether the needs of the disabled person call for the provision by the authority of any services in accordance with section 2(1) of the 1970 Act (provisions of welfare services).'

Counsel for Mr Barry founded on the separation of the first two subsections of section 47 to support his proposition that the regime for the provision of services for the disabled under section 2(1) of the Act of 1970 was distinct from that regarding the provision of services for others so that while in the other cases to which subsection 47(1) applied resources were a relevant consideration, the duty to provide for the disabled arose after a judgment had been made on the matter of necessity and resources played no part in the forming of that judgment. But it is essentially by reference to its own terms in the context in which it was enacted that section 2(1) of the Act of 1970 must be defined. So far as the twofold provision in section 47(1) and (2) is concerned the obligation on the local authority introduced by section 47(1) was to carry out an assessment on its own initiative and the separate provision made in subsection (2) cannot have been intended merely to achieve that purpose. It seems to me that there is sufficient reason for the making of a distinct provision in subsection (2) in the desire to recognise the distinct procedural situation relative to the disabled. But it does not follow that any distinction exists in the considerations which may or may not be taken into account in making an assessment in the case of the disabled as compared with any other case. What is significant is that section 2(1) is clearly embodied in the whole of the community care regime, distinct only in its particular procedure and the importing of an express duty of performance once the local authority has been satisfied regarding the necessity to make the arrangements.

We were referred to a number of publications which have emanated from central government sources containing views and guidance on the implementation of the Act of 1970 and, more recently, on the operation of the whole area of community care. I do not regard these as proper material for the construction of the critical provision but it is at least satisfactory that the view which I have formed of the section accords with what seems from these documents to have been a recognised opinion over the past years. It is also satisfactory that the view which I have taken avoids the considerable practical difficulties which the council would otherwise face in the provision of a coherent scheme of community care in its area.

These views may be compared with the analysis of Lord Lloyd of Berwick, for the minority:

It was as I have said common ground that the duty under section 2 is owed to the disabled person individually. It is not surprising, therefore, that the starting-point of the whole exercise is the assessment of his individual needs. The assessment is, to adopt the departmental jargon, 'needs-led.' The word 'need' like most English words has different shades of meaning. You can say to an overworked QC at the end of a busy term 'You look as though you need a holiday.' The word 'need' in section 2 is not used in that sense; which is not to say that there may not be disabled people living in very restricted circumstances who may not *need* a holiday in the sense which Parliament intended. To need is not the same as to want. 'Need' is the lack of what is essential for the ordinary business of living.

Who then is to decide what it is that the disabled person needs, and by what yardstick does he make his decision? I do not find the answer difficult. In the simplest case it is the individual social worker who decides. In more complicated cases there may have to be what is called a comprehensive assessment. But in every case, simple or complex, the need of the individual will be assessed against the standards of civilised society as we know them in the United Kingdom, or, in the more homely phraseology of the law, by the standards of the man on the Clapham omnibus. Those standards may vary over time. What was acceptable in Victorian England might not be acceptable today. Expectations have risen. But this does not pose any difficulty. The assessment of the needs of the disabled individual against contemporary standards is left to the professional judgment of the social worker concerned, just as the need for a bypass operation is left to the professional judgment of the heart specialist.

Who then decides what are the contemporary standards against which the social worker assesses the individual's needs? Again the answer seems straightforward. The standard is that set by the social services committee of the local authority in question. No doubt this was one of the reasons why social services committees were set up in the first place by section 2 of the Local Authority Social Services Act 1970, so as to represent the views of ordinary members of the public. Standards may vary from one local authority to another. But since the United Kingdom is relatively homogeneous, the standards may be expected to approximate to each other over time.

It is said that the standards of civilised society as interpreted by the social services committee of a particular local authority is too imprecise a concept to be of any practical value. I do not agree. But even if it were so, I do not see how it becomes less imprecise by bringing into consideration the availability of resources. Resources can, of course, operate to impose a cash limit on what is provided. But how can resources help to measure the need? This, as it seems to me, is the fallacy which lies at the heart of the council's argument.

The point can be illustrated by a simple example. Suppose there are two people with identical disabilities, living in identical circumstances, but in different parts of the country. Local authority A provides for his needs by arranging for meals on wheels four days a week. Local authority B might also be expected to provide meals on wheels four days a week, or its equivalent. It cannot, however, have been Parliament's intention that local authority B should be able to say 'because we do not have enough resources, we are going to reduce your needs.' His needs remain exactly the same. They cannot be affected by the local authority's inability to meet those needs. Every child needs a new pair of shoes from time to time. The need is not the less because his parents cannot afford them.

There was much discussion in the course of the hearing of the appeal about 'eligibility criteria.' This is the departmental way of describing the standard against which an individual's needs are judged. Local authorities are encouraged to publish their own eligibility criteria. The council has not fallen behind in this respect. There are elaborate tables included among our papers in which different degrees of disability are set against varying degrees of isolation from the community and other relevant factors. There are recommendations about the level of services which are appropriate for different combinations of disability and individual circumstances. Thus for a given degree of disability and a given degree of isolation (to take two of the relevant factors) the recommended home care might be for meals on wheels three times a week (or equivalent), cleaning twice a week and laundry once a fortnight. What is interesting about all this for present purposes is that nowhere in the tables is there any reference to resources. Nor is there any reason why there should be. The eligibility criteria work perfectly well without taking resources into account. With respect to those who take a different view, I can see no necessity on grounds of logic, and no advantage on grounds of practical convenience, in bringing resources into account as a relevant factor when assessing needs. Mr Pleming conceded that it is *possible* to assess need without taking resources into account.

Is it open to a local authority to raise the threshold artificially if it does not have sufficient resources to meet the previously assessed need? This is just what Parliament did *not* intend when enacting section 2 of the Act of 1970. If a local authority could arbitrarily reduce the assessed need by raising the eligibility criteria, the duty imposed by Parliament would, in Mr Gordon's graphic phrase, be collapsed into a power. The language of section 2 admits of no halfway house.

In the course of the argument it was suggested that 'needs' in section 2 might mean 'reasonable needs.' Mr Eccles, on behalf of the council, did not accept this suggestion. But I have no difficulty in reading 'needs' as meaning reasonable needs, in the sense that the social worker, in the exercise of his or her judgment, must act reasonably. In any event, if the needs are not reasonable it would not be necessary to make arrangements to meet the needs under the second of the three stages of the exercise. What I cannot accept is that the reasonable needs of the individual require consideration of the local authority's ability to meet those needs.

Mr Pleming put the same point a different way. He argued that all the relevant circumstances have to be taken into account in assessing an individual's needs, and that among the relevant circumstances are the resources of the local authority. I agree that all the circumstances relating to the individual are to be taken into account. But the local authority's resources are external to the individual. There is nothing in the language of the section which permits, let alone suggests, that external resources are to be taken into account when assessing the individual's needs.

Then it is said that section 2 must be construed in the light of section 29 of the Act of 1948, to which it refers. I agree. But a consideration of section 29, and the other provisions of Part III of the Act of 1948, which have been analysed in the very recent decision of the Court of Appeal in *Reg.* v *Hammersmith and Fulham London Borough Council, Ex parte M, The Times,* 19 February 1997 leads me in the exact opposite direction to that in which Mr Eccles would have me go.

Sections 21 to 28 of Part III as originally enacted cover the provision of accommodation. Under section 21 it was the *duty* of every local authority to provide residential accommodation for those in need of care and attention not otherwise available to them by reason of age, infirmity or any other circumstances. Sections 29 to 31 are concerned with welfare services. They conferred a *power* on local authorities to promote the welfare of the blind, deaf or dumb and other persons who are substantially and permanently handicapped by illness, injury, congenital deformities or other disabilities. By section 195(6) of and Schedule 23 to the Local Government Act 1972, section 21(1) of the Act of 1948 was amended. It now provides that the local authorities *may* provide residential accommodation and *shall* do so if directed by the Secretary of State. The Act of 1972 also made a similar amendment to section 29(1) of the Act of 1948. Thus there are now the same powers under both sections and the same duties if directed by the Secretary of State. But in the meantime Parliament had passed the Act of 1970. Like section 29 of the Act of 1948 sections 1 and 2 of the Act of 1970 are concerned with welfare services. It seems plain enough that the legislative purpose behind sections 1 and 2 was to impose a duty towards the disabled where hitherto there had been no more than a power. That duty was *not* made dependent on directions having been given by the Secretary of State. So far, therefore, from the inference being that the availability of resources was to remain a proper consideration, the inference is the other way.

It was pointed out that the Act of 1970 started life as a private member's Bill. So indeed it did. But it received strong all-party support. In any event the fact that the Act of 1970 owed its origin to the initiative of a private member Mr Alf Morris hardly throws light on its interpretation.

Simply looking at the language of section 2 of the Act of 1970, against the background of Part III of the Act of 1948, it is clear enough that Parliament did not intend that provision for the needs of the disabled should depend on the availability of resources. The intention was to treat disability as a special case. That is why the Act of 1970 has always been regarded as such an important landmark in the care of the disabled.

The decision and its implications are analysed in the following extracts from 'Needs: Resources and Abhorrent Choices' by Ellie Palmer and Maurice Sunkin [(1998) 61 Modern Law Review 401] which indicate the unpalatable choices left to local authorities as a result of the decision in *Barry*.

In every field of welfare provision, but particularly in the case of the chronically sick and disabled, there is a growing tide of need and competition for services which cannot be met by existing resources. Spiralling populations of elderly persons with increased life expectancy have exacerbated this problem. Treating people in the community, a goal which has been perceived by central government to provide a comparatively less expensive way of delivering care, has provided the impetus for a move away from institutional 'care' to community 'care'.

This policy, however, has not been presented as a purely cost driven exercise. Instead, the movement has been accompanied by language which has emphasised choice and the meeting of individual need. Indeed, escalating costs have not dampened the rhetoric. Despite the gap between the availability of resources and expectation-led demand, central government continued to place emphasis on the paramountcy of consumer choice. While Department of Health circulars and policy guidelines are replete with cautionary statements, which advise local authorities to keep within the limits of available resources, notions of choice, consumer sovereignty and entitlements have been more prominent and more public in documents such as the *Citizens Charter* and the Government White Paper, *Caring for People: Community Care in the Next Decade and Beyond*. While the latter trumpets a commitment to 'needs-led' provision, the gateway assessment provisions contained in section 47 of the National Health Service and Community Care Act (NHSCCA) 1990 have been carefully predicated on a discretion which allows that 'financial risk' may be taken into account when making decisions for the provision of services. Thus, at the heart of the current crisis in community care services lies a tension between two conflicting aspects of central government policy: financial cost cutting on the one hand and individual 'needs-led' provision on the other.

This tension has been sharpened by central government policy towards the financing of community care. Following the passing of the NHSCCA 1990, an increased financial burden was placed on local authorities. In addition to domiciliary care, the funding of placements in residential and nursing homes, previously supported, where necessary, on a national basis through the benefits system, was now to be funded by local authorities. To assist in meeting this new financial burden, central government provided funds in the form of a special transitional grant, which could only be used for community care. Nevertheless, as a result of a change in the basis of allocation, this grant for many authorities was substantially less than it would have been under the previous system. Gloucestershire County Council, for example, following the reduction in funding, sustained a cut in grant of £2.5million. How were such authorities to continue to perform their statutory functions in relation to community care? Could they, for example, justify reducing or even withdrawing care altogether on the grounds that their financial resources were now insufficient? This important question has been addressed by the courts in a series of cases in which the judiciary has become embroiled in some of the most sensitive issues in the field of social policy and central/local government relations. The decision of the House of Lords in *R v Gloucester County Council, ex parte Barry* is the most significant to date.

...

The challenge has importantly raised questions about the scope of the local authority's duty to a disabled person as contained in section 2 of the 1970 Act and the apparent conflict created by the distinction between that section and the assessment provisions introduced by section 47 of the NHSCCA 1990. While particular issues focused on the legal relevance of financial resources to assessment and provision decisions reached by local authorities in delivering services to the disabled, more general issues are raised by the case. These include the extent to which a relevant Government policy framework, which creates heightened expectations of 'needs-led' service provision, may be relied upon in order to challenge in court, a level of service provision which falls abysmally short of generated expectations. Perhaps most importantly, the case has provided a timely opportunity to appraise the way in which our judges deal with the relationship between fundamental concepts; in this case, the concept of 'individual need', on the one hand and financial imperatives on the other.

At first instance, Mr Barry obtained a declaration that the authority had acted unlawfully in withdrawing the services *solely* on the basis of the non-availability of financial resources and without first reassessing his needs. The Divisional Court also held, however, that the Council was entitled to *take resources into account* when assessing an individual's needs, provided that their decision was not *Wednesbury* unreasonable. As McCowan LJ put it: 'if no reasonable authority could conclude other than that *some* practical help was necessary, that would have to be its decision.' This left the way open for Gloucestershire, to take its own financial position into account in reassessing Mr Barry in order to reach the conclusion that his needs were reduced and that he did not qualify for a service.

Mr Barry appealed on the basis that resources should not have been taken into account in that reassessment. By a majority, the Court of Appeal held that a local authority was not entitled to take its resources into account at all in assessing whether to meet the needs of a disabled person under section 2(1) of the 1970 Act. However, on further appeal to the House of Lords, it has now been held, by a bare majority, that under section 2(1) of the Chronically Sick and Disabled Persons Act 1970, a local authority may always take its own resources into account in deciding whether to meet the needs of a disabled person, even in cases where a prior need has been established.

The majority
The majority in the House of Lords were more pragmatic in their approach, either seeking to interpret section 2(1) in the light of what they regarded as fundamental principles of social policy and financial reality (Lord Nicholls) or to rationalise the meaning of section 2(1) in the context of the general legislative framework which underpins the provision of community care (Lord Clyde). In this context the House seemed to assume that it had a quasi-legislative responsibility to render the various statutory systems coherent.

Lord Nicholls, influenced by general considerations of social policy of the kind which had influenced McCowan J at first instance and Hirst LJ in the Court of Appeal, observed that the finite nature of resources must always be taken into account in the distribution of wealth: 'a person's need for a particular type or level of service cannot be decided in a vacuum from which all considerations of cost have been expelled.' Like Lord Lloyd he described need as a relative concept, but his understanding of relative was significantly different. Not only do notions of what is necessary for living vary in time, they also vary across areas and between groups. He emphasised, for example, that because standards of living vary widely across the country notions of need might also differ from area to area. Like Lord Lloyd he also accepted that the standard for assessing need is to be determined by the local authority social services committee. However, he did not accept Lord Lloyd's more controversial contention that the local authority's financial resources should be left out of account in the setting of such standards. By merging the distinct decision making processes according to which standards are determined and needs assessed, and by adopting a geographically as well as a historically relative approach to need, it was possible for Lord Nicholls to reach the conclusion, that need may be determined using factors which are purely external to the individual. Having arrived at this point, for him, the only remaining challenge was to provide a convincing analysis of section 2(1).

Rejecting Lord Lloyd's clear textual analysis in favour of an analysis which is altogether more obscure, Lord Nicholls posited that costs and resources must be relevant at every stage of decision-making under section 2, whether in setting the criteria for measuring needs or in making professional decisions about whether it would be necessary to meet the assessed needs in an individual case: in every case the 'relative cost will be balanced against the relative benefit and the relative need for that benefit'. Conflating the process of assessment (Lord Lloyd's first stage) with subsequent decisions about whether it would be necessary to make arrangements to meet needs in a particular case (Lord Lloyd's second stage) he reasoned that if an individual's own resources can be taken into account in deciding what it is necessary to provide, it must surely follow that the council's resources are also relevant to the exercise.

At this stage it becomes particularly difficult to follow the logic of the argument. Even if it is accepted that an individual's own resources are relevant to decisions both at the assessment and provision stages, it certainly does not follow as Lord Nicholls suggests, that the council's resources should necessarily be taken into account as well.

Leaving aside the merits of this argument, we are left in little doubt about Lord Nicholls' conviction that section 2(1) affords an overriding discretion to a local authority at all stages of decision-making, permitting it to take account of matters both personal to and external to the individual. An authority's only duty is to act in 'a responsible fashion'. Should an authority act *Wednesbury* unreasonably (by which he seemed to mean absurdly, outrageously or irrationally) the disabled person would have a remedy in judicial review. Lord Nicholls complacently asserts, that far from emasculating the duty to meet the assessed needs of the disabled under section 2(1), such an approach enables the disabled to retain 'a valuable personal right to see that the authority acts reasonably'. Bearing in mind all the well known difficulties associated with access to judicial review, the forensic obstacles faced by applicants, and the generally discretionary nature of this process, this 'valuable right' is unlikely to provide substantial returns to those in possession of it, particularly in view of the breadth of the discretion now being accorded to authorities at the initial assessment stage.

Lord Clyde considered that it was unrealistic to assume that Parliament had intended anything more than a general safety net of provision in the comprehensive service list contained in section 2(1). In his textual analysis, like Lord Nicholls he conflated the two separate decision-making stages under the section. Moreover, conscious of the additional problems faced by local authorities if the disabled are to be treated as a distinct class, his main objective was to draw section 2(1) into the wider ambit of community care legislation. He therefore rejected the view that Parliament had accorded a unique status to the disabled, arguing that section 2(1) could be viewed merely as a procedural provision by which the discretionary services provided by section 29 of the NAA 1948 were to be delivered to the disabled. According to this view, local authorities would not be prevented from taking into account such external factors as their own resources, which they were clearly permitted to do when acting under other community care provisions. Moreover, he considered that section 47(2) of the NHSCCA 1990, thought by Lord Lloyd to trigger the unique rights afforded to the disabled by section 2(1), did no more than flag up the special procedures which allow for the assessment of the disabled under the CSDPA 1970 and the Disabled Persons (SCR) Act 1986. Section 2(1) could not therefore impose additional limitations on the discretionary powers of local authorities. Claiming to have reconciled section 2(1) with the gateway assessment provisions introduced by section 47, Lord Clyde expressed his satisfaction that the considerable practical difficulties which the council would otherwise face 'in the provision of a coherent scheme of community care in its area' could now be avoided. In seeking to provide such coherence there can be little doubt that he and his fellow judges in the majority have clearly signalled to local authorities that in future, in assessing and in reassessing the needs of the disabled, there can no longer be any question of a duty to provide services which an authority considers it cannot afford, provided that the authority does not act *Wednesbury* unreasonably.

From rhetoric to reality — when can citizens complain?

While the decision of the House of Lords serves the resource-led policy goals of central government, it also relieves local authorities of the increasingly insoluble dilemma with which they have been faced since the Court of Appeal had reached the opposite conclusion. The decision will be welcomed in the Treasury and will be received with relief by those responsible for local authority finance, although not necessarily by those social workers and social service committees who daily have to make choices considered by Lord Lloyd to be 'abhorrent' to them. In his analysis of section 2(1) Lord Lloyd remains convincingly faithful to the apparent intentions of the legislature, avoiding the level of sophistry which has been necessary to arrive at the comfortable conclusion that in one sense there can never be an 'unmet need'. Nevertheless, while rightly implying that responsibility for reforming the care system in the light of changing financial policy and local authority practice should reside with Parliament, a distinct lack of realism is evidenced by the inflexibility of his observation that a local authority should not be entitled to reduce its criteria of eligibility even in the light of changes in circumstances, including the possibility of diminished resources. It is certainly possible to argue that this conclusion can be avoided without violating the logic of section 2(1).

The majority approach on the other hand has once again highlighted the controversial role played by the judiciary in areas of social policy. Here their Lordships have sought to make policy work by allocating discretion; by finding coherence in complex legislative provisions; and, ultimately by allowing government financial policy towards local authorities to limit the scope of duties imposed by Parliament, even where Parliament has not expressly permitted this limitation to be achieved.

At the level of social policy, the decision in *Gloucester* has exposed the fundamental tensions which may arise in any system of welfare which, while purporting to provide a safety net of provision for those 'in need', uses individual demand to activate the process of delivery. By its interpretation of need as a relative concept in the context of the CSDPA, the House of Lords has resolved these tensions in favour of an externalised 'safety net' approach to the delivery of services, to be provided only within the limits of available resources. While the imposition of such a realistic solution may clearly be welcomed in many quarters, the absence of any uniformity of welfare provision throughout the UK must now give increasing cause for concern, particularly in the light of the clearly held majority view in *Gloucester*, that need is both a geographically and historically relative concept. An obvious concern must be that demographically disadvantaged authorities, bolstered by the knowledge that in relation to the disabled 'in one sense' there can never be an 'unmet need' and required by law to match the delivery of services to the availability of their own resources, may now be tempted to reduce even further the level of other community services.

The result of the decision of the majority of the House of Lords is expressed graphically in some comments quoted by Lord Lloyd of Berwick:

This brings me, last of all, to the wretched position in which the council now find themselves, through no fault of their own. I have read the affidavits of Mr Deryk Mead, the Director of Social Services, and Mr Honey, Chief Executive, with something approaching despair. Equally depressing is the evidence of Margaret Newland, chair of Age Concern, Gloucestershire, and the numerous letters written by the council to the Secretary of State. Most depressing of all are the minutes of the community care sub-committee of the social services committee, especially those of the meeting held on 14 October 1994, in which members expressed their abhorrence at the choices which the Social Services Department was being required to make. The chairman commented:

'It was deplorable that there was no other way forward apart from the exclusion of certain people from access to community care through the device of rationing services.'

Once a service has been provided, it cannot be withdrawn or altered without a fresh assessment of the person's needs, as the *Barry* case illustrates.

The local authority need not actually provide the service in question, but can instead provide financial assistance to enable a person to obtain the services for which a need has been assessed. A new regime, replacing that under the Community Care Direct Payment Act 1996, is created by the Health and Social Care Act 2001. The

Secretary of State is given power to make regulations governing the issue. At the time of writing, no regulations have been made.

57.(1) Regulations may make provision for and in connection with requiring or authorising the responsible authority in the case of a person of a prescribed description who falls within subsection (2) to make, with that person's consent, such payments to him as they may determine in accordance with the regulations in respect of his securing the provision of the service mentioned in paragraph (a) or (b) of that subsection.

(2) A person falls within this subsection if a local authority ('the responsible authority') have decided —

(a) under section 47 of the 1990 Act (assessment by local authorities of needs for community care services) that his needs call for the provision by them of a particular community care service (within the meaning of section 46 of that Act), or

(b) under section 2(1) of the Carers and Disabled Children Act 2000 (services for carers) to provide him with a particular service under that Act.

(3) Regulations under this section may, in particular, make provision —

(a) specifying circumstances in which the responsible authority are not required or authorised to make any payments under the regulations to a person, whether those circumstances relate to the person in question or to the particular service mentioned in paragraph (a) or (b) of subsection (2);

(b) for any payments required or authorised by the regulations to be made to a person by the responsible authority ('direct payments') to be made to that person ('the payee') as gross payments or alternatively as net payments;

(c) for the responsible authority to make for the purposes of subsection (4) or (5) such determination as to —
    (i) the payee's means, and
    (ii) the amount (if any) which it would be reasonably practicable for him to pay to the authority by way of reimbursement or contribution, as may be prescribed;

(d) as to the conditions falling to be complied with by the payee which must or may be imposed by the responsible authority in relation to the direct payments (and any conditions which may not be so imposed);

(e) specifying circumstances in which the responsible authority —
    (i) may or must terminate the making of direct payments,
    (ii) may require repayment (whether by the payee or otherwise) of the whole or part of the direct payments;

(f) for any sum falling to be paid or repaid to the responsible authority by virtue of any condition or other requirement imposed in pursuance of the regulations to be recoverable as a debt due to the authority;

(g) displacing functions or obligations of the responsible authority with respect to the provision of the service mentioned in subsection (2)(a) or (b) only to such extent, and subject to such conditions, as may be prescribed;

(h) authorising direct payments to be made to any prescribed person on behalf of the payee.

(4) For the purposes of subsection (3)(b) 'gross payments' means payments —

(a) which are made at such a rate as the authority estimate to be equivalent to the reasonable cost of securing the provision of the service concerned; but

(b) which may be made subject to the condition that the payee pays to the authority, by way of reimbursement, an amount or amounts determined under the regulations.

(5) For the purposes of subsection (3)(b) 'net payments' means payments —
  (a) which are made on the basis that the payee will himself pay an amount or amounts determined under the regulations by way of contribution towards the cost of securing the provision of the service concerned; and
  (b) which are accordingly made at such a rate below that mentioned in subsection (4)(a) as reflects any such contribution by the payee.

(6) Regulations under this section shall provide that, where direct payments are made in respect of a service which, apart from the regulations, would be provided under section 117 of the Mental Health Act 1983 (after-care) —
  (a) the payments shall be made at the rate mentioned in subsection (4)(a); and
  (b) subsection (4)(b) shall not apply.

(7) Regulations made for the purposes of subsection (3)(a) may provide that direct payments shall not be made in respect of the provision of residential accommodation for any person for a period in excess of a prescribed period.

(8) In this section 'prescribed' means specified in or determined in accordance with regulations under this section.

The decision whether a person needs community care services, and if so, what services that person needs is only part of the story. A further issue arises as to whether the authority may charge for the services provided.

Section 17 of the Health and Social Services and Social Security Adjudications Act 1983 states:

17.(1) Subject to subsection (3) below, an authority providing a service to which this section applies may recover such charge (if any) for it as they consider reasonable.
  (2) This section applies to services provided under the following enactments —
  (a) section 29 of the National Assistance Act 1948;
  (b) section 45(1) of the Health Services and Public Health Act 1968;
  (c) schedule 8 to the National Health Service Act 1977
  (d) section 8 of the Residential Homes Act 1980
  (e) paragraph 1 of Part II of Schedule 9 to this Act
  (f) section 2 of the Carers and Disabled Children Act 2000
other than the provision of services for which payment may be required under section 22 or 26 of the National Assistance Act 1948.

Some commentators believe that the law is in an unsatisfactory state and is in need of root and branch reform. Consider the following extracts from the article by Luke Clements quoted at the beginning of this chapter:

Community care law is, beyond peradventure, in a mess. The primary statutes contradict each other, give different rights to different service users and have been so amended as to contain many quite incomprehensible provisions. The product of this mess is that service users have little idea as to their service entitlement and social services departments are generally acting outside the law. The NHS & Community Care Act 1990 deceived much of the population into believing that the principles expounded in the White Paper 'Caring for People' had been enacted into law; the Act is however silent on the rights of carers, the right of individual choice, and the 'seamless service' with the NHS.

The problem goes beyond the mere fact that the legislation is riddled with inconsistencies and beyond the public policy 'resource issue' so prominent in the present Gloucestershire litigation. At its heart is the problem that we are dealing with a body of legislation enacted over a period of 50 years embodying differing philosophical attitudes and economic expectations. It is legislation which in large measure pre-dates the growth of public and administrative law; which was enacted at a time when the power and local democratic accountability of local government and health authorities was greater; it is legislation which contains a high proportion of statutes which originated as Private Members Bills — Acts which tend to be more 'rights based' energetic and provocative.

Community care law is in danger of becoming a lawyers playground. If Parliament does not take action to implement reform, then we must assume that it would prefer endless judicial review proceedings to the very obvious political difficulties which reform would pose.

...

Simple consolidation of the legislation is not possible. Such a procedure is generally only feasible where there are a number of different statutory provisions all embodying a coherent code of law; these are then repealed and re-enacted in one statute. It is self evident that community care law is not amenable to such treatment. More fundamental issues have to be tackled. A good example of this problem relates to the various statutory provisions governing domiciliary care services.

If home care assistance is assessed as being needed by

- *a disabled person*, the service is provided under s. 2 of the Chronically Sick and Disabled Persons Act 1970. The duty under this section is one owed to a specific individual and thus enforceable as a private law right, with the concomitant possibility of damages where there is a failure to provide the service.
- *an ill person*, the service will generally be provided under Schedule 8 of the NHS Act 1977. The duty under this provision is a 'target duty'; a failure to provide the service will not therefore give rise to a claim for damages nor (without more) would it necessarily constitute a breach of the duty.
- *an older person* the service will generally be provided under s. 45 Health Services and Public Health Act 1968, which merely gives the authority a power (but no duty) to provide such assistance. Being a matter of discretion alone, a failure to provide the service will not therefore (without more) give rise to any claim for damages.

These provisions cannot simply be 'consolidated'. If, as would appear desirable, the right to home care assistance is to be based upon need, rather than membership of any particular user group, one has then to decide what kind of legal right should attach to the service obligation. If (put crudely) the obligation is rounded down to the lowest common denominator (i.e. to a mere discretion) then ill and disabled people would lose tangible legal rights; if the obligation is rounded up, then the cost implications for the Exchequer could be substantial. Such issues are fundamental and have to be addressed by a fundamental reform.

Reform, does not of course, mean that everything in the existing legislation must be abandoned. The piece-meal development of community care law has the merit of being an organic response to developing social and economic needs. Many of the statutory provisions which have so emerged have proved to be reliable and represent (sometimes) the collective wisdom as to what is the most workable response to a particular problem. In this regard, the duty to assess under s. 47(l) of the National Health Service and Community Care Act 1990 is I believe a good example.

...

There appear, however, two significant constraints to the rather grand notion of a large reforming statute: one external and one internal.

The external constraint
The external constraint to wholesale reform lies in the legal interface between 'community care' and other adjoining social welfare fields. Since no complete definition of 'community care law' exists, it is indeed difficult to talk about legal interfaces — as opposed to overlapping fields. The

most significant area of overlap concerns the health care/social care boundary although clearly housing and to a lesser extent public health are also areas of significant overlap.

Inevitably there are situations where the community care element of such an overlapping area may be better dealt with separately. Grants for housing adaptations are an obvious example. There is no reason in principle why the statute governing such grants should be either a housing statute or a community care statute. The negative social consequences of inappropriate or poor housing are not unique to community care service users. There seems therefore, good reason to leave the situation as it is at present; with the question of grant support being dealt with in a housing statute whilst the duty to assess a need for (and then to 'facilitate') adaptations remaining a subject covered by the community care statute. This would also be in line with a major aim of any reform legislation (as discussed below): the separation of resource questions from service delivery obligations.

A more significant problem with the idea of one all embracing community care statute concerns 'remedies' (part 6 above). At present the main provisions concerning community care remedies are contained in the Local Authority Social Services Act 1970; s. 7B for complaints; s. 7D for the Secretary of State's default powers; and Part III Local Government Act 1974 for the Local Ombudsman procedures. There is an overwhelming logic in favour of merging the NHS and social services procedures; making them fully independent of both authorities and supervised by a merged NHS/local Ombudsman service — very much along the lines of the original North European model. This need not be seen as a particularly radical development; social services complaints units are becoming ever more independent and professional in their approach. A fundamental overhaul of the NHS complaints system has just occurred which mirrors many aspects of the social services system. Given the lack of democratic accountability within the NHS, the increasing focus on continuing health care eligibility criteria and discharge appeal procedures, such a merger is highly desirable. As reform would however raise many disparate questions it seems appropriate that the question of 'remedies' be left to a separate statute.

The issue of appropriate remedies is of course a major subject in its own right. Judicial review is in many respects a far from ideal remedy. What is often in issue is the way in which community resources are being divided, which is predominantly a socio-economic question rather than a classic individual civil matter. Such questions have historically been dealt with by collective action (i.e. in the political process) rather than by individual judicial action. The increased use of judicial review and the difficulty the judiciary is having getting to grips with the problems these cases raise, may be telling us that the lack of an appropriate community based remedy is as much a problem as is the contorted nature of the law.

The internal constraint

The significant internal constraint to wholesale reform is of course the 'resource question'. As Phyllida Parsloe has commented:

> 'The NHS & Community Care Act backs a whole field of horses, with the two front-runners being user choice and scarce resources. Local authorities are apparently expected to give equal weight to empowering users and keeping within their own budget. None of the official guidance even recognises the conflict, let alone shows how these two competing aims are to be balanced.'

The placing of enforceable legal obligations upon social services authorities presupposes the availability of sufficient resources to meet those obligations. Not surprisingly therefore the resource question runs like a fault line through the present structure of community care. As Sedley J put it

> 'even an unequivocal set of statutory duties cannot produce money where there is none or by itself repair gaps in the availability of finance.'

On one level it is difficult to envisage community care law reform which does not itself also reform the funding arrangements; the present legislation of course deals with both provision and funding. There are however powerful arguments in favour of any reform legislation separating the issues of 'charging' from 'service provision and assessment'.

Using a homely analogy, community care can be likened to a cake. Service users need to know how the cake is to be divided fairly between all those who are entitled to a share. Two of the three key values identified by Harding, Meredith and Wistow in 'Options for Long Term Care' were fairness and transparency. The legal mechanism for apportioning each person's share must be fair and the procedure adopted must be transparent. The size of the cake is however primarily a political rather than a legal question; a question of how much society is prepared to contribute to the collective kitty. Arguably therefore, community care law reform must concentrate on 'how the cake is cut'; the question of assessment of entitlement to services rather than the funding mechanisms. This approach is not only philosophically sound — it also has many other collateral/pragmatic advantages, including that:

- law reform can proceed without waiting for community care funding reform;
- law reform can accommodate most funding arrangements;
- it avoids the controversial question of charges for home care;
- it enables the legislation to concentrate upon rights/needs based principles.

There are however limits to the legal/political divide; a limit to how far one can separate resource questions from ostensible legal issues (such as assessment and equitable distribution). Two particular aspects of this point need emphasis:

(1)   Any system must ensure a basic provision; basic assistance to maintain personal safety and physical integrity, at this point of course the issue of provision becomes a civil and political right rather than merely socio-economic. This was expressed by McCowan LJ in *R* v *Gloucestershire County Council ex parte Mahfood* (1995) *The Times*, 21 June:

'I should stress, however, that there will, in my judgement, be situations where a reasonable authority could only conclude that some arrangements were necessary to meet the needs of a particular disabled person and in which it could not reasonably conclude that a lack of resources provided an answer. Certain persons would be at severe physical risk if they were unable to have some practical assistance in their own homes. In those situations, I cannot conceive that an authority would be held to have acted reasonably if it used shortage of resources as a reason for not being satisfied that some arrangement should be made to meet those persons' needs.'

(2)   The amount of public money society is prepared to contribute towards community care probably depends in part, upon how fair people perceive the assessment and distribution system to be. It is at least arguable that the more equitable, understandable and transparent the system becomes, the greater will be the public support and in turn the greater its willingness to contribute public resources to the community care kitty.

4.3 Residential care

The law recognises a range of residential accommodation and also the fact that such accommodation is run by both the public and private sectors. As with other areas of community care, financial matters loom large. The questions 'who pays?' and 'how much?' influence the operation of the law here as in other areas.

4.3.1 Part III accommodation

Part III of enables a local authority to arrange accommodation for those who are unable to cope at home and need a more supportive living environment which is not otherwise available.

Sections 21, 22, and 26 of the National Assistance Act (1984) (as amended) provide:

21.(1) Subject to and in accordance with the provisions of this Part of this Act, a local authority may with the approval of the Secretary of State, and to such extent as he may direct shall, make arrangements for providing —

(a) residential accommodation for persons aged eighteen or over who by reason of age, illness, disability or any other circumstances are in need of care and attention which is not otherwise available to them; and

(aa) residential accommodation for expectant or nursing mothers who are in need of care and attention which is not otherwise available to them;

...

(2) In making such arrangements a local authority shall have regard to the welfare of all persons for whom accommodation is provided, and in particular to the need for providing accommodation of different descriptions suited to different descriptions of such persons as are mentioned in the foregoing subsection.

(2A) In determining for the purposes of paragraph (a) or (aa) of subsection (1) of this section whether care and attention are otherwise available to a person, a local authority shall disregard so much of the person's resources as may be specified in, or determined in accordance with, regulations made by the Secretary of State for the purposes of this subsection.

(2B) In subsection (2A) of this section the reference to a person's resources is a reference to his resources within the meaning of regulations made for the purposes of that subsection.

(8) ... nothing in this section shall authorise or require a local authority to make any provision authorised or required to be made (whether by that or by any other authority) by or under any enactment not contained in this Part of this Act or authorised or required to be provided under the National Health Service Act 1977.

22.(1) Subject to section 26 of this Act, where a person is provided with accommodation under this Part of this Act the local authority the accommodation shall recover from him the amount of the payment he is liable to make in accordance with the following provisions of this section.

(2) Subject to the following provisions of this section, the payment which a person is liable to make for any such accommodation shall be in accordance with the standard rate fixed for that accommodation by the authority managing the premises in which it is provided and that standard rate shall represent the full cost to the authority of providing that accommodation.

(3) Where a person for whom accommodation in premises managed by any local authority is provided, or proposed to be provided, under this Part of this Act satisfies that local authority that he is unable to pay therefor at the standard rate, the authority shall assess his ability to pay and accordingly determine at what lower rate he shall be liable to pay for the accommodation.

(4) In assessing for the purposes of the last foregoing subsection a person's ability to pay, a local authority shall assume that he will need for his personal requirements such sum per week as may be prescribed by the Minister, or such other sum as in special circumstances the authority may consider appropriate.

(4A) Regulations made for the purposes of subsection (4) of this section may prescribe different sums for different circumstances.

(5) In assessing as aforesaid a person's ability to pay, a local authority shall give effect to regulations made by the Secretary of State for the purposes of this subsection.

(5A) If they think fit, an authority managing premises in which accommodation is provided for a person shall have power on each occasion when they provide accommodation for him, irrespective of his means, to limit to such amount as appears to them reasonable for him to pay the payments required from him for his accommodation during a period commencing when they begin to provide the accommodation for him and ending not more than eight weeks after that.

26.(1) … arrangements under section 21 of this Act may include arrangements made with a voluntary organisation or with any other person who is not a local authority where —

    (a) that organisation or person manages premises which provide for reward accommodation falling within subsection (1)(a) or (aa) of that section, and

    (b) the arrangements are for the provision of such accommodation in those premises.

The Health and Social Care Act 2001 adds some important provisions:

50(1) The following provisions, namely —

    (a) section 26A of the National Assistance Act 1948 (c. 29) (which prevents local authorities in England or Wales providing residential accommodation for persons who were in such accommodation on 31st March 1993), and

    (b) [corresponding provisions for Scotland, not reproduced here],

shall cease to have effect on the appointed day [i.e. the day these provisions come into force].

    (2) For the purposes of this section a 'qualifying person' is —

    (a) (in relation to any time before the appointed day) a person to whom section 26A(1) [or the Scottish provision] applies; or

    (b) (in relation to any later time) a person to whom either of those sections applied immediately before that day.

    (3) Where a qualifying person is immediately before the appointed day ordinarily resident in relevant premises in the area of a local authority ('the responsible authority'), that authority shall secure that —

    (a) as from that day, or

    (b) as soon thereafter as is reasonably practicable,

the person is provided with such community care services with respect to his accommodation as appear to the authority to be appropriate having regard to his needs as assessed under section 47(1)(a) of the National Health Service and Community Care Act 1990.

    (4) Each local authority shall accordingly —

    (a) use their best endeavours to identify every person ordinarily resident in relevant premises in their area who is a qualifying person; and

    (b) carry out such a programme of assessments under section 47(1)(a) [or Scottish equivalent] in respect of persons so identified as appears to the authority to be required for the purpose of enabling them to discharge their duty under subsection (3) in relation to such persons.

    (5) Where a person —

    (a) is a qualifying person immediately before the appointed day, and

    (b) is provided by the responsible authority with any community care services with respect to his accommodation in accordance with subsection his existing arrangements shall, by virtue of this subsection, terminate on the date as from which he is provided with those services.

    (6) Where any such person is not provided with any such services as from the appointed day, any liability of his to make any payment under his existing arrangements in respect of any period (or part of a period) falling within the period beginning with the appointed day and ending with —

    (a) the date as from which he is provided with any such services, or

    (b) the date on which he notifies (or is in accordance with regulations to be treated as notifying) the responsible authority that he does not wish to be provided with any such services,

shall instead be a liability of the responsible authority.

(7)   However, the responsible authority may, in respect of any payment made by them in pursuance of subsection (6), recover from the person such amount (if any) as may be prescribed; and any such amount shall be so recoverable in accordance with section 56 of the 1948 Act as if it were an amount due to the authority under that Act.

(8)   The provisions of subsections (3) to (7) do not apply, to such extent as may be prescribed, in relation to any person falling within any prescribed description of persons.

(9)   Regulations may also —
  (a) prescribe the circumstances in which persons are to be treated as ordinarily resident in any premises for the purposes of this section;
  (b) for the purpose of prescribing any such amount as is mentioned in subsection (7), provide for any provision made by or under section 22 or 26 of the 1948 Act to apply with or without modifications.

(10)   In this section —
'the appointed day' means the day appointed ... for the coming into force of subsection (1);

'existing arrangements', in relation to a person, means the arrangements for the provision of accommodation in the relevant premises mentioned in subsection (3), together with any arrangements for the provision of any services or facilities in connection with that accommodation;

'prescribed' means prescribed by regulations;

'relevant premises' —
  (a) in relation to England or Wales, has the same meaning as in section 26A of the 1948 Act;
  ...

'the responsible authority' shall be construed in accordance with subsection (3).

54(1)   Regulations may make provision for and in connection with the making, in respect of the provision of Part 3 accommodation, of additional payments —
  (a) by persons for whom such accommodation is provided ('residents'); or
  (b) by other persons (including persons liable to maintain residents by virtue of section 42 of the 1948 Act).

(2)   In this section 'additional payments', in relation to a resident, means payments which —
  (a) are made for the purpose of meeting all or part of the difference between the actual cost of his Part 3 accommodation and the amount that the local authority providing it would usually expect to pay in order to provide Part 3 accommodation suitable for a person with the assessed needs of the resident; and
  (b) (in the case of additional payments by the resident) are made out of such of his resources as may be specified in, or determined in accordance with, regulations under subsection (1);
and for this purpose 'resources' has the meaning given by such regulations.

(3)   In this Part 'Part 3 accommodation' means accommodation provided under sections 21 to 26 of the 1948 Act.

56(1)   Regulations may make provision for and in connection with authorising a local authority to make arrangements under section 21 of the 1948 Act for a person to be provided with residential accommodation in Scotland, Northern Ireland, any of the Channel Islands or the Isle of Man.

(2)   Regulations under this section may, in particular, make provision —
  (a) specifying conditions which must be satisfied before a local authority make any arrangements in pursuance of the regulations in respect of a person;

   (b) for the application of provisions of the 1948 Act in relation to —
     (i) any such arrangements, or
     (ii) the person in respect of whom any such arrangements are made, with or without modifications.

These provisions are supplemented by the Department of Health circular LAC (93) 10:

Residential accommodation for persons in need of care and attention
2.(1) The Secretary of State hereby —
   (a) approves the making by local authorities of arrangements under section 21(1)(a) of the Act in relation to persons with no settled residence and, to such extent as the authority may consider desirable, in relation to persons who are ordinarily resident in the area of another local authority, with the consent of that other authority; and
   (b) directs local authorities to make arrangements under section 21(1)(a) of the Act in relation to persons who are ordinarily resident in their area and other persons who are in urgent need thereof,
to provide residential accommodation for persons aged 18 or over who by reason of age, illness, disability or any other circumstance are in need of care and attention not otherwise available to them.

   (2) Without prejudice to the generality of sub-paragraph (1), the Secretary of State hereby directs local authorities to make arrangements under section 21(1)(a) of the Act to provide temporary accommodation for persons who are in urgent need thereof in circumstances where the need for that accommodation could not reasonably have been foreseen.

   (3) Without prejudice to the generality of sub-paragraph (1), the Secretary of State hereby directs local authorities to make arrangements under section 21(1)(a) of the Act to provide accommodation —
   (a) in relation to persons who are or have been suffering from mental disorder, or
   (b) for the purposes of the prevention of mental disorder,
for persons who are ordinarily resident in their area and for persons with no settled residence who are in the authority's area.

   (4) Without prejudice to the generality of sub-paragraph (1) and subject to section 24(4) of the Act, the Secretary of State hereby approves the making by local authorities of arrangements under section 21(1)(a) of the Act to provide residential accommodation —
   (a) in relation to persons who are or have been suffering from mental disorder; or
   (b) for the purposes of the prevention of mental disorder,
for persons who are ordinarily resident in the area of another local authority but who following discharge from hospital have become resident in the authority's area;

   (5) Without prejudice to the generality of sub-paragraph (1), the Secretary of State hereby approves the making by local authorities of arrangements under section 21(1)(a) of the Act to provide accommodation to meet the needs of persons for —
   (a) the prevention of illness;
   (b) the care of those suffering from illness; and
   (c) the aftercare of those so suffering.

   (6) Without prejudice to the generality of sub-paragraph (1), the Secretary of State hereby approves the making by local authorities of arrangements under section 21(1)(a) of the Act specifically for persons who are alcoholic or drug-dependent.

Residential accommodation for expectant and nursing mothers
3. The Secretary of State hereby approves the making by local authorities of arrangements under section 21(1)(aa) of the Act to provide residential accommodation (in particular mother

and baby homes) for expectant and nursing mothers (of any age) who are in need of care and attention which is not otherwise available to them.

Arrangements to provide services for residents
4.   The Secretary of State hereby directs local authorities to make arrangements in relation to persons provided with accommodation under section 21(1) of the Act for all or any of the following purposes —
  (a) for the welfare of all persons for whom accommodation is provided;
  (b) for the supervision of the hygiene of the accommodation so provided;
  (c) to enable persons for whom accommodation is provided to obtain —
      (i)   medical attention,
      (ii) nursing attention during illnesses of a kind which are ordinarily nursed at home, and
      (iii) the benefit of any services provided by the National Health Service of which they may from time to time be in need,
      but nothing in this paragraph shall require a local authority to make any provision authorised or required to be provided under the National Health Service Act 1977(a);
  (d) for the provision of board and such other services, amenities and requisites provided in connection with the accommodation, except where in the opinion of the authority managing the premises their provision is unnecessary (b);
  (e) to review regularly the provision made under the arrangements and to make such improvements as the authority considers necessary.

The local authority does not in fact have to provide any accommodation itself: all its arrangements for accommodation may be, for example, with voluntary organisations, despite what was said to the contrary in a Department of Health circular. As the following extract illustrates, the Act is the most authoritative source:

R v Wandsworth LBC ex p Beckwith [1996] 1 WLR 60
Lord Hoffmann.   My Lords, the appellant Mr Beckwith is 75. He lives in George Potter House in Battersea High Street. This is one of four homes for the elderly in the London Borough of Wandsworth. The borough council, which is respondent to this appeal, has a statutory duty to make arrangements for providing residential accommodation for old people in need of care and attention. Until recently the council managed the four homes itself. But on 7 December 1994 it decided to transfer the other three homes into private ownership, subject to arrangements for their continued use as homes for the elderly, and to close down George Potter House altogether. Mr Beckwith objected. He applied for judicial review on the ground that the council was under a legal duty to maintain some accommodation for the elderly in premises under its own management. Popplewell J accepted this submission and quashed the council's decision. Potts J quashed a later decision to the same effect. The Court of Appeal disagreed. It held that the council was entitled to discharge its statutory duty entirely by means of arrangements made with third parties. Mr Beckwith now appeals to this House.
  My Lords, the appeal turns on a very short point of construction on sections 21 and 26 of the National Assistance Act 1948. These sections have been amended a number of times, most recently by the National Health Service and Community Care Act 1990 (sections 42(1) and 66 and Schedule 9, paragraph 5(1)) and the Community Care (Residential Accommodation) Act 1992 (section 1(1)) respectively. These amendments came into force on 1 April 1993 and in consequence the relevant provisions of the two sections now read:
  '21(1)   Subject to and in accordance with the provisions of this Part of this Act, a local authority may with the approval of the Secretary of State, and to such extent as he may direct

shall, make arrangements for providing — (a) residential accommodation for persons aged 18 or over who by reason of age, illness, disability, or any other circumstances are in need of care and attention which is not otherwise available to them; and (aa) residential accommodation for expectant and nursing mothers who are in need of care and attention which is not otherwise available to them; ... (4) Subject to the provisions of section 26 of this Act accommodation provided by a local authority in the exercise of their functions under this section shall be provided in premises managed by the authority or, to such extent as may be determined in accordance with the arrangements under this section, in such premises managed by another local authority as may be agreed between the two authorities and on such terms, including terms as to the reimbursement of expenditure incurred by the said other authority, as may be so agreed ... 26(1) ... arrangements under section 21 of this Act may include arrangements made with a voluntary organisation or with any other person who is not a local authority where — (a) that organisation or person manages premises which provide for reward accommodation falling within subsection 1(a) or (aa) of that section, and (b) the arrangements are for the provision of such accommodation in those premises.'

By Local Authority Circular LAC(93)10 (Department of Health), which came into force on the same date as the amendments to the Act, the Secretary of State (Appendix 1, paragraph 2(1)(b)) directed local authorities to:

'make arrangements under section 21(1)(a) of the Act in relation to persons who are ordinarily resident in their area and other persons who are in urgent need thereof, to provide residential accommodation for persons aged 18 and over who by reason of age, illness, disability or any other circumstance are in need of care and attention not otherwise available to them.'

This direction triggered the statutory duty on which Mr Beckwith relies. The question is how that duty may be discharged. Section 26 says that arrangements under section 21 'may include' arrangements made with voluntary organisations or any other person. Mr Gordon, who appeared for Mr Beckwith, argued that 'may include' means that private sector arrangements may form part of a larger whole. It does not mean 'may wholly consist of.' If that had been intended, the Act would have used the expression 'may consist of or include' as it does in section 30 and other places.

In my view this argument does not allow for the many subtly different techniques which are open to the draftsman. If the Act had said that the accommodation to be provided by the council 'may include' homes in the private sector, I would have seen some force in Mr Gordon's argument. It could be argued that 'accommodation' was a collective noun for the homes which the council had to provide and that ordinarily something 'included' in a collective is a part rather than the whole. I do not say that even in this case the argument would have carried the day, because 'include' can mean 'consist of' and one might have adopted this construction rather than supposing that Parliament had meant something less than the whole without providing any clue about what proportion it should be.

In this case, however, the draftsman has adopted a different technique. The duty of the council under section 21 is to make 'arrangements' for providing residential accommodation for certain classes of people. Subsection (4) says that the accommodation must be managed by the local authority or by some other local authority. But this is expressed to be subject to section 26, which says that 'arrangements under section 21 of this Act' (not, notice, 'the arrangements made under section 21 of this Act') may include arrangements with the private sector. The draftsman is therefore not saying that homes in the private sector may be included in the collective of homes which the council has to provide. He is saying that the concept of 'arrangements' which has been used to define the council's duty in section 21 is to include arrangements with the private sector. This produces an altogether different result: it extends the meaning of the concept by which the council's duty is defined. Any arrangements which fall within the extended definition will satisfy the council's duty.

Mr Gordon attempted to support his construction by reference to the legislative pedigree of sections 21 and 26 and the policy guidance issued by the Department of Health. The legislative history was interesting but ultimately unhelpful. The earlier Acts, which say expressly that private sector accommodation may be provided in lieu of directly managed council homes, do not use the same drafting technique and one cannot therefore compare like with like. The policy guidance was issued under section 7 of the Local Authority Social Services Act 1970, which says:

'Local authorities shall, in the exercise of their social services functions, including the exercise of any discretion conferred by any relevant enactment, act under the general guidance of the Secretary of State.'

One source of such guidance was a booklet called 'Community Care in the Next Decade and Beyond' issued by the Department of Health to accompany the coming into force of the amended sections on 1 April 1993. It contains a number of references to a 'mixed economy of care' and it encourages local authorities to make more use of the private sector in arranging for the provision of social services. Mr Gordon says that wholly private provision can hardly be described as a mixed economy. But I find this phrase too vague to offer much help on the construction of the Act. What constitutes in this context a mixed economy? The Government could hardly have supposed that local authorities would be able to hand over all their care services to the private sector. The guidance contemplated that the move to greater private provision would take some time. It does not follow, however, that local authorities had to retain direct control of some unspecified proportion of every service. This would have been imposing a duty to make direct provision which had not existed before the amendments and which seems to me contrary to the general thrust of the Government's policy. It is true that paragraph 4 of LAC(93)10 says:

'It is the view of the Department that the amendments introduced into the Act of 1948 by section 1 of the Community Care (Residential Accommodation) Act 1992 will require authorities to make some provision for residential care under Part III of the Act of 1948.'

The opinion of the Department is entitled to respect, particularly since I assume that the Act was drafted upon its instructions. But in my view this statement is simply wrong. I would therefore dismiss the appeal.

4.3.2 Residential accommodation under the Care Standards Act 2000

The Care Standards Act 2000 creates a new legal framework for the registration and monitoring of residential homes and repeals the Residential Homes Act 1984. A major change is that the functions of registration and inspection, formerly carried out by local authorities, are now under the control of the National Care Standards Commission (NCSC) for England and the Welsh Assembly for establishments in Wales. The 2000 Act brings children's homes and a variety of agencies under the jurisdiction of the NCSC, with many of the provisions applying in common. In this section, we will concentrate on the provisions relating to residential care for older people. The Act establishes a legislative framework. More detailed regulation and guidance is provided in Regulations: the Care Homes Regulations 2001, National Care Standards Commission (Registration) Regulations 2001 and the National Care Standards Commission (Fees and Frequency of Inspections) Regulations 2001 have, at the time of writing, been issued. National minimum standards are explained and detailed in the Department of Health document *Care Homes for Older People* (2002).

The Care Standards Act does, however, retain many of the features of the earlier legislation in that the registration criteria continue to focus on the suitability of the applicant, the premises and the regime. The national minimum standards will, in effect, be reinforced by sanctions of deregistration, variation of conditions and/or prosecution.

The Act identifies the establishments to which it applies:

3.(1) For the purposes of this Act, an establishment is a care home if it provides accommodation, together with nursing or personal care, for any of the following persons.

(2) They are —
   (a) persons who are or have been ill;
   (b) persons who have or have had a mental disorder;
   (c) persons who are disabled or infirm;
   (d) persons who are or have been dependent on alcohol or drugs.

(3) But an establishment is not a care home if it is —
   (a) a hospital;
   (b) an independent clinic; or
   (c) a children's home,

or if it is of a description excepted by regulations.

It then identifies the registration authority and makes general provisions for the National Care Standards Commission and the National Assembly of Wales in this regard:

5. For the purposes of this Act —
   (a) the registration authority in relation to England is the National Care Standards Commission;
   (b) the registration authority in relation to Wales is the National Assembly for Wales (referred to in this Act as 'the Assembly').

6.(1) There shall be a body corporate, to be known as the National Care Standards Commission (referred to in this Act as 'the Commission'), which shall exercise in relation to England the functions conferred on it by or under this Act or any other enactment.

(2) The Commission shall, in the exercise of its functions, act —
   (a) in accordance with any directions in writing given to it by the Secretary of State; and
   (b) under the general guidance of the Secretary of State.

(3) Schedule 1 [which sets out the status, powers and membership of the Commission] shall have effect with respect to the Commission.

(4) The powers of the Secretary of State under this Part to give directions include power to give directions as to matters connected with the structure and organisation of the Commission, for example —
   (a) directions about the establishment of offices for specified areas or regions;
   (b) directions as to the organisation of staff into divisions.

7.(1) The Commission shall have the general duty of keeping the Secretary of State informed about the provision in England of Part II services and, in particular, about —
   (a) the availability of the provision; and
   (b) the quality of the services.

(2) The Commission shall have the general duty of encouraging improvement in the quality of Part II services provided in England.

(3) The Commission shall make information about Part II services provided in England available to the public.

(4)   When asked to do so by the Secretary of State, the Commission shall give the Secretary of State advice or information on such matters relating to the provision in England of Part II services as may be specified in the Secretary of State's request.

(5)   The Commission may at any time give advice to the Secretary of State on —

(a)   any changes which the Commission thinks should be made, for the purpose of securing improvement in the quality of Part II services provided in England, in the standards set out in statements under section 23; and

(b)   any other matter connected with the provision in England of Part II services.

(6)   The Secretary of State may by regulations confer additional functions on the Commission in relation to Part II services provided in England.

(7)   In this section and section 8, 'Part II services' means services of the kind provided by persons registered under Part II, other than the provision of —

(a)   medical or psychiatric treatment, or

(b)   listed services (as defined in section 2).

8.(1)   The Assembly shall have the general duty of encouraging improvement in the quality of Part II services provided in Wales.

(2)   The Assembly shall make information about Part II services provided in Wales available to the public.

(3)   In relation to Part II services provided in Wales, the Assembly shall have any additional function specified in regulations made by the Assembly; but the regulations may only specify a function corresponding to a function which, by virtue of section 7, is exercisable by the Commission in relation to Part II services provided in England.

(4)   The Assembly may charge a reasonable fee determined by it in connection with the exercise of any power conferred on it by or under this Act.

(5)   The Assembly may provide training for the purpose of assisting persons to attain standards set out in any statements published by it under section 23.

It is envisaged that the NCSC will work closely with the Commission for Health Improvement:

9.(1)   The Commission for Health Improvement ('CHI') and the National Care Standards Commission ('NCSC') may, if authorised to do so by regulations, arrange —

(a)   for prescribed functions of the NCSC to be exercised by CHI on behalf of the NCSC;

(b)   for prescribed functions of CHI, so far as exercisable in relation to England, to be exercised by the NCSC on behalf of CHI,

and accordingly CHI and the NCSC each have power to exercise functions of the other in accordance with arrangements under this subsection.

(2)   The Assembly and CHI may arrange for any functions of the Assembly mentioned in section 10(6) to be exercised by CHI on behalf of the Assembly; and accordingly CHI has power to exercise functions of the Assembly in accordance with arrangements under this subsection.

(3)   The Assembly and CHI may, if authorised to do so by regulations, arrange for prescribed functions of CHI, so far as exercisable in relation to Wales, to be exercised by the Assembly on behalf of CHI; and accordingly the Assembly has power to exercise functions of CHI in accordance with arrangements under this subsection.

(4)   References in this section to exercising functions include a reference to assisting with their exercise.

(5)   Regulations under this section shall be made by the Secretary of State; but the Secretary of State may not make regulations under subsection (3) without the agreement of the Assembly.

Part II of the Act then sets out the requirement to register:

11.(1)   Any person who carries on or manages an establishment or agency of any description without being registered under this Part in respect of it (as an establishment or, as the case may be, agency of that description) shall be guilty of an offence.

(2)   Where the activities of an agency are carried on from two or more branches, each of those branches shall be treated as a separate agency for the purposes of this Part.

(3)   The reference in subsection (1) to an agency does not include a reference to a voluntary adoption agency.

(4)   The Secretary of State may by regulations make provision about the keeping of registers by the Commission for the purposes of this Part.

(5)   A person guilty of an offence under this section shall be liable on summary conviction

(a)   if subsection (6) does not apply, to a fine not exceeding level five on the standard scale;

(b)   if subsection (6) applies, to imprisonment for a term not exceeding six months, or to a fine not exceeding level five on the standard scale, or to both.

(6)   This subsection applies if —

(a)   the person was registered in respect of the establishment or agency at a time before the commission of the offence but the registration was cancelled before the offence was committed; or

(b)   the conviction is a second or subsequent conviction of the offence and the earlier conviction, or one of the earlier convictions, was of an offence in relation to an establishment or agency of the same description.

12.(1)   A person seeking to be registered under this Part shall make an application to the registration authority.

(2)   The application —

(a)   must give the prescribed information about prescribed matters;

(b)   must give any other information which the registration authority reasonably requires the applicant to give,

and must be accompanied by a fee of the prescribed amount.

(3)   A person who applies for registration as the manager of an establishment or agency must be an individual.

(4)   A person who carries on or manages, or wishes to carry on or manage, more than one establishment or agency must make a separate application in respect of each of them.

13.(1)   Subsections (2) to (4) apply where an application under section 12 has been made with respect to an establishment or agency in accordance with the provisions of this Part.

(2)   If the registration authority is satisfied that —

(a)   the requirements of regulations under section 22; and

(b)   the requirements of any other enactment which appears to the registration authority to be relevant,

are being and will continue to be complied with (so far as applicable) in relation to the establishment or agency, it shall grant the application; otherwise it shall refuse it.

(3)   The application may be granted either unconditionally or subject to such conditions as the registration authority thinks fit.

(4)   On granting the application, the registration authority shall issue a certificate of registration to the applicant.

(5)   The registration authority may at any time —

(a)   vary or remove any condition for the time being in force in relation to a person's registration; or

(b)   impose an additional condition.

15.(1)   A person registered under this Part may apply to the registration authority —

(a)   for the variation or removal of any condition for the time being in force in relation to the registration; or

(b)   for the cancellation of the registration.

(2)   But a person may not make an application under subsection (1)(b) —

(a)   if the registration authority has given him notice under section 17(4)(a) of a proposal to cancel the registration, unless the registration authority has decided not to take that step; or

(b)   if the registration authority has given him notice under section 19(3)of its decision to cancel the registration and the time within which an appeal may be brought has not expired or, if an appeal has been brought, it has not been determined.

(3)   An application under subsection (1) shall be made in such manner and state such particulars as may be prescribed and, if made under paragraph (a) of that subsection, shall be accompanied by a fee of such amount as may be prescribed.

(4)   If the registration authority decides to grant an application under subsection (1)(a) it shall serve notice in writing of its decision on the applicant (stating, where applicable, the condition as varied) and issue a new certificate of registration.

(5)   If different amounts are prescribed under subsection (3), the regulations may provide for the registration authority to determine which amount is payable in a particular case.

An important feature of this process is the power of the Secretary of State to make regulations covering a wide range of issues, rather than providing for these in the Act itself:

22.(1)   Regulations may impose in relation to establishments and agencies any requirements which the appropriate Minister thinks fit for the purposes of this Part and may in particular make any provision such as is mentioned in subsection (2), (7) or (8).

(2)   Regulations may —

(a)   make provision as to the persons who are fit to carry on or manage an establishment or agency;

(b)   make provision as to the persons who are fit to work at an establishment or for the purposes of an agency;

(c)   make provision as to the fitness of premises to be used as an establishment or for the purposes of an agency;

(d)   make provision for securing the welfare of persons accommodated in an establishment or provided with services by an establishment, an independent medical agency or a domiciliary care agency;

(e)   make provision for securing the welfare of children placed, under section 23(2)(a) of the 1989 Act, by a fostering agency;

(f)   make provision as to the management and control of the operations of an establishment or agency;

(g)   make provision as to the numbers of persons, or persons of any particular type, working at an establishment or for the purposes of an agency;

(h)   make provision as to the management and training of such persons;

(i)   impose requirements as to the financial position of an establishment or agency;

(j)   make provision requiring the person carrying on an establishment or agency to appoint a manager in prescribed circumstances.

(3)   Regulations under subsection (2)(a) may, in particular, make provision for prohibiting persons from managing an establishment or agency unless they are registered in, or in a particular part of, one of the registers maintained under section 56(1).

(4) Regulations under subsection (2)(b) may, in particular, make provision for prohibiting persons from working in such positions as may be prescribed at an establishment, or for the purposes of an agency, unless they are registered in, or in a particular part of, one of the registers maintained under section 56(1).

(5) Regulations under paragraph (d) of subsection (2) may, in particular, make provision —

(a) as to the promotion and protection of the health of persons such as are mentioned in that paragraph;

(b) as to the control and restraint of adults accommodated in, or provided with services by, an establishment;

(c) as to the control, restraint and discipline of children accommodated in, or provided with services by, an establishment.

(6) Regulations under paragraph (e) of subsection (2) may, in particular, make provision —

(a) as to the promotion and protection of the health of children such as are mentioned in that paragraph;

(b) as to the control, restraint and discipline of such children.

(7) Regulations may make provision as to the conduct of establishments and agencies, and such regulations may in particular —

(a) make provision as to the facilities and services to be provided in establishments and by agencies;

(b) make provision as to the keeping of accounts;

(c) make provision as to the keeping of documents and records;

(d) make provision as to the notification of events occurring in establishments or in premises used for the purposes of agencies;

(e) make provision as to the giving of notice by the person carrying on an establishment or agency of periods during which he or (if he does not manage it himself) the manager proposes to be absent from the establishment or agency, and specify the information to be supplied in such a notice;

(f) provide for the making of adequate arrangements for the running of an establishment or agency during a period when the manager is absent from it;

(g) make provision as to the giving of notice by a person registered in respect of an establishment or agency of any intended change in the identity of the manager or the person carrying it on;

(h) make provision as to the giving of notice by a person registered in respect of an establishment or agency which is carried on by a body corporate of changes in the ownership of the body or the identity of its officers;

(i) make provision requiring the payment of a fee of such amount as may be prescribed in respect of any notification required to be made by virtue of paragraph (h);

(j) make provision requiring arrangements to be made by the person who carries on, or manages, an establishment or agency for dealing with complaints made by or on behalf of those seeking, or receiving, any of the services provided in the establishment or by the agency and requiring that person to take steps for publicising the arrangements;

(k) make provision requiring arrangements to be made by the person who carries on, or manages, an independent hospital, independent clinic or independent medical agency for securing that any medical or psychiatric treatment, or listed services, provided in or for the purposes of the establishment or (as the case may be) for the purposes of the agency are of appropriate quality and meet appropriate standards;

(l) make provision requiring arrangements to be made by the person who carries on, or manages, a care home for securing that any nursing provided by the home is of appropriate quality and meets appropriate standards.

(8) [*regulations regarding children's homes*]

(9) Before making regulations under this section, except regulations which amend other regulations made under this section and do not, in the opinion of the appropriate Minister, effect any substantial change in the provision made by those regulations, the appropriate Minister shall consult any persons he considers appropriate.

(10) References in this section to agencies do not include references to voluntary adoption agencies.

23.(1) The appropriate Minister may prepare and publish statements of national minimum standards applicable to establishments or agencies.

(2) The appropriate Minister shall keep the standards set out in the statements under review and may publish amended statements whenever he considers it appropriate to do so.

(3) Before issuing a statement, or an amended statement which in the opinion of the appropriate Minister effects a substantial change in the standards, the appropriate Minister shall consult any persons he considers appropriate.

(4) The standards shall be taken into account —
(a) in the making of any decision by the registration authority under this Part;
(b) in any proceedings for the making of an order under section 20;
(c) in any proceedings on an appeal against such a decision or order; and
(d) in any proceedings for an offence under regulations under this Part.

It is under these powers that the regulations detailed above and *Caring for Older People* have been made. It is too early to judge the impact of these provisions.

The Act is enforced through the power to cancel registration and the creation of criminal offences. The registration authority may cancel registration under one of two procedures: the normal procedure (s. 14) and the urgent procedure (s. 20).

14.(1) The registration authority may at any time cancel the registration of a person in respect of an establishment or agency —
(a) on the ground that that person has been convicted of a relevant offence;
(b) on the ground that any other person has been convicted of such an offence in relation to the establishment or agency;
(c) on the ground that the establishment or agency is being, or has at any time been, carried on otherwise than in accordance with the relevant requirements;
(d) on any ground specified by regulations.

(2) For the purposes of this section the following are relevant offences —
(a) an offence under this Part or regulations made under it;
(b) an offence under the Registered Homes Act 1984 or regulations made under it;
(c) an offence under the 1989 Act or regulations made under it;

...

(3) In this section 'relevant requirements' means —
(a) any requirements or conditions imposed by or under this Part; and
(b) the requirements of any other enactment which appear to the registration authority to be relevant.

20.(1) If —
(a) the registration authority applies to a justice of the peace for an order —
(i) cancelling the registration of a person in respect of an establishment or agency;
(ii) varying or removing any condition for the time being in force by virtue of this Part; or
(iii) imposing an additional condition; and

(b) it appears to the justice that, unless the order is made, there will be a serious risk to a person's life, health or well-being,

the justice may make the order, and the cancellation, variation, removal or imposition shall have effect from the time when the order is made.

(2) An application under subsection (1) may, if the justice thinks fit, be made without notice.

(3) As soon as practicable after the making of an application under this section, the registration authority shall notify the appropriate authorities of the making of the application.

(4) An order under subsection (1) shall be in writing.

(5) Where such an order is made, the registration authority shall, as soon as practicable after the making of the order, serve on the person registered in respect of the establishment or agency —

(a) a copy of the order; and

(b) notice of the right of appeal conferred by section 21.

(6) For the purposes of this section the appropriate authorities are —

(a) the local authority in whose area the establishment or agency is situated;

(b) the Health Authority in whose area the establishment or agency is situated; and

(c) any statutory authority not falling within paragraph (a) or (b) whom the registration authority thinks it appropriate to notify.

(7) In this section 'statutory authority' means a body established by or under an Act of Parliament.

There is an appeal to the Care Standards Tribunal against a decision of the registration authority:

21.(1) An appeal against —

(a) a decision of the registration authority under this Part; or

(b) an order made by a justice of the peace under section 20,

shall lie to the Tribunal.

(2) No appeal against a decision or order may be brought by a person more than 28 days after service on him of notice of the decision or order.

(3) On an appeal against a decision of the registration authority the Tribunal may confirm the decision or direct that it shall not have effect.

(4) On an appeal against an order made by a justice of the peace the Tribunal may confirm the order or direct that it shall cease to have effect.

(5) The Tribunal shall also have power on an appeal against a decision or order —

(a) to vary any condition for the time being in force in respect of the establishment or agency to which the appeal relates;

(b) to direct that any such condition shall cease to have effect; or

(c) to direct that any such condition as it thinks fit shall have effect in respect of the establishment or agency.

Again, it is too early in the life of the new regime to predict how the Tribunal will interpret the Act and regulations.

The offences are mainly technical, and those provisions are not reproduced. The Act provides for the inspection of premises, again with the Act creating a framework to be fleshed out by regulations.

31.(1) The registration authority may at any time require a person who carries on or manages an establishment or agency to provide it with any information relating to the establishment or agency which the registration authority considers it necessary or expedient to have for the purposes of its functions under this Part.

(2)   A person authorised by the registration authority may at any time enter and inspect premises which are used, or which he has reasonable cause to believe to be used, as an establishment or for the purposes of an agency.

(3)   A person authorised by virtue of this section to enter and inspect premises may —

(a)   make any examination into the state and management of the premises and treatment of patients or persons accommodated or cared for there which he thinks appropriate;

(b)   inspect and take copies of any documents or records (other than medical records) required to be kept in accordance with regulations under this Part, section 9(2) of the Adoption Act 1976, section 23(2)(a) or 59(2) of the 1989 Act or section 1(3) of the Adoption (Intercountry Aspects) Act 1999;

(c)   interview in private the manager or the person carrying on the establishment or agency;

(d)   interview in private any person employed there;

(e)   interview in private any patient or person accommodated or cared for there who consents to be interviewed.

(4)   The powers under subsection (3)(b) include —

(a)   power to require the manager or the person carrying on the establishment or agency to produce any documents or records, wherever kept, for inspection on the premises; and

(b)   in relation to records which are kept by means of a computer, power to require the records to be produced in a form in which they are legible and can be taken away.

(5)   Subsection (6) applies where the premises in question are used as an establishment and the person so authorised —

(a)   is a medical practitioner or registered nurse; and

(b)   has reasonable cause to believe that a patient or person accommodated or cared for there is not receiving proper care.

(6)   The person so authorised may, with the consent of the person mentioned in subsection (5)(b), examine him in private and inspect any medical records relating to his treatment in the establishment.

The powers conferred by this subsection may be exercised in relation to a person who is incapable of giving consent without that person's consent.

(7)   The Secretary of State may by regulations require the Commission to arrange for premises which are used as an establishment or for the purposes of an agency to be inspected on such occasions or at such intervals as may be prescribed.

(8)   A person who proposes to exercise any power of entry or inspection conferred by this section shall if so required produce some duly authenticated document showing his authority to exercise the power.

(9)   Any person who —

(a)   intentionally obstructs the exercise of any power conferred by this section or section 32; or

(b)   fails without a reasonable excuse to comply with any requirement under this section or that section,

shall be guilty of an offence and liable on summary conviction to a fine not exceeding level 4 on the standard scale.

32.(1)   A person authorised by virtue of section 31 to enter and inspect any premises may seize and remove any document or other material or thing found there which he has reasonable grounds to believe may be evidence of a failure to comply with any condition or requirement imposed by or under this Part.

(2)   A person so authorised —

(a)   may require any person to afford him such facilities and assistance with respect to matters within the person's control as are necessary to enable him to exercise his powers under section 31 or this section;

(b) may take such measurements and photographs and make such recordings as he considers necessary to enable him to exercise those powers.

(3)   A person authorised by virtue of section 31 to inspect any records shall be entitled to have access to, and to check the operation of, any computer and any associated apparatus which is or has been in use in connection with the records in question.

(4)   The references in section 31 to the person carrying on the establishment or agency include, in the case of an establishment or agency which is carried on by a company, a reference to any director, manager, secretary or other similar officer of the company.

(5)   Where any premises which are used as an establishment or for the purposes of an agency have been inspected under section 31, the registration authority —
   (a) shall prepare a report on the matters inspected; and
   (b) shall without delay send a copy of the report to each person who is registered in respect of the establishment or agency.

(6)   The registration authority shall make copies of any report prepared under subsection (5) available for inspection at its offices by any person at any reasonable time; and may take any other steps for publicising a report which it considers appropriate.

(7)   Any person who asks the registration authority for a copy of a report prepared under subsection (5) shall be entitled to have one on payment of a reasonable fee determined by the registration authority; but nothing in this subsection prevents the registration authority from providing a copy free of charge when it considers it appropriate to do so.

This process of registration and inspection is a very blunt instrument, though specific abuses may come to light through other means, such as complaints procedures or informal channels.

4.3.3 Removal from home

Finally, an extreme power is created under s. 47 of the National Assistance Act 1948. This provides for the removal of a person from her/his home. The fact that the power can only be exercised following an application to a magistrate is a recognition of the seriousness of the step involved.

47.   Removal to suitable premises of persons in need of care and attention
(1)   The following provisions of this section shall have effect for the purposes of securing the necessary care and attention for persons who —
   (a) are suffering from grave chronic disease or, being aged, infirm or physically incapacitated, are living in insanitary conditions, and
   (b) are unable to devote to themselves, and are not receiving from other persons, proper care and attention.

(2)   If the medical officer of health certifies in writing to the appropriate authority that he is satisfied after thorough inquiry and consideration that in the interests of any such person as aforesaid residing in the area of the authority, or for preventing injury to the health of, or serious nuisance to, other persons, it is necessary to remove any such person as aforesaid from the premises in which he is residing, the appropriate authority may apply to a court of summary jurisdiction having jurisdiction in the place where the premises are situated for an order under the next following subsection.

(3)   On any such application the court may, if satisfied on oral evidence of the allegations in the certificate, and that it is expedient so to do, order the removal of the person to whom the application relates, by such officer of the appropriate authority as may be specified in the order,

to a suitable hospital or other place in, or within convenient distance of, the area of the appropriate authority, and his detention and maintenance therein:

Provided that the court shall not order the removal of a person to any premises, unless either the person managing the premises has been heard in the proceedings or seven clear days' notice has been given to him of the intended application and of the time and place at which it is proposed to be made.

(4) An order under the last foregoing subsection may be made so as to authorise a person's detention for any period not exceeding three months, and the court may from time to time by order extend that period for such further period, not exceeding three months, as the court may determine.

(5) An order under subsection (3) of this section may be varied by an order of the court so as to substitute for the place referred to in that subsection such other suitable place in, or within convenient distance of, the area of the appropriate authority as the court may determine, so however that the proviso to the said subsection (3) shall with the necessary modification apply to any proceedings under this subsection.

(6) At any time after the expiration of six clear weeks from the making of an order under subsection (3) or (4) of this section an application may be made to the court by or on behalf of the person in respect of whom the order was made, and on any such application the court may, if in the circumstances it appears expedient so to do, revoke the order.

(7) No application under this section shall be entertained by the court unless, seven clear days before the making of the application, notice has been given of the intended application and of the time and place at which it is proposed to be made —

(a) where the application is for an order under subsection (3) or (4) of this section, to the person in respect of whom the application is made or to some person in charge of him;

(b) where the application is for the revocation of such an order, to the medical officer of health.

(8) Where in pursuance of an order under this section a person is maintained neither in hospital accommodation provided by the Minister of Health under the National Health Service Act 1977 or by the Secretary of State under the National Health Service (Scotland) Act 1978, nor in premises where accommodation is provided by, or by arrangement with, a local authority under Part III of this Act, the cost of his maintenance shall be borne by the appropriate authority.

(11) Any person who wilfully disobeys, or obstructs the execution of, an order under this section shall be guilty of an offence and liable on summary conviction to a fine not exceeding level 1 on the standard scale.

The National Assistance (Amendment) Act 1951 enables the process to be speeded up in urgent cases:

National Assistance (Amendment) Act 1951

1.(1) An order under subsection (3) of section forty-seven of the National Assistance Act 1948 for the removal of any such person as is mentioned in subsection (1) of that section may be made without notice required by subsection (7) if it is certified by the medical officer of health and another registered medical practitioner that in their opinion it is necessary in the interests of that person to remove him without delay.

(2) If in any such case it is shown by the applicant that the manager of any such hospital or place as is mentioned in the said subsection (3) agrees to accommodate therein the person in respect of whom the application is made, the proviso to that subsection (which requires that the manager of the premises to which a person is to be removed must be heard in the proceedings or receive notice of the application) shall not apply in relation to an order for the removal of that person to that hospital or place.

(3)   Any such order as is authorised by this section may be made on the application either of the appropriate authority within the meaning of the said section forty-seven or, if the medical officer of health is authorised by that authority to make such applications, by that officer, and may be made either by a court of summary jurisdiction having jurisdiction in the place where the premises are situated in which the person in respect of whom the application is made resides, or by a single justice having such jurisdiction; and the order may, if the court or justice thinks it necessary, be made ex parte.

(4)   In relation to any such order as is authorised by this section the provisions of the said section forty-seven shall have effect subject to the following modifications —

(a)   in subsection (4) (which specifies the period for which a person may be detained pursuant to an order) for the words 'three months' in the first place where those words occur, there shall be substituted the words 'three weeks' and subsection (6) (which enables an application to be made for the revocation of an order) shall not apply;

(b)   where the order is made by a single justice, any reference in subsections (4) and (5) to the court shall be construed as a reference to a court of summary jurisdiction having jurisdiction in the same place as that justice.

The following evaluation of the powers contained in s. 47 comes from a community physician writing in the *Journal of medical ethics* [1981 vol. 7 p. 146] some 20 years ago:

The compulsory hospitalisation of people who are mentally ill has received a great deal of attention in recent years because of the ethical issues involved. There is, however, one similar piece of legislation which is much more difficult to justify on ethical grounds but which has received much less attention — Section 47 of the National Assistance Act — for it allows the compulsory removal of people who are not mentally ill.

'Section 47', as it is known among doctors and social workers, concerns persons who:

(a)   are suffering from grave chronic disease or, being aged, infirm or physically incapacitated, are living in insanitary conditions, and

(b)   are unable to devote to themselves, and are not receiving from other persons, proper care and attention.

It lays down that they may be removed from their homes if it is in their 'interest', or if it is necessary to prevent 'injury to the health of, or serious nuisance to, other persons'. The power to approach a magistrate for a removal order was given to the Medical Officer of Health in 1948, and is now vested in the Medical Officer for Environmental Health to the District Council in which the elder lives, because, rather surprisingly, it was given to district councils in 1974 along with environmental responsibilities rather than to the authorities responsible for health or social services. The Medical Officer for Environmental Health, a community physician, has to apply to a court or a magistrate, giving seven days' notice of the intended removal. If an order is issued, the person can be detained for three months in 'a suitable hospital or other place'.

The National Assistance (Amendment) Act 1951 allows for immediate removal but the Medical Officer for Environmental Health must include the recommendation of another doctor, usually the person's general practitioner, that the person be removed without delay, but an order for immediate removal allows the person's detention for no more than three weeks. This Amendment Act was introduced as a Private Member's Bill, with government support, by the late Sir Alfred Broughton, a doctor, who was member for Batley and Morley. His constituents had been shocked by the death of a lady who had lain on the floor of her house, refusing all offers of help, watched by shocked neighbours and officials while the seven statutory days' notice expired, and who had developed a pressure sore and tetanus during this period.

The use of 'Section 47' powers

The Department of Health does not collect statistics on the number of times the powers are used, which is a serious deficiency in governmental statistics. I therefore conducted a survey of responsible community physicians in England, ninety per cent of whom replied, and have been able to calculate how often community physicians use these powers.

In England alone about 200 people are compulsorily removed from their homes each year. Ninety-seven per cent in my survey were over 65, although the legal provisions are not restricted to older people. In 94 per cent of cases the powers of immediate removal given by the 1951 Amendment Act were used and two-thirds of the people were removed to hospitals, most of the remainder being admitted to old people's homes.

Perhaps the most interesting finding is that the use of the powers varied widely. Thirty-five of the 141 community physicians who replied did not use the powers at all and among those who did the rate of use, calculated with respect to the number of people aged over sixty-five, varied six fold; that is some community physicians used it six times as often as others. This variation is not explained by social factors. For example 'Section 47' was not used more frequently in urban areas or 'retirement areas' and in my opinion the main factor is probably the attitude of the responsible community physician.

...

Four important ethical issues have to be considered by the community physician. Two of these are explicitly set out in 'Section 47', the other two are related to the implicit, or hidden, functions of the legislation.

The first explicit issue is the justifiability of removing an elderly person for prevention of 'injury to the health of, or serious nuisance to, other persons'. To remove an elderly person for the benefit of others would be difficult to justify but is rarely necessary because the Public Health Acts of 1936 and 1961 permit the compulsory cleaning of an old person's house and garden if either is in an insanitary condition. The risk of the elder starting a fire and harming other people is one situation which causes much concern and gives rise to some referrals but in my experience it is always possible to reduce the risk of fire by means other than the removal of the elder.

The second explicit ethical issue is the paternalistic removal of an old person from her home. The closest analogy is the removal of an elderly person using the powers of the Mental Health Act but the removal of someone who is mentally ill is justified by the concept of mental illness. However those who are removed with a 'Section 47' order are not insane, to use a legal term. Some are mentally disordered, usually as a result of dementia, and may be considered to be incompetent. That is, they are not so disturbed as to be removed using the Mental Health Act but sufficiently disordered to be deemed unfit to manage their own affairs just as many of the people whose cases are referred to the Court of Protection are more appropriately considered as incompetent rather than insane (1), (2). Others, however, are not in any way incompetent. They are mentally alert, being neither depressed nor demented, but refuse offers of help, and the ethical problems presented by this type of person is similar to that posed by the person who refuses consent to treatment (3). Some old people who refuse the services offered are ashamed of the dirt in which they live or are ashamed of their incontinence; some fear permanent institutionalisation and some still fear 'the workhouse' when offered a place in hospital.

The justifiability of the compulsory removal of people for paternalistic reasons has, like other pieces of paternalistic legislation, to be assessed by comparing the possible benefits with the certain infringement of liberty. Furthermore, the risks of removal have also to be considered because the very removal of a person from her home carries a risk of physical and mental deterioration and in some cases it will have fatal effects (4). Of the six people I have removed five improved and the one who died soon after admission was a lady whom I considered to be dying uncomfortably at home when I saw her who, in my opinion, died in greater comfort and dignity in hospital. The improvement was marked in every case. A survey of twenty-one cases in which elderly people had been removed compulsorily by colleagues working in the Oxford Region found that the average survival time was two years (5). Nevertheless, some people are adversely affected and some may die prematurely as a result of compulsory removal.

There are two other ethical issues which are implicit in the legislation which also have to be taken into consideration. Firstly, the community physician has to be aware that the principal reason why the elder is being referred for removal may be that there are insufficient resources to support her in her own home. Some people undoubtedly need treatment in hospital, the person with a fractured femur for example, but the need of others is for more frequent visits from the domiciliary services than are available in the area in which they live.

...

The second implicit issue is that one of the objectives of 'Section 47' is to control deviance. In the nineteenth century cleanliness, temperance and thrift — continent behaviour — was deserving behaviour; undeserving incontinent behaviour was deemed to need the control which 'the House' afforded. Both Majority and Minority Reports of the Royal Commission on the Poor Law recommended compulsory removal both to help and to control the individual who was incapable of maintaining 'proper' standards. 'Section 47' reflects the attitudes which prevailed in the nineteenth century towards old people who did not conform with conventional 'proper' standards and such attitudes still persist although they are less frequently expressed nowadays (6), (7).

Should 'Section 47' be repealed?

Since the legislation was first introduced as 'Section 56' of the Bradford Corporation Act 1925 much has changed although only minor alterations have been made to the wording of the law. Attitudes, values and beliefs have all changed considerably, and domiciliary services have grown, but I do not believe that it should be repealed, although I am sure that it should be amended.

What would happen if it were repealed? Would disabled elderly people, who were refusing to go to hospital for the treatment of some life-threatening disease or those who were refusing domiciliary services, be left at home? I do not think that they would. It is probable that the Mental Health Act would be used to remove some of them and I believe that the effects of this type of removal are even more serious than 'Section 47' removal. When I use 'Section 47' I am in effect saying 'I respect your opinion, I believe that you are sane and that it is a valid opinion but I also believe that it is wrong', whereas the Mental Health Act implies that the person is incapable of making decisions and that his opinions are invalid. The use of 'Section 47' is based on the legal concept of incompetence whereas the Mental Health Act is based on the premise of insanity and removal using the powers of the Mental Health Act may irreversibly label the individual as a 'psychogeriatric'. Not all would be removed using Mental Health Act powers, however. Others would be deceived, drugged, coerced or overpowered as many elders are today and I have evidence from many parts of the country that these practices take place. Deceit is still common with old people being told 'It's only for a holiday', or 'It's only for a few weeks'. Drugs are not commonly used for the sole purpose of overcoming a person's resistance, although that does happen, but the judgment of many older people is clouded by drugs.

Coercion is also used — 'if you won't agree to go, we can have you taken away', and the Medical Officer of Environmental Health sometimes finds that he has been used in this way, as the official who will take the elder away if she does not agree to go 'voluntarily'.

Finally, many people are overpowered; I don't mean physically overpowered — ambulancemen are too honest and cautious to go along with that sort of practice — but many elderly people give up and give in as a result of sustained pressure from friends, relatives, neighbours and sometimes from professionals, although the latter usually take the side of the old person. The term often used is 'persuasion' — 'she has been persuaded to go' — and in some cases the old person has been persuaded as a result of cool and rational argument; in others however she has been forced to change her mind as a result of sustained pressure.

In addition to the arguments put forward by Dr Muir Gray, there is also the question of whether s. 47 can survive the application of the Human Rights Act 1998, especially Arts. 5 and 6.

5

Mental health

5.1 Mental health

5.1.1 Introduction

The law relating to mental health has had a chequered history. It has to perform the impossible task of trying to accommodate a number of possibly irreconcilable interests. It has been recognised, officially as well as by practitioners and other commentators, that the present law is in need of reform. At the time of writing, legislation is promised as soon as the parliamentary timetable permits. The law, as currently constituted, is concerned to define basic concepts and to establish frameworks for decision making. It cannot provide a substitute for professional judgement as to whether a person does or does not fall within criteria established by the Act, nor does it attempt to do so. Rather, it seeks to facilitate professional functioning whilst ensuring that the rights of the individual are respected. Whether it achieves a suitable balance between these requirements will remain a matter of legitimate debate. Two short passages from *The Politics of Mental Health Legislation* by the late Clive Unsworth encapsulate the tensions underlying legislation in this area, whether present or future:

It is a characteristic of the debate surrounding the relationship between law and psychiatry that it tends to counterpose medical discretion — in the interests of maximizing therapeutic success — and legal intervention to control this discretion — in the interests of protecting civil liberty. However, law is also involved in the regulation of mental health practices in the less invasive sense of constituting and defining the discretionary domain of mental health professionals in the first place. The complex provisions of Part IV of the Mental Health Act 1983 headed 'Consent to Treatment', for example, have both a negative and a positive function with respect to psychiatric power. In their negative aspect, they perform the inhibitive and restrictive function intended by the critics of the psychiatric profession, of debarring the administration of certain of the more serious medical treatments for mental disorder without the patient's consent and/or (depending upon the gravity of the treatment) a second opinion. But at the same time, in their positive aspect, these provisions equip the appropriate professionals with a legal mandate to deploy their expertise in the treatment of the mentally disordered, subject to compliance with the specified substantive and procedural limitations. The Mental Health Act 1983 recognizes the psychiatric, the social work, and the nursing professions, and accords them specific areas of competence. Law actually constitutes the mental health system, in the sense that it authoritatively constructs, empowers, and regulates the relationships between the agents who perform mental health functions. It is indeed a precondition of the operation of the complex and intricate mechanisms of control, surveillance, discipline, and reconstruction which assemble into an advanced mental health system. As Paul Hirst affirms in a critique of Michel Foucault's de-emphasis of law in the characterization of 'disciplinary society': 'There is no opposition between law and discipline ... without a publicly assigned position and legally defined exclusiveness in the performance of their role, the key institutions and agents of the "disciplinary" region could not function: prisons, psychiatry, medicine, social work and so on.'

Alternatives to legal regulation even at this basic level are imaginable. Strict regulation of the exercise of mental health skills dependent upon recognized qualifications and membership of particular established professions could give way to a philosophy of 'let one hundred flowers bloom'. Exclusively voluntary and contractual relations could govern the supply of psychiatric services, with the public interest in controlling anti-social behaviour attributable to mental disorder being abandoned to the criminal law. Whatever the merits or demerits of such a marriage of anarchy and the market, the consequential social arrangements for solving the problem raised by mental pathology would not be recognizable as a mental health 'system' in its prevailing sense.

...

A number of general characteristics applicable to both professions suggest themselves. They include membership of the same social classes, a shared declaration of commitment to the ideals of professionalism and political conservatism. Toward the mentally disordered, both medical and legal approaches have traditionally adopted a posture of paternalism. In the legal approach this was the foundation of the jurisdiction over the person and property of lunatics and idiots originating in the medieval period. In medical approaches, it flows from the central contention that psychiatric patients are afflicted by an illness which has the special character of depriving them of the ability to calculate their own best interests. Both legal and medical approaches are founded upon moral positions, albeit opposed. The legal position is one of concern to protect liberty unless there is good justification for its suppression, while the medical position is one of concern to alleviate the mental suffering inflicted by mental disorder. Both can therefore claim to be rooted in humane traditions, although the legal position is liable to attack from the medical perspective for insensitively subjecting the insane to procedural ordeals designed to meet the needs of the sane, and the medical from the legal for presumptuously imposing its ministrations upon the resistant. Furthermore, there exists a space for the notion of patients' rights in both discourses. The legal approach is a natural resort for patients anxious to protect their civil liberty against medical or other professional encroachment supported by therapeutic legitimations, but can also unite with the medical perspective to the extent that patients, as psychiatric consumers, assert their rights to an improved quality and range of psychiatric services. Patients who accept that their treatment is a medical province and recognize their own need for psychiatric care can proclaim their entitlement to services through the medium of legal rights. The co-operation of patients and their relatives within the National Schizophrenia Fellowship provides an example of patients becoming organized politically to pursue interests no more corrosive of medical prerogatives than kidney patients demanding more kidney machines. Finally, however uneasy their alliance, psychiatry and law are intimately interconnected and interdependent in the apparatuses of modern criminal justice, a relationship traceable to the emergence of a penality based upon the principles of the Enlightenment. Psychiatric medicine has been one of the principal beneficiaries of what Michel Foucault describes as a fragmentation of the legal power to punish. Law and psychiatry function as intersecting modalities of judgment and disposition in the control of crime.

A second main function of law in the psychiatric arena is that of determining the therapeutic division of labour, allocating their respective roles to the different sets of personnel engaged in mental health practices. In doing so, it accommodates competing professional interests and establishes the hierarchy of professional authority in key areas of decision-making, especially those of commitment and treatment. For example, while it does not seriously threaten the hegemony of the medical profession, the Mental Health Act 1983 does reflect the weakened credibility of psychiatry since 1959 by subjecting psychiatric decisions in relation to commitment, continued detention, and treatment to closer scrutiny and increased review. By the same token, it accords new roles to other professions working in the mental health services — social workers, clinical psychologists, and nurses — in recognition of their growing strength and status enhancement. Via the principle of multidisciplinary review expressed in the consent to treatment provisions, and the complexion of the Mental Health Act Commission, the procedures and structures erected to place a check upon psychiatric practitioners for the protection of individual patients have simultaneously performed the function of elevating other mental health professions.

...

Thirdly, law performs that classic function most strongly advocated by lawyers and libertarians, of inhibiting and restricting psychiatric power in the interests of civil liberty and the accountability of the psychiatric profession as an agency of social control. The principle of the universality of the rule of law is pitted against a psychiatry characterized as a potentially arbitrary and oppressive concentration of power which threatens the legitimate autonomy of the individual.

In addition to the statutory provisions, there is also a Code of Practice, which, though not containing rules of law, explains how the principles of the Acts should be put into practice. The opening paragraph of the Code of Practice (Stationery Office, 1999) sets out the basic principles to be applied in respect of those subject to the Act:

1.1   The detailed guidance in the Code needs to be read in the light of the following broad principles, that people to whom the Act applies (including those being assessed for possible admission) should:

- receive recognition of their basic human rights under the European Convention on Human Rights (ECHR);
- be given respect for their qualities, abilities and diverse backgrounds as individuals and be assured that account will be taken of their age, gender, sexual orientation, social, ethnic, cultural and religious background, but that general assumptions will not be made on the basis of any one of these characteristics;
- have their needs taken fully into account, though it is recognised that, within available resources, it may not always be practicable to meet them in full;
- be given any necessary treatment or care in the least controlled and segregated facilities compatible with ensuring their own health or safety or the safety of other people;
- be treated and cared for in such a way as to promote to the greatest practicable degree their self determination and personal responsibility, consistent with their own needs and wishes;
- be discharged from detention or other powers provided by the Act as soon as it is clear that their application is no longer justified.

Note the reference to the European Convention on Human Rights and Fundamental Freedoms. As we have seen (in Chapter 2), by virtue of the Human Rights Act 1998, this became part of English law in October 2000. Articles 2, 3, 5 and 8 have particular relevance here. The new legal culture brought about by the Human Rights Act will mean that the third function of the law identified by Clive Unsworth, namely the protection of individual liberty and the rights of the patient, is thus likely to receive greater prominence. English law is further enriched by the addition of the case law of the European Court of Human Rights, which includes cases challenging the law and practices of other countries. One of the most important of these cases originated in the Netherlands. In this case, *Winterwerp v The Netherlands* (1979)2 EHRR387 the European Court of Human Rights discusses some fundamental principles affecting the compulsory admission and detention of patients which will need to be observed by practitioners and courts in the United Kingdom. The following excerpt concentrates on the Court's statements of principle, rather than on the actual facts and decision in the case, as these statements will impact on the content and operation of the mental health legislation in this country. A brief summary of the facts and decision is, however, included to provide a context for the Court's more general statements.

The applicant, who had been compulsorily detained under the relevant Netherlands legislation dealing with mentally ill persons, complained that Articles 5 (right to liberty) and 6 (right to a fair hearing in the determination of civil rights) of the European Convention on Human Rights had been violated. He had been detained by court orders renewed periodically, but had not been notified that the proceedings were in progress or allowed to appear or be represented. On several occasions, his requests for release were not forwarded to the court by the public prosecutor, who was entitled so to act in certain circumstances. As a result of his detention, the applicant automatically lost the capacity to administer his property. The Commission found a breach of Article 5, but decided to express no view as regards Article 6, and referred the case to the Court, as did the respondent Government.

Held (unanimously), (i) the applicant's inability to have his detention reviewed by a court and the failure to hear him constituted a violation of Article 5 (4); and (ii) the denial of capacity to administer his property without a proper judicial determination amounted to a determination of civil rights in violation of Article 6 (1).

In its judgment, the Court said:

37. The Convention does not state what is to be understood by the words 'persons of unsound mind'. This term is not one that can be given a definitive interpretation: as was pointed out by the Commission, the Government and the applicant, it is a term whose meaning is continually evolving as research in psychiatry progresses, an increasing flexibility in treatment is developing and society's attitudes to mental illness change, in particular so that a greater understanding of the problems of mental patients is becoming more widespread.

In any event, sub-paragraph (*e*) of Article 5 (1) obviously cannot be taken as permitting the detention of a person simply because his views or behaviour deviate from the norms prevailing in a particular society. To hold otherwise would not be reconcilable with the text of Article 5 (1), which sets out an exhaustive list of exceptions calling for a narrow interpretation. Neither would it be in conformity with the object and purpose of Article 5 (1), namely, to ensure that no one should be dispossessed of his liberty in an arbitrary fashion. Moreover, it would disregard the importance of the right to liberty in a democratic society.

...

39. The next issue to be examined is the 'lawfulness' of the detention for the purposes of Article 5 (1) (*e*). Such 'lawfulness' presupposes conformity with the domestic law in the first place and also, as confirmed by Article 18, conformity with the purpose of the restrictions permitted by Article 5 (1) (*e*); it is required in respect of both the ordering and the execution of the measures involving deprivation of liberty.

As regards the conformity with the domestic law, the Court points out that the term 'lawful' covers procedural as well as substantive rules. There thus exists a certain overlapping between this term and the general requirement stated at the beginning of Article 5 (1), namely, observance of 'a procedure prescribed by law' (see para. 45 below).

Indeed, these two expressions reflect the importance of the aim underlying Article 5 (1) (see para. 37 above): in a democratic society subscribing to the rule of law, no detention that is arbitrary can ever be regarded as 'lawful'.

The Commission likewise stresses that there must be no element of arbitrariness; the conclusion it draws is that no one may be confined as 'a person of unsound mind' in the absence of medical evidence establishing that his mental state is such as to justify his compulsory hospitalisation. The applicant and the Government both express similar opinions.

The Court fully agrees with this line of reasoning. In the Court's opinion, except in emergency cases, the individual concerned should not be deprived of his liberty unless he has been reliably shown to be of 'unsound mind'. The very nature of what has to be established before the competent national authority — that is, a true mental disorder — calls for objective medical expertise. Further, the mental disorder must be of a kind or degree warranting compulsory confinement. What is more, the validity of continued confinement depends upon the persistence of such a disorder.

...

45.   The Court for its part considers that the words 'in accordance with a procedure prescribed by law' essentially refer back to domestic law; they state the need for compliance with the relevant procedure under that law.

However, the domestic law must itself be in conformity with the Convention, including the general principles expressed or implied therein. The notion underlying the term in question is one of fair and proper procedure, namely, that any measure depriving a person of his liberty should issue from and be executed by an appropriate authority and should not be arbitrary. The Netherlands Mentally Ill Persons Act (described above at paras. 11 to 20) satisfies this condition.

46.   Whether the procedure prescribed by that Act was in fact respected in the applicant's case is a question that the Court has jurisdiction to examine. Whilst it is not normally the Court's task to review the observance of domestic law by the national authorities, it is otherwise in relation to matters where, as here, the Convention refers directly back to that law; for, in such matters, disregard of the domestic law entails breach of the Convention, with the consequence that the Court can and should exercise a certain power of review.

However, the logic of the system of safeguard established by the Convention sets limits upon the scope of this review. It is in the first place for the national authorities, notably the courts, to interpret and apply the domestic law, even in those fields where the Convention 'incorporates' the rules of that law: the national authorities are, in the nature of things, particularly qualified to settle the issues arising in this connection.

...

60.   The judicial proceedings referred to in Articles 5 (4) need not, it is true, always be attended by the same guarantees as those required under Article 6 (1) for civil or criminal litigation. Nonetheless, it is essential that the person concerned should have access to a court and the opportunity to be heard either in person or, where necessary, through some form of representation, failing which he will not have been afforded 'the fundamental guarantees of procedure applied in matters of deprivation of liberty'. Mental illness may entail restricting or modifying the manner of exercise of such a right, but it cannot justify impairing the very essence of the right. Indeed, special procedural safeguards may prove called for in order to protect the interests of persons who, on account of their mental disabilities, are not fully capable of acting for themselves.

As the law defines certain basic concepts and identifies key players in the legislative scheme, it is helpful to look at these first. The Act identifies certain key participants in the decision making process. The central focus is, of course, the patient. Confusingly, the Act uses this term in two senses. Section 145 provides:

'patient' (except in Part VII of this Act) means a person suffering or appearing to be suffering from mental disorder;

...

Whilst, for the purposes of Part VII, s. 94 provides:

(2)   The functions of the judge under this Part of this Act shall be exercisable where, after considering medical evidence, he is satisfied that a person is incapable, by reason of mental disorder, of managing and administering his property and affairs; and a person as to whom the judge is so satisfied is referred to in this Part of this Act as a patient.

The Act also identifies various professionals involved in making decisions and exercising powers under the Act. Again, the Act identifies different kinds of doctor. Section 12 provides:

(2)   Of the medical recommendations given for the purposes of any such application, one shall be given by a practitioner approved for the purposes of this section by the Secretary of State as having special experience in the diagnosis or treatment of mental disorder; and unless that practitioner has previous acquaintance with the patient, the other such recommendation shall, if practicable, be given by a registered medical practitioner who has such previous acquaintance.

...

Section 34 states:

'the responsible medical officer' means (except in the phrase the community responsible medical officer) —
    (a)   in relation to a patient who is liable to be detained by virtue of an application for admission for assessment or an application for admission for treatment, or who is to be subject to after-care supervision after leaving hospital the registered medical practitioner in charge of the treatment of the patient;
    (b)   in relation to a patient subject to guardianship, the medical officer authorised by the local social services authority to act (either generally or in any particular case or for any particular purpose) as the responsible medical officer.

Historically, the involvement of the patient's family in certain decision making processes has been a matter not without controversy: families having relatives 'put away' was one of the abuses of the system. Nevertheless, the involvement of the family is preserved by the roles assigned by the Act to the nearest relative. This term is defined in such a way as to enable a nearest relative to be identified in any given situation. The Act also provides for a nearest relative to be appointed if necessary:

26.   Definition of 'relative' and 'nearest relative'
(1)   In this Part of this Act 'relative' means any of the following persons: —
    (a)   husband or wife;
    (b)   son or daughter;
    (c)   father or mother;
    (d)   brother or sister;

    (e) grandparent;
    (f) grandchild;
    (g) uncle or aunt;
    (h) nephew or niece.

(2) In deducing relationships for the purposes of this section, any relationship of the half-blood shall be treated as a relationship of the whole blood, and an illegitimate person shall be treated as the legitimate child of his mother.

(3) In this Part of this Act, subject to the provisions of this section and to the following provisions of this Part of this Act, the 'nearest relative' means the person first described in subsection (1) above who is for the time being surviving, relatives of the whole blood being preferred to relatives of the same description of the half-blood and the elder or eldest of two or more relatives described in any paragraph of that subsection being preferred to the other or others of those relatives, regardless of sex.

(4) Subject to the provisions of this section and to the following provisions of this Part of this Act, where the patient ordinarily resides with or is cared for by one or more of his relatives (or, if he is for the time being an in-patient in a hospital, he last ordinarily resided with or was cared for by one or more of his relatives) his nearest relative shall be determined —

    (a) by giving preference to that relative or those relatives over the other or others; and
    (b) as between two or more such relatives, in accordance with subsection (3) above.

(5) Where the person who, under subsection (3) or (4) above, would be the nearest relative of a patient —

    (a) in the case of a patient ordinarily resident in the United Kingdom, the Channel Islands or the Isle of Man, is not so resident; or
    (b) is the husband or wife of the patient, but is permanently separated from the patient, either by agreement or under an order of a court, or has deserted or has been deserted by the patient for a period which has not come to an end; or
    (c) is a person other than the husband, wife, father or mother of the patient, and is for the time being under 18 years of age; the nearest relative of the patient shall be ascertained as if that person were dead.

(6) In this section 'husband' and 'wife' include a person who is living with the patient as the patient's husband or wife, as the case may be (or, if the patient is for the time being an in-patient in a hospital, was so living until the patient was admitted), and has been or had been so living for a period of not less than six months; but a person shall not be treated by virtue of this subsection as the nearest relative of a married patient unless the husband or wife of the patient is disregarded by virtue of paragraph (b) of subsection (5) above.

(7) A person, other than a relative, with whom the patient ordinarily resides (or, if the patient is for the time being an in-patient in a hospital, last ordinarily resided before he was admitted), and with whom he has or had been ordinarily residing for a period of not less than five years, shall be treated for the purposes of this Part of this Act as if he were a relative but —

    (a) shall be treated for the purposes of subsection (3) above as if mentioned last in subsection (1) above; and
    (b) shall not be treated by virtue of this subsection as the nearest relative of a married patient unless the husband or wife of the patient is disregarded by virtue of paragraph (b) of subsection (5) above.

…

29. Appointment by court of acting nearest relative

(1) The county court may, upon application made in accordance with the provisions of this section in respect of a patient, by order direct that the functions of the nearest relative of the patient under this Part of this Act and sections 66 and 69 below shall, during the continuance

in force of the order, be exercisable by the applicant, or by any other person specified in the application, being a person who, in the opinion of the court, is a proper person to act as the patient's nearest relative and is willing to do so.

(2)   An order under this section may be made on the application of —

(a)   any relative of the patient;

(b)   any other person with whom the patient is residing (or, if the patient is then an in-patient in a hospital, was last residing before he was admitted)); or

(c)   an approved social worker; but in relation to an application made by such a social worker, subsection (1) above shall have effect as if for the words 'the applicant' there were substituted the words 'the local social services authority'.

(3)   An application for an order under this section may be made upon any of the following grounds, that is to say —

(a)   that the patient has no nearest relative within the meaning of this Act, or that it is not reasonably practicable to ascertain whether he has such a relative, or who that relative is;

(b)   that the nearest relative of the patient is incapable of acting as such by reason of mental disorder or other illness;

(c)   that the nearest relative of the patient unreasonably objects to the making of an application for admission for treatment or a guardianship application in respect of the patient or;

(d)   that the nearest relative of the patient has exercised without due regard to the welfare of the patient or the interests of the public his power to discharge the patient from hospital or guardianship under this Part of this Act, or is likely to do so.

A particular type of social worker, with post qualification training, was created by the 1983 Act and is assigned a number of roles under the Act: this is the approved social worker (ASW). The local authority has a number of duties under the Act, one of which is to ensure that there are sufficient ASWs. The ASW has a number of functions under the legislation, for example in relation to decisions regarding compulsory admission (see below). Section 145 defines the ASW:

'approved social worker' means an officer of a local social services authority appointed to act as an approved social worker for the purposes of this Act;

...

114.   Appointment of approved social workers

(1)   A local social services authority shall appoint a sufficient number of approved social workers for the purpose of discharging the functions conferred on them by this Act.

(2)   No person shall be appointed by a local social services authority as an approved social worker unless he is approved by the authority as having appropriate competence in dealing with persons who are suffering from mental disorder.

(3)   In approving a person for appointment as an approved social worker a local social services authority shall have regard to such matters as the Secretary of State may direct.

As well as identifying key participants in decision making processes, the Act defines certain key concepts in s. 1:

(1)   The provisions of this Act shall have effect with respect to the reception, care and treatment of mentally disordered patients, the management of their property and other related matters.

(2)   In this Act —

'mental disorder' means mental illness, arrested or incomplete development of mind, psychopathic disorder and any other disorder or disability of mind and 'mentally disordered' shall be construed accordingly;

'severe mental impairment' means a state of arrested or incomplete development of mind which includes severe impairment of intelligence and social functioning and is associated with abnormally aggressive or seriously irresponsible conduct on the part of the person concerned and 'severely mentally impaired' shall be construed accordingly;

'mental impairment' means a state of arrested or incomplete development of mind (not amounting to severe mental impairment) which includes significant impairment of intelligence and social functioning and is associated with abnormally aggressive or seriously irresponsible conduct on the part of the person concerned and 'mentally impaired' shall be construed accordingly;

'psychopathic disorder' means a persistent disorder or disability of mind (whether or not including significant impairment of intelligence) which results in abnormally aggressive or seriously irresponsible conduct on the part of the person concerned;

and other expressions shall have the meanings assigned to them in section 145 below.

(3)   Nothing in subsection (2) above shall be construed as implying that a person may be dealt with under this Act as suffering from mental disorder, or from any form of mental disorder described in this section, by reason only of promiscuity or other immoral conduct, sexual deviancy or dependence on alcohol or drugs.

An underlying concept, and one which has been recognised as being in need of reform, is the question of the capacity to make decisions, as the following extract explains. It is important to remember that capacity is a legal concept in this context, and that medical evidence is merely evidential. It is difficult to find a clear workable test, as the following extract, in which the Law Commission in its report *Mental Incapacity* summarises the present position, the reasons why change is needed and its proposals, makes clear.

Introduction
3.1   ... The essence of our recommendations is that new legislation should provide a unified and comprehensive scheme within which people can make decisions on behalf of, and in the best interests of, people who lack capacity to make decisions for themselves. ...

(1)   Capacity and lack of capacity
Presumption of capacity and standard of proof
3.2   It is presumed at common law that an adult has full legal capacity unless it is shown that he or she does not. If a question of capacity comes before a court the burden of proof will be on the person seeking to establish incapacity, and the matter will be decided according to the usual civil standard, the balance of probabilities. We proposed in Consultation Paper No 128 that the usual civil standard should continue to apply and the vast majority of our respondents agreed with this proposal. A number, however, argued that it would be helpful if the new statutory provisions were expressly to include and restate both the presumption of capacity and the relevant standard of proof.

'We *recommend* that there should be a presumption against lack of capacity and that any question whether a person lacks capacity should be decided on the balance of probabilities.'

The functional approach
3.3   In our overview paper we described the variety of tests of capacity which already exist in our law, and we also discussed some medical and psychological tests of capacity. There are three broad approaches: the 'status', 'outcome' and 'functional' approaches. A 'status' test excludes all persons under eighteen from voting and used to exclude all married women from legal ownership of property. Under the present law, the status of being a 'patient' of the Court of Protection is used in a variety of enactments to trigger other legal consequences. Case-law also suggests that

the status of being a 'patient' has the extremely significant effect of depriving the patient of all contractual capacity, whether or not as a matter of fact the patient actually had such capacity. The status approach is quite out of tune with the policy aim of enabling and encouraging people to take for themselves any decision which they have capacity to take.

3.4   An assessor of capacity using the 'outcome' method focuses on the final content of an individual's decision. Any decision which is inconsistent with conventional values, or with which the assessor disagrees, may be classified as incompetent. This penalises individuality and demands conformity at the expense of personal autonomy. A number of our respondents argued that an 'outcome' approach is applied by many doctors; if the outcome of the patient's deliberations is to agree with the doctor's recommendations then he or she is taken to have capacity, while if the outcome is to reject a course which the doctor has advised then capacity is found to be absent.

3.5   We explained in Consultation Paper No 128 that most respondents to our overview paper strongly supported the 'functional' approach. This also has the merit of being the approach adopted by most of the established tests in English law. In this approach, the assessor asks whether an individual is able, at the time when a particular decision has to be made, to understand its nature and effects. Importantly, both partial and fluctuating capacity can be recognised. Most people, unless in a coma, are able to make at least some decisions for themselves, and many have levels of capacity which vary from week to week or even from hour to hour.

3.6   In view of the ringing endorsement of the 'functional' approach given by respondents to the overview paper, we formulated a provisional 'functional' test of capacity and set this out in all three of our 1993 consultation papers. This test focused on inability to understand or, in the alternative, inability to choose. We also made specific provision for those unable to communicate a decision they might in fact have made. We were encouraged to find that many respondents approved our draft test, and we have been able to build on it while taking into account suggestions made on consultation. Although one respondent argued that the whole idea of a test of capacity was ill-conceived and unhelpful, many said that it was vital to have a clear test, and one which catered explicitly for partial and fluctuating capacity. Professor Michael Gunn has referred to 'the virtue of certainty' and written that our proposals for a statutory test of capacity will be welcomed, 'if for no other reason than introducing certainty and clarity'.

3.7   The present law offers a number of tests of capacity depending on the type of decision in issue. Case-law has offered answers to some problems put to it; individual statutes include occasional definitions; the Mental Health Act Code of Practice deals in some detail with capacity to make medical treatment decisions; and Part VII of the 1983 Act addresses capacity in relation to the management of 'property and affairs'. For the purposes of our new legislative scheme, a single statutory definition should be adopted. We turn now to consider the terms of such a definition.

A diagnostic threshold

3.8   In the consultation papers we suggested that a person (other than someone unable to communicate) should not be found to lack capacity unless he or she is first found to be suffering from 'mental disorder' as defined in the Mental Health Act 1983. The arguments for and against such a diagnostic hurdle are very finely balanced and they are set out in full in Consultation Paper No 128. In the event, most respondents agreed with our preliminary view that a diagnostic hurdle did have a role to play in any definition of incapacity, in particular in ensuring that the test is stringent enough *not* to catch large numbers of people who make unusual or unwise decisions. There may also be a small number of cases where a finding of incapacity could lead to action which could amount to 'detention' as defined in the European Convention of Human Rights. The case-law of the European Court of Human Rights requires that any such detention should be pursuant to a finding of unsoundness of mind based on 'objective medical expertise'. Although we gave very careful consideration to the arguments against the inclusion of any diagnostic threshold, we have concluded that such a threshold would provide a significant protection and would in no sense prejudice or stigmatise those who are in need of help with decision-making.

3.9 That said, a significant number of respondents, including many who favoured a diagnostic threshold of some sort, expressed misgivings about the new legislation 'coat-tailing' on the statutory shorthand of 'mental disorder' and the definition set out in the Mental Health Act 1983. The full definition in the 1983 Act is that '"mental disorder" means mental illness, arrested or incomplete development of mind, psychopathic disorder *and any other disorder or disability of mind*'. Although this definition is extremely broad and may well cover all the conditions which a diagnostic threshold should cover we no longer favour its incorporation into the new legislation. We learned at first hand in working party meetings how 'mental disorder' is equated in many minds, both lay and professional, with the much narrower phenomenon of psychiatric illness or with the criteria for compulsory detention under the Mental Health Act 1983.

3.10 Many respondents raised these issues of 'mind-set' about the phrase 'mental disorder'. Medical professionals advised us that doctors who are not professionally involved with the treatment of psychiatric illnesses (surgeons, gynaecologists, obstetricians or intensive care specialists, for example) have no familiarity with the provisions or definitions of the Mental Health Act and assume that it is irrelevant to their own work. Those who work with people with learning disabilities argued that it would be rare for their clients to have any involvement with the psychiatric specialism. They suggested that the shorthand 'mental disorder' is not appropriate and that its adoption could discourage the use of the new scheme for this group of people, for whom it is in fact most specifically designed. A similar point was made in relation to people with brain damage, autism and sensory deficit.

3.11 There may, moreover, be an issue of substance here as well as one of 'mind-set'. Many respondents to our medical treatment consultation paper were concerned to ensure that all the conditions which can result in incapacity to take medical decisions should be included in the new definition. Some of these will have very little in common with psychiatric illnesses or congenital impairments of the kind addressed by the provisions of the 1983 Act. It was argued that some relevant conditions might not qualify as disorders or disabilities 'of mind' at all. Temporary toxic confusional states (whether resulting from prescription or illicit drugs, alcohol or other toxins) and neurological disorders were given as examples. Some doctors would argue that these are properly labelled disorders of *brain* rather than mind. One respondent pointed out that women can lack capacity to take obstetric decisions after prolonged labour, and queried whether the effects of pain and exhaustion were a disability 'of mind'. We are persuaded that there are many good reasons for departing from the 1983 Act definition.

3.12 We take the view that (except in cases where the person is unable to communicate) a new test of capacity should require that a person's inability to arrive at a decision should be linked to the existence of a 'mental disability'. The adoption of the phrase 'mental disability' will distinguish this requirement from the language of the Mental Health Act 1983 and will stress the importance of a mental condition which has a *disabling effect* on the person's capacity.

'We *recommend* that the expression "mental disability" in the new legislation should mean any disability or disorder of the mind or brain, whether permanent or temporary, which results in an impairment or disturbance of mental functioning.'

3.13 We took the provisional view in the consultation papers that those who cannot communicate decisions should be included within the scope of the new jurisdiction. We had in mind particularly those who are unconscious. In some rare conditions a conscious patient may be known to retain a level of cognitive functioning but the brain may be completely unable to communicate with the body or with the outside world. In other cases, particularly after a stroke, it may not be possible to say whether or not there is cognitive dysfunction. It can, however, be said that the patient cannot communicate any decision he or she may make. In either case, decisions may have to be made on behalf of such people, and only two respondents expressed the purist view that they should be excluded from our new jurisdiction because they do not suffer from true 'mental incapacity'. It appears to us appropriate that they should be brought within the scope of our new legislation rather than being left to fend for themselves within the uncertain and inadequate principles of the common law.

The definition of incapacity

3.14   The functional approach means that the new definition of incapacity should emphasise its decision-specific nature. A diagnostic threshold of 'mental disability' should be included, except in cases of inability to communicate.

'We *recommend* that legislation should provide that a person is without capacity if at the material time he or she is:

(1)   unable by reason of mental disability to make a decision on the matter in question, or

(2)   unable to communicate a decision on that matter because he or she is unconscious or for any other reason.'

(1)   Inability to make a decision

3.15   It would defeat our aim of offering clarity and certainty were no further guidance given as to the meaning of the phrase 'unable to make a decision'. In the consultation papers we identified two broad sub-sets within this category, one based on inability to understand relevant information and the other based on inability to make a 'true choice'. Although many respondents expressed disquiet about the elusiveness of the concept of 'true choice', there was broad agreement that incapacity cannot in every case be ascribed to an inability to understand information. It may arise from an inability to use or negotiate information which has been understood. In most cases an assessor of capacity will have to consider both the ability to understand information and the ability to use it in exercising choice, so that the two 'sub-sets' should not be seen as mutually exclusive. This was emphasised by Thorpe J in the very important High Court case of *Re C (Adult: Refusal of Treatment)*, perhaps the first reported case to give any clear guidance on questions of capacity in relation to medical treatment decisions. Thorpe J had to make a preliminary finding as to whether the patient concerned had capacity to refuse consent to amputation of his leg. He found it helpful to analyse decision-making capacity in three stages: first, comprehending and retaining information, second, believing it and, third, 'weighing it in the balance to arrive at choice.' He mentioned that we had proposed a similar approach in our consultation paper. Thorpe J adopted the same approach to the question of capacity in the later case of *B v Croydon District Health Authority*, while upholding a wide view of the scope of section 63 of the Mental Health Act 1983, which authorises treatment for mental disorder regardless of capacity and consent.

(a)   Understanding or retaining information

3.16   Respondents favoured our suggestion that it was more realistic to test whether a person can understand information, than to test whether he or she can understand 'the nature of' an action or decision. It was, however, suggested that an ability to 'appreciate' information about the likely consequences of a decision might be conceptually different from an ability to understand such information. We prefer to approach this question in a slightly different way, on the basis that information about consequences is one of the sorts of information which a person with capacity understands. Respondents supported the express mention of foreseeable consequences in our draft test, and we still see advantage in drawing attention to the special nature of information about likely consequences, as information which will in every case be relevant to the decision.

'We *recommend* that a person should be regarded as unable to make a decision by reason of mental disability if the disability is such that, at the time when the decision needs to be made, he or she is unable to understand or retain the information relevant to the decision, including information about the reasonably foreseeable consequences of deciding one way or another or failing to make the decision.'

(b) Using information

3.17 There are cases where the person concerned can understand information but where the effects of a mental disability prevent him or her from using that information in the decision-making process. We explained in Consultation Paper No 128 that certain compulsive conditions cause people who are quite able to absorb information to arrive, inevitably, at decisions which are unconnected to the information or their understanding of it. An example is the anorexic who always decides not to eat. There are also some people who, because of a mental disability, are unable to exert their will against some stronger person who wishes to influence their decisions or against some *force majeure* of circumstances. As Thorpe J said in *Re C*, some people can understand information but are prevented by their disability from being able to believe it. We originally suggested that such cases could be described as cases where incapacity resulted from inability to make a 'true choice'. Common to all these cases is the fact that the person's eventual decision is divorced from his or her ability to understand the relevant information. Emphasising that the person must be able to use the information which he or she has successfully understood in the decision-making process deflects the complications of asking whether a person needs to 'appreciate' information as well as understand it. A decision based on a compulsion, the overpowering will of a third party or any other inability to act on relevant information as a result of mental disability is not a decision made by a person with decision-making capacity.

'We *recommend* that a person should be regarded as unable to make a decision by reason of mental disability if the disability is such that, at the time when the decision needs to be made, he or she is unable to make a decision based on the information relevant to the decision, including information about the reasonably foreseeable consequences of deciding one way or another or failing to make the decision.'

Broad terms and simple language

3.18 In the draft test of incapacity which appeared in the consultation papers we suggested that a person should be found to lack capacity if he or she was unable to understand an explanation of the relevant information *in broad terms and simple language*. Many respondents supported this attempt to ensure that persons should not be found to lack capacity unless and until someone has gone to the trouble to put forward a suitable explanation of the relevant information. This focus requires an assessor to approach any apparent inability as something which may be dynamic and changeable. As one commentator on our original draft test has written, we chose 'to import the patient's right to information by implication into the test of capacity'. Further guidance on the way the new statutory language may impinge on the methods of assessing capacity in day to day practice should be given in a code of practice accompanying the legislation.

'We *recommend* that a person should not be regarded as unable to understand the information relevant to a decision if he or she is able to understand an explanation of that information in broad terms and simple language.'

Excluding imprudence

3.19 In the consultation papers we invited views on the need for a proviso stipulating that a person should not be regarded as lacking capacity because the decision made would not have been made by a person of ordinary prudence. We provisionally doubted the need for any such proviso. Those we consulted, however, overwhelmingly urged upon us the importance of making such an express stipulation. This would emphasise the fact that the 'outcome' approach to capacity has been rejected, while recognising that it is almost certainly in daily use.

'We *recommend* that a person should not be regarded as unable to make a decision by reason of mental disability merely because he or she makes a decision which would not be made by a person of ordinary prudence.'

(2)   Inability to communicate a decision
3.20   As most of our respondents appreciated, we intend the category of people unable to communicate a decision to be very much a residual category. This test will have no relevance if the person is known to be incapable of deciding (even if *also* unable to communicate) but will be available if the assessor does not know, one way or the other, whether the person is capable of deciding or not. Contrary to the views of one expert commentator, 'inability to communicate a decision' cannot be paraphrased as 'inability to express a view', nor should it be taken to apply to persons with the more severe forms of mental disability. This second category is a fall-back where the assessor cannot say whether any decision has been validly made or made at all but nonetheless can say that the person concerned cannot communicate any decision.
3.21   In relation to persons who are not simply unconscious, many respondents made the point that strenuous steps must be taken to assist and facilitate communication before any finding of incapacity is made. Specialists with appropriate skills in verbal and non-verbal communication should be brought in where necessary.

'We *recommend* that a person should not be regarded as unable to communicate his or her decision unless all practicable steps to enable him or her to do so have been taken without success.'

The assessment of incapacity: a code of practice
3.22   Many respondents who commented on our provisional tests of incapacity and were content with the broad outlines of the proposed test addressed themselves to technical questions about the methods of assessment and testing which should be applied. Some were insistent that outdated and discredited psychometric testing should not be used. There was grave concern about the concept of 'mental age'. We found the arguments against the use of any such concept extremely compelling. It is unhelpful to discuss, for example, the merits of sterilisation as opposed to barrier contraception for a mature woman with a learning disability on the basis that she is somehow 'equivalent' to a child of three. Particular professional bodies, for example the College of Speech and Language Therapists and the British Psychological Society, asserted that their members had the relevant skills to assess mental capacity. Others reminded us that cultural, ethnic and religious values should always be respected by any assessor of capacity. These are all very important matters, albeit not apt subjects for primary legislation. One of the matters which should certainly be covered by a code of practice is the way in which any assessment of capacity should be carried out.

'We *recommend* that the Secretary of State should prepare and from time to time revise a code of practice for the guidance of persons assessing whether a person is or is not without capacity to make a decision or decisions on any matters.'

Existing tests of capacity
3.23   The new test of incapacity in our draft Bill is expressed to apply 'for the purposes of [Part I of] this Act.' Schedule 8 to our draft Bill makes consequential amendments to existing statutes, inserting the new definition of what it means to be 'without capacity' into any provisions which currently depend on the test in Part VII of the Mental Health Act 1983. We did not consult on the need to replace any existing definitions of capacity *at common law* with the new statutory definition, and our draft Bill makes no attempt to do this. After implementation of the new statutory definition, it is likely that common law judges would consider it and then adopt it if they saw fit. The new definition expands upon, rather than contradicting, the terms of the existing common law tests. The only point of difference is the provision requiring an

explanation of the relevant information to have been made, if a finding of incapacity is to have prospective effect.

5.1.2 Informal admission and treatment

Before going on to examine compulsory powers under the Act, it is worth bearing in mind that the policy behind the Act is not to discourage individuals from seeking treatment on an informal basis. The legal background is explained by Dr Philip Fennell in the following extract from his article 'Doctor knows best? Therapeutic Detention under common law, the Mental Health Act, and the European Convention' [*Medical Law Review* vol. 6 (1998)]. This is followed by s. 131 Mental Health Act, the present provision relating to informal admission and treatment.

'Informal admission' was introduced in the Mental Health Act 1959 (the '1959 Act'). It meant that the person was admitted to hospital without using statutory powers of detention. It was intended to apply not only to patients with sufficient mental capacity actively and validly to consent to admission, but also to those who were incapable of giving a valid consent to admission and who were not actively resisting it. The thinking was that the latter group could be admitted without detention, as there was no detention unless the person was actively protesting against or resisting confinement. The crucial factor was not consent but *absence of dissent*. The intention behind the 1959 Act was to reserve detention under the Act for the minority of patients who were resisting hospital treatment.

The introduction of informal admission was the culmination of a process of de-regulation of psychiatry, freeing it from what has been described by Jones as the excessive legalism of the Lunacy Act 1890. Section 4 of the 1890 Act reflected a concern to ensure that all psychiatric admission would be subject to judicial control by providing that no-one could be received into a public hospital without first being certified as being insane and in need of care and treatment by a Justice of the Peace. There was limited provision under the 1890 Act for people to *remain* in hospital as voluntary boarders but, until 1930, there was a statutory prohibition on *admission* without certificate, subject only to limited exceptions, including a special exemption granted in 1915 to allow the newly founded Maudsley Hospital to admit patients voluntarily.

The Mental Treatment Act 1930 reflected an unprecedented acceptance of the profession's case for relaxation of the regulation imposed on it, most notably by the introduction of a *voluntary* admission procedure. This was done by way of exception to the prohibition on admission without certification in section 4 of the 1890 Act. Patients could be admitted voluntarily if they had the necessary capacity and agreed to enter hospital. Judicial certification was not abolished, but a 'counter-system' was set up which it was hoped would eventually take over from it in the majority of cases. Voluntary admission was by written application to the person in charge of the hospital. Voluntary patients effectively remained under doctors' orders because they had to give three days' notice before leaving the hospital, to allow for certification if it was considered necessary. Voluntary admissions rose from around 50 per cent of all admissions in 1947 until 1957 and 1958, when they accounted for between 82 and 85 per cent (73,000) of all admissions, with certifications running at around 14,000 per year.

Voluntary admission provided for those who were capable of consenting to admission, but thousands of in-patients lacked mental capacity. The 1930 Act also tried to take these latter patients out of the judicial certification net by providing for 'temporary' compulsory admission without judicial certification of patients who were 'incapable of expressing themselves willing or unwilling to receive such treatment.' These were called 'non-volitional' patients, ... In addition to being non-volitional the person had to be suffering from mental illness, and had to be likely to benefit from temporary treatment. A Board of Control Circular declared that a refusing patient, no matter how irrational, could not be temporarily admitted, but a person who was confused and incoherent to the extent that they were willing one minute and refusing the next could be. Applications were made not to a judicial authority but to the person in charge of the hospital. Even though there was no 'full certificate of insanity', patients temporarily admitted as non-volitional were still detained, and the maximum duration was one year. Despite the Board's, encouragement, there were only ever about 500 patients under temporary admission at any one time in England and Wales, and temporary admissions never exceeded four per cent of the total.

...

Section 5 of the Mental Health Act 1959 (now s. 131 of the 1983 Act) introduced informal admission. Section 4 of the 1890 Act was repealed. *The Royal Commission on the Law Relating to Mental Illness and Mental Deficiency 1954–1957* (the Percy Commission) reported that almost all the evidence put before them was 'in favour of reducing compulsory powers to a minimum and of treating mentally disordered patients on the same basis as other sick or handicapped patients, without certification.' The Percy Commission urged that non-resisting incapable patients with a learning disability or with a mental illness should be admitted informally without use of powers of compulsion.

'We ... recommend that the law and its administration should be altered, in relation to all forms of mental disorder, by abandoning the assumption that compulsory powers must be used unless the patient can express a positive desire for treatment and replacing this by the offer of care without deprivation of liberty, to all who need it and are not unwilling to receive it. All hospitals providing psychiatric treatment should be free to admit patients for any length of time without any legal formality and without power to detain.'

So when s. 5 of the 1959 Act allowed patients to '*be admitted* [rather than admit themselves] without any order or application rendering them liable to be detained', the intention was to amalgamate voluntary and 'non-volitional' status. Consent was no longer necessary for non-compulsory admission. Henceforth absence of dissent was the key concept, and the key indicia of dissent were physical resistance to admission, and persistent attempts to leave. There were several policy reasons for this approach. First, there was felt to be a stigma in detention (the pre-1959 phrase was certification — hence 'certifiable lunatic') and that this stigma ought not to be applied to people who were incapable and helpless. Families were reluctant to be involved in the process of compulsory admission, but they would be more willing to admit their relative without formality. Secondly, there had been a strong body of evidence to the Percy Commission from the medical professional bodies against the legalistic approach of the 1890 Act, to the effect that judicial certification procedures delayed necessary treatment in many cases. In future all informal admissions were to be arranged in the same way as admissions to general hospitals, with no need for a signed application from the patient.

Section 131 of the 1983 Act re-enacts section 5 of the 1959 Act.

Section 131 provides:
131. Informal admission of patients
(1) Nothing in this Act shall be construed as preventing a patient who requires treatment for mental disorder from being admitted to any hospital or mental nursing home in pursuance of arrangements made in that behalf and without any application, order or direction rendering him liable to be detained under this Act, or from remaining in any hospital or mental nursing home in pursuance of such arrangements after he has ceased to be so liable to be detained.
(2) In the case of a minor who has attained the age of 16 years and is capable of expressing his own wishes, any such arrangements as are mentioned in subsection (1) above may be made,

carried out and determined even though there are one or more persons who have parental responsibility for him (within the meaning of the Children Act 1989).

Fennell continues:

Nowadays the vast majority of patients admitted to psychiatric hospitals are informal. In 1996–7 24,200 patients were admitted under powers of detention. There are on average 270,000 informal admissions per year. In 1994–5 there were 216,240 informal admissions to the mental illness specialties, and 53,850 informal admissions to the mental handicap specialties. It is impossible to judge what proportion of informal admissions are of patients who are incapable of giving valid consent as opposed to truly voluntary patients.

Section 5 of the 1959 Act did not create any new admission powers, but it did create a new 'informal status' whereby 'non-volitional' patients may be admitted and retained without using compulsory powers, as long as they did not resist or try to leave. If they did they would have to be detained.

...

What does informal status mean? It does not entitle the patient to leave the hospital at will, contrary to the impression given by the Code of Practice on the Mental Health Act 1983 which affirms the importance of informal patients understanding 'their right to leave hospital'. The 'right' is subject to significant limitations. Under the 1983 Act, doctors have the power to detain any in-patient for up to 72 hours and mental health nurses can detain psychiatric in-patients for up to six hours pending an application for their compulsory admission. Even in-patients receiving treatment for a physical illness may be detained if the doctor in charge of their treatment considers that they ought to be detained for psychiatric treatment. Going into hospital for any form of in-patient treatment, physical or mental, in theory subjects a person to restrictions on their right to self-discharge, but obviously in practice the holding power is more likely to be and is predominantly used on in-patients receiving treatment for mental disorder. For informal patients truly to understand their 'right' to leave hospitals would have to tell them that it may be removed by decisions of doctors or nurses to restrain them from leaving hospital.

Even if there were an unlimited right for informal patients to leave hospital, to speak of mentally incapacitated patients having it makes little sense. There may be nowhere else capable of providing the care which the patient needs, he may have no home to go to and be too dependent to survive in sheltered accommodation. Any hospital or nursing home accepting responsibility for looking after mentally incapacitated informal patients thereby assumes a duty of care towards them. That duty of care extends to preventing them from leaving the hospital premises where to do so would put them at risk. Not being detained does not make an informal patient 'freer'. Paradoxically it may make them less free, because if formally detained, they would have access to statutory safeguards such as review of detention by a mental health review tribunal, the right to a second opinion if treated for mental disorder without consent, and the benefit of the complaints jurisdiction of the MHAC.

It is a general principle of law that treatment may only be given with the consent of the patient or on the basis of some legal justification, such as necessity in cases of emergency. Similarly, a person cannot be detained against his or her will without some legal justification, though, as the extract from Fennell indicates, powers are available to limit the right of discharge from hospital. But these principles presuppose a person with the capacity to make these decisions, and, as the *R v Bournewood Community and Mental Health NHS Trust ex parte L* [1999] 1 AC 458 illustrates, there are patients who lack such capacity yet can, it seems, be treated informally rather than admitted or treated under compulsory powers.

The facts are set out by Lord Goff:

My Lords, the respondent, Mr L ('L') is 48 years old. He is autistic, and is profoundly mentally retarded. He is unable to speak, and his level of understanding is severely limited. It follows that he has always been incapable of consenting to medical treatment. He is frequently agitated; he has no sense of danger, and has a history of self-harming behaviour.

From the age of 13, for a period of over 30 years, he was a resident at the Bournewood Hospital, which is now run by the appellant NHS Trust. In March 1994, however, he was discharged on a trial basis into the community. He went to live with paid carers, Mr and Mrs E; but since he had not been finally discharged, the trust remained responsible for his care and treatment. Mr and Mrs E became very fond of him and, with their children, regarded him as one of the family.

On 22 July 1997, at the Cranstock Day Centre which was regularly attended by him, L became particularly agitated, hitting himself on the head with his fists and banging his head against a wall. Mr and Mrs E could not be contacted. The day centre got in touch with a local doctor, who attended and administered a sedative. The social worker who had overall responsibility for him was also contacted. She attended and, on her recommendation, he was taken by ambulance to the accident and emergency department at the Bournewood Hospital. As a result of the sedative given to him, he became calm and relaxed; but while at the department he became increasingly agitated. He was assessed by a psychiatrist as being in need of in-patient treatment. He made no attempt to leave, and was transferred to the behavioural unit at the hospital. His consultant, Dr Manjubhashini, decided that his best interests required that he should be readmitted for in-patient treatment. She considered whether it was necessary to detain him under the provisions of the Mental Health Act 1983 but decided that this was not necessary because he appeared to be fully compliant and did not resist admission. I shall have to refer to her evidence in more detail at a later stage. He was therefore admitted informally.

The doctors and staff at the hospital responsible for treating L regarded it as very important for his future that he should be returned to live with Mr and Mrs E as soon as practical. But Mr and Mrs E have unfortunately not been satisfied as to the trust's motives. Dr Manjubhashini wrote to Mr and Mrs E explaining what was proposed, discussing meetings and visits by Mr and Mrs E to see L, but no programme of visits was achieved. In the result, proceedings were commenced in the name of L against the trust. I add in parenthesis that, when this matter was coming before the Court of Appeal, the court adjourned the hearing of the appeal to see if a suitable third party could achieve a reconciliation between Mr and Mrs E and those responsible for treating L; but Mr and Mrs E took the view that it would still be preferable if the legal position was clarified and so the appeal proceeded.

He then explains how the case had been determined in the lower courts. The decision of the Court of Appeal was particularly contentious, for reasons he explains:

Before Owen J and the Court of Appeal, the matter proceeded as follows. For L, it was submitted that he had been wrongfully detained in the hospital without his consent. In answer to that submission, the trust argued, first, that he had been informally admitted under section 131(1) of the Act of 1983, which provides:

'Nothing in this Act shall be construed as preventing a patient who requires treatment for mental disorder from being admitted to any hospital or mental nursing home in pursuance of arrangements made in that behalf and without any application, order or direction rendering him liable to be detained under this Act, or from remaining in any hospital or mental nursing home in pursuance of such arrangements after he has ceased to be so liable to be detained.'

It was further submitted that informal admission under section 131(1) does not require consent on the part of the patient, it being enough that he does not dissent from being admitted. Next, the trust submitted that, once L had been lawfully admitted, the treatment he received was lawful under the common law doctrine of necessity. For L, it was submitted that detention was a question of objective fact. On the evidence, he had in fact been detained. He had been physically taken to the hospital; and Dr Manjubhashini had made it plain that, if he had resisted admission, she would certainly have detained him under the Act. Furthermore the comprehensive statutory regime ousted any common law jurisdiction under the doctrine of necessity. The judge accepted the argument of the trust. He held that L had not in fact been detained; he had been informally admitted under section 131(1), which applied not only to persons who consented but also to those who, like him, did not dissent from their admission, and he had been free to leave until Dr Manjubhashini or somebody else took steps to 'section' him or otherwise prevent him from leaving. Furthermore, the statutory scheme under the Act of 1983 included section 131(1), which contemplated the exercise of common law powers.

The Court of Appeal, however, took a different view. They held that L had in fact been detained. They said, ante, p. 465:

'In our judgment a person is detained in law if those who have control over the premises in which he is have the intention that he shall not be permitted to leave those premises and have the ability to prevent him from leaving. We have concluded that this was and is the position of L.'

Next they concluded that the Act did indeed create a complete regime which excluded the application of the common law doctrine of necessity. In so holding, they invoked the decision of your Lordships' House in the Scottish case of *B v Forsey*, 1988 SC(HL) 28. Section 131(1), they held, did not assist the trust, because it addresses only the position of a patient who is admitted and treated with consent. This seemed to them to be implicit from the wording of section 131(2). They accordingly allowed L's appeal. It is from that decision that the trust now appeals to this House, with the leave of the Court of Appeal.

The impact of the Court of Appeal's judgment

There can be no doubt that the decision of the Court of Appeal has caused grave concern among those involved in the care and treatment of mentally disordered persons. As a result, three parties applied for, and were granted, leave to intervene in the appeal before this House. They were the Secretary of State for Health, the Mental Health Act Commission ('the Commission') and the Registered Nursing Home Association ('the RNHA'). At the hearing of the appeal, the Secretary of State and the RNHA were represented by counsel (though counsel for the RNHA was in the event content to adopt the argument of counsel for the Secretary of State), and the Commission provided a written submission for the assistance of the Appellate Committee. I wish to express the gratitude of the committee for the assistance provided to them in this way.

In the light of this assistance, I am able to summarise the position which has arisen following the Court of Appeal's judgment as follows. First and foremost, the effect of the judgment is that large numbers of mental patients who would formerly not have to be compulsorily detained under the Act of 1983 will now have to be so detained. Inquiries by the Commission suggest that 'there will be an additional 22,000 detained patients resident on any one day as a consequence of the Court of Appeal judgment plus an additional 48,000 admissions per year under the Act.' This estimate should be set against the background that the average number of detained patients resident on any one day in England and Wales is approximately 13,000. (Andrea Humphrey, a civil servant of the Department of Health, gave a figure of 11,000 for those detained under the Act at any time prior to the judgment.) The Commission considered it to be very likely that the majority of patients to whom the Court of Appeal judgment applied would be patients in need of long term care; and further considered that, if the judgment is held to apply to patients receiving medical treatment for mental disorder in mental nursing homes not registered to receive detained patients, the above estimates were likely to be very much higher. It is obvious that there would in the result be a substantial impact on the available resources; the Commission recorded that the resource implications were likely to be considerable, not only for the mental health services and professionals who have to implement the Act, but also for Mental Health Review Tribunals and for the Commission itself. These concerns were also reflected in the affidavit sworn by Andrea Humphrey of the Department of Health, following widespread consultation. Deep concern about the effect of the judgment was expressed, in particular, by the President of the Royal Society of Psychiatrists, and the Chairman of the Faculty for Psychiatry and Old Age of that Society; and also by the Executive Director of the Alzheimer's Disease Society. The various responses referred not only to the impact on the patients themselves, but also to the resource implications and to the effect on relatives and carers.

The Commission also stated that the Court of Appeal's judgment had given rise to a number of legal uncertainties. Two particular questions, described by the Commission as being 'of enormous practical importance,' arose with regard to mental nursing homes, viz whether such homes were required to be registered to receive patients detained under the Act of 1983 before receiving patients like L, and whether homes not so registered are now obliged to register or to discharge such patients from their care. The RNHA is particularly anxious about the position of elderly patients who lack the capacity to consent. The RNHA is concerned to know whether it is necessary for nursing homes who have or are likely to have such patients in their care to be so registered (which would have significant cost, staffing and other implications for the proprietors of such homes), or to decline to admit or keep such patients. Similar questions were raised by the Commission in relation to residential care homes, respite care and temporary care arrangements.

On the other hand, as the Commission stressed, another result of the Court of Appeal's judgment was that, if patients such as L had to be compulsorily detained under the Act of 1983 in order to be admitted to hospital, they would reap the benefit of the safeguards written into the Act for the protection of patients compulsorily detained. It appears from the Commission's written submission that the lack of statutory safeguards for patients informally admitted to hospital has been a matter of concern for the Commission, and that this concern has been expressed not only by the Commission itself but also by the authors of authoritative textbooks on the subject. However, under section 121(4) of the Act of 1983 there is vested in the Secretary of State the power to 'direct the Commission to keep under review the care and treatment, or any aspect of the care and treatment, in hospitals and mental nursing homes of patients who are not liable to be detained under this Act.' During the course of the hearing, the appellate committee was assured by counsel for the Secretary of State that he has had the matter under consideration, but that hitherto he has not thought it right to exercise his power in this respect. In this connection, it is plain that he has to have regard to the resource implications of extension of the statutory safeguards to the very much larger number of patients who are informally admitted. At all events, this is a matter which is entirely for the Secretary of State, and not for your Lordships' House whose task is to construe, and to apply, the Act as it stands. To that task, I now turn.

...

Central to the argument advanced by Mr Pleming on behalf of the Secretary of State was the submission that, under the Act of 1983, persons suffering from mental disorder who are treated for their condition as in-patients in hospital fall into two categories.
(1)   Those patients who are compulsorily, and formally, admitted into hospital, against their will or regardless of their will, who are detained or liable to be detained in hospital. This category may be called 'compulsory patients.' They may be admitted under section 2 of the Act of 1983 (admission for assessment); section 3 (admission for treatment); section 4 (admission for assessment in cases of emergency); or section 5 (admission of patients already in hospital).

(2) Those patients who enter hospital as in-patients for treatment either (a) who, having the capacity to consent, do consent ('voluntary patients') or (b) who, though lacking capacity to consent, do not object ('informal patients'). Both are admitted under section 131(1) without the formalities and procedures for admission necessary for detention under the Act. Strictly speaking, therefore, both groups could be described as informal patients, but it is convenient to confine that description to those who are not voluntary patients.

As Mr Pleming stressed, section 131(1) of the Act of 1983 is in identical terms to section 5(1) of the Mental Health Act 1959. Furthermore the Act of 1959 was enacted following the Report of the Royal Commission on the Law Relating to Mental Illness and Mental Deficiency 1954–1957 (1957) (Cmnd 169) ('the Percy Commission'), which recommended that compulsory detention should only be employed in cases where it was necessary to do so. The Percy Commission's views, and recommendation on this point are to be found at pp. 100–101, paras 289–291 of their Report, which read:

'289.   We consider compulsion and detention quite unnecessary for a large number, probably the great majority, of the patients at present cared for in mental deficiency hospitals, most of whom are childlike and prepared to accept whatever arrangements are made for them. There is no more need to have power to detain these patients in hospital than in their own homes or any other place which they have no wish to leave. We strongly recommend that the principle of treatment without certification should be extended to them. Such a step should help to alter the whole atmosphere of this branch of the mental health services. Many parents of severely sub-normal children at present feel that they lose all their rights as parents when their child is admitted to hospital and automatically becomes subject to compulsory detention there. We have no doubt that the element of coercion also increases the resentment of some feebleminded psychopaths, and of their parents, when they are placed under "statutory supervision" or admitted to mental deficiency hospitals after leaving school, and that this makes it even more difficult than it need be to persuade them to regard these services in the same way as other social services and other types of hospital treatment, as services which are provided for their own benefit. Equally important, if the procedures which authorise detention become the exception rather than the rule, the attitude towards compulsion on the part of those administering the services should change. These procedures will no longer be a formality which must be gone through before any patient can be given the care he needs. It will be possible to consider the need for care and the justification for compulsion as two quite separate questions in a way which is not possible at present.'

'290.   Admission to hospital without using compulsory powers should also be possible for considerably more mentally ill patients than are at present admitted as voluntary patients ...'

'291.   We therefore recommend that the law and its administration should be altered, in relation to all forms of mental disorder, by abandoning the assumption that compulsory powers must be used unless the patient can express a positive desire for treatment, and replacing this by the offer of care, without deprivation of liberty, to all who need it and are not unwilling to receive it. All hospitals providing psychiatric treatment should be free to admit patients for any length of time without any legal formality and without power to detain.'

Here we find a central recommendation of the Percy Commission, and the mischief which it was designed to cure. This recommendation was implemented, in particular, by section 5(1) of the Act of 1959. That the Bill was introduced with that recommendation in mind is confirmed by ministerial statements made in Parliament at the time: see Hansard (HL Debates, 4 June 1959, cols. 668–669).

Following the enactment of the Act of 1959, section 5(1) was duly implemented in the manner foreshadowed by the Percy Commission, a practice which (as is plain from the evidence before the committee) has been continued under section 131(1) of the Act of 1983, which is in identical terms. It is little wonder therefore that the judgment of the Court of Appeal in the present case, which restricts section 131(1) to voluntary patients, should have caused the grave concern which has been expressed in the evidence, both (1) about the need, following the Court of Appeal's judgment, to invoke the power of compulsory detention in many cases, numbered in their thousands each year, which for nearly 40 years had not been necessary and would, on the view expressed by the Percy Commission, be wholly inappropriate, and (2) about doubts whether some categories of patients would or would not, in consequence of the judgment, require compulsory detention.

> …

I should briefly refer to section 131(2) of the Act of 1983, which was relied on by the Court of Appeal in support of their construction of section 131(1). Subsection (2) reads:
> 'In the case of a minor who has attained the age of 16 years and is capable of expressing his own wishes, any such arrangements as are mentioned in subsection (1) above may be made, carried out and determined [even though there are one or more persons who have parental responsibility for him (within the meaning of the Children Act 1989)].'

The words which I have placed in square brackets were substituted by the Children Act 1989. The section in its original form was identical to section 5(2) of the Act of 1959, except that the word 'minor' was substituted in 1983 for the word 'infant.' It is plain, in my opinion, that subsection (2) can have no impact upon the admission of informal patients under subsection (1) which is concerned with patients who consent as well as those who do not object. It is the former category that subsection (2) addresses, with special reference to minors.

For these reasons, I am unable with all respect to accept the opinion of the Court of Appeal on the crucial question of the meaning of section 131(1). I wish to stress, however, that the statutory history of the subsection, which puts the matter beyond all doubt, appears not to have been drawn to the attention of the Court of Appeal, and that they did not have the benefit, as we have had, of assistance from counsel appearing for the Secretary of State.

> …

He then sets out the basis on which informal patients are treated and concludes:

I turn briefly to the basis upon which a hospital is entitled to treat, and to care for, patients who are admitted as informal patients under section 131(1) but lack the capacity to consent to such treatment or care. It was plainly the statutory intention that such patients would indeed be cared for, and receive such treatment for their condition as might be prescribed for them in their best interests. Moreover the doctors in charge would, of course, owe a duty of care to such a patient in their care. Such treatment and care can, in my opinion, be justified on the basis of the common law doctrine of necessity, as to which see the decision of your Lordships' House in *In re F (Mental Patient: Sterilisation)* [1990] 2 AC 1. It is not therefore necessary to find such justification in the statute itself, which is silent on the subject. It might, I imagine, be possible to discover an implication in the statute providing similar justification; but even assuming that to be right, it is difficult to imagine that any different result would flow from such a statutory implication. For present purposes, therefore, I think it appropriate to base justification for treatment and care of such patients on the common law doctrine.

It will be seen that, on Lord Goff's analysis, treatment of those unable to consent but not unwilling to be treated was permissible under the Act. On this, all the judges agreed. On the question whether L was detained, the judges were divided, with the majority deciding that L was not unlawfully detained. Lord Steyn, with whom Lord Nolan agreed, thought that L was in fact detained. His careful analysis of both issues is indicated in the following extract. His reluctant concurrence with the conclusion reached by the other judges is as noteworthy as his robust approach to the question of detention:

It is, of course, true that health care professionals will almost always act in the best interests of patients. But Parliament devised the protective scheme of the Act of 1983 as being necessary in order to guard amongst other things against misjudgment and lapses by the professionals involved in health care. This point requires some explanation. A hospital psychiatrist who decides that a patient ought to be admitted to hospital and treated makes a judgment which may be controversial. The clinical question may arise whether the patient is in truth incapacitated. The importance of this issue is described by *Grisso and Appelbaum, Assessing Competence to Consent to Treatment: A Guide to Physicians and Other Health Officials* (1998), p. 1:

'Competence is a pivotal concept in decision-making about medical treatment. Competent patients' decisions about accepting or rejecting proposed treatment are respected. Incompetent patients' choices, on the other hand, are put to one side, and alternative mechanisms for deciding about their care are sought. Thus, enjoyment of one of the most fundamental rights of a free society — the right to determine what shall be done to one's body — turns on the possession of those characteristics that we view as constituting decision-making competent.'

And the same authors have demonstrated how complex such an issue of competence may be: see also *Appelbaum, Almost a Revolution, Mental Health Law and The Limits of Change* (1994), ch. 4. Yet on the issue of competence depends a patient's right of autonomy: compare, however, the psychiatric argument for a 'trade-off' between competence and the consequences of treating or not treating: Eastman and Hope, 'The Ethics of Enforced Medical Treatment: The Balance Model.' Journal of Applied Philosophy (1998), Vol. 5, no. 1, p. 49. Moreover, the broad question of what is in an incompetent patient's best interests may involve a weighing of conflicting medical and social considerations. And, in regard to treatment, the moral right of the patient to be treated with dignity may pose acute problems. These are no doubt some of the reasons why Parliament thought it necessary to create a system of safeguards for those admitted under the Act of 1983. Parliament was not content in this complex and sensitive area to proceed on the paternalistic basis that the doctor is always right.

If the decision of the Court of Appeal is reversed almost all the basic protections under the Act of 1983 will be inapplicable to compliant incapacitated patients: see section 57(2) for an exception. The result would be an indefensible gap in our mental health law. In oral argument counsel for the Secretary of State for Health did not seek to justify such differential treatment on the grounds of resource implications. That is understandable. After all, how we address the intractable problems of mental health care for all classes of mentally incapacitated patients must be a touchstone of our maturity as a civilised society. Counsel for the Secretary of State did not seek to justify such differential treatment on the grounds of the views and wishes of health care professionals. That is also understandable. If protection is necessary to guard against misjudgment and professional lapses, the confident contrary views of professionals ought not to prevail. Professions are seldom enthusiastic about protective measures to guard against lapses by their members. And health care professionals are probably no different. But the law would be defective if it failed to afford adequate protective remedies to a vulnerable group of incapacitated mental patients.

For these reasons I would have wished to uphold the judgment of the Court of Appeal if that were possible. But as the issues were intensively probed in oral argument it became clear to me that, on a contextual interpretation of the Act of 1983, this course was not open to the House.

...

Detention
It is unnecessary to attempt a comprehensive definition of detention. In my view, this case falls on the wrong side of any reasonable line that can be drawn between what is or what is not

imprisonment or detention. The critical facts are as follows. (1) When on 22 July 1979 at the day centre L became agitated and started injuring himself, he was sedated and then physically supported and taken to the hospital. Even before sedation he was unable to express dissent to his removal to hospital. (2) Health care professionals exercised effective power over him. If L had physically resisted, the psychiatrist would immediately have taken steps to ensure his compulsory admission. (3) In hospital staff regularly sedated him. That ensured that he remained tractable. This contrasts with the position when he was with carers: they seldom resorted to medication and then only in minimal doses. (4) The psychiatrist vetoed visits by the carers to L. She did so, as she explained to the carers, in order to ensure that L did not try to leave with them. The psychiatrist told the carers that L would be released only when she, and other health care professionals, deemed it appropriate. (5) While L was not in a locked ward, nurses closely monitored his reactions. Nurses were instructed to keep him under continuous observation and did so.

Counsel for the trust and the Secretary of State argued that L was in truth always free not to go to the hospital and subsequently to leave the hospital. This argument stretches credulity to breaking point. The truth is that for entirely bona fide reasons, conceived in the best interests of L, any possible resistance by him was overcome by sedation, by taking him to hospital, and by close supervision of him in hospital. And, if L had shown any sign of wanting to leave, he would have been firmly discouraged by staff and, if necessary, physically prevented from doing so. The suggestion that L was free to go is a fairy tale.

At one stage counsel for the trust suggested that L was not detained because he lacked the necessary will, or more precisely the capacity to grant or refuse consent. That argument was misconceived. After all, an unconscious or drugged person can be detained: see *Meering* v *Grahame-White Aviation Co. Ltd* (1919) 122 L.T. 44, 53–54, *per* Atkin LJ (dictum approved in *Murray* v *Ministry of Defence* [1988] 1 WLR 692, 701–702, *per* Lord Griffiths). In my view L was detained because the health care professionals intentionally assumed control over him to such a degree as to amount to complete deprivation of his liberty.

Justification

It is now necessary to consider whether there was lawful authority to justify the detention and any treatment of L. This is a matter of statutory construction. But it is important to approach the mental health legislation against the context of the principles of the common law. The starting point of the common law is that when a person lacks capacity, for whatever reason, to take decisions about medical treatment, it is necessary for other persons, with appropriate qualifications, to take such decisions for him: *In re F. (Mental Patient: Sterilisation)* [1990] 2 AC 1, 55H, *per* Lord Brandon of Oakbrook. The principle of necessity may apply. For the purposes of the present case it has been assumed by all counsel that the requirements of the principle are simply that (1) there must be 'a necessity to act when it is not practicable to communicate with the assisted person' and (2) 'that the action taken must be such as a reasonable person would in all circumstances take, acting in the best interests of the assisted person:' *In re F.* [1990] 2 AC 1, 75H *per* Lord Goff of Chieveley. There was not unanimity on this point in *In re F.* But I am content to approach the matter in the same way as counsel did: see, however, *Feldman, Civil Liberties & Human Rights in England and Wales* (1993), pp. 147–150 for a critical appraisal of *In re F.* Against this common law background the Percy Report recommended a shift from the 'legalism' whereby hospital patients were 'certified' by special procedures, to a situation in which most patients would be 'informally' received in hospital, the term 'informally' signifying 'without any legal formality.' This was to be achieved by replacing the existing system 'by the offer of care, without deprivation of liberty, to all who need it and are not unwilling to receive it:' see the Report of the Royal Commission on the Law Relating to Mental Illness and Mental Deficiency 1954–1957 (1957) (Cmnd. 169), p. 101, para. 291. The desired objective was to avoid stigmatising patients and to avoid where possible the adverse effects of 'sectioning' patients. Where admission to hospital was required compulsion was to be regarded as a measure of last resort. The Mental Health Act 1959 introduced the recommended changes. Section 5(1) was the critical provision. The marginal note reads 'Informal admission of patients.' Section 5(1) provides:

'Nothing in this Act shall be construed as preventing a patient who requires treatment for mental disorder from being admitted to any hospital or mental nursing home in pursuance of arrangements made in that behalf and without any application, order or direction rendering him liable to be detained under this Act, or from remaining in any hospital or mental nursing home in pursuance of such arrangements after he has ceased to be so liable to be detained.'

Counsel appearing on behalf of L accepted that the effect of section 5 was to leave in place the common law principle of necessity as a justification for informally receiving in hospital or mental nursing homes compliant incapacitated patients.

In 1982 Parliament substantially amended the Act of 1959. In 1983 Parliament enacted a consolidating statute with amendments, namely the Mental Health Act 1983. By section 131(1) of the Act of 1983 the provisions of section 5(1) of the Act of 1959 were re-enacted verbatim. And the same marginal note appears next to section 131. Prima facie section 131(1) must be given the same meaning as section 5(1). On this basis, section 131(1) also preserved the common law principle of necessity as a means of admitting compliant incapacitated individuals. But counsel for L submitted that section 131(1), unlike its predecessor, only applies to consenting capacitated patients. He argued that contextual differences between the statutes of 1959 and 1983 required the court to interpret the language of section 131(1) of the Act of 1983 in a narrower sense than section 5(1) of the Act of 1959. He relied in particular on the provisions of Part IV of the Act which are set out under the heading 'Consent to Treatment.' Part IV undoubtedly contains safeguards going beyond those in the Act of 1959, and also expressly made some of its provisions only applicable to those 'liable to be detained under this Act,' and others applicable also to 'patients not liable to be detained under this Act.' These provisions are not inconsistent with the interpretation that the meaning of section 131(1) of the Act of 1983 is the same as the meaning of section 5(1) of the Act of 1959. Making due allowance for the improved safeguards for detained patients in the Act of 1983, the differences relied on do not in truth touch on the issue before the House and do not warrant a radical reinterpretation of identical statutory wording. On orthodox principles of statutory interpretation the conclusion cannot be avoided that section 131(1) permits the admission of compliant incapacitated patients where the requirements of the principle of necessity are satisfied. Having had the benefit of the fuller argument produced by the intervention of the Secretary of State, I have to accept that the view of the Court of Appeal on the meaning of section 131(1) cannot be upheld.

...

The effect of the decision of the House of Lords
The general effect of the decision of the House is to leave compliant incapacitated patients without the safeguards enshrined in the Act of 1983. This is an unfortunate result. The Mental Health Act Commission has expressed concern about such informal patients in successive reports. And in a helpful written submission the Commission has again voiced those concerns and explained in detail the beneficial effects of the ruling of the Court of Appeal. The common law principle of necessity is a useful concept, but it contains none of the safeguards of the Act of 1983. It places effective and unqualified control in the hands of the hospital psychiatrist and other health care professionals. It is, of course, true that such professionals owe a duty of care to patients and that they will almost invariably act in what they consider to be the best interests of the patient. But neither habeas corpus nor judicial review are sufficient safeguards against misjudgments and professional lapses in the case of compliant incapacitated patients. Given that

such patients are diagnostically indistinguishable from compulsory patients, there is no reason to withhold the specific and effective protections of the Act of 1983 from a large class of vulnerable mentally incapacitated individuals. Their moral right to be treated with dignity requires nothing less. The only comfort is that counsel for the Secretary of State has assured the House that reform of the law is under active consideration.

In the light of this decision, the Code now provides:

2.7   Where admission to hospital is considered necessary and the patient is willing to be admitted informally this should in general be arranged. Compulsory admission powers should only be exercised in the last resort. Informal admission is usually appropriate when a mentally capable patient consents to admission, but not if detention is necessary because of the danger the patient presents to him or herself or others. Compulsory admission should be considered where a mentally capable patient's current medical state, together with reliable evidence of past experience, indicates a strong likelihood that he or she will have a change of mind about informal admission prior to actually being admitted to hospital, with a resulting risk to their health or safety or to the safety of other people.

2.8   If at the time of admission, the patient is mentally incapable of consent, but does not object to entering hospital and receiving care or treatment, admission should be informal (see paras 15.9–15.10 for assessment of capacity and 15.18–15.22 for the treatment of mentally incapacitated patients). The decision to admit a mentally incapacitated patient informally should be made by the doctor in charge of the patient's treatment in accordance with what is in the patient's best interests and is justifiable on the basis of the common law doctrine of necessity (see para. 5.21). It a patient lacks capacity at the time of an assessment or review, it is particularly important that both clinical and social care requirements are considered, and that account is taken of the patient's ascertainable wishes and feelings and the views of their immediate relatives and carers on what would be in the patient's best interests.

The White Paper *Reforming the Mental Health Act* (Cm 5016 (2000)) proposes a new legislative scheme for such patients:

6.1   Under the 1983 Act the large majority of patients who are subject to formal powers are people who resist care or treatment. But some patients who need treatment for serious mental disorder are not able, because of long-term mental incapacity, to consent to care or treatment, although they do not resist it. It is estimated that at any time there may be as many as 44,000 people in this category who are being cared for by specialist mental health services.

6.2   The need to consider safeguards for this group of patients was highlighted in a recent case concerning the care of a patient with severe learning disability.

6.3   It is neither appropriate nor necessary to make a patient with long-term mental incapacity subject to care and treatment under compulsory powers unless he or she poses a risk of serious harm to other people or resists necessary care and treatment. But, under the 1983 Act, without the use of compulsory powers, these patients do not have access to the safeguards that are available to patients who are subject to compulsory care and treatment.

6.4   New legislation will introduce a separate framework of safeguards for this group of patients to ensure that care and treatment is provided in a way that is consistent with their best interests and to bring them within the remit of the Commission for Mental Health. There will be a right to apply to the Tribunal to challenge any detention and for a review where there are concerns about the quality or nature of the patient's care and treatment.

6.5   The aim is to protect the interests of patients who, because of the nature of their mental disorder or because of other disabilities, are not able fully to express their wishes. In many cases such patients are not capable of giving voice to concerns about care and treatment through the normal complaints procedures. The focus of the safeguards will, therefore, be on the quality of care and treatment the patient receives, in particular to ensure that it is provided in an appropriate setting and without unnecessary coercion or deprivation of liberty.

6.6   The new framework of safeguards will potentially apply to any patient with long-term mental incapacity who is assessed as needing long-term care and/or treatment for serious mental disorder from specialist mental health services in his or her best interests. This might include, for example, patients with dementia, severe learning disability or brain injury. The new framework will apply to patients admitted to a hospital, or resident in a care home or similar establishment but not to a patient who is living independently in his or her own home, with or without the support of carers and others. The considerations that a clinical team needs to take into account in deciding what care and treatment may be in a patient's best interests will be as described in Chapter 3.

6.7   Under the new legislation, where a patient appears to meet the criteria set out above, his or her clinical supervisor will be required to arrange a full assessment and develop a care plan on the basis of the Care Programme Approach and the Care Plan guidance in Wales. The plan would need to cover all aspects of care and treatment including any steps taken to restrict the patient's freedom involving locking doors or the routine administration of sedatives. Such steps will only be justifiable if they are in the patient's best interests. The assessment may be carried out in a hospital or any other appropriate establishment or facility, for example a nursing home or care home where the patient is resident at the time. The clinical supervisor will be required to arrange for a doctor drawn from the panel set up to provide expert evidence to the Tribunal to examine the patient. The second opinion doctor will discuss the proposed care and treatment plan with the clinical supervisor, and if appropriate, suggest changes to it. Before finalising the plan, the clinical supervisor will be under a duty to ensure that the patient's carers and close relatives are also consulted. He or she will also be required to consult with a social care representative who will nominate a person to represent the patient.

6.8   The clinical supervisor will be required to notify the Commission for Mental Health that a plan is being drawn up and, unless there are exceptional circumstances, finalise it within 28 days.

6.9   The clinical supervisor will be required to place on record with the care and treatment plan a note certifying that, in his or her opinion:

- the care and treatment plan is in the patient's best interests;
- that the patient is not actively resisting care and treatment; and,
- does not pose a significant risk of serious harm to other people.

6.10   He or she must also provide copies of the agreed care and treatment plan for the patient and the nominated person, and register it with the hospital or care home responsible for the patient's care and treatment. The clinical supervisor will be expected to keep the care and treatment plan under review in accordance with normal procedures under the Care Programme Approach. In the case of a patient with a learning disability and long-term mental incapacity there may be occasions when he or she is better able to understand the nature of the choices they are being asked to make in a particular situation and this should be taken into account by the clinical team. It is therefore essential that patients' needs are regularly assessed, including their capacity to make choices and decisions, so that care and treatment plans can be reviewed and updated accordingly.

6.11   At any stage, the patient or his or her representative will be able to apply to the Tribunal either to challenge detention or for a review of the care and treatment plan. This might be appropriate, where for example there were concerns about the content or whether it was being delivered in accordance with the patient's best interests. In such a case the Tribunal will be expected to commission an up to date report from a doctor drawn from the expert panel as well as considering evidence from the clinical team, the nominated person and, if appropriate, the patient's carers or close relatives. The clinical supervisor will be required to take account of any changes to the care plan suggested by the Tribunal and, if necessary, to submit a revised care plan for formal approval. However, the expectation is that any dispute would normally be resolved informally through discussion with the clinical team without recourse to the Tribunal. The patient and the nominated person will have access to support and advice from specialist independent advocates who may assist in this process (see Chapter 5 paragraphs 5.10–5.13).

6.12   Carers will have the right to ask the patient's clinical supervisor or doctor responsible for the patient's care to undertake a formal assessment under these procedures. If the clinical supervisor accepts, then the processes outlined above will apply. If the clinical supervisor rejects the request he or she will be required to provide a written reply setting out the reasons for the decision.

6.13   Because of the potentially large number of patients who may need to be assessed under the procedures at the time new legislation comes into force, transitional arrangements will be included to enable this to take place over a period of time.

5.1.3 Compulsory admission and treatment

The powers to compel admission or treatment remain among the most problematic powers in the Act. Two features of the powers stand out: first, the nature of the criteria triggering the use of such powers and, second, the procedural steps which need to be followed by the players involved. The Act allows for the exercise of independent judgement by the various parties involved in decisions under these provisions, whilst recognising that they also need to work together in the best interest of the patient. The ASW is given particular duties in relation to the assessment process:

13.   Duty of approved social workers to make applications for admission or guardianship
(1)   It shall be the duty of an approved social worker to make an application for admission to hospital or a guardianship application in respect of a patient within the area of the local social services authority by which that officer is appointed in any case where he is satisfied that such an application ought to be made and is of the opinion, having regard to any wishes expressed by relatives of the patient or any other relevant circumstances, that it is necessary or proper for the application to be made by him.
(2)   Before making an application for the admission of a patient to hospital an approved social worker shall interview the patient in a suitable manner and satisfy himself that detention in a hospital is in all the circumstances of the case the most appropriate way of providing the care and medical treatment of which the patient stands in need.
(3)   An application under this section by an approved social worker may be made outside the area of the local social services authority by which he is appointed.
(4)   It shall be the duty of a local social services authority, if so required by the nearest relative of a patient residing in their area, to direct an approved social worker as soon as practicable to take the patient's case into consideration under subsection (1) above with a view to making an application for his admission to hospital; and if in any such case that approved social worker decides not to make an application he shall inform the nearest relative of his reasons in writing.

The criteria for compulsory admission or treatment vary according to the process invoked:

2.   Admission for assessment
(1)   A patient may be admitted to a hospital and detained there for the period allowed by subsection (4) below in pursuance of an application (in this Act referred to as 'an application for admission for assessment') made in accordance with subsections (2) and (3) below.

(2)   An application for admission for assessment may be made in respect of a patient on the grounds that —

   (a) he is suffering from mental disorder of a nature or degree which warrants the detention of the patient in a hospital for assessment (or for assessment followed by medical treatment) for at least a limited period; and

   (b) he ought to be so detained in the interests of his own health or safety or with a view to the protection of other persons.

(3)   An application for admission for assessment shall be founded on the written recommendations in the prescribed form of two registered medical practitioners, including in each case a statement that in the opinion of the practitioner the conditions set out in subsection (2) above are complied with.

(4)   Subject to the provisions of section 29(4) below, a patient admitted to hospital in pursuance of an application for admission for assessment may be detained for a period not exceeding 28 days beginning with the day on which he is admitted, but shall not be detained after the expiration of that period unless before it has expired he has become liable to be detained by virtue of a subsequent application, order or direction under the following provisions this Act.

3. Admission for treatment

(1)   A patient may be admitted to a hospital and detained there for the period allowed by the following provisions of this Act in pursuance of an application (in this Act referred to as 'an application for admission for treatment') made in accordance with this section.

(2)   An application for admission for treatment may be made in respect of a patient on the grounds that —

   (a) he is suffering from mental illness, severe mental impairment, psychopathic disorder or mental impairment and his mental disorder is of a nature or degree which makes it appropriate for him to receive medical treatment in a hospital; and

   (b) in the case of psychopathic disorder or mental impairment, such treatment is likely to alleviate or prevent a deterioration of his condition; and

   (c) it is necessary for the health or safety of the patient or for the protection of other persons that he should receive such treatment and it cannot be provided unless he is detained under this section.

(3)   An application for admission for treatment shall be founded on the written recommendations in the prescribed form of two registered medical practitioners, including in each case a statement that in the opinion of the practitioner the conditions set out in subsection (2) above are complied with; and each such recommendation shall include —

   (a) such particulars as may be prescribed of the grounds for that opinion so far as it relates to the conditions set out in paragraphs (a) and (b) of that subsection; and

   (b) a statement of the reasons for that opinion so far as it relates to the conditions set out in paragraph (c) of that subsection, specifying whether other methods of dealing with the patient are available and, if so, why they are not appropriate.

4. Admission for assessment in cases of emergency

(1)   In any case of urgent necessity, an application for admission for assessment may be made in respect of a patient in accordance with the following provisions of this section, and any application so made is in this Act referred to as 'an emergency application'.

(2)   An emergency application may be made either by an approved social worker or by the nearest relative of the patient; and every such application shall include a statement that it is of urgent necessity for the patient to be admitted and detained under section 2 above, and that compliance with the provisions of this Part of this Act relating to applications under that section would involve undesirable delay.

(3)   An emergency application shall be sufficient in the first instance if founded on one of the medical recommendations required by section 2 above, given, if practicable, by a practitioner who has previous acquaintance with the patient and otherwise complying with the requirements of section 12 below so far as applicable to a single recommendation, and verifying the statement referred to in subsection (2) above.

(4)   An emergency application shall cease to have effect on the expiration of a period of 72 hours from the time when the patient is admitted to the hospital unless —

- (a) the second medical recommendation required by section 2 above is given and received by the managers within that period; and
- (b) that recommendation and the recommendation referred to in subsection (3) above together comply with all the requirements of section 12 below (other than the requirement as to the time of signature of the second recommendation).

(5)   In relation to an emergency application, section 11 below shall have effect as in subsection (5) of that section for the words 'the period of 14 days ending with the date of the application' there were substituted the words 'the previous 24 hours'.

...

11.   General provisions as to applications

(1)   Subject to the provisions of this section, an application for admission for assessment, an application for admission for treatment and a guardianship application may be made either by the nearest relative of the patient or by an approved social worker; and every such application shall specify the qualification of the applicant to make the application.

(2)   Every application for admission shall be addressed to the managers of the hospital to which admission is sought and every guardianship application shall be forwarded to the local social services authority named in the application as guardian, or, as the case may be, to the local social services authority for the area in which the person so named resides.

(3)   Before or within a reasonable time after an application for the admission of a patient for assessment is made by an approved social worker, that social worker shall take such steps as are practicable to inform the person (if any) appearing to be the nearest relative of the patient that the application is to be or has been made and of the power of the nearest relative under section 23 (2)(a) below.

(4)   Neither an application for admission for treatment nor a guardianship application shall be made by an approved social worker if the nearest relative of the patient has notified that social worker, or the local social services authority by whom that social worker is appointed, that he objects to the application being made and, without prejudice to the foregoing provision, no such application shall be made by such a social worker except after consultation with the person (if any) appearing to be the nearest relative of the patient unless it appears to that social worker that in the circumstances such consultation is not reasonably practicable or would involve unreasonable delay.

(5)   None of the applications mentioned in subsection (1) above shall be made by any person in respect of a patient unless that person has personally seen the patient within the period of 14 days ending with the date of the application.

(6)   An application for admission for treatment or a guardianship application, and any recommendation given for the purposes of such an application, may describe the patient as suffering from more than one of the following forms of mental disorder, namely mental illness, severe mental impairment, psychopathic disorder or mental impairment; but the application shall be of no effect unless the patient is described in each of the recommendations as suffering from the same form of mental disorder, whether or not he is also described in either of those recommendations as suffering from another form.

(7) Each of the applications mentioned in subsection (1) above shall be sufficient if the recommendations on which it is founded are given either as separate recommendations, each signed by a registered medical practitioner, or as a joint recommendations signed by two such practitioners.

...

12. General provisions as to medical recommendations

(1) The recommendations required for the purposes of an application for the admission of a patient under this Part of this Act (in this Act referred to as 'medical recommendations') shall be signed on or before the date of the application, and shall be given by practitioners who have personally examined the patient either together or separately, but where they have examined the patient separately not more than five days must have elapsed between the days on which the separate examination took place.

...

(5) A medical recommendation for the purposes of an application for the admission of a patient under this Part of this Act shall not be given by —
  (a) the applicant;
  (b) a partner of the applicant or of a practitioner by whom another medical recommendation is given for the purposes of the same application;
  (c) a person employed as an assistant by the applicant or by any such practitioner;
  (d) a person who receives or has an interest in the receipt of any payments made on account of the maintenance of the patient; or
  (e) except as provided by subsection (3) or (4) above, a practitioner on the staff of the hospital to which the patient is to be admitted,
or by the husband, wife, father, father-in-law, mother, mother-in-law, son, son-in-law, daughter, daughter-in-law, brother, brother-in-law, sister or sister-in-law of the patient, or of any person mentioned in paragraphs (a) to (e) above, or of a practitioner by whom another medical recommendation is given for the purposes of the same application.

The importance of the assessment process is emphasised in the Code of Practice, an important part of that being the identification of the appropriate course of action, but the Code also attempts to encourage proper decision making in relation to these provisions. It is worth setting out these parts of the Code at length:

General
2.1   This chapter is about the roles and responsibilities of ASWs and doctors when making assessments of the needs of a person with mental health problems, where the assessment may lead to an application for admission to hospital under the Act.
2.2   An individual should only be compulsorily admitted if the statutory criteria are met and other relevant factors have been considered as set out in para. 2.6 below. A decision *not* to apply for admission under the Act should be supported, where necessary, by an alternative framework of care and/or treatment. The decision should also be clearly recorded in the patient's medical notes.
2.3   Doctors and ASWs undertaking assessments need to apply professional judgment, and reach decisions independently of each other but in a framework of co-operation and mutual support. Good working relationships require knowledge and understanding by the members of each profession of the other's distinct role and responsibilities. Unless there are good reasons for undertaking separate assessments, assessments should be carried out jointly by the ASW and doctor(s).

It is essential that at least one of the doctors undertaking the medical assessment discusses the patient with the applicant (ASW or nearest relative) and desirable for both of them to do this.
2.4   Everyone involved in assessment should be alert to the need to provide support for colleagues, especially where there is a risk of the patient causing physical harm. Staff should be aware of circumstances where the police should be called to provide assistance, and how to use that assistance to minimise the risk of violence.

The objective of assessment under the Act
2.5   All those assessing for possible admission under the Act should ensure that:
- they take all relevant factors into account;
- they consider appropriate alternatives to compulsory admission;
- they comply with the legal requirements of the Act.

The factors to be taken into account at assessment
2.6   patient may be compulsorily admitted under the Act where this is necessary:
- in the interests of his or her own health, *or*
- in the interests of his or her own safety, *or*
- for the protection of other people.

Only one of the above ground needs to be satisfied (*in addition to those relating to the patient's mental disorder*). However, a patient may only be admitted for treatment under section 3 if the treatment cannot be provided unless he or she is detained under the section. In judging whether compulsory admission is appropriate, those concerned should consider not only the statutory criteria but should also take account of:
- the guiding principles in Chapter 1; [see above, p. 172]
- the patient's wishes and view of his or her own needs;
- the patient's social and family circumstances;
- the nature of the illness/behaviour disorder and its course;
- what may be known about the patient by his or her nearest relative, any other relatives or friends and professionals involved, assessing in particular how reliable this information is;
- other forms of care or treatment including, where relevant, consideration of whether the patient would be willing to accept medical treatment in hospital informally or as an out-patient and of whether guardianship would be appropriate (see Chapter 13);
- the needs of the patient's family or others with whom he or she lives;
- the need for others to be protected from the patient;
- the burden on those close to the patient of a decision not to admit under the Act.

Ordinarily only then should the applicant (in consultation with other professionals) judge whether the criteria stipulated in any of the admission sections are satisfied, and take the decision accordingly. In certain circumstances the urgency of the situation may curtail detailed consideration of all these factors.

Informal admission
2.7   Where admission to hospital is considered necessary and the patient is willing to be admitted informally this should in general be arranged. Compulsory admission powers should only be exercised in the last resort. Informal admission is usually appropriate when a mentally capable patient consents to admission, but not if detention is necessary because of the danger the patient presents to him or herself or others. Compulsory admission should be considered where a mentally capable patient's current medical state, together with reliable evidence of past experience, indicates a strong likelihood that he or she will have a change of mind about informal admission prior to actually being admitted to hospital, with a resulting risk to their health or safety or to the safety of other people.

2.8 If at the time of admission, the patient is mentally incapable of consent, but does not object to entering hospital and receiving care or treatment, admission should be informal (see paras 15.9–15.10 for assessment of capacity and 15.18–15.22 for the treatment of mentally incapacitated patients). The decision to admit a mentally incapacitated patient informally should be made by the doctor in charge of the patient's treatment in accordance with what is in the patient's best interests and is justifiable on the basis of the common law doctrine of necessity (see para. 15.21). If a patient lacks capacity at the time of an assessment or review, it is particularly important that both clinical and social care requirements are considered, and that account is taken of the patient's ascertainable wishes and feelings and the views of their immediate relatives and carers on what would be in the patient's best interests.

Protection of others

2.9 In considering the protection of others (see sections 2(2)(b) and 3(2)(c) of the Act) it is essential to assess both the nature and likelihood of risk and the level of risk others are entitled to be protected from, taking into account:
- reliability of evidence including any relevant details of the patient's clinical history and past behaviour including contact with other agencies;
- the degree of risk and its nature. A risk of physical harm, or serious persistent psychological harm, to others is an indicator of the need for compulsory admission;
- the willingness and ability to cope with the risk, by those with whom the patient lives, and whether there are alternative options available for managing the risk.

The health of the patient

2.10 A patient may be admitted under sections 2 or 3 solely in the interests of his or her own health or safety even if there is no risk to other people. Those assessing the patient must consider:
- any evidence suggesting that the patient's mental health will deteriorate if he or she does not receive treatment;
- the reliability of such evidence which may include the known history of the individual's mental disorder;
- the views of the patient and of any relatives or close friends, especially those living with the patient, about the likely course of the illness and the possibility of it improving;
- the impact that any future deterioration or lack of improvement would have on relatives or close friends, especially those living with the patient, including an assessment of their ability and willingness to cope;
- whether there are other methods of coping with the expected deterioration or lack of improvement.

Individual professional responsibility — the Approved Social Worker

2.11 It is important to emphasise that an ASW assessing a patient for possible admission under the Act has overall responsibility for co-ordinating the process of assessment and, where he or she decides to make an application, for implementing that decision. The ASW must, at the start of the assessment, identify him or herself to the person, members of the family or friends present and the other professionals involved in the assessment. They should explain in clear terms the ASW's own role and the purpose of the visit, and ensure that the other professionals have explained their roles. ASWs should carry with them at all times documents identifying them as ASWs.

2.12 The ASW must interview the patient in a 'suitable manner', taking account of the guiding principles in Chapter 1:
- a. It is not desirable for a patient to be interviewed through a closed door or window except where there is serious risk to other people. Where there is no immediate risk of physical danger to the patient or to others, powers in the Act to secure access (section 135) should be used.

b. Where the patient is subject to the effects of sedative medication, or the short-term effects of drugs or alcohol, the ASW should consult with the doctor(s) and, unless it is not possible because of the patient's disturbed behaviour and the urgency of the case, either wait until, or arrange to return when, the effects have abated before interviewing the patient. If it is not realistic, or the risk indicates that it would not be appropriate to wait, the assessment will have to be based on whatever information the ASW can obtain from all reliable sources. This should be made clear in the ASW's report.

2.13   The patient should ordinarily be given the opportunity of speaking to the ASW alone but if the ASW has reason to fear physical harm, he or she should insist that another professional be present. If the patient wants or needs another person (for example a friend, relative or an advocate) to be present during the assessment and any subsequent action that may be taken, then ordinarily the ASW should assist in securing that person's attendance unless the urgency of the case or some other reason makes it inappropriate to do so. Deaf or hearing impaired patients may feel more confident with a friend or advocate who is also deaf or hearing impaired.

2.14   The ASW must attempt to identify the patient's nearest relative as defined in section 26 of the Act. It is important to remember that the nearest relative for the purposes of the Act may not be the same person as the patient's 'next of kin', and also that the identity of the nearest relative is liable to change with the passage of time. The ASW must then ensure that the statutory obligations with respect to the nearest relative set out in section 11 of the Act are fulfilled. In addition, the ASW should where possible:

a. ascertain the nearest relative's views about both the patient's needs and the relative's own needs in relation to the patient;

b. inform the nearest relative of the reasons for considering an application for admission under the Act and the effects of making such an such an application.

Applications under section 2

2.15   It is a statutory requirement to take such steps as are practicable to inform the nearest relative about an application for admission under section 2 and of their power of discharge (section 11(3)). If the ASW has been unable to inform the nearest relative before the patient's admission, he or she should notify the hospital as soon as this has been done.

Applications under section 3

2.16   Consultation by the ASW with the nearest relative about possible application for admission under section 3 or reception into guardianship is a statutory requirement unless it is not reasonably practicable or would involve unreasonable delay (section 11(4)). Circumstances in which the nearest relative need not be informed or consulted include those where the ASW cannot obtain sufficient information to establish the identity or location of the nearest relative or where to do so would require an excessive amount of investigation. Practicability refers to the availability of the nearest relative and not to the appropriateness of informing or consulting the person concerned. If the ASW has been unable to consult the nearest relative before making an application for admission for treatment (section 3) he or she should persist in seeking to contact the nearest relative so as to inform the latter of his or her powers to discharge the patient under section 23. The ASW should inform the hospital as soon as this has been done.

Delegation of nearest relative's functions

2.17   If the nearest relative would find it difficult to undertake the functions defined in the Act, or is reluctant for any reason to do this, regulation 14 allows him or her to delegate those functions to another person. ASWs should consider proposing this in appropriate cases.

2.18   If the nearest relative objects to an application being made for admission for treatment or reception into guardianship it cannot proceed at that time. If, because of the urgency of the case, and the risks of not taking forward the application immediately, it is thought necessary to proceed with the application, the ASW will then need to consider applying to the county court for the nearest relative's 'displacement' (section 29), and Local Authorities must provide proper assistance, especially legal assistance, in such cases. It is desirable for social services authorities to provide clear practical guidance on the procedures, and this should be discussed with the relevant county courts.

2.19   In so far as the urgency of the case allows, an ASW who is the applicant for the admission of a patient to hospital should consult with other relevant relatives and should take their views into account.

2.20   The ASW should consult wherever possible with others who have been involved with the patient's care in the statutory, voluntary or independent services. Deaf patients may be known to one of the specialist hospital units for mental health and deafness.

2.21   Having decided whether or not to make an application for admission the ASW should tell (with reasons):

- the patient;
- the patient's nearest relative (whenever practicable);
- the doctor(s) involved in the assessment;
- the key worker, if the patient is on CPA;
- the patient's GP, if he or she was not involved in the assessment.

When an application for admission is to be made the ASW should plan how the patient is to be conveyed to hospital and take steps to make the necessary arrangements.

Individual professional responsibility — the doctor

2.22   The doctor should:

a.   decide whether the patient is suffering from mental disorder within the meaning of the Act (section 1) and assess its seriousness and the need for further assessment and/or medical treatment in hospital;

b.   consider the factors set out in para. 2.6, and discuss them with the applicant and the other doctor involved;

c.   specifically address the legal criteria for admission under the Act and, if satisfied that they are met, provide a recommendation setting out those aspects of the patient's symptoms and behaviour on which that conclusion is based;

d.   ensure that, where there is to be an application for admission, a hospital bed will be available.

Medical examination

2.23   A proper medical examination requires:

- direct personal examination of the patient's mental state;
- consideration of all available relevant medical information including that in the possession of others, professional or non-professional;
- that the guiding principles in Chapter 1 are taken into account.

by widening the discussion on the best way of meeting his or her needs. Doctors and ASWs should be ready to consult colleagues (especially keyworkers and other community care staff involved with the patient's care) while retaining for themselves the final responsibility. Where disagreements do occur, professionals should ensure that they discuss these with each other.

2.34   Where there is an unresolved dispute about an application for admission, it is essential that the professionals do not abandon the patient and the family. Rather, they should explore and agree an alternative plan, if necessary on a temporary basis, and ensure that the family is kept informed. Such a plan and the arrangements for reviewing it should be recorded in writing and copies made available to all those who need it (subject to the patient's right to confidentiality).

The choice of applicant for admission

2.35   The ASW is usually the right applicant, bearing in mind professional training, knowledge of the legislation and of local resources, together with the potential adverse effect that an application by the nearest relative might have on the latter's relationship with the patient. The doctor should therefore advise the nearest relative that it is preferable for an ASW to make an assessment of the need for a patient to be admitted under the Act, and for the ASW to make the application. When reasonably practicable the doctor should, however, advise the nearest relative of the rights set out in section 13(4) (see para. 2.38) and of his or her right to make an application.

2.36   The doctor should never advise the nearest relative to make an application in order to avoid involving an ASW in an assessment.

Agency responsibilities — the local authority

2.37   A nearest relative should not be put in the position of having to make an application for admission under the Act because it is not possible for an ASW to attend for assessment. Subject to resources, local authorities should provide a 24 hour ASW service to ensure that this does not happen.

Section 13(4)

2.38   Local Authorities are required, if requested by a nearest relative, to direct an ASW to make an assessment and:

 a.   should have explicit policies on how to respond to repeated requests for assessment where the condition of a patient has not changed significantly;

 b.   should give guidance to ASWs as to whether nearest relative requests can be accepted by way of GPs or other professions. (Such requests should certainly be accepted provided the GP or other professional has been so authorised by the nearest relative.)

Emergencies out of hours etc.

2.39   Arrangements should be made to ensure that information about applications is passed to professional colleagues who are next on duty. For example, where an application for admission is not immediately necessary but might be in the future, the necessary arrangements could be made for an ASW to attend the next day.

Agency responsibilities — the health authority

Doctors approved under section 12

2.40   The Secretary of State has delegated to Health Authorities the task of approving medical practitioners under section 12(2).

2.41   Health Authorities should:

 a.   take active steps to encourage sufficient doctors, including GPs and those working in the Health Care Service for Prisoners, to apply for approval;

 b.   seek to ensure a 24 hour on-call rota of approved doctors sufficient to cover the area;

 c.   maintain a regularly updated list of approved doctors which indicates how each approved doctor can be contacted and the hours that he or she is available;

4.5   Where the patient is currently receiving treatment from a doctor that doctor should be consulted by the doctor(s) providing the medical recommendation.

...

[*Chapter 5*]

The choice

5.1   Which admission section should be used? Professional judgment must be applied to the criteria in each section and only when this has been done can a decision be reached as to which, if either, section applies. Detention under section 3 can last for any period of time, and need not last its full course.

5.2 **Section 2 pointers:**
   a. the diagnosis and prognosis of a patient's condition is unclear;
   b. a need to carry out an in-patient assessment in order to formulate a treatment plan;
   c. a judgment is needed as to whether the patient will accept treatment on a voluntary basis following admission;
   d. a judgment has to be made as to whether a particular treatment proposal, which can only be administered to the patient under Part IV of the Act, is likely to be effective;
   e. the condition of a patient who has already been assessed, and who has been previously admitted compulsorily under the Act, is judged to have changed since the previous admission and further assessment is needed;
   f. the patient has not previously been admitted to hospital either compulsorily or informally and has not been in regular contact with the specialist psychiatric services.

5.3 **Section 3 pointers:**
   a. the patient is considered to need compulsory admission for the treatment of a mental disorder which is already known to his clinical team, and has been assessed in the recent past by that team. In these circumstances it may be right to use section 3 even where the patient has not previously been admitted as an in-patient;
   b. the patient is detained under section 2 and assessment indicates a need for treatment under the Act for a period beyond the 28 day detention under section 2. In such circumstances an application for detention under section 3 should be made at the earliest opportunity and should not be delayed until the end of section 2 detention. The change in detention status from section 2 to section 3 will not deprive the patient of a Mental Health Review Tribunal hearing if the change takes place after a valid application has been made to the Tribunal but before that application has been heard. The patient's rights to apply for a Tribunal under section 66(l)(b) in the first period of detention after his change of status are unaffected.

5.4 Decisions should not be influenced by the possibility that:
   a. a proposed treatment to be administered under the Act will last less than 28 days;
   b. a patient detained under section 2 will get quicker access to a Mental Health Review Tribunal than one detained under section 3;
   c. after-care under supervision will only be available if the patient has been admitted under section 3. The use of section 3 must be justified by the patient's need to be admitted for treatment under the terms of that section, not considerations about what is to happen after his or her eventual discharge;
   d. a patient's nearest relative objects to admission under section 3.

5.5 If the nearest relative unreasonably objects to admission under section 3 an application should be made to the county court under section 29 of the Act for the functions of the nearest relative to be transferred to the local Social Services Authority or another person. A further section 2 application cannot be made if the patient is already in hospital following admission under section 2. The section 29 application should be made as soon as it is clear that the patient will need to be detained under section 3 and that the nearest relative unreasonably objects to this.

...

[*Chapter 6*]

General

6.1 Application for admission for assessment under section 4 should be made only when:
   a. the criteria for admission for assessment are met (see para. 5.2); and

    b.   the matter is of urgent necessity and there is not enough time to get a second medical recommendation.

6.2   Section 4 should be used only in a genuine emergency, never for administrative convenience. 'Second doctors' should be available to assist with assessments prior to admission.

Admission

6.3   An emergency arises where those involved cannot cope with the mental state or behaviour of the patient. To be satisfied that an emergency has arisen, there must be evidence of:

- an immediate and significant risk of mental or physical harm to the patient or to others; and/or
- the danger of serious harm to property; and/or
- the need for physical restraint of the patient.

6.4   Patients should not be admitted under section 4 rather than section 2 because it is more convenient for the second doctor to examine the patient in, rather than outside, hospital. Those assessing an individual's need must be able to secure the attendance within a reasonable time of a second doctor and in particular an approved doctor.

6.5   If the ASW is considering an application for admission and no second doctor is available, he or she should discuss the case with the doctor providing the recommendation and seek to resolve the problem. If this is not possible he or she should have access to an officer in the local Social Services Authority who is sufficiently senior to take up the matter with the Health Authority or Trust. The ASW's Local Authority should make it clear that the ASW in these circumstances is under an obligation to report the matter in this way.

6.6   Hospital Managers should monitor the use of section 4 and seek to ensure that second doctors are available to visit a patient within a reasonable time after being so requested.

6.7   If a patient is admitted under section 4 an appropriate second doctor should examine him or her as soon as possible after admission, to decide whether the patient should be detained under section 2.

...

Purpose of guardianship

13.1   The purpose of guardianship is to enable patients to receive care in the community where it cannot be provided without the use of compulsory powers. It provides an authoritative framework for working with a patient, with a minimum of constraint, to achieve as independent a life as possible within the community. Where it is used it must be part of the patient's overall care and treatment plan.

13.2   After-care under supervision provides an alternative statutory framework for the after-care of patients who have been detained in hospital for treatment and meet the criteria set out in section 25A of the Act.

Assessment for guardianship

13.3   ASWs and doctors should consider guardianship as a possible alternative to admission to, or continuing care in, hospital.

13.4   An application for guardianship should be accompanied by a comprehensive care plan established on the basis of multi-disciplinary discussions. It is important that any procedures instituted by social services departments are no more than the minimum necessary to ensure the proper use of guardianship and that guardianship can be used in a positive and flexible manner.

Components of effective guardianship

13.5   A comprehensive care plan is required (under the Care Programme Approach (CPA) in England) which identifies the services needed by the patient and who will provide them.

The care plan should include care arrangements, suitable accommodation, treatment and personal support. For those subject to guardianship the care plan should also indicate which of the powers under the Act are necessary to achieve the plan. If no powers are required guardianship should not be used.

13.6   Key elements of the plan should include:
    a.   depending on the patient's level of 'capacity', his or her recognition of the 'authority' of, and willingness to work with, the guardian;
    b.   support from the Local Authority for the guardian;
    c.   suitable accommodation to help meet the patient's needs;
    d.   access to day care, education and training facilities;
    e.   effective co-operation and communication between all persons concerned in implementing the care plan.

The guardian should be willing to 'advocate' on behalf of the patient in relation to those agencies whose services are needed to carry out the care plan.

Duties of Social Services Departments

13.7   Each Local Authority should establish a policy setting out the arrangements for:
    a.   receiving, considering and scrutinising applications for guardianship. Such arrangements should ensure that applications are properly but speedily dealt with;
    b.   monitoring the progress of the guardianship including steps to be taken to fulfil the authority's statutory obligations in relation to private guardians and to arrange visits to the patient;
    c.   ensuring the suitability of any proposed private guardian, and that he or she is able to understand and carry out the statutory duties, including the appointment of a nominated medical attendant;
    d.   ensuring that patients under guardianship receive, both orally and in writing, relevant aspects of the information that Hospital Managers are required to give to detained patients under section 132 (patient leaflets 10 and 11);
    e.   ensuring that the patient is aware of his or her right to apply to a Mental Health Review Tribunal and that a named officer of the local authority will give any necessary assistance to the patient in making such an application;
    f.   maintaining detailed records relating to the person under guardianship;
    g.   ensuring the review of the guardianship towards the end of each period of guardianship;
    h.   discharging the patient from guardianship as soon as it is no longer required.

The powers of the guardian

13.8   Section 8 of the Act sets out the three powers of the guardian as follows:
    a.   to require the patient to live at a place specified by the guardian. This does not provide the legal authority to detain a patient physically or remove the patient against his or her wishes. A patient who is absent without leave from the specified place may be returned within the statutory time limit by those authorised to do so under the Act;
    b.   to require the patient to attend at specified places for medical treatment, occupation, education or training. If the patient refuses to attend, the guardian is not authorised to use force to secure such attendance, nor does the Act enable medical treatment to be administered in the absence of the patient's consent;
    c.   to require access to the patient to be given at the place where he or she is living to persons detailed in the Act. A refusal without reasonable cause to permit an authorised person to have access to the patient is an offence under section 129 but no force may be used to secure entry.

If the patient consistently resists the exercise of the guardian's powers it can be concluded that guardianship is not the most appropriate form of care for that person and the guardianship order should be discharged.

13.9   Points to remember:

    a. Guardianship does not restrict the patient's access to hospital services on an informal basis. A patient who requires treatment but does not need to be detained may be admitted informally.

    b. Guardianship can also remain in force if the patient is admitted to hospital under section 2 or 4 but not under section 3.

    c. It is possible in certain circumstances for a patient liable to be detained in hospital by virtue of an application under Part II of the Act to be transferred into guardianship and for a person subject to guardianship under Part II of the Act to be transferred into the guardianship of another local social services authority or person approved by such authority or to be transferred to hospital. (See section 19 and regulations 7–9 of the Mental Health (Hospital, Guardianship and Consent to Treatment) Regulations 1983).

13.10   Particular practice issues:

    a. Guardianship must not be used to require a patient to reside in hospital except where it is necessary for a very short time in order to provide shelter whilst accommodation in the community is being arranged.

    b. Where an adult is assessed as requiring residential care, but owing to mental incapacity is unable to make a decision as to whether he or she wishes to be placed in residential care, those who are responsible for his or her care should consider the applicability and appropriateness of guardianship for providing the framework within which decisions about his or her current and future care can be planned.

Guardianship under section 37

13.11   Guardianship may be used as an alternative to hospital orders by courts where the prescribed criteria, which are similar to those of a hospital order, are met. The court should be satisfied that the Local Authority or named person is willing to act as guardian. The Local Authority should be satisfied with the arrangements. In considering the appropriateness of guardianship they should be guided by the same principles as apply under Part II of the Act. The powers and duties conferred on the local authority or private guardian and the provisions as to duration, renewal and discharge are the same as in guardianship applications except that the power to discharge is not available to the nearest relative.

A particular concern is the avoidance of abuses of power, as the case of *St George's Healthcare NHS Trust* v *S* [1998] 3 All ER 673 (below) illustrates: a 'bizarre', 'irrational' or 'morally repugnant' decision does not of itself provide grounds for sectioning the person making it. The facts appear from the judgment of Judge LJ:

Introduction

On 25 April 1996 S, a single woman born in June 1967, working as a veterinary nurse, sought to register as a new patient at a local NHS practice in London. She was approximately 36 weeks pregnant. She had not sought antenatal care. Pre-eclampsia was rapidly diagnosed. She was advised that she needed urgent attention, with bedrest and admission to hospital for an induced delivery. Without this treatment her health and life and the health and life of her baby were in real danger. She fully understood the potential risks but rejected the advice. She wanted her baby to be born naturally.

She was seen by Louize Collins, a social worker approved under the Mental Health Act 1983, and two doctors, Dr Caroline Chill and Dr Siobhan Jeffreys, a duly qualified practitioner registered under s. 12(2) of the Act. They repeated the advice she had already been given.

She adamantly refused to accept it. An application was made under s. 2 of the Act by Louize Collins for her admission to Springfield Hospital 'for assessment'. Dr Chill and Dr Jeffreys signed the necessary written recommendations. That evening (25 April) S was admitted to Springfield Hospital against her will.

Shortly before midnight, again against her will, she was transferred to St George's Hospital. In view of her continuing adamant refusal to consent to treatment, an application was made ex parte on behalf of the hospital authority to Hogg J sitting in the Family Division in chambers, who granted a declaration which, in summary terms, dispensed with S's consent to treatment. Later that evening appropriate medical procedures were carried out and at 22.00 S was delivered of a baby girl by Caesarean section. When she recovered she developed strong feelings of revulsion and at first rejected her baby. Happily the natural bond between them has now been established.

On 30 April she was returned to Springfield Hospital. On 2 May her detention under s. 2 of the Act was terminated, and against medical advice, she immediately discharged herself from hospital.

During the period when she was a patient no specific treatment for mental disorder or mental illness was prescribed.

Virtually every step of the medical and legal procedures involving S between 25 April and 2 May is criticised and we have been required to consider important questions about the autonomy of a pregnant woman and the effect of her right to self-determination on her unborn child, the correct application of a number of provisions of the Act.

Judge LJ then deals with issues of principle:

...

Autonomy

Even when his or her own life depends on receiving medical treatment, an adult of sound mind is entitled to refuse it. This reflects the autonomy of each individual and the right of self-determination. Lest reiteration may diminish the impact of this principle, it is valuable to recognise the force of the language used when the right of self-determination was most recently considered in the House of Lords in *Airedale NHS Trust* v *Bland*:

'The first point to make is that it is unlawful, so as to constitute both the tort and crime of battery, to administer medical treatment to an adult, who is conscious and of sound mind, without his consent *see F* v *West Berkshire Health Authority (Mental Health Act Commission intervening)* [1989] 2 All ER 545; [1990] 2 AC 1. Such a person is completely at liberty to decline to undergo treatment, even if the result of his doing so will be that he will die.' (See [1993] 1 All ER 821 at 860, [1993] AC 789 at 857 per Lord Keith.)

'... it is established that the principle of self-determination requires that respect must be given to the wishes of the patient, so that, if an adult patient of sound mind refuses, however unreasonably, to consent to treatment or care by which his life would or might be prolonged, the doctors responsible for his care must give effect to his wishes, even ... though they do not consider it to be in his best interests to do so ... To this extent, the principle of the sanctity of human life must yield to the principle of self-determination ... and, for present purposes perhaps more important, the doctor's duty to act in the best interests of his patient must likewise be qualified.' (See [1993] 1 All ER 821 at 866, [1993] AC 789 at 864 per Lord Goff of Chieveley.)

'Any treatment given by a doctor to a patient which is invasive (ie involves any interference with the physical integrity of the patient) is unlawful unless done with the consent of the patient: it constitutes the crime of battery and the tort of trespass to the person. Thus, in the case of an adult who is mentally competent, the artificial feeding regime (and the attendant steps necessary to evacuate the bowels and bladder) would be unlawful unless the patient consented to it. A mentally competent patient can at any time put an end to life support systems by refusing his consent to their continuation.' (See [1993] 1 All ER 821 at 881–882, [1993] AC 789 at 882 per Lord Browne-Wilkinson.)

'Any invasion of the body of one person by another is potentially both a crime and a tort ... How is it that, consistently with the proposition just stated, a doctor can with immunity perform on a consenting patient an act which would be a very serious crime if done by someone else? The answer must be that bodily invasions in the course of proper medical treatment stand completely outside the criminal law. The reason why the consent of the patient is so important is not that it furnishes a defence in itself, but because it is usually essential to the propriety of medical treatment. Thus, if the consent is absent, and is not dispensed with in special circumstances by operation of law, the acts of the doctor lose their immunity ... If the patient is capable of making a decision whether to permit treatment and decides not to permit it his choice must be obeyed, even if on any objective view it is contrary to his best interests. A doctor has no right to proceed in the face of objection, even if it is plain to all, including the patient, that adverse consequences and even death will or may ensue.' (See [1993] 1 All ER 821 at 889, [1993] AC 789 at 891 per Lord Mustill.)

The speeches in *Airedale NHS Trust* v *Bland* did not establish the law, but rather underlined the principle found in a series of authoritative decisions. With the exception of one short passage from the observations of Lord Reid in *S* v *S, W* v *Official Solicitor* [1970] 3 All ER 107; [1972] AC 24 no further citation is necessary.

In that case the House of Lords considered whether it was right to order blood tests on two infants to help establish whether or not they were legitimate. Lord Reid examined the legal position and said ([1970] 3 All ER 107 at 111, [1972] AC 24 at 43):

'There is no doubt that a person of full age and capacity cannot be ordered to undergo a blood test against his will ... The real reason is that English law goes to great lengths to protect a person of full age and capacity from interference with his personal liberty. We have too often seen freedom disappear in other countries not only by coups d'état but by gradual erosion; and often it is the first step that counts. So it would be unwise to make even minor concessions.'

The importance of this salutary warning remains undiminished.

There are occasions when an individual lacks the capacity to make decisions about whether or not to consent to treatment. This may arise when he is unconscious or suffering from mental disability. This question will have to be examined more closely in due course, but dealing with it generally for the moment, where the adult patient is disabled from giving consent the medical practitioners must act in his best interests and if appropriate, may carry out major invasive surgery without express consent.

...

The Mental Health Act 1983

The Act cannot be deployed to achieve the detention of an individual against her will merely because her thinking process is unusual, even apparently bizarre and irrational, and contrary to the views of the overwhelming majority of the community at large. The prohibited reasoning is readily identified and easily understood. Here is an intelligent woman. She knows perfectly well that if she persists with this course against medical advice she is likely to cause serious harm, and possibly death, to her baby and to herself. No normal mother-to-be could possibly think like that. Although this mother would not dream of taking any positive steps to cause injury to herself or her baby, her refusal is likely to lead to such a result. Her bizarre thinking represents a danger to their safety and health. It therefore follows that she *must* be mentally disordered and detained in hospital in her own interests and those of her baby. The short answer is that she may be perfectly rational and quite outside the ambit of the Act, and will remain so notwithstanding her eccentric thought process.

Even when used by well-intentioned individuals for what they believe to be genuine and powerful reasons, perhaps shared by a large section of the community, unless the individual case falls within the prescribed conditions, the Act cannot be used to justify detention for mental disorder:

'... no adult citizen of the United Kingdom is liable to be confined in any institution against his will, save by the authority of the law. That is a fundamental constitutional principle, traceable back to Ch 29 of Magna Carta 1297(25 Edw 1 c l) and before that to Ch 39 of Magna Carta (1215) ... Powers therefore exist to ensure that those who suffer from mental illness may, in appropriate circumstances, be involuntarily admitted to mental hospitals and detained. But, and it is a very important but, the circumstances in which the mentally ill may be detained are very carefully prescribed by statute.' (See *Re S-C (mental patient: habeas corpus)* [1996] 1 All ER 532 at 534–535, [1996] QB 599 at 603 per Bingham MR.)

In *R* v *Hallstrom, ex p W (No. 2), R* v *Gardner, ex p L* [1986] 2 All ER 306 at 314, [1986] QB 1090 at 1104 McCullough J used language which encapsulated an axiomatic principle:

'There is ... no canon of construction which presumes that Parliament intended that people should, against their will, be subjected to treatment which others, however professionally competent, perceive, however sincerely and however correctly, to be in their best interests ... Parliament is presumed not to enact legislation which interferes with the liberty of the subject without making it clear that this was its intention. It goes without saying that, unless clear statutory authority to the contrary exists, no one is to be detained in hospital or to undergo medical treatment or even to submit himself to a medical examination without his consent. This is as true of a mentally disordered person as of anyone else.'

So even assuming lawful admission and detention in accordance with the 1983 Act, the patient is not deprived of all autonomy. Part IV of the Act provides a carefully structured scheme setting out the circumstances in which the patient's consent to treatment may be dispensed with. Section 63 of the Act may apply to the treatment of any condition which is integral to the mental disorder (*B* v *Croydon Health Authority* [1995] 1 All ER 683, [1995] Fam 133) provided the treatment is given by, or under the direction of, the responsible medical officer. The treatment administered to S was not so ordered; she was neither offered nor did she refuse treatment for mental disorder. Her detention under the Act did not undermine or restrict her right to self-determination unless she was deprived, 'either by long term mental capacity or retarded development or by temporary factors such as unconsciousness or confusion or the effects of fatigue, shock, pain or drugs', of her capacity to decide for herself. (See *Re JT(an adult: refusal of medical treatment)* [1998] 1 FLR 48.)

In *Re T (adult: refusal of medical treatment)* [1992] 4 All ER 649, [1993] Fam 95 Lord Donaldson MR set out a number of principles of general application for patients detained under the Act. Although these principles have been considered and extended in a number of subsequent cases, including *Re C (adult: refusal of medical treatment)* [1994] 1 All ER 819, [1994] 1 WLR 290, for present purposes it is sufficient to notice his observation:

'What matters is whether at that time the patient's capacity was reduced below the level needed in the case of a refusal of that importance, for refusals can vary in importance. Some may involve a risk to life or of irreparable damage to health. Others may not.' (See [1992] 4 All ER 649 at 6641; [1993] Fam 95 at 116.)

In the final analysis, a woman detained under the Act for mental disorder cannot be forced into medical procedures unconnected with her mental condition unless her capacity to consent to such treatment is diminished. When she retains her capacity her consent remains an essential prerequisite and whether she does, or not, must be decided on the basis of the evidence in each individual case, care being taken by those responsible for the detention of the patient, and indeed any court considering the problem, to ensure that the prohibited reasoning identified earlier in this judgment is avoided in relation to consent as it is with admission and detention under the Act.

He then concludes:

Application for admission under s. 2
It is clear that everyone involved in the process which led to S's admission, Louize Collins and both Dr Chill and Dr Jeffreys, was equally motivated by a genuine desire to achieve what, in their professional judgment, was best for S herself and for her baby. It is equally clear that S utterly rejected their well intentioned efforts to help her. She knew the risks. She was quite prepared to accept them. She was not willing to change her mind. She said that she saw birth as an entirely natural occurrence in which there was no place for medical or surgical intervention.

...

Under s. 13(1) of the Act it is the duty not of the doctors, but of an approved social worker, to make an application under s. 2, where satisfied 'that such an application ought to be made and ... of the opinion ... that it is necessary or proper for the application to be made'. Moreover the social worker must be satisfied that 'detention in a hospital is in all the circumstances of the case the most appropriate way of providing the care and medical treatment of which the patient stands in need' (see s. 13(2)).

These provisions make clear that the social worker must exercise her own independent judgment on the basis of all the available material, including her interview and assessment of the 'patient', and personally make the appropriate decision. When doing so she is required to take account of the recommendations made by the medical practitioners. Indeed the application must be 'founded' on their written recommendations (s. 2(3)). The doctors too are required to make their recommendations on the basis of their best judgment of the relevant facts and, while eschewing the prohibited reasoning, decide whether the conditions provided in s. 2(2) are satisfied. An application made for an improper or collateral purpose (*R* v *Wilson, ex p Williamson* [1996] COD 42), or flawed in the *Wednesbury* sense (see *Associated Provincial Picture Houses Ltd* v *Wednesbury Corp.* [1947] 2 All ER 680, [1948] 1 KB 223) (*R* v *South Western Hospital Managers, ex p M* [1994] 1 All ER 161 at 176, [1993] QB 683 at 700) would be susceptible to judicial review; so would similarly tainted recommendations by the medical practitioners.

...

The application for S's admission was made, not under s. 3, but under s. 2 of the Act. These are distinct provisions with significant differences between them. For present purposes it is sufficient to notice that the application under s. 3 is admission for treatment whereas under s. 2 the application is made for 'admission for assessment', and that whereas the basis for admission under s. 2 is mental disorder, under s. 3 treatment involves a more closely detailed diagnosis of the precise form of mental disorder from which the patient is suffering.

Before an application for assessment may be made, each of the specified grounds provided in s. 2(2) must be established. They are cumulative. There was considerable discussion whether s. 2(2)(a) required a final or provisional diagnosis of mental disorder. Section 2 is directed to admission for 'assessment' and not a final diagnosis. In *R* v *Kirklees Metropolitan BC, ex p C* [1993] 2 FCR 381 at 383, [1993] 2 FLR 187 at 190 Lloyd LJ commented:

'... there is, in my view, power to admit a patient for assessment under s. 2, if it appears to be suffering from mental disorder, on the ground that he or she is so suffering, even though it turns out on assessment that she is not. Any other construction would unnecessarily emasculate the beneficial power under s. 2 and confine assessment to choice of treatment.'

In our judgment at the time when the application for admission for assessment is made, the social worker should believe that the patient is suffering from mental disorder which warrants detention for such assessment. It cannot be a final concluded diagnosis. She is entitled to be wrong; so are the medical practitioners on whose recommendations her application is based. The final diagnosis may or may not confirm what can only be a provisional view formed, in the case of the social worker, by an individual who is not medically qualified. None of these considerations would vitiate an application made by a social worker who reasonably believed that the statutory conditions were fulfilled. The same principles apply to the medical practitioners.

...

We can now return to s. 2(2). The first requirement of s. 2(2)(a) is that the patient should be suffering from mental disorder. Mental disorder includes any 'disorder or disability of mind'. Conditions such as promiscuity or alcohol or drug dependency are excluded. We do not doubt that reactive depression (not merely a transient sense of being 'a little down' or 'fed up with everything') is capable of amounting to mental disorder. The second requirement is that even if the patient suffers from mental disorder it must be of 'such a nature or degree' that the patient's *detention* for assessment or assessment followed by treatment is warranted. For the purposes of s. 2(2)(a), such detention must be related to or linked with mental disorder. Treatment for the effects of pregnancy does not provide the necessary warrant. Turning to s. 2(2)(b), and assuming that the requirements of s. 2(2)(a) were otherwise fulfilled, for the reasons already given the unborn child is not a 'person' in need of protection. The only 'person' whose health and safety arose for consideration was S. Again, for the reasons already given, her health and safety could not be assessed on the basis that she was not 36 weeks pregnant and not suffering from pre-eclampsia. Those responsible have to deal in realities, and S was dangerously ill. Although the risks were caused by her pregnancy, the potential damage could have fallen within s. 2(2)(b).

We can now consider the submissions made by Mr Gordon in the light of the summary of the facts outlined earlier in this judgment. On the basis of the material available to them, Louize Collins and the doctors were entitled to conclude that S was suffering from mental disorder. Her refusal of treatment which would assist both her and her baby was unusual and unreasonable. Unassisted by human hands, nature's course involved the risk of death or disability for herself and her baby. She was profoundly indifferent to these consequences; an abnormal state of mind. Each doctor diagnosed depression. It was a view based on a report of earlier depression from another doctor who knew S and their own lengthy examination and discussion with her. Each completed the prescribed form because she believed that S 'was suffering from mental disorder' which warranted her admission for assessment and set out her reasons.

The contemporaneous documents themselves demonstrate that those involved in the decision to make an application for admission failed to maintain the distinction between the urgent need of S for treatment arising from her pregnancy, and the separate question whether her mental disorder (in the form of depression) warranted her detention in hospital. From the reasoning to be found in them, the conclusion that the detention was believed to be warranted in order that adequate provision could be made to deal with S's pregnancy and the safety of her unborn child is unavoidable. The reasoning process emerges most strongly from Louize Collins' assessment. She expressly acknowledged that a psychiatric ward was not 'the best place' for S (a judgment confirmed by the very brief period S remained in Springfield Hospital before being transferred to St George's). She believed, rightly, that S's condition was threatened by her very severe pre-eclampsia. At the time when she reached her conclusion she did not suggest that detention was required for the purpose of assessing S's mental condition or treating her depression. Put another way, if S had not been suffering from severe pre-eclampsia there is nothing in the contemporaneous documents to suggest that an application for her detention would have been considered, let alone justified.

We are satisfied that, notwithstanding our view that the requirements of s. 2(2)(b) might well have been fulfilled, the cumulative grounds prescribed in s. 2(2)(a) were not established. Therefore the application for admission was unlawful.

An additional power is provided enabling doctors and nurses to detain inpatients for a limited period:

5. Application in respect of patient already In hospital

(1)   An application for the admission of a patient to a hospital may be made under this Part of this Act notwithstanding that the patient is already an in-patient in that hospital or, in the case of an application for admission for treatment that the patient is for the time being liable to be detained in the hospital in pursuance of an application for admission for assessment; and where an application is so made the patient shall be treated for the purposes of this Part of this Act as if he had been admitted to the hospital, at the time when that application was received by the managers.

(2)   If, in the case of a patient who is an in-patient in a hospital, it appears to the registered medical practitioner in charge of the treatment of the patient that an application ought to be made under this Part of this Act for the admission of the patient to hospital, he may furnish to the managers a report in writing to that effect; and in any such case the patient may be detained in the hospital for a period of 72 hours from the time when the report is so furnished.

...

(4)   If, in the case of a patient who is receiving treatment for mental disorder as an in-patient in a hospital, it appears to a nurse of the prescribed class —

  (a)   that the patient is suffering from mental disorder to such a degree that it is necessary for his health or safety or for the protection of others for him to be immediately restrained from leaving the hospital; and

  (b)   that it is not practicable to secure the immediate attendance of a practitioner for the purpose of furnishing a report under subsection (2) above, the nurse may record that fact in writing; and in that event the patient may be detained in the hospital for a period of six hours from the time when that fact is so recorded or until the earlier arrival at the place where the patient is detained of a practitioner having power to furnish a report under that subsection.

(5)   A record made under subsection (4) above shall be delivered by the nurse (or by a person authorised by the nurse in that behalf) to the managers of the hospital as soon as possible after it is made; and where a record is made under that subsection the period mentioned in subsection (2) above shall begin at the time when it is made.

Powers of compulsory admission and detention are also available under Part III as a result of court proceedings for criminal offences and are not considered further here.

Guardianship provides the possibility of care being provided in the community rather than in an institutional setting:

7. Application for guardianship

(1)   A patient who has attained the age of 16 years may be received into guardianship, for the period allowed by the following provisions of this Act, in pursuance of an application (in this Act referred to as 'a guardianship application') made in accordance with this section.

(2)   A guardianship application may be made in respect of a patient on the grounds that —

  (a)   he is suffering from mental disorder, being mental illness, severe mental impairment, psychopathic disorder or mental impairment and his mental disorder is of a nature or degree which warrants his reception into guardianship under this section; and

  (b)   it is necessary in the interests of the welfare of the patient or for the protection of other persons that the patient should be so received.

(3) A guardianship application shall be founded on the written recommendations in the prescribed form of two registered medical practitioners, including in each case a statement that in the opinion of the practitioner the conditions set out in subsection (2) above are complied with; and each such recommendation shall include —

(a) such particulars as may be prescribed of the grounds for that opinion so far as it relates to the conditions set out in paragraph (a) of that subsection; and

(b) a statement of the reasons for that opinion so far as it relates to the conditions set out in paragraph (b) of that subsection.

(4) A guardianship application shall state the age of the patient or, if his exact age is not known to the applicant, shall state (if it be the fact) that the patient is believed to have attained the age of 16 years.

(5) The person named as guardian in a guardianship application may be either a local social services authority or any other person (including the applicant himself); but a guardianship application in which a person other than a local social services authority is named as guardian shall be of no effect unless it is accepted on behalf of that person by the local social services authority for the area in which he resides, and shall be accompanied by a statement in writing by that person that he is willing to act as guardian.

8. Effect of guardianship application, etc.

(1) Where a guardianship application, duly made under the provisions of this Part of this Act and forwarded to the local social services authority within the period allowed by subsection (2) below is accepted by that authority, the application shall, subject to regulations made by the Secretary of State, confer on the authority or person named in the application as guardian, to the exclusion of any other person —

(a) the power to require the patient to reside at a place specified by the authority or person named as guardian;

(b) the power to require the patient to attend at places and times so specified for the purpose of medical treatment, occupation, education or training;

(c) the power to require access to the patient to be given, at any place where the patient is residing, to any registered medical practitioner, approved social worker or other person so specified.

(2) The period within which a guardianship application is required for the purposes of this section to be forwarded to the local social services authority is the period of 14 days beginning with the date on which the patient was last examined by a registered medical practitioner before giving a medical recommendation for the purposes of the application.

(3) A guardianship application which appears to be duly made and to be founded on the necessary medical recommendations may be acted upon without further proof of the signature or qualification of the person by whom the application or any such medical recommendation is made or given, or of any matter of fact or opinion stated in the application.

(4) If within the period of 14 days beginning with the day on which a guardianship application has been accepted by the local social services authority the application, or any medical recommendation given for the purposes of the application, is found to be in any respect incorrect or defective, the application or recommendation may, within that period and with the consent of that authority, be amended by the person by whom it was signed; and upon such amendment being made the application or recommendation shall have effect and shall be deemed to have had effect as if it had been originally made as so amended.

(5) Where a patient is received into guardianship in pursuance of a guardianship application, any previous application under this Part of this Act by virtue of which he was subject to guardianship or liable to be detained in a hospital shall cease to have effect.

5.1.4 **Special treatments**

Part IV of the Act regulates the position regarding the giving of certain special treatments. As Judge LJ indicates in the passage quoted above, a person who is detained under the compulsory powers in the Mental Health Act does not, by virtue of this alone, lose all capacity to make decisions: under the law as it stands at present (see above), a person's capacity is determined in relation to each individual decision. This is recognised in relation to the treatments covered by ss. 57 and 58, in both of which reference is made to consent. Clearly, provisions such as ss. 57 and 58 would be meaningless if the patient lost all power to make decisions solely by virtue of compulsory admission. However, s. 58 increases the powers of medical practitioners to treat patients (though with limitations on its application), as the treatments specified there may be given either with consent or with a second opinion: the treatment may therefore be given without the consent of the patient. This may be contrasted with s. 57, which requires the consent of the patient as well as a second opinion and cannot, therefore, be given without consent: the power of the doctor is thus restricted. However, the key to this issue is the determination of whether the patient has or lacks capacity to make a decision about the matter. The treatments specified for the purposes of ss. 57 and 58 are indicated in the extract from the Mental Health (Hospital, Guardianship and Consent to Treatment) Regulations 1983 (SI 1983 893).

56.   Patients to whom Part IV applies
(1)   This Part of this Act applies to any patient liable to be detained under this Act except —
    (a)   a patient who is liable to be detained by virtue of an emergency application and in respect of whom the second medical recommendation referred to in section 4(4)(a) above has not been given and received;
    (b)   a patient who is liable to be detained by virtue of section 5(2) or (4) or 35 above or section 135 or 136 below or by virtue of a direction under section 37(4) above; and
    (c)   a patient who has been conditionally discharged under section 42(2) above or section 73 or 74 below and has not been recalled to hospital.
(2)   Section 57 and, so far as relevant to that section, sections 59, 60 and 62 below, apply also to any patient who is not liable to be detained under this Act.

57.   Treatment requiring consent and a second opinion
(1)   This section applies to the following forms of medical treatment for mental disorder —
    (a)   any surgical operation for destroying brain tissue or for destroying the functioning of brain tissue; and
    (b)   such other forms of treatment as may be specified for the purposes of this section by regulations made by the Secretary of State.
(2)   Subject to section 62 below, a patient shall not be given any form of treatment to which this section applies unless he has consented to it and —
    (a)   a registered medical practitioner appointed for the purposes of this Part of this Act by the Secretary of State (not being the responsible medical officer) and two other persons appointed for the purposes of this paragraph by the Secretary of State (not being registered medical practitioners) have certified in writing that the patient is capable of understanding the nature, purpose and likely effects of the treatment in question and has consented to it; and

(b) the registered medical practitioner referred to in paragraph (a) above has certified in writing that, having regard to the likelihood of the treatment alleviating or preventing a deterioration of the patient's condition, the treatment should be given.

(3) Before giving a certificate under subsection (2)(b) above the registered medical practitioner concerned shall consult two other persons who have been professionally concerned with the patient's medical treatment, and of those persons one shall be a nurse and the other shall be neither a nurse nor a registered medical practitioner.

(4) Before making any regulations for the purpose of this section the Secretary of State shall consult such bodies as appear to him to be concerned.

58. Treatment requiring consent or a second opinion

(1) This section applies to the following forms of medical treatment for mental disorder —

(a) such forms of treatment as may be specified for the purposes of this section by regulations made by the Secretary of State;

(b) the administration of medicine to a patient by any means (not being a form of treatment specified under paragraph (a) above or section 57 above) at any time during a period for which he is liable to be detained as a patient to whom this Part of this Act applies if three months or more have elapsed since the first occasion in that period when medicine was administered to him by any means for his mental disorder.

(2) The Secretary of State may by order vary the length of the period mentioned in subsection (l)(b) above.

(3) Subject to section 62 below, a patient shall not be given any form of treatment to which this section applies unless —

(a) he has consented to that treatment and either the responsible medical officer or a registered medical practitioner appointed for the purposes of this Part of this Act by the Secretary of State has certified in writing that the patient is capable of understanding its nature, purpose and likely effects and has consented to it; or

(b) a registered medical practitioner appointed as aforesaid (not being the responsible medical officer) has certified in writing that the patient is not capable of understanding the nature, purpose and likely effects of that treatment or has not consented to it but that, having regard to the likelihood of its alleviating or preventing a deterioration of his condition, the treatment should be given.

(4) Before giving a certificate under subsection (3)(b) above the registered medical practitioner concerned shall consult two other persons who have been professionally concerned with the patient's medical treatment, and of those persons one shall be a nurse and the other shall be neither a nurse nor a registered medical practitioner.

(5) Before making any regulations for the purposes of this section the Secretary of State shall consult such bodies as appear to him to be concerned.

...

The Regulations provide:

16.(1) For the purposes of section 57 (treatment requiring consent and a second opinion) —

(a) the form of treatment to which that section shall apply, in addition to the treatment mentioned in subsection (1)(a) of that section (any surgical operation for destroying brain tissue or for destroying the functioning of brain tissue), shall be the surgical implantation of hormones for the purpose of reducing male sexual drive;

(b) the certificates required for the purposes of subsection (2)(a) and (b) of that section shall be in the form set out in Form 37.

(2)   For the purposes of section 58 (treatment requiring consent or a second opinion) —

(a)   the form of treatment to which that section shall apply, in addition to the administration of medicine mentioned in subsection (1)(b) of that section, shall be electro-convulsive therapy; and

(b)   the certificates required for the purposes of subsection (3)(a) and (b) of that section shall be in the form set out in Forms 38 and 39 respectively.

5.1.5 Entry to premises and removal from public places

In addition to powers to compel admission and treatment, the Act also contains powers authorising entry to premises. The basic legal position in relation to entry to private premises is that a person may only enter the premises of another with the consent of that other or with some legal justification. This is as true of public officials as it is of ordinary citizens. When relying on legal justification, the person entering premises must be able to show that there is either a statutory provision or a rule of common law enabling that person to enter in the absence of consent. This is one of the most venerable principles in English law. In *Entick* v *Carrington* (1765) 19 St. Tr. 1029, the defendants argued that they had a right to enter premises on the basis of a general warrant (not specifying goods to be searched for) or on grounds of state necessity. The court held that the law did not recognise either of these as justifying entry to premises. The actions of the defendants were, therefore, unlawful. Lord Camden CJ said: 'If it is law, it will be found in our books. If it is not to be found there, it is not law'. Provisions, such as those contained in the Mental Health Act, authorising invasions of private property may only be used in the precise circumstances stated. So, for example, a social worker who is not an ASW would not be able to use the power of entry under s. 115:

115.   Powers of entry and inspection
An approved social worker of a local social services authority may at all reasonable times after producing, if asked to do so, some duly authenticated document showing that he is such a social worker, enter and inspect any premises (not being a hospital) in the area of that authority in which a mentally disordered patient is living, if he has reasonable cause to believe that the patient is not under proper care.

A further option is to apply to a magistrate for a warrant authorising entry:

135.   Warrant to search for and remove patients
(1)   If it appears to a justice of the peace, on information on oath laid by an approved social worker, that there is reasonable cause to suspect that a person believed to be suffering from mental disorder —

(a)   has been, or is being, ill-treated, neglected or kept otherwise than under proper control, in any place within the jurisdiction of the justice, or

(b)   being unable to care for himself, is living alone in any such place, the justice may issue a warrant authorising any constable to enter, if need be by force, any premises specified in the warrant in which that person is believed to be, and, if thought fit, to remove him to a place of safety with a view to the making of an application in respect of him under Part II of this Act, or of other arrangements for his treatment or care.

(2)   If it appears to a justice of the peace, on information on oath laid by any constable or other person who is authorised by or under this Act or under section 83 of the Mental Health

(Scotland) Act 1984 to take a patient to any place, or to take into custody or retake a patient who is liable under this Act or under the said section 83 to be so taken or retaken —

(a) that there is reasonable cause to believe that the patient is to be found on premises within the jurisdiction of the justice; and

(b) that admission to the premises has been refused or that a refusal of such admission is apprehended,

the justice may issue a warrant authorising any constable to enter the premises,

if need be by force, and remove the patient.

(3) A patient who is removed to a place of safety in the execution of a warrant issued under this section may be detained there for a period not exceeding 72 hours.

(4) In the execution of a warrant issued under subsection (1) above, a constable shall be accompanied by an approved social worker and by a registered medical practitioner, and in the execution of a warrant issued under subsection (2) above a constable may be accompanied —

(a) by a registered medical practitioner;

(b) by any person authorised by or under this Act or under section 83 of the Mental Health (Scotland) Act 1984 to take or retake the patient.

(5) It shall not be necessary in any information or warrant under subsection (1) above to name the patient concerned.

(6) In this section 'place of safety' means residential accommodation provided by a local social services authority under Part III of the National Assistance Act 1948, a hospital as defined by this Act, a police station, a mental nursing home or residential home for mentally disordered persons or any other suitable place the occupier of which is willing temporarily to receive the patient.

The Act also gives a constable the power to remove a person from a public place and take him or her to a place of safety. Note that this power exists in addition to other powers enjoyed by police officers under legislation such as the Police and Criminal Evidence Act 1984. The choice made by the constable as to whether to regard the person as a criminal suspect or a potential patient in any given situation can determine how and through which system — court or hospital — a person is processed.

136. Mentally disordered persons found in public places

(1) If a constable finds in a place to which the public have access a person who appears to him to be suffering from mental disorder and to be in immediate need of care or control, the constable may, if he thinks it necessary to do so in the interests of that person or for the protection of other persons, remove that person to a place of safety within the meaning of section 135 above.

(2) A person removed to a place of safety under this section may be detained there for a period not exceeding 72 hours for the purpose of enabling him to be examined by a registered medical practitioner and to be interviewed by an approved social worker and of making any necessary arrangements for his treatment or care.

5.1.6 Discharge from hospital

In accordance with basic principles under the Act, reinforced by the Code and the European Convention on Human Rights (especially Art. 5), a person should not continue to be detained as soon as the criteria for detention cease to apply in respect of that person. In theory, informal patients may discharge themselves at any time. However, as we have seen, doctors and nurses have the power to detain in-patients under s. 5. Detained patients should be discharged as soon as they are no longer suffering from mental disorder. This is even the case in respect of restricted patients, as

Johnson v *UK* makes clear. However, in some cases there may be a dispute as to whether the person is or is not still suffering from mental disorder. The nearest relative, the patient or the Secretary of State may apply to a Mental Health Review Tribunal for release of a patient who is no longer suffering from mental disorder. The Act also provides for automatic review by a Mental Health Review Tribunal.

[*Johnson* v *UK*]

7. The applicant was convicted at Leicester Crown Court on 8 August 1984 of causing actual bodily harm to a woman passer-by in a random and unprovoked attack. ... The applicant had previous convictions for unprovoked assaults:

...

8. While on remand in Leicester Prison the applicant was diagnosed as suffering from 'mental illness', manifested in delusions of conspiracy and victimisation and an obsession with astral projection. The precise diagnosis was of schizophrenia superimposed on a psychopathic personality. The applicant had a history of alcohol and drug abuse. He had never previously been diagnosed as mentally ill within the meaning of the Mental Health Act 1983 although, when on remand on a previous charge of actual bodily harm, he had been assessed for psychiatric treatment but had been found to be unsuitable.

9. The applicant's diagnosis (see paragraph 8 above) was confirmed by two psychiatrists. The Crown Court accordingly imposed a hospital order on him under section 37 of the 1983 Act. He was also made subject to a restriction order without limit in time under section 41 of the same Act, the court being satisfied that this order was necessary for the protection of the public from serious harm.

...

50. The applicant complained that his detention between 15 June 1989, the date when the Tribunal first found him to be no longer suffering from mental illness, and 12 January 1993, the date when his absolute discharge was ordered, was in violation of Article 5 Para. 1 of the Convention.

...

51. Mr Johnson in his primary submission maintained that the June 1989 Tribunal should have ordered his immediate and unconditional discharge. Having regard to the strength of the psychiatric evidence before it ... and to its own assessment of his condition, that Tribunal was satisfied that he was no longer suffering from mental illness. This finding was confirmed by three successive Tribunals before he was finally released from Rampton Hospital. Relying on the Court's *Winterwerp* v *the Netherlands* judgment of 24 October 1979 (Series A no. 33) he asserted that the authorities could not invoke any margin of appreciation to justify his continued detention beyond 15 June 1989 leaving aside any short period of time which might be needed to implement arrangements for his discharge. He had made a full recovery from the episode of mental illness specified in the hospital order which the domestic court had imposed on him (see paragraph 9 above). The Tribunal had not been justified in denying him an immediate and unconditional discharge on account of a possible risk of recurrence of mental illness given that any such risk had been neutralised by reason of the treatment he had received in Rampton Hospital.

52. While acknowledging by way of an alternative submission that the discharge of a person who is found to be no longer of unsound mind may be made subject to conditions, the applicant contended that any such conditions must not hinder immediate or near-immediate release and certainly not delay it excessively as occurred in his case. The imposition of the hostel residence

condition was not only an onerous, unnecessary and disproportionate requirement which could in itself be considered to be a breach of Article 5 para. 1 of the Convention if implemented, it was also causative of a delay of three years and seven months before he was eventually released. When imposing the hostel condition, the 1989 Tribunal had neither the legal powers to direct a hostel to accept him nor to specify a time-limit for the implementation of the condition. He maintained that the failure to secure a suitable hostel and the consequential delay in his discharge could not be attributed to him given that the hostels approached had all rejected him.

...

58.   The Court considers at the outset that it is appropriate to examine the lawfulness of the applicant's continued detention after 15 June 1989 under Article 5 para. 1(e) alone of the Convention, even if the lawfulness of his detention, at least up until that date, could also possibly be grounded on Article 5 para. 1(a) since it resulted from a 'conviction' by a 'competent court' within the meaning of that sub-paragraph. While the applicability of one ground listed in Article 5 para. 1 does not necessarily preclude the applicability of another and a detention may be justified under more than one sub-paragraph of that provision (see the *Eriksen v Norway* judgment of 27 May 1997, *Reports of Judgments and Decisions* 1997-III, pp. 861–62, para. 76), it is to be noted that the applicant was detained at Rampton Hospital on the basis of a hospital and a restriction order without limit in time made under the Mental Health Act 1983 in order to undergo psychiatric treatment (see paragraph 9 above). Indeed, it has not been disputed that the lawfulness of the applicant's detention after 15 June 1989 falls to be determined on the basis of Article 5 Para. 1(e) to the exclusion of Article 5 Para. 1(a).

59.   The Court also notes that those appearing before it have not contested that the applicant's continued detention was lawful under domestic law, having regard to the Tribunal's powers under section 73(2) and (7) of the 1983 Act to impose conditions on the discharge of patients who are no longer mentally ill within the meaning of section 1(2) of that Act and to defer a discharge until those conditions have been fulfilled. For its part, the Court sees no reason to find that the applicant's continued detention was not in conformity with the substantive and procedural rules governing the making of a conditional or deferred conditional discharge. It notes in fact that the Court of Appeal has considered that a Tribunal's competence to order the conditional rather than absolute discharge of a person no longer suffering from mental illness is an important discretionary power; moreover, a Tribunal's power to defer a conditional discharge without specifying a time-limit for the finalisation of the appropriate arrangements has been affirmed by the House of Lords.

60.   The Court stresses, however, that the lawfulness of the applicant's continued detention under domestic law is not in itself decisive. It must also be established that his detention after 15 June 1989 was in conformity with the purpose of Article 5 para. 1 of the Convention, which is to prevent persons from being deprived of their liberty in an arbitrary fashion (see, among many authorities, the *Wassink v the Netherlands* judgment of 27 September 1990, Series A no. 185-A, p. 11, para. 24) and with the aim of the restriction contained in sub-paragraph (e) (see the above-mentioned *Winterwerp* judgment, p. 17, para. 39). In this latter respect the Court recalls that, according to its established case-law, an individual cannot be considered to be of 'unsound mind' and deprived of his liberty unless the following three minimum conditions are satisfied: firstly, he must reliably be shown to be of unsound mind; secondly, the mental disorder must be of a kind or degree warranting compulsory confinement; thirdly, and of sole relevance to the case at issue, the validity of continued confinement depends upon the persistence of such a disorder (see the Winterwerp judgment cited above, pp. 21–22, para. 40; and the *Luberti v Italy* judgment of 23 February 1984, Series A no. 75, pp. 12–13, para. 27).

61.   By maintaining that the 1989 Tribunal was satisfied that he was no longer suffering from the mental illness which led to his committal to Rampton Hospital, Mr Johnson is arguing that

the above-mentioned third condition as to the persistence of mental disorder was not fulfilled and he should as a consequence have been immediately and unconditionally released from detention.

The Court cannot accept that submission. In its view it does not automatically follow from a finding by an expert authority that the mental disorder which justified a patient's compulsory confinement no longer persists, that the latter must be immediately and unconditionally released into the community.

Such a rigid approach to the interpretation of that condition would place an unacceptable degree of constraint on the responsible authority's exercise of judgment to determine in parti-cular cases and on the basis of all the relevant circumstances whether the interests of the patient and the community into which he is to be released would in fact be best served by this course of action. It must also be observed that in the field of mental illness the assessment as to whether the disappearance of the symptoms of the illness is confirmation of complete recovery is not an exact science. Whether or not recovery from an episode of mental illness which justified a patient's confinement is complete and definitive or merely apparent cannot in all cases be measured with absolute certainty. It is the behaviour of the patient in the period spent outside the confines of the psychiatric institution which will be conclusive of this.

62.   It is to be recalled in this respect that the Court in its Luberti judgment ... accepted that the termination of the confinement of an individual who has previously been found by a court to be of unsound mind and to present a danger to society is a matter that concerns, as well as that individual, the community in which he will live if released. Having regard to the pressing nature of the interests at stake, and in particular the very serious nature of the offence committed by Mr Luberti when mentally ill, it was accepted in that case that the responsible authority was entitled to proceed with caution and needed some time to consider whether to terminate his confinement, even if the medical evidence pointed to his recovery.

63.   In the view of the Court it must also be acknowledged that a responsible authority is enti-tled to exercise a similar measure of discretion in deciding whether in the light of all the relevant circumstances and the interests at stake it would in fact be appropriate to order the immediate and absolute discharge of a person who is no longer suffering from the mental disorder which led to his confinement. That authority should be able to retain some measure of supervision over the progress of the person once he is released into the community and to that end make his discharge subject to conditions. It cannot be excluded either that the imposition of a particular condition may in certain circumstances justify a deferral of discharge from detention, having regard to the nature of the condition and to the reasons for imposing it. It is, however, of para-mount importance that appropriate safeguards are in place so as to ensure that any deferral of discharge is consonant with the purpose of Article 5 para. 1 and with the aim of the restriction in sub-paragraph (e) (see paragraph 60 above) and, in particular, that discharge is not unreason-ably delayed.

64.   Having regard to the above considerations, the Court is of the opinion that the 1989 Tribunal could in the exercise of its judgment properly conclude that it was premature to order Mr Johnson's absolute and immediate discharge from Rampton Hospital. While it is true that the Tribunal was satisfied on the basis of its own assessment and the medical evidence before it ... that the applicant was no longer suffering from mental illness, it nevertheless considered that a phased conditional discharge was appropriate in the circumstances. It is to be noted that this approach was endorsed by Dr Cameron and Dr Wilson, the latter having been closely involved with the applicant's treatment since 3 November 1987 .... As an expert review body which included a doctor who had interviewed the applicant ... , the Tribunal could properly have regard to the fact that as recently as 10 February 1988 ... the applicant was still found to be suf-fering from mental illness and that his disorder had manifested itself prior to his confinement in acts of spontaneous and unprovoked violence against members of the public. It was not

therefore unreasonable for the Tribunal to consider, having regard to the views of Dr Wilson and Dr Cameron, that the applicant should be placed under psychiatric and social-worker supervision and required to undergo a period of rehabilitation in a hostel on account of the fact that 'the recurrence of mental illness requiring recall to hospital cannot be excluded' .... The Tribunal was also in principle justified in deferring the applicant's release in order to enable the authorities to locate a hostel which best suited his needs and provided him with the most appropriate conditions for his successful rehabilitation.

65.   As to the conditions imposed on Mr Johnson's discharge, it is to be noted that the requirement to remain under the psychiatric supervision of Dr Cameron and the social-worker supervision of Mr Patterson ... would not have hindered his immediate release from Rampton Hospital into the community and cannot be said to raise an issue under Article 5 para. 1 of the Convention.

66.   However, while imposing the hostel residence requirement on the applicant and deferring his release until the arrangements had been made to its satisfaction, the Tribunal lacked the power to guarantee that the applicant would be relocated to a suitable post-discharge hostel within a reasonable period of time. The onus was on the authorities to secure a hostel willing to admit the applicant. It is to be observed that they were expected to proceed with all reasonable expedition in finalising the arrangements for a placement .... While the authorities made considerable efforts to this end, these efforts were frustrated by the reluctance of certain hostels to accept the applicant as well as by the latter's negative attitude with respect to the options available .... They were also constrained by the limited number of available placements. Admittedly, a suitable hostel may have been located within a reasonable period of time had the applicant adopted a more positive approach to his rehabilitation. However, this cannot refute the conclusion that neither the Tribunal nor the authorities possessed the necessary powers to ensure that the condition could be implemented within a reasonable time. Furthermore, the earliest date on which the applicant could have had his continued detention reviewed was twelve months after the review conducted by the June 1989 Tribunal .... In between reviews the applicant could not petition the Tribunal to have the terms of the hostel residence condition reconsidered; nor was the Tribunal empowered to monitor periodically outside the annual reviews the progress made in the search for a hostel and to amend the deferred conditional discharge order in the light of the difficulties encountered by the authorities. While the Secretary of State could have referred the applicant's case to the Tribunal at any time ... it is to be noted that this possibility was unlikely to be effected in practice since even at the date of the January 1993 Tribunal the authorities maintained their opposition to the applicant's release from detention until he had fulfilled the hostel condition ....

67.   In these circumstances, it must be concluded that the imposition of the hostel residence condition by the June 1989 Tribunal led to the indefinite deferral of the applicant's release from Rampton Hospital, especially since the applicant was unwilling after October 1990 to cooperate further with the authorities in their efforts to secure a hostel, thereby excluding any possibility that the condition could be satisfied. While the 1990 and 1991 Tribunals considered the applicant's case afresh, they were obliged to order his continued detention since he had not yet fulfilled the terms of the conditional discharge imposed by the June 1989 Tribunal.

Having regard to the situation which resulted from the decision taken by the latter Tribunal and to the lack of adequate safeguards, including provision for judicial review to ensure that the applicant's release from detention would not be unreasonably delayed, it must be considered that his continued confinement after 15 June 1989 cannot be justified on the basis of Article 5 para. 1 (e) of the Convention (see paragraph 63 above).

For these reasons, the Court concludes that the applicant's continued detention after 15 June 1989 constituted a violation of Article 5 para. 1 of the Convention.

...

The Act provides:

23. Discharge of patients

(1)   Subject to the provisions of this section and section 25 below, a patient who is for the time being liable to be detained or subject to guardianship under this Part of this Act shall cease to be so liable or subject if an order in writing discharging him from detention or guardianship (in this Act referred to as 'an order for discharge') is made in accordance with this section.

(2)   An order for discharge may be made in respect of a patient —

(a)   where the patient is liable to be detained in a hospital in pursuance of an application for admission for assessment or for treatment by the responsible medical officer, by the managers or by the nearest relative of the patient;

(b)   where the patient is subject to guardianship, by the responsible medical officer, by the responsible local social services authority or by the nearest relative of the patient.

(3)   Where the patient is liable to be detained in a mental nursing home in pursuance of an application for admission for assessment or for treatment, an order for his discharge may, without prejudice to subsection (2) above, be made by the Secretary of State and, if the patient is maintained under a contract with a National Health Service trust, Health Authority or Special Health Authority, by that National Health Service Trust, Health Authority or Special Health Authority.

(4)   The powers conferred by this section on any authority, trust or body of persons may be exercised subject to subsection (5) below by any three or more members of that authority, trust or body authorised by them in that behalf or by three or more members of a committee or sub-committee of that authority, trust or body which has been authorised by them in that behalf.

(5)   The reference in subsection (4) above to the members of an authority, trust or body or the members of a committee or sub-committee of an authority, trust or body, —

(a)   in the case of a Health Authority or Special Health Authority or a committee or sub-committee of such a Health Authority or Special Health Authority, is a reference only to the chairman of the authority and such members (of the authority, committee or sub-committee, as the case may be) as are not also officers of the authority, within the meaning of the National Health Service Act 1977; and

(b)   in the case of a National Health Service trust or a committee or sub-committee of such a trust, is a reference only to the chairman of the trust and such directors or (in the case of a committee or sub-committee) members as are not also employees of the trust.

...

25. Restrictions on discharge by nearest relative

(1)   An order for the discharge of a patient who is liable to be detained in a hospital shall not be made by his nearest relative except after giving not less than 72 hours' notice in writing to the managers of the hospital; and if, within 72 hours after such notice has been given, the responsible medical officer furnishes to the managers a report certifying that in the opinion of that officer the patient, if discharged, would be likely to act in a manner dangerous to other persons or to himself —

(a)   any order for the discharge of the patient made by that relative in pursuance of the notice shall be of no effect; and

(b)   no further order for the discharge of the patient shall be made by that relative during the period of six months beginning with the date of the report.

(2)   In any case where a report under subsection (1) above is furnished in respect of a patient who is liable to be detained in pursuance of an application for admission for treatment the managers shall cause the nearest relative of the patient to be informed.

It may be noted that different considerations apply in respect of restricted patients: the relevant provisions are not reproduced here.

The general powers of the Mental Health Review Tribunal are set out in s. 72 and 73, which, in their original form read as follows:

72. Powers of tribunals

(1)   Where application is made to a Mental Health Review Tribunal by or in respect of a patient who is liable to be detained under this Act, the tribunal may in any case direct that the patient be discharged, and —

    (a) the tribunal shall direct the discharge of a patient liable to be detained under section 2 above if they are satisfied —

        (i) that he is not then suffering from mental disorder or from mental disorder of a nature or degree which warrants his detention in a hospital for assessment (or for assessment followed by medical treatment) for at least a limited period; or

        (ii) that his detention as aforesaid is not justified in the interests of his own health or safety or with a view to the protection of other persons;

    (b) the tribunal shall direct the discharge of a patient liable to be detained otherwise than under section 2 above if they are satisfied —

        (i) that he is not then suffering from mental illness, psychopathic disorder, severe mental impairment or mental impairment or from any of those forms of disorder of a nature or degree which makes it appropriate for him to be liable to be detained in a hospital for medical treatment; or

        (ii) that it is not necessary for the health or safety of the patient or for the protection of other persons that he should receive such treatment; or

        (iii) in the case of an application by virtue of paragraph (g) of section 66(1) above, that the patient, if released, would not be likely to act in a manner dangerous to other persons or to himself.

(2)   In determining whether to direct the discharge of a patient detained otherwise than under section 2 above in a case not falling within paragraph (b) of subsection (1) above, the tribunal shall have regard —

    (a) to the likelihood of medical treatment alleviating or preventing a deterioration of the patient's condition; and

    (b) in the case of a patient suffering from mental illness or severe mental impairment, to the likelihood of the patient, if discharged, being able to care for himself, to obtain the care he needs or to guard himself against serious exploitation.

(3)   A tribunal may under subsection (1) above direct the discharge of a patient on a future date specified in the direction; and where a tribunal do not direct the discharge of a patient under that subsection the tribunal may —

    (a) with a view to facilitating his discharge on a future date, recommend that he be granted leave of absence or transferred to another hospital or into guardianship; and

    (b) further consider his case in the event of any such recommendation not being complied with.

(3A)   Where, in the case of an application to a tribunal by or in respect of a patient who is liable to be detained in pursuance of an application for admission for treatment or by virtue of an order or direction for his admission or removal to hospital under Part III of this Act, the tribunal do not direct the discharge of the patient under subsection (1) above, the tribunal may —

    (a) recommend that the responsible medical officer consider whether to make a supervision application in respect of the patient; and

    (b) further consider his case in the event of no such application being made.

(4) Where application is made to a Mental Health Review Tribunal by or in respect of a patient who is subject to guardianship under this Act, the tribunal may in any case direct that the patient be discharged, and shall so direct if they are satisfied —
  (a) that he is not then suffering from mental illness, psychopathic disorder, severe 'mental impairment or mental impairment; or
  (b) that it is not necessary in the interests of the welfare of the patient, or for the protection of other persons, that the patient should remain under such guardianship.

(4A) Where application is made to a Mental Health Review Tribunal by or in respect of a patient who is subject to after-care under supervision (or, if he has not yet left hospital, is to be so subject after he leaves hospital), the tribunal may in any case direct that the patient shall cease to be so subject (or not become so subject), and shall so direct if they are satisfied —
  (a) in a case where the patient has not yet left hospital, that the conditions set out in section 25A(4) above are not complied with; or
  (b) in any other case, that the conditions set out in section 25G(4) above are not complied with.

(5) where application is made to a Mental Health Review Tribunal under any provision of this Act by or in respect of a patient and the tribunal do not direct that the patient be discharged, or, if he is (or is to be) subject to after-care under supervision, that he cease to be so subject (or not become so subject) the tribunal may, if satisfied that the patient is suffering from a form of mental disorder other than the form specified in the application, order or direction relating to him, direct that that application, order or direction be amended by substituting for the form of mental disorder specified in it such other form of mental disorder as appears to the tribunal to be appropriate.

(6) Subsections (1) to (5) above apply in relation to references to a Mental Health Review Tribunal as they apply in relation to applications made to such a tribunal by or in respect of a patient.

...

73(1) Where an application to a Mental Health Review Tribunal is made by a restricted patient who is subject to a restriction order, or where the case of such a patient is referred to such a tribunal, the tribunal shall direct the absolute discharge of the patient if satisfied —
  (a) as to the matters mentioned in paragraph (b)(i) or (ii) of section 72(1) above; and
  (b) that it is not appropriate for the patient to remain liable to be recalled to hospital for further treatment.

(2) Where in the case of any such patient as is mentioned in subsection (1) above the tribunal are satisfied as to the matters referred to in paragraph (a) of that subsection but not as to the matter referred to in paragraph (b) of that subsection the tribunal shall direct the conditional discharge of the patient.

(3) Where a patient is absolutely discharged under this section he shall thereupon cease to be liable to be detained by virtue of the relevant hospital order, and the restriction order shall cease to have effect accordingly.

However, ss. 72(1) and 73(1) have recently been declared incompatible with the Convention rights contained in the Human Rights Act 1998, insofar as they put the onus onto the patient to prove he should be discharged rather than on the hospital authorities to show that he should continue to be detained:

[*R(H)* v *London North and East Region Mental Health Review Tribunal* [2002] *QB 1*]
1 ... On 15 September 1988, the applicant, whom we shall call 'H', was convicted of manslaughter. He was ordered to be detained in a hospital and to be subject to special restrictions pursuant to sections 37 and 41 of the Mental Health Act 1983 ('the Act'). He was admitted to Broadmoor Hospital. On 22 December 1999, he applied to the mental health review tribunal

('the tribunal') for a discharge pursuant to section 73 of the Act. On 29 March 2000, the tribunal decided that he should not be discharged from liability to be detained. H applied for judicial review of the decision of the tribunal. On 15 September 2000, Crane J dismissed his application. Moreover, he refused to grant declaratory relief as to the compatibility of section 73 of the Act with article 5(1) and (4) of the European Convention for the Protection of Human Rights and Fundamental Freedoms. On 20 December 2000 the applicant obtained permission to appeal against these decisions from Laws LJ, who commented: 'the applicant should be allowed to argue his Human Rights Act 1998 points.' In the event the only issue that has been pursued before us has been the question of whether section 73 of the Act can be given an interpretation which is compatible with the Convention. That is a matter in which H has an interest. He is about to make a further application to the mental health review tribunal to be discharged from hospital. The true interpretation of section 73 may impact on the result of that application. The Secretary of State was given the requisite notice of an application by H for a declaration that section 73 is incompatible with H's rights under article 5 of the Convention. He has appeared at this appeal, through his counsel, Mr Rabinder Singh. Mr Singh has informed us that the Secretary of State wishes this court to make a declaration of incompatibility if it concludes that section 73 is not compatible with the Convention. The point is one of general importance and, in the circumstances, we have thought it right to entertain it.

...

The 1983 Act

11   H was admitted to hospital as a restricted patient pursuant to the provisions of sections 37 and 41 of the Act. For present purposes, however, it suffices to set out the following very similar provisions of the Act dealing with compulsory admission of an unrestricted patient for treatment in hospital under section 3(2). Section 3(2) reads:

'An application for admission for treatment may be made in respect of a patient on the grounds that — (a) he is suffering from mental illness, severe mental impairment, psychopathic disorder or mental impairment and his mental disorder is of a nature or degree which makes it appropriate for him to receive medical treatment in a hospital; and (b) in the case of psychopathic disorder or mental impairment, such treatment is likely to alleviate or prevent a deterioration of his condition; and (c) it is necessary for the health or safety of the patient or for the protection of other persons that he should receive such treatment and it cannot be provided unless he is detained under this section.'

12   The relevant provisions for discharge of an unrestricted patient are set out in section 72(1)(b):

'the tribunal shall direct the discharge of a patient liable to be detained otherwise than under section 2 above if they are satisfied — (i) that he is not then suffering from mental illness, psychopathic disorder, severe mental impairment or mental impairment or from any of those forms of disorder of a nature or degree which makes it appropriate for him to be liable to be detained in a hospital for medical treatment; or (ii) that it is not necessary for the health or safety of the patient or for the protection of other persons that he should receive such treatment...'

13   These apply to a restricted patient by virtue of section 73(1), which provides:

'Where an application to a mental health review tribunal is made by a restricted patient who is subject to a restriction order, or where the case of such a patient is referred to such a tribunal, the tribunal shall direct the absolute discharge of the patient if satisfied — (a) as to the matters mentioned in paragraph (b)(i) or (ii) of section 72(1) above; and (b) that it is not appropriate for the patient to remain liable to be recalled to hospital for further treatment.'

...

Are sections 72 and 73 compatible with the convention?

28   The written submission of the Secretary of State on this issue was as follows:

'Although the point about the burden of proof has not been directly decided by the European Court of Human Rights the Secretary of State accepts that to place the burden on a patient to prove that the conditions for detention are no longer met would be incompatible with article 5(1) of the Convention. This is ultimately a matter for the court but it appears to follow from cases such as *Winterwerp* v *The Netherlands* (1979) 2 EHRR 387, 402–403, paras 39–40, and *Johnson* v *United Kingdom* (1997) 27 EHRR 296, 322, para. 60. In those cases the European court has held that both the initial deprivation of a mental patient's liberty and the continued detention of a patient can only be lawful under article 5(1)(e) of the Convention if it can "reliably be shown" that he or she suffers from a mental disorder sufficiently serious to warrant detention.'

29   In oral argument Mr Singh suggested that this concession went no further than accepting that it was inappropriate to speak of the plaintiff having to discharge a 'burden of proof'. As indicated above, we do not find it possible to divorce the concept of 'burden of proof' from the question of the test that the tribunal has to apply when considering whether a patient is entitled to be discharged. We understand the Secretary of State to concede that the same approach has to be applied when considering whether to admit a patient as that which has to be applied when considering whether the continued detention of the patient is lawful. In either case the test is whether it can be 'reliably shown' that the patient suffers from a mental disorder sufficiently serious to warrant detention.

30   Mr Gordon's submission mirrored the written submission of the Secretary of State. He submitted that the continued detention of a patient who had been compulsorily admitted was not lawful under article 5(1) unless it could reliably be shown that the mental condition of the patient was such as to warrant detention. A test which allowed the continued detention of a patient simply because it could not be shown that his mental condition did not warrant detention violated article 5(1). Mr Gordon also submitted that such a test violated article 5(4), but invited us simply to record that he had taken this point rather than decide it.

31   We do not think it sensible to address the issue of compatibility without considering both the relevant paragraphs of article 5. So far as article 5(4) is concerned, it seems to us axiomatic that if the function of the tribunal is to consider whether the detention of the patient is lawful, it must apply the same test that the law required to be applied as a precondition to admission, unless it be the case that a patient once admitted can be lawfully detained provided that some other test is satisfied. We endorse the common submission of Mr Singh and Mr Gordon that it is contrary to the Convention compulsorily to detain a patient unless it can be shown that the patient is suffering from a mental disorder that warrants detention. Inasmuch as sections 72 and 73 do not require the tribunal to discharge a patient if this cannot be shown we have concluded that they are incompatible with both article 5(1) and article 5(4). We think that this follows from the following statement of principle in the seminal case of *Winterwerp* v *The Netherlands* (1979) 2 EHRR 387, 403, para. 39:

'In the court's opinion, except in emergency cases, the individual concerned should not be deprived of his liberty unless he has been reliably shown to be of "unsound mind" The very nature of what has to be established before the competent national authority — that is, a true mental disorder — calls for objective medical expertise. Further, the mental disorder must be of a kind or degree warranting compulsory confinement. What is more, the validity of continued confinement depends upon the persistence of such a disorder.'

Risk and uncertainty

32   There are some further observations that we wish to make although we should record that they relate to matters to which counsel for the applicant did not address detailed argument. It

does not follow from our conclusion that article 5 requires that a patient be discharged whenever any one of the three criteria in section 3 cannot be demonstrated on balance of probability. Detention cannot be justified under article 5(1)(e) unless the patient is 'of unsound mind', but once that is established we do not consider that the Convention restricts the right to detain a patient in hospital, as does section 3, to circumstances where medical treatment is likely to alleviate or prevent a deterioration of the condition. Nor is it necessary under the Convention to demonstrate that such treatment cannot be provided unless the patient is detained in hospital: see section 3(2)(c).

33   The circumstances of the present case, which are similar to those considered by Latham J in *Ex p Moyle* [2000] Lloyd's Rep Med 143, are not uncommon. A patient is detained who is unquestionably suffering from schizophrenia. While in the controlled environment of the hospital he is taking medication, and as a result of the medication is in remission. So long as he continues to take the medication he will pose no danger to himself or to others. The nature of the illness is such, however, that if he ceases to take the medication he will relapse and pose a danger to himself or to others. The professionals may be uncertain whether, if he is discharged into the community, he will continue to take the medication. We do not believe that article 5 requires that the patient must always be discharged in such circumstances. The appropriate response should depend upon the result of weighing the interests of the patient against those of the public having regard to the particular facts. Continued detention can be justified if, but only if, it is a proportionate response having regard to the risks that would be involved in discharge.

34   Having regard to these considerations, we believe that it is only rarely that the provisions of sections 72 and 73 constrain a mental health review tribunal to refuse an order of discharge where the continued detention of the patient infringes article 5. Indeed, in our experience where a tribunal refuses an application for a discharge it usually gives reasons for doing so that involve a positive finding that the patient is suffering from a mental disorder that warrants his or her continued detention. These may well be matters that the Secretary of State will wish to bear in mind when considering whether to take remedial action under section 10 of the Human Rights Act 1998. We have in mind the White Paper recently published on reforming the Mental Health Act and note that it does not appear to be proposed that the new mental health review tribunal will, when reviewing detention of a patient, apply a reversed burden of proof: see Reforming the Mental Health Act (Cm 5016-1/2000), Part 1, para. 3.42.

35   For the reasons that we have given we consider that H has made out his case for a declaration of incompatibility. We shall hear counsel on the precise form of the declaration.

As a result of this case, ss. 72(1) and 73(1) have been amended by the Mental Health Act 1983 (Remedial) Order 2001 (SI 2001/3712) and now read as follows:

72.(1)   Where application is made to a Mental Health Review Tribunal by or in respect of a patient who is liable to be detained under this Act, the tribunal may in any case direct that the patient be discharged, and —

   (a)   the tribunal shall direct the discharge of a patient liable to be detained under section 2 above if they are not satisfied —

   (i)   that he is suffering from mental disorder or from mental disorder of a nature or degree which warrants his detention in a hospital for assessment (or for assessment followed by medical treatment) for at least a limited period; or

   (ii)   that his detention as aforesaid is justified in the interests of his own health or safety or with a view to the protection of other persons;

   (b)   the tribunal shall direct the discharge of a patient liable to be detained otherwise than under section 2 above if they are not satisfied —

(i) that he is then suffering from mental illness, psychopathic disorder, severe mental impairment or mental impairment or from any of those forms of disorder of a nature or degree which makes it appropriate for him to be liable to be detained in a hospital for medical treatment; or

(ii) that it is necessary for the health or safety of the patient or for the protection of other persons that he should receive such treatment; ... .

73(1) Where an application to a Mental Health Review Tribunal is made by a restricted patient who is subject to a restriction order, or where the case of such a patient is referred to such a tribunal, the tribunal shall direct the absolute discharge of the patient if —

(a) the tribunal are not satisfied as to the matters mentioned in paragraph (b)(i) or (ii) of section 72(1) above; and

(b) the tribunal are satisfied that it is not appropriate for the patient to remain liable to be recalled to hospital for further treatment.

(2) Where in the case of any such patient as is mentioned in subsection (1) above —

(a) paragraph (a) of that subsection applies; but

(b) paragraph (b) of that subsection does not apply,

the tribunal shall direct the conditional discharge of the patient.

The Mental Health Review Tribunal is only concerned with the legality of continued detention and not with the legality of the initial admission. A person wishing to challenge the legality of the initial admission must either seek judicial review (see Chapter 1) or bring proceedings for habeas corpus: this is an action whereby a person detaining another (in this case a patient) must show legal justification for doing so. If such justification cannot be shown, the patient must be allowed to go free.

5.1.7 **After-care**

One of the major issues in recent years has been the question of treatment in the community and after-care. The provisions for after-care under s. 117 are of limited application, as they only apply to certain categories of patient, and to get a broader picture of services available, you should link these provisions with those in other community care legislation:

117. After-care

(1) This section applies to persons who are detained under section 3 above, or admitted to a hospital in pursuance of a hospital order made under section 37 above, or transferred to a hospital in pursuance of a transfer direction made under section 47 or 48 above, and then cease to be detained and (whether or not immediately after so ceasing) leave hospital.

(2) It shall be the duty of the Health Authority and of the local social services authority to provide, in co-operation with relevant voluntary agencies, after-care services for any person to whom this section applies until such time as the Health Authority and the local social services authority are satisfied that the person concerned is no longer in need of such services; but they shall not be so satisfied in the case of a patient who is subject to after-care under supervision at any time while he remains so subject.

(2A) It shall be the duty of the Health Authority to secure that at all times while a patient is subject to after-care under supervision—

(a) a person who is a registered medical practitioner approved for the purposes of section 12 above by the Secretary of State as having special experience in the diagnosis or treatment of mental disorder is in charge of the medical treatment provided for the patient as part of the after-care services provided for him under this section; and

(b) a person professionally concerned with any of the after-care services so provided is supervising him with a view to securing that he receives the after-care services so provided.

There are no powers under the 1983 Act to force a person in the community to receive treatment, though the powers accorded to a guardian may have this effect (see above). To go part of the way to remedying this perceived deficiency, the Mental Health (Patients in the Community) Act 1995 provides for a system of after-care under supervision. The Act inserts provisions into s. 25 of the Mental Health Act 1983:

25A. Application for supervision
(1)   Where a patient —
    (a) is liable to be detained in a hospital in pursuance of an application for admission for treatment; and
    (b) has attained the age of 16 years,
an application may be made for him to be supervised after he leaves hospital, for the period allowed by the following provisions of this Act, with a view to securing that he receives the after-care services provided for him under section 117 below.

(2)   In this Act an application for a patient to be so supervised is referred to as a 'supervision application'; and where a supervision application has been duly made and accepted under this Part of this Act in respect of a patient and he has left hospital, he is for the purposes of this Act 'subject to after-care under supervision' (until he ceases to be so subject in accordance with the provisions of this Act).

(3)   A supervision application shall be made in accordance with this section and sections 25B and 25C below.

(4)   A supervision application may be made in respect of a patient only on the grounds that —
    (a) he is suffering from mental disorder, being mental illness, severe mental impairment, psychopathic disorder or mental impairment;
    (b) there would be a substantial risk of serious harm to the health or safety of the patient or the safety of other persons, or of the patient being seriously exploited, if he were not to receive the after-care services to be provided for him under section 117 below after he leaves hospital; and
    (c) his being subject to after-care under supervision is likely to help to secure that he receives the after-care services to be so provided.

(5)   A supervision application may be made only by the responsible medical officer.

(6)   A supervision application in respect of a patient shall be addressed to the Health Authority which will have the duty under section 117 below to provide aftercare services for the patient after he leaves hospital.

(7)   Before accepting a supervision application in respect of a patient a Health Authority shall consult the local social services authority which will also have that duty.

(8)   Where a Health Authority accept a supervision application in respect of a patient the Health Authority shall —
    (a) inform the patient both orally and in writing —
        (i)   that the supervision application has been accepted; and
        (ii) of the effect in his case of the provisions of this Act relating to a patient subject to after-care under supervision (including, in particular, what rights of applying to a Mental Health Review Tribunal are available);

(b) inform any person whose name is stated in the supervision application in accordance with subparagraph (i) of paragraph (e) of section 25B(5) below that the supervision application has been accepted; and

(c) inform in writing any person whose name is so stated in accordance with sub-paragraph (ii) of that paragraph that the supervision application has been accepted.

(9)   Where a patient in respect of whom a supervision application is made is granted leave of absence from a hospital under section 17 above (whether before or after the supervision application is made), references in —

(a) this section and the following provisions of this Part of this Act; and

(b) Part V of this Act,

to his leaving hospital shall be construed as references to his period of leave expiring (otherwise than on his return to the hospital or transfer to another hospital).

25B.   Making of supervision application

(1)   The responsible medical officer shall not make a supervision application unless —

(a) subsection (2) below is complied with; and

(b) the responsible medical officer has considered the matters specified in subsection (4) below.

(2)   This subsection is complied with if —

(a) the following persons have been consulted about the making of the supervision application —

(i)   the patient;

(ii)   one or more persons who have been professionally concerned with the patient's medical treatment in hospital;

(iii)   one or more persons who will be professionally concerned with the after-care services to be provided for the patient under section 117 below; and

(iv)   any person who the responsible medical officer believes will play a substantial part in the care of the patient after he leaves hospital but will not be professionally concerned with any of the after-care services to be so provided;

(b) such steps as are practicable have been taken to consult the person (if any) appearing to be the nearest relative of the patient about the making of the supervision application; and

(c) the responsible medical officer has taken into account any views expressed by the persons consulted.

(3)   Where the patient has requested that paragraph (b) of subsection (2) above should not apply, that paragraph shall not apply unless —

(a) the patient has a propensity to violent or dangerous behaviour towards others; and

(b) the responsible medical officer considers that it is appropriate for steps such as are mentioned in that paragraph to be taken.

(4)   The matters referred to in subsection (1)(b) above are —

(a) the after-care services to be provided for the patient under section 117 below; and

(b) any requirements to be imposed on him under section 25D below.

(5)   A supervision application shall state —

(a) that the patient is liable to be detained in a hospital in pursuance of an application for admission for treatment;

(b) the age of the patient or, if his exact age is not known to the applicant, that the patient is believed to have attained the age of 16 years;

(c) that in the opinion of the applicant (having regard in particular to the patient's history) all of the conditions set out in section 25A(4) above are complied with;

(d) the name of the person who is to be the community responsible medical officer, and of the person who is to be the supervisor, in relation to the patient after he leaves hospital; and

(e) the name of —
- (i) any person who has been consulted under paragraph (a)(iv) of subsection (2) above; and
- (ii) any person who has been consulted under paragraph (b) of that subsection.

(6) A supervision application shall be accompanied by —
- (a) the written recommendation in the prescribed form of a registered medical practitioner who will be professionally concerned with the patient's medical treatment after he leaves hospital or, if no such practitioner other than the responsible medical officer will be so concerned, of any registered medical practitioner; and
- (b) the written recommendation in the prescribed form of an approved social worker.

(7) A recommendation under subsection (6)(a) above shall include a statement that in the opinion of the medical practitioner (having regard in particular to the patient's history) all of the conditions set out in section 25A(4) above are complied with.

(8) A recommendation under subsection (6)(b) above shall include a statement that in the opinion of the social worker (having regard in particular to the patient's history) both of the conditions set out in section 25A(4)(b) and (c) above are complied with.

(9) A supervision application shall also be accompanied by —
- (a) a statement in writing by the person who is to be the community responsible medical officer in relation to the patient after he leaves hospital that he is to be in charge of the medical treatment provided for the patient as part of the after-care services provided for him under section 117 below;
- (b) a statement in writing by the person who is to be the supervisor in relation to the patient after he leaves hospital that he is to supervise the patient with a view to securing that he receives the aftercare services so provided;
- (c) details of the after-care services to be provided for the patient under section 117 below; and
- (d) details of any requirements to be imposed on him under section 25D below.

(10) On making a supervision application in respect of a patient the responsible medical officer shall —
- (a) inform the patient both orally and in writing;
- (b) inform any person who has been consulted under paragraph (a)(iv) of subsection (2) above; and
- (c) inform in writing any person who has been consulted under paragraph (b) of that subsection, of the matters specified in subsection (11) below.

(11) The matters referred to in subsection (10) above are —
- (a) that the application is being made;
- (b) the after-care services to be provided for the patient under section 117 below;
- (c) any requirements to be imposed on him under section 25D below; and
- (d) the name of the person who is to be the community responsible medical officer, and of the person who is to be the supervisor, in relation to the patient after he leaves hospital.

25C. Supervision applications: supplementary

(1) Subject to subsection (2) below, a supervision application, and the recommendation under section 25B(6)(a) above accompanying it, may describe the patient as suffering from more than one of the following forms of mental disorder, namely, mental illness, severe mental impairment, psychopathic disorder and mental impairment.

(2) A supervision application shall be of no effect unless the patient is described in the application and the recommendation under section 25B(6)(a) above accompanying it as suffering from the same form of mental disorder, whether or not he is also described in the application or the recommendation as suffering from another form.

(3)   A registered medical practitioner may at any reasonable time visit a patient and examine him in private for the purpose of deciding whether to make a recommendation under section 25B(6)(a) above.

(4)   An approved social worker may at any reasonable time visit and interview a patient for the purpose of deciding whether to make a recommendation under section 25B(6)(b) above.

(5)   For the purpose of deciding whether to make a recommendation under section 25B(6) above in respect of a patient, a registered medical practitioner or an approved social worker may require the production of and inspect any records relating to the detention or treatment of the patient in any hospital or to any aftercare services provided for the patient under section 117 below.

(6)   If, within the period of 14 days beginning with the day on which a supervision application has been accepted, the application, or any recommendation accompanying it, is found to be in any respect incorrect or defective, the application or recommendation may, within that period and with the consent of the Health Authority which accepted the application, be amended by the person by whom it was made or given.

(7)   Where an application or recommendation is amended in accordance with subsection (6) above it shall have effect, and shall be deemed to have had effect, as if it had been originally made or given as so amended.

(8)   A supervision application which appears to be duly made and to be accompanied by recommendations under section 25B(6) above may be acted upon without further proof of —

- (a)   the signature or qualification of the person by whom the application or any such recommendation was made or given; or
- (b)   any matter of fact or opinion stated in the application or recommendation.

(9)   A recommendation under section 25B(6) above accompanying a supervision application in respect of a patient shall not be given by —

- (a)   the responsible medical officer;
- (b)   a person who receives or has an interest in the receipt of any payments made on account of the maintenance of the patient; or
- (c)   a close relative of the patient, of any person mentioned in paragraph (a) or (b) above or of a person by whom the other recommendation is given under section 25B(6) above for the purposes of the application.

(10)   In subsection (9)(c) above 'close relative' means husband, wife, father, father-in-law, mother, mother-in-law, son, son-in-law, daughter, daughter-in-law, brother, brother-in-law, sister or sister-in-law.

25D.   Requirements to secure receipt of after-care under supervision

(1)   Where a patient is subject to after-care under supervision (or, if he has not yet left hospital, is to be so subject after he leaves hospital), the responsible after-care bodies have power to impose any of the requirements specified in subsection, (3) below for the purpose of securing that the patient receives the after-care services provided for him under section 117 below.

(2)   In this Act 'the responsible after-care bodies', in relation to a patient, means the bodies which have (or will have) the duty under section 117 below to provide aftercare services for the patient.

(3)   The requirements referred to in subsection (1) above are —

- (a)   that the patient reside at a specified place;
- (b)   that the patient attend at specified places and times for the purpose of medical treatment, occupation, education or training; and
- (c)   that access to the patient be given, at any place where the patient is residing, to the supervisor, any registered medical practitioner or any approved social worker or to any other person authorised by the supervisor.

(4)   A patient subject to after-care under supervision may be taken and conveyed by, or by any person authorised by, the supervisor to any place where the patient is required to reside or to attend for the purpose of medical treatment, occupation, education or training.

(5)   A person who demands —

(a)   to be given access to a patient in whose case a requirement has been imposed under subsection (3)(c) above; or

(b)   to take and convey a patient in pursuance of subsection (4) above, shall, if asked to do so, produce some duly authenticated document to show that he is a person entitled to be given access to, or to take and convey, the patient.

25E.   Review of after-care under supervision

(1)   The after-care services provided (or to be provided) under section 117 below for a patient who is (or is to be) subject to after-care under supervision, and any requirements imposed on him under section 25D above, shall be kept under review, and (where appropriate) modified, by the responsible after-care bodies.

(2)   This subsection applies in relation to a patient who is subject to after-care under supervision where he refuses or neglects —

(a)   to receive any or all of the after-care services provided for him under section 117 below; or

(b)   to comply with any or all of any requirements imposed on him under section 25D above.

(3)   Where subsection (2) above applies in relation to a patient, the responsible after-care bodies shall review, and (where appropriate) modify —

(a)   the after-care services provided for him under section 117 below; and

(b)   any requirements imposed on him under section 25D above.

(4)   Where subsection (2) above applies in relation to a patient, the responsible after-care bodies shall also —

(a)   consider whether it might be appropriate for him to cease to be subject to after-care under supervision and, if they conclude that it might be, inform the community responsible medical officer; and

(b)   consider whether it might be appropriate for him to be admitted to a hospital for treatment and, if they conclude that it might be, inform an approved social worker.

(5)   The responsible after-care bodies shall not modify —

(a)   the after-care services provided (or to be provided) under section 117 below for a patient who is (or is to be) subject to after-care under supervision; or

(b)   any requirements imposed on him under section 25D above, unless subsection (6) below is complied with.

(6)   This subsection is complied with if —

(a)   the patient has been consulted about the modifications;

(b)   any person who the responsible after-care bodies believe plays (or will play) a substantial part in the care of the patient but is not (or will not be) professionally concerned with the after-care services provided for the patient under section 117 below has been consulted about the modifications;

(c)   such steps as are practicable have been taken to consult the person (if any) appearing to be the nearest relative of the patient about the modifications; and

(d)   the responsible after-care bodies have taken into account any views expressed by the persons consulted.

(7)   Where the patient has requested that paragraph (c) of subsection (6) above should not apply, that paragraph shall not apply unless —

(a)   the patient has a propensity to violent or dangerous behaviour towards others; and

    (b) the community responsible medical officer (or the person who is to be the community responsible medical officer) considers that it is appropriate for steps such as are mentioned in that paragraph to be taken.

(8)   Where the responsible after-care bodies modify the after-care services provided (or to be provided) for the patient under section 117 below or any requirements imposed on him under section 25D above, they shall —

    (a) inform the patient both orally and in writing;

    (b) inform any person who has been consulted under paragraph (b) of subsection (6) above; and

    (c) inform in writing any person who has been consulted under paragraph (c) of that subsection, that the modifications have been made.

(9)   Where —

    (a) a person other than the person named in the supervision application becomes the community responsible medical officer when the patient leaves hospital; or

    (b) when the patient is subject to after-care under supervision, one person ceases to be, and another becomes, the community responsible medical officer, the responsible after-care bodies shall comply with subsection (11) below.

(10)   Where —

    (a) a person other than the person named in the supervision application becomes the supervisor when the patient leaves hospital; or

    (b) when the patient is subject to after-care under supervision, one person ceases to be, and another becomes, the supervisor, the responsible after-care bodies shall comply with subsection (11) below.

(11)   The responsible after-care bodies comply with this subsection if they —

    (a) inform the patient both orally and in writing;

    (b) inform any person who they believe plays a substantial part in the care of the patient but is not professionally concerned with the after-care services provided for the patient under section 117 below; and

    (c) unless the patient otherwise requests, take such steps as are practicable to inform in writing the person (if any) appearing to be the nearest relative of the patient, of the name of the person who becomes the community responsible medical officer or the supervisor.

25F. Reclassifications of patient subject to after-care under supervision

(1)   If it appears to the community responsible medical officer that a patient subject to after-care under supervision is suffering from a form of mental disorder other than the form or forms specified in the supervision application made in respect of the patient, he may furnish a report to that effect to the Health Authority which have the duty under section 117 below to provide after-care services for the patient.

(2)   Where a report is so furnished the supervision application shall have effect as if that other form of mental disorder were specified in it.

(3)   Unless no-one other than the community responsible medical officer is professionally concerned with the patient's medical treatment, he shall consult one or more persons who are so concerned before furnishing a report under subsection (1) above.

(4)   Where a report is furnished under subsection (1) above in respect of a patient, the responsible after-care bodies shall —

    (a) inform the patient both orally and in writing; and

    (b) unless the patient otherwise requests, take such steps as are practicable to inform in writing the person (if any) appearing to be the nearest relative of the patient, that the report has been furnished.

25G. Duration and renewal of after-care under supervision

(1) Subject to sections 25H and 25I below, a patient subject to after-care under supervision shall be so subject for the period —

(a) beginning when he leaves hospital; and

(b) ending with the period of six months beginning with the day on which the supervision application was accepted, but shall not be so subject for any longer period except in accordance with the following provisions of this section.

(2) A patient already subject to after-care under supervision may be made so subject —

(a) from the end of the period referred to in subsection (1) above, for a further period of six months; and

(b) from the end of any period of renewal under paragraph (a) above, for a further period of one year, and so on for periods of one year at a time.

(3) Within the period of two months ending on the day on which a patient who is subject to after-care under supervision would (in default of the operation of subsection (7) below) cease to be so subject, it shall be the duty of the community responsible medical officer —

(a) to examine the patient; and

(b) if it appears to him that the conditions set out in subsection (4) below are complied with, to furnish to the responsible after-care bodies a report to that effect in the prescribed form.

(4) The conditions referred to in subsection (3) above are that —

(a) the patient is suffering from mental disorder, being mental illness, severe mental impairment, psychopathic disorder or mental impairment;

(b) there would be a substantial risk of serious harm to the health or safety of the patient or the safety of other persons, or of the patient being seriously exploited, if he were not to receive the after-care services provided for him under section 117 below;

(c) his being subject to after-care under supervision is likely to help to secure that he receives the after-care services so provided.

(5) The community responsible medical officer shall not consider whether the conditions set out in subsection (4) above are complied with unless —

(a) the following persons have been consulted —

(i) the patient;

(ii) the supervisor;

(iii) unless no-one other than the community responsible medical officer is professionally concerned with the patient's medical treatment, one or more persons who are so concerned;

(iv) one or more persons who are professionally concerned with the after-care services (other than medical treatment) provided for the patient under section 117 below; and

(v) any person who the community responsible medical officer believes plays a substantial part in the care of the patient but is not professionally concerned with the aftercare services so provided;

(b) such steps as are practicable have been taken to consult the person (if any) appearing to be the nearest relative of the patient; and

(c) the community responsible medical officer has taken into account any relevant views expressed by the persons consulted.

(6) Where the patient has requested that paragraph (b) of subsection (5) above should not apply, that paragraph shall not apply unless —

(a) the patient has a propensity to violent or dangerous behaviour towards others; and

(b) the community responsible medical officer considers that it is appropriate for steps such as are mentioned in that paragraph to be taken.

(7)   Where a report is duly furnished under subsection (3) above, the patient shall be thereby made subject to after-care under supervision for the further period prescribed in that case by subsection (2) above.

(8)   Where a report is furnished under subsection (3) above, the responsible after-care bodies shall —

  (a) inform the patient both orally and in writing —
    (i)   that the report has been furnished; and
    (ii) of the effect in his case of the provisions of this Act relating to making a patient subject to after-care under supervision for a further period (including, in particular, what rights of applying to a Mental Health Review Tribunal are available);
  (b) inform any person who has been consulted under paragraph (a)(v) of subsection (5) above that the report has been furnished; and
  (c) inform in writing any person who has been consulted under paragraph (b) of that subsection that the report has been furnished.

(9)   Where the form of mental disorder specified in a report furnished under subsection (3) above is a form of disorder other than that specified in the supervision application, that application shall have effect as if that other form of mental disorder were specified in it.

(10)   Where on any occasion a report specifying such a form of mental disorder is furnished under subsection (3) above the community responsible medical officer need not on that occasion furnish a report under section 25F above.

25H.   Ending of after-care under supervision

(1)   The community responsible medical officer may at any time direct that a patient subject to after-care under supervision shall cease to be so subject.

(2)   The community responsible medical officer shall not give a direction under subsection (1) above unless subsection (3) below is complied with.

(3)   This subsection is complied with if —

  (a) the following persons have been consulted about the giving of the direction —
    (i)   the patient;
    (ii) the supervisor;
    (iii) unless no-one other than the community responsible medical officer is professionally concerned with the patient's medical treatment, one or more persons who are so concerned;
    (iv) one or more persons who are professionally concerned with the after-care services (other than medical treatment) provided for the patient under section 117 below; and
    (v)   any person who the community responsible medical officer believes plays a substantial part in the care of the patient but is not professionally concerned with the aftercare services so provided;
  (b) such steps as are practicable have been taken to consult the person (if any) appearing to be the nearest relative of the patient about the giving of the direction; and
  (c) the community responsible medical officer has taken into account any views expressed by the persons consulted.

(4)   Where the patient has requested that paragraph (b) of subsection (3) above should not apply, that paragraph shall not apply unless —

  (a) the patient has a propensity to violent or dangerous behaviour towards others; and
  (b) the community responsible medical officer considers that it is appropriate for steps such as are mentioned in that paragraph to be taken.

(5)   A patient subject to after-care under supervision shall cease to be so subject if he —

  (a) is admitted to a hospital in pursuance of an application for admission for treatment; or
  (b) is received into guardianship.

(6) Where a patient (for any reason) ceases to be subject to after-care under supervision the responsible after-care bodies shall —
  (a) inform the patient both orally and in writing;
  (b) inform any person who they believe plays a substantial part in the care of the patient but is not professionally concerned with the after-care services provided for the patient under section 117 below; and
  (c) take such steps as are practicable to inform in writing the person (if any) appearing to be the nearest relative of the patient, that the patient has ceased to be so subject.

(7) Where the patient has requested that paragraph (c) of subsection (6) above should not apply, that paragraph shall not apply unless subsection (3)(b) above applied in his case by virtue of subsection (4) above.

However, some reservations concerning these provisions have been expressed. In the following extracts, Professor Herschel Prins explores some of the issues in an article entitled 'Can the law serve as the solution to social ills? The case of the Mental Health (Patients in the Community) Act, 1995' [from *Medicine, Science and the Law* vol. 36 No. 3 (1996)].

The intentions enshrined in the new legislation may seem, on first inspection, to be laudable.
  However, a number of questions are worth pondering.

1. The provisions require the active consent of the patient and, in some cases, his or her relatives. Experience dictates that, for a variety of reasons, this may not only be unforthcoming, but it may also fluctuate considerably because of the nature of the patient's illness.

2. The provisions only apply to patients who have been formally detained in hospital. The provisions do not apply to those offender-patients subject to condition discharge from a Hospital Order with restrictions under Sections 37/41 of the 1983 Mental Health Act. In the case of these patients there are, of course, sanctions that can be applied in respect of their non-co-operation. Under the 1995 Act there appear to be no sanctions for non-compliance. Indeed, the Act emphasizes the importance of patient co-operation and the fact that treatment under the relevant sections cannot itself be enforced.

  'A requirement to attend for medical treatment does not carry with it any power to impose medication or other treatment against the patient's wishes'.

3. There is no indication of the volume of work that will devolve upon an already overburdened MHRT system. The arrangements for interviewing patients are currently unclear, both in respect of the MHRT medical member's preliminary interview with the patient, and the actual Tribunal hearing. Since these patients, by definition, will be living in the community, one presumes that they will need to be recalled to the nearest hospital for the proceedings to take place. What will happen if the patient refuses to attend?

4. There are no reliable estimates as to how many patients will be involved in the new procedures: currently one can only make unreliable guesses.

5. It is also very clear that no additional resources are likely to be available; surely, this is a key requirement? The provisions also seem to exemplify a continuing trend in government, namely the increasing devolvement of responsibility on to local services. This has been very marked in the health and penal services in recent years. Those inclined to cynicism might observe that this could be seen less as a benevolent desire to place responsibility in the hand of the 'locals' and more of an attempt to off-load ministerial responsibility (see also Holloway, 1996).

General observation — iatrogenic and other consequences
It is my contention that the new Act is but one further illustration of the difficulties inherent in legislating for the amelioration of social and personal 'ills'. Perhaps the law should only be concerned with broad-based prescriptive constraints (for purposes of public and personal safety) aimed at

minimum legislative interference in the lives of others, provided that public safety and harm to self are not neglected. Mention has already been made of certain iatrogenic consequences of the 1983 Mental Health Act, notably the tendency not to admit certain patients who might really need 'asylum'. Voluntary mental health organizations, for example SANE and the NSF (National Schizophrenia Fellowship) have repeatedly attested to this. The 1983 Act has also probably led to an increasing degree of defensive psychiatry. In my view, the use of supervision registers and the new Act are likely to increase this trend (Prins, 1995). No fine-sounding piece of legislation, however attractive at first sight, can be a substitute for well-informed practice by adequately resourced professionals, both in terms of political recognition and encouragement and by economic support. Lack of support for professionals, and the work they do, is an important element that needs to be understood alongside the matters of concern about legislative trends already referred to.

5.2 Court of Protection

The Court has a statutory jurisdiction under Part VII Mental Health Act and becomes responsible for supervising the management of a person's affairs in circumstances where that person is incapable of doing so by reason of mental disorder. A person subject to the jurisdiction of the Court is called a patient. As we saw earlier in this chapter, the definition of 'patient' for the purposes of Part VII differs from that used in the rest of the Act. The Court has no automatic jurisdiction. It can only acquire jurisdiction on application, and a person can only be discharged from it on application. The administrative functions of the Court are handled by the Public Guardianship Office. The Court of Protection operates on an all-or-nothing basis. Once it assumes jurisdiction, the powers of the Court are extensive, as the following extract from the Act illustrates, and it takes over all running of the person's affairs:

93. Judicial authorities and Court of Protection
(1) The Lord Chancellor shall from time to time nominate one or more judges of the Supreme Court (in this Act referred to as 'nominated judges') to act for the purposes of this Part of this Act.
(2) There shall continue to be an office of the Supreme Court, called the Court of Protection, for the protection and management, as provided by this Part of this Act, of the property and affairs of persons under disability; and there shall continue to be a Master of the Court of Protection appointed by the Lord Chancellor under section 89 of the Supreme Court Act 1981.
(4) The Lord Chancellor may nominate other officers of the Court of Protection (in this Part of this Act referred to as 'nominated officers') to act for the purposes of this Part of this Act.

94. Exercise of the judge's functions: 'the patient'
(1) Subject to subsection (1A) below the functions expressed to be conferred by this Part of this Act on the judge shall be exercisable by the Lord Chancellor or by any nominated judge, and shall also be exercisable by the Master of the Court of Protection, by the Public Trustee, or by any nominated officer, but —
  (a) in the case of the Master, the Public Trustee or any nominated officer, subject to any express provision to the contrary in this Part of this Act or any rules made under this Part of this Act,
  (aa) in the case of the Public Trustee, subject to any directions of the Master and so far only is may be provided by any rules made under this Part of this Act or (subject to any such rules) by directions of the Master;

(b) in the case of any nominated officer, subject to any directions of the Master and so far only as may be provided by the instrument by which he is nominated; and references in this Part of this Act to the judge shall be construed accordingly.

(1A)   In such cases or circumstances as may be prescribed by any rules under this Part of this Act or (subject to any such rules) by directions of the Master, the functions of the judge under this Part of this Act shall be exercised by the Public Trustee (but subject to any directions of the Master as to their exercise).

...

95.   General functions of the judge with respect to property and affairs of patient

(1)   The judge may, with respect to the property and affairs of a patient, do or secure the doing of all such things as appear necessary or expedient —

(a) for the maintenance or other benefit of the patient,

(b) for the maintenance or other benefit of members of the patient's family,

(c) for making provision for other persons or purposes for whom or which the patient might be expected to provide if he were not mentally disordered, or

(d) otherwise for administering the patient's affairs.

(2)   In the exercise of the powers conferred by this section regard shall be had first of all to the requirements of the patient, and the rules of law which restricted the enforcement by a creditor of rights against property under the control of the judge in lunacy shall apply to property under the control of the judge; but, subject to the foregoing provisions of this subsection, the judge shall, in administering a patient's affairs, have regard to the interests of creditors and also to the desirability of making provision for obligations of the patient notwithstanding that they may not be legally enforceable.

The only exception is that the patient retains the power to make a will, as long as (s)he understands, in broad terms, the nature of the activity and can recall the extent of his/her property. The Court can make a will for a person who is unable to do so, as *Re C* [1991] 3 All ER 866 illustrates. The matter is not without controversy: how does the judge know what the person might have wanted to do?

96.   Powers of the judge as to patient's property and affairs

(1)   Without prejudice to the generality of section 95 above, the judge shall have power to make such orders and give such directions and authorities as he thinks fit for the purposes of that section and in particular may for those purposes make orders or give directions or authorities for —

(a) the control (with or without the transfer or vesting of property or the payment into or lodgment in the Supreme Court of money or securities) and management of any property of the patient;

(b) the sale, exchange, charging or other disposition of or dealing with any property of the patient;

(c) the acquisition of any property in the name or on behalf of the patient;

(d) the settlement of any property of the patient, or the gift of any property of the patient to any such persons or for any such purposes as are mentioned in paragraphs (b) and (c) of section 95(1) above;

(e) the execution for the patient of a will making any provision (whether by way of disposing of property or exercising a power or otherwise) which could be made by a will executed by the patient if he were not mentally disordered;

(f)   the carrying on by a suitable person of any profession, trade or business of the patient;

(g)   the dissolution of a partnership of which the patient is a member;

(h)   the carrying out of any contract entered into by the patient;

(i)   the conduct of legal proceedings in the name of the patient or on his behalf;

(j)   the reimbursement out of the property of the patient, with or without interest, of money applied by any person either in payment of the patient's debts (whether legally enforceable or not) or for the maintenance or other benefit of the patient or members of his family or in making provision for other persons or purposes for whom or which he might be expected to provide if he were not mentally disordered;

(k)   the exercise of any power (including a power to consent) vested in the patient, whether beneficially, or as guardian or trustee, or otherwise.

(2)   If under subsection (1) above provision is made for the settlement of any property of a patient, or the exercise of a power vested in a patient of appointing trustees or retiring from a trust, the judge may also make as respects the property settled or trust property such consequential vesting or other orders as the case may require, including (in the case of the exercise of such a power) any order which could have been made in such a case under Part IV of the Trustee Act 1925.

(3)   Where under this section a settlement has been made of any property of a patient, and the Lord Chancellor or a nominated judge is satisfied, at any time before the death of the patient, that any material fact was not disclosed when the settlement was made, or that there has been any substantial change in circumstances, he may by order vary the settlement in such manner as he thinks fit, and give any consequential directions.

(4)   The power of the judge to make or give an order, direction or authority for the execution of a will for a patient —

(a)   shall not be exercisable at any time when the patient is a minor, and

(b)   shall not be exercised unless the judge has reason to believe that the patient is incapable of making a valid will for himself.

(5)   The powers of a patient as patron of a benefice shall be exercisable by the Lord Chancellor only.

...

[Re C (a patient)]
A mental patient, who was born suffering from severe mental disability, lived at a hospital near London where she had been since the age of ten. She was now aged 75. Her mother died in 1918 and her father in 1953 leaving her property consisting of cash and investments valued at about £1,600,000. She had little memory, understanding or capacity to communicate, she was completely blind and could not dress, undress or bath herself. Nevertheless she enjoyed music, the sound of birds, the smell of flowers and outings or coach expeditions provided by the hospital. She was clearly incapable, and had always been incapable, of understanding the meaning or effect of a disposition of her property. Apart from the staff and other patients at the hospital, the only other person to take an interest in the patient had been a member of a voluntary organisation which befriended mental patients. The present gross annual income of the fund was about £57,000, from which had to be deducted £13,000 income tax and £3,500 costs of administration. Under an earlier order of the Court of Protection the patient made a covenanted annual payment of £3,000 to the hospital, leaving about £36,000 a year disposable income. An application was made to the Court of Protection for an order making a will for her and for immediate gifts to be made out of her property.

...

Hoffmann J   This is an application to the Court of Protection under ss. 95 and 96 of the Mental Health Act 1983 for an order making a will for a mental patient and for immediate gifts out of her property. The patient, whom I shall call Miss C, was born on 16 February 1916 and is therefore now aged 75. She has suffered since birth from severe mental disability and has lived at a hospital near London since the age of 10. Her mother died in 1918 and her father in 1953. It is not known whether her father maintained any contact with her, but few if any other members of her fairly extensive family appear to have been aware of her existence. Apart from the staff and other patients at the hospital, the only other person to take an interest in Miss C has been a Miss B who belongs to a voluntary organisation called Citizen Advocacy Alliance, which befriends mental patients. In that capacity Miss B has visited Miss C since 1984, taken her home for meals and out for drives and for holidays. The medical officer who has been responsible for Miss C said in 1988 that she had an excellent relationship with Miss B.

Miss C has little memory, understanding or capacity to communicate. She is completely blind and cannot dress, undress or bath herself. Nevertheless she enjoys music, the sound of birds, the smell of flowers and outings with Miss B or coach expeditions provided by the hospital. She is clearly incapable, and has always been incapable, of understanding the meaning or effect of a disposition of her property.

...

In this case, the patient has lacked capacity since birth. In all relevant respects, the record of her individual preferences and personality is a blank on which nothing has been written. Accordingly, there is no material on which to construct a subjective assessment of what the patient would have wanted to do. Mrs Harrison, appearing for one of the next of kin, submitted that in those circumstances it was very difficult for the court to be satisfied that any particular gift was something which the actual patient 'might be expected to provide'. There might be cases in which the moral obligation was so strong that one could say that the patient would have had to be extraordinarily insensitive not to recognise it. But there were no grounds for supposing that this patient would have wished, for example, to benefit a particular mental health charity, or even mental health charities in general. She might, but she might equally have wanted to benefit the victims of foreign disasters or any other good cause. There was no basis on which to form a view one way or the other.

I recognise the difficulty in forming a view of what might have been expected from a person who has never enjoyed a rational mind. But I think that in those circumstances the court must assume that she would have been a normal decent person, acting in accordance with contemporary standards of morality. In the absence of actual evidence to the contrary, no less should be assumed of any person and in this case there is nothing to displace such an assumption. A person in the position of Miss C, looking back over her life, would in my view have been influenced by two principal considerations. First, that she had spent the whole of her life in the care of the community, as embodied in the national health service, the hospital and voluntary mental health charities like the Friends of the Hospital and the Citizen Advocacy Alliance. Secondly, that she had derived her fortune from being a child of a family. She would therefore in my view have felt moral obligations to show recognition to the community and to her family. Once one has arrived at the conclusion that the disposition of her property would have been guided by these principles, I do not think it is necessary for the court to be satisfied that the patient would definitely have chosen one particular way of giving effect to them rather than another. A distribution which can be rationally justified as a way of giving effect to these principles would in my view be a provision which the patient 'might be expected to provide', even though a somewhat different distribution could also be so described. The court cannot of course indulge its own whims in these matters. The gifts and will it makes for the patient must be capable of being explained as something which the patient 'might be expected to provide'. But I observe that the statute, recognising the difficulty of arriving at any certainty in these matters, says 'might' rather than 'would be expected to provide'. In matters of detail, there must be a range of choices which would be equally valid.

The proportions in which a person in the position of Miss C would wish to give effect to these two principles must depend upon all the circumstances, including her relations with her family, the services which have been rendered to her by strangers and the size of her fortune. Miss C's estate is relatively large and this enables her to satisfy in full the claims of both community and family. I think that she would have recognised that although none of her family had ever been to see her, this was not on account of any lack of feeling on their part. None of them appear to have known of her existence. Taking her family as a whole, therefore, I think that she would have wished to distribute her estate equally between them and the community.

The recognition of the claims of the community would in my view have taken the form of gifts to mental health charities. I feel confident that a person in Miss C's position would have wished to benefit other people who had suffered from mental illness rather than wider or different charitable purposes. I am less confident about the particular choice which she would have made, but on the principle that people tend to prefer local and familiar causes to those which are more general and remote, I think that she would have wished primarily to benefit mentally handicapped people at the hospital or within the area which the hospital serves.

The Court only has powers over the person's property. It does not have any power over the person of the patient, for example, to give or withhold consent to medical treatment, as Lord Brandon explains in the following passage from Re F (Mental Patient: Sterilisation) [1990] 2 AC1:

I consider, secondly ... Part VII of the Mental Health Act 1983. That part of the Act has the heading 'Management of Property and Affairs of Patients' and comprises sections 93 to 113. The question which has to be considered is whether the expression 'the affairs of patients,' as used in the heading and various sections of Part VII, includes medical treatment such as an operation for sterilisation. In, order to answer that question, it is necessary to examine the following sections in Part VII which are mainly relevant to it:

...

The expression 'the affairs of patients,' taken by itself and without regard to the context in which it appears, is, in my view, capable of extending to medical treatment of patients other than treatment for their mental disorder. There is further an obvious attraction in construing that expression, as used in Part VII of the Act of 1983, as having that extended meaning ('the wider meaning'), since there would then be a judicial authority, namely, a judge nominated under section 93(1), who would have statutory power to authorise, or refuse to authorise, the sterilisation of an adult woman of unsound mind such as F. There are two passages in the sections of the Act set out above which, if they do not expressly support the wider meaning, are at least consistent with it. The first is the passage in section 95(1)(*a*) 'for the maintenance *or other benefit* of the patient' (my emphasis). The second is the passage in section 96(1)(*k*) 'the exercise of any power (*including a power to consent*) vested in the patient, whether beneficially, or as guardian or trustee, or otherwise' (again my emphasis). It seems to me, however, that, when one examines the general tenor of Part VII of the Act, and more particularly the context in which the two passages referred to above are to be found, the expression 'the affairs of patients' cannot properly be construed as having the wider meaning. It must rather be construed as including only business matters, legal transactions and other dealings of a similar kind.

I would, therefore, hold that Part VII of the Act of 1983 does not confer on a judge nominated under section 93(1) any jurisdiction to decide questions relating to the medical treatment of a patient, such as the question of F's sterilisation in the present case.

The Government has accepted that the Court of Protection should be reformed, as the following extract makes clear:

3.2   The Law Commission recommended that, in support of their proposals for a unified system of decision-making to cover financial, personal welfare and healthcare matters, there should be a single court jurisdiction, which would deal with all these issues together. It envisaged the court as being principally the option of last resort in cases of dispute.

3.3   *Who Decides?* supported the recommendation in principle, but identified the potential resource implications and sought views on whether the Court of Protection offered the most appropriate base for this jurisdiction.

3.4   Most respondents favoured a single court jurisdiction for all areas of decision-making. Although there were some concerns about the Court of Protection's perceived lack of accessibility and unsuitably for dealing with emergencies, no realistic alternatives were proposed, and a clear majority of respondents supported the Court of Protection exercising this jurisdiction.

The Government has decided that there will be a new single court jurisdiction, which will deal with all areas of decision-making for adults without capacity.

The new jurisdiction will be based at the Court of Protection, and concerns about accessibility will be met by a regionalised structure ...

Powers of the court

3.5   The Law Commission recommended that decision-making by the court should operate in the context of its key principles:
- decisions should be taken in the best interests of the person without capacity
- there should be minimal intervention in his or her affairs unless there is a demonstrable need to do so
- the option least restrictive of the person's freedom of action should be chosen.

3.6   The court would need to consider the nature and extent of the person's decision-making capacity in reaching a decision.

The Government has decided that the court will be able to make decisions on behalf of a person without capacity, or appoint a manager to make decisions.

The Government intends that the court should have the power to make declarations about capacity.

In exercising its powers, the court will follow two principles that support the aim of making the jurisdiction aimed at limiting intervention to the minimum possible:
- *the decision of the court is preferable to the appointment of a manager*
- *the appointment of a manager should be as limited in scope and duration as possible.*

Powers of the court in healthcare matters

3.7   The Law Commission recommended that the court's powers in this area should extend to:
- approving or refusing approval to particular forms of healthcare
- appointing a manager to consent, or refuse consent, to particular forms of healthcare
- requiring a person responsible for the healthcare of a patient to allow a different person to take over the healthcare of that patient
- obtaining access to healthcare records.

The Government agrees that the court should have these powers

3.8   The Government believes that certain serious healthcare decisions which can currently be made by a court, such as the withdrawal of artificial nutrition and hydration from a patient in a permanent vegetative state or similar condition, and questions of treatment where the patient has made an advance statement should remain a matter for the court, and should not be able to be delegated to a manager.

Powers of the court in welfare matters
3.9   The Law Commission recommended that the court's powers should extend in particular to matters relating to:
- where the person without capacity is to live
- what contact, if any, the person without capacity is to have with any specified persons (including the power to restrain a named person from having contact with or molesting the person without capacity)
- the exercise of the rights conferred on him or her by or under any enactment to obtain information
- obtaining the benefits and services to which the person without capacity is entitled or which are available to him or her.

The powers in relation to where the person is to live would not, however, extend to requiring or authorising admission against his or her will for assessment or treatment for mental disorder under the Mental Health Act 1983.
3.10   The Government indicated in *Who Decides?* that it accepted these recommendations in principle. It raised the question of whether explicit provision should also be made for the court to make other welfare-related orders in addition to residence and contact orders.

On the basis of the responses received, the Government's view is that as the list proposed by the Law Commission is not exhaustive, and gives the court flexibility to make orders relating to other welfare needs, an explicit list of those orders is not necessary.

...

3.17   *Who Decides?* asked whether the court should be able to appoint a manager; what the scope of the manager's responsibilities should be; and what criteria should be used to decide who should be a manager. The great majority of responses supported the court appointment of managers to deal with welfare, healthcare and property and financial decisions.
3.18   The Government's proposals are an extension of, and replacement for, the current receivership system. The court will be able to appoint a manager to make decisions on matters relating to the personal welfare, healthcare, property or financial affairs of a person without capacity.

...

3.20   The court will be able to appoint a suitable manager and set the scope of his or her responsibilities. The court will be able to appoint different managers for different areas of decision-making if appropriate.

Powers of a manager

Decisions that cannot be made by a manager
3.21   As is the case with the general authority to act reasonably, and with CPAs ..., a manager will not be able to take certain decisions on behalf of people without capacity. In addition, neither the court nor a manager should have power to make decisions which the person without capacity could not lawfully have made, if that person had retained capacity.

Powers of a manager to refuse consent to healthcare
3.22   *Who Decides?* expressed concern about the provision that would allow a court appointed manager to refuse consent to healthcare and asked the views of respondents on this point. The majority of responses opposed a manager having this power, although there was a substantial minority in favour, including the Law Society and Age Concern.

3.23   The Government takes the view that in most healthcare cases, a one-off decision about treatment will be needed. This could be made by the court without the need to appoint a manager. If a dispute then arose, the matter could be returned to court.

3.24   In cases where the court considered that the appointment of a manager was needed, it would take all relevant factors into account when making the appointment.

In making property and finance decisions managers appointed by the court will be able to deal with:
- *the control and management of any property, and its disposal or acquisition*
- *the carrying on of any business, trade or profession*
- *dissolution of any partnership*
- *carrying out of any contract*
- *discharge of any debt or obligation.*

3.25   The Law Commission recommended these powers, and *Who Decides?* indicated the Government's acceptance of these recommendations.

The Government will ensure that the following decisions, as recommended by the Law Commission, must be made by the court, and not delegated to a manager:
- *setting up a trust for the person concerned*
- *making a settlement of any property; whether with the person concerned or with others as beneficiaries*
- *making a will*
- *exercising powers vested in the person concerned, such as under a trust.*

The Government believes that, with the exception of these issues, the court should be able to decide the specific powers that a manager should have in each individual case.

...

The Government has decided that, when deciding who should be appointed as manager, and the need for security to protect the money of the person without capacity, the court should retain a wide discretion to deal with each case on its particular facts.

The following requirements will apply to all managers:
- *a manager will be obliged to act in the best interests of the person without capacity*
- *a manager must be an individual aged at least 18 or may, in relation to property and financial affairs (but not healthcare and welfare issues), be a trust corporation*
- *the holder of a specified office can be appointed provided there is no conflict of interest, except in relation to healthcare issues*
- *more than one manager can be appointed to act*
- *the court would be able to remove a manager on grounds of unsuitability or not acting in the best interests of the person without capacity*
- *a manager, acting in his or her capacity as such, will be regarded in law as a statutory agent of the person without capacity*
- *no manager will be able to do anything which is inconsistent with the decision of the attorney under a CPA acting within his or her authority.*

...

Monitoring of managers

3.35   The Law Commission recommended that:
- managers should continue to be asked for security and annual accounts as is currently the case for receivers under the Court of Protection, and that annual reports would still be appropriate even where the appointment related only to welfare or healthcare matters. It

envisaged the Public Trust Office taking on responsibility for monitoring welfare and health-care managers as well as financial ones; and

- the Public Trustee could continue to be appointed as financial manager of last resort as at present. The Public Trustee would have the power to raise questions on managers' reports, to direct a Lord Chancellor's Visitor to visit and report, and to inspect the person without capacity's property or direct an appropriate person to do so.

3.36   *Who Decides?* asked how practical these proposals would be. It highlighted the workload and training implications for the current Public Trust Office taking on the monitoring of welfare and healthcare matters, and the fact that many people requiring a welfare or healthcare man-ager would not have the resources to pay Public Trust Office fees. Most respondents agreed that the proposals were practical, subject to adequate staffing and resources being made available either to the PTO or to other bodies carrying out these functions.

The Government will ensure that appropriate arrangements are put in place to provide a practical and effective system to monitor healthcare, welfare and financial managers.

...

4.2   The Law Commission recommended that the new jurisdiction should be operated by the courts, which would provide an integrated forum and enable existing resources and expertise to be used.

The name of the court
4.3   The Law Commission recommended the establishment of a new superior court of record called the Court of Protection in place of the current Court of Protection, which would be an office of the Supreme Court, with a designated Senior Judge, and, if the future volume of work justified it, a President.
4.4   *Who Decides?* accepted this in principle, but sought views on whether the new forum should continue to be called the Court of Protection.
4.5   The majority of responses favoured the name remaining the same, although some, includ-ing the Bar Council, believed that a new name was needed to reflect the court's extended role. The Government will give further consideration to a possible new name for the court.

Regional presence for the court
4.6   The Law Commission noted that many respondents to their papers had criticised the Court of Protection's lack of regional presence and suggested that the new court should be based in London, with at least one other designated venue for each of the six other court circuits.
4.7   *Who Decides?* indicated that the Government was minded to adopt the approach taken with other specialist areas of the court system, centralising resources until the workload in a par-ticular area justified a new centre.
4.8   Although some respondents found this acceptable, others including the Law Society and MIND felt strongly that a regional presence was essential from the outset.

The Government now takes the view that there should be scope for healthcare, welfare and disputed financial cases to be dealt with locally rather than in London, where this is more convenient for the parties involved. A central administration will carry out support and administrative functions. High Court Judges, Circuit Judges and District Judges will be assigned to the Court of Protection.

4.9   The High Court will retain its inherent jurisdiction to make declarations on the lawfulness of certain medical actions.

Procedural matters
4.10   The usual civil appeals system will apply to the new jurisdiction.

4.11   The Court of Protection will be able to make an order or give directions pending a decision on whether the person concerned lacks capacity, and will be able to require an assessment of capacity to take place.

4.12   The Lord Chancellor will have the power to make Rules of Court governing proceedings under the new jurisdiction.

4.13   There will be provision for the transfer of proceedings in respect of 16–18 year olds between a court exercising the new jurisdiction, and a court exercising jurisdiction under the Children Act 1989.

4.14   The power of the Master of the Court of Protection to visit any patient, and to interview them in private, will be preserved and extended to the other nominated judges.

There will be no restrictions on the automatic right to apply to the court for orders under the new jurisdiction

4.15   The Law Commission recommended that there should be a leave requirement for certain categories of applicant. The majority of responses to consultation disagreed with this approach. The Government does not see a need to introduce restrictions initially, and will do so in future only if circumstances justify it.

The court will have the power to call for reports as necessary. The provider of the report could vary according to the issues involved.

4.16   Respondents to consultation suggested that a wide range of organisations could be appropriate to provide reports to the court in individual cases. The Government has decided that it would be sensible to allow the court discretion to decide who would be the most suitable agency in each case.

5.3 Powers of Attorney

Invoking the jurisdiction of the Court of Protection can be expensive and administratively cumbersome. One way of engaging in forward planning is to create a power of attorney, which authorises another person to act in the event of mental incapacity. The Powers of Attorney Act 1971 provided for this. The current Master of the Court of Protection, Denzil Lush, explains the nature of a power of attorney as follows: 'A power of attorney is a formal arrangement created by a deed in which one person ("the donor") gives another person ("the attorney") authority to act in his name and on his behalf'. (Lush *Cretney and Lush on Enduring Powers of Attorney* (Jordans, 2001), p. 1). He refers to a survey which found that the most common reasons for ordinary people using a power of attorney were health problems and foreign travel, with the power usually being granted by a parent to a grown up child.

Powers of Attorney Act 1971

1.(1)   An instrument creating a power of attorney shall be executed as a deed by the donor of the power.

...

    (3)   This section is without prejudice to any requirement in, or having effect under, any other Act as to the witnessing of instruments creating powers of attorney and does not affect the rules relating to the execution of instruments by bodies corporate.

10.(1)   Subject to subsection (2) of this section, a general power of attorney in the form set out in Schedule 1 to this Act, or in a form to the like effect but expressed to be made under this Act, shall operate to confer —

(a)   on the donee of the power; or

(b)   if there is more than one donee, on the donees acting jointly or acting jointly or severally, as the case may be,

authority to do on behalf of the donor anything which he can lawfully do by an attorney.

(2)   This section does not apply to functions which the donor has as a trustee or personal representative or as a tenant for life or statutory owner within the meaning of the Settled Land Act 1925.

Schedule 1 sets out the form in which a Power of Attorney under the Powers of Attorney Act 1971 should be made. To create a Power of Attorney, a person has to have capacity to do so, as Hoffmann J explains in *Re K* [1988] Ch 310 (though note the comments in *Re W* [2000] 1 All ER 175):

[In Re K]

The Act does not specify the mental capacity needed to execute an enduring power and the answer must therefore be found in the common law. It is well established that capacity to perform a juristic act exists when the person who purported to do the act had at the time the mental capacity, with the assistance of such explanation as he may have been given, to understand the nature and effect of that particular transaction: see *In re Beaney, decd.* [1978] 1 WLR 770. In principle, therefore, an understanding of the nature and effect of the power was sufficient for its validity.

At common law there is however the further rule that a power can no longer be validly exercised if the donor has lost the mental capacity to be a principal. The way in which this rule is usually expressed is to say that mental incapacity revokes the power. What is meant by mental incapacity for this purpose has not been fully explored in the authorities. The question is plainly different from the usual question about capacity to perform a juristic act. It is hypothetical rather than factual. The donor did not in fact exercise the power and one cannot therefore ask whether he actually understood the nature and effect of what he was doing. One can only ask whether he would have understood, and this requires one first to decide what he must be supposed to have done and the circumstances in which he must be supposed to have done it. In *Gibbons* v *Wright* (1954) 91 CLR 423, 445, it was said that a power is revoked if the donor ceases to have the mental capacity to perform the acts authorised by the power. This would seem to mean that, at any rate in the case of a general power, there will be revocation if the donor no longer has the general capacity to manage and administer his property and affairs. It is not necessary for me to discuss the question further because I am content to assume, as did the master, that the power executed by Miss K would at common law have been revoked, at latest, when she ceased to be able to manage and administer her property and affairs.

The main reason why the master held that Miss K's power was invalid was because in her view a person suffering from mental incapacity which would have revoked a power could not validly create one. There is at first sight a compelling logic about this reasoning. It is however important to bear in mind that in the rule that a power is revoked by the onset of mental incapacity, the term 'revoke' is used as a metaphor. To revoke a power ordinarily means intentionally to perform a juristic act which terminates its legal effect. But the donor who becomes mentally incapable has not performed any act. What happens is that at least for some purposes the power ceased to have effect *as if* he had revoked it. As in the case of all rules expressed as metaphors or analogies, there are dangers in reasoning from the metaphor as if it expressed a literal truth rather than from the underlying principle which the metaphor encapsulates.

...

The question is therefore whether, as a matter of construction, a power is 'valid' for the purposes of section 6(5)(*a*) of the Act only if the donor had the mental capacity which would have made it exercisable. This must be decided by having regard to the purpose of the Act as a whole, which is to enable powers to be exercised notwithstanding that the donor does not have the mental capacity required by the common law. There seems to me no logical reason why the validity of the power for the purposes of section 6(5)(*a*) should be affected by considerations of whether it would have been exercisable. The court is not concerned with whether the power has been validly exercised but whether as a juristic act it should be registered with a view to its future exercise notwithstanding the donor's loss of mental capacity.

...

Finally, I should say something about what is meant by understanding the nature and effect of the power. What degree of understanding is involved? Plainly one cannot expect that the donor should have been able to pass an examination on the provisions of the Act. At the other extreme, I do not think that it would be sufficient if he realised only that it gave Cousin William power to look after his property. Mr Rawson helpfully summarised the matters which the donor should have understood in order that he can be said to have understood the nature and effect of the power. First, (if such be the terms of the power) that the attorney will be able to assume complete authority over the donor's affairs. Secondly, (if such be the terms of the power) that the attorney will in general be able to do anything with the donor's property which he himself could have done. Thirdly, that the authority will continue if the donor should be or become mentally incapable. Fourthly, that if he should be or become mentally incapable, the power will be irrevocable without confirmation by the court. I do not wish to prescribe another form of words in competition with the explanatory notes prescribed by the Lord Chancellor, but I accept Mr Rawson's summary as a statement of the matters which should ordinarily be explained to the donor (whatever the precise language which may be used) and which the evidence should show he has understood.

[Re W]

In this case the essential facts were that at the time of the execution of the power (4 July 1996) Mrs W was 87 and by all accounts was physically well but suffering from a degree of memory impairment. Her GP, Dr H, had written a letter to her solicitor a fortnight before the execution of the power. The letter was dated 22 June 1996 and in it he said:

'I can confirm that I saw her recently with her daughter and found her to be suffering from a degree of memory impairment, however in my opinion she still has the necessary mental capacity to sign a power of attorney. I would add that her mental abilities are at their best in the early part of the day and tend to deteriorate as the day goes by.'

It seemed to me important for the court to see the doctor and ascertain precisely what he meant by the necessary mental capacity to sign a power of attorney and what tests he performed, if any, to reach this conclusion. However, I was told by Mr Jack, counsel for Mrs X, that the doctor had indicated that he could not now remember any detail whatsoever and that he was accordingly unable to help the court.

The hearing below proceeded in the total absence of Mrs X, who, unfortunately, was not served with appropriate notice of the hearing due to an error in the Public Trustee Office. That would of course have entitled Mrs X to have the proceedings below set aside as of right, but both counsel invited me, in the interest of saving costs, to treat the matter as effectively before me on the original as well as additional evidence put by Mrs X after the hearing before the master.

Against the doctor's evidence was the evidence of a chartered clinical psychologist to whom Mrs Y had taken Mrs W on 22 November and 13 December 1996. Mrs W had been taken from the residential home where she was then living to the psychologist without the knowledge of Mrs X, who first heard about the matter when the psychologist's report was produced in these proceedings.

As the master pointed out, the psychologist's report was extensive and detailed. He concluded that:

'... the above detected severity of deterioration across a number of vital areas of cognitive functioning suggests strongly that for the past period running into a number of years, Mrs W has not been in a position to deal properly with the intangible (non-concrete) or hypothetical, or to correctly comprehend, interpret, see implications in, judge, or to direct any business or operation, other than that which does not require weighing up the pros and cons, making comparisons, or seeing consequences of action beyond the immediate step.'

As the report did not specifically address the question whether or not Mrs W was capable of executing an enduring power of attorney, the psychologist wrote a supplemental note on 10 July 1998 in which he said: 'I believe that in no way was Mrs W in a condition on 4 July 1996 to execute an enduring power of attorney.' The doctor's evidence has the inestimable advantage of being that of the patient's GP, who saw her regularly, and of being more or less contemporaneous with the execution of the power. It would take a very strong opinion given as a result of an examination some five months later to persuade me positively that the patient did not have the necessary capacity. As it was, the psychologist recognised in his report that medication could make an assessment of the kind he was making problematic. Yet there is no record in his report of the various forms of medication (including morphine) that Mrs W was taking at the time. Mrs X has now given evidence of these: dothiepin for depression, inderalla for blood pressure, distalgesic co-proxamol for pain relief and merellil to keep her calm. Moreover, on 16 January 1997 Mrs W was rushed to hospital and treated for anaemia. The effect of anaemia on her performance of the psychometric tests is unclear.

I have taken into account all the evidence, on both sides, as to various incidents showing a certain degree of confusion over the years. There is no point in recording all the detail here. It is worth noting, however, that Mrs X had for many years handled her mother's financial affairs. Mrs X had been made a signatory on her bank account with Lloyds Bank. Mrs X arranged for the payment of her bills. When it was apparent in April 1996 that Mrs W's mental faculties were getting weaker she wrote, in her own handwriting, to her solicitor, in a perfectly intelligible way in connection with her will, a codicil and the division of what she called her 'household goods'. Mrs W herself, I am told, had been the attorney under an enduring power of attorney for her elder sister so I can assume that she probably knew what an enduring power of attorney was.

I have further evidence before me in the shape of a statement by one of the directors of the nursing home in which Mrs W now lives who says that as late as 12 April 1998, when the notice of intention to register the power was served on her, Mrs W understood the arrangements with Mrs X as the attorney and Mrs W said 'why would I want to change anything'. I have also been shown a letter written as late as April 1999 in a very shaky hand saying that she wanted the Public Trustee Office to stop interfering with her affairs. I must say that I was a little surprised at the coherence and vehemence of this letter and wondered to what extent it was influenced by others.

All in all, however, I am not satisfied that it has been established that Mrs W did not have the necessary understanding to execute an enduring power of attorney. That was the first ground put forward by the objectors, i.e. that the power was not valid as an enduring power because Mrs W did not understand the nature and effect of it. The degree of understanding and mental capacity necessary for this purpose has been laid down recently in *Re K, Re F* [1988] 1 All ER 358, [1988] Ch 310. The level of understanding required is less than that required to enable an individual to manage her affairs generally. What is required is that she understood that: (a) the attorney would be able to assume complete authority over her affairs; (b) that the attorney could do anything with her property that she could have done; (c) that that authority would continue if she became mentally incapable; and (d) would, in that event, become irrevocable without confirmation by the court.

I am not satisfied on the evidence that Mrs W did not have this understanding. This does not mean that I am satisfied that she did have it. The point of this judgment is that this last issue is not the question before me. If, as is the case, I am not satisfied that she lacked the necessary understanding, it seems to me that I am bid by the Act to register the power, and that, subject to consideration of the second ground of objection, is what I propose to do.

In *Re K* Hoffmann J (as he then was) added, after describing the above four elements, the following sentence:

'I do not wish to prescribe another form of words in competition with the explanatory notes prescribed by the Lord Chancellor, but I accept the summary of counsel as amicus curiae as a statement of the matters which should ordinarily be explained to the donor whatever the precise language which may be used and which the evidence should show he has understood.'
(See [1988] 1 All ER 358 at 363, [1988] Ch 310 at 316.)

This sentence forms no part of the reason for the decision. The learned judge was not concerned with an issue of onus or burden of proof. He inadvertently, in my judgment, turned the onus around so as to make it a requirement that the evidence should positively show the necessary understanding. The learned master concluded his judgment below thus:

'I must emphasise the final words of the passage I quoted earlier from Hoffmann J's judgment in *Re K* — "which the evidence should show that he has understood" — because they are often overlooked. The evidence in this case as it was presented to me prior to and at the hearing does not satisfy me that Mrs [W] understood the nature and effect of the enduring power of attorney she signed on 4 July 1996.'

In my judgment the master went wrong in following this part of Hoffmann J's judgment. To sustain the power Mrs X did not have to satisfy him that Mrs W understood the nature of the power: the master was bound to register it unless the objectors satisfied him that she did not.

However, a major weakness of the power created by this Act is that subsequent mental incapacity of the donor (the person granting the power) terminates the power of attorney. This is because the power of attorney is only valid if the donor retains the capacity to revoke it. The Enduring Powers of Attorney Act 1985 was passed to remedy this, as Vinelott J explains in *Re R* [1990] 2 All ER 893. It provides for a formal procedure to create a deed, which must be registered, whereby the power of attorney continues after the donor becomes mentally incapacitated:

[Enduring Powers of Attorney Act 1985]

1. Enduring power of attorney to survive mental incapacity of donor
(1) Where an individual creates a power of attorney which is an enduring power within the meaning of this Act then —
   (a) the power shall not be revoked by any subsequent mental incapacity of his; but
   (b) upon such incapacity supervening the donee of the power may not do anything under the authority of the power except as provided by subsection (2) below or as directed or authorised by the court under section 5 unless or, as the case may be, until the instrument creating the power is registered by the court under section 6; and
   (c) section 5 of the Powers of Attorney Act 1971 (protection of donee and third persons) so far as applicable shall apply if and so long as paragraph (b) above operates to suspend the donee's authority to act under the power as if the power had been revoked by the donor's mental incapacity.

(2)   Notwithstanding subsection (1)(b) above, where the attorney has made an application for registration of the instrument then, until the application has been initially determined, the attorney may take action under the power —
  (a) to maintain the donor or prevent loss to his estate; or
  (b) to maintain himself or other persons in so far as section 3(4) permits him to do so.

(3)   Where the attorney purports to act as provided by subsection (2) above then, in favour of a person who deals with him without knowledge that the attorney is acting otherwise than in accordance with paragraph (a) or (b) of that subsection, the transaction between them shall be as valid as if the attorney were acting in accordance with paragraph (a) or (b).

3.   Scope of authority etc. of attorney under enduring power

(1)   An enduring power may confer general authority (as defined in subsection (2) below) on the attorney to act on the donor's behalf in relation to all or a specified part of the property and affairs of the donor or may confer on him authority to do specified things on the donor's behalf and the authority may, in either case, be conferred subject to conditions and restrictions.

(2)   Where an instrument is expressed to confer general authority on the attorney it operates to confer, subject to the restriction imposed by subsection (5) below and to any conditions or restrictions contained in the instrument, authority to do on behalf of the donor anything which the donor can lawfully do by an attorney.

(3)   Subject to any conditions or restrictions contained in the instrument, an attorney under an enduring power, whether general or limited, may (without obtaining any consent) execute or exercise all or any of the trusts, powers or discretions vested in the donor as trustee and may (without the concurrence of any other person) give a valid receipt for capital or other money paid.

(4)   Subject to any conditions or restrictions contained in the instrument, an attorney under an enduring power, whether general or limited, may (without obtaining any consent) act under the power so as to benefit himself or other persons than the donor to the following extent but no further, that is to say —
  (a) he may so act in relation to himself or in relation to any other person if the donor might be expected to provide for his or that person's needs respectively; and
  (b) he may do whatever the donor might be expected to do to meet those needs.

(5)   Without prejudice to subsection (4) above but subject to any conditions or restrictions contained in the instrument, an attorney under an enduring power, whether general or limited, may (without obtaining any consent) dispose of the property of the donor by way of gift to the following extent but no further, that is to say —
  (a) he may make gifts of a seasonal nature or at a time, or on an anniversary, of a birth or marriage, to persons (including himself) who are related to or connected with the donor, and
  (b) he may make gifts to any charity to whom the donor made or might be expected to make gifts,
provided that the value of each such gift is not unreasonable having regard to all the circumstances and in particular the size of the donor's estate.

...

13.   Interpretation

(1)   'mentally incapable' or 'mental incapacity', except where it refers to revocation at common law, means, in relation to any person, that he is incapable by reason of mental disorder of managing and administering his property and affairs and 'mentally capable' and 'mental capacity' shall be construed accordingly; 'mental disorder' has the same meaning as it has in the Mental Health Act 1983;

(2)   Any question arising under or for the purposes of this Act as to what the donor of the power might at any time be expected to do shall be determined by assuming that he had full mental capacity at the time but otherwise by reference to the circumstances existing at that time.

[*Re R*]
The 1985 Act made a very remarkable change in the law. It creates a regime for the administration of the affairs of somebody who becomes incapable of managing their affairs which is supplemental to that provided by the Mental Health Act 1983. In effect the Act permits a person, while capable of managing his or her affairs, to select somebody who will be responsible for managing his or her affairs if there is a supervening incapacity, so avoiding the expense and (I think, possibly, in the minds of some) the embarrassment of invoking the full jurisdiction of the Court of Protection. A power of attorney has very limited effect until it is registered. When registered, it takes effect according to its terms. The scope of the attorney's authority is enlarged beyond that which it would bear under the general law by s. 3 (subject to any express restrictions in the power) and the court is given wide powers of supervision under s. 8. Section 3(4) provides:

'Subject to any conditions or restrictions contained in the instrument, an attorney under an enduring power ... may (without obtaining any consent) act under the power so as to benefit himself or other persons than the donor to the following extent but no further, that is to say — (a) he may so act in relation to himself or in relation to any other person if the donor might be expected to provide for his or that person's needs respectively; and (b) he may do whatever the donor might be expected to do to meet those needs.'

That extension is then further extended by sub-s (5), which gives the attorney power to 'dispose of the property of the donor by way of gift' in making gifts 'of a seasonal nature' or on a specified anniversary to 'persons ... who are related to or connected with the donor' subject to the proviso that 'the value of each such gift is not unreasonable having regard to all the circumstances and in particular the size of the donor's estate'.

The role of the court is set out in s. 8. Under sub-s (2)(a) the court has power to determine questions as to the meaning or effect of the instrument. Under sub-s(2)(b) the court has power to give directions with respect to —

'(i) the management or disposal by the attorney of the property and affairs of the donor; (ii) the rendering of accounts by the attorney and the production of the records kept by him for the purpose; (iii) the remuneration or expenses of the attorney, whether or not in default of or in accordance with any provision made by the instrument, including directions for the repayment of excessive or the payment of additional remuneration.'

Subsection (2)(c) gives the court power to require the attorney to furnish information or produce documents, and sub-s (2)(d) gives the court power to give any consent or authorisation to act which the attorney would have to obtain from a mentally capable donor. 1 must read sub-s (2)(e) in full:

'The court may ... (e) authorise the attorney to act as to benefit himself or other persons than the donor otherwise than in accordance with section 3(4) and (5) (but subject to any conditions or restrictions contained in the instrument).'

Subsection (2)(f) gives the court power to relieve the attorney wholly or partly from any liability which he has or may have incurred on account of a breach of his duties as attorney.

In its report *Mental Incapacity* the Law Commission has proposed the creation of a new Continuing Power of Attorney. This proposal has been accepted by the government. The view of the government is indicated in the following extract from the white paper *Making Decisions* (Cm 4465) (1999)

Background
2.2 There are currently two types of power of attorney:
- the first is the ordinary power, by which a person ('the donor') may delegate to another, decision-making on financial issues to be exercised on the donor's behalf. The donor may limit the power in time and make it subject to other conditions. This is used, for example, where a person goes abroad for a few years, and wants their property or financial affairs

looked after by somebody in their absence, on the understanding that control will return to the donor on the donor's return. This ordinary power of attorney only lasts for as long as the donor retains mental capacity. If the donor becomes incapable, the attorney loses his or her authority to act. Often a delegated decision-making power would be of most use at the point where the donor loses mental capacity;

- to overcome this difficulty the second type of power of attorney — the Enduring Power of Attorney (EPA) — was created, in the Enduring Powers of Attorney Act 1985. The Act specifically enables a person to delegate decision-making powers on financial matters, anticipating a time when the person will be mentally incapacitated and unable to make decisions for himself or herself. The 1985 Act requires an EPA to be made using a prescribed form, and to be drawn up at a time when the donor still has capacity. The attorney under the power is obliged to register the EPA when he has reason to believe that the donor is, or is becoming, mentally incapable. Before doing so, he is required by the statute to notify relatives of the donor.

Problems with the present system

2.3   The Government recognises that there are a number of problems with this system, and this view was reinforced in the consultation process. A number of concerns were raised, including the following:

The drafting or creation of the power:
- powers were used prior to the donor becoming incapacitated
- family members did not know about the existence of the EPA — some felt that it would be a safeguard if other people had to be alerted that the power had been created
- donors of EPAs were already without capacity by the time they signed their EPA.

The registration process:
- notification of others in the statutory list is inadequate, since the donor and relative may not see, or care anything for, one another
- there is no adequate system to compel the attorney to register the EPA when the donor becomes incapable.

The powers of the attorney:
- the court will not usually know about unregistered powers which are being exercised, where instances of financial abuse might occur.

The lack of a regional office:
- there is a lack of access for members of the public to speak to someone about EPAs.

2.4   The Law Commission recommended that EPAs, which are limited to financial affairs, should be replaced by Continuing Powers of Attorney (CPAs). CPAs would allow individuals to delegate decision-making powers on finance, healthcare, and personal welfare to a person of their choice. CPAs received very strong support on consultation from a wide range of individuals and organisations.

The Government intends to put in place a system of CPAs that would enable a person to delegate decision-making powers on finance, healthcare and personal welfare, where both the donor and donee are over 18.

2.5   A CPA may give general authority to take financial or welfare decisions but this principle is subject to reservations where the CPA relates to healthcare matters. A CPA should never be able to authorise the attorney to:
- consent or refuse consent to any treatment or procedure unless the donor is or is reasonably believed to be without capacity; or
- consent to the donor's compulsory treatment under the Mental Health Act 1983.

2.6   An attorney will not be able to make decisions on behalf of the person without capacity about the withdrawal of artificial nutrition and hydration unless the person has specifically given the authority to do this in the CPA. A general authority in the CPA to make health care decisions will be insufficient for this purpose.

2.7   An attorney will not be able to use the healthcare powers until the donor becomes incapacitated.

2.8   As is the case with the general authority to act reasonably … and managers …, there are a number of decisions which no one can take on behalf of the person without capacity …

Safeguards

There will be safeguards for those making CPAs.

2.9   As a result of the response to *Who Decides?*, the Government has decided that certain safeguards would be appropriate. These are intended to provide sufficient safeguards for people without capacity, while recognising that there should be minimal interference where things are working well.

2.10   Accordingly, the legislation will contain provisions about the form and manner of execution of the CPA, procedural requirements, and restrictions on who may be an attorney.

Making a CPA

- The form for making a CPA will be prescribed; and the terms of the CPA must be set out in writing. The document must be signed, witnessed and dated.
- The form must be accompanied by evidence that the donor was mentally capable at the time that it was created. That evidence could be provided by either a separate medical certificate or a signed statement by a doctor in the CPA form itself.
- Donors will be able to make more than one CPA and have more than one attorney. They may want to appoint different people to deal with different aspects, or they may wish to appoint joint attorneys for all decisions.
- Donors will be able to appoint substitute attorneys in case their first choice of attorney loses mental capacity or dies.
- It will not be possible to appoint the holder for the time being of a specified office to act as attorney.
- The donor must indicate whether he wishes to give to the attorney either general or specific powers in relation to finance, welfare and healthcare issues. As indicated at paragraph 2.6. above, certain healthcare powers can only be granted specifically.

Transitional arrangements

2.11   It will not be possible to convert an existing financial EPA into a CPA dealing with broader issues. Legislation will contain appropriate transitional arrangements in respect of EPAs to ensure a smooth transition.

Revocation and amendment of CPAs

2.12   Donors of CPAs will be able to revoke or amend them at any time while they have capacity, and to change their attorney. An attorney will be able to withdraw their consent to act under a CPA.

Powers of the court

The Government has decided that the Court of Protection will not be able to appoint a substitute attorney.

2.13   The aim of a CPA is to allow someone to choose another person to make decisions on their behalf. This process of selection will inevitably be highly personal. The nature of the relationship, and the level of trust that the donor has in the attorney, is crucial, given the wide range of powers that the attorney will have. But the original attorney may become unable, or unwilling, to perform his or her duties on behalf of the donor. If the donor has not nominated a substitute attorney, then the court will not be able to appoint a substitute itself. However, it will be able to appoint a manager, who will be subject to stricter controls than an attorney.

Compulsory registration of CPAs

There will be a compulsory Registration system and a Registering Authority. All CPAs must be registered before the attorney can use them.

2.14   Respondents strongly supported this on consultation. The authority will check whether the donor has already donated the same powers to another person under a valid, registered CPA, and, if necessary, refer the matter to the court for a ruling on validity. The legislation will set out the registration procedure.

2.15   Registration will be possible at any point following execution of the CPA until the time when the donor has become incapable. It will be possible for the attorney to exercise powers in relation to financial and welfare issues while the donor is still capable if that is the donor's wish. However, as noted at paragraph 2.7 above, it will only be possible for powers in relation to healthcare issues to be exercised when the donor has become incapable. This will ensure that the donor continues to make decisions about healthcare while capable of doing so, but would enable an attorney to make immediate decisions in the event of the donor becoming instantly incapable, for example as a result of receiving a head injury in a car accident.

Safeguards against abuse

2.16   As a safeguard against fraudulent registration and abuse, the Law Commission recommended that the attorney should be required to notify others of the application for registration *after* the CPA had been registered.

2.17   As a result of the response to consultation the Government has decided that notification should take place *before* registration. This would enable disputes and challenges to be settled by the court before the CPA has become effective. The attorney will have to provide evidence that notification had taken place or that best endeavours to contact those to be notified had failed.

2.18   The CPA form will allow donors to name specific people to be notified at the time of registration. This will replace the relationship provisions in relation to EPAs (see paragraphs 2.2.-2.3., above). The donor may specify on the CPA form that no one should be notified.

2.19   Except in unusual circumstances, a period of 28 days should elapse between notification and registration to allow time for objections to be lodged with the Registering Authority.

Emergency situations

2.20   The Government will make appropriate provision for emergency situations.

Recognition of CPAs

2.21   One current problem with the EPA system is that attorneys sometimes have problems with organisations or individuals who are unfamiliar with the EPA document, and are therefore suspicious of the attorney's claims to have authority to make decisions on the donor's behalf. It would be particularly problematic if this continued into the CPA system, when the attorney needed to make urgent medical decisions about a person's healthcare. The Government is looking at the most appropriate way of meeting the needs of the attorney in gaining recognition.

Role of the Court of Protection

2.22   The powers of the Court of Protection ('the court') in relation to CPAs will be similar to those held by the current court in relation to EPAs. These will include the power to determine questions about the meaning and effect of a CPA. The court will also have the power to revoke a CPA on the grounds of the unsuitability of an attorney, including where the attorney is not acting in the best interests of the donor.

Protection for attorneys and third parties

2.23   The Law Commission recommended protection for an attorney or third party who has acted in good faith using the powers contained in a CPA which had been revoked.

2.24   The Government agrees that an attorney or third party who acts in the belief that a revoked CPA is valid should be protected from liability, provided that their actions would otherwise be lawful.

Consent to treatment and civil liability

2.25   On healthcare matters, the Law Commission recommended that, as far as civil liability is concerned, consent to treatment given by the attorney in respect of an incapable adult should be regarded as if it was consent to treatment given by the individual patient. This recommendation was broadly supported in consultation and will be taken forward.

As with the Court of Protection, a power of attorney is limited to dealing with property and affairs. It cannot confer powers in relation to the person of the donor, such as the ability to consent to, or refuse, medical treatment. To do this, an advance statement is needed. 'Advance statement' is an umbrella term describing a formal document by means of which an individual can make provision for certain eventualities in advance to cover a time in the future when that person lacks the capacity to make decisions. They are sometimes called 'living wills', 'advance agreements' or 'advance directives'. Such documents are usually encountered in the context of health care and express a person's wishes regarding treatment in the event of losing capacity to do so.

The following extract from *Making Decisions* summarises the present legal status of such documents:

16.   The Government believes that a clear statement of the present legal position concerning advance statements would be helpful to lawyers, doctors and patients. The current law and medical practice is as follows. It is a general principle of law and medical practice that all adults have the right to consent to or refuse medical treatment. Advance statements are a means for patients to exercise that right by anticipating a time when they may lose the capacity to make or communicate a decision.

17.   An advance statement contains a person's instructions as to which medical treatment that person would or would not be prepared to accept if he or she should subsequently lose the capacity to decide for himself or herself. An advance statement can request specific treatments. It is an important principle that health professionals are not legally bound to provide that treatment if it conflicts with their professional judgement about the most appropriate treatment to give to a patient just as they would not be bound to give a treatment requested by a patient with capacity. However, the health professional may take the person's wishes into account when deciding the course of action.

18.   Advance statements are sometimes concerned with the refusal of life sustaining procedures in the event of terminal illness. They have nothing to do with euthanasia or suicide. They cannot authorise a doctor to do anything which is illegal or which a person with capacity could not request a doctor to do. Nor can they ask for treatment which is clinically inappropriate. Advance statements are simply a method whereby a person can exercise his or her right to accept or reject medical treatment. The Government wishes to make absolutely clear its complete opposition to euthanasia, which is and will remain illegal.

19.   Adults with capacity have the right to refuse or withdraw their consent to medical treatment. We do not accept that the decision has either to be reasonable or has to be justified to anyone apart from the individual who is making the decision. It follows that the Government respects the right

of people with capacity to be able to define, in advance, which medical procedures they will and will not consent to at a time when that individual has become incapable of making or communicating that decision. The courts have approved this principle and have determined that certain forms of advance statement already have full effect at common law. The judgments ... [of the courts] indicate that an advance refusal of treatment which is 'clearly established' and 'applicable in all the circumstances' is as effective as the decision of a capable adult. In [one] case, the High Court held that a refusal of treatment by a patient who had capacity to make that refusal was binding on his doctors for the present and the future until it was revoked. The Government accepts those decisions.

20. Given the division of opinion which exists on this complex subject and given the flexibility inherent in developing case law, the Government believes that it would not be appropriate to legislate at the present time, and thus fix the statutory position once and for all. The Government is satisfied that the guidance contained in case law, together with the Code of Practice Advance Statements about Medical Treatment published by the British Medical Association, provides sufficient clarity and flexibility to enable the validity and applicability of advance statements to be decided on a case by case basis. However, the Government intends to continue to keep the subject under consideration in the light of future medical and legal developments.

The matter is not, however, without controversy, especially where advance statements provide that treatment is not to be given in certain circumstances. Professor Hugh Collins succinctly identifies the issues:

Suppose that I am informed by doctors that I am suffering from a terminal illness, though I have a few months left. I then seek to make a bargain with my doctors specifying which treatments will be used and the point at which my life will be terminated, such as the moment when I become unable to savour ice-cream. The contract satisfies my preferences as a patient, and it states a measurable criterion for performance. Who could object to this arrangement? Who else does it concern? Nevertheless, to regard this as a valid transaction, necessarily requires elimination of the standards of homicide set by the criminal law, and the standards of professional conduct established by the medical profession. Moreover, the contract treats everyone else's preferences such as those of my family or other hospital workers as irrelevant. But to insist that the living will should be ineffective, to insist that this issue should not be within the scope of delegated powers to individuals, requires an affirmation of faith in public standards, of the right of organizations such as the medical profession to set standards of conduct, and it requires a deafness to the claims of others such as family to influence one's choices, all of which runs against the grain of the contractualization of social life.

[*Collins, H., The Sanctimony of Contract* in R. *Rawlings (ed.) Law, Society and Economy* (Clarendon Press, 1997).]

5.4 **Reform**

In recent years, a number of different reports have recommended reforms of various aspects of the mental health regime. The Law Commission's work on capacity has been largely accepted by the government. There is, thus, likely to be reform in respect of capacity, the Court of Protection, powers of attorney, procedures for detention and release and some rationalisation of the position regarding informal patients, though not yet in respect of advance statements, which, as indicated below, the government feels need further consideration. Quite when such reform might occur remains uncertain and is subject to the vagaries of political priorities.

The White Paper, *Reforming the Mental Health Act* (Cm 5016 (2000)) sets out the reasons identified by the government as suggesting that change is required, and indicates the government's thinking on some of the issues arising.

A brief extract from the foreword provides a summary of the government's assessment of the present law:

Millions of people face a mental illness at some point in their lives. That is why improving mental health services is a priority for the Government.

First we have made investment a priority. More staff, more beds and more services are being made available particularly for those with the most serious mental health problems. The *NHS Plan*, published in July, outlined further new resources and the development of further new services over the next few years including for those who are dangerous and severely personality disordered.

Second, we have made reform a priority. For the first time mental health services in all parts of England are having to operate to new national standards and similar measures will be introduced in Wales. While there are very real problems and pressures, progress is being made towards plugging gaps in provision and modernising services.

This White Paper details how we will now underpin these improvements in mental health services with reforms to mental health laws.

The current 1983 Mental Health Act is largely based on a review of mental health legislation which took place in the 1950s. Since then the way services are provided has dramatically changed. The current laws have failed properly to protect the public, patients or staff.

Under existing mental health laws, the only powers compulsorily to treat patients are if they are in hospital. The majority of patients today are treated in the community. But public confidence in care in the community has been undermined by failures in services and failures in the law. Too often, severely ill patients have been allowed to drift out of contact with mental health services. They have been able to refuse treatment. Sometimes, as the tragic toll of homicides and suicides involving such patients makes clear, lives have been put at risk. In particular existing legislation has also failed to provide adequate public protection from those whose risk to others arises from severe personality disorder. We are determined to remedy this.

Of course the vast majority of people with mental illness represents no threat to anyone. Many mentally ill patients are among the most vulnerable members of society. But the Government has a duty to protect individual patients and the public if a person poses a serious risk to themselves or to others.

The need for reform is emphasised in this extract from Chapter 1:

1.14 The last full review of mental health legislation took place in the 1950s under the chairmanship of Lord Eustace Percy. The Mental Health Act 1983 is largely based on that review. Since the time of the Percy review there have been major changes in mental health services. New drug treatments, different patterns of care which now see more people treated in the community rather than in institutions and a wider role for other therapeutic approaches have all contributed to a markedly different landscape. The 1983 Act, however, remains based on treatment within hospitals. Concerns are also being expressed about the way decisions relating to compulsory treatment are made under the Act. The Act itself is complex and in places, confusing, and its basic underlying principles have not been clearly set out.

1.15 The 1983 Act also fails to fully address the challenge posed by a minority of people with mental disorder who pose a significant risk to others as a result of their disorder. It has failed to properly protect the public, patients or staff. Severely mentally ill patients have been allowed to lose contact with services once they have been discharged into the community. Such patients have been able to refuse treatment in the community. And it is the community as well as those patients which has paid a heavy price. We also need to move away from the narrow concept of 'treatability' which applies to certain categories of mental disorder in the 1983 Act. New legislation must be clearly framed to allow all those who pose a significant risk of serious harm to others as a result of their mental disorder to be detained in a therapeutic environment where they can be offered care and treatment to manage their behaviour.

1.16 The Government commissioned a number of research projects into the working of the current Mental Health Act to help to inform us of weaknesses that new legislation should address. These research projects reported earlier this year and a summary of all of the projects was published in March.

1.17 We also commissioned a review of the existing legislation in 1998 led by Professor Genevra Richardson. The Government broadly accepted the framework for new legislation recommended by the Richardson Committee. Professor Richardson's report was published alongside a Green Paper last year where the Government began a process of consultation on a number of proposed changes to the Act.

1.18 The changes we intend to make to the Mental Health Act 1983 are described in some detail in the following chapters. In proposing these changes we are determined to make sure that the new legislation fully protects the rights of patients and the public, enhances the principles of fairness and equity, ensures consistency and supports the wider changes we are making to mental health services in England and Wales.

1.19 Finally, new mental health legislation will apply, as does the Mental Health Act 1983, to people with learning disabilities. However, we will be publishing a separate White Paper on the Government's wider approach to improving the life chances for this client group and the application of the legislation will be finalised in the context of that wider policy.

The next extract identifies the key areas that the government believes are in need of reform and the proposals for change:

2.1 The previous chapter sets out our strategy for improving services for the 630,000 people who, at any time, receive care and treatment from specialist mental health services. Good quality care and treatment is the key to making sure that most people with mental health problems will never need to fall within the scope of mental health legislation. This chapter explains why we need a modern framework of mental health legislation, why we need to reform the 1983 Act and the key changes we intend to introduce.

What are the objectives of mental health legislation?

2.2 People with mental illness or other mental disorders should as far as possible be treated in the same way as people with any other illnesses or medical conditions. Care and treatment needs should be properly assessed and, wherever possible, met on an informal basis with full agreement between the patient and the care team. However there will always be some people with mental disorder who are either unable or unwilling to seek care and treatment. They may not realise, or not accept, that such care and treatment will be in their best interests if it helps prevent their condition from getting worse or makes it less likely that they will harm themselves or take their own lives. In a small minority of cases, this may mean that not only will a patient pose a significant risk to him or herself but also to other people in their family or in the community.

2.3 In most other areas of health and social care, decisions are made under common law about whether to treat a person without their consent if they are unable to, or do not, seek necessary care and treatment voluntarily. But the principles of common law do not provide the sort of robust framework that is needed to protect people from the effects of mental disorder and to enable action necessary to prevent serious harm. The Government has a duty to set out a clear framework for determining when and how care and treatment for mental disorder must be provided, if necessary against the will of the patient, either in his or her best interest or to prevent serious harm to other people. The same framework should put in place safeguards to protect a patient's rights where care and treatment is given without consent.

What has gone before and what needs to change?

2.4 Legislation to address care of people with mental disorder in a comprehensive way was first introduced in England in the late eighteenth century and during the nineteenth century the issue was frequently reviewed by Parliament. There were over 20 Acts of Parliament passed between 1808 and 1891 dealing with the care of mentally disordered patients in public or private institutions. In 1959, legislation based on the recommendations of a Royal Commission chaired by Lord Eustace Percy, brought together for the first time in one Act a comprehensive framework of mental health law for England and Wales. That Act was amended and updated to become the Mental Health Act 1983.

2.5 Compulsory powers to detain patients in hospital for assessment and treatment for mental disorder under the 1983 Act are used on about 44,000 occasions each year. At any one time over 12,000 patients are detained for treatment in hospital. It is essential that legislation affecting the lives and liberty of so many people should reflect the values and priorities of society today.

2.6 Care and treatment for mental disorder has moved on a long way in the last 20 years and in many ways the 1983 Act falls short of what is needed. It does not command the confidence of patients and their carers or of the public. The procedures do not always support, and at worst, can frustrate good clinical practice. The processes of the 1983 Act are complex and have become more complex to apply as a result of amendments and development of case law over the past 20 years. Research shows lack of consistency about decisions made on use of powers in the Act between different groups of practitioners, and between hospitals in different parts of the country. The Act has failed to protect the public or patients, as the tragic toll of homicides and suicides by mentally ill people shows. That failure has undermined public confidence in mental health services.

Principles

2.7 One of our key aims is to ensure that the purpose and scope of new legislation are readily understood. This is important for patients, their carers, and the public. It is essential for the health and social care professionals and other practitioners who will use the new powers.

2.8 The fundamental principles that underpin new legislation will be set out in a way that provides a clear context for decisions about when and how the powers should be used. The areas that will be covered are described below.

2.9 New legislation will be fully compatible with the Human Rights Act 1998 and the emphasis throughout will be on ensuring that decisions taken are appropriate to each patient as an individual. An important aspect of this approach is that in deciding matters relating to the care and treatment of patients with mental disorder those responsible must act openly and fairly. This means that they must take account of the characteristics, abilities and diverse backgrounds of individual patients, including matters such as age, gender, sexual orientation, social, ethnic, cultural and religious background. They must not make general assumptions about how any one of those factors will impact on a particular patient's health and social care needs, or about the way that care and treatment should be provided.

2.10 Formal powers should not be used as an alternative to securing the agreement of people whose disabilities result in difficulties with communication. Formal powers should only involve imposition of such conditions as are necessary to ensure the patient's health or safety or the safety of other people. When decisions under mental health legislation affect a child the child's welfare should be paramount.

2.11 People with mental disorder should be treated in such a way as to promote to the greatest practicable degree their self-determination and personal responsibility. Steps should be taken to ensure that, so far as possible, patients are able to participate in decisions relating to their care and treatment. In some cases this will mean discussing with a patient when he or she is well what care and treatment they would prefer if the mental disorder deteriorates and they become acutely ill. Where a patient is required to comply with particular aspects of his or her care and treatment plan, services must be provided in a way that enables them to do so. Care and treatment should involve the least degree of compulsion that is consistent with ensuring that the objectives of the plan are met.

2.12   Mental health legislation makes provision for very significant curtailment of the freedom of individuals to refuse care and treatment and to determine how they live their lives. Formal powers should only be used with good cause and after alternatives have been considered.

Need for a new focus on the individual

2.13   Development of new therapies and drug treatments now means that the majority of people with serious mental disorder do not need long periods of hospital treatment. Most can, with appropriate supervision, be successfully and safely treated in the community. But successful treatment in the community will, for many, depend on compliance with treatment. All too often patients who have been discharged from hospital fail to comply with treatment and their condition relapses frequently resulting in unplanned readmission to hospital and, sometimes, serious harm to the patient or to other people. Over recent years there have been over 1,000 suicides each year by people with mental health problems, and about 40 homicides by people known to have been in recent contact with mental health services.

2.14   Under the 1983 Act powers to require compliance with treatment are linked to detention in hospital. This does not allow the flexibility for compulsory powers to be used in a way that fits with a patient's changing needs. Nor does it support the processes of individual care planning that are needed to ensure that compulsory treatment will result in good health outcomes for patients and reduced risk. At the moment clinicians have to wait until patients in the community become ill enough to need admission to hospital before compulsory treatment can be given. This prevents early intervention to reduce risk to both patients and the public.

2.15   New legislation will introduce statutory requirements that all patients treated under formal powers will be given a full assessment of their health and social care needs in accordance with the *Care Programme Approach* and the 1996 Welsh Office *Guidance on the Care of People in the Community with a Mental Illness*. Any proposals for compulsory care and treatment after the formal assessment period must be based on individual care and treatment plans.

2.16   Concerns of risk will always take precedence, but care and treatment provided under formal powers should otherwise reflect the best interests of the patient. Clinical teams will need to account for the steps they have taken to consider the needs and wishes of the patient in putting together a care and treatment plan.

2.17   Formal care and treatment of a patient with mental disorder will inevitably restrict his or her personal freedoms but should only do so to the extent justified by any risk that they pose to themselves or to other people. The possibility of informal, consensual care and treatment should always be considered before recourse to compulsory powers. Proposed plans for use of formal powers will be tested against the principle that necessary care and treatment should be provided in the least restrictive environment consistent with ensuring the safety of the patient and of other people. Government policy for people with learning disability or other disabilities is to promote independence, choice and inclusion. It is not intended that care and treatment under compulsory powers should be used as a means to prevent people taking the normal risks associated with daily life.

2.18   The new provisions will mean that compulsory care and treatment can, if appropriate, take place in the community rather than through detention in hospital. This would not be contemplated at a time when a patient was assessed as posing a significant risk of serious harm to him or herself or to other people — in these cases detention for treatment in hospital will be required. But otherwise if care in the community under compulsory powers offers the best prospect of a good therapeutic outcome it should be considered. Compliance with treatment and contact with services will both be enforced under the new legislation in a way that was never possible under the 1983 Act. That will help prevent patients relapsing and becoming subject to the distress of repeated unplanned admissions to acute wards and should achieve better outcomes for patients while minimising any risk they may pose to themselves or to other people. It will also help ensure that patients whose care, with proper supervision, can be well managed outside hospital without risk are not unnecessarily kept in hospital simply to ensure compliance with medication.

Need for better information for patients and their carers

2.19   Good information will often help ensure that patients get early access to care, sometimes avoiding the need for compulsory treatment. For patients who are subject to compulsory powers good information will help overcome misunderstandings between them and the clinicians who are responsible for their care. Misunderstandings that can sometimes get in the way of good health outcomes. The 1983 Act does not cover provision of information to patients and their carers outside use of compulsory powers. For patients who are subject to compulsory powers it requires that information is given but does not go beyond that to ensure that they get help in understanding the implications of that information or in communicating their views.

2.20   New legislation will include measures to ensure that patients and their carers get the information and support they need, when they need it. For some this may simply involve help in understanding how to access specialist mental health services. Primary Care Trusts, Primary Care Groups, and health and social services authorities will be required to make available advice and information about the services they commission for people with mental disorder, and about how patients and their carers can access those services. The information should be made available in an appropriate format, as required, for all patients. This will be backed up by the developments that are already taking place in England through implementation of the *Mental Health National Service Framework* and *NHS Plan* and which will be taken forward in Wales through the *All Wales Strategy* and the NSF for Wales.

2.21   In some circumstances, a family member or another person who knows a patient well, is better placed than the patient to recognise that he or she may need treatment for serious mental disorder. Patients suffering from first episode psychosis, for example, often fail to seek help before they become acutely ill. The Code of Practice on new legislation will include guidance for health and social care practitioners on the circumstances in which it may be appropriate to discuss a patient's care and treatment with a member of his or her family, or another person. This will include information about the action that a patient's GP should consider taking if he or she is asked by a relative or another person to assess the patient's mental state.

2.22   Patients who are subject to care and treatment under formal powers may also need help to understand how the legislation works including how to appeal against use of compulsory powers, and how to ensure that their views and wishes are properly represented.

2.23   New legislation will place a duty on those responsible for the care and treatment of patients under formal powers to ensure that, as far as possible, every patient is fully informed about the particular powers that apply in his or her case, and rights under the law. This will include the nomination of a person to represent him or her in discussions with their clinical team and in other matters relating to their care. This person, to be known as the 'nominated person', will replace the 'nearest relative' under the 1983 Act and take on some of the same functions. The patient may identify such a person in an advance agreement and it is likely that in most cases the nominated person will be a relative of the patient or their main carer.

Advocacy

2.24   As now, patients who want to challenge the use of compulsory powers will have the right to free legal representation and, if appropriate, to seek an independent medical opinion. But it is important that they have a right of access to advice and support from independent specialist advocacy services at other times. Access to independent specialist advocacy is already available in some areas; the Government is currently considering how best to extend the provision of such services, building on existing good practice. The aim is to ensure that patients who are subject to compulsory powers, and their carers, are better able to understand the purpose and scope of the legal powers that affect them. Specialist advocates will also be able to help represent any concerns that the patient has about his or her care and treatment.

2.25   The new Commission for Mental Health (see paragraph 2.33) will be responsible for monitoring the quality and overseeing the operation of these specialist advocacy services. The Patient Advocacy Liaison Service announced in the *NHS Plan* will be the gateway to specialist advocacy schemes.

Need for better decision-making

2.26   For mental health legislation to achieve its purpose patients, their carers and the public must be confident that the powers are used in a way that is equitable and consistent. The 1983 Act is complex. As a consequence, the reasons that patients are brought under, and discharged from, compulsory powers sometimes appear to reflect differences in practice between clinical teams rather than a consistent approach to decision-making under the Act. In addition, for most of the people who exercise key responsibilities the Act does not require any special training in the use of the powers it contains. Doctors are given responsibility for use of powers that allow patients to be detained for treatment for long periods of time with no provision for automatic independent scrutiny of their decisions.

2.27   The Mental Health Act Commission has responsibility for monitoring the operation of the Act but its remit is not clearly defined and nor is the interface between its responsibilities and those of the recently established Commission for Health Improvement and new National Commission for Care Standards. This lack of clarity is unhelpful for both patients and service providers.

2.28   A key aim in reviewing the 1983 Act has been to identify ways of improving the quality, openness and consistency of decisions that are made about use of compulsory powers. New legislation will significantly tighten up the procedures for assessment of patient needs and development of plans for continuing care and treatment. The same basic procedures will have to be followed for all patients who are subject to care and treatment under compulsory powers — a single pathway will replace the many different routes through the current Act. The aim is to require all practitioners to do what is already accepted as good professional practice. The new provisions will mean that there is a better record of why decisions are taken and what they entail.

2.29   Except for people before the Courts, proposals for use of compulsory powers beyond 28 days will require authorisation by a new independent Mental Health Tribunal. This will create greater openness and clearer accountability for decisions to use powers in the new legislation. It will also ensure that patient interests and the public interest are properly taken into account. The Tribunal will be required to seek advice from independent experts as well as taking evidence from the clinical team and the patient.

2.30   Practitioners who are responsible for using the powers in mental health legislation need to have a thorough understanding of its scope and purpose. They also need to know how their roles and responsibilities fit with the roles and responsibilities of others. Specialist training will be provided for all professional staff authorised to undertake specific functions under new legislation. Training and regular updating will be statutory requirements for those who are responsible for taking key decisions.

2.31   Professionals and agencies that have responsibility for patients who are subject to compulsory powers need to share relevant information to ensure that all those involved in a patient's care and treatment are properly informed. This is often important to ensuring the patient's best interests are met. It may sometimes be necessary in the public interest. According to independent inquiries a significant factor in many of the homicides and suicides that have taken place over the last decade has been a breakdown in communication and exchange of information between the local services charged with caring for and treating mentally ill patients. In the new legislation there will be a new duty covering the disclosure of information about patients suffering from mental disorder between health and social services agencies and other agencies, for example housing agencies or criminal justice agencies.

2.32   The new procedures to improve the process of making and recording decisions, including the procedures associated with presenting cases to the Tribunal, are important elements in providing high quality care and treatment for patients who are subject to formal powers. Managers of mental health services will be expected to ensure that this is recognised in the job descriptions for practitioners with key responsibilities under new legislation and that clinical teams get any necessary administrative support.

Commission for Mental Health

2.33   A new Commission for Mental Health will be established to look after the interests of people who are subject to care and treatment under powers in the new legislation. The new Commission, which will replace the Mental Health Act Commission, will, amongst other things, carry specific responsibilities for monitoring the use of formal powers, providing guidance on the operation of those powers, and assuring the quality of training provided for practitioners with key responsibilities under the legislation and for specialist advocacy services. The responsibility for inspecting and monitoring facilities in which detained patients are treated will in future rest with the Commission for Health Improvement and the National Care Standards Commission, allowing the Commission for Mental Health to focus more effectively on reviewing the use of the legislation. The Commission for Health Improvement or the National Care Standards Commission will however be able to ask the Commission for Mental Health to perform inspection and monitoring on its behalf.

Need for additional safeguards

2.34   In two areas the provisions of the 1983 Act do not sufficiently protect the interests of some of the most vulnerable patients who need treatment for mental disorder.

Children and young people

2.35   The provisions in new legislation, like the 1983 Act, will potentially apply to people of any age. In view of the special needs and status of children and young people, it is essential that special steps can be taken to safeguard and promote their welfare. But under the 1983 Act there are no special provisions about how the powers should be applied to children and young people. The new care and treatment order will provide flexibility, where the criteria for compulsory care and treatment are met, to ensure that the needs of a child or young person are reflected in a way that is consistent with his or her best interests.

2.36   Under new legislation the Tribunal will be required, in considering an application for a compulsory order for care and treatment of a child or young person, to obtain expert advice on both health and social care aspects of the proposed care plan. It will also be required to consider in particular whether the location of care is appropriate to his or her needs.

2.37   There will be changes in the provisions regarding the right of young people between the ages of 16 and 18 to refuse consent to care and treatment for mental disorder. This will clarify the circumstances in which use of compulsory powers under mental health legislation may be appropriate for this age group.

2.38   The Government will consider ways to further safeguard the rights of children and young people with serious mental disorder, including those who are treated informally.

Adult patients with long-term mental incapacity
2.39   New legislation will include provisions to protect the rights of people with long-term mental incapacity who need care and treatment for serious mental disorder. In many cases such patients do not resist care and treatment but nor are they able to consent to it. They are sometimes described as 'not uncompliant' and it is inappropriate to suggest that they should be subject to compulsory powers. But a patient with long-term mental incapacity who needs treatment for serious mental disorder is, potentially, particularly liable to abuse or neglect. This is an area where the human rights of a very vulnerable group of people have never been given sufficient consideration in mental health statute.
2.40   It is essential to ensure that the best interests of these patients are properly considered and protected and this can only be achieved through independent scrutiny. New legislation will place a duty on the clinical supervisor responsible for the care and treatment of a patient with long-term mental incapacity to refer the care plan to a member of the expert panel for a second opinion when the care and treatment for a mental disorder continues for longer than 28 days. These cases will come within the remit of the Commission for Mental Health and there will be a right to apply to the Tribunal to challenge detention and for a review where there are concerns about the quality and nature of the patient's care and treatment.

...

3.1   Mental health legislation establishes the framework for provision of care and treatment for mental disorder under formal powers. Within this framework, responsibility for decisions on what care and treatment a particular patient needs, and in what conditions it is provided, will generally rest with the clinicians concerned with his or her care. In the case of patients subject to compulsory care and treatment the responsibilities of the clinical team will, under new legislation, be subject to the jurisdiction of the new Mental Health Tribunal.
3.2   The provisions in new legislation will potentially apply to people of any age, but there will be special safeguards for children and young people under the age of 18 ... .

Definition of mental disorder
3.3   Powers in new legislation will be based on a broad definition of mental disorder covering — any disability or disorder of mind or brain, whether permanent or temporary, which results in an impairment or disturbance of mental functioning. This definition is consistent with the approach recommended by the Law Commission in considering legislation relating to mental incapacity. It is intended to ensure that the presence, or absence, of any one particular clinical condition does not limit the discretion of clinicians to consider whether a patient with mental disorder should be treated under compulsory powers.
3.4   In contrast to the 1983 Act, new legislation will not define particular categories of mental disorder. This means that no particular clinical diagnosis will have the effect of limiting the way that the powers are used. The same criteria will be used to determine whether an individual falls within the scope of the legislation whatever their diagnosis. ...
3.5   This change in approach will ensure the flexibility for compulsory powers to be used in whatever way best meets a particular patient's needs and is consistent with any risk that they pose to themselves or to other people. It will also help to ensure that patients who require care and treatment under mental health legislation are not excluded because of too narrow a definition of mental disorder. One of the effects of the change will be to move away from the narrow concept of 'treatability' that applies to certain categories of mental disorder in the 1983 Act. This will mean that new legislation will more clearly apply to any individual who has a personality disorder who poses a serious risk of significant harm to others as a result of their mental

disorder (see Part Two of the White Paper). Under the present Act we know that a significant number of people with a primary diagnosis of personality disorder who pose a risk to others are not detained in hospital because of uncertainty about whether their personality disorder can be 'treated' or not. The new criteria with specific references to risk will provide clarity. These powers will be matched by new services to provide assessment of patients' needs and care programmes designed to manage behaviours that lead to serious harm to other people.

3.6   But it is equally important that only those patients who need to be covered by the provisions of the legislation come within its scope. The wide definition of mental disorder will therefore be matched by criteria that set clear limits to the circumstances in which compulsory powers may be used .... A diagnosis of mental disorder alone would never be sufficient to justify use of compulsory powers.

3.7   The introduction of a new definition of mental disorder and new criteria for use of compulsory powers will have an impact on who comes within the scope of the new legislation and what provisions apply to them. Alongside the changes that are being introduced through the *Mental Health National Service Framework* and *NHS Plan* and their Welsh counterparts, this will mean more effective care and treatment for patients. The Government's objective is to reduce, wherever possible, the number of individuals who are subject to the use of powers for compulsory care and treatment in a way that is consistent with the objectives set out in the previous chapter.

Procedures for use of compulsory powers

3.8   A key aim of new legislation is to develop a framework that is fully compatible with the Human Rights Act 1998. The complexity of the matters that need to be covered make it essential that new legislation is straightforward for practitioners to use, and for patients and their carers to understand. It will be based on a common framework that will apply in all cases where there is a decision to use compulsory powers. New legislation will require those responsible for taking decisions about use of compulsory powers to make a written record, following a standard format, of what they decide and why.

3.9   The framework will set out a single pathway for compulsory care and treatment based on three distinct stages. The period of time that each stage takes will vary according to the needs of each patient, but all three stages will have to be followed consecutively in every case. If a patient is well known to the service the first and second stages of formal assessment and development of a care plan may be completed within a matter of days. But a patient will never be made subject to a care and treatment order beyond 28 days without first going through an initial period of formal assessment by specialist mental health services, either as an inpatient or in the community. Nor will any patient, other than a convicted prisoner, be subject to long-term compulsory care and treatment without authorisation by an independent Tribunal or the Court ... .

In a speech introducing the White Paper, *Making Decisions* (accessible at **http://www.open.gov.uk/lcd/speeches/1999/10-11-99.htm**), the Lord Chancellor stated that the government was committed to reform of the law on mental health and allied matters. He said that the government would bring forward legislation when parliamentary time became available. At the time of writing, no such reform has occurred. The government has, however, decided that it will not legislate in respect of advance statements for the time being. In the same speech, the Lord Chancellor said:

Let me summarise why we are not, at this time, taking forward legislation on advance statements, sometimes known as 'advance directives' or 'living wills'.

   The Government of course respects the right of people with capacity to be able to define, in advance, which medical procedures they will, and which they will not, consent to at a time when they have become incapable of making or communicating that decision. But the courts have already approved this principle and have determined that certain forms of advance statement have full effect at common law ... To fix into statute now a set of rules, when the case law, influenced by medical advances and the development of precedent, is still evolving, would not be sound.

The guidance contained in case law, together with the Code of Practice, Advance Statements about Medical Treatment, published by the BMA, provides sufficient flexibility to enable the validity and applicability of advance statements to be determined. The courts have a great advantage over any possible statute. They can provide an individualised assessment of the applicability of an advance statement, based on the individual circumstances of every case. No statute could do that, however complex. Unless the legislation were to say that all disputes over advance statements must be resolved in court, the legislation would risk making advance statements inappropriate and inflexible, with the obvious dangers to the best interests of individuals which that would involve.

PART III

Children

6

Children

6.1 Introduction

Prior to the enactment of the Children Act 1989, the law in this area was subject to the same flaws that continue to afflict the law in other areas of social service provision, such as community care: it was fragmented, with gaps in provision and administration, and it was not underpinned by clear statements of principle. That of itself would be sufficient to justify law reform, but another precipitant came from a series of child abuse scandals, in both domestic and residential settings. Amongst these may be listed the Cleveland Inquiry and the 'Pindown' Inquiry. The first, which predates the Children Act, was significant in that it was concerned with over zealous use of powers by social workers. Although superseded by the Children Act in many of its concerns, the following extracts from the *Report of the Inquiry into Child Abuse in Cleveland* [(1988) Cm 413] illustrate that the issues raised are still live. The first describes the events leading up to the Inquiry. You might like to consider whether the regime established under the Children Act and the procedures suggested in documents such as *Working Together* (see below) would have prevented the events described from taking place:

The story of the Cleveland 'crisis'
Prior to 1987
1.   In Cleveland during 1985 and 1986 a number of people had been expressing concern about the response of the agencies to child sexual abuse, notably Mrs Dunn a nursing officer responsible for dealing with child abuse in South Tees. A working party of the Area Review Committee under the chairmanship of the National Society for the Prevention of Cruelty to Children representative, Mr Michie, had experienced difficulties in gaining agreement to revised guidelines from all the agencies, particularly from the Police. The efforts of the working party had been protracted but an acceptable draft had been placed in October 1986 before the committee shortly before its demise.
2.   In June 1986 Cleveland County Council Social Services Department, as part of their programme to give child protection a greater priority, had appointed Mrs Richardson to the new post of Child Abuse Consultant.

January 1987
3.   On the 1st January 1987 Dr Higgs arrived in Cleveland on her appointment as a consultant paediatrician in South Tees Health District. She was based mainly at the Maternity Hospital and at Middlesbrough General Hospital. There she joined, among others, Dr Wyatt and Dr Morrell.

She also had sessions at North Tees General Hospital. Dr Higgs was concerned about the services available in Cleveland for deprived and abused children. Before her arrival in Middlesbrough, she had consulted Mrs Richardson on the prevalence of child abuse and the arrangements in Cleveland. She had expressed the hope of working in a community in a deprived area.

4.   Soon after her arrival Dr Higgs called on the Director of Social Services, Mr Bishop, and met Mr Walton, his Senior Assistant Director, and Mrs Richardson. She joined in various multi-disciplinary and community projects and became vice-chairman of the newly formed Joint Child Abuse Committee which took over from the Area Review Committee.

5.   Mrs Richardson was on the same committee and she was invited to chair a working party to bring up to date guidelines formulated in 1984 by the earlier committee, the Area Review Committee, for the various agencies to work together in the field of child abuse. The purpose of the new working party was to redraft the guidelines and to make more suitable arrangements for dealing with the special requirements of child sexual abuse.

6.   Dr Higgs had, in the summer of 1986 in her previous post in Newcastle, examined two Cleveland children in the care of the Cleveland County Council. She suspected sexual abuse and on examination saw for the first time the phenomenon of what has been termed 'reflex relaxation and anal dilatation'. She had recently learnt from Dr Wynne, a consultant paediatrician at Leeds, that this sign is found in children subject to anal abuse. On the basis of various physical findings, including this sign, she diagnosed anal abuse.

February

7.   Soon after her arrival in South Tees, her advice was sought about a little girl of 6 with vaginal bleeding. She had been taken by her mother to a doctor who as it happened was also a woman police surgeon. This doctor was concerned and consulted Mrs Richardson who initially recommended a police surgeon, but on learning that the referring doctor was herself a police surgeon, suggested Dr Higgs. Dr Higgs found evidence of vaginal and anal interference and the signs included anal dilatation. The child indicated that her grandfather was responsible. The police were called and arrested the grandfather, who denied the abuse. He was charged and bailed on the condition that he reside in a bail hostel, and the little girl returned home.

March

8.   In March Dr Higgs examined the little girl again and found the signs had reappeared; she diagnosed further abuse and informed Social Services. The grandfather on this occasion could not be the perpetrator, and the little girl said it was her father. Social Services informed the Police. The Police were embarrassed by this revelation and dropped charges against the grandfather. Inspector Whitfield consulted the senior police surgeon, Dr Irvine. The police wanted him to examine the child. He telephoned Dr Higgs. He said she refused to let him examine the child. He expressed the firm view that the sign was unreliable as a basis for diagnosis. On the following day both Dr Higgs and Dr Irvine were at the case conference on the child. Dr Irvine again said he could not accept the grounds for the diagnosis and that Dr Higgs was placing too much reliance upon the observations of Drs Hobbs and Wynne.

9.   Dr Irvine went away and consulted Dr Raine Roberts, a well-known police surgeon from Manchester; she supported his stand.

10.   The little girl was admitted to hospital and a week later the sign was observed again by Dr Higgs. Dr Higgs saw this child a fourth time in June, when the child was with foster parents, and again the sign was present. Dr Higgs concluded on each occasion that this indicated there had been further sexual abuse.

11.   Later in March a little boy of 2 was referred to hospital by his family practitioner as an emergency with constipation. Dr Higgs examined him and noted scars around the anus and the sign of anal dilatation. She considered the possibility of sexual abuse and asked his parents

to bring in the elder brother aged 10 and sister aged 9 for examination. They were seen at hospital that evening and Dr Higgs found signs of anal abuse in the boy and anal and vaginal abuse in the girl. This was the first time that Dr Higgs had diagnosed sexual abuse on the basis of the physical signs alone. She asked Dr Morrell to examine the three children and he agreed with her conclusions. None of the children had made any complaint of abuse. After a request for a second opinion, Dr Higgs directed the children be taken to Leeds to be examined by Dr Wynne. She confirmed the physical findings and endorsed the diagnoses of sexual abuse.

12.   Photographs of the children had been taken by a police photographer, and the Police later objected to the use of a police photographer for this purpose. Subsequently photographs of children were taken by a medical photographer.

13.   The Police decided to interview the two elder children and did so on Saturday and Sunday; no social worker was present when the children were seen. The elder boy was believed at one time to be the possible perpetrator. According to his father he was 'grilled' by the Police. The boy was upset. This was a matter of some concern to the social workers later involved in the case.

14.   Social workers obtained place of safety orders and the children were placed with separate foster parents. The two older children were interviewed on a number of occasions over a period of months, by social workers and a clinical psychologist, Mrs Bacon, who believed the children had been sexually abused and that they were making disclosures of abuse by their father. The children were made wards of court and after the hearing were returned home to their parents. The Judge held that they had not been sexually abused.

15.   Dr Wyatt who had little previous experience in child sexual abuse was shown the sign by Dr Higgs on one of these three children and found it striking.

16.   Some days later a seven year old girl was referred to Dr Higgs by her family practitioner because the child alleged that her father and his girl friend told her to take her clothes off, they played 'doctors' with her and squirted tea up her front. She had had a vaginal discharge for about 5 years. On examination there were abnormal signs relating to the vaginal opening.

April

17.   In early April, a 3 year old girl was brought to the Accident and Emergency Department because a school nurse had noticed excessive bruising. She was admitted under the care of Dr Wyatt. He found signs consistent with sexual abuse and asked to see the two elder children. The boy was fine, but the 6 year old girl had anal and vaginal signs, including anal dilatation. This was the first time that Dr Wyatt had observed the sign in one of his patients. All three children went to foster parents and later the elder girl made complaints to her teacher and the foster mother of interference by her step-father.

18.   The two children seen by Dr Higgs the previous summer in Newcastle had been placed with experienced foster parents in Cleveland. At the end of April Dr Higgs did a routine check-up preparatory to giving evidence in a pending Juvenile Court hearing. She found anal dilatation and diagnosed anal abuse. The parents had no access to the children for several months and suspicion fell on the foster family. The foster parents were asked to bring their three daughters to be examined in hospital and all were diagnosed as sexually abused.

19.   The Director of Social Services, Mr Bishop, was informed that children in the care of the Council had been abused in a foster home and he asked for a second opinion. The 2 foster children and the 3 children of the foster parents were taken to Leeds and examined by Dr Wynne who confirmed the physical signs of sexual abuse in each child.

20.   A number of children had gone through the foster household, both as foster children and some for whom the foster parents had acted as child minders. Social workers brought 6 more children to be examined by Dr Higgs. Together with the 2 foster children, the 3 children of the foster parents and these 6, 11 children in all were examined of which 10 were found by Dr Higgs to have signs of anal abuse and admitted to the ward.

21. Some of these children were no longer in the foster home or in contact with the foster father. None of the children in this group had made a complaint and no adult had made any allegation of sexual abuse. The children of the foster family became wards and were later returned home by the Judge.

May

22. The weekend after this group of children had been admitted to the ward happened to be the first Bank Holiday weekend in May and there was not the full complement of social workers available. Mrs Richardson helped social workers in the interviews of some of the children.

23. Other children entirely separate from those associated with the foster family were seen during the first week of May in Dr Higgs' outpatient clinic. On the 5th May, 7 of the children were diagnosed as sexually abused. One child, who suffered from a medical condition and was referred for excessive bruising, was a long term patient of Dr Wyatt. Dr Higgs found signs of anal and vaginal abuse and the child's two brothers were seen. A little girl of 1 was referred with rectal bleeding and bowel problems. On examination Dr Higgs found anal dilatation, fissures and a fresh scar. This child was seen by Dr Stanton and Dr Wynne who both confirmed Dr Higgs' findings. Another little girl of 2 was seen on a routine check-up for failure to thrive. She and two other related children were considered by Dr Higgs to have signs of anal abuse. She was already in care. The 3 children remained briefly on the ward and then went to a foster home. They became wards of court and later returned home on conditions by order of the Judge. A girl of 11 was referred by her family practitioner with poor weight gain and eating problems. Dr Higgs found signs of anal and vaginal abuse. Her young half-sister was called and was thought to have signs consistent with sexual abuse. The elder girl later made complaints against her step-father. After a wardship hearing she went to live with her natural father and his new wife. Her half sister went home. In total during the first week of May, 23 children were seen by Dr Higgs and diagnosed as sexually abused and admitted to the Middlesbrough General Hospital.

24. During May there was a steady stream of referrals to Dr Higgs and Dr Wyatt. These included children referred by social workers, health visitors, and a guardian ad litem. The reasons for referral included a mother who was worried that her boy friend might have sexually abused her child, who was found to have a very sore, red perineum, anal dilatation and multiple anal fissures. There were also several children with perineal injuries. In mid-May social workers brought in a family of 5 children for examination because of concern about sexual abuse. A boy aged 7 in the family had made a complaint to his mother and then to a social worker. That family was not admitted to hospital but went with their mother to a group home.

25. A week later social workers referred another family of 3 as a result of the comments of the eldest child of 10 at school and the concern of her headmistress. Dr Higgs examined the first child with the consent of the mother, and found signs she felt were consistent with sexual abuse. Before she could examine the second child, the father arrived on the ward and removed the 3 children. He took them to a secret address. He was at that time required to report daily to the police who were unable to persuade him to divulge the whereabouts of the children. However, he agreed to the examination of the children by a police surgeon, and Dr Beeby was taken to the secret address. He examined the children in an upstairs room and found no abnormality. They were then returned home by their father; removed on a place of safety order obtained by Social Services and taken back to hospital. This time Dr Higgs examined all 3 children and diagnosed sexual abuse in respect of all three. The following day Dr Irvine examined the 3 children and agreed with the conclusions of Dr Beeby. Two weeks later, Dr McCowen, paediatrician from Northallerton, considered the signs suspicious and later in June Dr Roberts and Dr Paul examined the children and considered there was no abnormality. These children were first dealt with, at a very prolonged hearing, on an interim care application before the Teesside Juvenile Court and thereafter in wardship. The children were returned home but remain wards. The Social

Services Department were extremely concerned at the removal of the children from the hospital ward by the father and the difficulties of tracing their whereabouts.

26. Also during May, there were referrals to Dr Higgs other than by Social Services; for example, a Senior House Officer while examining a child of 2 with a febrile fit noted an abnormal anus. Dr Higgs found signs of anal and vaginal abuse in this child and her 2 sisters. The father was charged with several sexual offences and committed suicide while awaiting trial. A Senior Clinical Medical Officer, as a result of concern in the neighbourhood about the possibility of sexual abuse, referred a family of 7 children, 4 of the children showed signs of sexual abuse and all 7 were admitted to the hospital. A nurse noticed an abnormal anus in a 2 year old boy admitted with asthma and Dr Higgs concluded that there were signs consistent with sexual abuse. He was examined by Dr Steiner who did not agree with Dr Higgs and the child returned home.

27. Over the second Bank Holiday weekend in May there was a new wave of admissions to Middlesbrough General Hospital. The numbers were augmented by the admission of the 7 children from one family and 3 children from another family. Altogether in May, 52 children from 17 families were examined for sexual abuse and 41 of them were considered to have physical signs of sexual abuse.

28. Most of the children had no medical problem requiring nursing or medical attention and their presence on the ward caused difficulties for the nurses. Social Services managed to place the children out of hospital with foster parents or in residential care, but their field workers were very stretched. Mrs de Lacy Dunne, the adoption and fostering officer, took control of all foster placements. By June she and her resources became overwhelmed and ran out of space for the children.

29. In May the hospital had the resources to cope, but it was an unprecedented number of children with an unfamiliar problem and alarm bells began to ring. Dr Drury, the Hospital Unit Manager had been informed of the numbers admitted in the first week of May. He got in touch with the Social Services Department to express his concern both at the numbers and the problems in the hospital, particularly for the nurses. Dr Drury met Dr Higgs and they discussed among other matters the disagreement between herself and Dr Irvine.

30. At a meeting in mid-May of the South Tees Community Health Council, Mr Urch, its Secretary, told Mr Bishop about mounting public anxiety over the admissions to hospital and the diagnosis of child sexual abuse.

31. Mrs Richardson, who had earlier predicted an increase in detection of sexual abuse, was alarmed by the numbers and the lack of resources to deal with them. On the 12th May, she wrote a memorandum to Mr Bishop referring to 'crisis', the likelihood that the numbers would increase and the need for more resources.

32. At the invitation of Mr Bishop she attended a meeting of the Social Services Directorate in mid-May. They discussed the alarming increase in referrals for child sexual abuse, but the differences between Dr Higgs and Dr Irvine and the controversy over the anal dilatation test and the diagnosis of sexual abuse were not referred to. Mrs Richardson did not recognise the importance of the dispute and did not inform the Director.

The Police in April and May

33. By the end of April and the beginning of May the Police were having doubts about the diagnosis of sexual abuse based upon the anal dilatation test. These doubts were reinforced by the strong views of Dr Irvine. At a meeting chaired by a Chief Superintendent on the 8th May, Dr Irvine was asked his views and made plain to senior police officers that he regarded the anal dilatation test as unreliable.

34. Also at the end of April, as a result of Dr Higgs requesting police photographers to photograph the ano-genital region of the 3 children in March, and on the instructions of Detective

Superintendent White, Inspector Walls, the head of the Scientific Aids Department went to see Dr Higgs and explain the concern his Department had at taking these photographs. His photographers were embarrassed and felt the children were upset. The meeting was more in the nature of a confrontation, with Inspector Walls telling Dr Higgs what he thought. It did not improve relations between the Police and Dr Higgs.

35.   Detective Superintendent White went twice in May to Middlesbrough General Hospital to discuss both the problem over the photographs and the difficulties caused by the diagnosis of child sexual abuse.

36.   In the absence of prompt medical statements and with these doubts the Police investigated but without much confidence in the outcome. There was also a feeling, expressed by Inspector Makepeace of the Community Relations Department, that the good relations which he believed existed between police officers and social workers on the ground had deteriorated since the appointment of Mrs Richardson in her new role. These feelings among the Police gathered momentum.

Joint Child Abuse Committee working party — meeting in May and its consequences

37.   The working party of the Joint Child Abuse Committee, chaired by Mrs Richardson (see paragraph 5 above), included a representative of the Police, Chief Inspector Taylor; a nursing officer, Mrs Dunn; Mr Michie from the NSPCC; an educational social worker, Mr Town and a probation officer. Between February and May they met on several occasions and agreed most of the outstanding issues which had troubled their predecessors on the Area Review Committee. The two main issues which remained were:

1.   the degree of co-operation between the police and social workers in the investigation of sexual abuse;
2.   who should perform the medical examination and whether the police surgeon should be consulted.

It was agreed that Mrs Richardson and Chief Inspector Taylor should arrange a meeting with Dr Higgs and Dr Irvine to try and come to an agreement on the issue which could be placed before the next meeting of the working party on the 1st June. The meeting was arranged for the 28th May.

38.   At that meeting in addition to Mrs Richardson and Dr Higgs there were Dr Irvine, Detective Superintendent White, Inspector Makepeace, and Chief Inspector Taylor. The previous day Dr Irvine had for the first time examined children found by Dr Higgs to have been sexually abused. His negative findings confirmed Dr Irvine in his view as to the unreliability of the anal dilatation test. Dr Higgs had by then diagnosed as anally abused a considerable number of children, some confirmed by other paediatricians, and was convinced of the reliability of the test. When the meeting began to discuss the medical aspects of sexual abuse, Mrs Richardson put forward some new proposals, the effect of which was to provide for examination in all cases by the paediatrician. When challenged on this it became clear that Mrs Richardson did not see any future for police surgeons in the examination of children said to be sexually abused. Dr Irvine then said that Dr Higgs was incompetent and misguided and that her 'mentors' in Leeds, Drs Wynne and Hobbs, were equally misguided. Dr Higgs was firm in her viewpoint. Inspector Makepeace supported Dr Irvine and Mrs Richardson supported Dr Higgs. The meeting became heated and all those present found it disagreeable.

39.   Detective Superintendent White expressed the Police conclusion that the police would treat the diagnosis of Dr Higgs with a degree of caution. Each group left the meeting with their preconceived ideas reinforced, and this led to a major breakdown in the relationship between the police and the social workers.

40.   After the meeting Mrs Richardson and Mr Hughes together drafted a memorandum for Mr Bishop. It was largely the work of Mrs Richardson. Mr Bishop was given this memorandum and signed it on the 29th May. Its main effects were to provide for routine applications for place

of safety orders in cases of suspected sexual abuse, to suspend access to the parents and to exclude the police surgeon from making a second examination.

41.   Detective Superintendent White on the 29th May sent out a Force circular in which he instructed the Police to view Dr Higgs' diagnosis on sexual abuse with caution, and to look for substantial corroboration of her findings before taking positive action.

Although Superintendent White had told Mrs Richardson of the police response, neither agency officially informed the other of the steps they were taking.

42.   The meeting of the working party of the Joint Child Abuse Committee was scheduled to take place on the 1st June. The Assistant Chief Constable Mr Smith instructed Chief Inspector Taylor not to attend. The working party went on in his absence and with no disagreement the proposals put forward on the 28th May were accepted by the working party as their recommendations to the Joint Child Abuse Committee on the medical issue. They included: that the hospital was the most appropriate setting for the examination of a child by a paediatrician, and where a consultant paediatrician is able to give a statement to the Police it is not necessary for a police surgeon to re-examine the child.

June

43.   In June children continued to be referred in ever growing numbers, mainly by Social Services. They included: children who had constipation, failure to thrive, an itchy bottom, urinary tract infection, bruised perineum, soiling etc. A nurse saw a gaping anus in a child admitted to hospital with tonsilitis and brought it to Dr Higgs' attention. There was a family of 7 children who had behavioural problems and poor growth, and several members of this family were diagnosed as showing signs of sexual abuse.

44.   Dr Wyatt was asked by Social Services to see 2 boys from a special school who had been found with others indulging in inappropriate sexual behaviour. Dr Wyatt found signs of anal interference in both boys and offered to examine all the children in the special school. In the event the situation was dealt with by the Education Department. 6 of the children from 2 of the families concerned were admitted to the ward. One boy of 11 had considerable behavioural problems and had been under the care of a child psychiatrist for several years. In 4 further families the index (first) child examined during June had behavioural problems and had previously been seen by a child psychiatrist. Also about this time Dr Higgs saw a 3 year old girl with a vaginal discharge caused by gonorrhoea. The infection was present in her rectum. Her 2 year old brother also had a sexually transmitted infection. The girl had vaginal signs, both had signs of anal abuse. The childrens' uncle and a friend were convicted of sexual offences. Another little girl had anal warts. She had been referred by her family practitioner on suspicion of sexual abuse. The Independent Panel which examined this child came to the conclusion that the child should return home. The anal warts were not shown to be sexually transmitted.

45.   During June children in two more foster homes were considered to have been sexually abused. In one case it was a handicapped child living with adoptive parents who was diagnosed as abused. Before informing the agencies Dr Higgs arranged for Dr Wynne to give a second opinion on the child and she confirmed the diagnosis. This child and his sister became wards and were returned home by the Judge on the basis that no sexual abuse had occurred.

46.   Also during June, members of the Emergency Duty Team of social workers were asked to obtain place of safety orders late at night mainly by Dr Wyatt. In one case there had been an agreement with the parents that the children would remain on the ward; in another the children had been allowed to go home and had gone to bed and then had to be brought back to hospital. On one evening Dr Wyatt asked for 11 place of safety orders, 7 relating to a family already well-known to the Social Services.

47.   On the evening of the 12th June Dr Wyatt was making a late evening round, a usual occurrence with him. Dr Higgs was on call and she went round the ward with him. The ward contained 12 children of 8 families where sexual abuse had been diagnosed. During that day

between them they had identified 4 index children as sexually abused. Late that evening nurses told them of abnormal anal findings in two further children. They examined the children and diagnosed sexual abuse. Those two children had between them 8 siblings. They examined in all 4 children that night because of the possibility of sexual abuse. They were dissuaded from examining a 5th child because the nurse said that mother and child were asleep. Some nurses became upset about these examinations and 2 nurses made a written complaint.

48.   The following day it was necessary to transfer 6 children to North Tees General Hospital because the wards in Middlesbrough General Hospital could not cope with the siblings of the children identified the night before.

49.   The events of the 12th June and the consequential intake of the siblings created the third large wave of admissions.

50.   On the 18th June there was a considerable number of parents at the hospital and there was a confrontation between Dr Wyatt and an angry father. The police were called and helped to calm the situation. The deputy administrator at the hospital took the parents to another building and helped them to set out their complaints for transmission to the hospital authorities.

51.   The following day Mr Stuart Bell MP was told of the situation at the hospital and paid it several visits during the following week. He heard the parents' complaints. Some parents had just begun to form themselves into a parents' support group with the assistance of the Rev. Michael Wright.

52.   During June there were meetings between professionals and the different disciplines to try to resolve the problems which arose.

— On the *1st June* Mr Bishop together with Mrs Richardson met Mr Donaldson, Dr Drury, Dr Ramiah, the new community physician, and Dr Higgs. Mr Bishop questioned Dr Higgs very closely on her diagnostic techniques and was satisfied that she was confident of what she was doing. None of the other doctors present queried her method of diagnosis.

— On the *5th June* the Chief Constable and the Assistant Chief Constable Mr Smith met Mr Bishop and Mr Walton, his senior Assistant Director, and they discussed the situation. Neither of the Chief Officers was entirely in the picture and the only suggestion made was for the deputies to meet the Crown Prosecution Service. This they did with no result. The Chief Constable and the Director made no arrangement to meet again and did not do so.

— Shortly after that Dr Higgs and Dr Wyatt called on Mr Bishop and refused to see anybody else. They praised him for his stand over child sexual abuse, and said that the detection of abuse was a breakthrough in the care of children and could explain many problems of child health which had previously not responded to treatment. He took the opportunity to tell them about the strain on the resources of the Department and asked them if they could proceed more slowly to allow Social Services to obtain more resources. They told him it was not professionally acceptable to them and that other agencies needed to recognise that this was a major development in child health.

— On the *11th June* Mr Cooke, the Clerk to the Justices went to see Mr Bishop. Many place of safety orders were expiring and applications were being made for interim care orders on the children. Two days before in the Teesside Juvenile Court there had been the unprecedented number of 45 applications for interim care orders. Mr Cooke asked Mr Bishop if he could arrange for 28 day applications for place of safety orders to be made to the magistrate. The numbers were compounded by the unusual opposition to the granting of the interim order. These applications were being contested and disputed medical evidence was having to be considered by the magistrates at an early stage in the proceedings. Mr Cooke noticed that this might have been due to the refusal or restriction of access to the parents which was also most unusual. A few days later Mr Cooke returned to see Mr Bishop, on this occasion accompanied by the Chairman of the Juvenile Panel, expressing the concerns of the Juvenile Bench about the numbers of cases which were threatening to overwhelm the Courts; the great concern of the magistrates at the refusal of access to parents; and the most unusual situation of disputed medical evidence. Again Mr Cooke suggested application for longer place of safety orders to relieve pressure on the courts. Later in June some disputed care applications were restarted in the High Court as wardship applications.

— On the *15th June* Mr Bishop consulted the Social Services Inspectorate as to whether second opinions might be obtained and was advised to go to the District Health Authority. He immediately got in touch with Mr Donaldson and asked him to arrange second opinions on the diagnoses of the two doctors.

— On the *16th June* Mr Donaldson consulted Dr Donaldson, the Regional Medical Officer of the Northern Regional Health Authority concerning the complaints of the two nurses about the evening of the 12th June and asked for advice and help. This was the first that Northern Region had heard of the crisis and they then became involved. Northern Region decided to deal with all the complaints about the two doctors. The following day Dr Donaldson and Mr Donaldson met and Mr Donaldson asked for help to deal with the request from Mr Bishop for second medical opinions.

— Also on the *16th June* there was a meeting of the Joint Child Abuse Consultative Committee at which senior representatives of Social Services and the Police attended. They did not tell the elected members about the difficulties being experienced between the two agencies. At the same time there were meetings between the Chief Executive and leading members of the County Council where the seriousness of the situation was fully explored.

— On the *18th June* after the incident with the parent on the ward, Mr Donaldson discussed the situation with both paediatricians and asked them to hold back. They refused and said that if they saw child sexual abuse they had a duty to act.

— Mr Donaldson then asked three senior consultants to interview the two doctors and find out if they were acting within the bounds of medical practice. At the meeting on the *23rd June* the two paediatricians assured the three consultants that they were acting correctly.

53. The Chairman of Northern Region, Professor Sir Bernard Tomlinson, became involved and he and Dr Donaldson invited the two paediatricians to the headquarters of the Regional Health Authority in Newcastle to find out if they were acting correctly. They had a four hour meeting. Drs Higgs and Wyatt were given the complaints and asked to comment on them, which they said they would do after they had consulted their legal advisers. After the meeting at which the two doctors were cross-examined at length by the two Regional Officers, both Professor Sir Bernard Tomlinson and Dr Donaldson could find no reason to recommend their suspension from duties to the Regional Committee. There were thereafter various meetings which included legal advisers to consider the complaints and the position of the doctors.

54. The Northern Regional Health Authority took over the arrangements for second opinions requested by Social Services and with the help of Professor Kolvin, Consultant Child Psychiatrist at Newcastle, set up a panel of paediatricians and child psychiatrists to see jointly the children who had been diagnosed as sexually abused. They started to see children at the end of June. Thereafter Northern Region set up a second panel called the Regional Reference Group, made up of paediatricians within the area of Northern Region, to see any children who were subsequently diagnosed as sexually abused, in South Tees District.

55. By the end of June parents had arranged their own second opinions and a number of doctors, principally Dr Roberts from Manchester, Dr Paul from London and Dr Clarke from Liverpool, saw many of the children concerned.

56.   On Friday *26th June* Dr Irvine was interviewed on television in the early evening and said that Dr Higgs was wrong in her diagnosis of sexual abuse in respect of a particular family.

57.   Later that evening on the television programme Nightline, Mr Bishop and Mr Bell MP were among those who were present. Dr Irvine's interview was shown. Mr Bishop said he had no alternative but to act on the diagnosis of the paediatrician.

58.   On the *29th June* Mr Bell put down a Private Notice Question in the House Of Commons asking the Minister if he would make a statement on the recent increase in the number of cases of alleged child abuse in Cleveland.

59.   At the request of the Minister of State for Health reports were provided very quickly by the Social Services Inspectorate, the Northern Regional Health Authority. The Police provided a report for the Home Office.

60.   At the end of June, with the help of Middlesbrough General Hospital, Social Services set up the Child Resource Centre in the grounds of the hospital and children and their parents were able to spend the day there and be interviewed there.

July

61.   On the *1st July* the Joint Child Abuse Committee met to consider the recommendations of the working party. Mr Walton with the help of Mr Smith took charge of the draft guidelines and in a few days secured agreement to a revised draft which was almost immediately put into effect both by the Social Services and the Police. The agreed guidelines included: that the hospital is often the most appropriate setting for medical examination; that the child should be referred as soon as possible to a consultant paediatrician; that the roles of the police surgeon and paediatrician are complementary; early consultation is essential; there should be joint examination where possible.

62.   Also on the *1st July* the Police set up the Child Abuse Unit at Yarm, to co-ordinate the investigation of child sexual abuse in the County.

63.   On the *7th July* Mr Bell gave the Minister a 'dossier' of cases he had investigated. On the *9th July* the Minister announced in a statement to the House of Commons the setting up of a Statutory Inquiry.

64.   In total 125 children were diagnosed as sexually abused between February and July 1987, 121 of them by Dr Higgs and Dr Wyatt — 78 by Dr Higgs, 43 by Dr Wyatt. 67 of the children became wards of court. In the wardship cases 27 were dewarded and went home with the proceedings dismissed; 24 went home on conditions which included supervision orders on the children and conditions as to medical examination of the children and 2 of them went home on interim care orders. 9 other children who are wards of court remain in the care of the County Council and away from their families. Of those children not made wards of court, a further 27 were the subject of place of safety orders. In all 21 children remain in care. We understand that out of the 121 children, 98 are now at home.

Much of the discussion in the Report is now dated and has been superseded by new laws and practices. The following extract contains some of the conclusions and recommendations from the Report:

1.   We have learned during the Inquiry that sexual abuse occurs in children of all ages, including the very young, to boys as well as girls, in all classes of society and frequently within the privacy of the family. The sexual abuse can be very serious and on occasions includes vaginal, anal and oral intercourse. The problems of child sexual abuse have been recognised to an increasing extent over the past few years by professionals in different disciplines. This presents new and particularly difficult problems for the agencies concerned in child protection. In Cleveland an honest attempt was made to address these problems by the agencies. In Spring 1987 it went wrong.

2.   The reasons for the crisis are complex. In essence they included:
— lack of a proper understanding by the main agencies of each others' functions in relation to child sexual abuse;
— a lack of communication between the agencies;
— differences of views at middle management level which were not recognised by senior staff. These eventually affected those working on the ground.

3.   These tensions came out into the open with Dr Higgs' appointment as a consultant paediatrician to the Middlesbrough General Hospital. She was known to have an interest in the problems of child abuse. As a result of her understanding of the work of Dr Hobbs and Dr Wynne in Leeds, she formed the view that physical signs could help to identify sexual abuse and assist those seeking to protect abused children. She referred the first few children in whom she made the diagnosis to Dr Wynne for a second opinion. In each she received confirmation of her diagnosis, and as a consequence she proceeded with increasing confidence. The presence of the physical signs was elevated from grounds of 'strong suspicion' to an unequivocal 'diagnosis' of sexual abuse.

4.   Dr Wyatt, another consultant paediatrician at Middlesbrough General Hospital, became equally convinced of the significance of the physical signs and he enthusiastically supported her.

5.   Dr Higgs and Dr Wyatt became the centre point of recognition of the problem. Between them in the five months, mainly in May and June they diagnosed sexual abuse in 121 children from 57 families. Children were referred to them in various ways; some were brought by social workers because of a suspicion of sexual abuse or allegations or complaints; others were referred by family practitioners, health visitors, or community medical officers because of a suspicion of sexual abuse; a few from within the hospital were referred by junior medical staff or by nurses. In some the diagnosis arose on children attending outpatient clinics with medical conditions in which the possibility of sexual abuse had not been previously raised. Many were siblings of or connected with these children.

6.   By reaching a firm conclusion on the basis of physical signs and acting as they would for non-accidental injury or physical abuse; by separating children from their parents and by admitting most of the children to hospital, they compromised the work of the social workers and the Police. The medical diagnosis assumed a central and determining role in the management of the child and the family.

7.   It was entirely proper for the two paediatricians to play their part in the identification of sexual abuse in children referred to them. They were responsible for the care of their patients. Nonetheless they had a responsibility to examine their own actions; to consider whether their practice was always correct and whether it was in the best interests of the children and their patients. They are to be criticised for not doing so and for the certainty and over-confidence with which they pursued the detection of sexual abuse in children referred to them. They were not solely nor indeed principally responsible for the subsequent management of the children concerned. However, the certainty of their findings in relation to children diagnosed by them without prior complaint, posed particular problems for the Police and Social Services.

8.   The response of the Social Services Department to the diagnoses of the two doctors was determined in the main by the newly appointed Child Abuse Consultant, Mrs Richardson, who supported and agreed with Dr Higgs' approach. She advised that immediately the diagnosis was made the child should be moved to a 'place of safety' for further investigation and evaluation and this was ensured by obtaining a place of safety order from a Magistrate. This practice was confirmed by the issuing of a memorandum by the Director of Social Services which in practice had the effect of endorsing the medical diagnoses of the two paediatricians. In most cases the social workers' own professional responsibilities required them to make a wider assessment before taking action. The number of children separated from their parents increased dramatically and required both the consultants and Social Services managers to reappraise their practice.

This they failed to do. They had a responsibility to look into the numbers of referrals and the method of diagnosis. As the crisis developed, both doctors and social workers had a duty to consider their priorities, particularity with children from families with long-standing problems who were well known to Social Services.

9.   Another element was the attitude of the Police encouraged by their senior police surgeon, Dr Irvine, who took the view that Dr Higgs was mistaken in her diagnoses. The Police retreated from the multi-disciplinary approach into an entrenched position. They can be criticised for allowing a rift to develop and taking no effective step to break the deadlock. There was no reaction at senior level to the problems being raised and passed on to them by operational officers. The Police blamed the attitude and approach of Mrs Richardson for their reactions. They should not have allowed personalities to stand in the way of an objective assessment of the situation and the need to resolve it. Their requirement that the diagnoses of Dr Higgs should be reviewed by the senior police surgeon was unhelpful in the circumstances.

10.   There was a failure by middle and senior managers in each agency to take action appropriate to the seriousness of the situation. The disagreements between the Police and Social Services were allowed to drift and the crisis to develop. In particular, the Chief Constable and the Director of Social Services failed to understand the depth of the disagreement between their staff and as a consequence failed to take some joint action to bring their two agencies together.

11.   The lack of appropriate legal advice at case conferences contributed to the failure of those most closely involved with the children to appreciate that the medical opinions they had acted upon might not provide a satisfactory basis for applications in care proceedings. This deprived them of an useful check in consideration of the advisability of the removal of the children from home.

12.   There was an understandable response from parents when the diagnosis of sexual abuse was made. Their child was admitted to hospital; a place of safety order was served on them; access was restricted for the purpose of 'disclosure work'. They were uncertain of their responsibilities, distressed and angry. They did not know what to do or where to turn. They were isolated. As the numbers grew many of them formed themselves into a support group and they then received increasing support from others both locally and nationally. The media reported the situation and the crisis became public knowledge.

13.   Most of the 121 children diagnosed by Drs Higgs and Wyatt as sexually abused, were separated from their parents and their home, 70% by place of safety orders. The majority have now returned home, some with all proceedings dismissed, others on conditions of medical examinations and supervision orders. A few children went to one parent or a different parent and a few children were committed to the care of the Council.

14.   It is unacceptable that the disagreements and failure of communication of adults should be allowed to obscure the needs of children both long term and short term in so sensitive, difficult and important a field. The children had unhappy experiences which should not be allowed to happen again.

15.   It is however important to bear in mind that those who have a responsibility to protect children at risk, such as social workers, health visitors, police and doctors have in the past been criticised for failure to act in sufficient time and to take adequate steps to protect children who are being damaged. In Cleveland the general criticism by the public has been of over-enthusiasm and zeal in the actions taken. It is difficult for professionals to balance the conflicting interests and needs in the enormously important and delicate field of child sexual abuse. We hope that professionals will not as a result of the Cleveland experience stand back and hesitate to act to protect the children.

16.   In many Inquiries it is social workers who are under scrutiny for their failure to act in time. We are concerned that in advising a calm, measured and considered approach to the problem of child sexual abuse, we are not seen to imply either that there are never occasions when

immediate action may need to be taken or that there is not a problem to be faced and children to be protected. It is a delicate and difficult line to tread between taking action too soon and not taking it soon enough. Social Services whilst putting the needs of the child first must respect the rights of the parents; they also must work if possible with the parents for the benefit of the children. These parents themselves are often in need of help. Inevitably a degree of conflict develops between those objectives.

17.   We are also concerned about the extent of the misplaced adverse criticism social workers have received from the media and elsewhere. There is a danger that social workers, including those in Cleveland, will be demoralised. Some may hesitate to do what is right. Social workers need the support of the public to continue in the job the public needs them to do. It is time the public and the press gave it to them.

18.   Whilst it was important to try and identify what went wrong, it is equally important not to let that identification impede progress in the future, in Cleveland and elsewhere. We make criticisms of individuals. Those criticisms must not be permitted to obscure the wider failings of agencies; nor would we wish to suggest that the identification and management of sexual abuse within the family is easy. It obviously is not.

19.   We hope that the troubles of 1987 will recede for those concerned with the protection of children in Cleveland, and that they will work together, to tackle the exacting task of helping children who are subject to sexual abuse to the lasting benefit of the children, the families and their community.

How society acknowledges the existence of, recognises and then handles child sexual abuse poses difficult and complex problems. There are some issues of importance upon which we did not receive evidence and which we have not addressed. These include specifically the nature of abusers and the reasons for sexual abuse of children; the effectiveness and appropriateness of the strategies used once the problem has been identified; and the response of society and the agencies to those who abuse.

...

We make the following recommendations:

Recommendations

1.   Recognition of sexual abuse
There is a need:
a.   To recognise and describe the extent of the problem of child sexual abuse;
b.   To receive more accurate data of the abuse which is identified.

2.   Children
There is a danger that in looking to the welfare of the children believed to be the victims of sexual abuse the children themselves may be overlooked. The child is a person and not an object of concern.
We recommend that:
a.   Professionals recognise the need for adults to explain to children what is going on. Children are entitled to a proper explanation appropriate to their age, to be told why they are being taken away from home and given some idea of what is going to happen to them.
b.   Professionals should not make promises which cannot be kept to a child, and in the light of possible court proceedings should not promise a child that what is said in confidence can be kept in confidence.
c.   Professionals should always listen carefully to what the child has to say and take seriously what is said.

d. Throughout the proceedings the views and the wishes of the child, particularly as to what should happen to him/her, should be taken into consideration by the professionals involved with their problems.
e. The views and the wishes of the child should be placed before whichever court deals with the case. We do not however, suggest that those wishes should predominate.
f. Children should not be subjected to repeated medical examinations solely for evidential purposes. Where appropriate, according to age and understanding, the consent of the child should be obtained before any medical examination or photography.
g. Children should not be subjected to repeated interviews nor to the probing and confrontational type of 'disclosure' interview for the same purpose, for it in itself can be damaging and harmful to them. The consent of the child should where possible be obtained before the interviews are recorded on video.
h. The child should be medically examined and interviewed in a suitable and sensitive environment, where there are suitably trained staff available.
i. When a child is moved from home or between hospital and foster home it is important that those responsible for the day-to-day care of the child not only understand the child's legal status but also have sufficient information to look after the child properly.
j. Those involved in investigation of child sexual abuse should make a conscious effort to ensure that they act throughout in the best interests of the child.

3. Parents
We recommend:
a. The parents should be given the same courtesy as the family of any other referred child. This applies to all aspects of the investigation into the suspicion of child sexual abuse, and should be recognised by all professionals concerned with the family.
b. Parents should be informed and where appropriate consulted at each stage of the investigation by the professional dealing with the child, whether medical, police or social worker. Parents are entitled to know what is going on, and to be helped to understand the steps that are being taken.
c. We discuss below the position of parents in case conferences.
d. Social Services should confirm all important decisions to parents in writing. Parents may not understand the implications of decisions made and they should have the opportunity to give the written decision to their lawyers.
e. Parents should always be advised of their rights of appeal or complaint in relation to any decisions made about them or their children.
f. Social Services should always seek to provide support to the family during the investigation. Parents should not be left isolated and bewildered at this difficult time.
g. The service of the place of safety order on parents should include a written explanation of the meaning of the order, the position of the parents, their continuing responsibilities and rights and advice to seek legal advice.

4. Social Services
We make the following recommendations with regard to Social Services:

Place of safety orders
a. Place of safety orders should only be sought for the minimum time necessary to ensure protection of the child.
b. Records related to the use of statutory powers on an emergency basis should be kept and monitored regularly by Social Services Departments.
c. A code of practice for the administration by social workers of emergency orders for the purposes of child protection including the provision of information to parents defining

their rights in clear simple language should be drawn up (see also recommendations on the courts).

Access

d.   Whenever and however children are received into care social workers should agree with parents the arrangements for access unless there are exceptional reasons related to the child's interests not to do so. In either event the parent should be notified in writing as soon as possible of the access arrangements and the avenues of complaint or appeal open to them if they are aggrieved.

Case conferences

e.   Parents should be informed of case conferences and invited to attend for all or part of the conference unless, in the view of the Chairman of the conference, their presence will preclude a full and proper consideration of the child's interests.

f.   Irrespective of whether parents attend the conferences, social workers have a primary responsibility to ensure that the case conference has information relating to the family background and the parents' views on the issues under consideration.

g.   In complex cases the Chairman of the conference must be able to call upon the attendance of a qualified lawyer to assist in the evaluation of evidence indicative of care proceedings.

h.   When a case conference is presented with medical opinions that are in conflict the doctors involved should be asked to review their findings jointly with the interests of the child in mind. If they are unable to establish common ground then they should be asked to identify the basis of their differences. It would then be for the case conference to consider their views in the context of the other information available.

Management

i.   Senior managers in Social Services Departments need to ensure that they have efficient systems available to allow accurate monitoring of service activity which will alert them to problems that need to be resolved.

j.   Staff engaged in social work practice in the field of child abuse and child sexual abuse need structured arrangements for their professional supervision and personal support. The work is stressful and it is important that their personal needs are not overlooked.

k.   We recommend that careful consideration be given to the provision of structured systems of support and supervision for staff undertaking work on Emergency Duty Teams. Operationally such teams should report to a senior line manager.

l.   Social Services Departments should maintain an open continuing relationship with the Police to review areas of mutual concern.

5.   Police

We make the following recommendations with regard to Police Forces:

a.   The Police should examine their organisation to ensure there is an adequate communication network to achieve the recognition and identification of problems at operational level and a system to develop remedies.

b.   The Police should develop, monitor and maintain communication and consultation with the other agencies concerned with child protection.

c.   The Police should develop and practise inter-agency working, including joint planning and interviews of children in investigation of sexual abuse within the family or caring agency.

d.   The Police should recognise and develop their responsibility for the protection of the child as extending beyond the collection of evidence for court proceedings. This should include their attendance at case conferences and assistance to the other child protection agencies.

6. The medical profession

We make the following recommendations with regard to the medical profession:

a. They should agree a consistent vocabulary to describe physical signs which may be associated with child sexual abuse.

b. There should be investigation of the natural history and the significance of signs and symptoms which may be associated with child sexual abuse.

c. Consideration be given to inquiring into the significance of the phenomonen of anal dilatation.

d. Doctors engaged in the care of a child in whom the suspicion of sexual abuse is raised must of course give the child the appropriate medical care, but should also recognise the importance of the forensic element.

   The doctor concerned should recognise the importance:

   i. of taking a full medical history and making a thorough medical examination.

   ii. of making where appropriate investigations for forensic purposes, for sexually transmitted diseases and for pregnancy in older girls.

   iii. of completing full and accurate medical records which should provide the information for the protective agencies and on occasions the courts .... Those records should be made at the time of examination.

   iv. of preparing statements for police purposes and/or for Social Services or NSPCC.

   We understand that the Standing Medical Advisory Committee to the DHSS are in the course of providing guidelines for the medical profession on this subject.

e. On a medical examination for forensic or other evidential purposes unconnected with the immediate care and treatment of the child the informed consent of the parents should be sought. This may present difficulties for the police surgeon or doctor from the approved panel on the specialist assessment team ... in cases of suspected sexual abuse within the family. This problem needs to be considered further.

f. Medical practitioners who have examined a child for suspected sexual abuse and disagree in their findings and conclusions should discuss their reports and resolve their differences where possible; in the absence of agreement identify the areas of dispute, recognising their purpose is to act in the best interests of the child.

7. Area Review Committees/Joint Child Abuse Committees

We make the following recommendations in respect of the Area Review Committees/Joint Child Abuse Committees:

a. They should review the arrangements for identifying and monitoring suitable training for professionals working with child sexual abuse;

b. The membership of these committees should include those who have the authority and responsibility to bind their agency to implementing the recommendations of the Committee, and to play a useful part in the decision-making process which accurately reflects the view of the agency they represent.

8. Inter-agency cooperation

We strongly recommend:

a. The development of inter-agency co-operation which acknowledges:

   i. no single agency — Health, Social Services, Police or voluntary organisation has the pre-eminent responsibility in the assessment of child abuse generally and child sexual abuse specifically. Each agency has a prime responsibility for a particular aspect of the problem. Neither childrens' nor parents' needs and rights can be adequately met or protected unless agencies agree a framework for their inter-action. The statutory duties of Social Service Departments must be recognised;

ii.   careful consideration must be given to the detail of working arrangements between doctors, nurses, social workers, police, teachers, staff of voluntary organisations and others responsible for the care of children;

iii. arrangements for collaboration between services must not inhibit prompt action by any professional or agency where this is demanded by the best interests of the child. Agreements over collaborative work should not inhibit or preclude doctors, social workers or policemen from carrying out their primary professional responsibilities. The responsibility for the decisions will remain theirs;

iv.   practical issues need to be recognised and resolved at local level in careful discussion between the respective agencies. For example:

— what the level of suspicion of physical or sexual abuse should be before the Police are informed that an offence appears to have been committed;

— when and what parents are told when doctors see signs that may be indicative of sexual abuse;

— in what circumstances social workers should delay seeing parents until they have been interviewed by the Police.

v.   managers should accept responsibility for ensuring that agreements reached are implemented in practice. Each agency should give an undertaking not to make unilateral changes in practice or policy without giving prior notice to the others;

vi.   the existence of bodies charged with the responsibility to co-ordinate practice between agencies does not relieve Chief Officers such as the Director of Social Services, the Chief Constable, the Director of Education and the Health Service District General Manager of their responsibility to ensure effective cooperation and collaboration between their services or to identify problems and seek solutions.

...

9. Training

Training is one of the major needs shown by the Cleveland experience. We recognise that training requirements are different for each profession. We strongly recommend:

a.   Those responsible for the educational programmes of all disciplines involved in the care of children immediately consider the introduction of some instruction on the subject of child sexual abuse in basic training at student level.

b.   There should be general continuing in-service training for practitioners concerned with child care.

c.   There is an urgent need to give immediate in-service training to professionals to bring them up-to-date on child sexual abuse.

d.   The investigation and the management of the child and the family where there is suspicion of sexual abuse needs considerable professional skill. We recommend specialised training for experienced professionals with immediate responsibility for the children and their families.

From the evidence presented to the Inquiry there were particular issues which arose and needed to be addressed.

1.   There is a need for inter-agency training and recognition of the role of other disciplines. For example police officers and social workers designated to interview children should have joint training in their approach to this task.

2.   Police training needs to be developed well beyond the acquisition of knowledge in respect of the criminal offences involved.

3.   The medical profession needs to appreciate the legal implications of and their responsibility for the evidential requirements of their work.

4.   Those who work in this field must have an empathy with children and 'their feet on the ground'. They must be able to cope with the stress that is experienced by all who deal with these children. It should not be seen as a failure for some to take the sensible course of saying that he/she is not suited to do that sort of work.

5.   In a rapidly changing and difficult area there is a need to review and evaluate the effectiveness of the programmes arranged.

6.   All lawyers engaged in this type of work including Judges and Magistrates should have a greater awareness of and inform themselves about the nature of child abuse and the management of children subjected to abuse and in particular sexual abuse.

...

11.   Issues for further consideration

We wish to raise the following matters for further thought and wider discussion, but not by way of specific recommendation.

1.   With the emphasis we place on the need to avoid the necessity of removing a child from home, Social Services Departments should consider the appropriateness of using their powers under s. 1 of the 1980 Act designed to prevent the reception of a child into care, to defray for a limited period additional costs incurred by the suspected abuser in leaving home on a temporary basis while initial assessment is completed.

2.   Samantha's story... leads us to advise that there needs to be more sensitive handling of teenagers who have been sexually abused.

3.   There is a need to recognise the problem of adults who disclose abuse they suffered as children and the lack of help generally available.

4.   There is a need to recognise the problems of an abuser who may wish to confess to the abuse but is inhibited from so doing by fear of the consequences. Some consideration might be given in certain circumstances to the wider interests of the child and the family and whether different arrangements might be made in suitable cases for those abusers who admit their guilt, who co-operate with the arrangements for the child and who are prepared to submit themselves to a programme of control.

5.   We suggest that consideration is given to creating a new Office of Child Protection for use in care proceedings in the Family Court with the following responsibilities:

    a.   To scrutinise the application of the Local Authority in care proceedings and ensure that it is well founded.

    b.   To call for additional investigation or reports.

    c.   To invite the Local Authority or the Police to reconsider the civil or criminal proceedings proposed.

    d.   To act as administrator of the guardian ad litem panel.

    e.   Further consideration should be given to whether the office holder should:

        i.   direct who should be parties to the care proceedings

        ii.   direct in which tier of the court it should be heard and

        iii.   have the power to take no further action.

How far do you think these objectives have been achieved?

The Pindown inquiry [Allan Levy and Barbara Kahan *The Pindown Experience and the Protection of Children* (1991)] reported after the enactment of the Children Act 1989 and illustrated that abuses could occur in residential settings as well as in domestic settings. It related to events that occurred before the Act was passed, and which were governed by a different legal regime. The first extract sets out the practices employed in four Staffordshire residential establishments in the 1980s — 245 Hartshill Road, Stoke-on-Trent; The Birches, Newcastle-under-Lyme; The Alders,

Tamworth; and Heron Cross House, Stoke-on-Trent:

1.1   On 2 October 1989 John Spurr, a deputy director of Staffordshire County Council's social services department was telephoned by a Stoke-on-Trent solicitor Kevin Williams who was extremely concerned about a 15 year old girl for whom he was acting in care proceedings. The solicitor had previously spoken to the chairman of the social services committee about the girl who was in the interim care of the local authority. She had indicated that whilst in a residential home at 245 Hartshill Road, Stoke-on-Trent a few days earlier she had been put in a room with a bed, a chair and a table, made to wear pyjamas the whole time, only allowed out of the room to go to the toilet after knocking on the door, had not gone to school, had nothing to read and had to be in bed at 7 p.m. She was also not allowed to communicate with other children. The following evening she had jumped out of the window of the room, a distance to the ground of about twenty feet, and had sprained her ankle. She had then gone in her pyjamas a considerable distance before she had been returned eventually by the police and had spent a further 10 days in the room. She described her experience as being in 'Pindown'.

1.2   On the following day, after various consultations, the then Director of Social Services, Barry O'Neill, issued instructions for the 'Pindown' system at 245 Hartshill Road to cease.

1.3   Subsequently, the 15 year old girl and a boy of the same age were made wards of court by Kevin Williams. On 13 October 1989 the High Court, exercising the wardship jurisdiction, granted injunctions prohibiting the use of Pindown by social services, and in relation to the boy's alleged experiences, restraining the employment of any child in care of school age during school hours other than in circumstances agreed in consultation with the Education Welfare Service. The actual terms of the injunction in respect of Pindown were: that no child or young person in the care of (the local authority) shall be subjected to the regime known as 'pin down' in any form whatsoever without the leave of the court save within the meaning of Regulation 10 of the Community Homes Regulations 1972. By agreement the Official Solicitor was appointed to act on behalf of the children and he was given permission by the court, as was the local authority, to disclose the papers in the proceedings to the Department of Health.

1.4   Over the next few months very considerable public concern was expressed and taken up by the media about the use of Pindown in Staffordshire residential homes. Pindown was variously alleged to be solitary confinement, a behaviour control method, and humiliating and degrading treatment. In addition there was further concern about the activities of a senior member of the social services department, Tony Latham, regarding the running of a number of private companies providing many services to the department under the general name of the Fundwell companies. He was also said to be the architect and leading exponent of Pindown. The origin of the word 'Pindown' was said to be the use by Tony Latham of the words, 'we must pin down the problem' whilst he gestured with his forefinger pointing towards the floor. The children began to speak of 'being in Pindown'.

...

The Nature of Pindown

12.2   When considering events in the past the bonus of having a wealth of contemporary documents is considerable. In the case of the practice of Pindown there is available, amongst other documentation, almost a complete set of log books and measures of control books together with Pindown unit books (under various titles) and books of so-called programmes. In addition the main practitioners of Pindown, Tony Latham and Philip Price, together with Glynis Mellors who played a significant part, have set out at various times between 1983 and 1989 their accounts of the 'philosophy' and practice of Pindown. There are also contributions by others which, for example, refer in detail to the 'rules' of Pindown. In respect of the various books of records kept in the residential units there is, as will have been noted from the numerous quotations in earlier chapters which speak for themselves, an extraordinary frankness and clarity in the vast majority of the entries relating to Pindown and the children who were put into the various units.

12.3   We also have had the advantage of hearing evidence from very many witnesses who could throw considerable light on the true nature of what took place over a period of almost six years. These included: children, adults who as children were in Pindown, parents, social workers, residential workers, managers, politicians, members of the public who lived near to residential units, and a number of distinguished experts. We also had the benefit of written evidence put in by many people. Our views based on the extensive evidence we received are set out below.

Documentation

12.4   The true nature of Pindown, in our view, emerges clearly from the writings of its practitioners. Prior to August 1984, Tony Latham and Philip Price produced 'Routine of the Intensive Training Unit' ... The message, in our view, is crystallised in the words 'DO AS IS TOLD' and in the observation on page 2 of the document, 'the philosophy behing (sic) the Intensive Training Unit is undermined if the "Rules of the Establishment" are not strictly adhered to'. It is made clear that 'privileges are to be earned through co-operation with staff and decided upon at specified review times. Failure to sustain co-operation will automatically lose the right for privileges and the basic programme will again be enforced.' One notes that throughout the Pindown era such matters as communicating with other children and/or the staff, going to school, taking exercise, having reading and writing materials, wearing ordinary clothing as opposed to night wear, being allowed to have visits, and going out of a room to go to the toilet without knocking on the door first and being given permission, are categorised and treated as 'privileges' which have to be earned.

12.5   About two years later, some time after July 1986, Glynis Mellors (then Bonnici) produced 'Intermediate Treatment in Newcastle Staffordshire Evaluation Report' .... Tony Latham approved the document which we were told was sent to Elizabeth Brennan, the principal area officer, who could not herself recall seeing it. Under a heading 'Intermediate Treatment — Preventative and Rehabilitation Work' Glynis Mellors wrote that, 'a unit was set up detached from the main part of the residential building based at 245 Hartshill Road. In those days it was referred to as the "special unit" (currently, known as the Intensive Training Unit). This section of the building soon became recognised as the place where problematical children were placed. Being totally isolated and self-contained it enabled its residents to be observed, assessed, appraised and programmes developed. *Above all, it enabled at times hard line punishment and reward tactics to be adopted without influence, prejudice or inconsistency*' (emphasis added). Glynis Mellors referred to the unit as having this 'so called "radical" practice of preventative and rehabilitation work'. Some attempts were made at the Inquiry to persuade us that the words quoted did not reflect the reality of the practice. We have, however, no doubt after considering the totality of the evidence that in the vast majority of cases the children perceived Pindown with its supposed panoply of meetings, reviews, contracts and attempts to establish a structure of understanding and trust, as a narrow, punitive and harshly restrictive experience. We think that their perceptions were correct.

12.6   On page 6 of her document Glynis Mellors wrote that 'care is presented as a totally negative experience'. What she referred to as 'negative I.T.' (Intermediate Treatment) was 'ensuring the participant clearly identifies, comes to terms with and works through his problems and is not allowed to take the easy way out'. On page 8 of the document, Glynis Mellors referred to a girl whose 'programme was structured on what was called a "heavy pin down", her only privilege being that of being allowed to attend school'. It should be noted that, as far as we are aware from the evidence, no contact was ever made with the relevant education department in respect of the use as a sanction of preventing children in care from attending school.

12.7   At the beginning of 1988, nearly two years after Glynis Mellors' Report, a set of 'rules' of Pindown was written down on the front cover of the 'Pindown — Other House' log book at The Birches ... The 'rules' are in the handwriting of Louise Doherty, a residential worker, who was acting on the instructions of Peter Nicol-Harper, who was in charge of The Birches. Four years after it commenced Pindown its traditional form is documented again: removal of clothes and personal possessions on admission; baths; wearing of night wear, underwear and dressing gown and 'no footwear of any description'; meals in the room; knocking on the door for permission to 'impart information' or go to the bathroom; no communication with other residents; no television, music, magazines, cigarettes or telephone calls; visits from social workers or parents are permitted 'by arrangement with team leader'; during the day any school work set should be completed and 'all books and writing materials should be removed after 4 o'clock; and rising at 7 a.m., bed 7 p.m. after having a bath'. The 'rules' are headed by the instruction 'it is essential that each child is made aware of these rules at the time of their admission'.

12.8   In the middle of 1988, after returning from a training course, Philip Price renewed the Pindown documentation ... . Some awareness of the legal implications and the basic nature of Pindown is apparent from the opening words 'while I recognise that most people working in the arena of Social Work may have difficulty in coming to terms with the working practices of a pin down unit i.e. possible infringements of rights, civil liberties etc. it has become necessary to devise such a unit within the structure of the 245 Community unit'.

12.9   Tony Latham after leaving The Alders, Tamworth, in August 1989 produced a report on the establishment ... . It eventually came into the hands of senior management. It was dated 12 September 1989 and dealt with the use of Pindown. On pages 12 and 13 of the document, Tony Latham wrote as follows: 'following the successful introduction some years ago of a specialised unit at 245 Hartshill Road, the profound problems being created by certain youngsters at Tamworth promoted an introduction of this case in Tamworth. Special unit with all its mystiques basically challenges the concept of positive care ideals and consequently is often misinterpreted and has been quoted as a lock up job!'

Basic philosophies

12.10   Tony Latham then described the 'basic philosophies' of the special unit: 'The isolation of a young person to a room away from the main care of the building, where loss of privileges are asserted. The young person is supervised 24 hours a day under a contract basis whereby issues, problems and relationships can be confronted. Care is presented as a totally negative experience initially ensuring that the participant can clearly identify their problems, come to terms with them through counselling and time out sessions with appointed staff, and is encouraged to work through the problems by not being allowed to take the easy way out. To ensure that work with the children on these lines is planned and clearly structured, it needs to include family contact, participation and agreement to the sanctions employed (where applicable) and the opportunity for the child to learn how privileges are earned and how co-operation brings rewards.'

12.11   In respect of the unit's use, Tony Latham wrote that the *'special unit should seldom be used. It should be a last resort and not be used liberally to exert heavy handed discipline or sanctions to children. Family Centre staff have worked with its philosophies and have seen what rewards and changes it brings in children when all else fails. Area Office Social Workers generally do not agree with its operation but are unable to offer alternatives, save secure units'* (emphasis added).

12.12   The actual use of Pindown, in our view, wandered far from its so-called 'philosophy'. Whilst a very few children who were in Pindown for a very short time were said to have benefitted from it, almost all who were in Pindown over the years suffered in varying degrees the despair and the potentially damaging effects of isolation, the humiliation of having to wear night clothes, knock on the door in order to 'impart information' as it was termed, and of having all their personal possessions removed; and the intense frustration and boredom from the lack of communication, companionship with others and recreation. To many Pindown must undoubtedly have appeared as 'heavy handed discipline'. It is not insignificant, in our view, that at the beginning of November 1983 when one of the first children was transferred from The Birches to 245 Hartshill Road to go into Pindown, the entry in the log book stated: 'R is at the secure unit at Hartshill'. Later on the 9 November 1983 John Aston recorded in the Hartshill log book: *'Tony please note ...* to keep the impression of a specail (sic)/secure unit going means no allowance of preveleges (sic) as it would defeat our "face" to other members of The Birches'. When Peter Nicol-Harper, who was an experienced practitioner of Pindown and who had tried to introduce a 'positive' form of it in early 1988 at The Birches, gave evidence he expressed the view that the Pindown unit had been used, at least on some occasions, as secure accommodation.

12.13   There are many references in the records to children being 'detained in the special unit' and to 'solitary confinement'. One particular example, noted in an earlier chapter, is not, in our view, unrepresentative. A boy, just fifteen years old, had 'absconded' from school and was put in the unit in early 1985 in 245 Hartshill Road. A log book entry states *'another week of solitary confinement* for (P.E.) has had some rather peculiar effects. He is talking to himself a great deal and we had tears several times during the course of the week. Sleeping in staff also report incidents of (P.E.) talking in his sleep' (emphasis added).

Definition

12.14   Pindown is referred to in many different ways in the documentation we received. The following is a list of some of the descriptions: 'Basic Pindown'; 'Total Pindown'; 'Full Pindown'; 'Heavy Pindown'; 'Strict Pindown'; 'Negative Pindown'; 'Nasty Pindown'; 'B-Plan Pindown'; 'Stage 2 Pindown'; 'Semi-Pindown'; 'Partial Pindown'; 'Relaxed Pindown'; 'Sympathetic Pindown'; 'Positive Pindown'; 'Therapeutic Pindown'; and 'Maisie'.

12.15   With some exceptions, the names in the main give a clue as to the approach used in the practice of Pindown. What, however, are the minimum criteria which qualify the practice as Pindown? It is almost impossible to be absolutely precise but we decided that four features were usually present: firstly, isolation for part of the time in a part of a children's home cordoned off as a 'special' or Pindown unit; secondly, removal of ordinary clothing for part of the time and the enforced wearing of shorts or night clothes; thirdly, being told of having to earn 'privileges'; and fourthly being allowed to attend school or a 'school room' in the unit, and changing back into shorts or night clothes after returning from school.

12.16   'Full' or 'Total' Pindown, in our view, must have the following features: firstly, persistent isolation in a part of a children's home cordoned off as a special or Pindown unit; secondly removal of ordinary clothing for lengthy periods and the enforced wearing of shorts or night clothes; thirdly, persistent loss of all 'privileges'; fourthly, having to knock on the door to 'impart information', for example, a wish to visit the bathroom; and fifthly, non-attendance at school, no writing or reading materials, no television, radio, cigarettes or visits.

12.17   The place in which Pindown was practised was variously called, 'the special unit', 'the Intensive Training Unit'; 'the structured unit'; the 'sculptured unit', the 'secure unit'; the 'time out area'; or 'the crash pad'.

12.18   As noted in chapter 1, the origin of the word 'Pindown' was said to be the use by Tony Latham of the words, 'we must pin down the problem' whilst he gestured with his forefinger pointing towards the floor. The children began to speak of 'being in Pindown'.

The regime

12.19   Tony Latham informed the Inquiry that 'the regime of Pindown which developed was based on the principle that we were re-establishing control of the young person. By taking away all privileges from that person for a short period we felt that we would firstly force the young person to face up to his or her difficulties, and secondly provide the mechanism for negotiation with that person since by taking responsibility for their actions they could earn the privileges previously denied to them, and by active participation in family meetings could have a say in their future'. He added that 'the Pindown unit was designed to concentrate on the specific issues to be addressed. The time spent in the unit, however, was seen as a very small part of a much wider process of formulating and developing care plans or contracts with each young person'. He pointed out that 'when the regime was first used it was a form of crisis intervention to deal with three particularly difficult youngsters at The Birches. However in order to avoid the intake of children coming into care inappropriately the model increasingly evolved into a preventative mode. ... This model of intervention was never envisaged as a punishment to young people but merely a method of containment for disruptive youngsters.' Tony Latham further indicated that 'the model was never a deliberate attempt to damage the children in any way or to restrict their liberty. No doors (were) ever locked, and the young people were always free to walk out of the building if that is what they chose to do albeit we would have tried to dissuade them from doing so.'

12.20   We were informed by Tony Latham that the review meeting 'was undoubtedly the most crucial element in the programme and they were often heated and charged with emotion by the young person and his or her family'. He encouraged accountability for everybody who attended the meeting. He acknowledged that 'by forcing people in a confrontational way to keep their part of any contract, I was not terribly popular amongst some of the area social workers'. Tony Latham chaired the meetings until September 1987. He also 'encouraged positive and negative role play with the idea that by creating conflict, people start saying what they think'.

12.21   A number of witnesses at the Inquiry told us that in their view the family meetings were an ordeal not only for parents and children but also for the social workers. They were centred on 'a powerful personality chairman' and one social worker, ... told us that she 'used to go in with butterflies in my stomach and feeling really worried and I really don't know what the child felt'. Others were offended by the bad language deliberately used. A child, for example, was told 'you are fucking useless'. Overall we formed a critical view of what we heard of the meetings. No proper documentation was apparently produced for the meeting and in the main no proper or any record kept of it. A great deal of play-acting by the Pindown practitioners appeared to be the order of the day. Additionally we heard that children often attended in their night clothes and girls who were wearing short night dresses felt very embarrassed and humiliated. Regarding 'contracts' and 'programmes', those produced to the Inquiry appeared to be extremely basic. Meetings in the early days of Pindown took place apparently once a week. Later at 245 Hartshill Road it would seem that they were not as frequent or as regular. At Heron Cross House and The Alders, however, during the short existence of Pindown in those establishments, there were frequent meetings.

12.22   Staff contact and nature of engagement

Lack of sufficient staff and lack of qualified and experienced people dictated the kind and quality of the contact with children in Pindown. The laudable aim of saturating the child with attention was in effect a pipe-dream. We formed the view that in the main staff in fact spent very little time with the Pindown residents. Complaints about the excruciating boredom of being alone without any means of recreation were legion. Other complaints related to being given such tasks as writing out a telephone directory or answering in writing very personal and difficult questions. Many examples are recorded in the log books of the occasions and the manner in which staff rebuffed attempts by the children to communicate with them. The instruction to staff in very many cases was 'strictly isolated no contact at all'. There were examples, however, of staff who literally took pity on the isolated child and broke the rules to speak to him or her. Our impression was that this was very much the exception rather than the rule. For those permitted some contact, some members of the staff seem to have made efforts to build up a kind of relationship with the child. The log books, however, are littered with examples of disparaging remarks by staff about individual children. One example catches the flavour of many: 'this little runt' wrote one residential worker.

...

Impact of Pindown

12.33 There is no doubt that Pindown was intended to have an impact on the children subjected to its regime. In Tony Latham's words, as noted above in paragraph 12.19 '(Pindown) was based on the principle that we were re-establishing control'. The whole approach, including the meetings, was confrontational and intended to cause conflict because then 'people start saying what they think'. As we have indicated above, no professional advice was taken either before or after the introduction of Pindown. The following list of the apparent reactions of children in Pindown is taken from numerous entries in the log books of the establishments: 'anger', 'depression', 'weeping', 'sobbing', 'anxiety', 'talking in sleep', 'talking to self', 'staring into space', 'lost confidence in people', 'frustrated', 'bored', 'banging on wall', 'loneliness', 'desperation', 'despair', 'could not eat', 'frantic attempts to get out', 'temper tantrums', and 'absconding'. In addition there were incidents of wrist-slashing and the taking of overdoses.

12.34 The extent, if any, to which the reactions listed above, and indeed any long term effects, were triggered wholly or partly by Pindown may well be the subject of debate in each particular case. A commonsense approach, however, in our view, can only point to the likely negative effects of the use of a regime intrinsically dependent on elements of isolation, humiliation and confrontation. The absence of professional advice in dealing with many children who were disturbed, depressed and in despair can only be described as inexplicable. More than one consultant psychiatrist later told us of the risks of some children suffering from post traumatic stress disorder.

The second extract gives some of the conclusions of the Inquiry. It begins by noting similarities to events such as those in Cleveland, and then goes on to suggest some issues raised by Pindown. In the present context, it is worth noting the failure to take legal advice prior to instituting the Pindown regime.

A combination of circumstances, certain individuals and a lack of effective safeguards brought fundamental problems to the surface in Cleveland and Rochdale. The same process, although in respect of a quite different problem, occurred in Staffordshire leading to the emergence of the unacceptable practice of Pindown. The kinds of difficulties disclosed are not resolved, however, by Inquiries and cases. We hope that those involved with the control of children in residential care, whether inside local and central government or outside, will maintain a heightened vigilance and concern in the future in the light of the events we have spent many months considering in Staffordshire.

...

12.55 Pindown, in our view, whether 'Total Pindown' or 'Sympathetic Pindown' involved elements of isolation, humiliation and confrontation to varying degrees. There was no satisfactory evidence before the Inquiry that doors were actually locked when children were in a Pindown room, although we accept that on at least one occasion at 245 Hartshill Road a door handle was probably removed and placed in an office drawer over night. We are quite satisfied, however, that saucepans and other objects were put on door handles as a warning signal; that staff remained and slept outside rooms in order to deter children from coming out; and very many children simply accepted that their liberty was restricted in that they had to knock on the door and make a request to leave the room. Some clearly demonstrated their understanding of the restraint by jumping out of the window of a Pindown room or attempting to do so. We have no doubt that children were humiliated in many ways, by, for example, being made to wear night clothes all the time, having their personal possessions removed and being denied any normal recreation. In addition during confrontational 'meetings' numerous children were harangued and referred to in grossly abusive terms.

...

(i) After considering the totality of the evidence we consider that the vast majority of children who underwent the regime perceived Pindown as a narrow, punitive and harshly restrictive experience. We think that their perceptions were correct;

(ii) The children who were in Pindown, in our view suffered in varying degrees the despair and the potentially damaging effects of isolation, the humiliation of having to wear night clothes, knock on the door in order to 'impart information' as it was termed, and of having all their personal possessions removed; and the intense frustration and boredom from the lack of communication, companionship with others and recreation;

(iii) Pindown contained the worst elements of institutional control: baths on admission, special clothing, strict routine, segregation and isolation, humiliation, and inappropriate bed-times;

(iv) Pindown, in our view, is likely to have stemmed initially from an ill-digested understanding of behavioural psychology; the regime had no theoretical framework and no safeguards;

(v) No psychiatric, psychological or educational advice was obtained before or during the time Pindown was used;

(vi) We regard the absence of professional advice in dealing with many children who were disturbed, depressed and in despair as inexplicable;

(vii) No legal advice was ever sought by social services despite the fact that in 1984 senior management were aware that some of the practices in the 'special unit' at 245 Hartshill Road, Stoke-on-Trent appeared to be in contravention of the Community Homes Regulations 1972;

(viii) We consider that one of the aims of the so-called 'philosophy' of Pindown, to saturate the child with attention, was never to any significant extent put into practice; and was in any event a pipe dream due to lack of sufficient staff and lack of qualified and experienced people. We are of the view that in the main staff spent very little time with the children in Pindown;

(ix) In the words of Tony Latham, the architect and prime practitioner of Pindown, the regime 'was based on the principle that we were establishing control'. The impact on the children was, in our view, likely to be wholly negative and was so in that the regime imposed was fundamentally dependent on elements of isolation, humiliation and confrontation;

(x) Pindown, in our view, falls decisively outside anything that could properly be considered as good child care practice. It was in all its manifestations intrinsically unethical, unprofessional and unacceptable;

Proving that the enactment of legislation is not a panacea for all ills, and notwithstanding the improvements in practice under the Children Act 1989, the recent murder of Victoria Climbie gives rise to a number of questions, currently the subject of a statutory inquiry.

One of the reasons for providing structures and powers of support and intervention is to create a framework within which the lives of children may be enhanced. A lesson emerging from the extracts above is that the effective operation of legal frameworks depends on human agencies. Any critical analysis of the effectiveness of the law must, therefore, take account of both the frameworks themselves and the people who operate them.

:e of legislation in this area is the Children Act 1989. Running to ad 15 Schedules, it impacts on the practice of child care social workers in a fundam... ntal way. Its concerns are wide ranging, though do not include adoption and fostering (not considered further here) and youth justice (see Chapter 7). The Act deals with both public law and private law matters. Private law matters are those initiated by individuals, such as divorce proceedings, whereas public law matters involve the exercise of statutory powers by public authorities, such as local authorities. A noteworthy feature of the Act is the attempt to identify some basic principles that underlie the legislation. However, much of the philosophy of the Act is expounded in the regulations and guidance issued with the Act. Thus, for example, there is no direct mention in the Act of the concept of partnership, though this is a theme running through many of the volumes of regulations and guidance (see below). Additionally, *Working Together to Safeguard Children* (Department of Health, Home Office and Department for Education and Employment, 1999) and *Framework for the Assessment of Children in Need and their Families* (Department of Health, Department for Education and Employment and Home Office, 2000), both of which are issued under s. 7 of the Local Authority Social Services Act 1970, and the companion volume to the latter, *Assessing Children in Need and their Families: Practice Guidance* (Department of Health, 2000), give guidance on practice in this area.

Whilst the 1989 Act represents a considerable improvement on the previous legal regime, tensions still remain, as the following extract from an article by Judith Timms entitled 'The Tension between Welfare and Justice' ([1997] Family Law 38) illustrates:

On the face of it, justice and welfare go hand in hand. The establishment of a fair and just legal system is a central plank of any democracy. If one defines 'justice' as a fair distribution of benefits and burdens and 'welfare' as a mixture of health, happiness and prosperity, then it would be reasonable to assume that where there is justice, welfare will follow. What then is this talk of tension? Children are involved in a wide range of proceedings in court. What is the purpose of those court proceedings? Is it to achieve 'justice', according to the law, or to arrive at a fair or impartial action or judgment? As the Roman comic dramatist Terence said 'extreme law is often extreme injustice'. Is it primarily about 'welfare', identifying a course of action most likely to lead to the long-term health and happiness of the child in question? Can justice and welfare, these two admirable aims, go hand in hand? In the final analysis, does one have to come down on the side of 'welfare' or 'justice'? Are the two mutually exclusive or compatible? If the latter, how do they relate to each other, not just in general but in relation to each individual case? If one takes 'justice' as a collection of rights, what rights do children and young people have? Should their rights take precedence over other people's rights because they are among the most vulnerable in society? Does the upholding of those rights always lead to outcomes which are in the long-term best interests of the child?

The aim of the family justice system

What does justice mean in the context of family law? The aim of the family justice system has been described by Peter Harris, the Official Solicitor, as to 'adjudicate upon disputes concerning family relationships and the care of children, including disputes relating to property and maintenance with a minimum of cost, delay and distress'. His view was that Parliament and Ministers have decided that the family justice system is required to do a number of things. It must:

• support marriage and the family;
• minimise conflict when relationships break down;
• protect children;
• listen to the children's wishes and feelings;
• avoid delay;
• do these things efficiently and cheaply.

The view taken here is that the best outcomes for children are achieved when there is a healthy balance of justice and welfare. That balance or synthesis is achieved through the medium of effective independent representation for children or their interests in all decision-making fora, both in and out of court. This is the requirement of Art. 12 of the UN Convention on the Rights of the Child 1989, also IRCHIN's mission statement:

'1.   States Parties shall assure to the child who is capable of forming his or her own views the right to express those views freely in all matters affecting the child, the views of the child being given due weight in accordance with the age and maturity of the child.

2.   For this purpose, the child shall in particular be provided the opportunity to be heard in any judicial and administrative proceedings affecting the child, either directly, or through a representative or an appropriate body, in a manner consistent with the procedural rules of national law.'

We are fortunate in that the Children Act 1989 and the UN Convention, together with the new European Convention on the Exercise of Children's Rights (Council of Europe, 1995), provide a framework which considerably strengthens the position of the child in relation to access to both justice and welfare and which may facilitate the development of new services to children and families, based on principles of participation and an acknowledgement of children's rights, including their right to protection. Whenever the balance is tipped, either too much in favour of 'justice' or adversarial rights or too much in favour of 'rampant' welfare, then both can have equally harmful results for children. This article will explore the broad working hypothesis that the balance in public law proceedings is being distorted by too heavy a reliance on imprecise concepts of welfare, while in private law proceedings the opposite is true. The adversarial apportionment of children in an atmosphere of implacable hostility between parents may or may not be just or fair to the adults involved but it gives rise to serious concerns about the long-term happiness and welfare of their children, and the protection of those children's longer-term interests. It must be stressed, at the outset, that there are many child care professionals struggling with scant resources and limited training, and producing many examples of excellent practice in spite of the areas of tension that will be highlighted.

Public law proceedings

While there is a general consensus about the importance of safeguarding the child's best interests, attempts to identify those best interests in the case of a particular child take practitioners into an ideological minefield, in which notions of protection and welfare jostle for position with those of natural justice and children's rights. The concept of the best interests of the child should be approached with caution by all concerned professionals, mindful that 'best interests' can quickly become a camouflage for 'vested interest' which may pave the way in turn for the insidious enactment of self-fulfilling prophecies. As every parent knows, there is no single invaluable formula for the successful bringing up of children. Rappaport and Strelitz (*Fathers, Mothers and Others* (Routledge, Kegan, Paul, 1977)) have drawn attention to the various influences which help to establish what is normal practice within society at any given time. These beliefs and practices may be communicated by child care professionals who have taken over where religion, the feudal system and extended family networks have left off. The culture thus produced is 'an amalgam of scientifically based knowledge, folk belief, plausible inference and extrapolation and sheer wish. Together they create expectations of parenthood, with variations for this or that social class, ethnic group or religion' ... Parents may be bombarded with the current received wisdom, but there is no science of parenting which can guarantee successful outcomes. Similarly, there is no universally acknowledged body of research which informs local authority decision making in relation to the best interests of children.

...

A central guiding philosophy of the Children Act 1989 is that children are generally best looked after within their family of origin without recourse to legal proceedings. To this end local authorities are required to provide the range of service provision necessary to achieve this objective. Families are to be supported in carrying out their responsibilities in relation to their children. One of the major components of justice must be an equitable distribution of available resources. Are children in need receiving their fair share of the cake? Part III of the Children Act 1989 covers local authority support for children and families and establishes two key principles which govern service provision. First, to safeguard and promote the welfare of children who are in need, and, secondly, 'so far as is consistent with that duty, to promote the upbringing of such children by their families, by providing a range and level of services appropriate to those children's needs' (s. 17(1)(a) and (b) of the Children Act 1989). The specific duties and powers of each local authority are set out in Part I of Sch. 2:

'Any service provided by an authority in the exercise of functions conferred on them by [section 17] may be provided for the family of a particular child in need or for any member of his family, if it is provided with a view to safeguarding or promoting the child's welfare.'

'The services provided by a local authority ... may include giving assistance in kind or, in exceptional circumstances, in cash' (s. 17(3) and (6)).

The definition of a child in need is set out in s. 17(10):

'A child shall be taken to be in need if —

(a) he is unlikely to achieve or maintain, or to have the opportunity of achieving or maintaining, a reasonable standard of health or development without the provision for him of services by a local authority under this Part;

(b) his health or development is likely to be significantly impaired, or further impaired, without the provision for him of such services; or

(c) he is disabled ...'

The definition of a child in need is therefore quite specific, yet extremely broad-ranging. The inclusion of further impairment as well as significant impairment gives considerable scope for the provision of supportive services. Children with disabilities are included in definitions of children in need and local authorities have significant responsibilities for the provision of services to them. The extensive range of services which may be offered to children and families is spelled out in Sch. 2, under local authority support for children and families. Section 27, which is arguably the most under-utilised of the Act, provides for co-operation between different local authority departments to ensure a co-ordinated provision of services through the resources of education, housing and health authorities, as well as social services departments.

The range of services theoretically available to children under the Act is impressive. While the Children Act 1989 has done a great deal to increase the potential provision of an extensive and welcome range of services for children and families, as the Audit Commission has pointed out, it has done little to increase the range of services available on the ground. There are some particular areas of deficit — in particular the lack of direct service provision for young people leaving care has left hundreds stranded at 16, lacking psychological, financial, educational and emotional support. The *Report of the Children Act Advisory Committee* (HMSO, 1992) found that nearly all the authorities questioned who had replied had adopted a common system for prioritising levels of need entitling access to services. It was clear that the highest priority was accorded to children for whom authorities already had some existing responsibility, i.e. children covered by Parts IV and V of the Act. The Act and the Guidance place great emphasis on services to children in need, not as a reactive response but as a proactive programme of support and preventive strategies to prevent children coming into care. These provisions are seen as an important innovation by the Department of Health; however, as the Audit Commission concluded:

'as yet there is little evidence of local quality assurance measures to test whether practice has been influenced by the new legislation and subsequent local policies. Nor is there much evidence of local mechanisms to ensure that policy developments locally reflect to any great extent the experience and requirements of the practitioners. In the absence of such mechanisms routinely applied the priority given to support for children in need and their families will vary, depending on the perception of professionals and their subjective judgements.'

Although the definition in the Act is admirably broad, each local authority has written its respective children in need documents to fit its own particular complex equations of tailoring definitions of need to existing available resources. In such a scenario resources for children and families in need are only being released in some areas where it is perceived that there is a significant risk of harm as other categorisations of need do not constitute an emergency and cannot be justified to social work managers.

...

Although in England and Wales we may be justly proud of our system of representation for children in public law proceedings, the situation for children involved in private law proceedings is very different, and it is questionable whether the present arrangements are either just or whether they could be said to protect adequately the interests of children involved in family breakdown. In private law proceedings the tensions between justice and welfare are particularly evident. In cases where there are long-running and acrimonious disputes over residence and particularly contact, where implacable hostility exists between the partners and there is no possibility of agreement, it is increasingly difficult for courts to reach just and fair solutions. Paradoxically here, it is an increased emphasis on the welfare of the child which can temper the just solutions that may involve crude apportionments of equal shares of the child's life to each parent. Unlike public law proceedings where we need a renaissance of rights to correct distortions arising from over-paternalistic policies of welfare, in private law proceedings we need to break up the adversarial dichotomy between the two parents by turning a direct spotlight on the welfare of the child concerned. Effective representation of the child's views can allow both parties to give in, in the interests of the child, rather than in the face of the other parent's demands. Although both the UN Convention on the Rights of the Child and the European Convention on the Exercise of Children's Rights stress the right of the child to be informed, consulted and, if necessary, represented in proceedings affecting them, the Family Law Bill (now the Family Law Act 1996) as first drafted was remarkable in that although one of its stated aims was to diminish the distress caused to children by the breakdown of their parents' relationship, in the clauses that followed any direct references to children were conspicuous by their absence. Instead, the Bill relied heavily on family mediation services in what is essentially an indirect method of protecting the best interests of children. This rests on two basic assumptions.

(1)   The best interests of children will always be served by the facilitation of agreement between their parents. This is in direct contrast to the position in public law proceedings when, in 1974, following the publication of the Field Fisher Report inquiring into the death of Maria Colwell, it was acknowledged that the agreement of adult parties to proceedings (in that case the parents and the local authority) was no guarantee of the protection of the child's interest. This acknowledgement of potential conflict of interest was reinforced by the early introduction of the

guardian ad litem service in November 1976 in uncontested cases only, which was seen at that time as an urgent priority.

(2)   Provided parents agree, the notion of agreement is in turn based on a concept of 'the reasonable parent'. It is assumed that parents involved in private law proceedings, unlike those in public law proceedings, are 'reasonable' and will therefore wish to come to an agreement about the residence and contact arrangements for their children at a time when even the most emotionally balanced people can become unreasonable during the stressful process of separation and divorce.

...

It is unfortunate that the increasingly sensitive areas of tension between justice and welfare have led to the emergence of children's rights and children's welfare lobbies. It is a paradox that the most successful advocates for the welfare of the child, in general terms, have the most difficulty with the concepts of rights and responsibility. Talk of 'empowering' children is extremely unpopular in today's society, which sees children as dangerous little adults much more in need of control than care, as current policies towards young offenders clearly demonstrate. However, there are practical and philosophical difficulties in espousing a mutually exclusive rights or welfare-based approach to the best interests of children. The child may not be capable of exercising his rights in his best interests in certain situations. Similarly, the imprecise science of best interests may itself constitute an abuse of children's rights if applied within a subjective, rather than objective framework of welfare. There are cogent reasons for allowing the child to participate in decision making while building in safeguards to prevent him being overwhelmed by both the responsibility for making the decision and the consequences of making a mistake. Responsibility is like a muscle, it has to be exercised in a safe environment. As Michael Freeman has pointed out:

> 'the framework for children's rights is very different from those of welfare which provide for the protection and is essentially paternalistic. A children's rights framework sees children as active participants in social processes. Rights are valuable commodities — important moral coinage. They enable us to stand with dignity, if necessary to demand what is our due without having to grovel, plead or beg. A world with claim rights is one in which all persons are dignified objects of respect. Love, compassion, having the child's best interests in mind are important values but they are no substitute for rights.'

Such rights are free-standing and are not within the gift of any individual or local authority. They make adults, carers, parents and professionals uneasy because they threaten the ability of adults to make unchallenged decisions and they require the professional to make a leap of trust in relinquishing some elements of control over children's lives. The essential weakness of children's rights, and one which undermines their access to justice, is that they remain dependent upon the goodwill of adults to enforce them, and so are particularly fragile. IRCHIN's work is based on the belief that a clear working knowledge of the rights of children and young people can act as the necessary corrective to imprecise definitions of 'best interests' and that the best practice is that which incorporates a core curriculum of rights within definitions of welfare at every stage of decision making, both in and out of court. On this analysis it is possible to forge a middle ground which incorporates the child's right of self-determination without sacrificing the child's right to be protected. Independent and effective representation is the mechanism through which a healthy synthesis of rights and welfare may be achieved. It is also the powerful force in motion which acts as the catalyst for change, debate and review. Finally, there are many features of a family justice system of which we should be justly proud. As George Soros said 'the stock market is the worst system of allocating resources apart from all the others'. Perhaps we can comfort ourselves with the thought that the same may be true of our system of family justice.

The Act, Regulations and Guidance now have to be read in the light of the Human Rights Act 1998. In relation to children, a key provision is Art. 8 which guarantees, amongst other things, the right to family life, though, like virtually all the other Articles in the Convention, this is qualified (see above Chapter 2). Article 5, the right to liberty (again qualified) may also be relevant when issues relating to restricting the liberty of children arise, as might Art. 6, the right to a fair trial. As we have seen, s. 3 requires that, so far as it is possible to do so, legislation is to be read and given effect in a way which is compatible with the Convention rights. It is further provided in s. 6 that a public authority must not act in a way which is incompatible with a Convention right. This duty, it will be recalled, applies to courts and means that they are not immune from falling foul of the Human Rights Act or, indeed, from using that Act in improper ways. In the case that reached the House of Lords as *In re S (Minors) (Care Order: Implementation of Care Plan)* [2002] UKHL 10; 2 WLR 720, the Court of Appeal had sought to rationalise the relationship between the courts and local authorities with regard to care plans, as Lord Nicholls of Birkenhead, giving the leading judgment, indicates:

17 Stated shortly, the two innovations fashioned by the Court of Appeal were these. First, the court enunciated guidelines intended to give trial judges a wider discretion to make an interim care order, rather than a final care order. The second innovation was more radical. It concerns the position after the court has made a care order. The Court of Appeal propounded a new procedure, by which at the trial the essential milestones of a care plan would be identified and elevated to a 'starred status'. If a starred milestone was not achieved within a reasonable time after the date set at trial, the local authority was obliged to 'reactivate the interdisciplinary process that contributed to the creation of the care plan'. At the least the local authority must inform the child's guardian of the position. Either the guardian or the local authority would then have the right to apply to the court for further directions.

Lord Nicholls then continues by explaining the structure laid down by the Children Act 1989 and the impetus for the view taken by the Court of Appeal:

23 Two preliminary points can be made at the outset. First, a cardinal principle of the Children Act 1989 is that when the court makes a care order it becomes the duty of the local authority designated by the order to receive the child into its care while the order remains in force. So long as the care order is in force the authority has parental responsibility for the child. The authority also has power to decide the extent to which a parent of the child may meet his responsibility for him: section 33. An authority might, for instance, not permit parents to change the school of a child living at home. While a care order is in force the court's powers, under its inherent jurisdiction, are expressly excluded: section 100(2)(c) and (d). Further, the court may not make a contact order, a prohibited steps order or a specific issue order: section 9(1).

24 There are limited exceptions to this principle of non-intervention by the court in the authority's discharge of its parental responsibility for a child in its care under a care order. The court retains jurisdiction to decide disputes about contact with children in care: section 34. The court may discharge a care order, either on an application made for the purpose under section 39 or as a consequence of making a residence order (sections 9(1) and 91(1)). The High Court's judicial review jurisdiction also remains available.

25 These exceptions do not detract significantly from the basic principle. The Act delineated the boundary of responsibility with complete clarity. Where a care order is made the responsibility for the child's care is with the authority rather than the court. The court retains no

supervisory role, monitoring the authority's discharge of its responsibilities. That was the intention of Parliament.

...

28 The Children Act, embodying what I have described as a cardinal principle, represents the assessment made by Parliament of the division of responsibility which would best promote the interests of children within the overall care system. The court operates as the gateway into care, and makes the necessary care order when the threshold conditions are satisfied and the court considers a care order would be in the best interests of the child. That is the responsibility of the court. Thereafter the court has no continuing role in relation to the care order. Then it is the responsibility of the local authority to decide how the child should be cared for.

29 My second preliminary point is this. The Children Act has now been in operation for 10 years. Over the last six years there has been a steady increase in the number of children looked after by local authorities in England and Wales. At present there are 36,400 children accommodated under care orders, compared with 28,500 in 1995, an increase of 27%. In addition local authorities provide accommodation for nearly 20,000 children under section 20 orders (children in need of accommodation). A decade's experience in the operation of the Act, at a time of increasing demands on local authorities, has shown that there are occasions when, with the best will in the world, local authorities' discharge of their parental responsibilities has not been satisfactory. The system does not always work well. Shortages of money, of suitable trained staff and of suitable foster carers and prospective adopters for difficult children are among the reasons. There have been delays in placing children in accordance with their care plans, unsatisfactory breakdown rates and delays in finding substitute placements.

30 But the problems are more deep-seated than shortage of resources. In November 1997 the Government published Sir William Utting's review of safeguards for children living away from home. Mr Frank Dobson, then Secretary of State for Health, summarised his reaction to the report: 'It covers the lives of children whose home circumstances were so bad that those in authority, to use the jargon, took them into care. The report reveals that in far too many cases not enough care was taken. Elementary safeguards were not in place or not enforced. Many children were harmed rather than helped. The review reveals that these failings were not just the fault of individuals — though individuals were at fault. It reveals the failure of a whole system.'

31 In autumn 1998 the Government published its response to the children's safeguards review (Cm 4105) and launched its 'Quality Protects' programme, aimed at improving the public care system for children. Conferences have also been held, and many research studies undertaken, both private and public, on particular aspects of the problems. Some of the problems were discussed at the biannual President's Interdisciplinary Conference on family law 1997, attended by judges, child psychiatrists, social workers, social services personnel and other experts. The proceedings of the conference were subsequently published in book form, *Divided Duties: Care Planning for Children within the Family Justice System* (1998). The sharpness of the divide between the court's powers before and after the making of a care order attracted criticism. The matters discussed included the need for a care plan to be open to review by the court in exceptional cases. One suggestion was that a court review could be triggered by failure to implement 'starred' key factors in the care plan within specified time-scales. The guardian ad litem would be the appropriate person to intervene.

32 This was the source of the innovation which found expression in the judgments of the Court of Appeal in the present appeals.

In the following extract, he goes on to explain why he does not agree with the approach taken by the Court of Appeal:

34 The judgments in the Court of Appeal are a clear and forceful statement of the continuing existence of serious problems in this field. In the nature of things, courts are likely to see more of

the cases which go wrong. But the view, widespread among family judges, is that all too often local authorities' discharge of their parental responsibilities falls short of an acceptable standard. A disturbing instance can be found in the recent case of *F v Lambeth London Borough Council* (unreported) 28 September 2001. Munby J said, in paragraph 38 of his judgment, that the 'blunt truth is that in this case the state has failed these parents and these boys'.

35   It is entirely understandable that the Court of Appeal should seek some means to alleviate these problems: some means by which the courts may assist children where care orders have been made but subsequently, for whatever reason, care plans have not been implemented as envisaged and, as a result, the welfare of the children is being prejudiced. This is entirely understandable. The courts, notably through their wardship jurisdiction, have long discharged an invaluable role in safeguarding the interests of children. But the question before the House is much more confined. The question is whether the courts have power to introduce into the working of the Children Act a range of rights and liabilities not sanctioned by Parliament.

36   On this I have to say at once, respectfully but emphatically, that I part company with the Court of Appeal. I am unable to agree that the court's introduction of a 'starring system' can be justified as a legitimate exercise in interpretation of the Children Act 1989 in accordance with section 3 of the Human Rights Act 1998. Even if the Children Act is inconsistent with articles 6 or 8 of the Convention, which is a question I will consider later, section 3 does not in this case have the effect suggested by the Court of Appeal.

37   Section 3(1) provides: 'So far as it is possible to do so, primary legislation ... must be read and given effect in a way which is compatible with the Convention rights.' This is a powerful tool whose use is obligatory. It is not an optional canon of construction. Nor is its use dependent on the existence of ambiguity. Further, the section applies retrospectively. So far as it is possible to do so, primary legislation 'must be read and given effect' to in a way which is compatible with Convention rights. This is forthright, uncompromising language.

38   But the reach of this tool is not unlimited. Section 3 is concerned with interpretation. This is apparent from the opening words of section 3(1): 'so far as it is possible to do so'. The side heading of the section is 'Interpretation of legislation'. Section 4 (power to make a declaration of incompatibility) and, indeed, section 3(2)(b) presuppose that not all provisions in primary legislation can be rendered Convention compliant by the application of section 3(1).

39   In applying section 3 courts must be ever mindful of this outer limit. The Human Rights Act reserves the amendment of primary legislation to Parliament. By this means the Act seeks to preserve parliamentary sovereignty. The Act maintains the constitutional boundary. Interpretation of statutes is a matter for the courts; the enactment of statutes, and the amendment of statutes, are matters for Parliament.

40   Up to this point there is no difficulty. The area of real difficulty lies in identifying the limits of interpretation in a particular case.

...

41   I should add a further general observation in the light of what happened in the present case. Section 3 directs courts on how legislation shall, as far as possible, be interpreted. When a court, called upon to construe legislation, ascribes a meaning and effect to the legislation pursuant to its obligation under section 3, it is important the court should identify clearly the particular statutory provision or provisions whose interpretation leads to that result. Apart from all else, this should assist in ensuring the court does not inadvertently stray outside its interpretation jurisdiction.

42   I return to the Children Act 1989. I have already noted, as a cardinal principle of the Act, that the courts are not empowered to intervene in the way local authorities discharge their parental responsibilities under final care orders. Parliament entrusted to local authorities, not the courts, the responsibility for looking after children who are the subject of care orders. To my mind the new starring system would depart substantially from this principle. Under the new

system the court, when making a care order, is empowered to impose an obligation on an authority concerning the future care of the child. In future, the authority must submit a progress report, in circumstances identified by the court, either to the court or to the Children and Family Court Advisory and Support Service ('CAFCASS'). This is only the first step. The next step is that the court, when seised of what has happened after the care order was made, may then call for action. If it considers this necessary in the best interests of the child, the court may intervene and correct matters which are going wrong. In short, under the starring system the court will exercise a newly-created supervisory function.

43   In his judgment [in the Court of Appeal] Thorpe LJ noted that the starring system 'seems to breach the fundamental boundary between the functions and responsibilities of the court and the local authority': ... I agree. I consider this judicial innovation passes well beyond the boundary of interpretation. I can see no provision in the Children Act which lends itself to the interpretation that Parliament was thereby conferring this supervisory function on the court. No such provision was identified by the Court of Appeal. On the contrary, the starring system is inconsistent in an important respect with the scheme of the Children Act. It would constitute amendment of the Children Act, not its interpretation. It would have far-reaching practical ramifications for local authorities and their care of children. The starring system would not come free from additional administrative work and expense. It would be likely to have a material effect on authorities' allocation of scarce financial and other resources. This in turn would affect authorities' discharge of their responsibilities to other children. Moreover, the need to produce a formal report whenever a care plan is significantly departed from, and then await the outcome of any subsequent court proceedings, would affect the whole manner in which authorities discharge, and are able to discharge, their parental responsibilities.

44   These are matters for decision by Parliament, not the courts. It is impossible for a court to attempt to evaluate these ramifications or assess what would be the views of Parliament if changes are needed.

...

In my view, in the present case the Court of Appeal exceeded the bounds of its judicial jurisdiction under section 3 in introducing this new scheme.

...

45   Sections 7 and 8 of the Human Rights Act 1998 have conferred extended powers on the courts. Section 6 makes it unlawful for a public authority to act in a way which is incompatible with a Convention right. Section 7 enables victims of conduct made unlawful by section 6 to bring court proceedings against the public authority in question. Section 8 spells out, in wide terms, the relief a court may grant in those proceedings. The court may grant such relief or remedy, or make such order, within its powers as it considers just and appropriate. Thus, if a local authority conducts itself in a manner which infringes the article 8 rights of a parent or child, the court may grant appropriate relief on the application of a victim of the unlawful act.

...

48   I do not think sections 7 and 8 can be pressed as far as would be necessary if they were to bring the introduction of the starring system within their embrace. Sections 7 and 8 are to be given a generous interpretation, as befits their human rights purpose. But, ... the starring system goes much further than provide a judicial remedy to victims of actual or proposed unlawful conduct by local authorities entrusted with the care of children.

49   Section 7 envisages proceedings, brought by a person who is or would be a victim, against a public authority which has acted or is proposing to act unlawfully. The question whether the authority has acted unlawfully, or is proposing to do so, is a matter to be decided in the

proceedings. Relief can be given against the authority only in respect of an act, or a proposed act, of the authority which the court finds is or would be unlawful. For this purpose an act includes a failure to act. But the starring system would impose obligations on local authorities in circumstances when there has been no such finding and when, indeed, the authority has committed no breach of a Convention right and is not proposing to do so. Unless an authority is acting in bad faith, the possibility or prospect of non-fulfilment, for example, of a placement for a child cannot by itself be evidence that the authority is 'proposing' to act unlawfully contrary to section 6. Nor can the non-fulfilment of a starred event, when the obligation to report arises, necessarily be equated with a breach or threatened breach of a Convention right. Failure to adhere to a care plan may be due to a change in circumstances which, in the best interests of the child, calls for a variation from the care plan which was approved by the court.

...

56   The possibility that something may go wrong with the local authority's discharge of its parental responsibilities or its decision making processes, and that this would be a violation of article 8 so far as the child or parent is concerned, does not mean that the legislation itself is incompatible, or inconsistent, with article 8. The Children Act imposes on a local authority looking after a child the duty to safeguard and promote the child's welfare. Before making any decision with respect to such a child the authority must, so far as reasonably practicable, ascertain the wishes and feelings of the child and his parents: section 22. Section 26 provides for periodic case reviews by the authority, including obtaining the views of parents and children. One of the required reviews is that every six months the local authority must actively consider whether it should apply to the court for a discharge of the care order: see the Review of Children's Cases Regulations 1991 (SI 1991/895). Every local authority must also establish a procedure for considering representations, including complaints, made to it by any child who is being looked after by it, or by his parents, about the discharge by the authority of its parental responsibilities for the child.

57   If an authority duly carries out these statutory duties, in the ordinary course there should be no question of infringement by the local authority of the article 8 rights of the child or his parents. Questions of infringement are only likely to arise if a local authority fails properly to discharge its statutory responsibilities. Infringement which then occurs is not brought about, in any meaningful sense, by the Children Act. Quite the reverse. Far from the infringement being compelled, or even countenanced, by the provisions of the Children Act, the infringement flows from the local authority's failure to comply with its obligations under the Act. True, it is the Children Act which entrusts responsibility for the child's care to the local authority. But that is not inconsistent with article 8. Local authorities are responsible public authorities, with considerable experience in this field. Entrusting a local authority with the sole responsibility for a child's care, once the 'significant harm' threshold has been established, is not of itself an infringement of article 8. There is no suggestion in the Strasbourg jurisprudence that absence of court supervision of a local authority's discharge of its parental responsibilities is itself an infringement of article 8.

58   Where, then, is the inconsistency which is alleged to exist? As I understand it, the principal contention is that the incompatibility lies in the absence from the Children Act of an adequate remedy if a local authority fails to discharge its parental responsibilities properly and, as a direct result, the rights of the child or his parents under article 8 are violated. The Children Act authorises the state to interfere with family life. The Act empowers courts to make care orders whose effect is to entrust the care of children to a public authority. But the selfsame Act, while conferring these wide powers of interference in family life, omits to provide any sufficient remedy, by way of a mechanism for controlling an erring local authority's conduct, if things go seriously wrong with the authority's care of the child. It is only to be expected, the submission runs, that

there will be occasions when the conduct of a local authority falls short of the appropriate standards. An Act which authorises state interference but makes no provision for external control when the body entrusted with parental responsibility fails in its responsibilities is not compatible with article 8. The extensive supervisory functions and responsibilities conferred on the Secretary of State in Part XI of the Act, including his default powers under section 84, are not sufficient in practice to provide an adequate and timely remedy in individual cases.

59   In my view this line of argument is misconceived. Failure by the state to provide an effective remedy for a violation of article 8 is not itself a violation of article 8. This is self-evident. So, even if the Children Act does fail to provide an adequate remedy, the Act is not for that reason incompatible with article 8. This is the short and conclusive answer to this point.

An important doctrine developed by the European Court of Human Rights and, as a result of the Human Rights Act now imported into English Law, is proportionality. This is the notion that any action by the state limiting the Convention right must be justified in terms of being 'necessary in a democratic society'. In other words, the state (in this context, the local authority) must be able to show that it has acted in a way that is proportionate to the legitimate aim it is pursuing. If it is limiting a Convention right more than is necessary and justifiable, it will now be acting unlawfully. This has implications, for example, for those working in child protection who will have to show that any decisions that involve removing a child from his or her family are proportionate, as the following case *Re C and B (children) (care order: future harm)* [2000] 2FCR614 illustrates:

In 1997 care orders were made under s. 31(2) of the Children Act 1989 in respect of the eldest child of the family, K, and her half-sister, CM. The care orders were made on the basis that K had suffered actual harm to her intellectual and emotional development, and the likelihood of such harm occurring to CM in the future, and the care plan was for both children to remain in long-term foster care. On 4 September 1998 the mother gave birth to a son, J. On 30 March 1999, at the instigation of the guardian ad litem in the proceedings concerning K and CM, a report under s. 37 of the 1989 Act was ordered into J's welfare. In the light of the social worker's conclusion that although there was no evidence that J was currently suffering any harm, 'it was highly likely that [J] will suffer similar significant harm as his sisters in the future', and that drastic intervention was required, the local authority applied for, and were granted, an interim care order in relation to him, and he was removed from his parents when he was ten months old. On 22 July 1999 the mother gave birth to the youngest child, C, and the local authority obtained an emergency protection order in respect of him the same day. On 27 September the county court made an interim care order in relation to C, and both children were placed with the same foster carers. On 20 October 1999 the judge found there was a likelihood of each child suffering significant emotional harm in the future and she made care orders under s. 31(2) of the 1989 Act in respect of them, and approved the local authority's care plan which was for adoption. The parents appealed.

Held — Where there was a real possibility of future harm to a child which could not sensibly be ignored, the action taken by the local authority in response had to be proportionate to the nature and gravity of that feared harm. The principle had to be that the local authority worked to support, and eventually to reunite, the family, unless the risks were so high that the child's welfare required alternative family care. Cases where intervention would be appropriate to protect the child from future harm were likely to involve long-standing problems interfering with the capacity to provide even 'good enough' parenting in a serious way, such as serious mental illness, or a serious personality disorder or intractable substance abuse, or evidence of past chronic neglect, or abuse, or evidence of serious ill-treatment and physical harm. None of those situations had arisen in the present case. The appeal in relation to J and C would be allowed, their care orders would be set aside, and the case would be remitted to a High Court judge for reconsideration. Hale LJ, in the course of her judgment, said this:

...

30. I have considerable sympathy for the local authority in this case. They had, in my view wisely, adopted a low profile in relation to J. They found themselves pushed by the guardian ad litem and the court into an application that they had not initially wanted to make. Once they had received Mr Williams' report, it was obviously difficult for them to do anything other than make such an application. I also accept that there are cases in which the local authority is not bound to wait until the inevitable happens: it can intervene to protect long before that. But there has to be a balance. The cases where it is appropriate to do that are likely to involve long-standing problems which interfere with the capacity to provide even 'good enough' parenting in a serious way, such as serious mental illness, or a serious personality disorder, or intractable substance abuse, or evidence of past chronic neglect, or abuse, or evidence of serious ill-treatment and physical harm. None of those was involved in this case. Nor can it follow that every case where there is any significant risk of harm to a young child should result in a care order in which the care plan is adoption. Again, one quite understands why this may be considered by the local authority to be the appropriate course of action because, if there is early intervention before problems have escalated, the chance of placing the child successfully for adoption are much increased. The prospects are much less favourable if the child remains and damage is in fact sustained.

31. Nevertheless one comes back to the principle of proportionality. The principle has to be that the local authority works to support, and eventually to reunite, the family, unless the risks are so high that the child's welfare requires alternative family care. I cannot accept Mr Dugdale's submission that this was a case for a care order with a care plan of adoption or nothing. There could have been other options. There could have been time taken to explore those other options. Even as between those two, it is not necessarily the case that the care order was the better option than nothing. All of this needed serious consideration and dealing with in the judgment. I do not necessarily blame the judge — much depends on the way in which the case was presented to her — but all she says about the matter is:

> 'I have applied the welfare check list and, after weighing all the evidence and the able submission of Miss Gilliatt, I have reached independently the conclusion that no other order, other than a care order in respect of both children, would provide them with a safe and emotionally secure childhood, with the potential to develop socially and emotionally without sustaining psychological damage. In those circumstances, I am compelled to approve the local authority's care plan.'

32. There are cases in which one can deal with the matter as shortly as that but, for the reasons I have tried to explain, that was not this case.

33. I would have reached that conclusion without reference to the Convention for the Protection of Human Rights and Fundamental Freedoms (the European Convention on Human Rights) (Rome, 4 November 1950; TS 71 (1953); Cmd 8969), but I do note that under art. 8 of the Convention both the children and the parents have the right to respect for their family and private life. If the state is to interfere with that there are three requirements: firstly, that it be in accordance with the law; secondly, that it be for a legitimate aim (in this case the protection of the welfare and interests of the children); and thirdly, that it be 'necessary in a democratic society.'

34. There is a long line of European Court of Human Rights jurisprudence on that third requirement, which emphasises that the intervention has to be proportionate to the legitimate aim. Intervention in the family may be appropriate, but the aim should be to reunite the family when the circumstances enable that, and the effort should be devoted towards that end. Cutting off all contact and the relationship between the child or children and their family is only justified by the overriding necessity of the interests of the child.

The structure of the Children Act should help in this respect. The Act provides for a range of measures to help children and their families, and the local authority can select the most appropriate course of action to follow in any individual case.

Part I of the Act outlines some key concepts. Section I sets out the principle that, when a court is making a decision in respect of certain of its powers under the Act, the welfare of the child is the paramount consideration. It is important to note that this is not the case in other contexts:

1. Welfare of the child

(1) When a court determines any question with respect to —
   (a) the upbringing of a child; or
   (b) the administration of a child's property or the application of any income arising from it,
the child's welfare shall be the court's paramount consideration.

(2) In any proceedings in which any question with respect to the upbringing of a child arises, the court shall have regard to the general principle that any delay in determining the question is likely to prejudice the welfare of the child.

(3) In the circumstances mentioned in subsection (4), a court shall have regard in particular to —
   (a) the ascertainable wishes and feelings of the child concerned (considered in the light of his age and understanding);
   (b) his physical, emotional and educational needs;
   (c) the likely effect on him of any change in his circumstances;
   (d) his age, sex, background and any characteristics of his which the court considers relevant;
   (e) any harm which he has suffered or is at risk of suffering;
   (f) how capable each of his parents, and any other person in relation to whom the court considers the question to be relevant, is of meeting his needs;
   (g) the range of powers available to the court under this Act in the proceedings in question.

(4) The circumstances are that —
   (a) the court is considering whether to make, vary or discharge a section 8 order, and the making, variation or discharge of the order is opposed by any party to the proceedings; or
   (b) the court is considering whether to make, vary or discharge an order under Part IV.

(5) Where a court is considering whether or not to make one or more orders under this Act with respect to a child, it shall not make the order or any of the orders unless it considers that doing so would be better for the child than making no order at all.

The important concept of parental responsibility, and the acquisition of it, is outlined in the following sections:

2. Parental responsibility for children

(1) Where a child's father and mother were married to each other at the time of his birth, they shall each have parental responsibility for the child.

(2) Where a child's father and mother were not married to each other at the time of his birth —
   (a) the mother shall have parental responsibility for the child;
   (b) the father shall not have parental responsibility for the child, unless he acquires it in accordance with the provisions of this Act.

(3) References in this Act to a child whose father and mother were, or (as the case may be) were not, married to each other at the time of his birth must be read with section 1 of the Family Law Reform Act 1987 (which extends their meaning).

(4) The rule of law that a father is the natural guardian of his legitimate child is abolished.

(5)   More than one person may have parental responsibility for the same child at the same time.

(6)   A person who has parental responsibility for a child at any time shall not cease to have that responsibility solely because some other person subsequently acquires parental responsibility for the child.

(7)   Where more than one person has parental responsibility for a child, each of them may act alone and without the other (or others) in meeting that responsibility; but nothing in this Part shall be taken to affect the operation of any enactment which requires the consent of more than one person in a matter affecting the child.

(8)   The fact that a person has parental responsibility for a child shall not entitle him to act in any way which would be incompatible with any order made with respect to the child under this Act.

(9)   A person who has parental responsibility for a child may not surrender or transfer any part of that responsibility to another but may arrange for some or all of it to be met by one or more persons acting on his behalf.

(10)   The person with whom any such arrangement is made may himself be a person who already has parental responsibility for the child concerned.

(11)   The making of any such arrangement shall not affect any liability of the person making it which may arise from any failure to meet any part of his parental responsibility for the child concerned.

3.   Meaning of 'parental responsibility'

(1)   In this Act 'parental responsibility' means all the rights, duties, powers, responsibilities and authority which by law a parent of a child has in relation to the child and his property.

(2)   It also includes the rights, powers and duties which a guardian of the child's estate (appointed, before the commencement of section 5, to act generally) would have had in relation to the child and his property.

(3)   The rights referred to in subsection (2) include, in particular, the right of the guardian to receive or recover in his own name, for the benefit of the child, property of whatever description and wherever situated which the child is entitled to receive or recover.

(4)   The fact that a person has, or does not have, parental responsibility for a child shall not affect —

    (a)   any obligation which he may have in relation to the child (such as a statutory duty to maintain the child); or

    (b)   any rights which, in the event of the child's death, he (or any other person) may have in relation to the child's property.

(5)   A person who —

    (a)   does not have parental responsibility for a particular child; but

    (b)   has care of the child,

may (subject to the provisions of this Act) do what is reasonable in all the circumstances of the case for the purpose of safeguarding or promoting the child's welfare.

4.   Acquisition of parental responsibility by father

(1)   Where a child's father and mother were not married to each other at the time of his birth —

    (a)   the court may, on the application of the father, order that he shall have parental responsibility for the child; or

    (b)   the father and mother may by agreement ('a parental responsibility agreement') provide for the father to have parental responsibility for the child.

(2)   No parental responsibility agreement shall have effect for the purposes of this Act unless —

    (a)   it is made in the form prescribed by regulations made by the Lord Chancellor; and

    (b)   where regulations are made by the Lord Chancellor prescribing the manner in which such agreements must be recorded, it is recorded in the prescribed manner.

(3)   Subject to section 12(4), an order under subsection (1)(a), or a parental responsibility agreement, may only be brought to an end by an order of the court made on the application —
(a) of any person who has parental responsibility for the child; or
(b) with leave of the court, of the child himself.
(4)   The court may only grant leave under subsection (3)(b) if it is satisfied that the child has sufficient understanding to make the proposed application.

This concept is explained in *An Introduction to the Children Act 1989* (HMSO 1989) as follows:

2.1   The law gives a collection of rights, powers, duties and responsibilities to parents. In the Act these are referred to collectively as 'parental responsibility'. Under the old law, the rules which governed who may acquire parental responsibility and when it could be exercised were unclear, particularly if a child was subject to a custody order. Only in certain matters, such as the right to withhold agreement to a child's adoption or the right to inherit property when a child dies, has the law been specific.
2.2   The courts have come to regard parental responsibility as a collection of powers and duties which follow from being a parent and bringing up a child, rather than as rights which may be enforced at law. The exercise of parental responsibility is left largely to the discretion of the adults involved, subject to two limitations. First, the criminal law imposes minimum standards of care and civil law provides remedies for the protection of children's welfare [*the Children and Young Persons Acts 1933–1969 and the Child Care Act 1980*]. Secondly, parental responsibility itself diminishes as the child acquires sufficient understanding to make his own decisions [*Gillick v West Norfolk and Wisbech Area Health Authority [1986] A.C. 112*]. It would not be realistic or desirable to attempt to prescribe in statute the content of parental responsibility. However, the Act does put on a consistent basis rules about who acquires parental responsibility, when it may be exercised and what effect an order under the Act will have upon this.
2.3   'Parental responsibility' is defined to include all the rights, powers, authority and duties of parents in relation to a child and his property [*section 3(1)*]. The value of the term parental responsibility is twofold. First, it unifies the many references in legislation to parental rights, powers and the rest. Secondly, it more accurately reflects that the true nature of most parental rights is of limited powers to carry out parental duties.
2.4   The effect of having parental responsibility is to empower a person to take most decisions in the child's life (subject to the limitations mentioned above). It does not make him a parent or relative of the child in law, for example to give him rights of inheritance, or to place him under a statutory duty to maintain a child [*section 3(4)*].

...

2.5   Where a child's parents were or have been married to each other at or after the time of his conception, they each have parental responsibility for him [*section 2(1), as extended by section 1 of the Family Law Reform Act 1987: section 2(3)*]. Otherwise, the mother alone has parental responsibility unless the father acquires it by a court order or an agreement under the Act [*section 2(2)*].
2.6   The father who does not have parental responsibility may acquire it in one of two ways:
(a) with the mother, he may make 'a parental responsibility agreement'; or
(b) he may apply to court for an order which gives him parental responsibility [*section 4(1)*].
2.7   A parental responsibility agreement was not available under the old law [*although a parent could make an agreement about the exercise of her parental rights and duties under section 1(2) of the Guardianship Act 1973*]. It is intended as a simple and cheap method by which unmarried parents may share parental responsibility without going to court. The agreement must be made in the form prescribed by regulations and, if further regulations are made, will have to be officially

recorded in the prescribed manner [*section 4(2)*]. The effect of a parental responsibility agreement is the same as a court order conferring parental responsibility. Both may only be brought to an end by a court order on the application of a person with parental responsibility for the child or (with the leave of the court) of the child himself, if he has sufficient understanding to make the application [*section 4(3) and (4)*].

2.8   A court order which gives a father parental responsibility is similar to an order which gave him parental rights and duties under section 4 of the Family Law Reform Act 1987. [*An order under the 1987 Act which was in force at the commencement of the Children Act is deemed to be an order under section 4 of the latter statute: Schedule 14, paragraph 4*]. An order under section 4 of the Children Act *must* be made if a residence order is made in favour of a father [*section 12(1)*]. This is to ensure that a father who is entitled to have the child live with him under a court order will always have parental responsibility for him. If that residence order is later discharged, the parental responsibility order will not come to an end unless the court specifically decides that it should [*section 12(4)*].

...

2.22   The fact that one person acquires parental responsibility does not in itself remove another's parental responsibility [*section 2(6)*]. After separation or divorce parents retain their parental responsibility. However, a person who has parental responsibility is not entitled to act incompatibly with a court order [*section 2(8)*]. In exceptional circumstances, he may be required to disobey an order which would otherwise put the child at risk. [*Pursuant to the duty not to cause unnecessary suffering in section 1 of the Children and Young Persons Act 1933*].

2.23   Parental responsibility for a child cannot be passed on to someone else or otherwise be given up [*section 2(9)*]. However, where he acquired parental responsibility under a court order (or parental responsibility agreement or private appointment of a guardian), the court may later bring that order (or agreement or appointment) to an end.

2.24   A person with parental responsibility may arrange for another person to meet that responsibility on his behalf [*section 2(9)*]. Such an arrangement might be useful while a person with parental responsibility is unable to act, perhaps due to a stay in hospital or a trip abroad. It does not affect any liability of the person with parental responsibility which follows from a failure to meet his parental responsibility [*section 2(11)*].

2.25   Where more than one person has parental responsibility for a child at the same time, one may act independently of the other or others to meet that responsibility [*section 2(5) and (7)*]. The Act does not repeat the old law in its attempts to impose a duty on one parent to consult the other or to give one a right of veto against the action of the other. If necessary, one person with parental responsibility may ask a court to make an order which would require another person to inform him before a particular step is taken or not taken [*Such an order may be made under Part II of the Act*]. ... The onus of applying to court should not generally fall on the person who is caring for the child. This person (who will usually be the child's mother) needs to be able to respond to circumstances as they arise in order to meet her parental responsibility.

2.26   The only exception to the rule which permits independent action to meet shared parental responsibility arises when a child is in care. Here, the local authority is given power to determine the extent to which another person with parental responsibility may act.

Parental responsibility may also be exercised by a guardian. The Act provides:

5.   Appointment of guardians

(1)   Where an application with respect to a child is made to the court by any individual, the court may by order appoint that individual to be the child's guardian if —

- (a) the child has no parent with parental responsibility for him; or
- (b) a residence order has been made with respect to the child in favour of a parent or guardian of his who has died while the order was in force.

(2)   The power conferred by subsection (1) may also be exercised in any family proceedings if the court considers that the order should be made even though no application has been made for it.

(3)   A parent who has parental responsibility for his child may appoint another individual to be the child's guardian in the event of his death.

(4)   A guardian of a child may appoint another individual to take his place as the child's guardian in the event of his death.

(5)   An appointment under subsection (3) or (4) shall not have effect unless it is made in writing, is dated and is signed by the person making the appointment or —

   (a)   in the case of an appointment made by a will which is not signed by the testator, is signed at the direction of the testator in accordance with the requirements of section 9 of the Wills Act 1837; or

   (b)   in any other case, is signed at the direction of the person making the appointment, in his presence and in the presence of two witnesses who each attest the signature.

(6)   A person appointed as a child's guardian under this section shall have parental responsibility for the child concerned.

(7)   Where —

   (a)   on the death of any person making an appointment under subsection (3) or (4), the child concerned has no parent with parental responsibility for him; or

   (b)   immediately before the death of any person making such an appointment, a residence order in his favour was in force with respect to the child,

the appointment shall take effect on the death of that person.

(8)   Where, on the death of any person making an appointment under subsection (3) or (4) —

   (a)   the child concerned has a parent with parental responsibility for him; and

   (b)   subsection (7)(b) does not apply,

the appointment shall take effect when the child no longer has a parent who has parental responsibility for him.

(9)   Subsections (1) and (7) do not apply if the residence order referred to in paragraph (b) of those subsections was also made in favour of a surviving parent of the child.

(10)   Nothing in this section shall be taken to prevent an appointment under subsection (3) or (4) being made by two or more persons acting jointly.

(11)   Subject to any provision made by rules of court, no court shall exercise the High Court's inherent jurisdiction to appoint a guardian of the estate of any child.

(12)   Where rules of court are made under subsection (11) they may prescribe the circumstances in which, and conditions subject to which, an appointment of such a guardian may be made.

(13)   A guardian of a child may only be appointed in accordance with the provisions of this section.

6.   Guardians: revocation and disclaimer

(1)   An appointment under section 5(3) or (4) revokes an earlier such appointment (including one made in an unrevoked will or codicil) made by the same person in respect of the same child, unless it is clear (whether as the result of an express provision in the later appointment or by any necessary implication) that the purpose of the later appointment is to appoint an additional guardian.

(2)   An appointment under section 5(3) or (4) (including one made in an unrevoked will or codicil) is revoked if the person who made the appointment revokes it by a written and dated instrument which is signed —

   (a)   by him; or

   (b)   at his direction, in his presence and in the presence of two witnesses who each attest the signature.

(3) An appointment under section 5(3) or (4) (other than one made in a will or codicil) is revoked if, with the intention of revoking the appointment, the person who made it —
  (a) destroys the instrument by which it was made; or
  (b) has some other person destroy that instrument in his presence.

(3A) An appointment under section 5(3) or (4) (including one made in an unrevoked will or codicil) is revoked if the person appointed is the spouse of the person who made the appointment and either —
  (a) a decree of a court of civil jurisdiction in England and Wales dissolves or annuls the marriage, or
  (b) the marriage is dissolved or annulled and the divorce or annulment is entitled to recognition in England and Wales by virtue of Part II of the Family Law Act 1986,
unless a contrary intention appears by the appointment.

(4) For the avoidance of doubt, an appointment under section 5(3) or (4) made in a will or codicil is revoked if the will or codicil is revoked.

(5) A person who is appointed as a guardian under section 5(3) or (4) may disclaim his appointment by an instrument in writing signed by him and made within reasonable time of his first knowing that the appointment has taken effect.

(6) Where regulations are made by the Lord Chancellor prescribing the manner in which such disclaimers must be recorded, no such disclaimer shall have effect unless it is recorded in the prescribed manner.

(7) Any appointment of a guardian under section 5 may be brought to an end at any time by order of the court —
  (a) on the application of any person who has parental responsibility for the child;
  (b) on the application of the child concerned, with leave of the court; or
  (c) in any family proceedings, if the court considers that it should be brought to an end even though no application has been made.

An Introduction to the Children Act 1989 explains this:

2.10   A guardian may be appointed to take over parental responsibility for a child when a parent with parental responsibility dies. A guardian may be any other individual (including a parent). A local authority or voluntary organisation cannot be a guardian, since they are not 'individuals'. He acquires parental responsibility (if he does not already have it) when the appointment takes effect and may appoint another guardian to act if he should die while the child is still under eighteen [*section 5(3), (4) and (6)*]. Guardians also acquire the right to agree (or to withhold agreement) to the child's adoption [*Adoption Act 1976, section 16*]. The Act clarifies the law of guardianship, enables appointments to be made more simply and introduces a number of new provisions which recognise that guardians are generally intended to take over the care of a child where he would not otherwise have a parent with parental responsibility.

2.11   Private appointments may be made by a parent who has parental responsibility for the child or a person who has already been appointed guardian [*section 5(3) and (4)*]. An appointment must be in writing, dated and signed by (or at the direction of) the maker [*section 5(5)*]. If it is made at the appointer's direction, the making must be attested by two witnesses. An appointment may be made in a will or by deed, as under the old law, but does not have to be made in these ways.

2.12   Private appointments will no longer always come into effect on the death of the maker. If, on the maker's death, the child still has a parent with parental responsibility, the appointment will not take effect until that parent also dies [*section 5(7) and (8)*]. The exception to this rule is that if, on the maker's death, there was a residence order in his favour, the appointment takes effect immediately (unless the residence order was also in favour of a surviving parent of the child) [*section 5(7) and (9)*]. Where a residence order was not in existence in favour of the appointing parent (or there was a joint residence order in favour of the appointer and a surviving parent), it is presumed that the surviving parent ought to be left to care for the child as he wishes. If he wants to seek the help or advice of the 'guardian' he may always do so. On his death, however, the guardian's appointment takes effect.

2.13 Private appointments may be made individually or by people acting together [*section 5(10)*]. More than one guardian may be appointed by the same person or persons. A later appointment of a guardian (which is not clearly additional) will revoke an earlier one by the same person [*section 6(1)*]. A private appointment may also be revoked, either in writing which is dated and signed by the maker (or at his direction) [*section 6(2)*]. If the revocation is signed at the maker's direction, the signature must be in his presence and that of two witnesses who attest or by destruction of the appointment by the maker (or in his presence and at his direction) with the intention of revocation [*section 6(3)*]. An appointment made in a will or a codicil is revoked if the will or codicil is revoked [*section 6(4)*].

2.14 The guardian may disclaim his appointment in signed writing provided that he acts within a reasonable time of learning that the appointment has taken effect [*section 6(5)*]. Regulations may be made prescribing the manner of recording disclaimers [*section 6(6)*]. He may also be discharged by a court order made on the application of any person who has parental responsibility for the child, the child (if he has sufficient understanding) or by the court of its own initiative in family proceedings [*section 6(7)*]. ...

2.15 A court may appoint a guardian in similar circumstances to those in which a private appointment may take effect, namely:

(a) where a child has no parent with parental responsibility for him; or

(b) where, even though he still has such a parent, his other parent or a guardian of his has died and, immediately before his death, the deceased had a residence order in his favour in respect of the child [*section 5(1)*].

2.16 No court appointment may be made under 2.15(b) if the residence order in question was also in favour of a surviving parent of the child [*section 5(9)*]. Court appointments may be made on the application of the person who would like to be guardian or by the court of its own initiative in family proceedings [*section 5(1) and (2)*].

2.17 Guardians appointed by the court may be discharged in the same circumstances as private appointments.

Aspects of the concept are explained in the following extract from *Re S (Parental Responsibility)* [1995] 3 FCR 225. This was an application by an unmarried father for a parental responsibility order, which was opposed by the mother. In the course of deciding the issue, both Ward LJ and Butler-Sloss LJ made some more general observations about parental responsibility:

[*Ward LJ*] ..., in essence, the granting of a parental responsibility order is the granting of status. It is unfortunate that the notion of 'parental responsibility' has still to be defined by s. 3 of the Children Act 1989 to mean 'all the rights, duties, powers, responsibilities and authorities which by law a parent has in relation to a child and his property', which gives out-moded pre-eminence to the 'rights' which are conferred. That it is unfortunate is demonstrated by the very fact that, when pressed in this case to define nature and effect of the order which was so vigorously opposed, counsel, for the mother, was driven to say that her rooted objection was to the rights to which it would entitle the father and power that it would give to him. That is a most unfortunate failure to appreciate the significant change that the Act has brought about where the emphasis is to move away from rights and to concentrate on responsibilities. She did not doubt, that if by unhappy chance this child falls ill whilst she was abroad, his father if then enjoying contact, would not deal responsibly with her welfare.

It would, therefore, be helpful if the mother could think calmly about the limited circumstances when the exercise of true parental responsibility is likely to be of practical significance. It is wrong to place undue and therefore false emphasis on the rights and duties and the powers comprised in parental responsibility and not to concentrate on the fact that what is at issue is conferring upon a committed father the status of parenthood for which nature has already ordained that he must bear responsibility. There seems to me to be all too frequently a failure to appreciate that the wide exercise of section 8 orders can control the abuse, if any, of the *exercise* of parental responsibility which is adverse to the welfare of the child. Those interferences with day-to-day management of the child's life have nothing to do with whether or not this order should be allowed.

There is another important emphasis I would wish to make. I have heard, up and down the land, psychiatrists tell me how important it is that children grow up with good self-esteem and how much they need to have a favourable positive image of the absent parent. It seems to me important, therefore, wherever possible, to ensure that the law confers upon a committed father that stamp of approval, lest the child grow up with some belief that he is in someway disqualified from fulfilling his role and that the reason for the disqualification is something inherent which will be inherited by the child, making her struggle to find her own identity all the more fraught.

[*Butler-Sloss LJ*] ... It is important for parents and it is important, indeed, for these parents to remember the emphasis placed by Parliament on the order which is applied for. It is that of duties and responsibilities as well as rights and powers. Indeed, the order itself is entitled 'Parental Responsibility'. A father who has shown real commitment to the child concerned and to whom there is a positive attachment, as well as a genuine *bona fide* reason for the application, ought, in a case such as the present, to assume the weight of those duties and cement that commitment and attachment by sharing the responsibilities for the child with the mother. This father is asking to assume that burden as well as that pleasure of looking after his child, a burden not lightly to be undertaken.

The concept of partnership is not, as indicated above, one found in the Act itself. It does, however, feature in the guidance and regulations as a principle on which action taken or contemplated under the Act should be founded. The following extracts from Vol. 2 of the Guidance and Regulations illustrate the point:

1.2. The Act brings together most private and public law about children, thereby replacing complex and fragmented legislation with a single statute. Part III together with Schedule 2 sets out the main responsibilities of local authorities for children in their area who are in need and their families and for children in need whom they look after. It also draws together local authorities' functions towards children which existed under the Child Care Act 1980, the National Assistance Act 1948 and Schedule 8 of the National Health Service Act 1977 in relation to children with disabilities and under fives. All these provisions reflect the Act's philosophy that the best place for the child to be brought up is usually in his own family and that the child in need (who includes the child with disabilities) can be helped most effectively if the local authority, working in partnership with the parents, provides a range and level of services appropriate to the child's needs. To this end the parents and the child (where he is of sufficient understanding) need to be given the opportunity to make their wishes and feelings known and to participate in decision-making.

...

1.13. The Act puts the responsibility firmly on local authorities to provide accommodation, advice and assistance for children and young people in certain circumstances where such measures are needed to safeguard and promote their welfare. This may involve a social services department of a local authority requesting help from a local housing authority which, under section 27 of the Act, shall comply with a request for help if it is compatible with their statutory functions and does not unduly prejudice the discharge of those functions. Under the same provision the department will on occasion turn to the education authority for assistance in meeting the duties placed on the social services department in respect of family support. Sections 17(5), 27, 28 and 30 provide duties and powers in relation to co-operation between and consultation with different authorities including social services, education departments and housing authorities, health authorities and independent organisations. In relation to a child who has special educational needs, the social services department is under a duty (section 27(4)) to help the education department in the provision of services, and to consult the education department maintaining a child's statement of special educational needs (made under the Education Act 1981) when placing a child at an establishment providing education (section 28(1)). A corporate policy and clear departmental procedures in respect of interdepartmental collaboration will ensure good co-operation at all levels.

1.14.   The local authority carries the principal responsibility for co-ordinating and providing services for children in need. In some cases their services will be supportive of other key agencies. The local authority and other relevant agencies remain responsible for decisions about their own service provision or legal and administrative issues assigned to them. They should, however, seek out and have available the best relevant help from other agencies. Similarly they must be available and prepared to contribute to the work of other key agencies in meeting the legitimate needs of children and their families. New organisational links between local authorities and health authorities will be needed in order to implement the Act fully in relation to chronically sick and disabled children and their parents.

1.15.   Policies on community care under the NHS and Community Care Act 1990 and service provision under the Children Act should be considered together in respect of the requirement in each case to assess need and deliver services in accordance with available resources. The more formalised approach in community care to assessment, planning and delivery of services and the greater emphasis on the statutory protective element in children's services may require different relationships with other agencies and different styles of working. However, the essential functions are not different in principle and should not lead to operational difficulties if all concerned have a clear understanding of the approach required in the respective areas of work.

1.16.   In the case of day care and education services for young children the importance of co-ordination between different local authority departments — particularly but not exclusively social services and education — has long been recognised. A co-ordinated approach is a means of ensuring that all children, whatever type of service they attend, have access to a good quality curriculum or programme with continuity of experience and smooth transition to other forms of day care or education. There are three levels at which co-ordination is needed: policy making, day-to-day operation of services and between staff working on different settings. A co-ordinated approach helps to create an environment where people with different qualifications and experience can share skills and expertise and ideas in a positive way. It is important for all departments within a local authority to find ways of encouraging staff to work with this in mind, so that all the appropriate skills are available in all settings.

1.17.   Some local authorities have developed policies which draw together services for young children and they have set up administrative arrangements for monitoring implementation. The new duty to review day care services involves a process of measurement or assessment, which means that the local authority as a whole should have aims and objectives for services for young children. Local authorities will wish to consider how best to achieve this and what the administrative structure should be.

A thread running through the Act and the Guidance and Regulations is that of obtaining the child's views in relation to matters affecting him or her. It features as part of the 'welfare checklist' in s. 1(3) (see above) and is explained further in *An Introduction to the Children Act 1989*:

1.24 The checklist of particular matters to which the court is to have regard in reaching decisions about the child is headed by the child's wishes and feelings and highlights the great importance attached to them.

In private proceedings
1.25 The Act in the area of private law seeks to strike a balance between the need to recognise the child as an independent person and to ensure that his views are fully taken into account, and the risk of casting on him the burden of resolving problems caused by his parents or requiring him to choose between them. As well as including his views in the checklist, the Act allows the child with the court's permission to seek an order about his own future. The child will also be able to be joined as a party if the court thinks fit even if he does not seek an order.
1.26 Whether or not the child is a party to proceedings, the court has the power to commission a welfare report and to ensure that it covers his wishes and feelings.

In local authority proceedings
1.27 In local authority proceedings, for example an application for a care order, the child is always to be a party. Generally the court will also appoint a trained social worker as his guardian *ad litem*. It will then be the guardian's duty to represent the child in these proceedings and safeguard the child's interests. The child will be entitled to separate legal representation and if the child and the guardian do not agree about the case, the solicitor will take his instructions from the child rather than the guardian.

Additionally, it is important to bear in mind the issue of the child's capacity to make decisions for him/herself. A person has full capacity at the age of 18. Below that age, the courts have laid down an approach to this issue which relies on the child's understanding, as the extract below from *Gillick v West Norfolk and Wisbech Area Health Authority and the DHSS* [1986] AC 112 illustrates. The case concerned a circular issued by the Department of Health on the provision of contraception to girls under the age of 16 (the age at which, by statute, children attain full capacity in relation to decisions regarding medical treatment), which was challenged by Mrs Gillick on various grounds, including the question of parental rights in such matters. These details need not concern us here. In the course of deciding this particular set of questions, however, the House of Lords made some general observations about the decision making capacity of children. Perhaps the clearest exposition comes from Lord Scarman:

Certainty is always an advantage in the law, and in some branches of the law it is a necessity. But it brings with it an inflexibility and a rigidity which in some branches of the law can obstruct justice, impede the law's development, and stamp upon the law the mark of obsolescence where what is needed is the capacity for development. The law relating to parent and child is concerned with the problems of the growth and maturity of the human personality. If the law should impose upon the process of 'growing up' fixed limits where nature knows only a continuous process, the price would be artificiality and a lack of realism in an area where the law must be sensitive to human development and social change. If certainty be thought desirable, it is better that the rigid demarcations necessary to achieve it should be laid down by legislation after a full consideration of all the relevant factors than by the courts confined as they are by the forensic process to the evidence adduced by the parties and to whatever may properly fall within the judicial notice of judges. Unless and until Parliament should think fit to intervene, the courts should establish a principle flexible enough to enable justice to be achieved by its application to the particular circumstances proved by the evidence placed before them.

The underlying principle of the law was exposed by Blackstone and can be seen to have been acknowledged in the case law. It is that parental right yields to the child's right to make his own decisions when he reaches a sufficient understanding and intelligence to be capable of making up his own mind on the matter requiring decision. Lord Denning MR captured the spirit and principle of the law when he said in *Hewer* v *Bryant* [1970] 1 QB 357, 369:

'I would get rid of the rule in *In re Agar-Ellis*, 24 ChD 317 and of the suggested exceptions to it. That case was decided in the year 1883. It reflects the attitude of a Victorian parent towards his children. He expected unquestioning obedience to his commands. If a son disobeyed, his father would cut him off with a shilling. If a daughter had an illegitimate child, he would turn her out of the house. His power only ceased when the child became 21. I decline to accept a view so much out of date. The common law can, and should, keep pace with the times. It should declare, in conformity with the recent Report of the Committee on the Age of Majority [Cmnd. 3342, 1967], that the legal right of a parent to the custody of a child ends at the 18th birthday: and even up till then, it is a dwindling right which the courts will hesitate to enforce against the wishes of the child, and the more so the older he is. It starts with a right of control and ends with little more than advice.'

But his is by no means a solitary voice. It is consistent with the opinion expressed by the House in *J* v *C* [1970] AC 668 where their Lordships clearly recognised as out of place the assertion in the *Agar-Ellis* cases, 10 ChD 49; 24 ChD 317 of a father's power bordering on 'patria potestas.' It is consistent with the view of Lord Parker CJ in *Reg.* v *Howard* [1966] 1 WLR 13, 14 where he ruled that in the case of a prosecution charging rape of a girl under 16 the Crown must *prove* either lack of her consent or that she was not in a position to decide whether to consent or resist and added the comment that 'there are many girls who know full well what it is all about and can properly consent.' And it is consistent with the views of the House in the recent criminal case where a father was accused of kidnapping his own child, *Reg.* v *D* [1984] AC 778, a case to which I shall return.

For the reasons which I have endeavoured to develop much of the case law of the 19th and earlier centuries is no guide to the application of the law in the conditions of today. The *Agar-Ellis* cases, 10 ChD 49; 24 ChD 317 (the power of the father) cannot live with the modern statute law. The habeas corpus 'age of discretion' cases are also no guide as to the limits which should be accepted today in marking out the bounds of parental right, of a child's capacity to make his or her own decision, and of a doctor's duty to his patient. Nevertheless the 'age of discretion' cases are helpful in that they do reveal the judges as accepting that a minor can in law achieve an age of discretion before coming of full age. The 'age of discretion' cases are cases in which a parent or guardian (usually the father) has applied for habeas corpus to secure the return of his child who has left home without his consent. The courts would refuse an order if the child had attained the age of discretion, which came to be regarded as 14 for boys and 16 for girls, and did not wish to return. The principle underlying them was plainly that an order would be refused if the child had sufficient intelligence and understanding to make up his own mind. A passage from the judgment of Cockburn CJ in *Reg.* v *Howes* (1860) 3 E. & E. 332, which Parker LJ quoted in the Court of Appeal, illustrates their reasoning and shows how a fixed age was used as a working rule to establish an age at which the requisite 'discretion' could be held to be achieved by the child. Cockburn CJ said, at pp. 336–337:

'Now the cases which have been decided on this subject shew that, although a father is entitled to the custody of his children till they attain the age of 21, this court will not grant a habeas corpus to hand a child which is below that age over to its father, provided that it has attained an age of sufficient discretion to enable it to exercise a wise choice for its own interests. The whole question is, what is that age of discretion? We repudiate utterly, as most dangerous, the notion that any intellectual precocity in an individual female child can hasten the period which appears to have been fixed by statute for the arrival of the age of discretion; for that very precocity, if uncontrolled, might very probably lead to her irreparable injury. The legislature has given us a guide, which we may safely follow, in pointing out 16 as the age up to which the father's right to the custody of his female child is to continue; and short of which such a child has no discretion to consent to leaving him.'

The principle is clear: and a fixed age of discretion was accepted by the courts by analogy from the Abduction Acts (the first being the Act of 1557, 4 & 5 Ph. & M. c.8). While it is unrealistic today to treat a 16th century Act as a safe guide in the matter of a girl's discretion, and while no modern judge would dismiss the intelligence of a teenage girl as 'intellectual precocity,' we can agree with Cockburn CJ as to the principle of the law — the attainment by a child of an age of sufficient discretion to enable him or her to exercise a wise choice in his or her own interests.

The modern law governing parental right and a child's capacity to make his own decisions was considered in *Reg.* v *D* [1984] AC 778. The House must, in my view, be understood as having in that case accepted that, save where statute otherwise provides, a minor's capacity to make his or her own decision depends upon the minor having sufficient understanding and intelligence to make the decision and is not to be determined by reference to any judicially fixed age limit. The House was faced with a submission that a father, even if he had taken his child away by force or fraud, could not be guilty of a criminal offence of any kind. Lord Brandon of Oakbrook, with whom their other Lordships agreed, commented that this might well have been the view of the legislature and the courts in the 19th century, but had this to say about parental right and a child's capacity in our time to give or withhold a valid consent, at pp. 804–805:

'This is because in those times both the generally accepted conventions of society, and the courts by which such conventions were buttressed and enforced, regarded a father as having absolute and paramount authority, as against all the world, over any children of his who were still under the age of majority (then 21), except for a married daughter. The nature of this view of a father's rights appears clearly from various reported cases, including, as a typical example, *In re Agar-Ellis* (1883) 24 ChD 317. The common law, however, while generally immutable in its principles, unless different principles are laid down by statute, is not immutable in the way in which it adapts, develops and applies those principles in a radically changing world and against the background of radically changed social conventions and conditions.'

And later, at p. 806:

'I see no good reason why, in relation to the kidnapping of a child, it should not in all cases be the absence of the child's consent which is material, whatever its age may be. In the case of a very young child, it would not have the understanding or the intelligence to give its consent, so that absence of consent would be a necessary inference from its age. In the case of an older child, however, it must, I think, be a question of fact for a jury whether the child concerned has sufficient understanding and intelligence to give its consent; if, but only if, the jury considers that a child has these qualities, it must then go on to consider whether it has been proved that the child did not give its consent. While the matter will always be for the jury alone to decide, I should not expect a jury to find at all frequently that a child under 14 had sufficient understanding and intelligence to give its consent.'

In the light of the foregoing I would hold that as a matter of law the parental right to determine whether or not their minor child below the age of 16 will have medical treatment terminates if and when the child achieves a sufficient understanding and intelligence to enable him or her to understand fully what is proposed. It will be a question of fact whether a child seeking advice has sufficient understanding of what is involved to give a consent valid in law. Until the child achieves the capacity to consent, the parental right to make the decision continues save only in exceptional circumstances. Emergency, parental neglect, abandonment of the child, or inability to find the parent are examples of exceptional situations justifying the doctor proceeding to treat the child without parental knowledge and consent: but there will arise, no doubt, other exceptional situations in which it will be reasonable for the doctor to proceed without the parent's consent.

When applying these conclusions to contraceptive advice and treatment it has to be borne in mind that there is much that has to be understood by a girl under the age of 16 if she is to have legal capacity to consent to such treatment. It is not enough that she should understand the nature of the advice which is being given: she must also have a sufficient maturity to understand what is involved. There are moral and family questions, especially her relationship with her parents; long-term problems associated with the emotional impact of pregnancy and its termination; and there are the risks to health of sexual intercourse at her age, risks which contraception may diminish but cannot eliminate. It follows that a doctor will have to satisfy himself that she is able to appraise these factors before he can safely proceed upon the basis that she has at law capacity to consent to contraceptive treatment. And it further follows that ordinarily the proper course will be for him, as the guidance lays down, first to seek to persuade the girl to bring her parents into consultation, and if she refuses, not to prescribe contraceptive treatment unless he is satisfied that her circumstances are such that he ought to proceed without parental knowledge and consent.

Like Woolf J [1984] QB 581, 597, I find illuminating and helpful the judgment of Addy J of the Ontario High Court in *Johnston* v *Wellesley Hospital* (1970) 17 DLR (3d) 139, a passage from which he quotes in his judgment. The key passage, at p. 143, bears repetition:

'But, regardless of modern trend, I can find nothing in any of the old reported cases, except where infants of tender age or young children were involved, where the courts have found that a person under 21 years of age was legally incapable of consenting to medical treatment. If a person under 21 years were unable to consent to medical treatment, he would also be incapable of consenting to other types of bodily interference. A proposition purporting to establish that any bodily interference acquiesced in by a youth of 20 years would nevertheless constitute an assault would be absurd. If such were the case, sexual intercourse with a girl under 21 years would constitute rape. Until the minimum age of consent to sexual acts was fixed at 14 years by a statute, the courts often held that infants were capable of consenting at a considerably earlier age than 14 years.'

'I feel that the law on this point is well expressed in the volume on *Medical Negligence* (1957), by Lord Nathan, p. 176: "It is suggested that the most satisfactory solution of the problem is to rule that an infant who is capable of appreciating fully the nature and consequences of a particular operation or of particular treatment can give an effective consent thereto, and in such cases the consent of the guardian is unnecessary; but that where the infant is without that capacity, any apparent consent by him or her will be a nullity, the sole right to consent being vested in the guardian." '

I am, therefore, satisfied that the department's guidance can be followed without involving the doctor in any infringement of parental right. Unless, therefore, to prescribe contraceptive treatment for a girl under the age of 16 is either a criminal offence or so close to one that to prescribe such treatment is contrary to public policy, the department's appeal must succeed.

As a result of this case, a child who is able in law to make his/her own decisions is said to be 'Gillick competent.'

Part II of the Act gives the court jurisdiction to make certain orders in the context of 'family proceedings', most notably, though not exclusively, in relation to divorce. Section 8 sets out the orders that can be made in such proceedings, and the subsequent sections make more detailed provision for the making of such orders.

8. Residence, contact and other orders with respect to children

(1) In this Act —

'a contact order' means an order requiring the person with whom a child lives, or is to live, to allow the child to visit or stay with the person named in the order, or for that person and the child otherwise to have contact with each other;

'a prohibited steps order' means an order that no step which could be taken by a parent in meeting his parental responsibility for a child, and which is of a kind specified in the order, shall be taken by any person without the consent of the court;

'a residence order' means an order settling the arrangements to be made as to the person with whom a child is to live; and

'a specific issue order' means an order giving directions for the purpose of determining a specific question which has arisen, or which may arise, in connection with any aspect of parental responsibility for a child.

(2) In this Act 'a section 8 order' means any of the orders mentioned in subsection (1) and any order varying or discharging such an order.

(3) For the purposes of this Act 'family proceedings' means any proceedings

    (a) under the inherent jurisdiction of the High Court in relation to children; and

    (b) under the enactments mentioned in subsection (4),

but does not include proceedings on an application for leave under section 100(3).

(4) The enactments are —

    (a) Parts I, II and IV of this Act;

    (b) the Matrimonial Causes Act 1973;

    (d) the Adoption Act 1976;

    (e) the Domestic Proceedings and Magistrates' Courts Act 1978;

    (g) Part III of the Matrimonial and Family Proceedings Act 1984;

    (h) the Family Law Act 1996;

    (i) sections 11 and 12 of the Crime and Disorder Act 1998.

9. Restrictions on making section 8 orders

(1) No court shall make any section 8 order, other than a residence order, with respect to a child who is in the care of a local authority.

(2) No application may be made by a local authority for a residence order or contact order and no court shall make such an order in favour of a local authority.

(3) A person who is, or was at any time within the last six months, a local authority foster parent of a child may not apply for leave to apply for a section 8 order with respect to the child unless —

    (a) he has the consent of the authority;

    (b) he is a relative of the child; or

    (c) the child has lived with him for at least three years preceding the application.

(4) The period of three years mentioned in subsection (3)(c) need not be continuous but must have begun not more than five years before the making of the application.

(5) No court shall exercise its powers to make a specific issue order or prohibited steps order —

    (a) with a view to achieving a result which could be achieved by making a residence or contact order; or

    (b) in any way which is denied to the High Court (by section 100 (2)) in the exercise of its inherent jurisdiction with respect to children.

(6) No court shall make any section 8 order which is to have effect for a period which will end after the child has reached the age of sixteen unless it is satisfied that the circumstances of the case are exceptional.

(7) No court shall make any section 8 order, other than one varying or discharging such an order, with respect to a child who has reached the age of sixteen unless it is satisfied that the circumstances of the case are exceptional.

10. Power of court to make section 8 orders

(1) In any family proceedings in which a question arises with respect to the welfare of any child, the court may make a section 8 order with respect to the child if —

    (a) an application for the order has been made by a person who —

        (i) is entitled to apply for a section 8 order with respect to the child; or

        (ii) has obtained the leave of the court to make the application; or

    (b) the court considers that the order should be made even though no such application has been made.

(2) The court may also make a section 8 order with respect to any child on the application of a person who —

    (a) is entitled to apply for a section 8 order with respect to the child; or

    (b) has obtained the leave of the court to make the application.

(3) This section is subject to the restrictions imposed by section 9.

(4) The following persons are entitled to apply to the court for any section 8 order with respect to a child —

    (a) any parent or guardian of the child;

    (b) any person in whose favour a residence order is in force with respect to the child.

(5) The following persons are entitled to apply for a residence or contact order with respect to a child

    (a) any party to a marriage (whether or not subsisting) in relation to whom the child is a child of the family;

    (b) any person with whom the child has lived for a period of at least three years;

    (c) any person who

        (i) in any case where a residence order is in force with respect to the child, has the consent of each of the persons in whose favour the order was made;

        (ii) in any case where the child is in the care of a local authority, has the consent of that authority; or

        (iii) in any other case, has the consent of each of those (if any) who have parental responsibility for the child.

(6) A person who would not otherwise be entitled (under the previous provisions of this section) to apply for the variation or discharge of a section 8 order shall be entitled to do so if —

    (a) the order was made on his application; or

    (b) in the case of a contact order, he is named in the order.

(7) Any person who falls within a category of person prescribed by rules of court is entitled to apply for any such section 8 order as may be prescribed in relation to that category of person.

(8) Where the person applying for leave to make an application for a section 8 order is the child concerned, the court may only grant leave if it is satisfied that he has sufficient understanding to make the proposed application for the section 8 order.

(9) Where the person applying for leave to make an application for a section 8 order is not the child concerned, the court shall, in deciding whether or not to grant leave, have particular regard to —

    (a) the nature of the proposed application for the section 8 order;

    (b) the applicant's connection with the child;

    (c) any risk there might be of that proposed application disrupting the child's life to such an extent that he would be harmed by it; and

    (d) where the child is being looked after by a local authority —

        (i) the authority's plans for the child's future; and

        (ii) the wishes and feelings of the child's parents.

(10) The period of three years mentioned in subsection (5)(b) need not be continuous but must not have begun more than five years before, or ended more than three months before, the making of the application.

11. General principles and supplementary provisions

(1)   In proceedings in which any question of making a section 8 order, or any other question with respect to such an order arises, the court shall (in the light of any rules made by virtue of subsection (2)) —

   (a) draw up a timetable with a view to determining the question without delay; and

   (b) give such directions as it considers appropriate for the purpose of ensuring, so far as is reasonably practicable, that that timetable is adhered to.

(2)   Rules of court may —

   (a) specify periods within which specified steps must be taken in relation to proceedings in which such questions arise; and

   (b) make other provision with respect to such proceedings for the purpose of ensuring, so far as is reasonably practicable, that such questions are determined without delay.

(3)   Where a court has power to make a section 8 order, it may do so at any time during the course of the proceedings in question even though it is not in a position to dispose finally of those proceedings.

(4)   Where a residence order is made in favour of two or more persons who do not themselves all live together, the order may specify the periods during which the child is to live in the different households concerned.

(5)   Where —

   (a) a residence order has been made with respect to a child; and

   (b) as a result of the order the child lives, or is to live, with one of two parents who each have parental responsibility for him,

the residence order shall cease to have effect if the parents live together for a continuous period of more than six months.

(6)   A contact order which requires the parent with whom a child lives to allow the child to visit, or otherwise have contact with, his other parent shall cease to have effect if the parents live together for a continuous period of more than six months.

(7)   A section 8 order may —

   (a) contain directions about how it is to be carried into effect;

   (b) impose conditions which must be complied with by any person —

      (i)   in whose favour the order is made;

      (ii) who is a parent of the child concerned;

      (iii) who is not a parent of his but who has parental responsibility for him; or

      (iv) with whom the child is living,

and to whom the conditions are expressed to apply;

   (c) be made to have effect for a specified period, or contain provisions which are to have effect for a specified period;

   (d) make such incidental, supplemental or consequential provision as the court thinks fit.

12. Residence orders and parental responsibility

(1)   Where the court makes a residence order in favour of the father of a child it shall, if the father would not otherwise have parental responsibility for the child, also make an order under section 4 giving him that responsibility.

(2)   Where the court makes a residence order in favour of any person who is not the parent or guardian of the child concerned that person shall have parental responsibility for the child, while the residence order remains in force.

(3)   Where a person has parental responsibility for a child as a result of subsection (2), he shall not have the right —

   (a) to consent, or refuse to consent, to the making of an application with respect to the child under section 18 of the Adoption Act 1976;

    (b) to agree, or refuse to agree, to the making of an adoption order, or an order under section 55 of the Act of 1976 with respect to the child; or

    (c) to appoint a guardian for the child.

(4)   Where subsection (1) requires the court to make an order under section 4 in respect of the father of a child, the court shall not bring that order to an end at any time while the residence order concerned remains in force.

13. Change of child's name or removal from jurisdiction

(1)   Where a residence order is in force with respect to a child, no person may —

    (a) cause the child to be known by a new surname; or

    (b) remove him from the United Kingdom;

without either the written consent of every person who has parental responsibility for the child or the leave of the court.

(2)   Subsection (1)(b) does not prevent the removal of a child, for a period of less than one month, by the person in whose favour the residence order is made.

(3)   In making a residence order with respect to a child the court may grant the leave required by subsection (1)(b), either generally or for specified purposes.

There are limits to the making of such orders, however. For example, in addition to the limitations expressed in ss. 9–13, the 'no order' principle applies to s. 8 orders (see s. 1(5) above). An important lesson emerges from the case of *Nottinghamshire CC* v *P* [1994] Fam. 18, which is that a local authority may not apply for orders under s. 8 (see s. 9(2)) and, in any event cannot use s. 8 orders as a way of getting the same result as a care order but by a different route. If a care order is appropriate, then the authority should apply for one rather than, as here, seeking to achieve the same result through s. 8. Indeed, by failing to do so it could be in breach of its duties under Part IV (see below). The court was obviously unhappy at the outcome of the case, for it left children at risk from an abusive parent. But a court cannot rewrite the law to achieve a result that is not permissible under the legislation as it stands. These issues are discussed in the following extract from the judgment of Sir Stephen Brown, speaking for the Court of Appeal:

Counsel for the mother, the father and the guardian ad litem all supported the judge's ruling on the application of the local authority for a prohibited steps order. They all submitted that the application was misconceived and that leave to make the application should not have been granted particularly by means of an ex parte application to a single justice of a family proceedings court. Miss Parker for the mother submitted that the structure and scheme of the Children Act 1989 made it clear that applications made by local authorities were governed principally by Part IV of the Act under which local authorities might apply for care or supervision orders which gave them statutory responsibilities. Part II of the Act principally concerned private law remedies and the remedies provided by section 8 were essentially private law remedies. Furthermore, local authorities were specifically prohibited from applying for residence and contact orders although they were not debarred with leave from seeking specific issue and prohibited steps orders. However, these were subject to the restrictions contained in section 9(5) of the Act. Miss Parker supported the judge's decision that the application made in this instance by the local authority fell foul of the restrictions contained in section 9(5). It was an application which patently sought to determine the residence of the children and the degree of contact which the children might have with the father. Miss Parker also submitted that, in any event, a prohibited steps order could not in fact operate as an exclusion order or much less an order requiring a father to leave his home at the instance of a local authority. She drew to the attention of the court the report in Hansard (H.C. Debates), 27 October 1989, col. 1314, with regard to a proposal to introduce a clause into the Children Bill during its passage through the House of Commons. Hansard records that a member sought to introduce a new clause 34 headed 'Removal of Adults' and the clause as drafted provided:

'(1) Where the court has made: (a) an emergency protection order; or (b) an interim care order; and it is satisfied that the child's welfare would be satisfactorily safeguarded or promoted if a person who is resident in the child's household were removed from that household the court may in addition — (i) make an order (exclusion order) requiring that person to vacate that household; or (ii) accept an undertaking from that person that he shall vacate the household. (2) For the purposes of the section the term exclusion order shall include the term undertaking. (3) Where an exclusion order is made under this section the child shall not be removed from the household.'

This clause was not approved and therefore was not incorporated in the Act which received the Royal Assent. It is suggested by Miss Parker that the local authority's application erroneously assumes that such a power nevertheless exists.

Miss Parker also pointed out that when a care order is made under section 31 a local authority assumes parental responsibility and, inter alia, has power to place a child with its parent or parents under the provisions of section 23(5) of the Act and the Placement of Children with Parents, etc. Regulations 1991 (SI 1991 No. 893). In such circumstances the child need not be taken from her home and the local authority is afforded wide powers to supervise the placement. Furthermore section 34 of the Act of 1989 gives wide powers with regard to contact.

Section 31 gives power to the court to make a supervision order as an alternative to making a care order. Schedule 3 to the Act of 1989 gives detailed powers to the supervisor to impose obligations and to give directions.

In this case it appears that from the time when the application first came before a circuit judge all the parties other than the local authority were willing to submit to the making of a supervision order under section 31. The court has been told by Miss Scotland, for the father, that he was prepared to consent to a number of requirements being included in a supervision order. Section 9(5) of the Act of 1989 provides:

'No court shall exercise its power to make a specific issue order or prohibited steps order — (a) with a view to achieving a result which could be achieved by making a residence or contact order; or (b) in any way which is denied to the High Court [by section 100(2)] in the exercise of its inherent jurisdiction with respect to children.'

In the view of this court the application for a prohibited steps order by this local authority was in reality being made with a view to achieving a result which could be achieved by making a residence or contact order. Section 9(2) specifically provides:

'No application may be made by a local authority for a residence order or contact order and no court shall make such an order in favour of a local authority.'

The court is satisfied that the local authority was indeed seeking to enter by the 'back door' as it were. It agrees with Ward J that he had no power to make a prohibited steps order in this case.

Submissions were made to the court to the effect that a contact order in any event necessarily implied a positive order and that an order which merely provided for 'no contact' could not be construed as a contact order. There are certain passages in editorial comment which seem to support that view. We do not share it. We agree with the judge that the sensible and appropriate construction of the term contact order includes a situation where a court is required to consider whether any contact should be provided for. An order that there shall be 'no contact' falls within the general concept of contact and common sense requires that it should be considered to fall within the definition of 'contact order' in section 8(1). We agree with the reasoning of Ward J and would therefore dismiss the appeal of the local authority against his refusal of its application for a prohibited steps order.

A wider question arises as to policy. We consider that this court should make it clear that the route chosen by the local authority in this case was wholly inappropriate. In cases where children are found to be at risk of suffering significant harm within the meaning of section 31 of the Children Act 1989 a clear duty arises on the part of local authorities to take steps to protect them. In such circumstances a local authority is required to assume responsibility and to intervene in the family arrangements in order to protect the child. Part IV specifically provides them with wide powers and a wide discretion. As already pointed out the Act envisages that local authorities may place children with their parents even though they may have a care order under section 31.

...

In our judgment these orders cannot stand. Even if the judge had a theoretical power to assume authority by reason of section 10 of the Act of 1989, the orders were plainly not appropriate even in the unhappy circumstances of this case. In the result the appeals against these orders must be allowed.

In the result there are now no orders in force which are capable of regulating and safeguarding the position of these children. In point of fact the elder has now reached the age of 16 but the younger is now still only 13 years of age. The situation remains that they are at risk and the local authority is under a statutory obligation to take steps to protect them and to seek to ensure their welfare. The court has been told that as a result of action taken by the regional health authority prompted by the judge, the father did in fact go to the Gracewell Clinic following the proceedings before Ward J. However the court has also now been told by Miss Scotland that he has since left the clinic. The court has not been told the circumstances under which that occurred. Since the fact of the risk of significant harm to the children has been established and not contradicted there remains upon the local authority the clear duty to take steps to safeguard the welfare of these children. It should not shrink from taking steps under Part IV of the Act. It appears from submissions made by all counsel in this court that the mother, the father and the children by their guardian ad litem would not resist the making of a supervision order in favour of the local authority pursuant to section 31 of the Act. That at least would afford a basis for the local authority to take some constructive steps in order to protect these children.

This court is deeply concerned at the absence of any power to direct this authority to take steps to protect the children. In the former wardship jurisdiction it might well have been able to do so. The operation of the Children Act 1989 is entirely dependent upon the full co-operation of all those involved. This includes the courts, local authorities, social workers, and all who have to deal with children. Unfortunately, as appears from this case, if a local authority doggedly resists taking the steps which are appropriate to the case of children at risk of suffering significant harm it appears that the court is powerless. The authority may perhaps lay itself open to an application for judicial review but in a case such as this the question arises, at whose instance? The position is one which it is to be hoped will not recur and that lessons will be learnt from this unhappy catalogue of errors.

For the reasons set out in this judgment, the court dismisses the appeal of the local authority and allows the appeals of the other appellants.

Note however, that, under s. 37, a court can give directions to a local authority:

37. Powers of court in certain family proceedings
(1)   Where, in any family proceedings in which a question arises with respect to the welfare of any child, it appears to the court that it may be appropriate for a care or supervision order to be made with respect to him, the court may direct the appropriate authority to undertake an investigation of the child's circumstances.

(2)   Where the court gives a direction under this section the local authority concerned shall, when undertaking the investigation, consider whether they should —
    (a)   apply for a care order or for a supervision order with respect to the child;
    (b)   provide services or assistance for the child or his family; or
    (c)   take any other action with respect to the child.

(3)   Where a local authority undertake an investigation under this section, and decide not to apply for a care order or supervision order with respect to the child concerned, they shall inform the court of —
    (a)   their reasons for so deciding;
    (b)   any service or assistance which they have provided, or intend to provide, for the child and his family; and
    (c)   any other action which they have taken, or propose to take, with respect to the child.

(4)   The information shall be given to the court before the end of the period of eight weeks beginning with the date of the direction, unless the court otherwise directs.

(5)   The local authority named in a direction under subsection (1) must be —
    (a)   the authority in whose area the child is ordinarily resident; or
    (b)   where the child is not ordinarily resident in the area of a local authority, the authority within whose area any circumstances arose in consequence of which the direction is being given.

(6)   If, on the conclusion of any investigation or review under this section, the authority decide not to apply for a care order or supervision order with respect to the child —
    (a)   they shall consider whether it would be appropriate to review the case at a later date; and
    (b)   if they decide that it would be, they shall determine the date on which that review is to begin.

Services provided under Part III of the Act are voluntary and preventive, with the ultimate aim of keeping families together. They are often provided to children in their own home and in partnership with the parents. There are however provisions for accommodation of children under this Part. The key concept under Part III is that of the 'child in need'. This is the threshold for the availability of such services and is defined in s. 17, as are the general duties relating to the local authority:

17.   Provision of services for children in need, their families and others
(1)   It shall be the general duty of every local authority (in addition to the other duties imposed on them by this Part) —
    (a)   to safeguard and promote the welfare of children within their area who are in need; and
    (b)   so far as is consistent with that duty, to promote the upbringing of such children by their families,
by providing a range and level of services appropriate to those children's needs.

(2)   For the purpose principally of facilitating the discharge of their general duty under this section, every local authority shall have the specific duties and powers set out in Part 1 of Schedule 2.

(3)   Any service provided by an authority in the exercise of functions conferred on them by this section may be provided for the family of a particular child in need or for any member of his family, if it is provided with a view to safeguarding or promoting the child's welfare.

(4)   The Secretary of State may by order amend any provision of Part I of Schedule 2 or add any further duty or power to those for the time being mentioned there.

(5) Every local authority —
  (a) shall facilitate the provision by others (including in particular voluntary organisations) of services which the authority have power to provide by virtue of this section, or section 18, 20, 23, 23B to 23D, 24A or 24B; and
  (b) may make such arrangements as they see fit for any person to act on their behalf in the provision of any such service.

(6) The services provided by a local authority in the exercise of functions conferred on them by this section may include giving assistance in kind or, in exceptional circumstances, in cash.

(7) Assistance may be unconditional or subject to conditions as to the repayment of the assistance or of its value (in whole or in part).

(8) Before giving any assistance or imposing any conditions, a local authority shall have regard to the means of the child concerned and of each of his parents.

(9) No person shall be liable to make any repayment of assistance or of its value at any time when he is in receipt of income support, working families' tax credit or disabled person's tax credit under Part VII of the Social Security Contributions and Benefits Act 1992 or of an income-based jobseeker's allowance.

(10) For the purposes of this Part a child shall be taken to be in need if —
  (a) he is unlikely to achieve or maintain, or to have the opportunity of achieving or maintaining, a reasonable standard of health or development without the provision for him of services by a local authority under this Part;
  (b) his health or development is likely to be significantly impaired, or further impaired, without the provision for him of such services; or
  (c) he is disabled,
and 'family', in relation to such a child, includes any person who has parental responsibility for the child and any other person with whom he has been living.

(11) For the purposes of this Part, a child is disabled if he is blind, deaf or dumb or suffers from mental disorder of any kind or is substantially and permanently handicapped by illness, injury or congenital deformity or such other disability as may be prescribed; and in this Part —
'development' means physical, intellectual, emotional, social or behavioural development; and
'health' means physical or mental health.

17A. Direct payments

(1) The Secretary of State may by regulations make provision for and in connection with requiring or authorising the responsible authority in the case of a person of a prescribed description who falls within subsection (2) to make, with that person's consent, such payments to him as they may determine in accordance with the regulations in respect of his securing the provision of the service mentioned in that subsection.

(2) A person falls within this subsection if he is —
  (a) a person with parental responsibility for a disabled child,
  (b) a disabled person with parental responsibility for a child, or
  (c) a disabled child aged 16 or 17,
and a local authority ('the responsible authority') have decided for the purposes of section 17 that the child's needs (or, if he is such a disabled child, his needs) call for the provision by them of a service in exercise of functions conferred on them under that section.

(3) Subsections (3) to (5) and (7) of section 57 of the 2001 Act shall apply, with any necessary modifications, in relation to regulations under this section as they apply in relation to regulations under that section.

(4) Regulations under this section shall provide that, where payments are made under the regulations to a person falling within subsection (5) —
  (a) the payments shall be made at the rate mentioned in subsection (4)(a) of section 57 of the 2001 Act (as applied by subsection (3)); and

(b) subsection (4)(b) of that section shall not apply.

(5) A person falls within this subsection if he is —

(a) a person falling within subsection (2)(a) or (b) and the child in question is aged 16 or 17, or

(b) a person who is in receipt of income support, working families' tax credit or disabled person's tax credit under Part 7 of the Social Security Contributions and Benefits Act 1992 (c. 4) or of an income-based jobseeker's allowance.

(6) In this section —

'the 2001 Act' means the Health and Social Care Act 2001;

'disabled' in relation to an adult has the same meaning as that given by section 17(11) in relation to a child;

'prescribed' means specified in or determined in accordance with regulations under this section (and has the same meaning in the provisions of the 2001 Act mentioned in subsection (3) as they apply by virtue of that subsection).

17B. Vouchers for persons with parental responsibility for disabled children

(1) The Secretary of State may by regulations make provision for the issue by a local authority of vouchers to a person with parental responsibility for a disabled child.

(2) 'Voucher' means a document whereby, if the local authority agrees with the person with parental responsibility that it would help him care for the child if the person with parental responsibility had a break from caring, that person may secure the temporary provision of services for the child under section 17.

(3) The regulations may, in particular, provide —

(a) for the value of a voucher to be expressed in terms of money, or of the delivery of a service for a period of time, or both;

(b) for the person who supplies a service against a voucher, or for the arrangement under which it is supplied, to be approved by the local authority;

(c) for a maximum period during which a service (or a service of a prescribed description) can be provided against a voucher.

The concept of the child in need is explained in Volume 2 of the Guidance and Regulations:

2.4.   The definition of 'need' in the Act is deliberately wide to reinforce the emphasis on preventive support and services to families. It has three categories: a reasonable standard of health or development; significant impairment of health or development; and disablement. It would not be acceptable for an authority to exclude any of these three — for example, by confining services to children at risk of significant harm which attracts the duty to investigate under section 47. The child's needs will include physical, emotional and educational needs according to his age, sex, race, religion, culture and language and the capacity of the current carer to meet those needs. This guidance does not lay down firm criteria or set general priorities because the Act requires each authority to decide their own level and scale of services appropriate to the children in need in their area. However, because the definition is in the Act, a local authority cannot lawfully substitute any other definition for the purposes of Part III.

2.5.   In assessing individual need, authorities must assess the existing strengths and skills of the families concerned and help them overcome identified difficulties and enhance strengths. Sometimes the needs will be found to be intrinsic to the child; at other times however it may be that parenting skills and resources are depleted or under-developed and thus threaten the child's well-being. For example, a chronically sick parent may need continuing practical and emotional support of varying degrees of intensity according to the incidence of acute phases of his illness and the developing needs of the child. At times, a sick parent may seek short periods of local authority accommodation for the child so as to have a period of recuperation and avoid stress for the child; in these cases social workers should consider whether a package of support services provided in the home would be the better form of provision. Children should not necessarily be identified as in need because one or both parents are disabled, although this could of course be a factor. It may be that the provision of services to the parent, either under adult disabled persons legislation or under section 17(3) of the Act may safeguard the welfare of the child sufficiently to enable the parent to continue looking after him at home. In other cases social problems, relationship problems, unemployment or bereavement, for example, may temporarily reduce the quality of care of children in the family. A package of support and prompt use of respite care may sustain the child's longer term well-being within the family.

2.6.   The Act envisages family support services being offered to members of a family of a child in need where the service is provided with a view to safeguarding and promoting the child's welfare (section 17(3)). Any person who has parental responsibility for the child and any other person with whom the child is living is included so that a local authority may put together a package of services for a family which could include home help, day care provision for a family member other than the child in need (e.g. another child in the household) or a short-term, temporary placement for the child to relieve the carer. The outcome of any service provision under this power should be evaluated to see whether it has met the primary objective, namely to safeguard or promote the child's welfare.

Assessment

2.7.   Good practice requires that the assessment of need should be undertaken in an open way and should involve those caring for the child, the child and other significant persons. Families with a child in need, whether the need results from family difficulties or the child's circumstances, have the right to receive sympathetic support and sensitive intervention in their family's life. Paragraph 3 of Schedule 2 to the Act provides that 'a local authority may assess a child's needs for the purpose of this Act at the same time as any assessment under:

   (a)   the Chronically Sick and Disabled Persons Act 1970;
   (b)   the Education Act 1981;
   (c)   the Disabled Persons (Services, Consultation and Representation) Act 1986; or
   (d)   any other enactment.'

2.8.   In making an assessment, the local authority should take account of the particular needs of the child — that is in relation to health, development, disability, education, religious persuasion, racial origin, cultural and linguistic background, the degree, (if any) to which these needs are being met by existing services to the family or child and which agencies' services are best suited to the child's needs. In the case of a child with disabilities or a child with a parent with communication difficulties provision of a sign language interpreter, large print, tape and braille may need to be made if communication is to be effective. The need for an interpreter should be considered where the family's first language is not English.

2.9.   Assessment must identify and find a way to provide as helpful a guide as possible to the child's needs. Necessary experience and expertise should be provided for in staffing of services and through relationships with other professions and services and with the community. In some areas the local community may include too great a variety of ethnic groups to be reflected fully in composition of staff. In others, local authorities may be called on only rarely to provide a service for a child or family from a minority ethnic group. In both these circumstances, local authorities will need to identify sources of advice and help so that the necessary experience, expertise and resources are available when needed. Care is needed to ensure that the terms 'black' and 'black family' are not used in isolation or in such a way as to obscure characteristics and needs.

This is the gateway to the provision of services, as the Guidance and Regulations explain. Chapter 3 of Volume 2 (not reproduced here but referred to in the extract below) gives examples of services that may be provided, by way of expanding on the provisions in ss. 18–23.

2.11.　Section 17 and Part 1 of Schedule 2 to the Act set out in considerable detail the specific duties and powers of the local authorities in relation to support services for children with families. Under section 17(1) local authorities have a general duty to provide a range and level of services appropriate to the children in their area who are 'in need' so as to safeguard and promote their welfare and, so far as is consistent with that aim, promote their upbringing by their families. Local authorities are not expected to meet every individual need, but they are asked to identify the extent of need and then make decisions on the priorities for service provision in their area in the context of that information and their statutory duties. Local authorities will have to ensure that a range of services is available to meet the extent and nature of need identified within their administrative areas. In addition to day care provision for pre-school and school age children, it is likely that a range of services designed to support and improve the strengths and skills of parents in their own homes and neighbourhoods will be required. It is also likely that a vigorous foster care service will be required, offering a range of placements which reflects the racial, cultural, linguistic and religious needs of children requiring accommodation, and is responsive to the amount of short term, longer term, or permanent placements which the children may need. It remains likely that some children will need special forms of residential care. In many areas these services exist already, provided by statutory, voluntary and independent sources. It is important to recognise the benefits of developing packages of services appropriate to the assessed needs of individual children and their families, rather than directing them to existing services which may not be appropriate. Chapter 3 describes the range of services which are likely to be needed but this is not an exhaustive list; others may need to be provided according to the local authority's assessment of need in their own area.

2.12.　Local authorities are also expected to act as facilitators of provision of the services covered by section 17, 18 (day care) and 20, 23 (accommodation) and 24 (advice and assistance to certain young persons aged under 21) by others as well as being the principal providers themselves (section 17(5)). They must publicise the availability of such services and they should monitor and evaluate the availability of all those services which can be viewed as family support. In undertaking these tasks the local authority will have to ensure that they are properly informed about the different racial groups to which children within their area who are in need belong (paragraph 11 of Schedule 2). The development of information systems will assist local authorities in this task. When they have assembled the information they will be able to decide on priorities and allocate resources for services such as family support, day care and fostering and consider how to deal with the consequential staffing and recruitment issues. Local authorities should provide a range of services which should reflect (in scale as well as type) the needs of children and families from ethnic minority groups. More detailed guidance on issues of race and culture and placement of children is contained in volume 3 in this series (Family Placements).

...

2.13.　The effect of the provision of services to support families may often be to avoid the need to take the child into long-term compulsory care. Section 1 of the Child Care Act 1980 was formulated in a way that implied that the aim of supportive work is to prevent admission to care. This has contributed to a negative interpretation of local authority interaction with families. The direct link between preventive work and reducing the need for court procedures found in section 1 of the Child Care Act 1980 is reproduced in the Children Act in paragraph 7 of Schedule 2 but only as one of a range of local authority duties and powers. The accommodation of a child by a local authority is now to be viewed as a service providing positive support to a child and his family.

2.14.　In general, families have the capacity to cope with their own problems, or to identify and draw upon resources in the community for support. Some families however reach a stage where they are not able to resolve their own difficulties, and are therefore providing inadequate care for their child or are afraid of doing so. They may look to social services for support and assistance. If they do this they should receive a positive response which reduces any fears they may have of stigma or loss of parental responsibility.

2.15. The Act gives a positive emphasis to identifying and providing for the child's needs rather than focusing on parental shortcomings in a negative manner. The responsibility on local authorities to provide accommodation for children in need who require it — because, for example, the parents are prevented from providing appropriate care during the illness of one parent — replaces 'reception into care' with its unhelpful associations of parental shortcomings. Where, for example, parents who usually provide good and devoted care for their child need a break, the provision of additional help in the home or suitable accommodation for the child for a short time should be seen as a service to the child and family without pressure or prejudice. Children accommodated are 'looked after' by the local authority in partnership with the parents. The Act also emphasises that partnership with parents should not become weaker if it becomes necessary to provide the child with accommodation.

2.16. In putting together packages of services, local authorities should take account of services provided by the voluntary sector and other agencies. Some examples of supportive services provided under section 17 are advice on such matters as local facilities, social security benefits, housing or education, domiciliary support in the form of family aides, befriending schemes, play facilities and specialist services such as counselling, parent-craft training, family centres, respite care and the provision of accommodation for longer periods. In appropriate circumstances assistance given may be in kind or, exceptionally, in cash (section 17(6)).

The Act itself provides:

18. Day care for pre-school and other children

(1) Every local authority shall provide such day care for children in need within their area who are —
> (a) aged five or under; and
> (b) not yet attending schools,

as is appropriate.

(2) A local authority may provide day care for children within their area who satisfy the conditions mentioned in subsection (1)(a) and (b) even though they are not in need.

(3) A local authority may provide facilities (including training, advice, guidance and counselling) for those —
> (a) caring for children in day care; or
> (b) who at any time accompany such children while they are in day care.

(4) In this section 'day care' means any form of care or supervised activity provided for children during the day (whether or not it is provided on a regular basis).

(5) Every local authority shall provide for children in need within their area who are attending any school such care or supervised activities as is appropriate —
> (a) outside school hours; or
> (b) during school holidays.

(6) A local authority may provide such care or supervised activities for children within their area who are attending any school even though those children are not in need.

(7) In this section 'supervised activity' means an activity supervised by a responsible person.

19. Review of provision for day care, child minding etc.

(1) Every local authority in England and Wales shall review —
> (a) the provision which they make under section 18;
> (b) the extent to which the services of child minders are available within their area with respect to children under the age of eight; and
> (c) the provision for day care within their area made for children under the age of eight by persons other than the authority required to register under Part XA.

(2) A review under subsection (1) shall be conducted —
> (a) together with the appropriate local education authority; and
> (b) at least once in every review period.

(4)   In conducting any such review the two authorities or, in Scotland, the authority shall have regard to the provision made with respect to children under the age of eight in relevant establishments within their area.

(5)   In this section —
'relevant establishment' means —

...

    (b)   in relation to England and Wales, any establishment which is mentioned in paragraphs 1 and 2 of Schedule 9A (establishments exempt from the registration requirements which apply in relation to the provision of day care in England and Wales);

'review period' means the period of one year beginning with the commencement of this section and each subsequent period of three years beginning with an anniversary of that commencement.

(6)   Where a local authority have conducted a review under this section they shall publish the result of the review —

    (a)   as soon as is reasonably practicable;

    (b)   in such form as they consider appropriate; and

    (c)   together with any proposals they may have with respect to the matters reviewed.

(7)   The authorities conducting any review under this section shall have regard to —

    (a)   any representations made to any one of them by any relevant Health Authority, Special Health Authority, Primary Care Trust, or health board; and

    (b)   any other representations which they consider to be relevant.

Provision of accommodation for children

20.   Provision of accommodation for children: general

(1)   Every local authority shall provide accommodation for any child in need within their area who appears to them to require accommodation as a result of —

    (a)   there being no person who has parental responsibility for him;

    (b)   his being lost or having been abandoned; or

    (c)   the person who has been caring for him being prevented (whether or not permanently, and for whatever reason) from providing him with suitable accommodation or care.

(2)   Where a local authority provide accommodation under subsection (1) for a child who is ordinarily resident in the area of another local authority, that other local authority may take over the provision of accommodation for the child within —

    (a)   three months of being notified in writing that the child is being provided with accommodation; or

    (b)   such other longer period as may be prescribed.

(3)   Every local authority shall provide accommodation for any child in need within their area who has reached the age of sixteen and whose welfare the authority consider is likely to be seriously prejudiced if they do not provide him with accommodation.

(4)   A local authority may provide accommodation for any child within their area (even though a person who has parental responsibility for him is able to provide him with accommodation) if they consider that to do so would safeguard or promote the child's welfare.

(5)   A local authority may provide accommodation for any person who has reached the age of sixteen but is under twenty-one in any community home which takes children who have reached the age of sixteen if they consider that to do so would safeguard or promote his welfare.

(6)   Before providing accommodation under this section, a local authority shall, so far as is reasonably practicable and consistent with the child's welfare —

    (a)   ascertain the child's wishes regarding the provision of accommodation; and

    (b)   give due consideration (having regard to his age and understanding) to such wishes of the child as they have been able to ascertain.

(7)   A local authority may not provide accommodation under this section for any child if any person who —
  (a) has parental responsibility for him;
  (b) is willing and able to —
      (i)   provide accommodation for him; or
      (ii) arrange for accommodation to be provided for him,
objects.

(8)   Any person who has parental responsibility for a child may at any time remove the child from accommodation provided by or on behalf of the local authority under this section.

(9)   Subsections (7) and (8) do not apply while any person —
  (a) in whose favour a residence order is in force with respect to the child; or
  (b) who has care of the child by virtue of an order made in the exercise of the High Court's inherent jurisdiction with respect to children,
agrees to the child being looked after in accommodation provided by or on behalf of the local authority.

(10)   Where there is more than one such person as is mentioned in subsection (9), all of them must agree.

(11)   Subsections (7) and (8) do not apply where a child who has reached the age of sixteen agrees to being provided with accommodation under this section.

21.   Provision of accommodation for children in police protection or detention or on remand, etc.

(1)   Every local authority shall make provision for the reception and accommodation of children who are removed or kept away from home under Part V.

(2)   Every local authority shall receive, and provide accommodation for, children —
  (a) in police protection whom they are requested to receive under section 46(3)(f);
  (b) whom they are requested to receive under section 38(6) of the Police and Criminal Evidence Act 1984;
  (c) who are —
      (i)   on remand (within the meaning of the section) under paragraph 7(5) of Schedule 7 to the Powers of Criminal Courts (Sentencing) Act 2000 or section 23(1) of the Children and Young Persons Act 1969; or
      (ii) the subject of a supervision order imposing a local authority residence requirement under paragraph 5 of Schedule 6 to that Act of 2000, and with respect to whom they are the designated authority.

(3)   Where a child has been —
  (a) removed under Part V; or
  (b) detained under section 38 of the Police and Criminal Evidence Act 1984,
and he is not being provided with accommodation by a local authority or in a hospital vested in the Secretary of State or a Primary Care Trust or otherwise made available pursuant to arrangements made by a Health Authority or a Primary Care Trust, any reasonable expenses of accommodating him shall be recoverable from the local authority in whose area he is ordinarily resident.

Duties of local authorities in relation to children looked after by them

22.   General duty of local authority in relation to children looked after by them

(1)   In this Act, any reference to a child who is looked after by a local authority is a reference to a child who is —
  (a) in their care; or
  (b) provided with accommodation by the authority in the exercise of any functions (in particular those under this Act) which are social services functions within the meaning

of the Local Authority Social Services Act 1970, apart from functions under sections 23B and 24B.

(2) In subsection (1) 'accommodation' means accommodation which is provided for a continuous period of more than 24 hours.

(3) It shall be the duty of a local authority looking after any child —

 (a) to safeguard and promote his welfare; and

 (b) to make such use of services available for children cared for by their own parents as appears to the authority reasonable in his case.

(4) Before making any decision with respect to a child whom they are looking after, or proposing to look after, a local authority shall, so far as is reasonably practicable, ascertain the wishes and feelings of —

 (a) the child;

 (b) his parents;

 (c) any person who is not a parent of his but who has parental responsibility for him; and

 (d) any other person whose wishes and feelings the authority consider to be relevant,

regarding the matter to be decided.

(5) In making any such decision a local authority shall give due consideration —

 (a) having regard to his age and understanding, to such wishes and feelings of the child as they have been able to ascertain;

 (b) to such wishes and feelings of any person mentioned in subsection (4)(b) to (d) as they have been able to ascertain; and

 (c) to the child's religious persuasion, racial origin and cultural and linguistic background.

(6) If it appears to a local authority that it is necessary, for the purpose of protecting members of the public from serious injury, to exercise their powers with respect to a child whom they are looking after in a manner which may not be consistent with their duties under this section, they may do so.

(7) If the Secretary of State considers it necessary, for the purpose of protecting members of the public from serious injury, to give directions to a local authority with respect to the exercise of their powers with respect to a child whom they are looking after, he may give such directions to the authority.

(8) Where any such directions are given to an authority they shall comply with them even though doing so is inconsistent with their duties under this section.

23. Provision of accommodation and maintenance by local authority for children whom they are looking after

(1) It shall be the duty of any local authority looking after a child —

 (a) when he is in their care, to provide accommodation for him; and

 (b) to maintain him in other respects apart from providing accommodation for him

(2) A local authority shall provide accommodation and maintenance for any child whom they are looking after by —

 (a) placing him (subject to subsection (5) and any regulations made by the Secretary of State) with —

 (i) a family;

 (ii) a relative of his; or

 (iii) any other suitable person,

 on such terms as to payment by the authority and otherwise as the authority may determine:

 (aa) maintaining him in an appropriate children's home; or

 (f) making such other arrangements as —

 (i) seem appropriate to them; and

 (ii) comply with any regulations made by the Secretary of State.

(2A)   Where under subsection (2)(aa) a local authority maintains a child in a home provided, equipped and maintained by the Secretary of State under section 82(5), it shall do so on such terms as the Secretary of State may from time to time determine.

(3)   Any person with whom a child has been placed under subsection (2)(a) is referred to in this Act as a local authority foster parent unless he falls within subsection (4).

(4)   A person falls within this subsection if he is —
   (a) a parent of the child;
   (b) a person who is not a parent of the child but who has parental responsibility for him; or
   (c) where the child is in care and there was a residence order in force with respect to him immediately before the care order was made, a person in whose favour the residence order was made.

(5)   Where a child is in the care of a local authority, the authority may only allow him to live with a person who falls within subsection (4) in accordance with regulations made by the Secretary of State.

(5A) For the purposes of subsection (5) a child shall be regarded as living with a person if he stays with that person for a continuous period of more than 24 hours.

(6)   Subject to any regulations made by the Secretary of State for the purposes of this subsection, any local authority looking after a child shall make arrangements to enable him to live with —
   (a) a person falling within subsection (4); or
   (b) a relative, friend or other person connected with him,
unless that would not be reasonably practicable or consistent with his welfare.

(7)   Where a local authority provide accommodation for a child whom they are looking after, they shall, subject to the provisions of this Part and so far as is reasonably practicable and consistent with his welfare, secure that —
   (a) the accommodation is near his home; and
   (b) where the authority are also providing accommodation for a sibling of his, they are accommodated together.

(8)   Where a local authority provide accommodation for a child whom they are looking after and who is disabled, they shall, so far as is reasonably practicable, secure that the accommodation is not unsuitable to his particular needs.

(9)   Part II of Schedule 2 shall have effect for the purposes of making further provision as to children looked after by local authorities and in particular as to the regulations that may be made under subsections (2)(a) and (f) and (5).

(10)   In this Act —
   'appropriate children's home' means a children's home in respect of which a person is registered under Part II of the Care Standards Act 2000; and

   'children's home' has the same meaning as in that Act.

Advice and assistance for certain children and young persons

23A.   The responsible authority and relevant children
(1)   The responsible local authority shall have the functions set out in section 23B in respect of a relevant child.

(2)   In subsection (1) 'relevant child' means (subject to subsection (3)) a child who —
   (a) is not being looked after by any local authority;
   (b) was, before last ceasing to be looked after, an eligible child for the purposes of paragraph 19B of Schedule 2; and
   (c) is aged sixteen or seventeen.

(3)   The Secretary of State may prescribe —
   (a)   additional categories of relevant children; and
   (b)   categories of children who are not to be relevant children despite falling within subsection (2).
(4)   In subsection (1) the 'responsible local authority' is the one which last looked after the child.
(5)   If under subsection (3)(a) the Secretary of State prescribes a category of relevant children which includes children who do not fall within subsection (2)(b) (for example, because they were being looked after by a local authority in Scotland), he may in the regulations also provide for which local authority is to be the responsible local authority for those children.

23B.   Additional functions of the responsible authority in respect of relevant children
(1)   It is the duty of each local authority to take reasonable steps to keep in touch with a relevant child for whom they are the responsible authority, whether he is within their area or not.
(2)   It is the duty of each local authority to appoint a personal adviser for each relevant child (if they have not already done so under paragraph 19C of Schedule 2).
(3)   It is the duty of each local authority, in relation to any relevant child who does not already have a pathway plan prepared for the purposes of paragraph 19B of Schedule 2 —
   (a)   to carry out an assessment of his needs with a view to determining what advice, assistance and support it would be appropriate for them to provide him under this Part; and
   (b)   to prepare a pathway plan for him.
(4)   The local authority may carry out such an assessment at the same time as any assessment of his needs is made under any enactment referred to in sub-paragraphs (a) to (c) of paragraph 3 of Schedule 2, or under any other enactment.
(5)   The Secretary of State may by regulations make provision as to assessments for the purposes of subsection (3).
(6)   The regulations may in particular make provision about —
   (a)   who is to be consulted in relation to an assessment;
   (b)   the way in which an assessment is to be carried out, by whom and when;
   (c)   the recording of the results of an assessment;
   (d)   the considerations to which the local authority are to have regard in carrying out an assessment.
(7)   The authority shall keep the pathway plan under regular review.
(8)   The responsible local authority shall safeguard and promote the child's welfare and unless they are satisfied that his welfare does not require it, support him by —
   (a)   maintaining him;
   (b)   providing him with or maintaining him in suitable accommodation; and
   (c)   providing support of such other descriptions as may be prescribed.
(9)   Support under subsection (8) may be in cash.
(10)   The Secretary of State may by regulations make provision about the meaning of 'suitable accommodation' and in particular about the suitability of landlords or other providers of accommodation.
(11)   If the local authority have lost touch with a relevant child, despite taking reasonable steps to keep in touch, they must without delay —
   (a)   consider how to re-establish contact; and
   (b)   take reasonable steps to do so,
and while the child is still a relevant child must continue to take such steps until they succeed.
(12)   Subsections (7) to (9) of section 17 apply in relation to support given under this section as they apply in relation to assistance given under that section.
(13)   Subsections (4) and (5) of section 22 apply in relation to any decision by a local authority for the purposes of this section as they apply in relation to the decisions referred to in that section.

23C. Continuing functions in respect of former relevant children

(1) Each local authority shall have the duties provided for in this section towards —

    (a) a person who has been a relevant child for the purposes of section 23A (and would be one if he were under eighteen), and in relation to whom they were the last responsible authority; and

    (b) a person who was being looked after by them when he attained the age of eighteen, and immediately before ceasing to be looked after was an eligible child, and in this section such a person is referred to as a 'former relevant child'.

(2) It is the duty of the local authority to take reasonable steps —

    (a) to keep in touch with a former relevant child whether he is within their area or not; and

    (b) if they lose touch with him, to re-establish contact.

(3) It is the duty of the local authority —

    (a) to continue the appointment of a personal adviser for a former relevant child; and

    (b) to continue to keep his pathway plan under regular review.

(4) It is the duty of the local authority to give a former relevant child —

    (a) assistance of the kind referred to in section 24B(1), to the extent that his welfare requires it;

    (b) assistance of the kind referred to in section 24B(2), to the extent that his welfare and his educational or training needs require it;

    (c) other assistance, to the extent that his welfare requires it.

(5) The assistance given under subsection (4)(c) may be in kind or, in exceptional circumstances, in cash.

(6) Subject to subsection (7), the duties set out in subsections (2), (3) and (4) subsist until the former relevant child reaches the age of twenty-one.

(7) If the former relevant child's pathway plan sets out a programme of education or training which extends beyond his twenty-first birthday —

    (a) the duty set out in subsection (4)(b) continues to subsist for so long as the former relevant child continues to pursue that programme; and

    (b) the duties set out in subsections (2) and (3) continue to subsist concurrently with that duty.

(8) For the purposes of subsection (7)(a) there shall be disregarded any interruption in a former relevant child's pursuance of a programme of education or training if the local authority are satisfied that he will resume it as soon as is reasonably practicable.

(9) Section 24B(5) applies in relation to a person being given assistance under subsection (4)(b) as it applies in relation to a person to whom section 24B(3) applies.

(10) Subsections (7) to (9) of section 17 apply in relation to assistance given under this section as they apply in relation to assistance given under that section.

Personal advisers and pathway plans

23D. Personal advisers

(1) The Secretary of State may by regulations require local authorities to appoint a personal adviser for children or young persons of a prescribed description who have reached the age of sixteen but not the age of twenty-one who are not —

    (a) children who are relevant children for the purposes of section 23A;

    (b) the young persons referred to in section 23C; or

    (c) the children referred to in paragraph 19C of Schedule 2.

(2) Personal advisers appointed under or by virtue of this Part shall (in addition to any other functions) have such functions as the Secretary of State prescribes.

23E. Pathway plans
(1) In this Part, a reference to a 'pathway plan' is to a plan setting out —
  (a) in the case of a plan prepared under paragraph 19B of Schedule 2 —
    (i) the advice, assistance and support which the local authority intend to provide a child under this Part, both while they are looking after him and later; and
    (ii) when they might cease to look after him; and
  (b) in the case of a plan prepared under section 23B, the advice, assistance and support which the local authority intend to provide under this Part,
and dealing with such other matters (if any) as may be prescribed.
(2) The Secretary of State may by regulations make provision about pathway plans and their review.

Detailed supplementary provision is made in Schedule 2:

Identification of children in need and provision of information
1.(1) Every local authority shall take reasonable steps to identify the extent to which there are children in need within their area.
  (2) Every local authority shall —
    (a) publish information —
      (i) about services provided by them under sections 17, 18, 20, 23B to 23D, 24A and 24B; and
      (ii) where they consider it appropriate, about the provision by others (including, in particular, voluntary organisations) of services which the authority have power to provide under those sections; and
    (b) take such steps as are reasonably practicable to ensure that those who might benefit from the services receive the information relevant to them.

Children's services plans
1A.(1) Every local authority shall, on or before 31st March 1997 —
  (a) review their provision of services under sections 17, 20, 21, 23 and 24; and
  (b) having regard to that review and to their most recent review under section 19, prepare and publish a plan for the provision of services under Part III.
  (2) Every local authority —
  (a) shall, from time to time review the plan prepared by them under sub-paragraph (1)(b) (as modified or last substituted under this sub-paragraph), and
  (b) may, having regard to that review and to their most recent review under section 19, prepare and publish —
    (i) modifications (or, as the case may be, further modifications) to the plan reviewed; or
    (ii) a plan in substitution for that plan.
  (3) In carrying out any review under this paragraph and in preparing any plan or modifications to a plan, a local authority shall consult —
  (a) every Health Authority and Primary Care Trust the whole or any part of whose area lies within the area of the local authority;
  (b) every National Health Service trust which manages a hospital, establishment or facility (within the meaning of the National Health Service and Community Care Act 1990) in the authority's area;
  (c) if the local authority is not itself a local education authority, every local education authority the whole or any part of whose area lies within the area of the local authority;
  (d) any organisation which represents schools in the authority's area which are grant-maintained schools or grant-maintained special schools (within the meaning of the Education Act 1993);

(e) the governing body of every such school in the authority's area which is not so represented;

(f) such voluntary organisations as appear to the local authority —

    (i) to represent the interests of persons who use or are likely to use services provided by the local authority under Part III; or

    (ii) to provide services in the area of the local authority which, were they to be provided by the local authority, might be categorised as services provided under that Part.

(g) the chief constable of the police force for the area;

(h) the probation committee for the area;

(i) such other persons as appear to the local authority to be appropriate; and

(j) such other persons as the Secretary of State may direct.

(4) Every local authority shall, within 28 days of receiving a written request from the Secretary of State, submit to him a copy of —

(a) the plan prepared by them under sub-paragraph (1); or

(b) where that plan has been modified or substituted, the plan as modified or last substituted.

Maintenance of a register of disabled children

2.(1) Every local authority shall open and maintain a register of disabled children within their area.

(2) The register may be kept by means of a computer.

Assessment of children's needs

3. Where it appears to a local authority that a child within their area is in need, the authority may assess his needs for the purposes of this Act at the same time as any assessment of his needs is made under —

(a) the Chronically Sick and Disabled Persons Act 1970;

(b) Part IV of the Education Act 1996;

(c) the Disabled Persons (Services, Consultation and Representation) Act 1986; or

(d) any other enactment.

Prevention of neglect and abuse

4.(1) Every local authority shall take reasonable steps, through the provision of services under Part III of this Act, to prevent children within their area suffering ill-treatment or neglect.

(2) Where a local authority believe that a child who is at any time within their area —

(a) is likely to suffer harm; but

(b) lives or proposes to live in the area of another local authority

they shall inform that other local authority.

(3) When informing that other local authority they shall specify —

(a) the harm that they believe he is likely to suffer; and

(b) (if they can) where the child lives or proposes to live.

Provision of accommodation in order to protect child

5.(1) Where —

(a) it appears to a local authority that a child who is living on particular premises is suffering, or is likely to suffer, ill treatment at the hands of another person who is living on those premises; and

(b) that other person proposes to move from the premises,

the authority may assist that other person to obtain alternative accommodation.

(2) Assistance given under this paragraph may be in cash.

(3) Subsections (7) to (9) of section 17 shall apply in relation to assistance given under this paragraph as they apply in relation to assistance given under that section.

Provision for disabled children

6.   Every local authority shall provide services designed —
   (a) to minimise the effect on disabled children within their area of their disabilities; and
   (b) to give such children the opportunity to lead lives which are as normal as possible.

Provision to reduce need for care proceedings etc.

7.   Every local authority shall take reasonable steps designed —
   (a) to reduce the need to bring —
      (i)   proceedings for care or supervision orders with respect to children within their area;
      (ii) criminal proceedings against such children;
      (iii) any family or other proceedings with respect to such children which might lead to them being placed in the authority's care; or
      (iv) proceedings under the inherent jurisdiction of the High Court with respect to children;
   (b) to encourage children within their area not to commit criminal offences; and
   (c) to avoid the need for children within their area to be placed in secure accommodation.

Provision for children living with their families

8.   Every local authority shall make such provision as they consider appropriate for the following services to be available with respect to children in need within their area while they are living with their families —
   (a) advice, guidance and counselling;
   (b) occupational, social, cultural or recreational activities;
   (c) home help (which may include laundry facilities);
   (d) facilities for, or assistance with, travelling to and from home for the purpose of taking advantage of any other service provided under this Act or of any similar service;
   (e) assistance to enable the child concerned and his family to have a holiday.

Family centres

9.(1)   Every local authority shall provide such family centres as they consider appropriate in relation to children within their area.
   (2)   'Family centre' means a centre at which any of the persons mentioned in sub-paragraph (3) may —
   (a) attend for occupational, social, cultural or recreational activities;
   (b) attend for advice, guidance and counselling; or
   (c) be provided with accommodation while he is receiving advice, guidance or counselling.
   (3)   The persons are —
   (a) a child;
   (b) his parents;
   (c) any person who is not a parent of his but who has parental responsibility for him;
   (d) any other person who is looking after him.

Maintenance of the family home

10.   Every local authority shall take such steps as are reasonably practicable, where any child within their area who is in need and whom they are not looking after is living apart from his family —
   (a) to enable him to live with his family; or
   (b) to promote contact between him and his family,
if, in their opinion, it is necessary to do so in order to safeguard or promote his welfare.

Duty to consider racial groups to which children in need belong

11.   Every local authority shall, in making any arrangements —
   (a) for the provision of day care within their area; or
   (b) designed to encourage persons to act as local authority foster parents,
have regard to the different racial groups to which children within their area who are in need
belong.

...

Regulations as to placing of children with local authority foster parents

12.   Regulations under section 23(2)(a) may, in particular, make provision —
   (a) with regard to the welfare of children placed with local authority foster parents;
   (b) as to the arrangements to be made by local authorities in connection with the health
        and education of such children;
   (c) as to the records to be kept by local authorities;
   (d) for securing that a child is not placed with a local authority foster parent unless that
        person is for the time being approved as a local authority foster parent by such local
        authority as may be prescribed;
   (e) for securing that where possible the local authority foster parent with whom a child is
        to be placed is —
        (i)   of the same religious persuasion as the child; or
        (ii) gives an undertaking that the child will be brought up in that religious persuasion;
   (f) for securing that children placed with local authority foster parents, and the premises in
        which they are accommodated, will be supervised and inspected by a local authority and
        that the children will be removed from those premises if their welfare appears to require it;
   (g) as to the circumstances in which local authorities may make arrangements for duties
        imposed on them by the regulations to be discharged, on their behalf.

Regulations as to arrangements under section 23(2)(f)

13.   Regulations under section 23(2)(f) may, in particular, make provision as to —
   (a) the persons to be notified of any proposed arrangements;
   (b) the opportunities such persons are to have to make representations in relation to the
        arrangements proposed;
   (c) the persons to be notified of any proposed changes in arrangements;
   (d) the records to be kept by local authorities;
   (e) the supervision by local authorities of any arrangements made.

Regulations as to conditions under which child in care is allowed to live with parent, etc.

14.   Regulations under section 23(5) may, in particular, impose requirements on a local authority
as to —
   (a) the making of any decision by a local authority to allow a child to live with any person
        falling within section 23(4) (including requirements as to those who must be consulted
        before the decision is made, and those who must be notified when it has been made);
   (b) the supervision or medical examination of the child concerned;
   (c) the removal of the child, in such circumstances as may be prescribed, from the care of
        the person with whom he has been allowed to live;
   (d) the records to be kept by local authorities.

Promotion and maintenance of contact between child and family

15.(1)   Where a child is being looked after by a local authority, the authority shall, unless it is
not reasonably practicable or consistent with his welfare, endeavour to promote contact between
the child and —
   (a) his parents;
   (b) any person who is not a parent of his but who has parental responsibility for him; and

(c) any relative, friend or other person connected with him.
(2)   Where a child is being looked after by a local authority —
(a) the authority shall take such steps as are reasonably practicable to secure that —
(i)   his parents; and
(ii)   any person who is not a parent of his but who has parental responsibility for him,
are kept informed of where he is being accommodated; and
(b) every such person shall secure that the authority are kept informed of his or her address.
(3)   Where a local authority ('the receiving authority') take over the provision of accommodation for a child from another local authority ('the transferring authority') under section 20(2) —
(a) the receiving authority shall (where reasonably practicable) inform —
(i)   the child's parents; and
(ii)   any person who is not a parent of his but who has parental responsibility for him;
(b) sub-paragraph (2)(a) shall apply to the transferring authority, as well as the receiving authority, until at least one such person has been informed of the change; and
(c) sub-paragraph (2)(b) shall not require any person to inform the receiving authority of his address until he has been so informed.
(4)   Nothing in this paragraph requires a local authority to inform any person of the whereabouts of a child if —
(a) the child is in the care of the authority; and
(b) the authority has reasonable cause to believe that informing the person would prejudice the child's welfare.
(5)   Any person who fails (without reasonable excuse) to comply with sub-paragraph (2)(b) shall be guilty of an offence and liable on summary conviction to a fine not exceeding level 2 on the standard scale.
(6)   It shall be a defence in any proceedings under sub-paragraph (5) to prove that the defendant was residing at the same address as another person who was the child's parent or had parental responsibility for the child and had reasonable cause to believe that the other person had informed the appropriate authority that both of them were residing at that address.

Visits to or by children: expenses
16.(1)   This paragraph applies where —
(a) a child is being looked after by a local authority; and
(b) the conditions mentioned in sub-paragraph (3) are satisfied.
(2)   The authority may —
(a) make payments to —
(i)   a parent of the child;
(ii)   any person who is not a parent of his but who has parental responsibility for him; or
(iii)   any relative, friend or other person connected with him,
in respect of travelling, subsistence or other expenses incurred by that person in visiting the child; or
(b) make payments to the child, or to any person on his behalf, in respect of travelling, subsistence or other expenses incurred by or on behalf of the child in his visiting —
(i)   a parent of his;
(ii)   any person who is not a parent of his but who has parental responsibility for him; or
(iii)   any relative, friend or other person connected with him.
(3)   The conditions are that —
(a) it appears to the authority that the visit in question could not otherwise be made without undue financial hardship; and
(b) the circumstances warrant the making of the payments.

Appointment of visitor for child who is not being visited

17.(1) Where it appears to a local authority in relation to any child that they are looking after that —

(a) communication between the child and —
(i) a parent of his; or
(ii) any person who is not a parent of his but who has parental responsibility for him,

has been infrequent; or

(b) he has not visited or been visited by (or lived with) any such person during the preceeding twelve months,

and that it would be in the child's best interests for an independent person to be appointed to be his visitor for the purposes of this paragraph, they shall appoint such a visitor.

(2) A person so appointed shall —

(a) have the duty of visiting, advising and befriending the child; and
(b) be entitled to recover from the authority who appointed him any reasonable expenses incurred by him for the purposes of his functions under this paragraph.

(3) A person's appointment as a visitor in pursuance of this paragraph shall be determined if —

(a) he gives notice in writing to the authority who appointed him that he resigns the appointment; or
(b) the authority give him notice in writing that they have terminated it.

(4) The determination of such an appointment shall not prejudice any duty under this paragraph to make a further appointment.

(5) Where a local authority propose to appoint a visitor for a child under this paragraph, the appointment shall not be made if —

(a) the child objects to it; and
(b) the authority are satisfied that he has sufficient understanding to make an informed decision.

(6) Where a visitor has been appointed for a child under this paragraph, the local authority shall determine the appointment if —

(a) the child objects to its continuing; and
(b) the authority are satisfied that he has sufficient understanding to make an informed decision.

(7) The Secretary of State may make regulations as to the circumstances in which a person appointed as a visitor under this paragraph is to be regarded as independent of the local authority appointing him.

Arrangements to assist children to live abroad

19.(1) A local authority may only arrange for, or assist in arranging for, any child in their care to live outside England and Wales with the approval of the court.

(2) A local authority may, with the approval of every person who has parental responsibility for the child arrange for, or assist in arranging for, any other child looked after by them to live outside England and Wales.

(3) The court shall not give its approval under sub-paragraph (1) unless it is satisfied that —

(a) living outside England and Wales would be in the child's best interests;
(b) suitable arrangements have been, or will be, made for his reception and welfare in the country in which he will live;
(c) the child has consented to living in that country; and
(d) every person who has parental responsibility for the child has consented to his living in that country.

(4) Where the court is satisfied that the child does not have sufficient understanding to give or withhold his consent, it may disregard sub-paragraph (3)(c) and give its approval if the child is to live in the country concerned with a parent, guardian, or other suitable person.

(5)　Where a person whose consent is required by sub-paragraph (3)(d) fails to give his consent, the court may disregard that provision and give its approval if it is satisfied that that person —

(a)　cannot be found;

(b)　is incapable of consenting; or

(c)　is withholding his consent unreasonably.

(6)　Section 56 of the Adoption Act 1976 (which requires authority for the taking or sending abroad for adoption of a child who is a British subject) shall not apply in the case of any child who is to live outside England and Wales with the approval of the court given under this paragraph.

(7)　Where a court decides to give its approval under this paragraph it may order that its decision is not to have effect during the appeal period.

(8)　In sub-paragraph (7) 'the appeal period' means —

(a)　where an appeal is made against the decision, the period between the making of the decision and the determination of the appeal; and

(b)　otherwise, the period during which an appeal may be made against the decision.

Preparation for ceasing to be looked after

19A.　It is the duty of the local authority looking after a child to advise, assist and befriend him with a view to promoting his welfare when they have ceased to look after him.

19B.(1)　A local authority shall have the following additional functions in relation to an eligible child whom they are looking after.

(2)　In sub-paragraph (1) 'eligible child' means, subject to sub-paragraph (3), a child who —

(a)　is aged sixteen or seventeen; and

(b)　has been looked after by a local authority for a prescribed period, or periods amounting in all to a prescribed period, which began after he reached a prescribed age and ended after he reached the age of sixteen.

(3)　The Secretary of State may prescribe —

(a)　additional categories of eligible children; and

(b)　categories of children who are not to be eligible children despite falling within sub-paragraph (2).

(4)　For each eligible child, the local authority shall carry out an assessment of his needs with a view to determining what advice, assistance and support it would be appropriate for them to provide him under this Act —

(a)　while they are still looking after him; and

(b)　after they cease to look after him,

and shall then prepare a pathway plan for him.

(5)　The local authority shall keep the pathway plan under regular review.

(6)　Any such review may be carried out at the same time as a review of the child's case carried out by virtue of section 26.

(7)　The Secretary of State may by regulations make provision as to assessments for the purposes of sub-paragraph (4).

(8)　The regulations may in particular provide for the matters set out in section 23B(6).

Personal advisers

19C.　A local authority shall arrange for each child whom they are looking after who is an eligible child for the purposes of paragraph 19B to have a personal adviser.

Death of children being looked after by local authorities

20.(1)　If a child who is being looked after by a local authority dies, the authority —

(a)　shall notify the Secretary of State;

(b)　shall, so far as is reasonably practicable, notify the child's parents and every person who is not a parent of his but who has parental responsibility for him;

(c) may, with the consent (so far as it is reasonably practicable to obtain it) of every person who has parental responsibility for the child, arrange for the child's body to be buried or cremated; and

(d) may, if the conditions mentioned in sub-paragraph (2) are satisfied, make payments to any person who has parental responsibility for the child, or any relative, friend or other person connected with the child, in respect of travelling, subsistence or other expenses incurred by that person in attending the child's funeral.

(2) The conditions are that —

(a) it appears to the authority that the person concerned could not otherwise attend the child's funeral without undue financial hardship; and

(b) that the circumstances warrant the making of the payments.

(3) Sub-paragraph (1) does not authorise cremation where it does not accord with the practice of the child's religious persuasion.

(4) Where a local authority have exercised their power under sub-paragraph (1)(c) with respect to a child who was under sixteen when he died, they may recover from any parent of the child any expenses incurred by them.

(5) Any sums so recoverable shall, without prejudice to any other method of recovery, be recoverable summarily as a civil debt.

(6) Nothing in this paragraph affects any enactment regulating or authorising the burial, cremation or anatomical examination of the body of a deceased person.

...

Liability to contribute

21.(1) Where a local authority are looking after a child (other than in the cases mentioned in sub-paragraph (7)) they shall consider whether they should recover contributions towards the child's maintenance from any person liable to contribute ('a contributor').

(2) An authority may only recover contributions from a contributor if they consider it reasonable to do so.

(3) The persons liable to contribute are —

(a) where the child is under sixteen, each of his parents;

(b) where he has reached the age of sixteen, the child himself.

(4) A parent is not liable to contribute during any period when he is in receipt of income support, working families' tax credit or disabled person's tax credit under Part VII of the Social Security Contributions and Benefits Act 1992 or of an income-based jobseeker's allowance.

(5) A person is not liable to contribute towards the maintenance of a child in the care of a local authority in respect of any period during which the child is allowed by the authority (under section 23(5)) to live with a parent of his.

(6) A contributor is not obliged to make any contribution towards a child's maintenance except as agreed or determined in accordance with this Part of this Schedule.

(7) The cases are where the child is looked after by a local authority under —

(a) section 21;

(b) an interim care order;

(c) section 92 of the Powers of Criminal Courts (Sentencing) Act 2000.

Agreed contributions

22.(1) Contributions towards a child's maintenance may only be recovered if the local authority have served a notice ('a contribution notice') on the contributor specifying —

(a) the weekly sum which they consider that he should contribute; and

(b) arrangements for payment.

(2) The contribution notice must be in writing and dated.

(3) Arrangements for payment shall, in particular, include —
- (a) the date on which liability to contribute begins (which must not be earlier than the date of the notice);
- (b) the date on which liability under the notice will end (if the child has not before that date ceased to be looked after by the authority); and
- (c) the date on which the first payment is to be made.

(4) The authority may specify in a contribution notice a weekly sum which is a standard contribution determined by them for all children looked after by them.

(5) The authority may not specify in a contribution notice a weekly sum greater than that which they consider —
- (a) they would normally be prepared to pay if they had placed a similar child with local authority foster parents; and
- (b) it is reasonably practicable for the contributor to pay (having regard to his means).

(6) An authority may at any time withdraw a contribution notice (without prejudice to their power to serve another).

(7) Where the authority and the contributor agree —
- (a) the sum which the contributor is to contribute; and
- (b) arrangements for payment,

(whether as specified in the contribution notice or otherwise) and the contributor notifies the authority in writing that he so agrees, the authority may recover summarily as a civil debt any contribution which is overdue and unpaid.

(8) A contributor may, by serving a notice in writing on the authority, withdraw his agreement in relation to any period of liability falling after the date of service of the notice.

(9) Sub-paragraph (7) is without prejudice to any other method of recovery.

Contribution orders

23.(1) Where a contributor has been served with a contribution notice and has —
- (a) failed to reach any agreement with the local authority as mentioned in paragraph 22(7) within the period of one month beginning with the day on which the contribution notice was served; or
- (b) served a notice under paragraph 22(8) withdrawing his agreement,

the authority may apply to the court for an order under this paragraph.

(2) On such an application the court may make an order ('a contribution order') requiring the contributor to contribute a weekly sum towards the child's maintenance in accordance with arrangements for payment specified by the court.

(3) A contribution order —
- (a) shall not specify a weekly sum greater than that specified in the contribution notice; and
- (b) shall be made with due regard to the contributor's means.

(4) A contribution order shall not —
- (a) take effect before the date specified in the contribution notice; or
- (b) have effect while the contributor is not liable to contribute (by virtue of paragraph 21); or
- (c) remain in force after the child has ceased to be looked after by the authority who obtained the order.

(5) An authority may not apply to the court under sub-paragraph (1) in relation to a contribution notice which they have withdrawn.

(6) Where —
- (a) a contribution order is in force;
- (b) the authority serve another contribution notice; and
- (c) the contributor and the authority reach an agreement under paragraph 22(7) in respect of that other contribution notice,

the effect of the agreement shall be to discharge the order from the date on which it is agreed that the agreement shall take effect.

(7) Where an agreement is reached under sub-paragraph (6) the authority shall notify the court —

   (a) of the agreement; and

   (b) of the date on which it took effect.

(8) A contribution order may be varied or revoked on the application of the contributor or the authority.

(9) In proceedings for the variation of a contribution order, the authority shall specify —

   (a) the weekly sum which, having regard to paragraph 22, they propose that the contributor should contribute under the order as varied; and

   (b) the proposed arrangements for payment.

(10) Where a contribution order is varied, the order —

   (a) shall not specify a weekly sum greater than that specified by the authority in the proceedings for variation; and

   (b) shall be made with due regard to the contributor's means.

(11) An appeal shall lie in accordance with rules of court from any order made under this paragraph.

Enforcement of contribution orders etc.

24.(1) A contribution order made by a magistrates' court shall be enforceable as a magistrates' court maintenance order (within the meaning of section 150(1) of the Magistrates' Courts Act 1980).

(2) Where a contributor has agreed, or has been ordered, to make contributions to a local authority, any other local authority within whose area the contributor is for the time being living may —

   (a) at the request of the local authority who served the contribution notice; and

   (b) subject to agreement as to any sum to be deducted in respect of services rendered,

collect from the contributor any contributions due on behalf of the authority who served the notice.

...

(4) The power to collect sums under sub-paragraph (2) includes the power to —

   (a) receive and give a discharge for any contributions due; and

   (b) (if necessary) enforce payment of any contributions,

even though those contributions may have fallen due at a time when the contributor was living elsewhere.

(5) Any contribution collected under sub-paragraph (2) shall be paid (subject to any agreed deduction) to the local authority who served the contribution notice.

(6) In any proceedings under this paragraph, a document which purports to be —

   (a) a copy of an order made by a court under or by virtue of paragraph 23; and

   (b) certified as a true copy by the justices' chief executive for the court,

shall be evidence of the order.

(7) In any proceedings under this paragraph, a certificate which —

   (a) purports to be signed by the clerk or some other duly authorised officer of the local authority who obtained the contribution order; and

   (b) states that any sum due to the authority under the order is overdue and unpaid,

shall be evidence that the sum is overdue and unpaid.

Regulations

25. The Secretary of State may make regulations —
   (a) as to the considerations which a local authority must take into account in deciding —
      (i) whether it is reasonable to recover contributions; and
      (ii) what the arrangements for payment should be;
   (b) as to the procedures they must follow in reaching agreements with —
      (i) contributors (under paragraphs 22 and 23); and
      (ii) any other local authority (under paragraph 23).

Additional duties are now imposed on local authorities in respect of children leaving their care under the Children (Leaving Care) Act 2000 (not reproduced here).

By contrast with Part III, Parts IV and V contain compulsory measures, which, with the exception of s. 46, require application to a court. Part IV deals with care and supervision, whilst Part V is concerned with child protection. The key concept for both parts lies in the concept of 'significant harm', which is defined in s. 31, which also contains provisions for the making of care and supervision orders:

31. Care and supervision orders

(1) On the application of any local authority or authorised person, the court may make an order —
   (a) placing the child with respect to whom the application is made in the care of a designated local authority; or
   (b) putting him under the supervision of a designated local authority.

(2) A court may only make a care order or supervision order if it is satisfied —
   (a) that the child concerned is suffering, or is likely to suffer, significant harm; and
   (b) that the harm, or likelihood of harm, is attributable to —
      (i) the care given to the child, or likely to be given to him if the order were not made, not being what it would be reasonable to expect a parent to give to him; or
      (ii) the child's being beyond parental control.

(3) No care order or supervision order may be made with respect to a child who has reached the age of seventeen (or sixteen, in the case of a child who is married).

(4) An application under this section may be made on its own or in any other family proceedings.

(5) The court may —
   (a) on an application for a care order, make a supervision order;
   (b) on an application for a supervision order, make a care order.

(6) Where an authorised person proposes to make an application under this section he shall —
   (a) if it is reasonably practicable to do so; and
   (b) before making the application,
consult the local authority appearing to him to be the authority in whose area the child concerned is ordinarily resident.

(7) An application made by an authorised person shall not be entertained by the court if, at the time when it is made, the child concerned is —
   (a) the subject of an earlier application for a care order, or supervision order, which has not been disposed of; or
   (b) subject to —
      (i) a care order or supervision order;
      (ii) an order under section 63(1) of the Powers of Criminal Courts (Sentencing) Act 2000; ...

(8) The local authority designated in a care order must be —
   (a) the authority within whose area the child is ordinarily resident; or
   (b) where the child does not reside in the area of a local authority, the authority within whose area any circumstances arose in consequence of which the order is being made.
(9) In this section —
   'authorised person' means —
   (a) the National Society for the Prevention of Cruelty to Children and any of its officers; and
   (b) any person authorised by order of the Secretary of State to bring proceedings under this section and any officer of a body which is so authorised.
   'harm' means ill-treatment or the impairment of health or development;

   'development' means physical, intellectual, emotional, social or behavioural development;

   'health' means physical or mental health; and

   'ill-treatment' includes sexual abuse and forms of ill-treatment which are not physical.

(10) Where the question of whether harm suffered by a child is significant turns on the child's health or development, his health or development shall be compared with that which could reasonably be expected of a similar child.
(11) In this Act —
   'a care order' means (subject to section 105(1)) an order under subsection (1)(a) and (except where express provision to the contrary is made) includes an interim care order made under section 38; and

   'a supervision order' means an order under subsection (1)(b) and (except where express provision to the contrary is made) includes an interim supervision order made under section 38.

Working Together notes:

2.16   The Children Act 1989 introduced the concept of significant harm as the threshold that justifies compulsory intervention in family life in the best interests of children. The local authority is under a duty to make enquiries, or cause enquiries to be made, where it has reasonable cause to suspect that a child is suffering, or likely to suffer significant harm (s. 47). A court may only make a care order (committing the child to the care of the local authority) or supervision order (putting the child under the supervision of a social worker, or a probation officer) in respect of a child if it is satisfied that:
   • the child is suffering, or is likely to suffer, significant harm; *and*
   • that the harm or likelihood of harm is attributable to a lack of adequate parental care or control (s. 31).

2.17   There are no absolute criteria on which to rely when judging what constitutes significant harm. Consideration of the severity of ill-treatment may include the degree and the extent of physical harm, the duration and frequency of abuse and neglect, and the extent of premeditation, degree of threat and coercion, sadism, and bizarre or unusual elements in child sexual abuse. Each of these elements has been associated with more severe effects on the child, and/or relatively greater difficulty in helping the child overcome the adverse impact of the ill-treatment. Sometimes, a single traumatic event may constitute significant harm, e.g. a violent assault, suffocation or poisoning. More often, significant harm is a compilation of significant events, both acute and long-standing, which interrupt, change or damage the child's physical and psychological development. Some children live in family and social circumstances where their health and development are neglected. For them, it is the corrosiveness of long-term emotional, physical or sexual abuse that causes impairment to the extent of constituting significant harm. In each case, it is necessary to consider any ill-treatment alongside the family's strengths and supports.

2.18   To understand and establish significant harm, it is necessary to consider:
* the family context;
* the child's development within the context of their family and wider social and cultural environment;
* any special needs, such as a medical condition, communication difficulty or disability that may affect the child's development and care within the family;
* the nature of harm, in terms of ill-treatment or failure to provide adequate care;
* the impact on the child's health and development; *and*
* the adequacy of parental care.

It is important always to take account of the child's reactions, and his or her perceptions, according to the child's age and understanding.

As the extract from *Working Together* illustrates, a key matter is the nature and weight of evidence needed to decide whether a child is 'likely to suffer significant harm'. This was the issue for the House of Lords to decide in *Re H and others (Minors)(Sexual Abuse: Standard of Proof)* [1996] AC 563. The facts and issues appear in the judgment of Lord Nicholls of Birkenhead:

My Lords, the subject of this appeal is the care of children. Section 31 of the Children Act 1989 empowers the court to make an order placing a child in the care of a local authority or putting a child under the supervision of a local authority or a probation officer. Section 31(2) provides that a court may only make such an order:
'if it is satisfied — (a) that the child concerned is suffering, or is likely to suffer, significant harm; and (b) that the harm, or likelihood of harm, is attributable to — (i) the care given to the child, or likely to be given him if the order were not made, not being what it would be reasonable to expect a parent to give to him; or (ii) the child's being beyond parental control.'
In short, the court must be satisfied of the existence or likelihood of harm attributable either to the care the child is receiving or likely to receive or to the child being beyond parental control. Harm means ill-treatment or impairment of health or development: see section 31(9). This appeal concerns the need for the court to be 'satisfied' that the child is suffering significant harm or is 'likely' to do so.
For present purposes I can summarise [the facts] shortly. The mother has four children, all girls. D1 and D2 were children of her marriage to Mr H in 1979. D1 was born in June 1978 and D2 in August 1981. Mr H and the mother then separated. In 1984 she commenced living with Mr R and they had two children: D3, born in March 1985, and D4, born in April 1992.
In September 1993, when she was 15, D1 made a statement to the police. She said she had been sexually abused by Mr R ever since she was 7 or 8 years old. She was then accommodated with foster-parents, and Mr R was charged with having raped her. In February 1994 the local authority applied for care orders in respect of the three younger girls. Interim care orders were made, followed by interim supervision orders.
In October 1994 Mr R was tried on an indictment containing four counts of rape of D1. D1 was the principal witness for the Crown. The jury acquitted Mr R on all counts after a very short retirement. Despite this the local authority proceeded with the applications for care orders in respect of D2, D3 and D4. These girls were then aged 13, 8 and 2 years. The local authority's case, and this is an important feature of these proceedings, was based solely on the alleged sexual abuse of D1 by Mr R. Relying on the different standard of proof applicable in civil and criminal matters, the local authority asked the judge still to find that Mr R had sexually abused D1, or at least that there was a substantial risk he had done so, thereby, so it was said, satisfying the section 31(2) conditions for the making of a care order in respect of the three younger girls.

The applications were heard by Judge Davidson QC sitting in the Nottingham County Court. On 23 November, after a hearing lasting seven days, he dismissed the applications. He was not impressed by the evidence of Mr R or of the mother. Nevertheless he concluded he could not be sure 'to the requisite high standard of proof' that D1's allegations were true. He added:

'It must follow that the statutory criteria for the making of a care order are not made out. This is far from saying that I am satisfied the child's complaints are untrue. I do not brush them aside as the jury seem to have done. I am, at the least, more than a little suspicious that [Mr R] has abused her as she says. If it were relevant, I would be prepared to hold that there is a real possibility that her statement and her evidence are true, nor has [Mr R] by his evidence and demeanour, not only throughout the hearing but the whole of this matter, done anything to dispel those suspicions, but this in the circumstances is nihil ad rem.'

By a majority, comprising the President and Millett LJ, the Court of Appeal dismissed an appeal by the local authority. Kennedy LJ disagreed.

He then goes on to discuss the resolution of those issues in a closely argued judgment which bears extended quotation:

'Likely' to suffer harm

I shall consider first the meaning of 'likely' in the expression 'likely to suffer significant harm' in section 31. In your Lordships' House Mr Levy advanced an argument not open in the courts below. He submitted that likely means probable, and that the decision of the Court of Appeal to the contrary in *Newham London Borough Council* v *AG* [1993] 1 FLR 281 was wrong. I cannot accept this contention.

In everyday usage one meaning of the word likely, perhaps its primary meaning, is probable, in the sense of more likely than not. This is not its only meaning. If I am going walking on Kinder Scout and ask whether it is likely to rain, I am using likely in a different sense. I am inquiring whether there is a real risk of rain, a risk that ought not to be ignored. In which sense is likely being used in this subsection?

In section 31(2) Parliament has stated the prerequisites which must exist before the court has power to make a care order. These prerequisites mark the boundary line drawn by Parliament between the differing interests. On one side are the interests of parents in caring for their own child, a course which prima facie is also in the interests of the child. On the other side there will be circumstances in which the interests of the child may dictate a need for his care to be entrusted to others. In section 31(2) Parliament has stated the minimum conditions which must be present before the court can look more widely at all the circumstances and decide whether the child's welfare requires that a local authority shall receive the child into their care and have parental responsibility for him. The court must be satisfied that the child is already suffering significant harm. Or the court must be satisfied that, looking ahead, although the child may not yet be suffering such harm, he or she is likely to do so in the future. The court may make a care order if, but only if, it is satisfied in one or other of these respects.

In this context Parliament cannot have been using likely in the sense of more likely than not. If the word likely were given this meaning, it would have the effect of leaving outside the scope of care and supervision orders cases where the court is satisfied there is a real possibility of significant harm to the child in the future but that possibility falls short of being more likely than not. Strictly, if this were the correct reading of the Act, a care or supervision order would not be available even in a case where the risk of significant harm is as likely as not. Nothing would suffice short of proof that the child will probably suffer significant harm.

The difficulty with this interpretation of section 31(2)(a) is that it would draw the boundary line at an altogether inapposite point. What is in issue is the prospect, or risk, of the child suffering significant harm. When exposed to this risk a child may need protection just as much when the risk is considered to be less than 50–50 as when the risk is of a higher order.

Conversely, so far as the parents are concerned, there is no particular magic in a threshold test based on a probability of significant harm as distinct from a real possibility. It is otherwise if there is no real possibility. It is eminently understandable that Parliament should provide that where there is no real possibility of significant harm, parental responsibility should remain solely with the parents. That makes sense as a threshold in the interests of the parents and the child in a way that a higher threshold, based on probability, would not.

In my view, therefore, the context shows that in section 31(2)(a) likely is being used in the sense of a real possibility, a possibility that cannot sensibly be ignored having regard to the nature and gravity of the feared harm in the particular case. By parity of reasoning the expression likely to suffer significant harm bears the same meaning elsewhere in the Act; for instance, in sections 43, 44 and 46. Likely also bears a similar meaning, for a similar reason, in the requirement in section 31(2)(b) that the harm or likelihood of harm must be attributable to the care given to the child or 'likely' to be given him if the order were not made.

The burden of proof

The power of the court to make a care or supervision order only arises if the court is 'satisfied' that the criteria stated in section 31(2) exist. The expression 'if the court is satisfied,' here and elsewhere in the Act, envisages that the court must be judicially satisfied on proper material. There is also inherent in the expression an indication of the need for the subject matter to be affirmatively proved. If the court is left in a state of indecision the matter has not been established to the level, or standard, needed for the court to be 'satisfied.' Thus in section 31(2), in order for the threshold to be crossed, the conditions set out in paragraphs (a) and (b) must be affirmatively established to the satisfaction of the court. The legal burden of establishing the existence of these conditions rests on the applicant for a care order. The general principle is that he who asserts must prove. Generally, although there are exceptions, a plaintiff or applicant must establish the existence of all the preconditions and other facts entitling him to the order he seeks. There is nothing in the language or context of section 31(2) to suggest that the normal principle should not apply to the threshold conditions.

The standard of proof

Where the matters in issue are facts the standard of proof required in non-criminal proceedings is the preponderance of probability, usually referred to as the balance of probability. This is the established general principle. There are exceptions such as contempt of court applications, but I can see no reason for thinking that family proceedings are, or should be, an exception. By family proceedings I mean proceedings so described in the Act of 1989, sections 105 and 8(3). Despite their special features, family proceedings remain essentially a form of civil proceedings. Family proceedings often raise very serious issues, but so do other forms of civil proceedings.

The balance of probability standard means that a court is satisfied an event occurred if the court considers that, on the evidence, the occurrence of the event was more likely than not. When assessing the probabilities the court will have in mind as a factor, to whatever extent is appropriate in the particular case, that the more serious the allegation the less likely it is that the event occurred and, hence, the stronger should be the evidence before the court concludes that the allegation is established on the balance of probability. Fraud is usually less likely than negligence. Deliberate physical injury is usually less likely than accidental physical injury. A stepfather is usually less likely to have repeatedly raped and had non-consensual oral sex with his under age stepdaughter than on some occasion to have lost his temper and slapped her. Built into the preponderance of probability standard is a generous degree of flexibility in respect of the seriousness of the allegation.

Although the result is much the same, this does not mean that where a serious allegation is in issue the standard of proof required is higher. It means only that the inherent probability or improbability of an event is itself a matter to be taken into account when weighing the probabilities and deciding whether, on balance, the event occurred. The more improbable the event, the stronger must be the evidence that it did occur before, on the balance of probability, its occurrence will be established. Ungoed-Thomas J expressed this neatly in *In re Dellow's Will Trusts* [1964] 1 WLR 451, 455: 'The more serious the allegation the more cogent is the evidence required to overcome the unlikelihood of what is alleged and thus to prove it.'

...

The threshold conditions

There is no difficulty in applying [the ordinary civil] standard to the threshold conditions. The first limb of section 31(2)(a) predicates an existing state of affairs: that the child is suffering significant harm. The relevant time for this purpose is the date of the care order application or, if temporary protective arrangements have been continuously in place from an earlier date, the date when those arrangements were initiated. This was decided by your Lordships' House in *In re M (A Minor) (Care Orders: Threshold Conditions)* [1994] 2 AC 424. Whether at that time the child was suffering significant harm is an issue to be decided by the court on the basis of the facts admitted or proved before it. The balance of probability standard applies to proof of the facts.

The same approach applies to the second limb of section 31(2)(a). This is concerned with evaluating the risk of something happening in the future: aye or no, is there a real possibility that the child will suffer significant harm? Having heard and considered the evidence, and decided any disputed questions of relevant fact upon the balance of probability, the court must reach a decision on how highly it evaluates the risk of significant harm befalling the child, always remembering upon whom the burden of proof rests.

Suspicion and the threshold conditions

This brings me to the most difficult part of the appeal. The problem is presented in stark form by the facts in this case. The local authority do not suggest that the first limb of section 31(2)(a) is satisfied in respect of D2, D3 or D4. They do not seek a finding that any of the three younger girls is suffering harm. Their case for the making of a care order is based exclusively on the second limb. In support of the allegation that D2, D3 and D4 are likely to suffer significant harm, the local authority rely solely upon the allegation that over many years D1 was subject to repeated sexual abuse by Mr R.

The judge held that the latter allegation was not made out. Mr R did not establish that abuse did not occur. The outcome on this disputed serious allegation of fact was that the local authority, upon whom the burden of proof rested, failed to establish that abuse did occur. However, the judge remained suspicious and, had it been relevant, he would have held there was a reasonable possibility that D1's allegations were true. The question arising from these conclusions can be expressed thus: when a local authority assert but fail to prove past misconduct, can the judge's suspicions or lingering doubts on that issue form the basis for concluding that the second limb of section 31(2)(a) has been established?

In many instances where misconduct is alleged but not proved this question will not arise. Other allegations may be proved. The matters proved may suffice to show a likelihood of future harm. However, the present case is not unique. *In re P (A Minor) (Care: Evidence)* [1994] 2 FLR 751 is another instance where the same problem arose. There the only matter relied upon was the death of the child's baby brother while in the care of the parents. Douglas Brown J held that it was for the local authority to prove that the death was non-accidental and that, since they failed to do so, there was no factual basis for a finding of likelihood of harm to the surviving child.

In the Court of Appeal [1995] 1 FLR 643 in the present case the President adopted the same approach, at p. 652. Since the judge rejected the only allegation which gave rise to the applications for care orders, it was not then open to him to go on and consider the likelihood of harm to the children. Millett LJ agreed. He said, at p. 657:

> 'where the risk of harm depends on the truth of disputed allegations, the court must investigate them and determine whether they are true or false. Unless it finds that they are true, it cannot be satisfied that the child is likely to suffer significant harm if the order is not made.'

A conclusion based on facts

The starting point here is that courts act on evidence. They reach their decisions on the basis of the evidence before them. When considering whether an applicant for a care order has shown that the child is suffering harm or is likely to do so, a court will have regard to the undisputed evidence. The judge will attach to that evidence such weight, or importance, as he considers appropriate. Likewise with regard to disputed evidence which the judge accepts as reliable. None of that is controversial. But the rejection of a disputed allegation as not proved on the balance of probability leaves scope for the possibility that the non-proven allegation may be true after all. There remains room for the judge to have doubts and suspicions on this score. This is the area of controversy.

In my view these unresolved judicial doubts and suspicions can no more form the basis of a conclusion that the second threshold condition in section 31(2)(a) has been established than they can form the basis of a conclusion that the first has been established. My reasons are as follows.

Evidence is the means whereby relevant facts are proved in court. What the evidence is required to establish depends upon the issue the court has to decide. At some interlocutory hearings, for instance, the issue will be whether the plaintiff has a good arguable case. The plaintiff may assert he is at risk of the defendant trespassing on his land or committing a breach of contract and that, in consequence, he will suffer serious damage. When deciding whether to grant an interlocutory injunction the court will not be concerned to resolve disputes raised by the parties, conflicting affidavit evidence.

At trials, however, the court normally has to resolve disputed issues of relevant fact before it can reach its conclusion on the issue it has to decide. This is a commonplace exercise, carried out daily by courts and tribunals throughout the country. This exercise applies as much where the issue is whether an event may happen in the future as where the issue is whether an event did or did not happen in the past. To decide whether a car was being driven negligently, the court will have to decide what was happening immediately before the accident and how the car was being driven and why. Its findings on these facts form the essential basis for its conclusion on the issue of whether the car was being driven with reasonable care. Likewise, if the issue before the court concerns the possibility of something happening in the future, such as whether the name or get-up under which goods are being sold is likely to deceive future buyers. To decide that issue the court must identify and, when disputed, decide the relevant facts about the way the goods are being sold and to whom and in what circumstances. Then, but only then, can the court reach a conclusion on the crucial issue. A decision by a court on the likelihood of a future happening must be founded on a basis of present facts and the inferences fairly to be drawn therefrom.

The same, familiar approach is applicable when a court is considering whether the threshold conditions in section 31(2)(a) are established. Here, as much as anywhere else, the court's conclusion must be founded on a factual base. The court must have before it facts on which its conclusion can properly be based. That is clearly so in the case of the first limb of section 31(2)(a). There must be facts, proved to the court's satisfaction if disputed, on which the court can properly conclude that the child is suffering harm. An alleged but non-proven fact is not a fact for this purpose. Similarly with the second limb: there must be facts from which the court can properly conclude there is a real possibility that the child will suffer harm in the future. Here also, if the facts are disputed, the court must resolve the dispute so far as necessary to reach a proper conclusion on the issue it has to decide.

There are several indications in the Act that when considering the threshold conditions the court is to apply the ordinary approach, of founding its conclusion on facts, and that nothing less will do. The first pointer is the difference in the statutory language when dealing with earlier stages in the procedures which may culminate in a care order. Under Part V of the Act a local authority are under a duty to investigate where they have 'reasonable cause to suspect' that a child is suffering or is likely to suffer harm. The court may make a child assessment order if satisfied that the applicant has 'reasonable cause to suspect' that the child is suffering or is likely to suffer harm. The police may take steps to remove or prevent the removal of a child where a constable has 'reasonable cause to believe' that the child would otherwise be likely to suffer harm. The court may make an emergency protection order only if satisfied there is 'reasonable cause to believe' that the child is likely to suffer harm in certain eventualities. Under section 38 the court may make an interim care order or an interim supervision order if satisfied there are 'reasonable grounds for believing' that the section 31(2) circumstances exist.

In marked contrast is the wording of section 31(2). The earlier stages are concerned with pre-liminary or interim steps or orders. Reasonable cause to believe or suspect provides the test. At those stages, as in my example of an application for an interlocutory injunction, there will usu-ally not have been a full court hearing. But when the stage is reached of making a care order, with the far-reaching consequences this may have for the child and the parents, Parliament pre-scribed a different and higher test: 'a court may only make a care order or supervision order if it is satisfied ... that ... the child ... is suffering, or is likely to suffer, significant harm; ...'

This is the language of proof, not suspicion. At this stage more is required than suspicion, however reasonably based.

The next pointer is that the second threshold condition in paragraph (a) is cheek by jowl with the first. Take a case where a care order is sought in respect of a child on the ground that for some time his parents have been maltreating him. Having heard the evidence, the court finds the alle-gation is not proved. No maltreatment has been established. The evidence is rejected as insuffi-cient. That being so, the first condition is not made out, because there is no factual basis from which the court could conclude that the child is suffering significant harm attributable to the care being given to him. Suspicion that there may have been maltreatment clearly will not do. It would be odd if, in respect of the selfsame non-proven allegations, the self-same insufficient evidence could nonetheless be regarded as a sufficient factual basis for satisfying the court there is a real possibility of harm to the child in the future.

The third pointer is that if indeed this were the position, this would effectively reverse the bur-den of proof in an important respect. It would mean that once apparently credible evidence of misconduct has been given, those against whom the allegations are made must disprove them. Otherwise it would be open to a court to hold that, although the misconduct has not been proved, it has not been disproved and there is a real possibility that the misconduct did occur. Accordingly there is a real possibility that the child will suffer harm in the future and, hence, the threshold criteria are met. I do not believe Parliament intended that section 31(2) should work in this way.

Thus far I have concentrated on explaining that a court's conclusion that the threshold con-ditions are satisfied must have a factual base, and that an alleged but unproved fact, serious or trivial, is not a fact for this purpose. Nor is judicial suspicion, because that is no more than a judi-cial state of uncertainty about whether or not an event happened.

I must now put this into perspective by noting, and emphasising, the width of the range of facts which may be relevant when the court is considering the threshold conditions. The range of facts which may properly be taken into account is infinite. Facts include the history of mem-bers of the family, the state of relationships within a family, proposed changes within the mem-bership of a family, parental attitudes, and omissions which might not reasonably have been expected, just as much as actual physical assaults. They include threats, and abnormal behav-iour by a child, and unsatisfactory parental responses to complaints or allegations. And facts, which are minor or even trivial if considered in isolation, when taken together may suffice to satisfy the court of the likelihood of future harm. The court will attach to all the relevant facts the appropriate weight when coming to an overall conclusion on the crucial issue.

I must emphasise a further point. I have indicated that unproved allegations of maltreatment cannot form the basis for a finding by the court that either limb of section 31(2)(a) is established.

It is, of course, open to a court to conclude there is a real possibility that the child will suffer harm in the future although harm in the past has not been established. There will be cases where, although the alleged maltreatment itself is not proved, the evidence does establish a combination of profoundly worrying features affecting the care of the child within the family. In such cases it would be open to a court in appropriate circumstances to find that, although not satisfied the child is yet suffering significant harm, on the basis of such facts as are proved there is a likelihood that he will do so in the future.

That is not the present case. The three younger girls are not at risk unless D1 was abused by Mr R in the past. If she was not abused, there is no reason for thinking the others may be. This is not a case where Mr R has a history of abuse. Thus the one and only relevant fact is whether DI was abused by Mr R as she says. The other surrounding facts, such as the fact that D1 made a complaint and the fact that her mother responded unsatisfactorily, lead nowhere relevant in this case if they do not lead to the conclusion that D1 was abused. To decide that the others are at risk because there is a possibility that D1 was abused would be to base the decision, not on fact, but on suspicion: the suspicion that D1 may have been abused. That would be to lower the threshold prescribed by Parliament.

Conclusion

I am very conscious of the difficulties confronting social workers and others in obtaining hard evidence, which will stand up when challenged in court, of the maltreatment meted out to children behind closed doors. Cruelty and physical abuse are notoriously difficult to prove. The task of social workers is usually anxious and often thankless. They are criticised for not having taken action in response to warning signs which are obvious enough when seen in the clear light of hindsight. Or they are criticised for making applications based on serious allegations which, in the event, are not established in court. Sometimes, whatever they do, they cannot do right.

I am also conscious of the difficulties facing judges when there is conflicting testimony on serious allegations. On some occasions judges are left deeply anxious at the end of a case. There may be an understandable inclination to 'play safe' in the interests of the child. Sometimes judges wish to safeguard a child whom they fear may be at risk without at the same time having to fasten a label of very serious misconduct on to one of the parents.

These are among the difficulties and considerations Parliament addressed in the Children Act 1989 when deciding how, to use the fashionable terminology, the balance should be struck between the various interests. As I read the Act, Parliament decided that the threshold for a care order should be that the child is suffering significant harm, or there is a real possibility that he will do so. In the latter regard the threshold is comparatively low. Therein lies the protection for children. But, as I read the Act, Parliament also decided that proof of the relevant facts is needed if this threshold is to be surmounted. Before the section 1 welfare test and the welfare 'checklist' can be applied, the threshold has to be crossed. Therein lies the protection for parents. They are not to be at risk of having their child taken from them and removed into the care of the local authority on the basis only of suspicions, whether of the judge or of the local authority or anyone else. A conclusion that the child is suffering or is likely to suffer harm must be based on facts, not just suspicion.

It follows that I would dismiss this appeal. In his judgment, when deciding that the alleged sexual abuse was not proved, the judge referred to the headnote in *In re W (Minors) (Sexual Abuse: Standard of Proof)* [1994] 1 FLR 419 and the need for a higher than ordinary standard of proof. Despite these references the Court of Appeal were satisfied that the judge applied the right test. I agree. Reading his judgment overall, I am not persuaded he adopted a materially different standard of proof from the standard I have mentioned above. Sexual abuse not having been proved, there were no facts upon which the judge could properly conclude there was a likelihood of harm to the three younger girls.

The circumstances for the creation, variation, operation, and discharge of care orders and supervision orders are outlined in the following sections.

32. Period within which application for order under this Part must be disposed of

(1)   A court hearing an application for an order under this Part shall (in the light of any rules made by virtue of subsection (2)) —

   (a)   draw up a timetable with a view to disposing of the application without delay; and

   (b)   give such directions as it considers appropriate for the purpose of ensuring, so far as is reasonably practicable, that that timetable is adhered to.

(2)   Rules of court may —

   (a)   specify periods within which specified steps must be taken in relation to such proceedings; and

   (b)   make other provision with respect to such proceedings for the purpose of ensuring, so far as is reasonably practicable, that they are disposed of without delay.

Care orders

33. Effect of care order

(1)   Where a care order is made with respect to a child it shall be the duty of the local authority designated by the order to receive the child into their care and to keep him in their care while the order remains in force.

(2)   Where —

   (a)   a care order has been made with respect to a child on the application of an authorised person; but

   (b)   the local authority designated by the order was not informed that that person proposed to make the application,

the child may be kept in the care of that person until received into the care of the authority.

(3)   While a care order is in force with respect to a child, the local authority designated by the order shall —

   (a)   have parental responsibility for the child; and

   (b)   have the power (subject to the following provisions of this section) to determine the extent to which a parent or guardian of the child may meet his parental responsibility for him.

(4)   The authority may not exercise the power in subsection (3)(b) unless they are satisfied that it is necessary to do so in order to safeguard or promote the child's welfare.

(5)   Nothing in subsection (3)(b) shall prevent a parent or guardian of the child who has care of him from doing what is reasonable in all the circumstances of the case for the purpose of safeguarding or promoting his welfare.

(6)   While a care order is in force with respect to a child, the local authority designated by the order shall not —

   (a)   cause the child to be brought up in any religious persuasion other than that in which he would have been brought up if the order had not been made; or

   (b)   have the right —

      (i)   to consent or refuse to consent to the making of an application with respect to the child under section 18 of the Adoption Act 1976;

      (ii)   to agree or refuse to agree to the making of an adoption order, or an order under section 55 of the Act of 1976 with respect to the child; or

      (iii)   to appoint a guardian for the child.

(7)   while a care order is in force with respect to a child, no person may —

   (a)   cause the child to be known by a new surname; or

   (b)   remove him from the United Kingdom,

without either the written consent of every person who has parental responsibility for the child or the leave of the court.

(8) Subsection (7)(b) does not —
  (a) prevent the removal of such a child, for a period of less than one month, by the authority in whose care he is; or
  (b) apply to arrangements for such a child to live outside England and Wales (which are governed by paragraph 19 of Schedule 2).

(9) The power in subsection (3)(b) is subject (in addition to being subject to the provisions of this section) to any right, duty, power, responsibility or authority which a parent or guardian of the child has in relation to the child and his property by virtue of any other enactment.

34. Parental contact etc. with children in care

(1) Where a child is in the care of a local authority, the authority shall (subject to the provisions of this section) allow the child reasonable contact with —
  (a) his parents;
  (b) any guardian of his;
  (c) where there was a residence order in force with respect to the child immediately before the care order was made; the person in whose favour the order was made; and
  (d) where, immediately before the care order was made, a person had care of the child by virtue of an order made in the exercise of the High Court's inherent jurisdiction with respect to children, that person.

(2) On the application made by the authority or the child, the court may make such order as it considers appropriate with respect to the contact which is to be allowed between the child and any named person.

(3) On an application made by —
  (a) any person mentioned in paragraphs (a) to (d) of subsection (1); or
  (b) any person who has obtained the leave of the court to make the application, the court may make such order as it considers appropriate with respect to the contact which is to be allowed between the child and that person.

(4) On an application made by the authority or the child, the court may make an order authorising the authority to refuse to allow contact between the child and any person who is mentioned in paragraphs (a) to (d) of subsection (1) and named in the order.

(5) When making a care order with respect to a child, or in any family proceedings in connection with a child who is in the care of a local authority, the court may make an order under this section, even though no application for such an order has been made with respect to the child, if it considers that the order should be made.

(6) An authority may refuse to allow the contact that would otherwise be required by virtue of subsection (1) or an order under this section if —
  (a) they are satisfied that it is necessary to do so in order to safeguard, or promote the child's welfare; and
  (b) the refusal —
    (i) is decided upon as a matter of urgency; and
    (ii) does not last for more than seven days.

(7) An order under this section may impose such conditions as the court considers appropriate.

(8) The Secretary of State may by regulations make provision as to —
  (a) the steps to be taken by a local authority who have exercised their powers under subsection (6);
  (b) the circumstances in which, and conditions subject to which, the terms of any order made under this section may be departed from by agreement between the local authority and the person in relation to whom this order is made;

    (c) notification by a local authority of any variation or suspension of arrangements made (otherwise than under an order under this section) with a view to affording any person contact with a child to whom this section applies.

(9)   The court may vary or discharge any order made under this section on the application of the authority, the child concerned or the person named in the order.

(10)   An order under this section may be made either at the same time as the care order itself or later.

(11)   Before making a care order with respect to any child the court shall —

    (a) consider the arrangements which the authority have made, or propose to make, for affording any person contact with a child to whom this section applies; and

    (b) invite the parties to the proceedings to comment on those arrangements.

Supervision orders

35. Supervision orders

(1)   While a supervision order is in force it shall be the duty of the supervisor —

    (a) to advise, assist and befriend the supervised child;

    (b) to take such steps as are reasonably necessary to give effect to the order; and

    (c) where —

        (i)   the order is not wholly complied with; or

        (ii)   the supervisor considers that the order may no longer be necessary,

to consider whether or not to apply to the court for its variation or discharge.

(2)   Parts I and II of Schedule 3 make further provision with respect to supervision orders.

36. Education supervision orders

(1)   On the application of any local education authority, the court may make an order putting the child with respect to whom the application is made under the supervision of a designated local education authority.

(2)   In this Act 'an education supervision order' means an order under subsection (1).

(3)   A court may only make an education supervision order if it is satisfied that the child concerned is of compulsory school age and is not being properly educated.

(4)   For the purposes of this section, a child is being properly educated only if he is receiving efficient full-time education suitable to his age, ability and aptitude and any special educational needs he may have.

(5)   Where a child is —

    (a) the subject of a school attendance order which is in force under section 437 of the Education Act 1996 and which has not been complied with; or

    (b) a registered pupil at a school which he is not attending regularly within the meaning of section 444 of that Act,

then, unless it is proved that he is being properly educated, it shall be assumed that he is not.

(6)   An education supervision order may not be made with respect to a child who is in the care of a local authority.

(7)   The local education authority designated in an education supervision order must be —

    (a) the authority within whose area the child concerned is living or will live; or

    (b) where —

        (i)   the child is a registered pupil at a school; and

        (ii)   the authority mentioned in paragraph (a) and the authority within whose area the school is situated agree,

the latter authority.

(8)   Where a local education authority propose to make an application for an education supervision order they shall, before making the application, consult the appropriate local authority.

(9)   The appropriate local authority is —

    (a)   in the case of a child who is being provided with accommodation by, or on behalf of a local authority, that authority;

...

38.   Interim orders

(1)   Where —

    (a)   in any proceedings on an application for a care order or supervision order, the proceedings are adjourned; or

    (b)   the court gives a direction under section 37(1),

the court may make an interim care order or an interim supervision order with respect to the child concerned.

(2)   A court shall not make an interim care order or interim supervision order under this section unless it is satisfied that there are reasonable grounds for believing that the circumstances with respect to the child are as mentioned in section 31(2).

(3)   Where, in any proceedings on an application for a care order or supervision order, a court makes a residence order with respect to the child concerned, it shall also make an interim supervision order with respect to him unless satisfied that his welfare will he satisfactorily safeguarded without an interim order being made.

(4)   An interim order made under or by virtue of this section shall have effect for such period as may be specified in the order, but shall in any event cease to have effect on whichever of the following events first occurs —

    (a)   the expiry of the period of eight weeks beginning with the date on which the order is made:

    (b)   if the order is the second or subsequent such order made with respect to the same child in the same proceedings, the expiry of the relevant period;

    (c)   in a case which falls within subsection (l)(a), the disposal of the application;

    (d)   in a case which falls within subsection (l)(b), the disposal of an application for a care order or supervision order made by the authority with respect to the child;

    (e)   in a case which falls within subsection (l)(b) and in which —

        (i)   the court has given a direction under section 37(4), but

        (ii)   no application for a care order or supervision order has been made with respect to the child,

the expiry of the period fixed by that direction.

(5)   In subsection (4)(b) 'the relevant period' means —

    (a)   the period of four weeks beginning with the date on which the order in question is made; or

    (b)   the period of eight weeks beginning with the date on which the first order was made if that period ends later than the period mentioned in paragraph (a).

(6)   Where the court makes an interim care order, or interim supervision order, it may give such directions (if any) as it considers appropriate with regard to the medical or psychiatric examination or other assessment of the child; but if the child is of sufficient understanding to make an informed decision he may refuse to submit to the examination or other assessment.

(7)   A direction under subsection (6) may be to the effect that there is to be —

    (a)   no such examination or assessment; or

    (b)   no such examination or assessment unless the court directs otherwise.

(8)   A direction under subsection (6) may be —

    (a)   given when the interim order is made or at any time while it is in force; and

    (b)   varied at any time on the application of any person falling within any class of person prescribed by rules of court for the purposes of this subsection.

(9)   Paragraphs 4 and 5 of Schedule 3 shall not apply in relation to an interim supervision order.

(10)   Where a court makes an order under or by virtue of this section it shall, in determining the period for which the order is to be in force, consider whether any party who was, or might have been, opposed to the making of the order was in a position to argue his case against the order in full.

38A.   Power to include exclusion requirement in interim care order

(1)   Where —
- (a)   on being satisfied that there are reasonable grounds for believing that the circumstances with respect to a child are as mentioned in section 31(2) (a) and (b)(i), the court makes an interim care order with respect to a child, and
- (b)   the conditions mentioned in subsection (2) are satisfied,

the court may include an exclusion requirement in the interim care order.

(2)   The conditions are —
- (a)   that there is reasonable cause to believe that, if a person ('the relevant person') is excluded from a dwelling-house in which the child lives, the child will cease to suffer, or cease to be likely to suffer, significant harm, and
- (b)   that another person living in the dwelling-house (whether a parent of the child or some other person) —
  - (i)   is able and willing to give to the child the care which it would be reasonable to expect a parent to give him, and
  - (ii)   consents to the inclusion of the exclusion requirement.

(3)   For the purposes of this section an exclusion requirement is any one or more of the following —
- (a)   a provision requiring the relevant person to leave a dwelling-house in which he is living with the child,
- (b)   a provision prohibiting the relevant person from entering a dwelling-house in which the child lives, and
- (c)   a provision excluding the relevant person from a defined area in which a dwelling-house in which the child lives is situated.

(4)   The court may provide that the exclusion requirement is to have effect for a shorter period than the other provisions of the interim care order.

(5)   Where the court makes an interim care order containing an exclusion requirement, the court may attach a power of arrest to the exclusion requirement.

(6)   Where the court attaches a power of arrest to an exclusion requirement of an interim care order, it may provide that the power of arrest is to have effect for a shorter period than the exclusion requirement.

(7)   Any period specified for the purposes of subsection (4) or (6) may be extended by the court (on one or more occasions) on an application to vary or discharge the interim care order.

(8)   Where a power of arrest is attached to an exclusion requirement of an interim care order by virtue of subsection (5), a constable may arrest without warrant any person whom he has reasonable cause to believe to be in breach of the requirement.

(9)   Sections 47(7), (11) and (12) and 48 of, and Schedule 5 to, the Family Law Act 1996 shall have effect in relation to a person arrested under subsection (8) of this section as they have effect in relation to a person arrested under section 47(6) of that Act.

(10)   If, while an interim care order containing an exclusion requirement is in force, the local authority have removed the child from the dwelling-house from which the relevant person is excluded to other accommodation for a continuous period of more than 24 hours, the interim care order shall cease to have effect in so far as it imposes the exclusion requirement.

38B.   Undertakings relating to interim care orders

(1)   In any case where the court has power to include an exclusion requirement in an interim care order, the court may accept an undertaking from the relevant person.

(2)   No power of arrest may be attached to any undertaking given under subsection (1).

(3)   An undertaking given to a court under subsection (1) —

(a)   shall be enforceable as if it were an order of the court, and

(b)   shall cease to have effect if, while it is in force, the local authority have removed the child from the dwelling-house from which the relevant person is excluded to other accommodation for a continuous period of more than 24 hours.

(4)   This section has effect without prejudice to the powers of the High Court and county court apart from this section.

(5)   In this section 'exclusion requirement' and 'relevant person' have the same meaning as in section 38A.

39. Discharge and variation etc. of care orders and supervision orders

(1)   A care order may be discharged by the court on the application of —

(a)   any person who has parental responsibility for the child;

(b)   the child himself; or

(c)   the local authority designated by the order.

(2)   A supervision order may be varied or discharged by the court on the application of —

(a)   any person who has parental responsibility for the child;

(b)   the child himself; or

(c)   the supervisor.

(3)   On the application of a person who is not entitled to apply for the order to be discharged, but who is a person with whom the child is living, a supervision order may be varied by the court in so far as it imposes a requirement which affects that person.

(3A)   On the application of a person who is not entitled to apply for the order to be discharged, but who is a person to whom an exclusion requirement contained in the order applies, an interim care order may be varied or discharged by the court in so far as it imposes the exclusion requirement.

(3B)   Where a power of arrest has been attached to an exclusion requirement of an interim care order, the court may, on the application of any person entitled to apply for the discharge of the order so far as it imposes the exclusion requirement, vary or discharge the order in so far as it confers a power of arrest (whether or not any application has been made to vary or discharge any other provision of the order).

(4)   Where a care order is in force with respect to a child the court may, on the application of any person entitled to apply for the order to be discharged, substitute a supervision order for the care order.

(5)   When a court is considering whether to substitute one order for another under subsection (4) any provision of this Act which would otherwise require section 31(2) to be satisfied at the time when the proposed order is substituted or made shall be disregarded.

More detailed provision appears in Schedule 3:

Meaning of 'responsible person'

1.   In this Schedule, 'the responsible person', in relation to a supervised child, means —

(a)   any person who has parental responsibility for the child; and

(b)   any other person with whom the child is living.

Power of supervisor to give directions to supervised child

2.(1)   A supervision order may require the supervised child to comply with any directions given from time to time by the supervisor which require him to do all or any of the following things —

(a)   to live at a place or places specified in the directions for a period or periods so specified;

(b) to present himself to a person or persons specified in the directions at a place or places and on a day or days so specified;

(c) to participate in activities specified in the directions on a day or days so specified.

(2) It shall be for the supervisor to decide whether, and to what extent, he exercises his power to give directions and to decide the form of any directions which he gives.

(3) Sub-paragraph (1) does not confer on a supervisor power to give directions in respect of any medical or psychiatric examination or treatment (which are matters dealt with in paragraphs 4 and 5).

Imposition of obligations on responsible person

3.(1) With the consent of any responsible person, a supervision order may include a requirement —

(a) that he take all reasonable steps to ensure that the supervised child complies with any direction given by the supervisor under paragraph 2;

(b) that he take all reasonable steps to ensure that the supervised child complies with any requirement included in the order under paragraph 4 or 5;

(c) that he comply with any directions given by the supervisor requiring him to attend at a place specified in the directions for the purpose of taking part in activities so specified.

(2) A direction given under sub-paragraph (1)(c) may specify the time at which the responsible person is to attend and whether or not the supervised child is required to attend with him.

(3) A supervision order may require any person who is a responsible person in relation to the supervised child to keep the supervisor informed of his address, if it differs from the child's.

Psychiatric and medical examinations

4.(1) A supervision order may require the supervised child —

(a) to submit to a medical or psychiatric examination; or

(b) to submit to any such examination from time to time as directed by the supervisor.

(2) Any such examination shall be required to be conducted —

(a) by, or under the direction of, such registered medical practitioner as may be specified in the order;

(b) at a place specified in the order and at which the supervised child is to attend as a non-resident patient; or

(c) at —

(i) a health service hospital; or

(ii) in the case of a psychiatric examination, a hospital, independent hospital or care home,

at which the supervised child is, or is to attend as, a resident patient.

(3) A requirement of a kind mentioned in sub-paragraph (2)(c) shall not be included unless the court is satisfied, on the evidence of a registered medical practitioner, that —

(a) the child may be suffering from a physical or mental condition that requires, and may be susceptible to, treatment; and

(b) a period as a resident patient is necessary if the examination is to be carried out properly.

(4) No court shall include a requirement under this paragraph in a supervision order unless it is satisfied that —

(a) where the child has sufficient understanding to make an informed decision, he consents to its inclusion; and

(b) satisfactory arrangements have been, or can be, made for the examination.

Psychiatric and medical treatment

5.(1) Where a court which proposes to make or vary a supervision order is satisfied, on the evidence of a registered medical practitioner approved for the purposes of section 12 of the

Mental Health Act 1983, that the mental condition of the supervised child —
    (a) is such as requires, and may be susceptible to, treatment; but
    (b) is not such as to warrant his detention in pursuance of a hospital order under Part III of that Act,
the court may include in the order a requirement that the supervised child shall, for a period specified in the order, submit to such treatment as is so specified.

(2) The treatment specified in accordance with sub-paragraph (1) must be —
    (a) by, or under the direction of, such registered medical practitioner as may be specified in the order;
    (b) as a non-resident patient at such a place as may be so specified; or
    (c) as a resident patient in a hospital, independent hospital or care home.

(3) Where a court which proposes to make or vary a supervision order is satisfied, on the evidence of a registered medical practitioner, that the physical condition of the supervised child is such as requires, and may be susceptible to, treatment, the court may include in the order a requirement that the supervised child shall, for a period specified in the order, submit to such treatment as is so specified.

(4) The treatment specified in accordance with sub-paragraph (3) must be —
    (a) by, or under the direction of, such registered medical practitioner as may be specified in the order;
    (b) as a non-resident patient at such place as may be so specified; or
    (c) as a resident patient in a health service hospital.

(5) No court shall include a requirement under this paragraph in a supervision order unless it is satisfied —
    (a) where the child has sufficient understanding to make an informed decision, that he consents to its inclusion; and
    (b) that satisfactory arrangements have been, or can be, made for the treatment.

(6) If a medical practitioner by whom or under whose direction a supervised person is being treated in pursuance of a requirement included in a supervision order by virtue of this paragraph is unwilling to continue to treat or direct the treatment of the supervised child or is of the opinion that —
    (a) the treatment should be continued beyond the period specified in the order;
    (b) the supervised child needs different treatment;
    (c) he is not susceptible to treatment; or
    (d) he does not require further treatment,
the practitioner shall make a report in writing to that effect to the supervisor.

Life of supervision order
6.(1) Subject to sub-paragraph (2) and section 91, a supervision order shall cease to have effect at the end of the period of one year beginning with the date on which it was made.

(2) A supervision order shall also cease to have effect if an event mentioned in section 25(1)(a) or (b) of the Child Abduction and Custody Act 1985 (termination of existing orders) occurs with respect to the child.

(3) Where the supervisor applies to the court to extend, or further extend, a supervision order the court may extend the order for such period as it may specify.

(4) A supervision order may not be extended so as to run beyond the end of the period of three years beginning with the date on which it was made.

Information to be given to supervisor etc.
8.(1) A supervision order may require the supervised child —
    (a) to keep the supervisor informed of any change in his address; and
    (b) to allow the supervisor to visit him at the place where he is living.

(2)   The responsible person in relation to any child with respect to whom a supervision order is made shall —
- (a)   if asked by the supervisor, inform him of the child's address (if it is known to him); and
- (b)   if he is living with the child, allow the supervisor reasonable contact with the child.

Selection of supervisor

9.(1)   A supervision order shall not designate a local authority as the supervisor unless —
- (a)   the authority agree; or
- (b)   the supervised child lives or will live within their area.

Effect of supervision order on earlier orders

10.   The making of a supervision order with respect to any child brings to an end any earlier care or supervision order which —
- (a)   was made with respect to that child; and
- (b)   would otherwise continue in force.

Local authority functions and expenditure

11.(1)   The Secretary of State may make regulations with respect to the exercise by a local authority of their functions where a child has been placed under their supervision by a supervision order.

(2)   Where a supervision order requires compliance with directions given by virtue of this section, any expenditure incurred by the supervisor for the purposes of the directions shall be defrayed by the local authority designated in the order.

...

Effect of orders

12.(1)   Where an education supervision order is in force with respect to a child, it shall be the duty of the supervisor —
- (a)   to advise, assist and befriend, and give directions to —
  - (i)   the supervised child; and
  - (ii)   his parents,

in such a way as will, in the opinion of the supervisor, secure that he is properly educated;
- (b)   where any such directions given to —
  - (i)   the supervised child; or
  - (ii)   a parent of his,

have not been complied with, to consider what further steps to take in the exercise of the supervisor's powers under this Act.

(2)   Before giving any directions under sub-paragraph (1) the supervisor shall, so far as is reasonably practicable, ascertain the wishes and feelings of —
- (a)   the child; and
- (b)   his parents,

including, in particular, their wishes as to the place at which the child should be educated.

(3)   When settling the terms of any such directions, the supervisor shall give due consideration —
- (a)   having regard to the child's age and understanding, to such wishes and feelings of his as the supervisor has been able to ascertain; and
- (b)   to such wishes and feelings of the child's parents as he has been able to ascertain.

(4)   Directions may be given under this paragraph at any time while the education supervision order is in force.

13.(1)   Where an education supervision order is in force with respect to a child, the duties of the child's parents under sections 7 and 444 of the Education Act 1996 (duties to secure education of children and to secure regular attendance of registered pupils) shall be superseded by their duty to comply with any directions in force under the education supervision order.

(2) Where an education supervision order is made with respect to a child —

(a) any school attendance order —

(i) made under section 437 of the Education Act 1996 with respect to the child; and

(ii) in force immediately before the making of the education supervision order,

shall cease to have effect; and

(b) while the education supervision order remains in force, the following provisions shall not apply with respect to the child —

(i) section 437 of that Act (school attendance orders);

(ii) section 9 of that Act (pupils to be educated in accordance with wishes of their parents);

(iii) sections 411 and 423 of that Act (parental preference and appeals against admission decisions);

(c) a supervision order made with respect to the child in criminal proceedings, while the education supervision order is in force, may not include an education requirement of the kind which could otherwise be included under paragraph 7 of Schedule 6 to the Powers of Criminal Courts (Sentencing) Act 2000;

(d) any education requirement of a kind mentioned in paragraph (c), which was in force with respect to the child immediately before the making of the education supervision order, shall cease to have effect.

Effect where child also subject to supervision order

14.(1) This paragraph applies where an education supervision order and a supervision order, or order under section 63(1) of the Powers of Criminal Courts (Sentencing) Act 2000, are in force at the same time with respect to the same child.

(2) Any failure to comply with a direction given by the supervisor under the education supervision order shall be disregarded if it would not have been reasonably practicable to comply with it without failing to comply with a direction given under the other order.

Duration of orders

15.(1) An education supervision order shall have effect for a period of one year, beginning with the date on which it is made.

(2) An education supervision order shall not expire if, before it would otherwise have expired, the court has (on the application of the authority in whose favour the order was made) extended the period during which it is in force.

(3) Such an application may not be made earlier than three months before the date on which the order would otherwise expire.

(4) The period during which an education supervision order is in force may be extended under sub-paragraph (2) on more than one occasion.

(5) No one extension may be for a period of more than three years.

(6) An education supervision order shall cease to have effect on —

(a) the child's ceasing to be of compulsory school age; or

(b) the making of a care order with respect to the child;

and sub-paragraphs (1) to (4) are subject to this sub-paragraph.

Information to be given to supervisor etc.

16.(1) An education supervision order may require the child

(a) to keep the supervisor informed of any change in his address; and

(b) to allow the supervisor to visit him at the place where he is living.

(2)   A person who is the parent of a child with respect to whom an education supervision order has been made shall —
- (a) if asked by the supervisor, inform him of the child's address (if it is known to him); and
- (b) if he is living with the child, allow the supervisor reasonable contact with the child.

Discharge of orders
17.(1)   The court may discharge any education supervision order on the application of —
- (a) the child concerned;
- (b) a parent of his; or
- (c) the local education authority concerned.

(2)   On discharging an education supervision order, the court may direct the local authority within whose area the child lives, or will live, to investigate the circumstances of the child.

Offences
18.(1)   If a parent of a child with respect to whom an education supervision order is in force persistently fails to comply with a direction given under the order he shall be guilty of an offence.

(2)   It shall be a defence for any person charged with such an offence to prove that
- (a) he took all reasonable steps to ensure that the direction was complied with;
- (b) the direction was unreasonable; or
- (c) he had complied with —
  - (i)   a requirement included in a supervision order made with respect to the child; or
  - (ii) directions given under such a requirement,

and that it was not reasonably practicable to comply both with the direction and with the requirement or directions mentioned in this paragraph.

(3)   A person guilty of an offence under this paragraph shall be liable on summary conviction to a fine not exceeding level 3 on the standard scale.

Persistent failure of child to comply with directions
19.(1)   Where a child with respect to whom an education supervision order is in force persistently fails to comply with any direction given under the order, the local education authority concerned shall notify the appropriate local authority.

(2)   Where a local authority have been notified under sub-paragraph (1) they shall investigate the circumstances of the child.

(3)   In this paragraph 'the appropriate local authority' has the same meaning as in section 36.

Miscellaneous
20.   The Secretary of State may by regulations make provision modifying, or displacing, the provisions of any enactment about education in relation to any child with respect to whom an education supervision order is in force to such extent as appears to the Secretary of State to be necessary or expedient in consequence of the provision made by this Act with respect to such orders.

Interpretation
21.   In this Part of this Schedule 'parent' has the same meaning as in the Education Act 1996.

...

Part V is concerned with child protection. Again, the key concept is that of 'significant harm', which then provides the gateway for local authority intervention. However, when exercising these powers, especially if they involve the removal of children from their families, local authorities must bear in mind not only the position of the child but also the provisions of the Human Rights Act. In particular, it must have in mind the doctrine of proportionality, referred to above, and Art. 8 of the European Convention on Human Rights, the right to family life. The Children Act creates the following framework:

43. Child assessment orders

(1) On the application of a local authority or authorised person for an order to be made under this section with respect to a child, the court may make the order if, but only if, it is satisfied that —
- (a) the applicant has reasonable cause to suspect that the child is suffering, or is likely to suffer, significant harm;
- (b) an assessment of the state of the child's health or development, or of the way in which he has been treated, is required to enable the applicant to determine whether or not the child is suffering, or is likely to suffer, significant harm; and
- (c) it is unlikely that such an assessment will be made, or be satisfactory, in the absence of an order under this section.

(2) In this Act 'a child assessment order' means an order under this section.

(3) A court may treat an application under this section as an application for an emergency protection order.

(4) No court shall make a child assessment order if it is satisfied —
- (a) that there are grounds for making an emergency protection order with respect to the child; and
- (b) that it ought to make such an order rather than a child assessment order.

(5) A child assessment order shall —
- (a) specify the date by which the assessment is to begin; and
- (b) have effect for such period, not exceeding 7 days beginning with that date, as may be specified in the order.

(6) Where a child assessment order is in force with respect to a child it shall be the duty of any person who is in a position to produce the child —
- (a) to produce him to such person as may be named in the order; and
- (b) to comply with such directions relating to the assessment of the child as the court thinks fit to specify in the order.

(7) A child assessment order authorises any person carrying out the assessment, or any part of the assessment, to do so in accordance with the terms of the order.

(8) Regardless of subsection (7), if the child is of sufficient understanding to make an informed decision he may refuse to submit to a medical or psychiatric examination or other assessment.

(9) The child may only be kept away from home —
- (a) in accordance with directions specified in the order;
- (b) if it is necessary for the purposes of the assessment; and
- (c) for such period or periods as may be specified in the order.

(10) Where the child is to be kept away from home, the order shall contain such directions as the court thinks fit with regard to the contact that he must be allowed to have with other persons while away from home.

(11) Any person making an application for a child assessment order shall take such steps as are reasonably practicable to ensure that notice of the application is given to —
- (a) the child's parents;
- (b) any person who is not a parent of his but who has parental responsibility for him;
- (c) any other person caring for the child;
- (d) any person in whose favour a contact order is in force with respect to the child;
- (e) any person who is allowed to have contact with the child by virtue of an order under section 34; and
- (f) the child, before the hearing of the application.

(12) Rules of court may make provision as to the circumstances in which —
  (a) any of the persons mentioned in subsection (11); or
  (b) such other person as may be specified in the rules, may apply to the court for a child assessment order to be varied or discharged.
(13) In this section 'authorised person' means a person who is an authorised person for the purposes of section 31.

44. Orders for emergency protection of children
(1) Where any person ('the applicant') applies to the court for an order to be made under this section with respect to a child, the court may make the order if, but only if, it is satisfied that —
  (a) there is reasonable cause to believe that the child is likely to suffer significant harm if —
    (i) he is not removed to accommodation provided by or on behalf of the applicant; or
    (ii) he does not remain in the place in which he is then being accommodated;
  (b) in the case of an application made by a local authority —
    (i) enquiries are being made with respect to the child under section 47(1)(b); and
    (ii) those enquiries are being frustrated by access to the child being unreasonably refused to a person authorised to seek access and that the applicant has reasonable cause to believe that access to the child is required as a matter of urgency; or
  (c) in the case of an application made by an authorised person —
    (i) the applicant has reasonable cause to suspect that a child is suffering, or is likely to suffer, significant harm;
    (ii) the applicant is making enquiries with respect to the child's welfare; and
    (iii) those enquiries are being frustrated by access to the child being unreasonably refused to a person authorised to seek access and the applicant has reasonable cause to believe that access to the child is required as a matter of urgency.
(2) In this section
  (a) 'authorised person' means a person who is an authorised person for the purposes of section 31; and
  (b) 'a person authorised to seek access' means —
    (i) in the case of an application by a local authority, an officer of the local authority or a person authorised by the authority to act on their behalf in connection with the enquiries; or
    (ii) in the case of an application by an authorised person, that person.
(3) Any person —
  (a) seeking access to a child in connection with enquiries of a kind mentioned in subsection (1); and
  (b) purporting to be a person authorised to do so, shall, on being asked to do so, produce some duly authenticated document as evidence that he is such a person.
(4) While an order under this section ('an emergency protection order') is in force it —
  (a) operates as a direction to any person who is in a position to do so to comply with any request to produce the child to the applicant;
  (b) authorises —
    (i) the removal of the child at any time to accommodation provided by or on behalf of the applicant and his being kept there; or
    (ii) the prevention of the child's removal from any hospital, or other place, in which he was being accommodated immediately before the making of the order; and
  (c) gives the applicant parental responsibility for the child.
(5) Where an emergency protection order is in force with respect to a child, the applicant —
  (a) shall only exercise the power given by virtue of subsection (4)(b) in order to safeguard the welfare of the child;

(b) shall take, and shall only take, such action in meeting his parental responsibility for the child as is reasonably required to safeguard or promote the welfare of the child (having regard in particular to the duration of the order); and

(c) shall comply with the requirements of any regulations made by the Secretary State for the purposes of this subsection.

(6) Where the court makes an emergency protection order, it may give such directions (if any) as it considers appropriate with respect to —

(a) the contact which is, or is not, to be allowed between the child and any named person;

(b) the medical or psychiatric examination or other assessment of the child.

(7) Where any direction is given under subsection (6)(b), the child may, if he is of sufficient understanding to make an informed decision, refuse to submit to the examination or other assessment.

(8) A direction under subsection (6)(a) may impose conditions and one under subsection (6)(b) may be to the effect that there is to be —

(a) no such examination or other assessment; or

(b) no such examination or assessment unless the court directs otherwise.

(9) A direction under subsection (6) may be —

(a) given when the emergency protection order is made or at any time while it is in force; and

(b) varied at any time on the application of any person falling within any class of person prescribed by rules of court for the purposes of this subsection.

(10) Where an emergency protection order is in force with respect to a child and

(a) the applicant has exercised the power given by subsection (4)(b)(i) but it appears to him that it is safe for the child to be returned; or

(b) the applicant has exercised the power given by subsection (4)(b)(ii) but it appears to him that it is safe for the child to be allowed to be removed from the place in question,

he shall return the child or (as the case may be) allow him to be removed.

(11) Where he is required by subsection (10) to return the child the applicant shall —

(a) return him to the care of the person from whose care he was removed; or

(b) if that is not reasonably practicable, return him to the care of —

(i) a parent of his;

(ii) any person who is not a parent of his but who has parental responsibility for him; or

(iii) such other person as the applicant (with the agreement of the court) considers appropriate.

(12) Where the applicant has been required by subsection (10) to return the child, or to allow him to be removed, he may again exercise his powers with respect to the child (at any time while the emergency protection order remains in force) if it appears to him that a change in the circumstances of the case makes it necessary for him to do so.

(13) Where an emergency protection order has been made with respect to a child, the applicant shall, subject to any direction given under subsection (6), allow the child reasonable contact with —

(a) his parents;

(b) any person who is not a parent of his but who has parental responsibility for him;

(c) any person with whom he was living immediately before the making of the order;

(d) any person in whose favour a contact order is in force with respect to him;

(e) any person who is allowed to have contact with the child by virtue of an order under section 34; and

(f) any person acting on behalf of any of those persons.

(14) Wherever it is reasonably practicable to do so, an emergency protection order shall name the child; and where it does not name him it shall describe him as clearly as possible.

(15) A person shall be guilty of an offence if he intentionally obstructs any person exercising the power under subsection (4)(b) to remove, or prevent the removal of, a child.

(16) A person guilty of an offence under subsection (15) shall be liable on summary conviction to a fine not exceeding level 3 on the standard scale.

44A. Power to include exclusion requirement in emergency protection order

(1) Where —
- (a) on being satisfied as mentioned in section 44(1)(a), (b) or (c), the court makes an emergency protection order with respect to a child, and
- (b) the conditions mentioned in subsection (2) are satisfied, the court may include an exclusion requirement in the emergency protection order.

(2) The conditions are —
- (a) that there is reasonable cause to believe that, if a person ('the relevant person') is excluded from a dwelling-house in which the child lives, then —
  - (i) in the case of an order made on the ground mentioned in section 44(1)(a), the child will not be likely to suffer significant harm, even though the child is not removed as mentioned in section 44(1)(a)(i) or does not remain as mentioned in section 44(1)(a)(ii), or
  - (ii) in the case of an order made on the ground mentioned in paragraph (b) or (c) of section 44(1), the enquiries referred to in that paragraph will cease to be frustrated, and
- (b) that another person living in the dwelling-house (whether a parent of the child or some other person) —
  - (i) is able and willing to give to the child the care which it would be reasonable to expect a parent to give him, and
  - (ii) consents to the inclusion of the exclusion requirement.

(3) For the purposes of this section an exclusion requirement is any one or more of the following —
- (a) a provision requiring the relevant person to leave a dwelling-house in which he is living with the child,
- (b) a provision prohibiting the relevant person from entering a dwelling-house in which the child lives, and
- (c) a provision excluding the relevant person from a defined area in which a dwelling-house in which the child lives is situated.

(4) The court may provide that the exclusion requirement is to have effect for a shorter period than the other provisions of the order.

(5) Where the court makes an emergency protection order containing an exclusion requirement, the court may attach a power of arrest to the exclusion requirement.

(6) Where the court attaches a power of arrest to an exclusion requirement of an emergency protection order, it may provide that the power of arrest is to have effect for a shorter period than the exclusion requirement.

(7) Any period specified for the purposes of subsection (4) or (6) may be extended by the court (on one or more occasions) on an application to vary or discharge the emergency protection order.

(8) Where a power of arrest is attached to an exclusion requirement of an emergency protection order by virtue of subsection (5), a constable may arrest without warrant any person whom he has reasonable cause to believe to be in breach of the requirement.

(9) Sections 47(7), (11) and (12) and 48 of, and Schedule 5 to, the Family Law Act 1996 shall have effect in relation to a person arrested under subsection (8) of this section as they have effect in relation to a person arrested under section 47(6) of that Act.

(10)   If, while an emergency protection order containing an exclusion requirement is in force, the applicant has removed the child from the dwelling-house from which the relevant person is excluded to other accommodation for a continuous period of more than 24 hours, the order shall cease to have effect in so far as it imposes the exclusion requirement.

44B.   Undertakings relating to emergency protection orders

(1)   In any case where the court has power to include an exclusion requirement in an emergency protection order, the court may accept an undertaking from the relevant person.

(2)   No power of arrest may be attached to any undertaking given under subsection (1).

(3)   An undertaking given to a court under subsection (1) —
  (a)   shall be enforceable as if it were an order of the court, and
  (b)   shall cease to have effect if, while it is in force, the applicant has removed the child from the dwelling-house from which the relevant person is excluded to other accommodation for a continuous period of more than 24 hours.

(4)   This section has effect without prejudice to the powers of the High Court and county court apart from this section.

(5)   In this section 'exclusion requirement' and 'relevant person' have the same meaning as in section 44A.

45.   Duration of emergency protection orders and other supplemental provisions

(1)   An emergency protection order shall have effect for such period, not exceeding eight days, as may be specified in the order.

(2)   Where —
  (a)   the court making an emergency protection order would, but for this subsection, specify a period of eight days as the period for which the order is to have effect; but
  (b)   the last of those eight days is a public holiday (that is to say, Christmas Day, Good Friday, a bank holiday or a Sunday),
the court may specify a period which ends at noon on the first later day which is not such a holiday.

(3)   Where an emergency protection order is made on an application under section 46(7), the period of eight days mentioned in subsection (1) shall begin with the first day on which the child was taken into police protection under section 46.

(4)   Any person who —
  (a)   has parental responsibility for a child as the result of an emergency protection order; and
  (b)   is entitled to apply for a care order with respect to the child, may apply to the court for the period during which the emergency protection order is to have effect to be extended.

(5)   On an application under subsection (4) the court may extend the period during which the order is to have effect by such period, not exceeding seven days, as it thinks fit, but may do so only if it has reasonable cause to believe that the child concerned is likely to suffer significant harm if the order is not extended.

(6)   An emergency protection order may only be extended once.

(7)   Regardless of any enactment or rule of law which would otherwise prevent it from doing so, a court hearing an application for, or with respect to, an emergency protection order may take account of —
  (a)   any statement contained in any report made to the court in the course of, or in connection with, the hearing; or
  (b)   any evidence given during the hearing,
which is, in the opinion of the court, relevant to the application.

(8) Any of the following may apply to the court for an emergency protection order to be discharged —

    (a) the child;

    (b) a parent of his;

    (c) any person who is not a parent of his but who has parental responsibility for him; or

    (d) any person with whom he was living immediately before the making of the order.

(8A) On the application of a person who is not entitled to apply for the order to be discharged, but who is a person to whom an exclusion requirement contained in the order applies, an emergency protection order may be varied or discharged by the court in so far as it imposes the exclusion requirement.

(8B) Where a power of arrest has been attached to an exclusion requirement of an emergency protection order, the court may, on the application of any person entitled to apply for the discharge of the order so far as it imposes the exclusion requirement, vary or discharge the order in so far as it confers a power of arrest (whether or not any application has been made to vary or discharge any other provision of the order). '

(9) No application for the discharge of an emergency protection order shall be heard by the court before the expiry of the period of 72 hours beginning with the making of the order.

(10) No appeal may be made against —

    (a) the making of, or refusal to make, an emergency protection order;

    (b) the extension of, or refusal to extend, the period during which such an order is to have effect;

    (c) the discharge of, or refusal to discharge, such an order; or

    (d) the giving of, or refusal to give, any direction in connection with such an order.

(11) Subsection (8) does not apply —

    (a) where the person who would otherwise be entitled to apply for the emergency protection order to be discharged —

        (i) was given notice (in accordance with rules of court) of the hearing at which the order was made; and

        (ii) was present at that hearing; or

    (b) to any emergency protection order the effective period of which has been extended under subsection (5).

(12) A court making an emergency protection order may direct that the applicant may, in exercising any powers which he has by virtue of the order, be accompanied by a registered medical practitioner, registered nurse or registered health visitor, if he so chooses.

46. Removal and accommodation of children by police in cases of emergency

(1) Where a constable has reasonable cause to believe that a child would otherwise be likely to suffer significant harm, he may —

    (a) remove the child to suitable accommodation and keep him there; or

    (b) take such steps as are reasonable to ensure that the child's removal from any hospital, or other place, in which he is then being accommodated is prevented.

(2) For the purposes of this Act, a child with respect to whom a constable has exercised his powers under this section is referred to as having been taken into police protection.

(3) As soon as is reasonably practicable after taking a child into police protection, the constable concerned shall —

    (a) inform the local authority within whose area the child was found of the steps that have been, and are proposed to be, taken with respect to the child under this section and the reasons for taking them;

    (b) give details to the authority within whose area the child is ordinarily resident ('the appropriate authority') of the place at which the child is being accommodated;

   (c) inform the child (if he appears capable of understanding) —
      (i) of the steps that have been taken with respect to him under this section and of the reasons for taking them; and
      (ii) of the further steps that may be taken with respect to him under this section;
   (d) take such steps as are reasonably practicable to discover the wishes and feelings of the child;
   (e) secure that the case is inquired into by an officer designated for the purposes of this section by the chief officer of the police area concerned; and
   (f) where the child was taken into police protection by being removed to accommodation which is not provided —
      (i) by or on behalf of a local authority; or
      (ii) as a refuge, in compliance with the requirements of section 51,
     secure that he is moved to accommodation which is so provided.

(4)   As soon as is reasonably practicable after taking a child into police protection, the constable concerned shall take such steps as are reasonably practicable to inform —
   (a) the child's parents;
   (b) every person who is not a parent of his but who has parental responsibility for him; and
   (c) any other person with whom the child was living immediately before being taken into police protection,
of the steps that he has taken under this section with respect to the child, the reasons for taking them and the further steps that may be taken with respect to him under this section.

(5)   On completing any inquiry under subsection (3)(e), the officer conducting it shall release the child from police protection unless he considers that there is still reasonable cause for believing that the child would be likely to suffer significant harm if released.

(6)   No child may be kept in police protection for more than 72 hours.

(7)   While a child is being kept in police protection, the designated officer may apply on behalf of the appropriate authority for an emergency protection order to be made under section 44 with respect to the child.

(8)   An application may be made under subsection (7) whether or not the authority know of it or agree to its being made.

(9)   While a child is being kept in police protection —
   (a) neither the constable concerned nor the designated officer shall have parental responsibility for him; but
   (b) the designated officer shall do what is reasonable in all the circumstances of the case for the purpose of safeguarding or promoting the child's welfare (having regard in particular to the length of the period during which the child will be so protected).

(10)   Where a child has been taken into police protection, the designated officer shall allow —
   (a) the child's parents;
   (b) any person who is not a parent of the child but who has parental responsibility for him;
   (c) any person with whom the child was living immediately before he was taken into police protection;
   (d) any person in whose favour a contact order is in force with respect to the child;
   (e) any person who is allowed to have contact with the child by virtue of an order under section 34; and
   (f) any person acting on behalf of any of those persons, to have such contact (if any) with the child as, in the opinion of the designated officer, is both reasonable and in the child's best interests.

(11)   Where a child who has been taken into police protection is in accommodation provided by, or on behalf of, the appropriate authority, subsection (10) shall have effect as if it referred to the authority rather than to the designated officer.

47. Local authority's duty to investigate

(1)   Where a local authority —
   (a)   are informed that a child who lives, or is found, in their area —
      (i)   is the subject of an emergency protection order; or
      (ii)   is in police protection; or
      (iii) has contravened a ban imposed by a curfew notice within the meaning of Chapter I of Part I of the Crime and Disorder Act 1998; or
   (b)   have reasonable cause to suspect that a child who lives, or is found, in their area is suffering, or is likely to suffer, significant harm,
the authority shall make, or cause to be made, such enquiries as they consider necessary to enable them to decide whether they should take any action to safeguard or promote the child's welfare.
(2)   Where a local authority have obtained an emergency protection order with respect to a child, they shall make, or cause to be made, such enquiries as they consider necessary to enable them to decide what action they should take to safeguard or promote the child's welfare.
(3)   The enquiries shall, in particular, be directed towards establishing —
   (a)   whether the authority should make any application to the court, or exercise any of their other powers under this Act or section 11 of the Crime and Disorder Act 1998 (child safety orders), with respect to the child;
   (b)   whether, in the case of a child —
      (i)   with respect to whom an emergency protection order has been made; and
      (ii)   who is not in accommodation provided by or on behalf of the authority,
      it would be in the child's best interests (while an emergency protection order remains in force) for him to be in such accommodation; and
   (c)   whether, in the case of a child who has been taken into police protection, it would be in the child's best interests for the authority to ask for an application to be made under section 46(7).
(4)   Where enquiries are being made under subsection (1) with respect to a child, the local authority concerned shall (with a view to enabling them to determine what action, if any, to take with respect to him) take such steps as are reasonably practicable —
   (a)   to obtain access to him; or
   (b)   to ensure that access to him is obtained, on their behalf, by a person authorised by them for the purpose,
unless they are satisfied that they already have sufficient information with respect to him.
(5)   Where, as a result of any such enquiries, it appears to the authority that there are matters connected with the child's education which should be investigated, they shall consult the relevant local education authority.
(6)   Where, in the course of enquiries made under this section —
   (a)   any officer of the local authority concerned; or
   (b)   any person authorised by the authority to act on their behalf in connection with those enquiries —
      (i)   is refused access to the child concerned; or
      (ii)   is denied information as to his whereabouts,
the authority shall apply for an emergency protection order, a child assessment order, a care order or a supervision order with respect to the child unless they are satisfied that his welfare can be satisfactorily safeguarded without their doing so.
(7)   If, on the conclusion of any enquiries or review made under this section, the authority decide not to apply for an emergency protection order, a child assessment order, a care order or a supervision order they shall —
   (a)   consider whether it would be appropriate to review the case at a later date; and
   (b)   if they decide that it would be, determine the date on which that review is to begin.

(8)   Where, as a result of complying with this section, a local authority conclude that they should take action to safeguard or promote the child's welfare they shall take that action (so far as it is both within their power and reasonably practicable for them to do so).

(9)   Where a local authority are conducting enquiries under this section, it shall be the duty of any person mentioned in subsection (11) to assist them with those enquiries (in particular by providing relevant information and advice) if called upon by the authority to do so.

(10)   Subsection (9) does not oblige any person to assist a local authority where doing so would be unreasonable in all the circumstances of the case.

(11)   The persons are —

(a)   any local authority;

(b)   any local education authority;

(c)   any local housing authority;

(d)   any Health Authority, Special Health Authority, Primary Care Trust or National Health Service trust; and

(e)   any person authorised by the Secretary of State for the purposes of this section.

(12)   Where a local authority are making enquiries under this section with respect to a child who appears to them to be ordinarily resident within the area of another authority, they shall consult that other authority, who may undertake the necessary enquiries in their place.

48.   Powers to assist in discovery of children who may be in need of emergency protection

(1)   Where it appears to a court making an emergency protection order that adequate information as to the child's whereabouts —

(a)   is not available to the applicant for the order; but

(b)   is available to another person,

it may include in the order a provision requiring that other person to disclose, if asked to do so by the applicant, any information that he may have as to the child's whereabouts.

(2)   No person shall be excused from complying with such a requirement on the ground that complying might incriminate him or his spouse of an offence; but a statement or admission made in complying shall not be admissible in evidence against either of them in proceedings for any offence other than perjury.

(3)   An emergency protection order may authorise the appliant to enter premises specified by the order and search for the child with respect to whom the order is made.

(4)   Where the court is satisfied that there is reasonable cause to believe that there may be another child on those premises with respect to whom an emergency protection order ought to be made, it may make an order authorising the applicant to search for that other child on those premises.

(5)   Where —

(a)   an order has been made under subsection (4);

(b)   the child concerned has been found on the premises; and

(c)   the applicant is satisfied that the grounds for making an emergency protection order exist with respect to him,

the order shall have effect as if it were an emergency protection order.

(6)   Where an order has been made under subsection (4), the applicant shall notify the court of its effect.

(7)   A person shall be guilty of an offence if he intentionally obstructs any person exercising the power of entry and search under subsection (3) or (4).

(8)   A person guilty of an offence under subsection (7) shall be liable on summary conviction to a fine not exceeding level 3 on the standard scale.

(9)   Where, on an application made by any person for a warrant under this section, it appears to the court —

    (a)   that a person attempting to exercise powers under an emergency protection order has been prevented from doing so by being refused entry to the premises concerned or access to the child concerned; or

    (b)   that any such person is likely to be so prevented from exercising any such powers,

it may issue a warrant authorising any constable to assist the person mentioned in paragraph (a) or (b) in the exercise of those powers using reasonable force if necessary.

(10)   Every warrant issued under this section shall be addressed to, and executed by, a constable who shall be accompanied by the person applying for the warrant if —

    (a)   that person so desires; and

    (b)   the court by whom the warrant is issued does not direct otherwise.

(11)   A court granting an application for a warrant under this section may direct that the constable concerned may, in executing the warrant, be accompanied by a registered medical practitioner, registered nurse or registered health visitor if he so chooses.

(12)   An application for a warrant under this section shall be made in the manner and form prescribed by rules of court.

(13)   Wherever it is reasonably practicable to do so, an order under subsection (4), an application for a warrant under this section and any such warrant shall name the child; and where it does not name him it shall describe him as clearly as possible.

These provisions do not tell local authorities how to go about their tasks under Part V. They do not, for example, mention the case conference. Such guidance does, however, appear in *Working Together to Safeguard Children*. This also makes clear that there is an expectation of the local authority working in partnership with other agencies as well as with the family in this area. This is summarised in the first chapter:

Supporting children and families

1.1   All children deserve the opportunity to achieve their full potential. They should be enabled to:

- be as physically and mentally healthy as possible;
- gain the maximum benefit possible from good-quality educational opportunities;
- live in a safe environment and be protected from harm;
- experience emotional well-being;
- feel loved and valued, and be supported by a network of reliable and affectionate relationships;
- become competent in looking after themselves and coping with everyday living;
- have a positive image of themselves, and a secure sense of identity including cultural and racial identity;
- develop good inter-personal skills and confidence in social situations.

If they are denied the opportunity to achieve their potential in this way, children are at risk not only of an impoverished childhood, but they are also more likely to experience disadvantage and social exclusion in adulthood.

1.2   Patterns of family life vary and there is no one, perfect way to bring up children. Good parenting involves caring for children's basic needs, showing them warmth and love and providing the stimulation needed for their development, within a stable environment where they experience consistent guidance and boundaries.

1.3   All parents — supported by friends and family, the wider community and statutory and voluntary services — need to be able to ensure that their children grow up adequately cared for and safe from harm and to promote their children's health and development and help them achieve their potential.

1.4   Parenting can be challenging. It often means juggling with competing priorities to balance work and home life as well as trying to understand how best to meet children's needs at all stages of their development. Parents themselves require and deserve support. Asking for help should be seen as a sign of responsibility rather than as a parenting failure.

1.5   A wide range of services and professionals provide support to families in bringing up children. Both statutory and voluntary services can support families: by helping all children develop to their full potential — for example, through universal education and health services; by providing specialist help to those who need it; and by providing support, or otherwise intervening, at times of adversity or crisis. In the great majority of cases, it should be the decision of parents when to ask for help and advice on their children's care and upbringing. Only in exceptional cases should there be compulsory intervention in family life: for example, where this is necessary to safeguard a child from significant harm. Such intervention should — provided this is consistent with the safety and welfare of the child — support families in making their own plans for the welfare and protection of their children.

1.6   Some children have particular needs, because they are disabled, or because they need certain services in order to achieve or maintain a reasonable standard of health or development, or to prevent their development being impaired. These children are described in the Children Act 1989 as being 'children in need'. They, and possibly also their families may need, or benefit from, a range of extra support and services.

1.7   Some children may be suffering, or at risk of suffering, significant harm, either as a result of a deliberate act, or of a failure on the part of a parent or carer to act or to provide proper care, or both. These children need to be made safe from harm, alongside meeting their other needs.

An integrated approach

1.8   Children have varying needs which change over time. Judgements on how best to intervene when there are concerns about harm to a child will often and unavoidably entail an element of risk — at the extreme, of leaving a child for too long in a dangerous situation or of removing a child unnecessarily from their family. The way to proceed in the face of uncertainty is through competent professional judgements based on a sound assessment of the child's needs, the parents' capacity to respond to those needs — including their capacity to keep the child safe from significant harm — and the wider family circumstances.

1.9   Effective measures to safeguard children should not be seen in isolation from the wider range of support and services available to meet the needs of children and families:

- many of the families who become the subject of child protection concerns suffer from multiple disadvantages. Providing services and support to children and families under stress may strengthen the capacity of parents to respond to the needs of their children before problems develop into abuse;
- child protection enquiries may reveal significant unmet needs for support and services among children and families. These should always be explicitly considered, even where concerns are not substantiated about significant harm to a child if the family so wishes;
- if child protection processes are to result in improved outcomes for children, then effective plans for safeguarding children and promoting their welfare should be based on a wide ranging assessment of the needs of the child and their family circumstances;
- all work with children and families should retain a clear focus on the welfare of the child. Just as child protection processes should always consider the wider needs of the child and family, so broad-based family support services should always be alert to, and know how to respond quickly and decisively to potential indicators of abuse and neglect.

A shared responsibility

1.10   Promoting children's well-being and safeguarding them from significant harm depends crucially upon effective information sharing, collaboration and understanding between agencies and professionals. Constructive relationships between individual workers need to be supported by a strong lead from elected or appointed authority members, and the commitment of chief officers.

1.11   At the strategic level, agencies and professionals need to work in partnership with each other and with service users, to plan comprehensive and co-ordinated children's services.

1.12   Individual children, especially some of the most vulnerable children and those at greatest risk of social exclusion, will need co-ordinated help from health, education, social services, and quite possibly the voluntary sector and other agencies, including youth justice services.

1.13   For those children who are suffering, or at risk of suffering significant harm, joint working is essential, to safeguard the child/ren and — where necessary — to help bring to justice the perpetrators of crimes against children. All agencies and professionals should:

- be alert to potential indicators of abuse or neglect;
- be alert to the risks which individual abusers, or potential abusers, may pose to children;
- share and help to analyse information so that an informed assessment can be made of the child's needs and circumstances;
- contribute to whatever actions are needed to safeguard the child and promote his or her welfare;
- regularly review the outcomes for the child against specific shared objectives; *and*
- work co-operatively with parents unless this is inconsistent with the need to ensure the child's safety.

Additionally, powers are given to a Magistrates' Court to make a child safety order under ss. 11 and 12 Crime and Disorder Act 1998: see Chapter 7. A further safeguard to protect children is the listing of those unsuitable to work with children. Lists previously held by the Department of Health and the Department for Education and Employment (as it then was) were put on a statutory footing by the Protection of Children Act 1999. These provisions are not reproduced here.

Parts VI, VII and VIII deal with the availability and regulation of various forms of home for children: see also Care Standards Act 2000. These provisions are not reproduced here.

PART IV

Criminal justice

7

Social workers in the justice system

Your main statutory roles are to do with children: preventing youth crime; supporting children (and also vulnerable adults) during police investigations; providing reports to courts for sentencing; diverting children in trouble away from the criminal courts; carrying out community sentences; accommodating children on remand or after sentence; and supporting children as witnesses in criminal cases. Not all of these roles are mentioned in the Local Authorities Social Services Act, Sch. 1, but those that are not mentioned will fall within the broader frameworks of providing social work support to children in need (see Chapter 8) and vulnerable adults (see Chapters 4 and 5).

We have organised these topics into four broad headings:

(a) philosophy, statutory framework, issues, and role of the social worker;
(b) procedures before charge, including quasi-criminal orders (this section is relevant to vulnerable suspects of all ages);
(c) procedures after charge — remand, bail and appearance in court;
(d) court procedures and sentencing options for child offenders;

7.1 Philosophy, statutory framework, issues, and role of the social worker

7.1.1 Philosophy of the youth justice system

The Crime and Disorder Act 1998, s. 42 defines the youth justice system as:

the system of criminal justice in so far as it relates to children and young persons.

'Children' in the criminal justice legislation means aged below 14, and 'young persons' means 14 through to 17. The distinction is not significant or helpful, and for simplicity, unless we are quoting, we will talk of children or juveniles.

Is the justice system about the welfare of the child or holding children and families responsible? Sue Bandalli writing in *Childright* [1997] vol. 141, 2, explores these issues in 'Juvenile Justice: a new government but the same direction.'

The 'welfare' approach can be illustrated by the Children and Young Persons Act 1969, which reflected the 1960s consensus that the causes of juvenile delinquency lay in family problems and social deprivation. The solution was treatment, advice, information and assistance aimed at both the juvenile and his family, which would continue until the problems were solved. Juvenile justice would be largely decriminalised for under 14s and restricted for under 16s, with increased use of civil care proceedings. Most of the Act was not implemented owing to a change of government. The criminal justice system, designed to allocate responsibility and punishment, has long been uncertain about the place of the child's welfare. With the failure to enact the decriminalisation provisions, welfare became largely meaningless. The remaining provisions were used to produce consequences entirely unforeseen by the architects of the legislation, with large numbers of juveniles being drawn into the criminal justice system and in particular, being incarcerated.

The 1980s, a Conservative era, was a time of unexpected enlightenment in the practice of juvenile justice. Whilst politicians still proclaimed the benefits of the short, sharp, shock and swift and certain punishment, in 1982 the Criminal Justice Act placed restrictions on the power of courts to lock young people away. Numbers fell dramatically, due to falling numbers of juveniles in the population, the publication of research about the damaging effects of custody and its high reconviction rates, together with mounting concern about the cost of financing incarceration. Schemes providing community alternatives received significant funding and a consensus emerged that children should be diverted from the criminal justice system by cautions and informal measures. There was increasing concern for the rights of young people which resulted in a more legalistic 'justice' approach. The 1980s were a time of success in the administration of juvenile justice.

The 1990s saw another change of direction. The criminal justice system became driven by retribution and deterrence. In 1992, the country was shocked and horrified when the murder of a two year old child by two 10 year old boys, Thompson and Venables, hit the headlines and stayed there for the trial and after-math. A wave of media-led despair followed which widened the focus onto the dreadful behaviour of some juveniles. Incidents were broadened and exaggerated, causing moral panic which evoked exuberant political rhetoric about being tough on crime.

The Conservative Government responded to the demands for something to be done. The momentum which built up resulted in one of the most retributive systems in Western Europe, unfortunately at odds with the principles of the UN Convention on the Rights of the Child. Even before the recent spate of new measures, the UN Committee, in its concluding observations on the administration of juvenile justice in England and Wales, had voiced 'general concern'.

The UN Convention on the Rights of the Child was ratified by the UK in 1991. The principles connected with the approach of the criminal justice system to young offenders advocate responses taking due account of the child's age, the desirability of working towards his re-integration and his assumption of a constructive role in society, using judicial proceedings and imprisonment for the shortest period of time only as a last resort (articles 40 and 37). These exist within the umbrella principle of the best interests of the child as a primary consideration (article 3).

The policies of the Conservative Government from 1993 onwards demonstrate that these principles have not been influential in government thinking. Retribution was the keyword in adult criminal justice with harsher penalties, longer sentences and a philosophy of 'prison works'. The measures against young offenders took a similar direction and resulted in many new provisions for young offenders. These included changing the Home Office Guidelines on cautioning so that most juveniles would have only one chance before being prosecuted (Home Office Circular 18/1994 para. 8); omitting the presumption in favour of not prosecuting juveniles from the Public Interest Considerations in the Guidelines; omitting youth as a category of vulnerable offenders in the Code for Crown Prosecutors (1994). Provisions in the Criminal Justice and Public Order Act 1994 include abolishing the right of silence of a juvenile questioned or charged (s. 34); increasing the maximum sentence for young offenders from 12 to 24 months (s. 17); extending the special sentencing provisions for serious offences to 10–13 year olds (s. 16(3)); establishing secure training units for non-serious but persistent offenders aged 12–14 (s. 1) and the naming and shaming of young convicted offenders by removing their anonymity (s. 49).

Section 37 of the Crime and Disorder Act 1998 sets out the statutory philosophy:

(1)   It shall be the principal aim of the youth justice system to prevent offending by children and young persons.
(2)   In addition to any other duty to which they are subject, it shall be the duty of all persons and bodies carrying out functions in relation to the youth justice system to have regard to that aim.

The 'other duties' referred to in section 37 include:

Every court in dealing with a child or young person who is brought before it, either as ... an offender or otherwise, shall have regard to the welfare of the child or young person ... (Children and Young Persons Act 1933, s. 44(1))
   Every local authority shall take reasonable steps designed to ... reduce the need to bring ... criminal proceedings against such children ... [and] to encourage children within their area not to commit criminal offences. (Children Act 1989, Schedule 2 para. 7)

A fuller statement of the approach which governs much of the recent legislation and guidance in the present chapter can be found in the Home Office Framework Document on the Crime and Disorder Act 1998. The full text can be found at **http://www.homeoffice.gov.uk/cdact/youjust.htm**

7.   The response to a child or young person's offending needs to be constructive and appropriate. Whether intervention following an admission of guilt or conviction is community-based or a custodial sentence, the emphasis should be on taking effective action to prevent further offending and on carrying out the groundwork needed to allow the child or young person to be effectively re-integrated into the community and to stay away from further crime. A nationwide youth justice system should have the capacity to reduce offending rates of all the children and young people with whom it deals and not only of those whose offending behaviour is easiest to tackle or of those who live in areas where local youth justice services have developed further than others.
8.   Many young people who offend can be dealt with effectively in the community and all areas need to ensure that a full range of community penalties are available, delivered and enforced in line with legislation and national standards. The Crime and Disorder Act provides for a new police final warning scheme and a range of new court powers which strengthen and widen the scope for effective community-based intervention when children and young people first offend.
9.   For those whose offending is serious or persistent, custody may, however, be the only way of protecting the public from further offending. It may be the best way of bringing home to the young person the seriousness of his or her behaviour and the best way of preventing the young person from continuing to offend. Placing a young person in a secure environment that

provides discipline, structure, education and training, as well as programmes to tackle offending behaviour, may provide a vital opportunity for the young person to break out of a pattern of offending and regain control of his or her behaviour. Good quality custodial facilities, as well as community based provision, need to be an integral part of youth justice services so that the youth justice system can intervene effectively with all children and young people who offend.

There is a complex interrelationship between political mood and legal principle. The age of criminal responsibility is a good topic to illustrate this issue.

The Children and Young Persons Act 1933 s 50, as amended in 1963, states:

It shall be conclusively presumed that no child under the age of ten years can be guilty of any offence.

Until 1963 the age was eight. As we see in the next article, in other jurisdictions it can be as high as 18 or as low as seven. But until 1998 there existed a rule known as '*doli incapax*' for 10 to 13 year olds. These children could not be convicted unless the prosecution could prove they knew that they were doing wrong. Many commentators are unhappy with the abolition of this rule. In an article in *Child and Family Law Quarterly* [1998] 209, 'Much Ado about Nothing — a critical comment on key provisions relating to children in the Crime and Crime and Disorder Act 1998', Loraine Gelsthorpe and Allison Morris write:

The age of criminal responsibility, set at 10 in England and Wales, is one of the lowest in Europe and, indeed, worldwide. It is, for example, 18 in Belgium and Luxembourg, 16 in Spain and Portugal, and 15 in Denmark, Finland and Sweden. This does not, of course, mean that children mature somewhat quicker in England than elsewhere. The age of criminal responsibility is a social and legal construct which reflects the age at which a particular society deems it appropriate to criminalise children. This young age of criminal responsibility in England, however used to be softened somewhat by the use of the presumption of *doli incapax* — the presumption that children under the age of 14 were incapable of crime. In effect, this meant that the prosecution of children was restricted until the age of 14 since, before that age, the prosecution had to establish not only that the child had the required *mens rea* for the specific crime charged, but also that the child knew that what s/he had done was *seriously* wrong and not merely naughty or mischievous.

... The importance of the presumption lay in its *symbolism*: it was a statement about the nature of childhood, the vulnerability of children and the appropriateness of *criminal justice sanctions* for children.

...

The abolition of *doli incapax* is also in breach of the UN Convention on the Rights of the Child which defines children as those under the age of 18. Indeed, in January 1995, the Committee on the Rights of the Child was critical of the extent to which the British Government had complied with this Convention. Specifically, it invited the then Government to give serious consideration to *raising* the age of criminal responsibility. Instead, the Government has effectively lowered it by making it easier to prosecute younger children. Also, as we will see in the next section, the Government has effectively lowered it by criminalising the activities of those below the age of 10. Further, Article 40(3) of the Convention provides that children's legal safeguards should be fully respected. By removing the safeguard of proving that children subject to penal measures actually understood that their offending was 'seriously wrong', the Government is again in breach of the Convention. The Home Office believes otherwise on the basis that the courts are likely to deal with 10 year olds differently from 17 year olds. Only time will tell.

7.1.2 Statutory framework

Youth courts (formerly juvenile courts) deal with all criminal trials of children, unless the child is jointly charged with an adult (see the following extract) or unless the offence is a 'grave crime' (see below page 444 where we deal with sentencing for grave crimes, and also page 394 below in relation to the Bulger case).

Special arrangements for dealing with children in court or during police investigation are set out in the legislation. Unless otherwise stated the Act from which these extracts are taken is the 1933 Children and Young Persons Act.

31(1)   Arrangements shall be made for preventing a child or young person while detained in a police station, or while being conveyed to or from any criminal court, or while waiting before or after attendance in any criminal court, from associating with an adult (not being a relative) who is charged with any offence other than an offence with which the child or young person is jointly charged, and for ensuring that a girl (being a child or young person) shall while so detained, being conveyed, or waiting, be under the care of a woman.

...

34(2)   Where a child or young person is in police detention, such steps as are practicable shall be taken to ascertain the identity of a person responsible for his welfare.

(3)   If it is practicable to ascertain the identity of a person responsible for the welfare of the child or young person, that person shall be informed, unless it is not practicable to do so —

(a)   that the child or young person has been arrested;

(b)   why he has been arrested; and

(c)   where he is being detained.

(4)   Where information falls to be given under subsection (3) above, it shall be given as soon as it is practicable to do so.

(5)   For the purposes of this section the persons who may be responsible for the welfare of a child or young person are —

(a)   his parent or guardian; or

(b)   any other person who has for the time being assumed responsibility for his welfare.

(6)   If it is practicable to give a person responsible for the welfare of the child or young person the information required by subsection (3) above, that person shall be given it as soon as it is practicable to do so.

If the child is under a supervision order or in local authority accommodation, the supervisor or the authority must also be notified under subsections (7) and 7(A) (not reproduced).

34A.(1)   Where a child or young person is charged with an offence or is for any other reason brought before a court, the court —

(a)   may in any case; and

(b)   shall in the case of a child or a young person who is under the age of sixteen years, require a person who is a parent or guardian of his to attend at the court during all the stages of the proceedings, unless and to the extent that the court is satisfied that it would be unreasonable to require such attendance, having regard to the circumstances of the case.

(2)   In relation to a child or young person for whom a local authority have parental responsibility and who —

(a)   is in their care; or

(b) is provided with accommodation by them in the exercise of any functions (in particular those under the Children Act 1989) which stand referred to their social services committee under the Local Authority Social Services Act 1970,

the reference in subsection (1) above to a person who is a parent or guardian of his shall be construed as a reference to that authority or, where he is allowed to live with such a person, as including such a reference.

The 1969 Children and Young Persons Act requires that:
5(8)   It shall be the duty of a person who decides to lay an information in respect of an offence in a case where he has reason to believe that the alleged offender is a young person to give notice of the decision to the appropriate local authority unless he is himself that authority.

A child defendant should not normally be identified to the public. This provision derives from the welfare approach to youth justice.

47(2)   ... No person shall be present at any sitting of a youth court except —
   (a) members and officers of the court;
   (b) parties to the case before the court, their solicitors and counsel, and witnesses and other persons directly concerned in that case;
   (c) bona fide representatives of newspapers or news agencies
[the broader words 'news gathering or reporting organisations' will be substituted under the Youth Justice and Criminal Evidence Act 1999, but the substitution is not yet in force];
   (d) such other persons as the court may specially authorise to be present;
39(1)   In relation to any proceedings in any court ... the court may direct that —
   (a) no newspaper report of the proceedings shall reveal the name, address, or school, or include any particulars calculated to lead to the identification, of any child or young person concerned in the proceedings, either as being the person by or against or in respect of whom the proceedings are taken, or as being a witness therein;
   (b) no picture shall be published in any newspaper as being or including a picture of any child or young person so concerned in the proceedings as aforesaid;
except in so far (if at all) as may be permitted by the direction of the court.
49(1)   The following prohibitions apply (subject to subsection (5) below) in relation to any proceedings to which this section applies, that is to say —
   (a) no report shall be published which reveals the name, address or school of any child or young person concerned in the proceedings or includes any particulars likely to lead to the identification of any child or young person concerned in the proceedings; and
   (b) no picture shall be published or included in a programme service as being or including a picture of any child or young person concerned in the proceedings.
   (2)   The proceedings to which this section applies are —
   (a) proceedings in a youth court;
   (b) proceedings on appeal from a youth court (including proceedings by way of case stated);
   (c) proceedings under section 15 or 16 of the Children and Young Persons Act 1969 (proceedings for varying or revoking supervision orders); and
   (d) [not reproduced]
   (3)   The reports to which this section applies are reports in a newspaper and reports included in a programme service; and similarly as respects pictures.
   (4)   For the purposes of this section a child or young person is 'concerned' in any proceedings whether as being the person against or in respect of whom the proceedings are taken or as being a witness in the proceedings.

(5)   Subject to subsection (7) below, a court may, in relation to proceedings before it to which this section applies, by order dispense to any specified extent with the requirements of this section in relation to a child or young person who is concerned in the proceedings if it is satisfied —

(a) that it is appropriate to do so for the purpose of avoiding injustice to the child or young person; or

(b) that, as respects a child or young person to whom this paragraph applies who is unlawfully at large, it is necessary to dispense with those requirements for the purpose of apprehending him and bringing him before a court or returning him to the place in which he was in custody.

(6)   Paragraph (b) of subsection (5) above applies to any child or young person who is charged with or has been convicted of —

(a) a violent offence,

(b) a sexual offence, or

(c) an offence punishable in the case of a person aged 21 or over with imprisonment for fourteen years or more.

Can a child be tried in the adult magistrates courts?

46(1)   Subject as hereinafter provided, no charge against a child or young person ... shall be heard by a court of summary jurisdiction which is not a youth court:
Provided that —

(a) a charge made jointly against a child or young person and a person who has attained the age of eighteen years shall be heard by a court of summary jurisdiction other than a youth court; and

(b) where a child or young person is charged with an offence, the charge may be heard by a court of summary jurisdiction which is not a youth court if a person who has attained the age of eighteen years is charged at the same time with aiding, abetting, causing, procuring, allowing or permitting that offence; and

(c) where, in the course of any proceedings before any court of summary jurisdiction other than a youth court, it appears that the person to whom the proceedings relate is a child or young person, nothing in this subsection shall be construed as preventing the court, if it thinks fit so to do, from proceeding with the hearing and determination of those proceedings.

The following section is from the Children and Young Persons Act 1969
18.   Notwithstanding section 46(1) of the principal Act (which restricts the jurisdiction of magistrates' courts which are not youth courts in cases where a child or young person is charged with an offence) a magistrates' court which is not a youth court may hear an information against a child or young person if he is charged —

(a) with aiding, abetting, causing, procuring, allowing or permitting an offence with which a person who has attained the age of eighteen is charged at the same time; or

(b) with an offence arising out of circumstances which are the same as or connected with those giving rise to an offence with which a person who has attained the age of eighteen is charged at the same time.

Can a child be sent to a Crown Court for trial? This is governed by the Magistrates Courts Act 1980 s. 24.

24(1)   Where a person under the age of 18 years appears or is brought before a magistrates' court on an information charging him with an indictable offence other than homicide, he shall be tried summarily unless —
   (a)   the offence is such as is mentioned in subsection (1) or (2) of section 91 of the Powers of Criminal Courts (Sentencing) Act 2000 (under which young persons convicted on indictment of certain grave crimes may be sentenced to be detained for long periods) and the court considers that if he is found guilty of the offence it ought to be possible to sentence him in pursuance of subsection (3) of that section; or
   (b)   he is charged jointly with a person who has attained the age of 18 years and the court considers it necessary in the interests of justice to commit them both for trial;
and accordingly in a case falling within paragraph (a) or (b) of this subsection the court shall commit the accused for trial if either it is of opinion that there is sufficient evidence to put him on trial or it has power under section 6(2) above so to commit him without consideration of the evidence.

[Grave crimes and homicide must be tried in the Crown Court whatever the age of the defendant. These will be mentioned in relation to the *Bulger* case (below); the 2000 Act is covered below when we look at sentencing. The reference to section 6 is to the committal process for the magistrates, court to decide, in either way cases, if there is a case to put to the jury in Crown Court.]

24(1A)   Where a magistrates' court —
   (a)   commits a person under the age of 18 for trial for an offence of homicide; or
   (b)   in a case falling within subsection (1)(a) above, commits such a person for trial for an offence,
the court may also commit him for trial for any other indictable offence with which he is charged at the same time if the charges for both offences could be joined in the same indictment.

(2)   Where, in a case falling within subsection (1)(b) above, a magistrates' court commits a person under the age of 18 years for trial for an offence with which he is charged jointly with a person who has attained that age, the court may also commit him for trial for any other indictable offence with which he is charged at the same time (whether jointly with the person who has attained that age or not) if the charges for both offences could be joined in the same indictment.

7.1.3 **The Bulger case — an example of difficult issues in youth justice**

This case aroused and still commands enormous public and press interest. As a charge of murder, the trial took place in the Crown Court. The boys were ten at the time of the murder, and 11 when sentenced to detention during Her Majesty's Pleasure. Julia Fionda identifies some of the issues in '*R v Secretary of State for the Home Department ex p Thompson and Venables* "The age of innocence? The concept of childhood in the punishment of young offender" ', *Child and Family Law Quarterly* [1998] 77:

The Children Act 1908, which created the juvenile court, marked the birth of the juvenile justice system in England and Wales. The early nineteenth century had been marked by its punitive stance towards youth crime. The punishment approach drew no distinction between children and adults in the attribution of blame and the infliction of penalties, being founded on an almost religious equation of crime and sin for which retribution was the only response. The Children Act 1908 gave legislative form to the welfare approach which had developed throughout the previous 50 years. The new juvenile court, now renamed the Youth Court, was symbolic of the emergence of a separate and distinct criminal justice system which was to deal with all but the most heinous of youth crime. The foundation of such a court was based upon a widespread belief that children who offend require, and are worthy of, a response from criminal justice authorities which recognises their immaturity, their sensitivity and their lack of full awareness of the consequences of their behaviour. In short, this new court was to recognise the nature of childhood (as it was then perceived) and structure its system of punishment accordingly.

...

However, the 1990s have witnessed a fundamental reversal of this approach to youth crime. A series of legislative changes, major judicial decisions and reformulations of policy have in common an almost stubborn blindness towards the incapacity of children. Political expediency and a long-standing media panic over how youth crime should be dealt with have dictated a redefinition of the nature of childhood and, in some cases, a complete refusal to recognise it as a concept at all in the development of policy and practice in this field. The theme which underpins this turbulent and dynamic period in the history of youth justice is the lack of emphasis on 'youth' and the greater emphasis on 'justice'. The Court of Appeal and House of Lords' judgments in *R v Secretary of State for the Home Department ex parte Venables and Thompson* are the latest in this line of developments which fail to acknowledge that a discrete approach to the punishment of young offenders is the keystone of the youth justice system.

Background to the case
On 12 February 1993 James Bulger, aged two, was abducted from a shopping centre [in Bootle] and was later found murdered. Shortly afterwards, Jon Venables and Robert Thompson (both aged 10 at the time) were arrested and charged with the murder. On 24 November 1993, after a very public Crown Court trial, the two defendants were found guilty and sentenced to detention during Her Majesty's pleasure — a mandatory penalty in respect of children convicted of murder by virtue of CYPA 1933, section 53(1).

The arrest, trial, conviction and sentencing of the two defendants gave rise to an almost unprecedented degree of media commentary and speculation. However, not only was the amount of press coverage unusually high, but it was also virtually unanimous and dogmatic in its vilification of the two boys, their parents and the causative factors attributed to the violent killing. The defendants were labelled with descriptions such as 'monsters', 'freaks', and 'animals' and the trial judge contributed to this melting pot of critique when he described the killing as 'an act of unparalleled evil and barbarity' and told the boys that their conduct was 'both cunning and very wicked'. Analysis of this case added fuel to an existing media debate over youth crime generally; the problem of joyriding had already sparked discussion of fears over the increased incidence and persistence of youth crime. The conviction of Venables and Thompson added a new facet to the discussion — whether young offenders were becoming increasingly violent at an earlier age.

The judicial review was about the Home Secretary's apparently politically motivated decision to increase the tariff. The House of Lords, by a majority, ruled that the setting of a punitive tariff, which closed the door to release based on a child offender's progress, was illegal. Fionda concludes her analysis:

This tough, justice-based rhetoric signifies a return to the nineteenth century punishment approach. Former Home Secretary Michael Howard's assessment that 'crime is caused by criminals' mirrors this approach based on classicist criminology. Since all crime, according to this model, is a product of free will and volition, the appropriate response is retribution proportionate to society's condemnation, and punishment proportionate to the gravity of the crime. Hence, there is no material difference between the child offender and the adult offender since both are deemed to have rationally chosen to commit the crime and both are therefore fully accountable for their actions.

This view is very evident within the decision of the Court of Appeal and the minority in the House of Lords in *R v Secretary of State for the Home Department ex parte Venables and Thompson*. Their approach was to justify the use of adult procedures in the punishment of two 11-year-old offenders through the heinousness of the offence, which precluded any other approach. The majority in the House of Lords preferred to follow the welfare model, as illustrated by their emphasis on the relevance of section 44 of the CYPA 1933. This, more recent model focuses on the underlying sociological disorders of the offender, of which crime is symptomatic, and on offering assistance or treatment to the individual as a response to their offending behaviour. Although widely criticised in the 1960s and 1970s for its non-proportionate and over-interventionist approach which undermined the autonomy and rights of the child, this model at least recognised the relevance of a child's incomplete development and his potential to reform and change within the punishment process. The potential for change in the character of the offender was the basis of the House of Lords' concern about the rigidity of the very long tariff set by the Home Secretary.

At the time, the Human Rights Act (see Chapter 2) was not in force, so Thompson and Venables brought an appeal to the European Court of Human Rights. The full case report of *V v United Kingdom*, 0002488/94, heard 6.12.99, can be read at: **http://hudoc.echr.coe.int/hudoc/**

51.   The applicant applied to the Commission on 20 May 1994. He alleged that, in view of his young age, his trial in public in an adult Crown Court and the punitive nature of his sentence constituted violations of his right not to be subjected to inhuman or degrading treatment or punishment as guaranteed under Article 3 of the European Convention on Human Rights. He further complained that he had been denied a fair trial in breach of Article 6 of the Convention, that he had suffered discrimination in breach of Article 14 in that a child aged younger than ten at the time of the alleged offence would not have been held criminally responsible; that the sentence imposed on him of detention during Her Majesty's pleasure amounted to a breach of his right to liberty under Article 5; and that the fact that a government minister, rather than a judge, was responsible for setting the tariff violated his rights under Article 6. Finally, he complained under Article 5 para. 4 of the Convention that he had not had the opportunity to have the continuing lawfulness of his detention examined by a judicial body, such as the Parole Board.

The European Court of Human Rights took into account the international texts relating to trials of children. The commentaries are from the original documents, not the judgment of the Court:

45.   The Beijing Rules were adopted by the United Nations General Assembly on 29 November 1985. These Rules are not binding in international law; in the Preamble, States are invited, but not required, to adopt them. They provide, as relevant:

4.   Age of criminal responsibility
4.1   In those legal systems recognising the concept of the age of criminal responsibility for juveniles, the beginning of that age shall not be fixed at too low an age level, bearing in mind the facts of emotional, mental and intellectual maturity.

Commentary
The minimum age of criminal responsibility differs widely owing to history and culture. The modern approach would be to consider whether a child can live up to the moral and

psychological components of criminal responsibility; that is, whether a child, by virtue of her or his individual discernment and understanding, can be held responsible for essentially anti-social behaviour. If the age of criminal responsibility is fixed too low or if there is no lower age limit at all, the notion of criminal responsibility would become meaningless. In general, there is a close relationship between the notion of responsibility for delinquent or criminal behaviour and other social rights and responsibilities (such as marital status, civil majority, etc.).

Efforts should therefore be made to agree on a reasonable lowest age limit that is applicable internationally.

...

8. Protection of privacy
8.1   The juvenile's privacy shall be respected at all stages in order to avoid harm being caused to her or him by undue publicity or by the process of labelling.
8.2   In principle, no information that may lead to the identification of a juvenile offender shall be published.

...

17. Guiding principles in adjudication and disposition
17.1   The disposition of the competent authorities shall be guided by the following principles:
  (a) The reaction taken shall always be in proportion not only to the circumstances and gravity of the offence but also to the circumstances and the needs of the child as well as to the needs of the society;
  (b) Restrictions on the personal liberty of the juvenile shall be imposed only after careful consideration and shall be limited to the possible minimum;

...

  (d) The well-being of the juvenile shall be the guiding factor in the consideration of her or his case.

...

Commentary

...

Rule 17.1(b) implies that strictly punitive approaches are not appropriate. Whereas in adult cases, and possibly also in cases of severe offences by juveniles, just desert and retributive sanctions might be considered to have some merit, in juvenile cases such considerations should always be outweighed by the interest of safeguarding the well-being and future of the young person.

...'

B. The United Nations Convention on the Rights of the Child (1989)
46.   This treaty (hereafter 'the UN Convention'), adopted by the General Assembly of the United Nations on 20 November 1989, has binding force under international law on the Contracting States, including all of the member States of the Council of Europe.
Article 3 para. 1 of the UN Convention states:
'In all actions concerning children, whether undertaken by public or private social welfare institutions, courts of law, administrative, authoritative, or legislative bodies, the best interest of the child shall be a primary consideration.'
Article 37 (a) and (b) provides:
'States Parties shall ensure that:
  (a) No child shall be subjected to torture or other cruel, inhuman or degrading treat-ment or punishment. Neither capital punishment nor life imprisonment without the

possibility of release shall be imposed for offences committed by persons below eighteen years of age;

(b) No child shall be deprived of his or her liberty unlawfully or arbitrarily. The arrest, detention or imprisonment of a child shall be in conformity with the law and shall be used only as a measure of last resort and for the shortest appropriate period of time ...'

Article 40 provides, as relevant:

1. States Parties recognise the right of every child alleged as, accused of, or recognised as having infringed the penal law to be treated in a manner consistent with the promotion of the child's sense of dignity and worth, which reinforces the child's respect for the human rights and fundamental freedoms of others and which takes into account the child's age and the desirability of promoting the child's reintegration and the child's assuming a constructive role in society.

2. To this end ... the States Parties shall, in particular, ensure that:

...

(b) Every child alleged as or accused of having infringed the penal law has at least the following guarantees:

...

(vii) To have his or her privacy fully respected at all stages of the proceedings.

3. States Parties shall seek to promote the establishment of laws, procedures, authorities and institutions, specifically applicable to children alleged as, accused of, or recognised as having infringed the penal law, and, in particular:

(a) The establishment of a minimum age below which children shall be presumed not to have the capacity to infringe the penal law;

(b) Whenever appropriate and desirable, measures for the dealing with such children without resorting to judicial proceedings, providing that human rights and legal safeguards are fully respected.

...'

C.   Report on the United Kingdom by the Committee on the Rights of the Child

47.   In its concluding observations in respect of the United Kingdom (CRC/C/15/add. 34) dated 15 February 1995, the Committee set up by the United Nations to monitor compliance with the UN Convention stated, *inter alia*:

35.   The Committee recommends that law reform be pursued to ensure that the system of the administration of juvenile justice is child-oriented ...

36.   More specifically, the Committee recommends that serious consideration be given to raising the age of criminal responsibility throughout the areas of the United Kingdom ...

D.   International Covenant on Civil and Political Rights (1966)

48.   The Covenant provides in Article 14 para. 4, which broadly corresponds to Article 6 of the European Convention, that:

'In the case of juvenile persons, the procedure shall be such as will take account of their age and the desirability of promoting their rehabilitation.'

E.   Recommendation no. R (87) 20 of the Committee of Ministers of the Council of Europe

49.   The above recommendation, adopted by the Committee of Ministers on 17 September 1987, states, *inter alia*:

'The Committee of Ministers, under the terms of Article 15.*b* of the Statute of the Council of Europe,

...

Considering that social reactions to juvenile delinquency should take account of the personality and specific needs of minors, and that the latter need specialised interventions and, where appropriate, specialised treatment, based in particular on the principles embodied in the United Nations Declaration of the Rights of the Child;

Convinced that the penal system for minors should continue to be characterised by its objective of education and social integration ...;

...

Having regard to the United Nations Standard Minimum Rules for the Administration of Juvenile Justice (the Beijing Rules),

Recommends the governments of member states to review, if necessary, their legislation and practice with a view:

...

4. to ensuring that minors are tried more rapidly, avoiding undue delay, so as to ensure effective educational action;
5. to avoiding committing minors to adult courts, where juvenile courts exist;

...

8. to reinforcing the legal position of minors throughout the proceedings ... by recognising, *inter alia*:

...

the right of juveniles to respect for their private lives;

...'

We now turn to the court's deliberations over the trial of the two boys. Space permits only key paragraphs to be selected.

69.   The Court observes at the outset that Article 3 enshrines one of the most fundamental values of democratic society. It prohibits in absolute terms torture or inhuman or degrading treatment or punishment, irrespective of the victim's conduct (see the *Chahal v the United Kingdom* judgment of 15 November 1996, Reports 1996-V, p. 1855, para. 79). The nature of the crime committed by T. and the applicant is, therefore, immaterial to the consideration under Article 3.

74.   The Court does not consider that there is at this stage any clear common standard amongst the member States of the Council of Europe as to the minimum age of criminal responsibility. Even if England and Wales is among the few European jurisdictions to retain a low age of criminal responsibility, the age of ten cannot be said to be so young as to differ disproportionately from the age-limit followed by other European States. The Court concludes that the attribution of criminal responsibility to the applicant does not in itself give rise to a breach of Article 3 of the Convention.

75.   The second part of the applicant's complaint under Article 3 concerning the trial relates to the fact that the criminal proceedings took place over three weeks in public in an adult Crown Court with attendant formality, and that, after his conviction, his name was permitted to be published.

78.   The Court recognises that the criminal proceedings against the applicant were not motivated by any intention on the part of the State authorities to humiliate him or cause him suffering. Indeed, special measures were taken to modify the Crown Court procedure in order to attenuate the rigours of an adult trial in view of the defendants' young age ... .

79.   Even if there is evidence that proceedings such as those applied to the applicant could be expected to have a harmful effect on an eleven-year-old child ..., the Court considers that any proceedings or inquiry to determine the circumstances of the acts committed by T. and the applicant, whether such inquiry had been carried out in public or in private, attended by the formality of the Crown Court or informally in the youth court, would have provoked in the applicant feelings of guilt, distress, anguish and fear. The psychiatric evidence shows that before the trial commenced he was suffering from the post-traumatic effects of the offence; that he cried inconsolably and found it difficult and distressing when asked to talk about what he and T. had done to the two-year-old, and that he suffered fears of punishment and terrible retribution ... Whilst the public nature of the proceedings may have exacerbated to a certain extent these feelings in the applicant, the Court is not convinced that the particular features of the trial process as applied to him caused, to a significant degree, suffering going beyond that which would inevitably have been engendered by any attempt by the authorities to deal with the applicant following the commission by him of the offence in question ... .

80.   In conclusion, therefore, the Court does not consider that the applicant's trial gave rise to a violation of Article 3 of the Convention.

C.   Article 6 para. 1 of the Convention

81.   'In addition, the applicant complained that he had been denied a fair trial in breach of Article 6, para. 1 of the Convention, which states:

'In the determination of ... any criminal charge against him, everyone is entitled to a fair and public hearing within a reasonable time by an independent and impartial tribunal established by law. Judgment shall be pronounced publicly but the press and public may be excluded from all or part of the trial in the interests of morals, public order or national security in a democratic society, where the interests of juveniles or the protection of the private life of the parties so require, or to the extent strictly necessary in the opinion of the court in special circumstances where publicity would prejudice the interests of justice.'

82.   The applicant submitted that the right to a fair trial under Article 6 para. 1 of the Convention implies the right of an accused to be present so that he can participate effectively in the conduct of his case (he relied upon the *Stanford* v *the United Kingdom* judgment of 23 February 1994, Series A no. 282-A, pp. 10–11, para. 26). He referred to psychiatric and other evidence which established that the applicant was no more emotionally mature than an eight- or nine-year-old, that he did not fully attend to or understand the proceedings and that he was too traumatised and intimidated to give his own account of events, either to his lawyers, the psychiatrist who interviewed him, or to the court ...

83.   The Government disputed that the public nature of the trial breached the applicant's rights. They emphasised that a public trial serves to protect the interests of defendants as a guarantee that proceedings will be conducted fairly and by encouraging witnesses to come forward. Moreover, hearings of grave charges should take place in open court because of the legitimate public interest in knowing what has occurred and why, and to maintain confidence in the administration of justice. They pointed out that the applicant was represented by highly experienced leading counsel and that the procedure was modified as far as possible to facilitate his understanding and participation ...

86.   The Court recalls its above findings that there is not at this stage any clear common standard amongst the member States of the Council of Europe as to the minimum age of criminal responsibility and that the attribution of criminal responsibility to the applicant does not in itself give rise to a breach of Article 3 of the Convention (see paragraph 74 above). Likewise, it cannot be said that the trial on criminal charges of a child, even one as young as eleven, as such violates the fair trial guarantee under Article 6, para. 1. The Court does, however, agree with the Commission that it is essential that a child charged with an offence is dealt with in a manner

which takes full account of his age, level of maturity and intellectual and emotional capacities, and that steps are taken to promote his ability to understand and participate in the proceedings.

87.   It follows that, in respect of a young child charged with a grave offence attracting high levels of media and public interest, it would be necessary to conduct the hearing in such a way as to reduce as far as possible his or her feelings of intimidation and inhibition. In this connection it is noteworthy that in England and Wales children charged with less serious crimes are dealt with in special youth courts, from which the general public is excluded and in relation to which there are imposed automatic reporting restrictions on the media ... Moreover, the Court has already referred to the international tendency towards the protection of the privacy of child defendants (see paragraph 77 above). It has considered carefully the Government's argument that public trials serve the general interest in the open administration of justice (see paragraph 83 above), and observes that, where appropriate in view of the age and other characteristics of the child and the circumstances surrounding the criminal proceedings, this general interest could be satisfied by a modified procedure providing for selected attendance rights and judicious reporting.

88.   The Court notes that the applicant's trial took place over three weeks in public in the Crown Court. Special measures were taken in view of the applicant's young age and to promote his understanding of the proceedings: for example, he had the trial procedure explained to him and was taken to see the courtroom in advance, and the hearing times were shortened so as not to tire the defendants excessively. Nonetheless, the formality and ritual of the Crown Court must at times have seemed incomprehensible and intimidating for a child of eleven, and there is evidence that certain of the modifications to the courtroom, in particular the raised dock which was designed to enable the defendants to see what was going on, had the effect of increasing the applicant's sense of discomfort during the trial, since he felt exposed to the scrutiny of the press and public. The trial generated extremely high levels of press and public interest, both inside and outside the courtroom, to the extent that the judge in his summing-up referred to the problems caused to witnesses by the blaze of publicity and asked the jury to take this into account when assessing their evidence ...

90.   In such circumstances the Court does not consider that it was sufficient for the purposes of Article 6 para. 1 that the applicant was represented by skilled and experienced lawyers. This case is different from that of *Stanford* (cited in paragraph 82 above), where the Court found no violation arising from the fact that the accused could not hear some of the evidence given at trial, in view of the fact that his counsel, who could hear all that was said and was able to take his client's instructions at all times, chose for tactical reasons not to request that the accused be seated closer to the witnesses. Here, although the applicant's legal representatives were seated, as the Government put it, 'within whispering distance', it is highly unlikely that the applicant would have felt sufficiently uninhibited, in the tense courtroom and under public scrutiny, to have consulted with them during the trial or, indeed, that, given his immaturity and his disturbed emotional state, he would have been capable outside the courtroom of cooperating with his lawyers and giving them information for the purposes of his defence.

91.   In conclusion, the Court considers that the applicant was unable to participate effectively in the criminal proceedings against him and was, in consequence, denied a fair hearing in breach of Article 6 para. 1.

The Court also dealt with the issue of the tariff, which had gone to the House of Lords, and held that, under Art. 6(1), this should be a judicial decision, not one for the Home Secretary. We have not reproduced this part of the court's judgment.

The Lord Chief Justice, Lord Woolf, had the task of putting the European Court of Human Rights ruling into effect, and has now ruled that Venables and Thompson should serve eight years in total (*Re Thompson and Another (Tariff Recommendations)*

[2001] 1 All ER 737.) He also issued a practice direction: *Crown Court: Young Defendants, reported at* [2000] 1 WLR 659.

The overriding principle

3.   Some young defendants accused of committing serious crimes may be very young and very immature when standing trial in the Crown Court. The purpose of such trial is to determine guilt (if that is in issue) and decide the appropriate sentence if the young defendant pleads guilty or is convicted. The trial process should not itself expose the young defendant to avoidable intimidation, humiliation or distress. All possible steps should be taken to assist the young defendant to understand and participate in the proceedings. The ordinary trial process should so far as necessary be adapted to meet those ends. Regard should be had to the welfare of the young defendant as required by Section 44 of the Children and Young Persons Act 1933.

Before trial

4.   If a young defendant is indicted jointly with an adult defendant, the court should consider at the plea and directions hearing whether the young defendant should be tried on his own and should ordinarily so order unless of opinion that a joint trial would be in the interests of justice and would not be unduly prejudicial to the welfare of the young defendant. If a young defendant is tried jointly with an adult the ordinary procedures will apply subject to such modifications (if any) as the court may see fit to order.

5.   At the plea and directions hearing before trial of a young defendant, the court should consider and so far as practicable give directions on the matters covered in paragraphs 9 to 15 below inclusive.

6.   It may be appropriate to arrange that a young defendant should visit, out of court hours and before the trial, the courtroom in which the trial is to be held so that he can familiarise himself with it.

7.   If any case against a young defendant has attracted or may attract widespread public or media interest, the assistance of the police should be enlisted to try and ensure that a young defendant is not, when attending for the trial, exposed to intimidation, vilification or abuse.

8.   The court should be ready at this stage (if it has not already done so) to give a direction under section 39 of the Children and Young Persons Act 1933 or, as the case may be, section 45 of the Youth Justice and Criminal Evidence Act 1999. Any such order, once made, should be reduced to writing and copies should on request be made available to anyone affected or potentially affected by it.

[These relate to orders prohibiting identification of the child — see above.]

The trial

9.   The trial should, if practicable, be held in a courtroom in which all the participants are on the same or almost the same level.

10.   A young defendant should normally, if he wishes, be free to sit with members of his family or others in a like relationship and in a place which permits easy, informal communication with his legal representatives and others with whom he wants or needs to communicate.

11.   The court should explain the course of proceedings to a young defendant in terms he can understand, should remind those representing a young defendant of their continuing duty to explain each step of the trial to him and should ensure, so far as practicable, that the trial is conducted in language which the young defendant can understand.

12.   The trial should be conducted according to a timetable which takes full account of a young defendant's inability to concentrate for long periods. Frequent and regular breaks will often be appropriate.

13.   Robes and wigs should not be worn unless the young defendant asks that they should or the court for good reason orders that they should. Any person responsible for the security of a

young defendant who is in custody should not be in uniform. There should be no recognisable police presence in the courtroom save for good reason.

14.   The court should be prepared to restrict attendance at the trial to a small number, perhaps limited to some of those with an immediate and direct interest in the outcome of the trial. The court should rule on any challenged claim to attend.

15.   Facilities for reporting the trial (subject to any direction given under section 39 of the 1933 Act or section 45 of the 1999 Act) must be provided. But the court may restrict the number of those attending in the courtroom to report the trial to such number as is judged practicable and desirable. In ruling on any challenged claim to attend the courtroom for the purpose of reporting the trial the court should be mindful of the public's general right to be informed about the administration of justice in the Crown Court. Where access to the courtroom by reporters is restricted, arrangements should be made for the proceedings to be relayed, audibly and if possible visually, to another room in the same court complex to which the media have free access if it appears that there will be a need for such additional facilities.

7.1.4 **The social worker's place in the statutory framework**

The framework for youth justice is established by the 1998 Crime and Disorder Act. Interestingly, social work roles in the 1998 Act were not added to the list of statutory duties of social services department under the Local Authority Social Services Act (LASSA) 1970 (Chapter 1 above). But there remains the overarching duty to keep children from committing or being charged with crimes under the Children Act 1989 schedule 2, and this *is* listed as a statutory duty under LASSA, Sch. 1.

5.(1)   Subject to the provisions of this section, the functions conferred by section 6 below shall be exercisable in relation to each local government area by the responsible authorities, that is to say —

   (a)   the council for the area and, where the area is a district and the council is not a unitary authority, the council for the county which includes the district; and

   (b)   every chief officer of police any part of whose police area lies within the area.

(2)   In exercising those functions, the responsible authorities shall act in cooperation with the following persons and bodies, namely —

   (a)   every police authority any part of whose police area lies within the area;

   (b)   every probation committee or health authority any part of whose area lies within the area; and

   (c)   every person or body of a description which is for the time being prescribed by order of the Secretary of State under this subsection;

and it shall be the duty of those persons and bodies to co-operate in the exercise by the responsible authorities of those functions.

(3)   The responsible authorities shall also invite the participation in their exercise of those functions of at least one person or body of each description which is for the time being prescribed by order of the Secretary of State under this subsection.

(4)   In this section and sections 6 and 7 below 'local government area' means —

   (a)   in relation to England, each district or London borough, the City of London, the Isle of Wight and the Isles of Scilly;

   (b)   in relation to Wales, each county or county borough.

6.(1)   The responsible authorities for a local government area shall, in accordance with the provisions of section 5 above and this section, formulate and implement, for each relevant period, a strategy for the reduction of crime and disorder in the area.

    (2)   Before formulating a strategy, the responsible authorities shall —

        (a) carry out a review of the levels and patterns of crime and disorder in the area (taking due account of the knowledge and experience of persons in the area);

        (b) prepare an analysis of the results of that review;

        (c) publish in the area a report of that analysis; and

        (d) obtain the views on that report of persons or bodies in the area (including those of a description prescribed by order under section 5(3) above), whether by holding public meetings or otherwise.

Part III of the 1998 Act then requires each social services authority to establish a Youth Offending Team with defined objectives (under s. 37, the overriding one is to reduce offending — see above). The YOT will work with children of all ages, but since a child under ten cannot, by definition, be an offender, the name given to these teams — in referring to 'offending' — may be inaccurate:

38.(1)   It shall be the duty of each local authority, acting in cooperation with the persons and bodies mentioned in subsection (2) below, to secure that, to such extent as is appropriate for their area, all youth justice services are available there.

    (2)   It shall be the duty of —

        (a) every chief officer of police or police authority any part of whose police area lies within the local authority's area; and

        (b) every probation committee or health authority any part of whose area lies within that area, to co-operate in the discharge by the local authority of their duty under subsection (1) above.

    (3)   The local authority and every person or body mentioned in subsection (2) above shall have power to make payments towards expenditure incurred in the provision of youth justice services —

        (a) by making the payments directly; or

        (b) by contributing to a fund, established and maintained by the local authority, out of which the payments may be made.

    (4)   In this section and sections 39 to 41 below 'youth justice services' means any of the following, namely —

        (a) the provision of persons to act as appropriate adults to safeguard the interests of children and young persons detained or questioned by police officers;

        (b) the assessment of children and young persons, and the provision for them of rehabilitation programmes, for the purposes of section 66(2) below;

        (c) the provision of support for children and young persons remanded or committed on bail while awaiting trial or sentence;

        (d) the placement in local authority accommodation of children and young persons remanded or committed to such accommodation under section 23 of the Children and Young Persons Act 1969 ('the 1969 Act');

        (e) the provision of reports or other information required by courts in criminal proceedings against children and young persons;

        (f) the provision of persons to act as responsible officers in relation to parenting orders, child safety orders, reparation orders and action plan orders;

        (g) the supervision of young persons sentenced to a community rehabilitation order, a community punishment order or a community punishment and rehabilitation order;

        (h) the supervision of children and young persons sentenced to a detention and training order or a supervision order;

        (i) the post-release supervision of children and young persons under section 37(4A) or 65 of the 1991 [release on licence — not reproduced] Act or section 31 of the Crime (Sentences) Act 1997 ('the 1997 Act') [release of life prisoners on licence — not reproduced];

(j) the performance of functions under subsection (1) of section 75 below by such persons as may be authorised by the Secretary of State under that subsection.

(5) The Secretary of State may by order amend subsection (4) above so as to extend, restrict or otherwise alter the definition of 'youth justice services' for the time being specified in that subsection.

39.(1) Subject to subsection (2) below, it shall be the duty of each local authority, acting in cooperation with the persons and bodies mentioned in subsection (3) below, to establish for their area one or more youth offending teams.

(2) Two (or more) local authorities acting together may establish one or more youth offending teams for both (or all) their areas; and where they do so —

(a) any reference in the following provisions of this section (except subsection (4)(b)) to, or to the area of, the local authority or a particular local authority shall be construed accordingly, and

(b) the reference in subsection (4)(b) to the local authority shall be construed as a reference to one of the authorities.

(3) It shall be the duty of —

(a) every chief officer of police any part of whose police area lies within the local authority's area; and

(b) every probation committee or health authority any part of whose area lies within that area,

to co-operate in the discharge by the local authority of their duty under subsection (1) above.

(4) The local authority and every person or body mentioned in subsection (3) above shall have power to make payments towards expenditure incurred by, or for purposes connected with, youth offending teams —

(a) by making the payments directly; or

(b) by contributing to a fund, established and maintained by the local authority, out of which the payments may be made.

(5) A youth offending team shall include at least one of each of the following, namely —

(a) a probation officer;

(b) a social worker of a local authority social services department;

(c) a police officer;

(d) a person nominated by a health authority any part of whose area lies within the local authority's area;

(e) a person nominated by the chief education officer appointed by the local authority under section 532 of the Education Act 1996.

(6) A youth offending team may also include such other persons as the local authority thinks appropriate after consulting the persons and bodies mentioned in subsection (3) above.

(7) It shall be the duty of the youth offending team or teams established by a particular local authority —

(a) to co-ordinate the provision of youth justice services for all those in the authority's area who need them; and

(b) to carry out such functions as are assigned to the team or teams in the youth justice plan formulated by the authority under section 40(1) below.

40.(1) It shall be the duty of each local authority, after consultation with the relevant persons and bodies, to formulate and implement for each year a plan (a 'youth justice plan') setting out —

(a) how youth justice services in their area are to be provided and funded; and

(b) how the youth offending team or teams established by them (whether alone or jointly with one or more other local authorities) are to be composed and funded, how they are to operate, and what functions they are to carry out.

(2) In subsection (1) above 'the relevant persons and bodies' means the persons and bodies mentioned in section 38(2) above and, where the local authority is a county council, any district councils whose districts form part of its area.

(3) The functions assigned to a youth offending team under subsection (1)(b) above may include, in particular, functions under paragraph 7(b) of Schedule 2 to the 1989 [Children] Act (local authority's duty to take reasonable steps designed to encourage children and young persons not to commit offences).

(4) A local authority shall submit their youth justice plan to the Board established under section 41 below, and shall publish it in such manner and by such date as the Secretary of State may direct.

These sections are explained by Home Office guidance on the legislation (Home Office Crime and Disorder Act 1998 Framework Document — **www.homeoffice.gov.uk/ cdact/youjust.htm**, not reproduced.)

7.2 Investigation of crime and procedures before charge

7.2.1 The child in the police station

The word 'juvenile' in the Police and Criminal Evidence Act means a child under the age of 17. A child of 17 is dealt with as an adult during police investigation, even though then dealt with (normally) by the youth court.

The provision of 'appropriate adult' services during questioning is a duty for social services departments under the Crime and Disorder Act s. 38 (above). This includes appropriate adult services for vulnerable adult suspects.

We look first at police powers to detain a suspect, either for questioning or after charge. They are governed by the Police and Criminal Evidence Act 1984.

34(1) A person arrested for an offence shall not be kept in police detention except in accordance with the provisions of this Part of this Act.

(2) Subject to subsection (3) below, if at any time a custody officer —
   (a) becomes aware, in relation to any person in police detention, that the grounds for the detention of that person have ceased to apply; and
   (b) is not aware of any other grounds on which the continued detention of that person could be justified under the provisions of this Part of this Act,
it shall be the duty of the custody officer, subject to subsection (4) below, to order his immediate release from custody.

(5) A person whose release is ordered under subsection (2) above shall be released without bail unless it appears to the custody officer —
   (a) that there is need for further investigation of any matter in connection with which he was detained at any time during the period of his detention; or
   (b) that, in respect of any such matter, proceedings may be taken against him or he may be reprimanded or warned under section 65 of the Crime and Disorder Act 1998,
and, if it so appears, he shall be released on bail.

37(1)   Where —
    (a)   a person is arrested for an offence —

        ...

    the custody officer at each police station where he is detained after his arrest shall determine whether he has before him sufficient evidence to charge that person with the offence for which he was arrested and may detain him at the police station for such period as is necessary to enable him to do so.

  (2)   If the custody officer determines that he does not have such evidence before him, the person arrested shall be released either on bail or without bail, unless the custody officer has reasonable grounds for believing that his detention without being charged is necessary to secure or preserve evidence relating to an offence for which he is under arrest or to obtain such evidence by questioning him.

  (3)   If the custody officer has reasonable grounds for so believing, he may authorise the person arrested to be kept in police detention.

  (7)   Subject to section 41(7) below, if the custody officer determines that he has before him sufficient evidence to charge the person arrested with the offence for which he was arrested, the person arrested —
    (a)   shall be charged; or
    (b)   shall be released without charge, either on bail or without bail.

  (10)   The duty imposed on the custody officer under subsection (1) above shall be carried out by him as soon as practicable after the person arrested arrives at the police station or, in the case of a person arrested at the police station, as soon as practicable after the arrest.

If the suspect is charged, s. 38 sets out the grounds for continued detention. For a juvenile, under s. 38(1)(b)(i) these are when:

the custody officer has reasonable grounds for believing that he ought to be detained in his own interests

or

38(1)(a)
    (i)   his name or address cannot be ascertained or the custody officer has reasonable grounds for doubting whether a name or address furnished by him as his name or address is his real name or address;
    (ii)   the custody officer has reasonable grounds for believing that the person arrested will fail to appear in court to answer to bail;
    (iii)   in the case of a person arrested for an imprisonable offence, the custody officer has reasonable grounds for believing that the detention of the person arrested is necessary to prevent him from committing an offence;
    (iv)   in the case of a person arrested for an offence which is not an imprisonable offence, the custody officer has reasonable grounds for believing that the detention of the person arrested is necessary to prevent him from causing physical injury to any other person or from causing loss of or damage to property;
    (v)   the custody officer has reasonable grounds for believing that the detention of the person arrested is necessary to prevent him from interfering with the administration of justice or with the investigation of offences or of a particular offence;

Refusal of bail for a juvenile normally leads to social services having to accommodate the child, and this allows the authority to detain the child in secure accommodation if she or he is over 12:

...

38(6) Where a custody officer authorises an arrested juvenile to be kept in police detention under subsection (1) above, the custody officer shall, unless he certifies —
   (a) that, by reason of such circumstances as are specified in the certificate, it is impracticable for him to do so; or
   (b) in the case of an arrested juvenile who has attained the age of 12 years, that no secure accommodation is available and that keeping him in other local authority accommodation would not be adequate to protect the public from serious harm from him,
secure that the arrested juvenile is moved to local authority accommodation.

...

   (6B) Where an arrested juvenile is moved to local authority accommodation under subsection (6) above, it shall be lawful for any person acting on behalf of the authority to detain him.

The social services department is required to operate appropriate adult services (s. 38 of the Crime and Disorder Act 1998 above). The Code of Practice for the detention, treatment and questioning of persons by police officers, which follows, covers the role of the appropriate adult as well as the general powers of the police:

1.1 All persons in custody must be dealt with expeditiously, and released as soon as the need for detention has ceased to apply.

...

1.4 If an officer has any suspicion, or is told in good faith, that a person of any age may be mentally disordered or mentally handicapped, or mentally incapable of understanding the significance of questions put to him or his replies, then that person shall be treated as a mentally disordered or mentally handicapped person for the purposes of this code.

1.5 If anyone appears to be under the age of 17 then he shall be treated as a juvenile for the purposes of this code in the absence of clear evidence to show that he is older.

1.6 If a person appears to be blind or seriously visually handicapped, deaf, unable to read, unable to speak or has difficulty orally because of a speech impediment, he should be treated as such for the purposes of this code in the absence of clear evidence to the contrary.

1.7 In this code 'the appropriate adult' means:
   (a) in the case of a juvenile:
      (i) his parent or guardian (or, if he is in care, the care authority or voluntary organisation. The term 'in care' is used in this code to cover all cases in which a juvenile is 'looked after' by a local authority under the terms of the Children Act 1989);
      (ii) a social worker;
      (iii) failing either of the above, another responsible adult aged 18 or over who is not a police officer or employed by the police.
   (b) in the case of a person who is mentally disordered or mentally handicapped:
      (i) a relative, guardian or other person responsible for his care or custody;
      (ii) someone who has experience of dealing with mentally disordered or mentally handicapped people but is not a police officer or employed by the police (such as an approved social worker as defined by the Mental Health Act 1983 or a specialist social worker); or
      (iii) failing either of the above, some other responsible adult aged 18 or over who is not a police officer or employed by the police.

...

1C   A person, including a parent or guardian, should not be an appropriate adult if he is suspected of involvement in the offence in question, is the victim, is a witness, is involved in the investigation or has received admissions prior to attending to act as the appropriate adult. If the parent of a juvenile is estranged from the juvenile, he should not be asked to act as the appropriate adult if the juvenile expressly and specifically objects to his presence.

1D   If a juvenile admits an offence to or in the presence of a social worker other than during the time that the social worker is acting as the appropriate adult for that juvenile, another social worker should be the appropriate adult in the interest of fairness.

1E   In the case of people who are mentally disordered or mentally handicapped, it may in certain circumstances be more satisfactory for all concerned if the appropriate adult is someone who has experience or training in their care rather than a relative lacking such qualifications. But if the person himself prefers a relative to a better qualified stranger or objects to a particular person as the appropriate adult, his wishes should if practicable be respected.

1EE   A person should always be given an opportunity, when an appropriate adult is called to the police station, to consult privately with a solicitor in the absence of the appropriate adult if they wish to do so.

...

1I   It is important that the custody officer reminds the appropriate adult and the detained person of the right to legal advice and records any reasons for waiving it in accordance with section 6 of this code.

...

2.4   A solicitor or appropriate adult must be permitted to consult the custody record of a person detained as soon as practicable after their arrival at the police station. When a person leaves police detention or is taken before a court, he or his legal representative or his appropriate adult shall be supplied on request with a copy of the custody record as soon as practicable. This entitlement lasts for 12 months after his release.

...

3.7   If the person is a juvenile, the custody officer must, if it is practicable, ascertain the identity of a person responsible for his welfare. That person may be his parent or guardian (or, if he is in care, the care authority or voluntary organisation) or any other person who has, for the time being, assumed responsibility for his welfare. That person must be informed as soon as practicable that the juvenile has been arrested, why he has been arrested and where he is detained. This right is in addition to the juvenile's right in section 5 of the code not to be held incommunicado.

...

3.11   If the appropriate adult is already at the police station, then the provisions of paragraphs 3.1 to 3.5 above must be complied with in his presence. If the appropriate adult is not at the police station when the provisions of paragraphs 3.1 to 3.5 above are complied with, then these provisions must be complied with again in the presence of the appropriate adult once that person arrives.

3.12   The person shall be advised by the custody officer that the appropriate adult (where applicable) is there to assist and advise him and that he can consult privately with the appropriate adult at any time.

3.13   If, having been informed of the right to legal advice under paragraph 3.11 above, either the appropriate adult or the person detained wishes legal advice to be taken, then the provisions of section 6 of this code apply.

3.14   If the person is blind or seriously visually handicapped or is unable to read, the custody officer should ensure that his solicitor, relative, the appropriate adult or some other person likely to take an interest in him (and not involved in the investigation) is available to help in checking any documentation. Where this code requires written consent or signification then the person who is assisting may be asked to sign instead if the detained person so wishes.

...

3A   The notice of entitlements is intended to provide detained persons with brief details of their entitlements over and above the statutory rights which are set out in the notice of rights. The notice of entitlements should list the entitlements contained in this code, including visits and contact with outside parties (including special provisions for Commonwealth citizens and foreign nationals), reasonable standards of physical comfort, adequate food and drink, access to toilets and washing facilities, clothing, medical attention, and exercise where practicable. It should also mention the provisions relating to the conduct of interviews, the circumstances in which an appropriate adult should be available to assist the detained person and his statutory rights to make representation whenever the period of his detention is reviewed.

3B   In addition to the notices in English, translations should be available in Welsh, the main ethnic minority languages and the principal European languages whenever they are likely to be helpful.

3C   If the juvenile is in the care of a local authority or voluntary organisation but is living with his parents or other adults responsible for his welfare then, although there is no legal obligation on the police to inform them, they as well as the authority or organisation should normally be contacted unless suspected of involvement in the offence concerned. Even if a juvenile in care is not living with his parents, consideration should be given to informing them as well.

3D   Most local authority Social Services Departments can supply a list of interpreters who have the necessary skills and experience to interpret for the deaf at police interviews. The local Community Relations Council may be able to provide similar information in cases where the person concerned does not understand English.

...

3F   Blind or seriously visually handicapped persons may be unwilling to sign police documents. The alternative of their representative signing on their behalf seeks to protect the interests of both police and detained people.

3G   The purpose of paragraph 3.13 is to protect the rights of a juvenile, mentally disordered or mentally handicapped person who may not understand the significance of what is being said to him. If such a person wishes to exercise the right to legal advice the appropriate action should be taken straightaway and not delayed until the appropriate adult arrives.

...

5.1   Any person arrested and held in custody at a police station or other premises may on request have one person known to him or who is likely to take an interest in his welfare informed at public expense of his whereabouts as soon as practicable. If the person cannot be contacted the person who has made the request may choose up to two alternatives. If they too cannot be contacted the person in charge of detention or of the investigation has discretion to allow further attempts until the information has been conveyed.

...

6.1   Subject to the provisos in Annex B all people in police detention must be informed that they may at any time consult and communicate privately, whether in person, in writing or by telephone with a solicitor, and that independent legal advice is available free of charge from the duty solicitor.

...

6.8   Where a person has been permitted to consult a solicitor and the solicitor is available (i.e. present at the station or on his way to the station or easily contactable by telephone) at the time the interview begins or is in progress, the solicitor must be allowed to be present while he is interviewed.

...

6.15   If a solicitor arrives at the station to see a particular person, that person must ... be informed of the solicitor's arrival whether or not he is being interviewed and asked whether he would like to see him. This applies even if the person concerned has already declined legal advice or having requested it, subsequently agreed to be interviewed without having received advice. The solicitor's attendance and the detained person's decision must be noted in the custody record.

...

6B   A person who asks for legal advice should be given an opportunity to consult a specific solicitor or another solicitor from that solicitor's firm or the duty solicitor. If advice is not available by these means, or he does not wish to consult the duty solicitor, the person should be given an opportunity to choose a solicitor from a list of those willing to provide legal advice. If this solicitor is unavailable, he may choose up [to] two alternatives. If these attempts to secure legal advice are unsuccessful, the custody officer has discretion to allow further attempts until a solicitor has been contacted and agrees to provide legal advice. Apart from carrying out his duties under Note 6B, a police officer must not advise the suspect about any particular firm of solicitors.

...

6D   A detained person has a right to free legal advice and to be represented by a solicitor. The solicitor's only role in the police station is to protect and advance the legal rights of his client. On occasions this may require the solicitor to give advice which has the effect of his client avoiding giving evidence which strengthens a prosecution case. The solicitor may intervene in order to seek clarification or to challenge an improper question to his client or the manner in which it is put, or to advise his client not to reply to particular questions, or if he wishes to give his client further legal advice. ...

...

7.1   Any citizen of an independent Commonwealth country or a national of a foreign country (including the Republic of Ireland) may communicate at any time with his High Commission, Embassy or Consulate. He must be informed of this right as soon as practicable. He must also be informed as soon as practicable of his right, upon request to have his High Commission, Embassy or Consulate told of his whereabouts and the grounds for his detention. Such a request should be acted upon as soon as practicable.

...

8.8   A juvenile shall not be placed in a police cell unless no other secure accommodation is available and the custody officer considers that it is not practicable to supervise him if he is not placed in a cell or the custody officer considers that a cell provides more comfortable accommodation than other secure accommodation in the police station. He may not be placed in a cell with a detained adult.

...

9.1   If a complaint is made by or on behalf of a detained person about his treatment since his arrest, or it comes to the notice of any officer that he may have been treated improperly, a report must be made as soon as practicable to an officer of the rank of inspector or above who is not connected with the investigation. If the matter concerns a possible assault or the possibility of the unnecessary or unreasonable use of force then the police surgeon must also be called as soon as practicable.

...

10.1   A person whom there are grounds to suspect of an offence must be cautioned before any questions about it (or further questions if it is his answers to previous questions which provide the grounds for suspicion) are put to him regarding his involvement or suspected involvement in that offence if his answers or his silence (i.e. failure or refusal to answer a question or to answer satisfactorily) may be given in evidence to a court in a prosecution.

...

10.4   The caution shall be in the following terms:
'You do not have to say anything. But it may harm your defence if you do not mention when questioned something which you later rely on in court. Anything you do say may be given in evidence.'

...

11.1   Following a decision to arrest a suspect he must not be interviewed about the relevant offence except at a police station or other authorised place of detention unless the consequent delay would be likely:
  (a) to lead to interference with or harm to evidence connected with an offence or inter-ference with or physical harm to other people; or
  (b) to lead to the alerting of other people suspected of having committed an offence but not yet arrested for it; or
  (c) to hinder the recovery of property obtained in consequence of the commission of an offence.
Interviewing in any of these circumstances shall cease once the relevant risk has been averted or the necessary questions have been put in order to attempt to avert that risk.

...

11.2A   At the beginning of an interview carried out in a police station, the interviewing officer, after cautioning the suspect, shall put to him any significant statement or silence which occurred before his arrival at the police station, and shall ask him whether he confirms or denies that earlier statement or silence and whether he wishes to add anything. A 'significant' state-ment or silence is one which appears capable of being used in evidence against the suspect, in particular a direct admission of guilt, or failure or refusal to answer a question or to answer it sat-isfactorily, which might give rise to an inference under part III of the Criminal Justice and Public Order Act 1994.

11.3   No police officer may try to obtain answers to questions or to elicit a statement by the use of oppression. Except as provided for in paragraph 10.5C, no police officer shall indicate, except in answer to a direct question, what action will be taken on the part of the police if the person being interviewed answers questions, makes a statement or refuses to do either. If the person asks the officer directly what action will be taken in the event of his answering questions, mak-ing a statement or refusing to do either, then the officer may inform the person what action the police propose to take in that event provided that action is itself proper and warranted.

11.4   As soon as a police officer who is making enquiries of any person about an offence believes that a prosecution should be brought against him and that there is sufficient evidence for it to succeed, he should ask the person if he has anything further to say. If the person indicates that he has nothing more to say the officer shall without delay cease to question him about that offence.

...

11.14   A juvenile or a person who is mentally disordered or mentally handicapped, whether suspected or not, must not be interviewed or asked to provide or sign a written statement in the absence of the appropriate adult unless paragraph 11.1 or Annex C applies.

11.15   Juveniles may only be interviewed at their places of education in exceptional circumstances and then only where the principal or his nominee agrees. Every effort should be made to notify both the parent(s) or other person responsible for the juvenile's welfare and the appropriate adult (if this is a different person) that the police want to interview the juvenile and reasonable time should be allowed to enable the appropriate adult to be present at the interview. Where awaiting the appropriate adult would cause unreasonable delay and unless the interviewee is suspected of an offence against the educational establishment, the principal or his nominee can act as the appropriate adult for the purposes of the interview.

11.16   Where the appropriate adult is present at an interview, he should be informed that he is not expected to act simply as an observer; and also that the purposes of his presence are, first, to advise the person being questioned and to observe whether or not the interview is being conducted properly and fairly, and secondly, to facilitate communication with the person being interviewed.

...

11B   It is important to bear in mind that, although juveniles or people who are mentally disordered or mentally handicapped are often capable of providing reliable evidence, they may, without knowing or wishing to do so, be particularly prone in certain circumstances to provide information which is unreliable, misleading or self-incriminating. Special care should therefore always be exercised in questioning such a person, and the appropriate adult should be involved, if there is any doubt about a person's age, mental state or capacity. Because of the risk of unreliable evidence it is also important to obtain corroboration of any facts admitted whenever possible.

11C   It is preferable that a juvenile is not arrested at his place of education unless this is unavoidable. Where a juvenile is arrested at his place of education, the principal or his nominee must be informed.

...

16.1   When an officer considers that there is sufficient evidence to prosecute a detained person, and that there is sufficient evidence for a prosecution to succeed, and that the person has said all that he wishes to say about the offence, he shall without delay (and subject to the following qualification) bring him before the custody officer who shall then be responsible for considering whether or not he should be charged. When a person is detained in respect of more than one offence it is permissible to delay bringing him before the custody officer until the above conditions are satisfied in respect of all the offences (but see paragraph 11.4). Any resulting action should be taken in the presence of the appropriate adult if the person is a juvenile or mentally disordered or mentally handicapped.

...

16.6   Where a juvenile is charged with an offence and the custody officer authorises his continued detention he must try to make arrangements for the juvenile to be taken into the care of a local authority to be detained pending appearance in court unless he certifies that it is impracticable to do so, or, in the case of a juvenile of at least 12 years of age, no secure accommodation is available and there is a risk to the public of serious harm from that juvenile, in accordance with section 38(6) of the Police and Criminal Evidence Act 1984, as amended by section 59 of the Criminal Justice Act 1991 and section 24 of the Criminal Justice and Public Order Act 1994.

...

16B   Except as provided for in 16.6 above, neither a juvenile's behaviour nor the nature of the offence with which he is charged provides grounds for the custody officer to decide that it is impracticable to seek to arrange for his transfer to the care of the local authority. Similarly, the lack of secure local authority accommodation shall not make it impracticable for the custody officer to transfer him. The availability of secure accommodation is only a factor in relation to a juvenile aged 12 or over when the local authority accommodation would not be adequate to protect the public from serious harm from the juvenile. The obligation to transfer a juvenile to local authority accommodation applies as much to a juvenile charged during the daytime as it does to a juvenile to be held overnight, subject to a requirement to bring the juvenile before a court under section 46 of the Police and Criminal Evidence Act 1984.

The role of the appropriate adult requires skill and training. Research cited in the following paper, 'PACE ten years on: a review of the research', *Home Office Research Study* 155 (1977) (Chapters 9 and 10) suggests that not all appropriate adults fulfill the role required:

The appropriate adult's role

Several commentators have drawn attention to the difficulties and conflicts attached to the appropriate adult's task, particularly where that person is a parent or relative who is unlikely to be aware of the law or police procedures. Dixon (1990) and Brown et al (1992) point out that parents may often be disorientated, scared and compliant with police requests. Parents of first-time offenders are particularly likely to be shocked, anxious and intimidated (Evans and Rawstorne, 1994). Few are articulate and well-informed enough to provide commonsense advice. A study of detective work by Thornton (1989) notes how CID officers may co-opt appropriate adults to their side against the juvenile. Thomas (1988) notes that the Codes give scanty guidance about how adults should fulfil their role, while Evans (1993) and Evans and Rawstorne (1994) are doubtful whether adults are actually told by the police what their role is, other than in very general terms. Some confirmation of this view is provided by Irving and McKenzie (1989), who observed no cases involving juveniles in their Brighton research in which such information was given. Where the adult is a social worker, the police may assume that he or she is aware of their role — an assumption that may not necessarily be justified.

Dixon (1990) argues that the current provisions reflect an uneasy mix between a parent's right to be with their child when in trouble and the child's need for effective advice and support. Irving and McKenzie (1989) doubt whether a parent is likely to know that an interview is being conducted fairly. It is not surprising, therefore, that in 75 per cent of cases they make no contribution at all (Evans, 1993). Nor are they always supportive of their children: Evans (ibid.), with Dixon et al (1990b) and Fennell (1994), note that parents sometimes see their role as to extract a confession, using methods that would have amounted to contraventions of the Codes of Practice if used by the police. Evans and Rawstorne (1994) found that custody and interviewing officers tended to prefer parents rather than social workers as appropriate adults precisely because they were more likely to get the truth out of their child. They were also less likely to ask for a solicitor.

Evans (1993) and others (for example, Dixon, 1990; Brown et al, 1992) point out that the adult's role in facilitating communication between police and suspect during interviews may detract from exercise of the juvenile's right to silence. Dixon (1990) notes too that, should adults take the more active role in advising juveniles which Code C envisages, they may rapidly come into conflict with the police who are content with the presence of adults only so long as they remain passive observers or assist the interview.

Brown et al (1992) and Evans and Rawstorne (1994) both make the point that the competence with which social work staff perform the role of appropriate adult may vary depending on how appropriate adult provision is organised by social services departments. Dedicated Youth Justice

Teams, who often provided cover during office hours, have the advantage that they are conversant with police station procedure and PACE. Out of normal office hours, however, the quality of provision may vary, depending on the degree of specialism of the teams providing emergency cover.

...

Some difficulties may persist, regardless of the form of organisation. Dixon (1990), Kay and Quao (1987) and Evans and Rawstorne (1994) refer to tensions between control and welfare ideologies in social work. Juveniles may view social workers as reflecting the former. Social workers who seek to look after the juvenile's best interests — perhaps advising silence during interview — may rapidly find themselves in conflict with the police. They may also, as Thomas (1988) notes, experience difficulties in assessing what are acceptable interviewing tactics. These are not defined in PACE or the Codes and the question has by no means been settled in the courts. Since social workers have to maintain good working relationships with the police, they may find the easiest course is to act as passive witnesses to police interviews rather than to provide strong and confident intervention where required (Evans, 1993; Evans and Rawstorne, 1994). Evans and Rawstorne (ibid.) have suggested that the general acquiescence of appropriate adults, social workers included, suits the police well. For their presence gives police actions the gloss of legality and protects the admissibility of confession evidence, while allowing them to carry on with their work relatively unimpeded.

One key issue is that of potential conflict where social work professionals are also acting as appropriate adults for their own clients. A problem arises in relation to information about the offence confided by the suspect and whether this should remain confidential (RCCJ, 1993; Fennell, 1994; Evans and Rawstorne, 1994). Bean and Nemitz (1994) suggest that social workers' duty of care and control towards their clients may point towards disclosure, while the advocate/supportive role of appropriate adult may indicate the opposite. In law, it would appear that, unlike information passed to legal advisers, that imparted to appropriate adults is not legally privileged (Evans and Rawstorne, 1994).

...

The demands made on mental health professionals raise the question of how well their organisations are geared up to respond. Evans and Rawstorne (1994) examined this question in relation to the work of local authority social services departments. They found that, during the day, Mental Health Teams were able to respond to calls to police stations. Outside of office hours, however, it was not always the case that a specialist social worker would be available, since Emergency Duty Teams sometimes consist of a range of personnel with different types of expertise. As is the case with juveniles, some social workers dealing with the mentally disordered have received little or no training on PACE.

...

The suspect's response to questioning

A study in the Metropolitan Police suggests that, even where the correct action is taken and some kind of independent expert is summoned, difficulties of dealing with mentally abnormal suspects at the police station persist (Cahill and Grebler, 1988). Particular problems occur in assessing whether the suspect had the appropriate *mens rea* for the offence in question.

Tully and Cahill (1984), in a study of the interviewing of the mentally handicapped, have drawn attention to the varying response of this group of suspects to police questioning. In some cases, they may be extremely resistant, but in others they may perceive the situation as one demanding obedience and be over-ready to answer questions in a way which they believe will please the interviewer, irrespective of the truth. They also draw attention to other features of interviews with the mentally handicapped which may render statements unreliable. Thus, questioning designed to portray the suspect in a bad light may lead the interviewee to respond in ways that avoid him or her looking foolish rather than representing the truth. Pressure to respond may also reduce the accuracy of replies. These problems would not be so significant if it were easy to identify and quantify degrees of mental handicap but, unfortunately, this is not the case.

The same study found that, while police officers recognised that there were problems associated with mentally handicapped suspects' responses to questioning, they consistently overestimated the reliability of information provided by them. Furthermore, officers took suspects' co-operativeness and confidence to imply reliability, probably because in normal cases these qualities are linked. They categorised a variety of ways in which erroneous responses to questions might be produced, a common element to which was that positive answers reduced the risk of the suspect appearing incompetent.

...

References

Bean, P. and Nemitz, T. (1994). *Out of depth and out of sight*. Final report of research commissioned by Mencap on the implementation of the appropriate adult scheme. Midlands Centre for Criminology: University of Loughborough.

Bottomley, K., Coleman, C., Dixon, D., Gill, M. and Wall, D. (1989). *The Impact of Aspects of the Police and Criminal Evidence Act 1984 on Policing in a Force in the North of England*. Final report to ESRC. Unpublished.

Brown, D. (1989). *Detention at the Police Station under the Police and Criminal Evidence Act 1984*. Home Office Research Study No. 104. London: HMSO.

Brown, D., Ellis, T. and Larcombe, K. (1992). *Changing the Code: Police Detention under the Revised PACE Codes of Practice*. Home Office Research Study No. 129. London: HMSO.

Cahill, D. and Grebler, G. (1988). *Vulnerable testimony*. Report to MENCAP and the Metropolitan Police. Unpublished.

Clare, I.C.H. and Gudjunsson, G.H. (1992). *Devising and Piloting an Experimental Version of the 'Notice to Detained Persons'*. Royal Commission on Criminal Justice Research Study No. 7. London: HMSO.

Dixon, D. (1990). 'Juvenile suspects and the Police and Criminal Evidence Act'. In Freestone, D. (ed). *Children and the Law: essays in honour of Professor H. K. Bevan*. Hull: Hull University Press.

Dixon, D., Coleman, C. and Bottomley, K. (1990a). 'Consent and the legal regulation of policing'. *Journal of Law and Society*, 17(3), 345–362.

Evans, R. (1993). *The Conduct of Police Interviews with Juveniles*. Royal Commission on Criminal Justice Research Study No. 8. London: HMSO.

Evans, R. and Rawstorne, S. (1994). *The Protection of Vulnerable Suspects*. A report to the Home Office Research and Planning Unit. Unpublished.

Fennell, P.W.H. (1994). 'Mentally disordered suspects in the Criminal Justice System'. *In Justice and Efficiency? The Royal Commission on Criminal Justice*. S. Field and P.A. Thomas (Eds.). Oxford: Blackwell.

Gudjunsson, G.H. (1992). *The Psychology of Interrogations, Confessions and Testimony*. Chichester: Wiley.

Gudjunsson, G., Clare, I., Rutter, S. and Pearse, J. (1993). *Persons at Risk during Interviews in Police Custody: the identification of vulnerabilities*. Royal Commission on Criminal Justice Research Study No. 12. London: HMSO.

Irving, B.L. (1980). *Police Interrogation*. Royal Commission on Criminal Procedure Research Study 1. London: HMSO.

Irving, B.L. and McKenzie, I. (1989). *Police Interrogation: the effects of the Police and Criminal Evidence Act 1984*. London: Police Foundation.

Justice. (1994). *Unreliable Evidence?: confessions and the safety of convictions*. London: Justice.

Kay, N. and Quao, S. (1987). 'To be or not to be an appropriate adult'. *Community Care*, No. 688, 20–2.

Morgan, R., Reiner, R. and McKenzie, I.K. (1991). *Police Powers and Police: a study of the work of custody officers*. Full final report to the ESRC. Unpublished.

Parker, C. (1992). *Confessions and the Mentally Vulnerable Suspect*. Thesis submitted for L.L.M. in Human Rights and Civil Liberties. Unpublished.

Phillips, C. and Brown, D., with the assistance of Goodrich, P. and James, Z. *Entry into the Criminal Justice System: a survey of police arrests and their outcomes*. Home Office Research Study. London: HMSO.

Robertson, G. (1992). *The Role of Police Surgeons*. Royal Commission on Criminal Justice Research Study No. 6. London: HMSO.

Sanders, A., Bridges, L., Mulvaney, A. and Crozier, G. (1989). *Advice and Assistance at Police Stations and the 24 hour Duty Solicitor Scheme*. London: Lord Chancellor's Department.

Thomas, T. (1988). 'The Police and Criminal Evidence Act 1984: the social work role'. *The Howard Journal of Criminal Justice*, Vol. 27, No. 4, pp. 256–265.

Thornton, G.L. (1989). *The Role of the Criminal Investigation Department: Present Performance and Future prospects*. M.A. thesis submitted to University of Manchester, Faculty of Social and Economic Studies. (Unpublished).

Tully, B. and Cahill, D. (1984). *Police Interviewing of the Mentally Handicapped: an Experimental Study*. London: Police Foundation.

[*Chapters 9 and 10 of PACE ten years on: a review of the research. Home Office Research Study 155(1997)*.]

7.2.2 **Should the child be charged?**

The decision on how to proceed normally requires consultation by police with social services.

A warning or reprimand

These replace cautioning. The provisions are set out in a criminal justice statute (Crime and Disorder Act 1998), although warnings and reprimands are intended to keep a person *out* of the criminal justice system.

65.(1) Subsections (2) to (5) below apply where —
- (a) a constable has evidence that a child or young person ('the offender') has committed an offence;
- (b) the constable considers that the evidence is such that, if the offender were prosecuted for the offence, there would be a realistic prospect of his being convicted;
- (c) the offender admits to the constable that he committed the offence;
- (d) the offender has not previously been convicted of an offence; and
- (e) the constable is satisfied that it would not be in the public interest for the offender to be prosecuted.

(2)   Subject to subsection (4) below, the constable may reprimand the offender if the offender has not previously been reprimanded or warned.

(3)   The constable may warn the offender if —

(a)   the offender has not previously been warned; or

(b)   where the offender has previously been warned, the offence was committed more than two years after the date of the previous warning and the constable considers the offence to be not so serious as to require a charge to be brought;

but no person may be warned under paragraph (b) above more than once.

(4)   Where the offender has not been previously reprimanded, the constable shall warn rather than reprimand the offender if he considers the offence to be so serious as to require a warning.

(5)   The constable shall —

(a)   give any reprimand or warning at a police station and, where the offender is under the age of 17, in the presence of an appropriate adult; and

(b)   explain to the offender and, where he is under that age, the appropriate adult in ordinary language —

(i)   in the case of a reprimand, the effect of subsection (5)(a) of section 66 below;

(ii)   in the case of a warning, the effect of subsections (1), (2), (4) and (5)(b) and (c) of that section, and any guidance issued under subsection (3) of that section.

66.(1)   Where a constable warns a person under section 65 above, he shall as soon as practicable refer the person to a youth offending team.

(2)   A youth offending team —

(a)   shall assess any person referred to them under subsection (1) above; and

(b)   unless they consider it inappropriate to do so, shall arrange for him to participate in a rehabilitation programme.

(4)   Where a person who has been warned under section 65 above is convicted of an offence committed within two years of the warning, the court by or before which he is so convicted —

(a)   shall not make an order under subsection (1)(b) (conditional discharge) of section 1A of the 1973 Act in respect of the offence unless it is of the opinion that there are exceptional circumstances relating to the offence or the offender which justify its doing so; and

(b)   where it does so, shall state in open court that it is of that opinion and why it is.

(5)   The following, namely —

(a)   any reprimand of a person under section 65 above;

(b)   any warning of a person under that section; and

(c)   any report on a failure by a person to participate in a rehabilitation programme arranged for him under subsection (2) above,

may be cited in criminal proceedings in the same circumstances as a conviction of the person may be cited.

Guidance to youth offending teams on reprimands and warnings was published by the Home Office in April 2000. We do not have space to reproduce the whole document, which may be found at **www.homeoffice.gov.uk/cdact/yotguide.htm** and should be referred to to get an understanding of concepts like restorative justice and involvement of the victim of crime. (Guidance to the police is also worth reading — see **www.homeoffice.gov.uk/cdact/police.htm**).

(ix)   Decision to deliver the warning
48.   The young offender's behaviour at the delivery of the warning (whether that be through a restorative process or not) is relevant to the police officer's decision as to whether a warning is an

appropriate response. Up to the point that the police officer delivers the warning there is still the option for proceedings to be taken against the young offender.

49. However, the failure by a young person to turn up for, or participate constructively in, a restorative conference or warning will not be a reason in itself for a charge to be brought. The young offender's behaviour may be the result of circumstances not related to the offence itself, for example fear of meeting the victim. In the exceptional circumstances where it is not possible to deliver a warning at the conclusion of a restorative conference or warning session (either because the young offender has failed to appear or the session has broken down) the young offender should be given the opportunity to receive a standard warning. Only if the young offender's behaviour clearly demonstrates that a warning will not be appropriate, or he or she fails to answer bail to receive a standard warning would a charge be considered.

(xii) Delivering the warning

50. Where possible a member of the youth offending team should be present for the delivery of a warning. The youth offending team member will be able to explain to the young person and his or her parent(s) or guardian(s) the likely nature of the rehabilitation (change) programme. The police officer should ensure that the young offender and his or her parents or appropriate adult are given written information which clearly explains the implications of the warning. A standard information leaflet is attached at Annex C [not reproduced].

51. In issuing the warning, the police should specify the offence(s) which have resulted in the warning. They should also make clear that:

- the warning is a serious matter
- any further offending behaviour will result in charges being brought, in all but the most exceptional circumstance
- a record of the warning will be kept by the police until the offender is 18 or the warning is more than two years old, whichever is later
- the warning may be cited in any future criminal proceedings
- if the young person is convicted of a further offence within two years of getting the warning, the option of conditional discharge will only be open to the courts in exceptional circumstances. The young person can in most cases expect a more serious sentence
- if the offence is one covered by the Sex Offenders Act 1997, the young person is required to register with the police for inclusion on the sex offenders register (paragraphs 54 and 55 below)
- the warning will trigger referral to a local youth offending team
- the youth offending team will assess the young person and, unless they consider it inappropriate, prepare a rehabilitation (change) programme designed to tackle the reasons for the young person's offending behaviour, to prevent reoffending and to help repair some of the harm done
- unreasonable non-compliance with the rehabilitation (change) programme would be recorded and could be cited in any future criminal proceedings
- referral to the youth offending team will be immediate and the young person can expect to be contacted by the team within five working days
- any questions about what will happen next should be put to the youth offending team (the officer should also give contact details for the team).

(xiv) Referral following a warning

57. The police have a statutory duty to refer all offenders who have been given a warning to the youth offending team. Whether or not a member of the youth offending team is present when a warning is issued, the police should notify the youth offending team manager, or an individual nominated by the manager, within one working day of the names, addresses and telephone numbers of those young people who have received a reprimand or warning, along

with information about the nature of their offence(s) and (where the victim has consented) contact details for the victim(s), if any. The police should give details of what contact has been made with the victim (including a copy of a victim statement where one has been taken) and whether they have been involved in the delivery of the warning. The police may also pass on any additional information obtained during the course of the investigation or through the delivery of the warning which may be relevant to the assessment or the development of a rehabilitation programme.

58. The youth offending team has a statutory duty to assess any young offender who has been referred following a warning and, unless they consider it inappropriate to do so, to arrange for the offender to participate in a rehabilitation (change) programme. On receipt of the referral notice from the police, the youth offending team manager, or a person nominated by him or her, should allocate a member of staff to deal with the assessment of each young person. Where possible, this should be same team member who carried out any prior assessment.

(xix) Non-compliance with rehabilitation (change) programmes

88. The young offender will be expected to attend and take a satisfactory part in the rehabilitation activity. Failure to complete a rehabilitation programme delivered as part of a warning is not in itself an offence. However successful programmes need sufficient incentive for young offenders and their parents to co-operate. For some young offenders the intrinsic benefits of the scheme will be enough; for others the legislation provides that failure to comply with the rehabilitation (change) programme may be cited in court in the event of the young person being prosecuted for a subsequent offence.

89. The youth offending team should also note any non-compliance with the rehabilitation programme by the young person's parents, and take early action to identify and address the reasons.

(xx) Reasonable non-compliance

90. If a young offender is not complying with the terms of his or her rehabilitation (change) programme, the case worker must first decide whether this is deliberate, premeditated and intended to go against the expectations of the programme. If there was a good reason, such as illness, this should not be treated as non-compliance and the team should consider whether the programme requires modification to take account of the reasons for non-compliance. If the reasons appear to relate to wider family problems which require specific action, the youth offending team may also need to alert the local authority social services department to the circumstances.

(xxi) Unreasonable non-compliance

91. If it appears that non-compliance is unreasonable the case worker should notify the young person and his or her family immediately, in writing, that if the failure continues or is repeated it will be noted and may be taken into account by a court when sentencing for any subsequent offence. The case worker should also consider whether the programme requires modification or extension to improve future compliance.

92. If unreasonable non-compliance continues after such an initial written warning, the case worker must record further instances. The records should be kept on the case file of the young offender and should indicate:
- the date of the written warning and the reasons for the warning
- the nature of the continuing non-compliance
- when it took place and the date it was recorded.

93.   A copy of the record should be sent to:
- the police force responsible for administering the warning which triggered the rehabilitation programme, for their records, and (where different) to the police force in the young person's home town
- the young person and his or her parent(s) or guardian(s).

Is prosecution in the public interest?

You will have noted in the guidance on deciding whether to charge that difficult cases are referred to the Crown Prosecution Service for advice. The CPS is governed by a Code for Crown Prosecutors (see **www.cps.gov.uk/cpsb/whatdoes.htm**), which contains guidance on whether the public interest demands a prosecution or not.

1.1   The decision to prosecute an individual is a serious step. Fair and effective prosecution is essential to the maintenance of law and order. Even in a small case a prosecution has serious implications for all involved — victims, witnesses and defendants. The Crown Prosecution Service applies the Code for Crown Prosecutors so that it can make fair and consistent decisions about prosecutions.

5.   The evidential test
5.1   Crown Prosecutors must be satisfied that there is enough evidence to provide a 'realistic prospect of conviction' against each defendant on each charge. They must consider what the defence case may be, and how that is likely to affect the prosecution case.

5.2   A realistic prospect of conviction is an objective test. It means that a jury or bench of magistrates, properly directed in accordance with the law, is more likely than not to convict the defendant of the charge alleged. This is a separate test from the one that the criminal courts themselves must apply. A jury or magistrates' court should only convict if satisfied so that it is sure of a defendant's guilt.

5.3   When deciding whether there is enough evidence to prosecute, Crown Prosecutors must consider whether the evidence can be used and is reliable. There will be many cases in which the evidence does not give any cause for concern. But there will also be cases in which the evidence may not be as strong as it first appears. Crown Prosecutors must ask themselves the following questions:

Can the evidence be used in court?
a   Is it likely that the evidence will be excluded by the court? There are certain legal rules which might mean that evidence which seems relevant cannot be given at a trial. For example, is it likely that the evidence will be excluded because of the way in which it was gathered or because of the rule against using hearsay as evidence? If so, is there enough other evidence for a realistic prospect of conviction?

Is the evidence reliable?
b   Is there evidence which might support or detract from the reliability of a confession? Is the reliability affected by factors such as the defendant's age, intelligence or level of understanding?
c   What explanation has the defendant given? Is a court likely to find it credible in the light of the evidence as a whole? Does it support an innocent explanation?
d   If the identity of the defendant is likely to be questioned, is the evidence about this strong enough?

e Is the witness's background likely to weaken the prosecution case? For example, does the witness have any motive that may affect his or her attitude to the case, or a relevant previous conviction?

f Are there concerns over the accuracy or credibility of a witness? Are these concerns based on evidence or simply information with nothing to support it? Is there further evidence which the police should be asked to seek out which may support or detract from the account of the witness?

6. The public interest test

The following lists of some common public interest factors, both for and against prosecution, are not exhaustive. The factors that apply will depend on the facts in each case.

Some common public interest factors in favour of prosecution

6.4   The more serious the offence, the more likely it is that a prosecution will be needed in the public interest. A prosecution is likely to be needed if:

a   a conviction is likely to result in a significant sentence;

b   a weapon was used or violence was threatened during the commission of the offence;

c   the offence was committed against a person serving the public (for example, a police or prison officer, or a nurse);

d   the defendant was in a position of authority or trust;

e   the evidence shows that the defendant was a ringleader or an organiser of the offence;

f   there is evidence that the offence was premeditated;

g   there is evidence that the offence was carried out by a group;

h   the victim of the offence was vulnerable, has been put in considerable fear, or suffered personal attack, damage or disturbance;

i   the offence was motivated by any form of discrimination against the victim's ethnic or national origin, sex, religious beliefs, political views or sexual orientation, or the suspect demonstrated hostility towards the victim based on any of those characteristics;

j   there is a marked difference between the actual or mental ages of the defendant and the victim, or if there is any element of corruption;

k   the defendant's previous convictions or cautions are relevant to the present offence;

l   the defendant is alleged to have committed the offence whilst under an order of the court;

m   there are grounds for believing that the offence is likely to be continued or repeated, for example, by a history of recurring conduct; or

n   the offence, although not serious in itself, is widespread in the area where it was committed.

Some common public interest factors against prosecution

6.5   A prosecution is less likely to be needed if:

a   the court is likely to impose a nominal penalty;

b   the defendant has already been made the subject of a sentence and any further conviction would be unlikely to result in the imposition of an additional sentence or order, unless the nature of the particular offence requires a prosecution;

c   the offence was committed as a result of a genuine mistake or misunderstanding (these factors must be balanced against the seriousness of the offence);

d   the loss or harm can be described as minor and was the result of a single incident, particularly if it was caused by a misjudgement;

e   there has been a long delay between the offence taking place and the date of the trial, unless:
  • the offence is serious;
  • the delay has been caused in part by the defendant;
  • the offence has only recently come to light; or
  • the complexity of the offence has meant that there has been a long investigation;
f   a prosecution is likely to have a bad effect on the victim's physical or mental health, always bearing in mind the seriousness of the offence;
g   the defendant is elderly or is, or was at the time of the offence, suffering from significant mental or physical ill health, unless the offence is serious or there is a real possibility that it may be repeated. The Crown Prosecution Service, where necessary, applies Home Office guidelines about how to deal with mentally disordered offenders. Crown Prosecutors must balance the desirability of diverting a defendant who is suffering from significant mental or physical ill health with the need to safeguard the general public;
h   the defendant has put right the loss or harm that was caused (but defendants must not avoid prosecution solely because they pay compensation).
i   details may be made public that could harm sources of information, international relations, or national security.

7.2.3 Quasi-criminal orders under the Crime and Disorder Act 1998

Anti-social behaviour orders (ASBOs)

These are not criminal orders. However a breach is a criminal offence:

(1)   An application for an order under this section may be made by a relevant authority if it appears to the authority that the following conditions are fulfilled with respect to any person aged 10 or over, namely —
  (a) that the person has acted, since the commencement date, in an anti-social manner, that is to say, in a manner that caused or was likely to cause harassment, alarm or distress to one or more persons not of the same household as himself; and
  (b) that such an order is necessary to protect persons in the local government area in which the harassment, alarm or distress was caused or was likely to be caused from further anti-social acts by him;
and in this section 'relevant authority' means the council for the local government area or any chief officer of police any part of whose police area lies within that area.
(2)   A relevant authority shall not make such an application without consulting each other relevant authority.
(3)   Such an application shall be made by complaint to the magistrates' court whose commission area includes the place where it is alleged that the harassment, alarm or distress was caused or was likely to be caused.
(4)   If, on such an application, it is proved that the conditions mentioned in subsection (1) above are fulfilled, the magistrates' court may make an order under this section (an 'anti-social behaviour order') which prohibits the defendant from doing anything described in the order.
(5)   For the purpose of determining whether the condition mentioned in subsection (1)(a) above is fulfilled, the court shall disregard any act of the defendant which he shows was reasonable in the circumstances.

(6) The prohibitions that may be imposed by an anti-social behaviour order are those necessary for the purpose of protecting from further anti-social acts by the defendant —

  (a) persons in the local government area; and

  (b) persons in any adjoining local government area specified in the application for the order;
and a relevant authority shall not specify an adjoining local government area in the application without consulting the council for that area and each chief officer of police any part of whose police area lies within that area.

(7) An anti-social behaviour order shall have effect for a period (not less than two years) specified in the order or until further order.

(8) Subject to subsection (9) below, the applicant or the defendant may apply by complaint to the court which made an anti-social behaviour order for it to be varied or discharged by a further order.

(9) Except with the consent of both parties, no anti-social behaviour order shall be discharged before the end of the period of two years beginning with the date of service of the order.

(10) If without reasonable excuse a person does anything which he is prohibited from doing by an anti-social behaviour order, he shall be liable —

  (a) on summary conviction, to imprisonment for a term not exceeding six months or to a fine not exceeding the statutory maximum, or to both; or

  (b) on conviction on indictment, to imprisonment for a term not exceeding five years or to a fine, or to both.

Subsection 12 (not reproduced) provides that it is the district authority which makes the application. From LASSA (Chapter 1) you may recall that social services are run by county councils where there is a two tier system of government. So the anti-social behaviour order application cannot be a social service function. As the guidance makes clear, social services are to be consulted.

Guidance on the ASBO is provided at **www.homeoffice.gov.uk/cdact/asbo.htm**

Consultation with other agencies

3.6 It is important that a multi-agency approach is adopted and that all agencies who may have some knowledge of the individual being considered for an order are drawn into the discussion at an early stage. Where appropriate a case conference approach should be adopted. For example, the probation service, social services department, health services and voluntary organisations may already be involved with the individual, or with other members of his or her family. Registered Social Landlords may need to be drawn into discussion on certain cases. Part of the local strategies could include a checklist of agencies that might be notified or consulted if an order is being considered.

3.9 In broad terms an anti-social behaviour order is likely to be relevant where there is behaviour of a criminal nature which causes or is likely to cause harassment, alarm or distress to other people ... . Examples of cases where an anti-social behaviour order might be appropriate include:

  – where individuals intimidate neighbours and others through threats or violence or a mixture of unpleasant actions;

  – where there is persistent unruly behaviour by a small group of individuals on a housing estate or other local area, who may dominate others and use minor damage to property and fear of retaliation, possibly at unsociable hours, as a means of intimidating other people;

  – where there are families whose anti-social behaviour, when challenged, leads to verbal abuse, vandalism, threats and graffiti, sometimes using children as the vehicle for action against neighbouring families;

– where there is persistent abusive behaviour towards elderly people or towards mentally ill or disabled people causing them fear and distress;
– where there is serious and persistent bullying of children on an organised basis in public recreation grounds or on the way to school or within the school grounds if normal school disciplinary procedures do not stop the behaviour;
– where there is persistent racial harassment or homophobic behaviour;
– where there is persistent anti-social behaviour as a result of drugs or alcohol misuse.

3.15   There is a duty under the Children Act 1989 generally, and under section 17 in particular, for local authorities to assess and meet the needs of children in need in their area. Under the Act, local authority social services departments may, in addition, seek care and supervision orders, for example for children at risk of significant harm or beyond parental control. If an application for an anti-social behaviour order in relation to a child or young person aged 10 up to their 18th birthday is being considered, local authority social services departments need to be consulted although the decision to seek an order is one for the applying authority alone. In areas where there are two tiers of local government, the relevant department will be the county council social services department. The social services departments should give careful consideration to the implications for the child or young person in question. The court hearing the application should satisfy itself that Social Services have been consulted, and that the child's needs have been assessed before deciding whether an ASBO is appropriate.

3.16   Local authorities also have a duty under the NHS and Community Care Act 1990 to assess any person who may be in need of community care services. If there is any evidence to suggest that the person against whom the order is being sought may be suffering from drug and/or alcohol problems and/or mental health problems, advice should be sought through the relevant social services department. In some cases it may be appropriate to consider whether the individual should be admitted to hospital under the Mental Health Act 1983 rather than pursuing an anti-social behaviour order.

Vulnerable and intimidated witnesses

4.8   An application for an order, although made in the magistrates' court, is a civil proceeding, and civil rules of evidence and the civil burden of proof i.e. on 'the balance of probabilities' will apply, although the exact level of that test may vary on a case by case basis (see paragraph 5.2 below). Sections 1–4 of the Civil Evidence Act 1995, which permit the use of hearsay evidence in civil proceedings, apply to proceedings for applications for orders.

4.9   In addition, where those affected by the defendant's behaviour are too frightened to be identified and to give evidence, the police or local authority may decide to use professional witnesses to observe the misconduct at first hand and give evidence of what has taken place. Such witnesses should be able to give evidence from their own direct observations of the behaviour, not from hearsay. Care needs to be taken to ensure that any professional witness does not inadvertently enable the vulnerable or intimidated witnesses to be identified, for example from their home address.

5.3   A separate application must be made against each single named individual, even though that person may be one of a larger group, each of whom is summonsed ...

6.4   Part III of the Children and Young Persons Act 1933 applies to children and young persons in such summary proceedings in magistrates' courts. Under Section 34A of this Act the court must in relation to an under 16, and may in other cases, require the attendance of a parent or guardian (which may include the local authority social services department). Every effort should be made in advance of a hearing to ensure this takes place, so that the court does not need to adjourn to require their attendance. When assigning magistrates for anti-social behaviour order hearings, Justices' clerks should consider magistrates with relevant experience (in, for example, the youth courts) or qualifications to deal with applications for orders against children and young persons.

Parenting orders

These are also dealt with under the 1998 Act.

8(1) This section applies where, in any court proceedings —

(a) a child safety order is made in respect of a child;

(b) an anti-social behaviour order or sex offender order is made in respect of a child or young person;

(c) a child or young person is convicted of an offence; or

(d) a person is convicted of an offence under section 443 (failure to comply with school attendance order) or section 444 (failure to secure regular attendance at school of registered pupil) of the Education Act 1996.

(2) Subject to subsection (3) and section 9(1) below and to section 19(5) of, and paragraph 13(5) of Schedule 1 to, the Powers of Criminal Courts (Sentencing) Act 2000, [conviction following a referral order — see below] if in the proceedings the court is satisfied that the relevant condition is fulfilled, it may make a parenting order in respect of a person who is a parent or guardian of the child or young person or, as the case may be, the person convicted of the offence under section 443 or 444 ('the parent').

(3) A court shall not make a parenting order unless it has been notified by the Secretary of State that arrangements for implementing such orders are available in the area in which it appears to the court that the parent resides or will reside and the notice has not been withdrawn.

(4) A parenting order is an order which requires the parent —

(a) to comply, for a period not exceeding twelve months, with such requirements as are specified in the order; and

(b) subject to subsection (5) below, to attend, for a concurrent period not exceeding three months and not more than once in any week, such counselling or guidance sessions as may be specified in directions given by the responsible officer;

and in this subsection 'week' means a period of seven days beginning with a Sunday.

(5) A parenting order may, but need not, include such a requirement as is mentioned in subsection (4)(b) above in any case where such an order has been made in respect of the parent on a previous occasion.

(6) The relevant condition is that the parenting order would be desirable in the interests of preventing —

(a) in a case falling within paragraph (a) or (b) of subsection (1) above, any repetition of the kind of behaviour which led to the child safety order, anti-social behaviour order or sex offender order being made;

(b) in a case falling within paragraph (c) of that subsection, the commission of any further offence by the child or young person;

(c) in a case falling within paragraph (d) of that subsection, the commission of any further offence under section 443 or 444 of the Education Act 1996.

(7) The requirements that may be specified under subsection (4)(a) above are those which the court considers desirable in the interests of preventing any such repetition or, as the case may be, the commission of any such further offence.

(8) In this section and section 9 below 'responsible officer', in relation to a parenting order, means one of the following who is specified in the order, namely —

(a) a probation officer an officer of a local probation board;

(b) a social worker of a local authority social services department; and

(bb) a person nominated by a person appointed as chief education officer under section 532 of the Education Act 1996;

(c) a member of a youth offending team.

9(1)   Where a person under the age of 16 is convicted of an offence, the court by or before which he is so convicted —

(a) if it is satisfied that the relevant condition is fulfilled, shall make a parenting order; and

(b) if it is not so satisfied, shall state in open court that it is not and why it is not.

(1A) Subsection (1) above has effect subject to section 19(5) of, and paragraph 13(5) of Schedule 1 to, the Powers of Criminal Courts (Sentencing) Act 2000.

(2)   Before making a parenting order —

(a) in a case falling within paragraph (a) of subsection (1) of section 8 above;

(b) in a case falling within paragraph (b) or (c) of that subsection, where the person concerned is under the age of 16; or

(c) in a case falling within paragraph (d) of that subsection, where the person to whom the offence related is under that age,

a court shall obtain and consider information about the person's family circumstances and the likely effect of the order on those circumstances.

(3)   Before making a parenting order, a court shall explain to the parent in ordinary language —

(a) the effect of the order and of the requirements proposed to be included in it;

(b) the consequences which may follow (under subsection (7) below) if he fails to comply with any of those requirements; and

(c) that the court has power (under subsection (5) below) to review the order on the application either of the parent or of the responsible officer.

(4)   Requirements specified in, and directions given under, a parenting order shall, as far as practicable, be such as to avoid —

(a) any conflict with the parent's religious beliefs; and

(b) any interference with the times, if any, at which he normally works or attends an educational establishment.

(5)   If while a parenting order is in force it appears to the court which made it, on the application of the responsible officer or the parent, that it is appropriate to make an order under this subsection, the court may make an order discharging the parenting order or varying it —

(a) by cancelling any provision included in it; or

(b) by inserting in it (either in addition to or in substitution for any of its provisions) any provision that could have been included in the order if the court had then had power to make it and were exercising the power.

(6)   Where an application under subsection (5) above for the discharge of a parenting order is dismissed, no further application for its discharge shall be made under that subsection by any person except with the consent of the court which made the order.

(7)   If while a parenting order is in force the parent without reasonable excuse fails to comply with any requirement included in the order, or specified in directions given by the responsible officer, he shall be liable on summary conviction to a fine not exceeding level 3 on the standard scale.

Guidance on parenting orders can be found at **www.homeoffice.gov.uk/cdact/ parent.htm**:

3.1   The parenting order can consist of two elements. The first imposes a requirement on the parent or guardian to attend counselling or guidance sessions where they will receive help and support in dealing with their child. This element will normally form the core of the parenting order and must, with one exception, be imposed in all cases when an order is made. (The exception is where the parent or guardian has previously received a parenting order — section 8(5)).

They will be able to learn, for example, how to set and enforce consistent standards of behaviour, and how to respond more effectively to challenging adolescent demands. Section 8(4)(b) provides that parents can be required to attend a counselling or guidance session no more than once a week for up to three months.

3.2 The second element, which is discretionary, is requirements on the parent or guardian to exercise control over their child's behaviour. These could include seeing that the child gets to school every day, or ensuring that he or she is home by a certain time at night. Section 8(4)(a) provides that this element can last for up to 12 months; it will be for the court to decide how long such requirements should run taking account of the circumstances of the case. For example, if the order is made where a young person is convicted of an offence and the court makes the young person subject to a court order, the length of the parenting order could be linked to that order.

3.3 All elements of the parenting order will be supervised by the responsible officer, who will generally be a member of the local youth offending team. It is the duty of the youth offending team to co-ordinate the provision of persons to act as responsible officers under a parenting order (section 38(4)(f)) and how this is to be delivered should be set out in the local youth justice plan (section 40(1)). The responsible officer will have responsibility for, amongst other things, arranging the provision of counselling or guidance sessions and ensuring that the parent complies with any other requirements which the court may impose.

3.4 The operation of the parenting order, in the family proceedings court or in a magistrates' court acting under civil jurisdiction, may fall outside the formal youth justice system, that is the system of criminal justice for offenders aged 10–17. However, the parenting order is intended, by reinforcing or securing proper parental responsibility, to prevent offending, which section 37 of the 1998 Act establishes as the principal aim of the youth justice system. That section also requires all those working within the youth justice system, in addition to any other duties to which they are subject, to have regard to that aim. It therefore helps set the overall framework within which work with young offenders, and their parents, is to be undertaken.

4.11 The Government believes that parents have an important role to play in supporting their children when they are involved in any court proceedings. Magistrates' courts, including youth courts, have powers to enforce parental attendance at court where appropriate.

The guidance then considers the powers to order parents to attend, some of which are set out under the 1933 Children and Young Persons Act above. This part is not reproduced.

4.16 There is no requirement for the court to consider an oral or written report before making a parenting order, but in some circumstances the court has to obtain and consider information about the family circumstances. How and in what form the court obtains and considers that information is for the court to determine.

4.19 What form the information about family circumstances should take — whether it should be presented orally or in writing — will be for the court to determine depending on the circumstances of the case. There is no requirement for a written report, but the information could be incorporated in such a report (e.g. a reparation or action plan order report or presentence report) if one has been commissioned or provided in a separate written assessment. Alternatively, the court may rely on an oral report in court (e.g. where the family circumstances are known to the youth offending team), or ask questions of the parent or guardian or of the child or young person if they are present in court.

4.25 The court should only consider imposing a parenting order where the child is in the care of a local authority or living in local authority accommodation where it believes that the parent or guardian of the child or young person would benefit from the help and support which would be offered by a parenting order. The core element of the order is the requirement under section 8(4)(b) to attend counselling or guidance sessions and it is this element which could be imposed on the child or young person's parent or guardian in the expectation that it might help lead to the eventual return of the child or young person to their parent or guardian. It would be inappropriate to impose this element of the order on the local authority or those acting on its behalf, including foster parents. But the court may consider that, in *exceptional* circumstances, in addition to a requirement on the parent(s) of the child or young person to attend counselling or guidance sessions, there could be a need to impose specific requirements under section 8(4)(a) on the local authority, or those acting on its behalf, to help address, for example, the child or young person's offending behaviour or any other reason why the child or young person was before the court.

Child safety orders

These relate to criminal-type activities — actual or feared — by a child too young to be prosecuted and are governed by the Crime and Disorder Act ss. 11 and 12:

11(1)   Subject to subsection (2) below, if a magistrates' court, on the application of a local authority, is satisfied that one or more of the conditions specified in subsection (3) below are fulfilled with respect to a child under the age of 10, it may make an order (a 'child safety order') which —

(a)   places the child, for a period (not exceeding the permitted maximum) specified in the order, under the supervision of the responsible officer; and

(b)   requires the child to comply with such requirements as are so specified.

(2)   A court shall not make a child safety order unless it has been notified by the Secretary of State that arrangements for implementing such orders are available in the area in which it appears that the child resides or will reside and the notice has not been withdrawn.

(3)   The conditions are —

(a)   that the child has committed an act which, if he had been aged 10 or over, would have constituted an offence;

(b)   that a child safety order is necessary for the purpose of preventing the commission by the child of such an act as is mentioned in paragraph (a) above;

(c)   that the child has contravened a ban imposed by a curfew notice; and

(d)   that the child has acted in a manner that caused or was likely to cause harassment, alarm or distress to one or more persons not of the same household as himself.

(4)   The maximum period permitted for the purposes of subsection (1)(a) above is 3 months or, where the court is satisfied that the circumstances of the case are exceptional, 12 months.

(5)   The requirements that may be specified under subsection (1)(b) above are those which the court considers desirable in the interests of —

(a)   securing that the child receives appropriate care, protection and support and is subject to proper control; or

(b)   preventing any repetition of the kind of behaviour which led to the child safety order being made.

(6)   Proceedings under this section or section 12 below shall be family proceedings for the purposes of the 1989 Act or section 65 of the Magistrates' Courts Act 1980 ('the 1980 Act'); and the standard of proof applicable to such proceedings shall be that applicable to civil proceedings.

(7)   In this section 'local authority' has the same meaning as in the 1989 Act.

(8)   In this section and section 12 below, 'responsible officer', in relation to a child safety order, means one of the following who is specified in the order, namely —

(a)   a social worker of a local authority social services department; and

(b)   a member of a youth offending team.

12(1)   Before making a child safety order, a magistrates' court shall obtain and consider information about the child's family circumstances and the likely effect of the order on those circumstances.

(2)   Before making a child safety order, a magistrates' court shall explain to the parent or guardian of the child in ordinary language —

(a)   the effect of the order and of the requirements proposed to be included in it;

(b)   the consequences which may follow (under subsection (6) below) if the child fails to comply with any of those requirements; and

(c)   that the court has power (under subsection (4) below) to review the order on the application either of the parent or guardian or of the responsible officer.

(3)   Requirements included in a child safety order shall, as far as practicable, be such as to avoid —

(a)   any conflict with the parent's religious beliefs; and

(b)   any interference with the times, if any, at which the child normally attends school.

(4)   If while a child safety order is in force in respect of a child it appears to the court which made it, on the application of the responsible officer or a parent or guardian of the child, that it is appropriate to make an order under this subsection, the court may make an order discharging the child safety order or varying it —

(a)   by cancelling any provision included in it; or

(b)   by inserting in it (either in addition to or in substitution for any of its provisions) any provision that could have been included in the order if the court had then had power to make it and were exercising the power.

(5)   Where an application under subsection (4) above for the discharge of a child safety order is dismissed, no further application for its discharge shall be made under that subsection by any person except with the consent of the court which made the order.

(6)   Where a child safety order is in force and it is proved to the satisfaction of the court which made it or another magistrates' court acting for the same petty sessions area, on the application of the responsible officer, that the child has failed to comply with any requirement included in the order, the court —

(a)   may discharge the order and make in respect of him a care order under subsection (1)(a) of section 31 of the 1989 [Children] Act; or

(b)   may make an order varying the order —

(i)   by cancelling any provision included in it; or

(ii)   by inserting in it (either in addition to or in substitution for any of its provisions) any provision that could have been included in the order if the court had then had power to make it and were exercising the power.

(7)   Subsection (6)(a) above applies whether or not the court is satisfied that the conditions mentioned in section 31(2) of the 1989 [Children] Act are fulfilled.

Guidance on the child safety order is to be found in The Crime and Disorder Act 1998 Guidance Document: Child Safety Order at **www.homeoffice.gov.uk/cdact/ csorddft.htm**:

2.3   The child safety order is available for those under the age of 10 and can be made in a family proceedings court. It can be made in respect of a named child following an application by a local authority with social services (and education) responsibilities. The standard of proof in such proceedings is the civil standard, that is the balance of probabilities. The conditions which can trigger such an application are contained in section 11(3) and are set out in paragraph 4.5 below.

2.4   The child safety order is a new form of intervention available to local authority social services departments to help them deal with children with problems. The order supplements the existing welfare provisions under the Children Act 1989 (see Annex B [not reproduced]) and should be seen in that context. Local authority social services departments will need to decide which power within its widened range it should make use of to deal with the problems of a particular child. The increased scope of these welfare powers should help practitioners to tailor their response more effectively to the needs of the child.

2.5 As these are family proceedings as defined by section 8(3) and (4) of the Children Act 1989, the court may make orders under that Act of its own volition or by application. These include an order under section 8 dealing with contact, prohibited steps, residence and specific issues, and the option under section 37 of directing the local authority to undertake an investigation of the child's circumstances. As with any proceedings which involve issues relating to the upbringing of a child, the child's welfare is the court's paramount consideration under section 1 of the 1989 Act. Similarly, the court should bear in mind the underlying 'no order' principle set out in section 1(5) of that Act when considering child safety order applications.

2.6 Under a child safety order, the court is able to impose requirements on the child so as to ensure that he or she receives appropriate care, protection and support and is subject to proper control, in order to prevent any repetition of the kind of behaviour which led to the order being made. The child is placed under the supervision of a responsible officer who will be a social worker from the local authority social services department or a member of a youth offending team.

2.7 Normally, the maximum length of an order will be three months. However, where the court is satisfied that the circumstances of the case are exceptional, then the maximum period may be up to 12 months. This allows the court discretion to help it tailor an order to meet the needs and circumstances of a particular child and vary the length of the order accordingly.

Section 3: Multi-agency working

3.1 The child safety order needs to be seen in the context of other work to safeguard and promote the welfare of children and take into account the contribution which a number of agencies can make to preventing offending. In particular:

- A close connection needs to be made between the consideration of child safety order applications and multi-agency child protection work under the new 'Working Together' guidance. Local authority child protection investigations under section 47 of the 1989 Act may give rise to child safety order referrals. Likewise, investigations of cases in which children are or appear to be involved in serious anti-social behaviour or at risk of offending may give rise to concerns about the child's welfare which need to be addressed through child protection procedures. Local referral and case conference arrangements should take account of these links.
- A wide range of local agencies may give rise to referrals of young children involved in anti-social or offending-type behaviour, including social services, schools, the police and housing authorities. How such referrals are managed is a matter for local decision but there should be a clear focal point for them to be appropriately assessed and investigated. Given its multi-agency composition, the youth offending team may be well placed to take this on. Other work undertaken by the local authority to prevent children becoming involved in crime, including in discharging its duty under paragraph 7(b) of Schedule 2 to the 1989 Act to encourage children in its area not to commit offences, also needs to be taken into account.

4.6 In applying for a child safety order, the local authority will need to provide the court with information in support of its application, as it does now with applications for other welfare orders. The nature of that information will depend upon the circumstances of the case and

which of the four conditions described above are applicable. For example:
- under section 11(3)(a) information should involve evidence of the 'offence' and the child's involvement, together with a commentary of the likely causes for this 'offending' behaviour, such as negative peer group pressure, poor parental supervision, etc;
- under section 11(3)(b) information should cover the factors which suggest that the child is at risk of committing an act which, but for their age, would constitute a criminal offence. There may be evidence of truancy, poor educational attainment or exclusion, for example, and a report may need to be commissioned from the school or local education authority;
- under section 11(3)(c) there would need to be evidence of the breach of the local child curfew, the report of the follow-up investigation by the local authority under section 47(1)(a)(iii) of the 1989 Act, and some explanation of why in that case a child safety order might usefully be imposed as a result of the breach; and
- under section 11(3)(d) there would need to be evidence of the anti-social behaviour by the child and the harassment, alarm or distress it caused or was likely to cause to the person(s) concerned. Some commentary on the causes of that behaviour might also be appropriate. Further information on the type of behaviour that might constitute alarm, harassment or distress can be found in the guidance document issued to support the anti-social behaviour order (available for those aged 10 and over), though typically it might include serious vandalism or persistent intimidation of elderly people.

Each case will have to be addressed on its own merits and any information provided to the courts suitably tailored. In all cases, the application should advise the court as to how the child safety order might best be used to address the identified problems.

(b) The court hearing
4.7   Proceedings for child safety order applications are not specified proceedings for the purposes of section 41 of the Children Act 1989. As such there is no requirement to appoint a guardian ad litem when the application is considered. If a child safety order is breached, the proceedings that follow allow for the child to be made subject to a care order. Existing arrangements which apply in the case of applications for care orders made under the 1989 Act should then be followed. This would include consideration of the appointment of a guardian ad litem and the production of a care plan, etc ....

4.26   The requirements imposed under a child safety order will need to be proportionate and tailored to the problems or behaviour of the child which caused the court to make the order. Requirements which might be included are:
- attendance at school or other relevant educational activities, such as mentoring in literacy or numeracy or a homework club;
- avoiding contact with disruptive and possibly older children;
- not visiting areas, such as shopping centres, unsupervised;
- being home during certain hours at night and being effectively supervised; and
- attending a programme or course to address specific behavioural or other problems.

4.27   Examples of a child safety order might be:
- an 8 year old girl is found shoplifting with a group of older girls in the local shopping centre and has been referred by the police to social services. The local authority then applies to the court for a child safety order. The order requires her to stay away from the shopping centre, not mix with the older girls and (with the agreement of the organisers) attend a local youth programme to make constructive use of her leisure time.
- a 9 year old boy is found riding in a stolen car with a group of older boys. The incident occurred during school hours. After the case has been referred to it by the police, the local authority applies for a child safety order. The boy's school advises that he is not attending regularly and has fallen well behind in acquiring basic skills. The order requires the boy to

attend school regularly and to take part in after school literacy and numeracy classes. It also requires him not to mix with the older boys and to be home by 7 p.m. at night.

10.4   [Any] breach application is made by the responsible officer. The parent(s) or guardian of the child should also be present at the hearing. The responsible officer will clearly have a view about what may be an appropriate response if the court is satisfied that the order has been breached and will be expected to provide advice to the court on this.

10.5   The court may decide that the only solution open to it is to make a care order under section 31(1)(a) of the 1989 Act. In such cases there is no requirement for the court to be satisfied that the conditions set out in section 31(2) of the 1989 Act are fulfilled. These limit the making of a care order to those situations where the child concerned is suffering or is likely to suffer significant harm, and that the harm or likelihood of harm is attributable to the care given to the child not being what it would be reasonable to expect a parent to give or to the child being beyond parental control. Given the conditions which need to be met for a child safety order to be made, its breach may in itself be sufficient to trigger care action by the local authority. In considering the making of a care order in such circumstances, the court is, however, bound by the welfare and 'no order' principles contained in section 1 of the 1989 Act.

Child curfew schemes

As with the other quasi-criminal orders above, this one is not a social services responsibility — where there is a two tier system of local government it is initiated by a district council. The child curfew is an administrative act, not involving the courts unless there is a breach:

14(1)   A local authority may make a scheme (a 'local child curfew scheme') for enabling the authority —
  (a)   subject to and in accordance with the provisions of the scheme; and
  (b)   if, after such consultation as is required by the scheme, the authority considers it necessary to do so for the purpose of maintaining order,
to give a notice imposing, for a specified period (not exceeding 90 days), a ban to which subsection (2) below applies.

  (2)   This subsection applies to a ban on children of specified ages (under 16) being in a public place within a specified area —
  (a)   during specified hours (between 9 p.m. and 6 a.m.); and
  (b)   otherwise than under the effective control of a parent or a responsible person aged 18 or over.

  (3)   Before making a local child curfew scheme, a local authority shall consult —
  (a)   every chief officer of police any part of whose police area lies within its area; and
  (b)   such other persons or bodies as it considers appropriate.

  (4)   A local child curfew scheme shall be made under the common seal of the local authority and shall not have effect until it is confirmed by the Secretary of State.

  (5)   The Secretary of State —
  (a)   may confirm, or refuse to confirm, a local child curfew scheme submitted under this section for confirmation; and
  (b)   may fix the date on which such a scheme is to come into operation;
and if no date is so fixed, the scheme shall come into operation at the end of the period of one month beginning with the date of its confirmation.

  (6)   A notice given under a local child curfew scheme (a 'curfew notice') may specify different hours in relation to children of different ages.

(7)   A curfew notice shall be given —
   (a) by posting the notice in some conspicuous place or places within the specified area; and
   (b) in such other manner, if any, as appears to the local authority to be desirable for giving publicity to the notice.

Government guidance on the curfew scheme — not reproduced here — can be found at **www.homeoffice.gov.uk/cdact/curfews.htm**

7.3 What happens after charge — remand, bail, and appearance in court

We saw under s. 38 of the Police and Criminal Evidence Act that a custody officer may refuse bail to a child. Under the same Act, accommodation must normally be arranged with the local authority:

46(1) Where a person —
   (a) is charged with an offence; and
   (b) after being charged —
      (i)   is kept in police detention; or
      (ii) is detained by a local authority in pursuance of arrangements made under section 38(6) above,
he shall be brought before a magistrates' court in accordance with the provisions of this section.
   (2)   If he is to be brought before a magistrates' court for the petty sessions area in which the police station at which he was charged is situated, he shall be brought before such a court as soon as is practicable and in any event not later than the first sitting after he is charged with the offence.

Children awaiting trial or sentence may be remanded in between hearings. If the court does remand, will bail be granted? The 1976 Bail Act, s. 4(1) states that:

A person ... shall be granted bail except as provided in Schedule 1 to this Act.

The meaning of bail and the power of the court to impose conditions on bail are set out in s. 3 (not reproduced). Schedule 1 of the Act lays down the grounds on which bail can be refused or made subject to conditions:

2   The defendant need not be granted bail if the court is satisfied that there are substantial grounds for believing that the defendant, if released on bail (whether subject to conditions or not) would —
   (a) fail to surrender to custody, or
   (b) commit an offence while on bail, or
   (c) interfere with witnesses or otherwise obstruct the course of justice, whether in relation to himself or any other person.
2A   The defendant need not be granted bail if —
   (a) the offence is an indictable offence or an offence triable either way; and
   (b) it appears to the court that he was on bail in criminal proceedings on the date of the offence.

3   The defendant need not be granted bail if the court is satisfied that the defendant should be kept in custody for his own protection or, if he is a child or young person, for his own welfare.

...

5   The defendant need not be granted bail where the court is satisfied that it has not been practicable to obtain sufficient information for the purpose of taking the decisions required by this Part of this Schedule for want of time since the institution of the proceedings against him.

6   The defendant need not be granted bail if, having been released on bail in or in connection with the proceedings for the offence, he has been arrested in pursuance of section 7 of this Act.

7   Where his case is adjourned for inquiries or a report, the defendant need not be granted bail if it appears to the court that it would be impracticable to complete the inquiries or make the report without keeping the defendant in custody.

Paragraph 8 of Sch. 1 provides that the court can make bail conditional for the same reasons.

9   In taking the decisions required by paragraph 2 or 2A of this Part of this Schedule, the court shall have regard to such of the following considerations as appear to it to be relevant, that is to say —
  (a) the nature and seriousness of the offence or default (and the probable method of dealing with the defendant for it),
  (b) the character, antecedents, associations and community ties of the defendant,
  (c) the defendant's record as respects the fulfilment of his obligations under previous grants of bail in criminal proceedings,
  (d) except in the case of a defendant whose case is adjourned for inquiries or a report, the strength of the evidence of his having committed the offence or having defaulted,
as well as to any others which appear to be relevant.

If bail is refused, the Children and Young Persons Act 1969 requires the court to remand the defendant to local authority accommodation, unless he is a boy of 15 or 16, in which case he can be remanded to prison or remand centre. (This will also apply to any 17 year old child, who is not treated as a child for remand purposes). Section 23 of the 1969 Act is unusual: it has two versions, one for boys of 15 to 16 and one for all other children under 17. Exceptionally, we have not cited the legislation because of its length and complexity, and have used instead the guidance document, *Implementation Guidance: Court-Ordered Secure Remands*, to explain these provisions. Both versions of section 23 are available on the website **www.homeoffice. gov.uk/ cdact/secrem.htm**:

(ii) Summary
2.6   From 1 June 1999, the courts will have the following powers available to them:

10–11 year olds   Courts may decide to bail the child, with or without conditions, or remand to local authority accommodation. If the child is remanded to local authority accommodation, conditions may be attached. Paragraphs 3.1–3.5 describe the procedure in detail. The local authority may then apply to hold the child in secure accommodation under section 25 of the Children Act 1989, if the criteria in the Children (Secure Accommodation) Regulations 1991 are met. Paragraphs 3.8–3.10 deal more fully with such applications.

12–14 year olds Courts may decide to bail the child or young person, with or without conditions, or remand to local authority accommodation. If the child or young person is remanded to local authority accommodation, conditions may be attached. As with 10–11 year olds, the local authority may then apply to the court to hold the child or young person in secure accommodation under section 25 of the 1989 Act. The court may, however, itself decide to remand the child or young person to local authority secure accommodation under section 23 of the Children and Young Persons Act 1969 if the criteria in section 23(5) of the 1969 Act are met. Paragraphs 3.11–3.18 describe the procedure in more detail.

15–16 year old girls Courts may decide to bail the young person, with or without conditions, or remand to local authority accommodation. If the young person is remanded to local authority accommodation, conditions may be attached. As with the younger age groups, the local authority may then apply to the court to hold the young person in secure accommodation under the provisions in section 25 of the 1989 Act. The court may, however, itself decide to remand the young person to local authority secure accommodation under section 23 of the 1969 Act if the criteria in section 23(5) are met. Again these matters are dealt with in more detail in paragraphs 3.11–3.18.

15–16 year old boys Courts may decide to bail the young person, with or without conditions, or remand to local authority accommodation. If the young person is remanded to local authority accommodation, conditions may be attached. Like 15–16 year old girls, the local authority may then apply to the court to hold the young person in secure accommodation under provisions in section 25 of the 1989 Act. If the court judges the young person to be particularly vulnerable it may remand to local authority secure accommodation under section 23 of the 1969 Act if the criteria in section 23(5) are met, and provided that a secure place has been identified *in advance*. Paragraphs 3.18–3.24 describe the procedure in detail. Alternatively, courts may decide to remand to Prison Service accommodation under section 23 of 1969 Act again if the criteria in section 23(5) are met. Paragraphs 3.26–3.28 describe the procedure in detail.

Section 3: Procedure

(i) Remands to local authority accommodation (10–16 year olds)
3.1   When children and young persons (aged 10–16 years — 17 year olds are regarded as adults for remand purposes) are charged and not released on bail, they are remanded to local authority accommodation (section 23(1) of the 1969 Act). The remanding court must designate the relevant local authority (section 23(2) of the 1969 Act). In the case of a child or young person already being looked after by a local authority, that authority is to be the designated authority. In any other case, it will be the local authority for the area where the court believes the child or young person resides, or where the alleged offence was committed.

3.2   Where a child or young person is remanded to local authority accommodation, the local authority has the same powers and duties towards that child or young person under the Children Act 1989 as for any other child whom the local authority is looking after and for whom it does not have parental responsibility by virtue of the 1989 Act. However, the way in which the local authority deals with the remanded child or young person is subject to the following existing powers available to the court. These are:

• a power to impose conditions upon the child or young person; and
• a power to impose requirements upon the local authority.

3.3   The court may, whether on the application of the local authority or otherwise, impose on the child or young person on remand any conditions that can be imposed under section 3(6) of the Bail Act 1976 on a defendant granted bail (section 23(10) of the 1969 Act). The placement of the defendant, in these cases, is a matter for the discretion of the local authority, subject to the court's specific power to stipulate that the child or young person is not to be placed with a named person (see paragraph 3.4); the power to impose conditions on a child or young person does *not*, therefore, include the power to impose a condition as to place of residence. The court must explain to the defendant in open court and in ordinary language why it is imposing the conditions (section 23(8) of the 1969 Act); and in the case of a magistrates' court (including a youth court), the reasons must be specified in the warrant of commitment and entered in the register.

3.4   The requirements which the court may impose upon the local authority are of two kinds. First, the court may stipulate that the child or young person shall not be placed (i.e. accommodated) with a named person (section 23(9)(b) of the 1969 Act). For example, the court may take the view that the fact that the defendant has been living at home with his or her parents has contributed to the circumstances which have led to the court appearance. The court may decide, therefore, to require the local authority not to allow the child or young person to return to live at home. Subject to this requirement, the local authority retains full responsibility for deciding where a child or young person remanded to local authority accommodation should be placed. Second, the court may impose on the local authority requirements needed to ensure that the defendant complies with any conditions imposed upon him or her (section 23(9)(a) of the 1969 Act).

3.5   The court must consult the designated authority before imposing any conditions or requirements. The requirement to consult is waived only where consultation is not reasonably practicable in all the circumstances. Conditions or requirements may be revoked or varied by a court on the application of the designated local authority or the defendant (section 23(11) of the 1969 Act).

(iv) Remands to local authority secure accommodation (12–14 year olds, 15–16 year old girls)

3.11   Section 97 of the 1998 Act amends section 23 of the 1969 Act to allow courts to remand certain alleged juvenile offenders direct to local authority secure accommodation. The provisions apply to any 12, 13 or 14 year old, and any 15 or 16 year old girl. They will also apply to 15 or 16 year old boys who are adjudged by the court to fall within the vulnerability definition in section 98(3) of the 1998 Act and where a place has been identified in advance. The powers in relation to this latter group of boys are dealt with in more detail in paragraphs 3.19–3.24.

3.12   The court may remand a child or young person of relevant age and sex to local authority secure accommodation when one of two particular criteria are met (section 23(5) of the 1969 Act). These are:

- the child or young person is charged with, or has been convicted of, a violent or sexual offence, or of an offence punishable in the case of an adult with imprisonment for a term of 14 years or more; or
- the child or young person has a recent history of absconding while remanded to local authority accommodation, and is charged or has been convicted of an imprisonable offence alleged or found to have been committed while he has been so remanded,

and in either case the court must be of an opinion that only remanding the child or young person to local authority secure accommodation would be adequate to protect the public from serious harm from them.

3.13   The first limb covers the most serious offenders. The second limb covers young people who are remanded to local authority accommodation and who persistently abscond and allegedly commit further less serious imprisonable offences. It is intended to be used for those young people whose repeated absconding and alleged offending together constitute a serious problem.

3.14   In either case the court must be of an opinion that remanding him or her to local authority secure accommodation would be the only adequate way to protect the public from serious harm from him or her. In relation to sexual or violent offences, 'serious harm' means death or serious personal injury, whether physical or psychological, occasioned by further such offences committed by the young person. 'Serious harm' is not defined in relation to other offences. However, the definition for sexual and violent offences gives an indication of the gravity of the harm to which the public would need to be exposed from a young person in other circumstances before the test was likely to be satisfied.

3.15 Much of the practical detail is the same as that which applies in the case of a remand to local authority accommodation. For example, the court is required to designate the relevant authority which, in the case of a child or young person who is being looked after by an authority, is that authority (section 23(2) of the 1969 Act); no such secure remand shall take place without the child or young person being given the opportunity to apply for legal aid (section 23(5A) of the 1969 Act); the court must state in open court that it is of the opinion that only a secure remand is adequate to protect the public from serious harm from him or her; it must explain to him or her in open court and in ordinary language why it is of that opinion; and in the case of a magistrates' court (including a youth court), the reasons must be specified in the warrant of commitment and entered in the register (section 23(6) of the 1969 Act).

3.16 Under section 23(4) of the 1969 Act there is a requirement on the court to consult the designated local authority before it imposes a security requirement. The purpose of such consultation is to allow the local authority to provide the court with information so that the court is best placed to make an appropriate decision depending on the circumstances of the case. Such information should include:

- the nature and availablity of local provision to support a remand in the community; and
- the nature and availability of secure and non-secure accommodation.

3.17 When a court remands a child or young person to local authority secure accommodation, the designated local authority will be required to find a place in local authority secure accommodation (section 23(4) of the 1969 Act). This duty may be exercised on behalf of the local authority either by a local authority social worker or a probation officer. In future, this duty is likely to be exercised by youth offending team members.

3.18 Under section 61 of the Criminal Justice Act 1991, local authorities are under a duty to comply with any security requirement imposed on them under section 23(4) of the Children and Young Persons Act 1969. This duty may be discharged by a local authority by providing their own secure accommodation or ensuring access to secure accommodation provided elsewhere.

(v) Remands to local authority secure accommodation (15 or 16 year old boys)

3.19 Section 98 of the 1998 Act modifies section 23 of the 1969 Act to apply specifically to 15 or 16 year old boys and those not prescribed by an order under section 97 of the 1998 Act. Paragraphs 3.26–3.28 describe the procedure in relation to prison remands for a 15 or 16 year old boy. Within the 15 or 16 year old age group there will be some boys who, because of their physical or emotional immaturity or propensity to harm themselves, should not be remanded to Prison Service accommodation. Following consultation with a probation officer, a local authority social worker or a member of a youth offending team a court may remand such a 15 or 16 year old boy to local authority secure accommodation (section 23 (4) of the 1969 Act) provided that:

- the criteria at subsection (5) (and described in detail at paragraph 3.12 above) are met;
- the young person is someone to whom subsection (5A) of the *modified* provisions applies; *and*
- it has been notified by the local authority that such secure accommodation is available for him.

3.20 It is the responsibility of the designated local authority to provide the court with information as to the young person's likely 'vulnerability'. Each case will need to be considered on its own merits. However, the local authority and the court may wish to take into account such things as the young person's physical immaturity, or any psychological evidence or any evidence of self harm. The local authority may consider it appropriate to provide supporting material in the form of medical or psychological reports.

3.21   The onus is on the local authority to find a place in local authority secure accommodation. This duty may be exercised on behalf of the local authority either by a local authority social worker or a probation officer. In future, this duty is likely to be exercised by youth offending team members. At the time that the court considers information concerning the 'vulnerability' of the young person, the local authority needs to be in a position to inform the court that local authority secure accommodation is available. It is clearly in the interests of both the young person and justice to ensure that any delay is minimised.

3.22   There may be situations when despite the fact that the court may feel that the remanded young person would meet the definition of 'vulnerability', there is no local authority secure accommodation available at the time of the hearing. Should this be the case the initial remand will be to prison. Sections 128 and 128A of the Magistrates' Courts Act 1980 allow a court to remand a juvenile in custody in the first instance for a period of up to eight days. Second and subsequent remands can be for a period of up to 28 days. Courts are, therefore, free to set shorter remand periods if, in the circumstances of the case, they judge that this would be desirable. Setting a shorter remand period, which would allow the local authority time to find a suitable secure place, may be an option which the court would consider appropriate in such a case.

3.23   There is, of course, a general duty on courts under section 44 of the Children and Young Persons Act 1933 to have regard to the welfare of children and young people who appear before them. In particular, the courts should be aware of the need to keep cases involving juveniles remanded in custody under constant review and to minimise delays.

3.24   The court is required to designate the relevant authority which, in the case of a young person who is being looked after by an authority, is that authority (section 23(2) of the 1969 Act); no such secure remand shall take place without the young person being given the opportunity to apply for legal aid (section 23(4A) of the 1969 Act); the court must state in open court that it is of the opinion that only a secure remand is adequate to protect the public from serious harm from him; it must explain to him in open court and in ordinary language why it is of that opinion; and in the case of a magistrates' court (including a youth court), the reasons must be specified in the warrant of commitment and entered in the register (section 23(6) of the 1969 Act).

3.25   Where a young person has been remanded to local authority accommodation, the designated local authority may apply to the court for him to be remanded to local authority secure accommodation. In such cases the court will need to be satisfied that the provisions in section 23(4), described in paragraph 3.19 above, apply (section 23(9A) of the 1969 Act).

(vi)   Remands to prison (15 or 16 year old boys)

3.26   *Fifteen or sixteen year old boys* may be remanded by the court direct to prison, but only if strict conditions are met (section 23(5) of the 1969 Act). A 15 or 16 year old boy may be remanded by the court to prison where the following criteria are met;

- the boy is charged with, or has been convicted of, a violent or sexual offence, or of an offence punishable in the case of an adult with imprisonment for a term of 14 years or more; *or*
- the boy has a recent history of absconding while remanded to local authority accommodation, and is charged with or has been convicted of an imprisonable offence alleged or found to have been committed while he has been so remanded.

and in either case the court *must* be of an opinion that only remanding the young person to prison would be adequate to protect the public from serious harm from them.

3.27   The court is required to consult a local authority social worker or a probation officer, that is normally the court duty officer, before remanding a young person to prison. In future, this duty is likely to be exercised by a youth offending team member. No young person may be remanded to prison without having been given the opportunity of applying for legal aid (section 23(4A) of the 1969 Act). When a young person is remanded to prison, the court must state in open court that it is of the opinion that only a prison remand is adequate to protect the public from serious harm from him; and it must explain to him in open court and in ordinary language why it is of that opinion. In the case of a magistrates' court (including a youth court), the reasons must be specified in the warrant of commitment and entered in the register (section 23(6) of the 1969 Act)

3.28   Where a young person has been remanded to local authority accommodation, the designated local authority may apply to the court for him to be remanded to prison (section 23(9A) of the 1969 Act).

7.4 **Trial and sentencing options for child offenders**

The procedures are set out in the Magistrates Courts (Children and Young Persons) Rules 1992 (SI 1992/2071):

Assistance in conducting case

5.(1)   Except where the relevant minor is legally represented, the court shall allow his parent or guardian to assist him in conducting his case.

(2)   Where the parent or guardian cannot be found or cannot in the opinion of the court reasonably be required to attend, the court may allow any relative or other responsible person to take the place of the parent or guardian for the purposes of this Part.

Duty of court to explain nature of proceedings etc.

6.(1)   The court shall explain to the relevant minor the nature of the proceedings and, where he is charged with an offence, the substance of the charge.

(2)   The explanation shall be given in simple language suitable to his age and understanding.

Duty of court to take plea to charge

7.   Where the relevant minor is charged with an offence the court shall, after giving the explanation required by rule 6, ask him whether he pleads guilty or not guilty to the charge.

Evidence in support of charge or application

8.(1)   Where —
- (a) the relevant minor is charged with an offence and does not plead guilty, or
- (b) the proceedings are of a kind mentioned in rule 4(2)(a), (b) or (c) [breach of a community sentence],

    the court shall hear the witnesses in support of the charge or, as the case may be, the application.

(2)   Except where —
- (a) the proceedings are of a kind mentioned in rule 4(2)(a), (b) or (c), and
- (b) the relevant minor is the applicant,

each witness may at the close of his evidence-in-chief be cross-examined by or on behalf of the relevant minor.

(3)   If in any case where the relevant minor is not legally represented or assisted as provided by rule 5, the relevant minor, instead of asking questions by way of cross- examination, makes assertions, the court shall then put to the witness such questions as it thinks necessary on behalf of the relevant minor and may for this purpose question the relevant minor in order to bring out or clear up any point arising out of any such assertions.

Evidence in reply

9.   If it appears to the court after hearing the evidence in support of the charge or application that a prima facie case is made out, the relevant minor shall, if he is not the applicant and is not legally represented, be told that he may give evidence or address the court, and the evidence of any witnesses shall be heard.

Procedure after finding against minor

10.(1)   This rule applies where —

(a)   the relevant minor is found guilty of an offence, whether after a plea of guilty or otherwise, or

(b)   in proceedings of a kind mentioned in rule 4(2)(a), (b) or (c) the court is satisfied that the case for the applicant —

(i)   if the relevant minor is not the applicant, has been made out, or

(ii)   if he is the applicant, has not been made out.

(2)   Where this rule applies —

(a)   the relevant minor and his parent or guardian, if present, shall be given an opportunity of making a statement,

(b)   the court shall take into consideration all available information as to the general conduct, home surroundings, school record and medical history of the relevant minor and, in particular, shall take into consideration such information as aforesaid which is provided in pursuance of section 9 of the Act of 1969,

(c)   if such information as aforesaid is not fully available, the court shall consider the desirability of adjourning the proceedings for such inquiry as may be necessary,

(d)   any written report of a probation officer, local authority, local education authority, educational establishment or registered medical practitioner may be received and considered by the court without being read aloud, and

(e)   if the court considers it necessary in the interests of the relevant minor, it may require him or his parent or guardian, if present, to withdraw from the court.

(3)   The court shall arrange for copies of any written report before the court to be made available to —

(a)   the legal representative, if any, of the relevant minor,

(b)   any parent or guardian of the relevant minor who is present at the hearing, and

(c)   the relevant minor, except where the court otherwise directs on the ground that it appears to it impracticable to disclose the report having regard to his age and understanding or undesirable to do so having regard to potential serious harm which might thereby be suffered by him.

(4)   In any case in which the relevant minor is not legally represented and where a report which has not been made available to him in accordance with a direction under paragraph (3)(c) has been considered without being read aloud in pursuance of paragraph (2)(d) or where he or his parent or guardian has been required to withdraw from the court in pursuance of paragraph (2)(e), then —

(a)   the relevant minor shall be told the substance of any part of the information given to the court bearing on his character or conduct which the court considers to be material to the manner in which the case should be dealt with unless it appears to it impracticable so to do having regard to his age and understanding, and

(b)   the parent or guardian of the relevant minor, if present, shall be told the substance of any part of such information which the court considers to be material as aforesaid and which has reference to his character or conduct or to the character, conduct, home surroundings or health of the relevant minor, and if such a person, having been told the substance of any part of such information, desires to produce further evidence with reference thereto, the court, if it thinks the further evidence would be material, shall adjourn the proceedings for the production thereof and shall, if necessary in the case of a report, require the attendance at the adjourned hearing of the person who made the report.

Duty of court to explain manner in which it proposes to deal with case and effect of order

11.(1) Before finally disposing of the case or before remitting the case to another court in pursuance of section 56 of the Act of 1933 [sending case to Crown Court for grave crimes — see p. 467 below], the court shall inform the relevant minor and his parent or guardian, if present, or any person assisting him in his case, of the manner in which it proposes to deal with the case and allow any of those persons so informed to make representations; but the relevant minor shall not be informed as aforesaid if the court considers it undesirable so to do.

(2) On making any order, the court shall explain to the relevant minor the general nature and effect of the order unless, in the case of an order requiring his parent or guardian to enter into a recognizance, it appears to it undesirable so to do.

Duty of court to explain nature of proceedings

17. Except where, by virtue of any enactment, the court may proceed in the absence of the relevant minor, before proceeding with the hearing the court shall inform him of the general nature both of the proceedings and of the grounds on which they are brought, in terms suitable to his age and understanding, or if by reason of his age and understanding or his absence it is impracticable so to do, shall so inform any parent or guardian of his present at the hearing.

Conduct of case on behalf of relevant minor

18.(1) Except where the relevant minor or his parent or guardian is legally represented, the court shall, unless the relevant minor otherwise requests, allow his parent or guardian to conduct the case on his behalf, subject, however, to the provisions of rule 19(2).

(2) If the court thinks it appropriate to do so it may, unless the relevant minor otherwise requests, allow a relative of his or some other responsible person to conduct the case on his behalf.

Power of court to hear evidence in absence of relevant minor and to require parent or guardian to withdraw

19.(1) Where the evidence likely to be given is such that in the opinion of the court it is in the interests of the relevant minor that the whole, or any part, of the evidence should not be given in his presence, then, unless he is conducting his own case, the court may hear the whole or part of the evidence, as it thinks appropriate, in his absence; but any evidence relating to his character or conduct shall be heard in his presence.

(2) If the court is satisfied that it is appropriate so to do, it may require a parent or guardian of the relevant minor to withdraw from the court while the relevant minor gives evidence or makes a statement; but the court shall inform the person so excluded of the substance of any allegations made against him by the relevant minor.

Duty of court to explain procedure to relevant minor at end of applicant's case

20. If it appears to the court after hearing the evidence in support of the applicant's case that he has made out a prima facie case it shall tell the relevant minor or the person conducting the case on his behalf under rule 18 that he may give evidence or make a statement and call witnesses.

Duty of court to explain manner in which it proposes to deal with case and effect of order

22.(1) Before finally disposing of the case, the court shall in simple language inform the relevant minor, any person conducting the case on his behalf, and his parent or guardian, if present, of the manner in which it proposes to deal with the case and allow any of those persons so informed to make representations; but the relevant minor shall not be informed as aforesaid if the court considers it undesirable or, having regard to his age and understanding, impracticable so to inform him.

(2)   On making any order, the court shall in simple language suitable to his age and understanding explain to the relevant minor the general nature and effect of the order unless it appears to it impracticable so to do having regard to his age and understanding and shall give such an explanation to the relevant minor's parent or guardian, if present.

Virtually all sentencing legislation has been consolidated into one Act, the Powers of Criminal Courts (Sentencing) Act 2000 (PCCSA). In what follows the legislation is take from this Act unless otherwise stated.

7.4.1 Which court should sentence a child?

Children are generally sentenced by youth courts (CYPA 1933, s. 46 above). Sometimes an adult court deals with the case because the juvenile is charged with an adult:

8.(1)   Subsection (2) below applies where a child or young person (that is to say, any person aged under 18) is convicted by or before any court of an offence other than homicide.

(2)   The court may and, if it is not a youth court, shall unless satisfied that it would be undesirable to do so, remit the case —

  (a)   if the offender was committed for trial or sent to the Crown Court for trial under section 51 of the Crime and Disorder Act 1998, to a youth court acting for the place where he was committed for trial or sent to the Crown Court for trial;

[Section 51 of the Crime and Disorder Act allows the court to commit a juvenile for trial where the offence is jointly charged with an adult. The Crown Court can then try summary as well as indictable offences.]

  (b)   in any other case, to a youth court acting either for the same place as the remitting court or for the place where the offender habitually resides;
but in relation to a magistrates' court other than a youth court this subsection has effect subject to subsection (6) below.

(3)   Where a case is remitted under subsection (2) above, the offender shall be brought before a youth court accordingly, and that court may deal with him in any way in which it might have dealt with him if he had been tried and convicted by that court.

...

(6)   Without prejudice to the power to remit any case to a youth court which is conferred on a magistrates' court other than a youth court by subsections (1) and (2) above, where such a magistrates' court convicts a child or young person of an offence it must exercise that power unless the case falls within subsection (7) or (8) below.

(7)   The case falls within this subsection if the court would, were it not so to remit the case, be required by section 16(2) below to refer the offender to a youth offender panel (in which event the court may, but need not, so remit the case).

(8)   The case falls within this subsection if it does not fall within subsection (7) above but the court is of the opinion that the case is one which can properly be dealt with by means of —

  (a)   an order discharging the offender absolutely or conditionally, or

  (b)   an order for the payment of a fine, or

  (c)   an order (under section 150 below) requiring the offender's parent or guardian to enter into a recognizance to take proper care of him and exercise proper control over him,
with or without any other order that the court has power to make when absolutely or conditionally discharging an offender.

7.4.2 **The range of possible sentences**

The powers of the court to defer sentence (PCCSA, s. 1) or to discharge the offender without punishment (s. 12) are theoretically available for convicted children. In practice, such a disposal is unlikely and the legislation is not reproduced. The sentences below will all be within the powers of both a youth court and the Crown Court. The only exception is where a sentence can only be imposed by the Crown Court for grave crimes under PCCSA, ss. 90–92 (reproduced below, and also discussed in relation to the *Bulger* case above).

Referral orders and reparation orders

New orders called referral orders, reparation orders and action plan orders were introduced by the Crime and Disorder Act and the Youth Justice and Criminal Evidence Act (now consolidated into PCCSA, though the guidance reproduced below will refer to the original legislation). They all enable the offender to be dealt with within the community. (The action plan order is a community sentence and is dealt with under that heading.)

Referral orders

The referral order is the disposition of first choice for a first time offender pleading guilty. Guidance on the referral order is available at **www.homeoffice.gov.uk/yousys/dgyot.htm**, but is not reproduced here.

16.(1) This section applies where a youth court or other magistrates' court is dealing with a person aged under 18 for an offence and —

(a) neither the offence nor any connected offence is one for which the sentence is fixed by law;

(b) the court is not, in respect of the offence or any connected offence, proposing to impose a custodial sentence on the offender or make a hospital order (within the meaning of the Mental Health Act 1983) in his case; and

(c) the court is not proposing to discharge him absolutely in respect of the offence.

(2) If —

(a) the compulsory referral conditions are satisfied in accordance with section 17 below, and

(b) referral is available to the court,

the court shall sentence the offender for the offence by ordering him to be referred to a youth offender panel.

(3) If —

(a) the discretionary referral conditions are satisfied in accordance with section 17 below, and

(b) referral is available to the court,

The court may sentence the offender for the offence by ordering him to be referred to a youth offender panel.

(4) For the purposes of this Part an offence is connected with another if the offender falls to be dealt with for it at the same time as he is dealt with for the other offence (whether or not he is convicted of the offences at the same time or by or before the same court).

(5) For the purposes of this section referral is available to a court if —

(a) the court has been notified by the Secretary of State that arrangements for the implementation of referral orders are available in the area in which it appears to the court that the offender resides or will reside; and

(b) the notice has not been withdrawn.

(6)   An order under subsection (2) or (3) above is in this Act referred to as a 'referral order'.

(7)   ...

17.(1)   For the purposes of section 16(2) above the compulsory referral conditions are satisfied in relation to an offence if the offender —

(a)   pleaded guilty to the offence and to any connected offence;

(b)   has never been convicted by or before a court in the United Kingdom of any offence other than the offence and any connected offence; and

(c)   has never been bound over in criminal proceedings in England and Wales or Northern Ireland to keep the peace or to be of good behaviour.

(2)   For the purposes of section 16(3) above the discretionary referral conditions are satisfied in relation to an offence if —

(a)   the offender is being dealt with by the court for the offence and one or more connected offences;

(b)   although he pleaded guilty to at least one of the offences mentioned in paragraph (a) above, he also pleaded not guilty to at least one of them;

(c)   he has never been convicted by or before a court in the United Kingdom of any offence other than the offences mentioned in paragraph (a) above; and

(d)   he has never been bound over in criminal proceedings in England and Wales or Northern Ireland to keep the peace or to be of good behaviour.

18.(1)   A referral order shall —

(a)   specify the youth offending team responsible for implementing the order;

(b)   require the offender to attend each of the meetings of a youth offender panel to be established by the team for the offender; and

(c)   specify the period for which any youth offender contract taking effect between the offender and the panel under section 23 below is to have effect (which must not be less than three nor more than twelve months).

(2)   The youth offending team specified under subsection (1)(a) above shall be the team having the function of implementing referral orders in the area in which it appears to the court that the offender resides or will reside.

(3)   On making a referral order the court shall explain to the offender in ordinary language —

(a)   the effect of the order; and

(b)   the consequences which may follow —

(i)   if no youth offender contract takes effect between the offender and the panel under section 23 below; or

(ii)   if the offender breaches any of the terms of any such contract.

20.(1)   A court making a referral order may make an order requiring —

(a)   the appropriate person, or

(b)   in a case where there are two or more appropriate persons, any one or more of them, to attend the meetings of the youth offender panel.

(2)   Where an offender is aged under 16 when a court makes a referral order in his case —

(a)   the court shall exercise its power under subsection (1) above so as to require at least one appropriate person to attend meetings of the youth offender panel; and

(b)   if the offender falls within subsection (6) below, the person or persons so required to attend those meetings shall be or include a representative of the local authority mentioned in that subsection.

(3)   The court shall not under this section make an order requiring a person to attend meetings of the youth offender panel —

(a)   if the court is satisfied that it would be unreasonable to do so; or

(b)   to an extent which the court is satisfied would be unreasonable.

(4) Except where the offender falls within subsection (6) below, each person who is a parent or guardian of the offender is an 'appropriate person' for the purposes of this section.

(5) Where the offender falls within subsection (6) below, each of the following is an 'appropriate person' for the purposes of this section —

(a) a representative of the local authority mentioned in that subsection; and

(b) each person who is a parent or guardian of the offender with whom the offender is allowed to live.

(6) An offender falls within this subsection if he is (within the meaning of the Children Act 1989) a child who is looked after by a local authority.

(7) If, at the time when a court makes an order under this section —

(a) a person who is required by the order to attend meetings of a youth offender panel is not present in court, or

(b) a local authority whose representative is so required to attend such meetings is not represented in court,

the court must send him or (as the case may be) the authority a copy of the order forthwith.

21.(1) Where a referral order has been made in respect of an offender (or two or more associated referral orders have been so made), it is the duty of the youth offending team specified in the order (or orders) —

(a) to establish a youth offender panel for the offender;

(b) to arrange for the first meeting of the panel to be held for the purposes of section 23 below; and

(c) subsequently to arrange for the holding of any further meetings of the panel required by virtue of section 25 below (in addition to those required by virtue of any other provision of this Part).

(2) A youth offender panel shall —

(a) be constituted,

(b) conduct its proceedings, and

(c) discharge its functions under this Part (and in particular those arising under section 23 below),

in accordance with guidance given from time to time by the Secretary of State.

(3) At each of its meetings a panel shall, however, consist of at least —

(a) one member appointed by the youth offending team from among its members; and

(b) two members so appointed who are not members of the team.

22.(1) The specified team shall, in the case of each meeting of the panel established for the offender, notify —

(a) the offender, and

(b) any person to whom an order under section 20 above applies,

of the time and place at which he is required to attend that meeting.

(2) If the offender fails to attend any part of such a meeting the panel may —

(a) adjourn the meeting to such time and place as it may specify; or

(b) end the meeting and refer the offender back to the appropriate court; and subsection (1) above shall apply in relation to any such adjourned meeting.

(3) One person aged 18 or over chosen by the offender, with the agreement of the panel, shall be entitled to accompany the offender to any meeting of the panel (and it need not be the same person who accompanies him to every meeting).

(4) The panel may allow to attend any such meeting —

(a) any person who appears to the panel to be a victim of, or otherwise affected by, the offence, or any of the offences, in respect of which the offender was referred to the panel;

(b) any person who appears to the panel to be someone capable of having a good influence on the offender.

(2) Where the panel allows any such person as is mentioned in subsection (4)(a) above ('the victim') to attend a meeting of the panel, the panel may allow the victim to be accompanied to the meeting by one person chosen by the victim with the agreement of the panel.

23.(1) At the first meeting of the youth offender panel established for an offender the panel shall seek to reach agreement with the offender on a programme of behaviour the aim (or principal aim) of which is the prevention of re-offending by the offender.

(2) The terms of the programme may, in particular, include provision for any of the following —

(a) the offender to make financial or other reparation to any person who appears to the panel to be a victim of, or otherwise affected by, the offence, or any of the offences, for which the offender was referred to the panel;

(b) the offender to attend mediation sessions with any such victim or other person;

(c) the offender to carry out unpaid work or service in or for the community;

(d) the offender to be at home at times specified in or determined under the programme;

(e) attendance by the offender at a school or other educational establishment or at a place of work;

(f) the offender to participate in specified activities (such as those designed to address offending behaviour, those offering education or training or those assisting with the rehabilitation of persons dependent on, or having a propensity to misuse, alcohol or drugs);

(g) the offender to present himself to specified persons at times and places specified in or determined under the programme;

(h) the offender to stay away from specified places or persons (or both);

(i) enabling the offender's compliance with the programme to be supervised and recorded.

(3) The programme may not, however, provide —

(a) for the electronic monitoring of the offender's whereabouts; or

(b) for the offender to have imposed on him any physical restriction on his movements.

(4) No term which provides for anything to be done to or with any such victim or other affected person as is mentioned in subsection (2)(a) above may be included in the programme without the consent of that person.

(5) Where a programme is agreed between the offender and the panel, the panel shall cause a written record of the programme to be produced forthwith —

(a) in language capable of being readily understood by, or explained to, the offender; and

(b) for signature by him.

(6) Once the record has been signed —

(a) by the offender, and

(b) by a member of the panel on behalf of the panel,

the terms of the programme, as set out in the record, take effect as the terms of a 'youth offender contract' between the offender and the panel; and the panel shall cause a copy of the record to be given or sent to the offender.

25.(1) Where it appears to a youth offender panel to be appropriate to do so, the panel may —

(a) end the first meeting (or any further meeting held in pursuance of paragraph (b) below) without having reached agreement with the offender on a programme of behaviour of the kind mentioned in section 23(1) above; and

(b) resume consideration of the offender's case at a further meeting of the panel.

(2)   If, however, it appears to the panel at the first meeting or any such further meeting that there is no prospect of agreement being reached with the offender within a reasonable period after the making of the referral order (or orders) —

(a)   subsection (1)(b) above shall not apply; and

(b)   instead the panel shall refer the offender back to the appropriate court.

(3)   If at a meeting of the panel —

(a)   agreement is reached with the offender but he does not sign the record produced in pursuance of section 23(5) above, and

(b)   his failure to do so appears to the panel to be unreasonable,

the panel shall end the meeting and refer the offender back to the appropriate court.

26.(1)   At any time —

(a)   after a youth offender contract has taken effect under section 23 above, but

(b)   before the end of the period for which the contract has effect,

the specified team shall, if so requested by the panel, arrange for the holding of a meeting of the panel under this section ('a progress meeting').

(2)   The panel may make a request under subsection (1) above if it appears to the panel to be expedient to review —

(a)   the offender's progress in implementing the programme of behaviour contained in the contract; or

(b)   any other matter arising in connection with the contract.

(3)   The panel shall make such a request if —

(a)   the offender has notified the panel that —

(i)   he wishes to seek the panel's agreement to a variation in the terms of the contract; or

(ii)   he wishes the panel to refer him back to the appropriate court with a view to the referral order (or orders) being revoked on account of a significant change in his circumstances (such as his being taken to live abroad) making compliance with any youth offender contract impractical; or

(b)   it appears to the panel that the offender is in breach of any of the terms of the contract.

(4)   At a progress meeting the panel shall do such one or more of the following things as it considers appropriate in the circumstances, namely —

(a)   review the offender's progress or any such other matter as is mentioned in subsection (2) above;

(b)   discuss with the offender any breach of the terms of the contract which it appears to the panel that he has committed;

(c)   consider any variation in the terms of the contract sought by the offender or which it appears to the panel to be expedient to make in the light of any such review or discussion;

(d)   consider whether to accede to any request by the offender that he be referred back to the appropriate court.

(5)   Where the panel has discussed with the offender such a breach as is mentioned in subsection (4)(b) above —

(a)   the panel and the offender may agree that the offender is to continue to be required to comply with the contract (either in its original form or with any agreed variation in its terms) without being referred back to the appropriate court; or

(b)   the panel may decide to end the meeting and refer the offender back to that court.

(6)   Where a variation in the terms of the contract is agreed between the offender and the panel, the panel shall cause a written record of the variation to be produced forthwith —

(a)   in language capable of being readily understood by, or explained to, the offender; and

(b)   for signature by him.

(7)   Any such variation shall take effect once the record has been signed —

(a)   by the offender; and

(b)   by a member of the panel on behalf of the panel;

and the panel shall cause a copy of the record to be given or sent to the offender.

(8)   If at a progress meeting —

(a)   any such variation is agreed but the offender does not sign the record produced in pursuance of subsection (6) above, and

(b)   his failure to do so appears to the panel to be unreasonable, the panel may end the meeting and refer the offender back to the appropriate court.

27.(1)   Where the compliance period in the case of a youth offender contract is due to expire, the specified team shall arrange for the holding, before the end of that period, of a meeting of the panel under this section ('the final meeting').

(2)   At the final meeting the panel shall —

(a)   review the extent of the offender's compliance to date with the terms of the contract; and

(b)   decide, in the light of that review, whether his compliance with those terms has been such as to justify the conclusion that, by the time the compliance period expires, he will have satisfactorily completed the contract;

and the panel shall give the offender written confirmation of its decision.

(3)   Where the panel decides that the offender's compliance with the terms of the contract has been such as to justify that conclusion, the panel's decision shall have the effect of discharging the referral order (or orders) as from the end of the compliance period.

(4)   Otherwise the panel shall refer the offender back to the appropriate court.

Schedule 1
Youth offender panels: further court proceedings
Part I
Referral back to appropriate court

Power of court where it upholds panel's decision
5.(1)   If it is proved to the satisfaction of the appropriate court as regards any decision of the panel which resulted in the offender being referred back to the court —

(a)   that, so far as the decision relied on any finding of fact by the panel, the panel was entitled to make that finding in the circumstances, and

(b)   that, so far as the decision involved any exercise of discretion by the panel, the panel reasonably exercised that discretion in the circumstances,

the court may exercise the power conferred by sub-paragraph (2) below.

(2)   That power is a power to revoke the referral order (or each of the referral orders).

(3)   The revocation under sub-paragraph (2) above of a referral order has the effect of revoking any related order under paragraph 11 or 12 below.

(4)   Where any order is revoked under sub-paragraph (2) above or by virtue of sub-paragraph (3) above, the appropriate court may deal with the offender in accordance with sub-paragraph (5) below for the offence in respect of which the revoked order was made.

(5)   In so dealing with the offender for such an offence, the appropriate court —

(a)   may deal with him in any way in which (assuming section 16 of this Act had not applied) he could have been dealt with for that offence by the court which made the order; and

(b) shall have regard to —
  (i) the circumstances of his referral back to the court; and
  (ii) where a contract has taken effect under section 23 of this Act between the offender and the panel, the extent of his compliance with the terms of the contract.

(6) The appropriate court may not exercise the powers conferred by sub-paragraph (2) or (4) above unless the offender is present before it; but those powers are exercisable even if, in a case where a contract has taken effect under section 23, the period for which the contract has effect has expired (whether before or after the referral of the offender back to the court).

[Note that parts of this Schedule, not reproduced, give powers to arrest and remand the juvenile.]

Appeal

6. Where the court in exercise of the power conferred by paragraph 5(4) above deals with the offender for an offence, the offender may appeal to the Crown Court against the sentence.

Court not revoking referral order or orders

7.(1) This paragraph applies —
  (a) where the appropriate court decides that the matters mentioned in paragraphs (a) and (b) of paragraph 5(1) above have not been proved to its satisfaction; or
  (b) where, although by virtue of paragraph 5(1) above the appropriate court —
    (i) is able to exercise the power conferred by paragraph 5(2) above, or
    (ii) would be able to do so if the offender were present before it,
  the court (for any reason) decides not to exercise that power.

(2) If either —
  (a) no contract has taken effect under section 23 of this Act between the offender and the panel, or
  (b) a contract has taken effect under that section but the period for which it has effect has not expired,

the offender shall continue to remain subject to the referral order (or orders) in all respects as if he had not been referred back to the court.

(3) If —
  (a) a contract had taken effect under section 23 of this Act, but
  (b) the period for which it has effect has expired (otherwise than by virtue of section 24(6)),

the court shall make an order declaring that the referral order (or each of the referral orders) is discharged.

Exception where court satisfied as to completion of contract

8. If, in a case where the offender is referred back to the court under section 27(4) of this Act, the court decides (contrary to the decision of the panel) that the offender's compliance with the terms of the contract has, or will have, been such as to justify the conclusion that he has satisfactorily completed the contract, the court shall make an order declaring that the referral order (or each of the referral orders) is discharged.

Part II of the Schedule deals with extension of referral for further offences, and is not reproduced.

Reparation Orders

Guidance on the reparation order (not reproduced) is available at **www.homeoffice. gov.uk/cdact.repord.htm**

73.(1) Where a child or young person (that is to say, any person aged under 18) is convicted of an offence other than one for which the sentence is fixed by law, the court by or before which he is convicted may make an order requiring him to make reparation specified in the order —

(a) to a person or persons so specified; or

(b) to the community at large;

and any person so specified must be a person identified by the court as a victim of the offence or a person otherwise affected by it.

(2) An order under subsection (1) above is in this Act referred to as a 'reparation order'.

(3) In this section and section 74 below 'make reparation', in relation to an offender, means make reparation for the offence otherwise than by the payment of compensation; and the requirements that may be specified in a reparation order are subject to section 74(1) to (3).

(4) The court shall not make a reparation order in respect of the offender if it proposes —

(a) to pass on him a custodial sentence; or

(b) to make in respect of him a community punishment order, a community punishment and rehabilitation order, a supervision order which includes requirements authorised by Schedule 6 to this Act, an action plan order or a referral order.

(5) Before making a reparation order, a court shall obtain and consider a written report by a probation officer, a social worker of a local authority social services department or a member of a youth offending team indicating —

(a) the type of work that is suitable for the offender; and

(b) the attitude of the victim or victims to the requirements proposed to be included in the order.

(6) The court shall not make a reparation order unless it has been notified by the Secretary of State that arrangements for implementing such orders are available in the area proposed to be named in the order under section 74(4) below and the notice has not been withdrawn.

(7) Before making a reparation order, the court shall explain to the offender in ordinary language —

(a) the effect of the order and of the requirements proposed to be included in it;

(b) the consequences which may follow (under Schedule 8 to this Act) if he fails to comply with any of those requirements; and

(c) that the court has power (under that Schedule) to review the order on the application either of the offender or of the responsible officer;

and 'responsible officer' here has the meaning given by section 74(5) below.

(8) The court shall give reasons if it does not make a reparation order in a case where it has power to do so.

74.(1) A reparation order shall not require the offender —

(a) to work for more than 24 hours in aggregate; or

(b) to make reparation to any person without the consent of that person.

(2) Subject to subsection (1) above, requirements specified in a reparation order shall be such as in the opinion of the court are commensurate with the seriousness of the offence, or the combination of the offence and one or more offences associated with it.

(3) Requirements so specified shall, as far as practicable, be such as to avoid —

(a) any conflict with the offender's religious beliefs or with the requirements of any community order to which he may be subject; and

(b) any interference with the times, if any, at which he normally works or attends school or any other educational establishment.

(4) A reparation order shall name the petty sessions area in which it appears to the court making the order (or to the court amending under Schedule 8 to this Act any provision included in the order in pursuance of this subsection) that the offender resides or will reside.

(5) In this Act 'responsible officer', in relation to an offender subject to a reparation order, means one of the following who is specified in the order, namely —

    (a) a probation officer;

    (b) a social worker of a local authority social services department;

    (c) a member of a youth offending team.

(6) Where a reparation order specifies a probation officer under subsection (5) above, the officer specified must be an officer appointed for or assigned to the petty sessions area named in the order.

(7) Where a reparation order specifies under that subsection —

    (a) a social worker of a local authority social services department, or

    (b) a member of a youth offending team,

the social worker or member specified must be a social worker of, or a member of a youth offending team established by, the local authority within whose area it appears to the court that the offender resides or will reside.

(8) Any reparation required by a reparation order —

    (a) shall be made under the supervision of the responsible officer; and

    (b) shall be made within a period of three months from the date of the making of the order.

Schedule 8 spells out the consequences of a breach of the reparation order (it also refers to breach of the action plan order — these are covered below):

Schedule 8
Breach, revocation and amendment of action plan orders and reparation orders

Breach of requirement of action plan order or reparation order
2.(1) This paragraph applies if while an action plan order or reparation order is in force in respect of an offender it is proved to the satisfaction of the appropriate court, on the application of the responsible officer, that the offender has failed to comply with any requirement included in the order.

(2) Where this paragraph applies, the court —

    (a) whether or not it also makes an order under paragraph 5(1) below (revocation or amendment of order) —

        (i) may order the offender to pay a fine of an amount not exceeding £1,000; or

        (ii) subject to paragraph 3 below, may make a curfew order in respect of him; or

        (iii) subject to paragraph 4 below, may make an attendance centre order in respect of him; or

    (b) if the action plan order or reparation order was made by a magistrates' court, may revoke the order and deal with the offender, for the offence in respect of which the order was made, in any way in which he could have been dealt with for that offence by the court which made the order if the order had not been made; or

    (c) if the action plan order or reparation order was made by the Crown Court, may commit him in custody or release him on bail until he can be brought or appear before the Crown Court.

(4) Where —

    (a) by virtue of sub-paragraph (2)(c) above the offender is brought or appears before the Crown Court, and

    (b) it is proved to the satisfaction of the court that he has failed to comply with the requirement in question,

that court may deal with him, for the offence in respect of which the order was made, in any way in which it could have dealt with him for that offence if it had not made the order.

(7)   In dealing with an offender under this paragraph, a court shall take into account the extent to which he has complied with the requirements of the action plan order or reparation order.

Paragraphs 3 and 4 of Schedule 8 provide for curfew orders and attendance centre orders to be imposed where a child is in breach of the action plan or the reparation order. These are not reproduced.

Revocation and amendment of action plan order or reparation order
5.(1)   If while an action plan order or reparation order is in force in respect of an offender it appears to the appropriate court, on the application of the responsible officer or the offender, that it is appropriate to make an order under this sub-paragraph, the court may —
  (a)   make an order revoking the action plan order or reparation order; or
  (b)   make an order amending it —
    (i)   by cancelling any provision included in it; or
    (ii)   by inserting in it (either in addition to or in substitution for any of its provisions) any provision which could have been included in the order if the court had then had power to make it and were exercising the power.

Community sentences

Seriousness test

Community sentences are more serious than those we have considered so far. In fact they are not available unless a seriousness threshold is first considered.
35.(1)   A court shall not pass a community sentence on an offender unless it is of the opinion that the offence, or the combination of the offence and one or more offences associated with it, was serious enough to warrant such a sentence.
(3)   Subject to subsection (2) above and to section 69(5) below (which limits the community orders that may be combined with an action plan order), where a court passes a community sentence —
  (a)   the particular order or orders comprising or forming part of the sentence shall be such as in the opinion of the court is, or taken together are, the most suitable for the offender; and
  (b)   the restrictions on liberty imposed by the order or orders shall be such as in the opinion of the court are commensurate with the seriousness of the offence, or the combination of the offence and one or more offences associated with it.
36.(1)   In forming any such opinion as is mentioned in subsection (1) or (3)(b) of section 35 above, a court shall take into account all such information as is available to it about the circumstances of the offence or (as the case may be) of the offence and the offence or offences associated with it, including any aggravating or mitigating factors.
(2)   In forming any such opinion as is mentioned in subsection (3)(a) of that section, a court may take into account any information about the offender which is before it.
(3)   The following provisions of this section apply in relation to —
  (a)   a community rehabilitation order which includes additional requirements authorised by Schedule 2 to this Act;
  (b)   a community punishment order;
  (c)   a supervision and community punishment order;
  (d)   a drug treatment and testing order;
  (e)   a supervision order which includes requirements authorised by Schedule 6 to this Act.
(4)   Subject to subsection (5) below, a court shall obtain and consider a pre-sentence report before forming an opinion as to the suitability for the offender of one or more of the orders mentioned in subsection (3) above.

(5)   Subsection (4) above does not apply if, in the circumstances of the case, the court is of the opinion that it is unnecessary to obtain a pre-sentence report.

(6)   In a case where the offender is aged under 18 and the offence is not triable only on indictment and there is no other offence associated with it that is triable only on indictment, the court shall not form such an opinion as is mentioned in subsection (5) above unless —

(a)   there exists a previous pre-sentence report obtained in respect of the offender; and
(b)   the court has had regard to the information contained in that report, or, if there is more than one such report, the most recent report.

(7)   No community sentence which consists of or includes such an order as is mentioned in subsection (3) above shall be invalidated by the failure of a court to obtain and consider a pre-sentence report before forming an opinion as to the suitability of the order for the offender, but any court on an appeal against such a sentence —

(a)   shall, subject to subsection (8) below, obtain a pre-sentence report if none was obtained by the court below; and
(b)   shall consider any such report obtained by it or by that court.

(8)   Subsection (7)(a) above does not apply if the court is of the opinion —

(a)   that the court below was justified in forming an opinion that it was unnecessary to obtain a pre-sentence report; or
(b)   that, although the court below was not justified in forming that opinion, in the circumstances of the case at the time it is before the court, it is unnecessary to obtain a pre-sentence report.

(9)   In a case where the offender is aged under 18 and the offence is not triable only on indictment and there is no other offence associated with it that is triable only on indictment, the court shall not form such an opinion as is mentioned in subsection (8) above unless —

(a)   there exists a previous pre-sentence report obtained in respect of the offender; and
(b)   the court has had regard to the information contained in that report, or, if there is more than one such report, the most recent report.

Action plan orders

This is the first community sentence we consider. It is like the referral order, but the Court, not the Youth Offending Panel, makes the decision on what the offender has to do.

Guidance (not reproduced) is available at
www.homeoffice.gov.uk/cdact/acplnord.htm

69.(1)   Where a child or young person (that is to say, any person aged under 18) is convicted of an offence and the court by or before which he is convicted is of the opinion mentioned in subsection (3) below, the court may (subject to sections 34 to 36 above) make an order which —

(a)   requires the offender, for a period of three months beginning with the date of the order, to comply with an action plan, that is to say, a series of requirements with respect to his actions and whereabouts during that period;
(b)   places the offender for that period under the supervision of the responsible officer; and
(c)   requires the offender to comply with any directions given by the responsible officer with a view to the implementation of that plan;

and the requirements included in the order, and any directions given by the responsible officer, may include requirements authorised by section 70 below.

(2)   An order under subsection (1) above is in this Act referred to as an 'action plan order'.

(3)   The opinion referred to in subsection (1) above is that the making of an action plan order is desirable in the interests of —

(a)   securing the rehabilitation of the offender; or
(b)   preventing the commission by him of further offences.

(4)   In this Act 'responsible officer', in relation to an offender subject to an action plan order, means one of the following who is specified in the order, namely —

(a)   a probation officer;

(b)   a social worker of a local authority social services department;

(c)   a member of a youth offending team.

(5)   The court shall not make an action plan order in respect of the offender if —

(a)   he is already the subject of such an order; or

(b)   the court proposes to pass on him a custodial sentence or to make in respect of him a community rehabilitation order, a community punishment order, a community punishment and rehabilitation order, an attendance centre order, a supervision order or a referral order.

(6)   Before making an action plan order, the court shall obtain and consider —

(a)   a written report by a probation officer, a social worker of a local authority social services department or a member of a youth offending team indicating —

(i)   the requirements proposed by that person to be included in the order;

(ii)   the benefits to the offender that the proposed requirements are designed to achieve; and

(iii)   the attitude of a parent or guardian of the offender to the proposed requirements; and

(b)   where the offender is aged under 16, information about the offender's family circumstances and the likely effect of the order on those circumstances.

(7)   The court shall not make an action plan order unless it has been notified by the Secretary of State that arrangements for implementing such orders are available in the area proposed to be named in the order under subsection (8) below and the notice has not been withdrawn.

(11)   Before making an action plan order, the court shall explain to the offender in ordinary language —

(a)   the effect of the order and of the requirements proposed to be included in it;

(b)   the consequences which may follow (under Schedule 8 to this Act) if he fails to comply with any of those requirements; and

(c)   that the court has power (under that Schedule) to review the order on the application either of the offender or of the responsible officer.

70.(1)   Requirements included in an action plan order, or directions given by a responsible officer, may require the offender to do all or any of the following things, namely —

(a)   to participate in activities specified in the requirements or directions at a time or times so specified;

(b)   to present himself to a person or persons specified in the requirements or directions at a place or places and at a time or times so specified;

(c)   subject to subsection (2) below, to attend at an attendance centre specified in the requirements or directions for a number of hours so specified;

(d)   to stay away from a place or places specified in the requirements or directions;

(e)   to comply with any arrangements for his education specified in the requirements or directions;

(f)   to make reparation specified in the requirements or directions to a person or persons so specified or to the community at large; and

(g)   to attend any hearing fixed by the court under section 71 below.

(2)   Subsection (1)(c) above applies only where the offence committed by the offender is an offence punishable with imprisonment.

(3)   In subsection (1)(f) above 'make reparation', in relation to an offender, means make reparation for the offence otherwise than by the payment of compensation.

(4) A person shall not be specified in requirements or directions under subsection (1)(f) above unless —
  (a) he is identified by the court or (as the case may be) the responsible officer as a victim of the offence or a person otherwise affected by it; and
  (b) he consents to the reparation being made.

(5) Requirements included in an action plan order and directions given by a responsible officer shall, as far as practicable, be such as to avoid —
  (a) any conflict with the offender's religious beliefs or with the requirements of any other community order to which he may be subject; and
  (b) any interference with the times, if any, at which he normally works or attends school or any other educational establishment.

71.(1) Immediately after making an action plan order, a court may —
  (a) fix a further hearing for a date not more than 21 days after the making of the order; and
  (b) direct the responsible officer to make, at that hearing, a report as to the effectiveness of the order and the extent to which it has been implemented.

(2) At a hearing fixed under subsection (1) above, the court —
  (a) shall consider the responsible officer's report; and
  (b) may, on the application of the responsible officer or the offender, amend the order —
    (i) by cancelling any provision included in it; or
    (ii) by inserting in it (either in addition to or in substitution for any of its provisions) any provision that the court could originally have included in it.

We saw above (page 452) that breach of the order means the offender is referred back to the Court under Schedule 8.

Supervision orders

Supervision orders are also available under the Children Act 1989 Part IV, but criminal supervision orders contain a range of powers to control the activities of the child, which the civil orders lack.

63.(1) Where a child or young person (that is to say, any person aged under 18) is convicted of an offence, the court by or before which he is convicted may (subject to sections 34 to 36 above) make an order placing him under the supervision of
  (a) a local authority designated by the order;
  (b) a probation officer; or
  (c) a member of a youth offending team.

                                        ...

  (6) A supervision order —
  (b) may contain such prescribed provisions as the court making the order .... considers appropriate for facilitating the performance by the supervisor of his functions under section 64(4) below, including any prescribed provisions for requiring visits to be made by the offender to the supervisor;
and in paragraph (b) above 'prescribed' means prescribed by rules under section 144 of the Magistrates' Courts Act 1980 [not reproduced].

  (7) A supervision order shall, unless it has previously been revoked, cease to have effect at the end of the period of three years, or such shorter period as may be specified in the order, beginning with the date on which the order was originally made.

(8)   A court which makes a supervision order shall forthwith send a copy of its order —

(a)   to the offender and, if the offender is aged under 14, to his parent or guardian;

(b)   to the supervisor;

(c)   to any local authority who are not entitled by virtue of paragraph (b) above to such a copy and whose area is named in the supervision order in pursuance of subsection (6) above;

(d)   where the offender is required by the order to reside with an individual or to undergo treatment by or under the direction of an individual or at any place, to the individual or the person in charge of that place; and

...

(9)   If a court makes a supervision order while another such order made by any court is in force in respect of the offender, the court making the new order may revoke the earlier order ...

...

64.(1)   A court shall not designate a local authority as the supervisor by a provision of a supervision order unless —

(a)   the authority agree; or

(b)   it appears to the court that the offender resides or will reside in the area of the authority.

...

(3)   Where a provision of a supervision order places the offender under the supervision of a member of a youth offending team, the supervisor shall be a member of a team established by the local authority within whose area it appears to the court that the offender resides or will reside.

(4)   While a supervision order is in force, the supervisor shall advise, assist and befriend the offender.

Schedule 6
Requirements which may be included in supervision orders

Requirement to reside with named individual
1.   A supervision order may require the offender to reside with an individual named in the order who agrees to the requirement, but a requirement imposed by a supervision order in pursuance of this paragraph shall be subject to any such requirement of the order as is authorised by paragraph 2, 3, 6 or 7 below.

Requirement to comply with directions of supervisor
2.(1)   Subject to sub-paragraph (2) below, a supervision order may require the offender to comply with any directions given from time to time by the supervisor and requiring him to do all or any of the following things —

(a)   to live at a place or places specified in the directions for a period or periods so specified;

(b)   to present himself to a person or persons specified in the directions at a place or places and on a day or days so specified;

(c)   to participate in activities specified in the directions on a day or days so specified.

(2)   A supervision order shall not require compliance with directions given by virtue of sub-paragraph (1) above unless the court making it is satisfied that a scheme under section 66 of this Act (local authority schemes) [not reproduced] is in force for the area where the offender resides or will reside; and no such directions may involve the use of facilities which are not for the time being specified in a scheme in force under that section for that area.

(3) A requirement imposed by a supervision order in pursuance of sub-paragraph (1) above shall be subject to any such requirement of the order as is authorised by paragraph 6 below (treatment for offender's mental condition).

(4) It shall be for the supervisor to decide —

   (a) whether and to what extent he exercises any power to give directions conferred on him by virtue of sub-paragraph (1) above; and

   (b) the form of any directions.

(5) The total number of days in respect of which an offender may be required to comply with directions given by virtue of paragraph (a), (b) or (c) of sub-paragraph (1) above shall not exceed 90 or such lesser number, if any, as the order may specify for the purposes of this sub-paragraph.

(6) For the purpose of calculating the total number of days in respect of which such directions may be given, the supervisor shall be entitled to disregard any day in respect of which directions were previously given in pursuance of the order and on which the directions were not complied with.

(7) Directions given by the supervisor by virtue of sub-paragraph (1)(b) or (c) above shall, as far as practicable, be such as to avoid —

   (a) any conflict with the offender's religious beliefs or with the requirements of any other community order to which he may be subject; and

   (b) any interference with the times, if any, at which he normally works or attends school or any other educational establishment.

Requirements as to activities, reparation, night restrictions etc.
3.(1) This paragraph applies to a supervision order unless the order requires the offender to comply with directions given by the supervisor under paragraph 2(1) above.

(2) Subject to the following provisions of this paragraph and paragraph 4 below, a supervision order to which this paragraph applies may require the offender —

   (a) to live at a place or places specified in the order for a period or periods so specified;

   (b) to present himself to a person or persons specified in the order at a place or places and on a day or days so specified;

   (c) to participate in activities specified in the order on a day or days so specified;

   (d) to make reparation specified in the order to a person or persons so specified or to the community at large;

   (e) to remain for specified periods between 6 p.m. and 6 a.m. —

      (i)   at a place specified in the order; or

      (ii) at one of several places so specified;

   (f) to refrain from participating in activities specified in the order —

      (i)   on a specified day or days during the period for which the supervision order is in force; or

      (ii) during the whole of that period or a specified portion of it;

      and in this paragraph 'make reparation' means make reparation for the offence otherwise than by the payment of compensation.

(3) The total number of days in respect of which an offender may be subject to requirements imposed by virtue of paragraph (a), (b), (c), (d) or (e) of sub-paragraph (2) above shall not exceed 90.

(4) The court may not include requirements under sub-paragraph (2) above in a supervision order unless —

   (a) it has first consulted the supervisor as to —

      (i)   the offender's circumstances, and

      (ii) the feasibility of securing compliance with the requirements,

and is satisfied, having regard to the supervisor's report, that it is feasible to secure compliance with them;

(b) having regard to the circumstances of the case, it considers the requirements necessary for securing the good conduct of the offender or for preventing a repetition by him of the same offence or the commission of other offences; and

(c) if the offender is aged under 16, it has obtained and considered information about his family circumstances and the likely effect of the requirements on those circumstances.

(5)   The court shall not by virtue of sub-paragraph (2) above include in a supervision order —

(a) any requirement that would involve the cooperation of a person other than the supervisor and the offender, unless that other person consents to its inclusion;

(b) any requirement to make reparation to any person unless that person —

(i)   is identified by the court as a victim of the offence or a person otherwise affected by it; and

(ii)   consents to the inclusion of the requirement;

(c) any requirement requiring the offender to reside with a specified individual; or

(d) any such requirement as is mentioned in paragraph 6(2) below (treatment for offender's mental condition).

(6)   Requirements included in a supervision order by virtue of sub-paragraph (2)(b) or (c) above shall, as far as practicable, be such as to avoid —

(a) any conflict with the offender's religious beliefs or with the requirements of any other community order to which he may be subject; and

(b) any interference with the times, if any, at which he normally works or attends school or any other educational establishment;

and sub-paragraphs (7) and (8) below are without prejudice to this sub-paragraph.

(7)   Subject to sub-paragraph (8) below, a supervision order may not by virtue of sub-paragraph (2) above include —

(a) any requirement that would involve the offender in absence from home —

(i)   for more than two consecutive nights, or

(ii)   for more than two nights in any one week, or

(b) if the offender is of compulsory school age, any requirement to participate in activities during normal school hours,

unless the court making the order is satisfied that the facilities whose use would be involved are for the time being specified in a scheme in force under section 66 of this Act for the area in which the offender resides or will reside.

(8)   Sub-paragraph (7)(b) above does not apply to activities carried out in accordance with arrangements made or approved by the local education authority in whose area the offender resides or will reside.

4.(1)   The place, or one of the places, specified in a requirement under paragraph 3(2)(e) above ('a night restriction') shall be the place where the offender lives.

(2)   A night restriction shall not require the offender to remain at a place for longer than ten hours on any one night.

(3)   A night restriction shall not be imposed in respect of any day which falls outside the period of three months beginning with the date when the supervision order is made.

(4)   A night restriction shall not be imposed in respect of more than 30 days in all.

(5)   A night restriction imposed in respect of a period of time beginning in the evening and ending in the morning shall be treated as imposed only in respect of the day upon which the period begins.

(6)   An offender who is required by a night restriction to remain at a place may leave it if he is accompanied —

(a) by his parent or guardian;

(b) by his supervisor; or

(c) by some other person specified in the supervision order.

Requirement to live for specified period in local authority accommodation

5.(1)   Where the conditions mentioned in sub-paragraph (2) below are satisfied, a supervision order may impose a requirement ('a local authority residence requirement') that the offender shall live for a specified period in local authority accommodation (as defined by section 163 of this Act).

(2)   The conditions are that —

(a)   a supervision order has previously been made in respect of the offender;

(b)   that order imposed —

   (i)   a requirement under paragraph 1, 2, 3 or 7 of this Schedule; or

   (ii)   a local authority residence requirement;

(c)   the offender fails to comply with that requirement, or is convicted of an offence committed while that order was in force; and

(d)   the court is satisfied that —

   (i)   the failure to comply with the requirement, or the behaviour which constituted the offence, was due to a significant extent to the circumstances in which the offender was living; and

   (ii)   the imposition of a local authority residence requirement will assist in his rehabilitation;

   except that sub-paragraph (i) of paragraph (d) above does not apply where the condition in paragraph (b)(ii) above is satisfied.

(3)   A local authority residence requirement shall designate the local authority who are to receive the offender, and that authority shall be the authority in whose area the offender resides.

(4)   The court shall not impose a local authority residence requirement without first consulting the designated authority.

(5)   A local authority residence requirement may stipulate that the offender shall not live with a named person.

(6)   The maximum period which may be specified in a local authority residence requirement is six months.

(7)   A court shall not impose a local authority residence requirement in respect of an offender who is not legally represented at the relevant time in that court unless —

(a)   he was granted a right to representation funded by the Legal Services Commission as part of the Criminal Defence Service for the purposes of the proceedings but the right was withdrawn because of his conduct; or

(b)   he has been informed of his right to apply for such representation for the purposes of the proceedings and has had the opportunity to do so, but nevertheless refused or failed to apply.

(9)   A supervision order imposing a local authority residence requirement may also impose any of the requirements mentioned in paragraphs 2, 3, 6 and 7 of this Schedule.

Requirements as to treatment for mental condition

6.(1)   This paragraph applies where a court which proposes to make a supervision order is satisfied, on the evidence of a registered medical practitioner approved for the purposes of section 12 of the Mental Health Act 1983, that the mental condition of the offender —

(a)   is such as requires and may be susceptible to treatment; but

(b)   is not such as to warrant the making of a hospital order or guardianship order within the meaning of that Act.

(2)   Where this paragraph applies, the court may include in the supervision order a requirement that the offender shall, for a period specified in the order, submit to treatment of one of the following descriptions so specified, that is to say —

(a)   treatment as a resident patient in a hospital or mental nursing home within the meaning of the Mental Health Act 1983, but not a hospital at which high security psychiatric services within the meaning of that Act are provided;

(b) treatment as a non-resident patient at an institution or place specified in the order;

(c) treatment by or under the direction of a registered medical practitioner specified in the order; or

(d) treatment by or under the direction of a chartered psychologist specified in the order.

(3) A requirement shall not be included in a supervision order by virtue of sub-paragraph (2) above —

(a) in any case, unless the court is satisfied that arrangements have been or can be made for the treatment in question and, in the case of treatment as a resident patient, for the reception of the patient;

(b) in the case of an order made or to be made in respect of a person aged 14 or over, unless he consents to its inclusion;

and a requirement so included shall not in any case continue in force after the offender attains the age of 18.

Requirements as to education

7.(1) This paragraph applies to a supervision order unless the order requires the offender to comply with directions given by the supervisor under paragraph 2(1) above.

(2) Subject to the following provisions of this paragraph, a supervision order to which this paragraph applies may require the offender, if he is of compulsory school age, to comply, for as long as he is of that age and the order remains in force, with such arrangements for his education as may from time to time be made by his parent, being arrangements for the time being approved by the local education authority.

(3) The court shall not include such a requirement in a supervision order unless —

(a) it has consulted the local education authority with regard to its proposal to include the requirement; and

(b) it is satisfied that in the view of the local education authority arrangements exist for the offender to receive efficient full-time education suitable to his age, ability and aptitude and to any special educational need he may have.

...

(5) The court may not include a requirement under sub-paragraph (2) above unless it has first consulted the supervisor as to the offender's circumstances and, having regard to the circumstances of the case, it considers the requirement necessary for securing the good conduct of the offender or for preventing a repetition by him of the same offence or the commission of other offences.

Schedule 7 deals with breach, revocation and amendment of supervision orders. Paragraphs 1 and 2 deal with administrative issues and are not reproduced. Paragraphs 3 and 4 (not reproduced) set out powers to impose curfew and attendance centre orders where there has been a breach of the supervision order.

Revocation and amendment of supervision order

5.(1) If while a supervision order is in force in respect of an offender it appears to a relevant court, on the application of the supervisor or the offender, that it is appropriate to make an order under this sub-paragraph, the court may —

(a) make an order revoking the supervision order; or

(b) make an order amending it —

(i) by cancelling any requirement included in it in pursuance of Schedule 6 to, or section 63(6)(b) of, this Act; or

(ii) by inserting in it (either in addition to or in substitution for any of its provisions) any provision which could have been included in the order if the court had then had power to make it and were exercising the power.

(2) Sub-paragraph (1) above has effect subject to paragraphs 7 to 9 below.

(3) The powers of amendment conferred by sub-paragraph (1) above do not include power —

(a) to insert in the supervision order, after the end of three months beginning with the date when the order was originally made, a requirement in pursuance of paragraph 6 of Schedule 6 to this Act (treatment for mental condition), unless it is in substitution for such a requirement already included in the order; or

(b) to insert in the supervision order a requirement in pursuance of paragraph 3(2)(e) of that Schedule (night restrictions) in respect of any day which falls outside the period of three months beginning with the date when the order was originally made.

Paragraph 6 covers revocation and amendment where there is a requirement to obtain medical treatment, and 7 deals with the presence of the offender in court and remands following alleged breach of the supervision order. These are not reproduced.

Restrictions on court's powers to revoke or amend order

8.(1) A youth court shall not —

(a) exercise its powers under paragraph 5(1) above to make an order —

(i) revoking a supervision order, or

(ii) inserting in it a requirement authorised by Schedule 6 to this Act, or

(iii) varying or cancelling such a requirement,

except in a case where the court is satisfied that the offender either is unlikely to receive the care or control he needs unless the court makes the order or is likely to receive it notwithstanding the order;

Curfew orders

These community sentences are governed by ss. 37–40 and Sch. 3 of PCCSA. As with any community sentence, the seriousness requirement applies:

37.(1) Where a person is convicted of an offence, the court by or before which he is convicted may (subject to sections 34 to 36 above) make an order requiring him to remain, for periods specified in the order, at a place so specified.

(2) An order under subsection (1) above is in this Act referred to as a 'curfew order'.

(3) A curfew order may specify different places or different periods for different days, but shall not specify —

(a) periods which fall outside the period of six months beginning with the day on which it is made; or

(b) periods which amount to less than two hours or more than twelve hours in any one day.

(4) In relation to an offender aged under 16 on conviction, subsection (3)(a) above shall have effect as if the reference to six months were a reference to three months.

(5) The requirements in a curfew order shall, as far as practicable, be such as to avoid —

(a) any conflict with the offender's religious beliefs or with the requirements of any other community order to which he may be subject; and

(b) any interference with the times, if any, at which he normally works or attends school or any other educational establishment.

(6) A curfew order shall include provision for making a person responsible for monitoring the offender's whereabouts during the curfew periods specified in the order; and a person who is made so responsible shall be of a description specified in an order made by the Secretary of State.

(7) A court shall not make a curfew order unless the court has been notified by the Secretary of State that arrangements for monitoring the offender's whereabouts are available in the area in which the place proposed to be specified in the order is situated and the notice has not been withdrawn.

(8)   Before making a curfew order, the court shall obtain and consider information about the place proposed to be specified in the order (including information as to the attitude of persons likely to be affected by the enforced presence there of the offender).

(9)   Before making a curfew order in respect of an offender who on conviction is under 16, the court shall obtain and consider information about his family circumstances and the likely effect of such an order on those circumstances.

(10)   Before making a curfew order, the court shall explain to the offender in ordinary language —

(a)   the effect of the order (including any additional requirements proposed to be included in the order in accordance with section 38 below (electronic monitoring));

(b)   the consequences which may follow (under Part II of Schedule 3 to this Act) if he fails to comply with any of the requirements of the order; and

(c)   that the court has power (under Parts III and IV of that Schedule) to review the order on the application either of the offender or of the responsible officer.

(11)   The court by which a curfew order is made shall give a copy of the order to the offender and to the responsible officer.

(12)   In this Act, 'responsible officer', in relation to an offender subject to a curfew order, means the person who is responsible for monitoring the offender's whereabouts during the curfew periods specified in the order.

38.(1)   Subject to subsection (2) below, a curfew order may in addition include requirements for securing the electronic monitoring of the offender's whereabouts during the curfew periods specified in the order.

(2)   A court shall not make a curfew order which includes such requirements unless the court —

(a)   has been notified by the Secretary of State that electronic monitoring arrangements are available in the area in which the place proposed to be specified in the order is situated; and

(b)   is satisfied that the necessary provision can be made under those arrangements.

(3)   Electronic monitoring arrangements made by the Secretary of State under this section may include entering into contracts with other persons for the electronic monitoring by them of offenders' whereabouts.

Schedule 3, not reproduced here, covers breach of a curfew order.

Other community sentences

A number of sentences can only be imposed where the child is at least 16: community rehabilitation order (formerly probation); community punishment (formerly community service); community punishment and supervision order (formerly combination order); attendance centre, and drug treatment and testing order. The responsible officer involved in the supervision of orders where the offender is 16 or over is normally a probation officer; for reasons of space the legislation is not copied here. See however Brayne, Martin and Carr, Chapter 12 for a summary, and PCCSA ss. 41–59.

Custodial sentences

Seriousness requirements for custody
Under s. 79 there is a seriousness requirement (similar to that applying to community sentences).
Detention and training orders under PCCSA, ss. 100–107 have replaced all other forms of custody for children, save custody for life and custody during Her Majesty's pleasure under PCCSA, ss. 90–93.

79.(2)   Subject to subsection (3) below, the court shall not pass a custodial sentence on the offender unless it is of the opinion —

   (a) that the offence, or the combination of the offence and one or more offences associated with it, was so serious that only such a sentence can be justified for the offence; or

   (b) where the offence is a violent or sexual offence, that only such a sentence would be adequate to protect the public from serious harm from him.

(3)   Nothing in subsection (2) above shall prevent the court from passing a custodial sentence on the offender if he fails to express his willingness to comply with —

   (a) a requirement which is proposed by the court to be included in a community rehabilitation order or supervision order and which requires an expression of such willingness; or

   (b) a requirement which is proposed by the court to be included in a drug treatment and testing order or an order under section 52(4) above (order to provide samples).

(4)   Where a court passes a custodial sentence, it shall —

   (a) in a case not falling within subsection (3) above, state in open court that it is of the opinion that either or both of paragraphs (a) and (b) of subsection (2) above apply and why it is of that opinion; and

   (b) in any case, explain to the offender in open court and in ordinary language why it is passing a custodial sentence on him.

Detention and training orders

These are governed by PCCSA ss. 100–107.

Guidance on the detention and training order (not reproduced) is available at **www.homeoffice.gov.uk/cdact/dto0902.htm**

100.(1)   Subject to sections 90, 91 and 93 [sentencing for grave crimes] above and subsection (2) below, where —

   (a) a child or young person (that is to say, any person aged under 18) is convicted of an offence which is punishable with imprisonment in the case of a person aged 21 or over, and

   (b) the court is of the opinion that either or both of paragraphs (a) and (b) of section 79(2) above apply or the case falls within section 79(3),

the sentence that the court is to pass is a detention and training order.

(2)   A court shall not make a detention and training order —

   (a) in the case of an offender under the age of 15 at the time of the conviction, unless it is of the opinion that he is a persistent offender;

   (b) in the case of an offender under the age of 12 at that time, unless —

      (i)   it is of the opinion that only a custodial sentence would be adequate to protect the public from further offending by him; and

(3)   A detention and training order is an order that the offender in respect of whom it is made shall be subject, for the term specified in the order, to a period of detention and training followed by a period of supervision.

   (4)   On making a detention and training order in a case where subsection (2) above applies, it shall be the duty of the court (in addition to the duty imposed by section 79(4) above) to state in open court that it is of the opinion mentioned in paragraph (a) or, as the case may be, paragraphs (a) and (b)(i) of that subsection.

101.(1)   Subject to subsection (2) below, the term of a detention and training order made in respect of an offence (whether by a magistrates' court or otherwise) shall be 4, 6, 8, 10, 12, 18 or 24 months.

(2)   The term of a detention and training order may not exceed the maximum term of imprisonment that the Crown Court could (in the case of an offender aged 21 or over) impose for the offence.

(3)   Subject to subsections (4) and (6) below, a court making a detention and training order may order that its term shall commence on the expiry of the term of any other detention and training order made by that or any other court.

(4)   A court shall not make in respect of an offender a detention and training order the effect of which would be that he would be subject to detention and training orders for a term which exceeds 24 months.

(5)   Where the term of the detention and training orders to which an offender would otherwise be subject exceeds 24 months, the excess shall be treated as remitted.

(6)   A court making a detention and training order shall not order that its term shall commence on the expiry of the term of a detention and training order under which the period of supervision has already begun (under section 103(1) below).

(7)   Where a detention and training order ('the new order') is made in respect of an offender who is subject to a detention and training order under which the period of supervision has begun ('the old order'), the old order shall be disregarded in determining —

(a)   for the purposes of subsection (4) above whether the effect of the new order would be that the offender would be subject to detention and training orders for a term which exceeds 24 months; and

(b)   for the purposes of subsection (5) above whether the term of the detention and training orders to which the offender would (apart from that subsection) be subject exceeds 24 months.

(8)   In determining the term of a detention and training order for an offence, the court shall take account of any period for which the offender has been remanded in custody in connection with the offence, or any other offence the charge for which was founded on the same facts or evidence.

(9)   Where a court proposes to make detention and training orders in respect of an offender for two or more offences —

(a)   subsection (8) above shall not apply; but

(b)   in determining the total term of the detention and training orders it proposes to make in respect of the offender, the court shall take account of the total period (if any) for which he has been remanded in custody in connection with any of those offences, or any other offence the charge for which was founded on the same facts or evidence.

(10)   Once a period of remand has, under subsection (8) or (9) above, been taken account of in relation to a detention and training order made in respect of an offender for any offence or offences, it shall not subsequently be taken account of (under either of those subsections) in relation to such an order made in respect of the offender for any other offence or offences.

102.(1)   An offender shall serve the period of detention and training under a detention and training order in such secure accommodation as may be determined by the Secretary of State or by such other person as may be authorised by him for that purpose.

(2)   Subject to subsections (3) to (5) below, the period of detention and training under a detention and training order shall be one-half of the term of the order.

(3)   The Secretary of State may at any time release the offender if he is satisfied that exceptional circumstances exist which justify the offender's release on compassionate grounds.

(4)   The Secretary of State may release the offender —

(a)   in the case of an order for a term of 8 months or more but less than 18 months, one month before the half-way point of the term of the order; and

(b)   in the case of an order for a term of 18 months or more, one month or two months before that point.

(5)   If a youth court so orders on an application made by the Secretary of State for the purpose, the Secretary of State shall release the offender —

   (a)   in the case of an order for a term of 8 months or more but less than 18 months, one month after the half-way point of the term of the order; and

   (b)   in the case of an order for a term of 18 months or more, one month or two months after that point.

(6)   An offender detained in pursuance of a detention and training order shall be deemed to be in legal custody.

103.(1)   The period of supervision of an offender who is subject to a detention and training order —

   (a)   shall begin with the offender's release, whether at the half-way point of the term of the order or otherwise; and

   (b)   subject to subsection (2) below, shall end when the term of the order ends.

(2)   The Secretary of State may by order provide that the period of supervision shall end at such point during the term of a detention and training order as may be specified in the order under this subsection.

(3)   During the period of supervision, the offender shall be under the supervision of —

   (a)   a probation officer;

   (b)   a social worker of a local authority social services department; or

   (c)   a member of a youth offending team;

and the category of person to supervise the offender shall be determined from time to time by the Secretary of State.

(4)   Where the supervision is to be provided by a probation officer, the probation officer shall be an officer appointed for or assigned to the petty sessions area within which the offender resides for the time being.

(5)   Where the supervision is to be provided by —

   (a)   a social worker of a local authority social services department, or

   (b)   a member of a youth offending team,

the social worker or member shall be a social worker of, or a member of a youth offending team established by, the local authority within whose area the offender resides for the time being.

104.(1)   Where a detention and training order is in force in respect of an offender and it appears on information to a justice of the peace acting for a relevant petty sessions area that the offender has failed to comply with requirements under section 103(6)(b) above, the justice —

   (a)   may issue a summons requiring the offender to appear at the place and time specified in the summons before a youth court acting for the area; or

   (b)   if the information is in writing and on oath, may issue a warrant for the offender's arrest requiring him to be brought before such a court.

(2)   ...

(3)   If it is proved to the satisfaction of the youth court before which an offender appears or is brought under this section that he has failed to comply with requirements under section 103(6)(b) above, that court may —

   (a)   order the offender to be detained, in such secure accommodation as the Secretary of State may determine, for such period, not exceeding the shorter of three months or the remainder of the term of the detention and training order, as the court may specify; or

   (b)   impose on the offender a fine not exceeding level 3 on the standard scale.

105.(1)   This section applies to a person subject to a detention and training order if —

   (a)   after his release and before the date on which the term of the order ends, he commits an offence punishable with imprisonment in the case of a person aged 21 or over ('the new offence'); and

   (b)   whether before or after that date, he is convicted of the new offence.

(2)   Subject to section 8(6) above (duty of adult magistrates' court to remit young offenders to youth court for sentence), the court by or before which a person to whom this section applies is convicted of the new offence may, whether or not it passes any other sentence on him, order him to be detained in such secure accommodation as the Secretary of State may determine for the whole or any part of the period which —

(a)   begins with the date of the court's order; and

(b)   is equal in length to the period between the date on which the new offence was committed and the date mentioned in subsection (1) above.

(3)   The period for which a person to whom this section applies is ordered under subsection (2) above to be detained in secure accommodation —

(a)   shall, as the court may direct, either be served before and be followed by, or be served concurrently with, any sentence imposed for the new offence; and

(b)   in either case, shall be disregarded in determining the appropriate length of that sentence.

(4)   Where the new offence is found to have been committed over a period of two or more days, or at some time during a period of two or more days, it shall be taken for the purposes of this section to have been committed on the last of those days.

(5)   A person detained in pursuance of an order under subsection (2) above shall be deemed to be in legal custody.

107.(1)   In sections 102, 104 and 105 above 'secure accommodation' means —

(a)   a secure training centre;

(b)   a young offender institution;

(c)   accommodation provided by a local authority for the purpose of restricting the liberty of children and young persons;

(d)   accommodation provided for that purpose under subsection (5) of section 82 of the Children Act 1989 (financial support by the Secretary of State); or

(e)   such other accommodation provided for the purpose of restricting liberty as the Secretary of State may direct.

At the time of writing only three secure training centres have been built (See generally *A Second Chance: A Review of Education and Supporting Arrangements within Units for Juveniles Managed by HM Prison Service: A Thematic Review* by HM Chief Inspector of Prisons Nov 2001, **www.homeoffice.gov.uk/hmipris/inspects/ a_second_chance.pdf**)

Custodial sentences for grave crimes

The power to sentence for grave crimes is contained in PCCSA sections 90–92:

90.   Where a person convicted of murder appears to the court to have been aged under 18 at the time the offence was committed, the court shall (notwithstanding anything in this or any other Act) sentence him to be detained during Her Majesty's pleasure.

91.(1)   Subsection (3) below applies where a person aged under 18 is convicted on indictment of —

(a)   an offence punishable in the case of a person aged 21 or over with imprisonment for 14 years or more, not being an offence the sentence for which is fixed by law; or

(b)   an offence under section 14 of the Sexual Offences Act 1956 (indecent assault on a woman); or

(c)   an offence under section 15 of that Act (indecent assault on a man) ...

(3)   If the court is of the opinion that none of the other methods in which the case may legally be dealt with is suitable, the court may sentence the offender to be detained for such

period, not exceeding the maximum term of imprisonment with which the offence is punishable in the case of a person aged 21 or over, as may be specified in the sentence.

92.(1) A person sentenced to be detained under section 90 or 91 above shall be liable to be detained in such place and under such conditions —

(a) as the Secretary of State may direct; or

(b) as the Secretary of State may arrange with any person.

93. Where a person aged under 21 is convicted of murder or any other offence the sentence for which is fixed by law as imprisonment for life, the court shall sentence him to custody for life unless he is liable to be detained under Section 90 above.

Power to fine the child or the parent/guardian

The powers of magistrates and youth courts to impose a fine are set out in PCCSA, ss. 135–138. These courts have a limit on the level of fine they are able to impose. Crown Courts have no such limit, but if a case is before the Crown Court because of its gravity (PCCSA, ss. 90–93 above) the sentencing judge will not be considering a fine anyway:

135.(1) Where a person aged under 18 is found guilty by a magistrates' court of an offence for which, apart from this section, the court would have power to impose a fine of an amount exceeding £1,000, the amount of any fine imposed by the court shall not exceed £1,000.

(2) In relation to a person aged under 14, subsection (1) above shall have effect as if for '£1,000', in both places where it occurs, there were substituted '£250'.

136.(1) Before exercising its powers under section 137 below (power to order parent or guardian to pay fine, costs or compensation) against the parent or guardian of an individual who has been convicted of an offence, the court may make a financial circumstances order with respect to the parent or (as the case may be) guardian.

137.(1) Where —

(a) a child or young person (that is to say, any person aged under 18) is convicted of any offence for the commission of which a fine or costs may be imposed or a compensation order may be made, and

(b) the court is of the opinion that the case would best be met by the imposition of a fine or costs or the making of such an order, whether with or without any other punishment, the court shall order that the fine, compensation or costs awarded be paid by the parent or guardian of the child or young person instead of by the child or young person himself, unless the court is satisfied —

(i) that the parent or guardian cannot be found; or

(ii) that it would be unreasonable to make an order for payment, having regard to the circumstances of the case.

(2) Where but for this subsection a court would impose a fine on a child or young person under —

(a) paragraph 4(1)(a) or 5(1)(a) of Schedule 3 to this Act (breach of curfew, probation, community punishment, combination or drug treatment and testing order),

(b) paragraph 2(1)(a) of Schedule 5 to this Act (breach of attendance centre order or attendance centre rules),

(c) paragraph 2(2)(a) of Schedule 7 to this Act (breach of supervision order),

(d) paragraph 2(2)(a) of Schedule 8 to this Act (breach of action plan order or reparation order),

(e) section 104(3)(b) above (breach of requirements of supervision under a detention and training order), or

(f) section 4(3)(b) of the Criminal Justice and Public Order Act 1994 (breach of requirements of supervision under a secure training order),

the court shall order that the fine be paid by the parent or guardian of the child or young person instead of by the child or young person himself, unless the court is satisfied —

(i) that the parent or guardian cannot be found; or

(ii) that it would be unreasonable to make an order for payment, having regard to the circumstances of the case.

(3) In the case of a young person aged 16 or over, subsections (1) and (2) above shall have effect as if, instead of imposing a duty, they conferred a power to make such an order as is mentioned in those subsections.

(4) Subject to subsection (5) below, no order shall be made under this section without giving the parent or guardian an opportunity of being heard.

(5) An order under this section may be made against a parent or guardian who, having been required to attend, has failed to do so.

(8) In relation to a child or young person for whom a local authority have parental responsibility and who —

(a) is in their care,

(b) is provided with accommodation by them in the exercise of any functions (in particular those under the Children Act 1989) which stand referred to their social services committee under the Local Authority Social Services Act 1970

references in this section to his parent or guardian shall be construed as references to that authority.

Compensation order

A compensation order can be made under ss. 130–134 PCCSA. These sections are not reproduced. See Brayne Martin and Carr, Chapter 12.

Requirement to bind over the parent or guardian

Under PCCSA courts have a power — indeed are under an expectation — to bind over an offender's parent or guardian when punishing a child.

150.(1) Where a child or young person (that is to say, any person aged under 18) is convicted of an offence, the powers conferred by this section shall be exercisable by the court by which he is sentenced for that offence, and where the offender is aged under 16 when sentenced it shall be the duty of that court —

(a) to exercise those powers if it is satisfied, having regard to the circumstances of the case, that their exercise would be desirable in the interests of preventing the commission by him of further offences; and

(b) if it does not exercise them, to state in open court that it is not satisfied as mentioned in paragraph (a) above and why it is not so satisfied; but this subsection has effect subject to section 19(5) above and paragraph 13(5) of Schedule 1 to this Act (cases where referral orders made or extended).

(2) The powers conferred by this section are as follows —

(a) with the consent of the offender's parent or guardian, to order the parent or guardian to enter into a recognizance to take proper care of him and exercise proper control over him; and

(b) if the parent or guardian refuses consent and the court considers the refusal unreasonable, to order the parent or guardian to pay a fine not exceeding £1,000; and where the court has passed a community sentence on the offender, it may include in the recognizance a provision that the offender's parent or guardian ensure that the offender complies with the requirements of that sentence.

(3) An order under this section shall not require the parent or guardian to enter into a recognizance for an amount exceeding £1,000.

(4) An order under this section shall not require the parent or guardian to enter into a recognizance —

(a) for a period exceeding three years; or

(b) where the offender will attain the age of 18 in a period shorter than three years, for a period exceeding that shorter period.

(7) In fixing the amount of a recognizance under this section, the court shall take into account among other things the means of the parent or guardian so far as they appear or are known to the court; and this subsection applies whether taking into account the means of the parent or guardian has the effect of increasing or reducing the amount of the recognizance.

(11) For the purposes of this section, taking 'care' of a person includes giving him protection and guidance and 'control' includes discipline.

8

Children as victims of crime

8.1 Offences against children

Social workers are involved with child abuse victims as part of their duties of protecting children under Children Act 1989, Parts II and IV, including co-operation with the police and Crown Prosecution Service. This chapter looks at some of the criminal offences which may be committed against children, and how to bring the child's evidence before the court. The alleged perpetrator may, of course, him or herself be a child, in which case, issues relating to avoiding proceeding, (Chapter 6) or supporting that child through the justice process (Chapter 7) also arise.

8.1.1 Sexual crimes

Sexual Offences Act 1993
1. The presumption of criminal law that a boy under the age of fourteen is incapable of sexual intercourse (whether natural or unnatural) is hereby abolished.

Sexual Offences Act 1956
1.(1) It is an offence for a man to rape a woman or another man.
  (2) A man commits rape if —
    (a) he has sexual intercourse with a person (whether vaginal or anal) who at the time of the intercourse does not consent to it; and
    (b) at the time he knows that the person does not consent to the intercourse or is reckless as to whether that person consents to it.
5. It is felony for a man to have unlawful sexual intercourse with a girl under the age of thirteen.

[Crimes used to be divided into felonies and misdemeanors — the distinction no longer exists.]

6.(1) It is an offence, subject to the exceptions mentioned in this section, for a man to have unlawful sexual intercourse with a girl under the age of sixteen.
  (3) A man is not guilty of an offence under this section because he has unlawful sexual intercourse with a girl under the age of sixteen, if he is under the age of twenty-four and has not previously been charged with a like offence, and he believes her to be of the age of sixteen or over and has reasonable cause for the belief.
  In this subsection, 'a like offence' means an offence under this section or an attempt to commit one ...

10.(1)   It is an offence for a man to have sexual intercourse with a woman whom he knows to be his grand-daughter, daughter, sister or mother.

(2)   In the foregoing subsection 'sister' includes half-sister, and for the purposes of that subsection any expression importing a relationship between two people shall be taken to apply notwithstanding that the relationship is not traced through lawful wedlock.

12.(1)   It is felony for a person to commit buggery with another person otherwise than in the circumstances described in subsection (1A) or (1AA) below or with an animal.

(1A)   The circumstances first referred to in subsection (1) are that the act of buggery takes place in private and both parties have attained the age of sixteen.

(1AA)   The other circumstances so referred to are that the person is under the age of sixteen and the other person has attained that age.

(1B)   An act of buggery by one man with another shall not be treated as taking place in private if it takes place —

(a)   when more than two persons take part or are present; or

(b)   in a lavatory to which the public have or are permitted to have access, whether on payment or otherwise.

13.   It is an offence for a man to commit an act of gross indecency with another man otherwise than in the circumstances described below, whether in public or private, or to be a party to the commission by a man of an act of gross indecency with another man, or to procure the commission by a man of an act of gross indecency with another man.

The circumstances referred to above are that the man is under the age of sixteen and the other man has attained that age.

14.(1)   It is offence, subject to the exception mentioned in subsection (3) of this section, for a person to make an indecent assault on a woman.

(2)   A girl under the age of sixteen cannot in law give any consent which would prevent an act being an assault for the purposes of this section.

(4)   A woman who is a defective cannot in law give any consent which would prevent an act being an assault for the purposes of this section, but a person is only to be treated as guilty of an indecent assault on a defective by reason of that incapacity to consent, if that person knew or had reason to suspect her to be a defective.

15.(1)   It is an offence for a person to make an indecent assault on a man.

(2)   A boy under the age of sixteen cannot in law give any consent which would prevent an act being an assault for the purposes of this section.

(3)   A man who is a defective cannot in law give any consent which would prevent an act being an assault for the purposes of this section, but a person is only to be treated as guilty of an indecent assault on a defective by reason of that incapacity to consent, if that person knew or had reason to suspect him to be a defective.

16.(1)   It is an offence for a person to assault another person with intent to commit buggery.

17.(1)   It is felony for a person to take away or detain a woman against her will with the intention that she shall marry or have unlawful sexual intercourse with that or any other person, if she is so taken away or detained either by force or for the sake of her property or expectations of property.

(2)   In the foregoing subsection, the reference to a woman's expectations of property relates only to property of a person to whom she is next of kin or one of the next of kin, and 'property' includes any interest in property.

19.(1)   It is an offence, subject to the exception mentioned in this section, for a person to take an unmarried girl under the age of eighteen out of the possession of her parent or guardian against his will, if she is so taken with the intention that she shall have unlawful sexual intercourse with men or with a particular man.

(2)   A person is not guilty of an offence under this section because he takes such a girl out of the possession of her parent or guardian as mentioned above, if he believes her to be of the age of eighteen or over and has reasonable cause for the belief.

(3)   In this section 'guardian' means any person having parental responsibility for or care of the girl.

46.   The use in any provision of this Act of the word 'man' without the addition of the word 'boy', or vice versa, shall not prevent the provision applying to any person to whom it would have applied if both words had been used, and similarly with the words 'woman' and 'girl'.

The maximum punishments for the offences in the 1956 Act are set out in Sch. 2, which we have not reproduced.

The 1956 legislation left a couple of gaps — indecent behaviour with a child without the use or threat of force — which was filled by the 1960 Indecency with Children Act — and inciting a girl to have sexual intercourse with her father, brother or grandfather — now covered by the Criminal Law Act 1977.

Indecency with Children Act 1960

1.(1)   Any person who commits an act of gross indecency with or towards a child under the age of sixteen, or who incites a child under that age to such an act with him or another, shall be liable on conviction on indictment to imprisonment for a term not exceeding ten years, or on summary conviction to imprisonment for a term not exceeding six months, to a fine not exceeding the prescribed sum, or to both.

Criminal Law Act 1977

54.(1)   It is an offence for a man to incite to have sexual intercourse with him a girl under the age of sixteen whom he knows to be his grand-daughter, daughter or sister.

(2)   In the preceding subsection 'man' includes boy, 'sister' includes half-sister, and for the purposes of that subsection any expression importing a relationship between two people shall be taken to apply notwithstanding that the relationship is not traced through lawful wedlock.

8.1.2 Assault and neglect

Children are also frequently the subject of crimes of physical abuse, neglect and assault. We have reproduced below the main statutory offences.

Offences Against the Person Act 1861

27.   Whosoever shall unlawfully abandon or expose any child, being under the age of two years, whereby the life of such child shall be endangered, or the health of such child shall have been or shall be likely to be permanently injured, shall be guilty of a misdemeanor, and being convicted thereof shall be liable to be kept in penal servitude.

Children and Young Persons Act 1933

1(1)   If any person who has attained the age of sixteen years and has responsibility for any child or young person under that age, wilfully assaults, ill-treats, neglects, abandons, or exposes him, or causes or procures him to be assaulted, ill-treated, neglected, abandoned, or exposed, in a manner likely to cause him unnecessary suffering or injury to health (including injury to or loss of sight, or hearing, or limb, or organ of the body, and any mental derangement), that person shall be guilty of a misdemeanour...

(2)   For the purposes of this section —

(a)   a parent or other person legally liable to maintain a child or young person, or the legal guardian of a child or young person, shall be deemed to have neglected him in a manner likely to cause injury to his health if he has failed to provide adequate food, clothing, medical aid or lodging for him, or if, having been unable otherwise to provide such food, clothing, medical aid or lodging, he has failed to take steps to procure it to be provided under the enactments applicable in that behalf;

(b) where it is proved that the death of an infant under three years of age was caused by suffocation (not being suffocation caused by disease or the presence of any foreign body in the throat or air passages of the infant) while the infant was in bed with some other person who has attained the age of sixteen years, that other person shall, if he was, when he went to bed, under the influence of drink, be deemed to have neglected the infant in a manner likely to cause injury to its health.

(3)   A person may be convicted of an offence under this section —

(a) notwithstanding that actual suffering or injury to health, or the likelihood of actual suffering or injury to health, was obviated by the action of another person;

(b) notwithstanding the death of the child or young person in question.

(7)   Nothing in this section shall be construed as affecting the right of any parent, or (subject to section 548 of the Education Act 1996) any other person, having the lawful control or charge of a child or young person to administer punishment to him.

S 1(7) restates the common law right of 'reasonable chastisement'. This 'right' to beat children has been the subject of proceedings in the European Court of Human Rights. The Education Act 1986, s. 47 and the School Standards and Framework Act 1998, s. 131 now outlaw physical punishment in all schools, state and private respectively. In *A v UK* [1998] 2 FLR 959, A was the nine year old victim of a severe beating with a cane by his step father, who had been acquitted by a jury using section 1(7) CYPA above as his defence. The case was heard before the European Convention could be applied in English courts. The European Court of Human Rights held that a law which protected an abuser from conviction for such a brutal attack was a breach of A's human right not to suffer inhuman and degrading treatment (Art. 3). The government has promised to amend the law to restrict the type of punishment which will be lawful, but, adhering to the quaint but dangerous notion of the 'loving smack', has ruled out making all physical punishment an offence. See **http://www.doh.gov.uk/scg/pcspresponse/**

8.2 Children as witnesses in criminal cases

Lawyers for the alleged abuser have a professional duty to seek an acquittal. Destroying the credibility of the principal witness for the prosecution is their unfortunate but legitimate task. So if a child has suffered abuse, testifying in court not only re-opens the painful experience, but because of the child feeling attacked on her or his credibility, this can be itself a further form of abuse. This is not all. Merely waiting for the trial can delay therapeutic help being provided, for fear of the child's evidence being seen as contaminated. The law has made tentative steps to protect the child in this situation, while maintaining the civil liberties of the accused.

The new statutory framework for witnesses under 17 (and other vulnerable witnesses) is set out under the Youth Justice and Criminal Evidence Act 1999, which we cite below. In any particular court the provisions will only be in force when the relevant facilities are available.

A useful introduction to the relevant issues is provided by Phil Bates, The Youth Justice and Criminal Evidence Act — the Evidence of children and vulnerable adults, (1999) 11(3) *Child and Family Law Quarterly* 289:

Traditionally, the law has placed a series of obstacles in the path of child witnesses in criminal proceedings. These rules appear to have been based on the idea that children are fundamentally unreliable witnesses, who are prone to fantasy and falsehood. However, more recently, there has been an increasing recognition of the ability of children to give coherent accounts of their experiences. The public interest in allowing children to testify has also been recognised, particularly in the context of child abuse prosecutions, where the child concerned may be the only witness. In recent years, the vulnerability to abuse of disabled adults has also been recognised. While the needs of vulnerable adult witnesses received relatively little attention, a series of legislative measures has attempted to clarify the circumstances in which children can give evidence, and to ease the trauma involved. However, there has been continuing criticism of the legal system's treatment of vulnerable witnesses, both children and adults, and yet another reform of the law has been introduced. Part II of the Youth Justice and Criminal Evidence Act 1999 reforms the law relating to the evidence of children and vulnerable adults. ...

Competence to give sworn evidence
Under the common law, all testimony, whether from children or adults, had to be on oath. In *R* v *Brasier* it was said that 'there is no precise or fixed rule as to the time within which infants are excluded from giving evidence, but the admissibility of their evidence depends upon the sense and reason they entertain of the danger and impiety of falsehood, which is to be collected from their answers to questions propounded to them by the court'. This test was based upon the child's understanding of the oath's religious significance. However, the extent to which a witness's sincerity is reinforced by the threat of divine retribution has probably declined since the eighteenth century, and a more secular approach to the understanding of the oath emerged in *R* v *Hayes*. The Court of Appeal decided that the trial judge had been wrong to question a 12-year-old boy, about his religious instruction at school and his belief in God. It was said that the important consideration is 'whether the child has a sufficient appreciation of the solemnity of the occasion and the added responsibility to tell the truth, which is involved in taking an oath, over and above the duty to tell the truth which is an ordinary duty of normal social conduct'. The court suggested that 'the watershed dividing young children who are normally considered old enough to take the oath and children normally considered too young to take the oath, probably falls between the ages of eight and ten'.

...

The test in *R* v *Hayes* was also applied where mental illness or learning disabilities have reduced a witness's ability to understand the nature of the oath. For example, in *R* v *Bellamy* the defendant was charged with the rape of a woman who was 33 years old, but she was said to have a 'mental age' of 10 years. The Court of Appeal decided that the trial judge had been correct to inquire into her competence before she gave evidence, but that it was not necessary to inquire into her belief in God. The judge's inquiry should be directed to ascertaining whether the witness had a sufficient understanding of the solemnity of the occasion and the responsibility to tell the truth. Although many adults with learning disabilities may be perfectly able to satisfy this test, it is likely that prosecutions are sometimes not brought because of uncertainty about the ability of the witness to satisfy the test. The needs of vulnerable adults have received little legislative attention until recently, whereas there have been various changes which have been made to the position of child witnesses. ...

Previous statutory reform for child witnesses

The inability of young children to take the oath led to legislation to allow children to give evidence 'unsworn', without taking an oath. For example, section 38(1) of the Children and Young Persons Act 1933 provided that where a child of 'tender years' called as a witness in criminal proceedings did not understand the nature of the oath, his evidence could be received unsworn if, in the opinion of the court, he possessed sufficient intelligence to justify the reception of the evidence, and understood the duty of speaking the truth. Although this test no longer applies in criminal proceedings, a similar test still governs the ability of child witnesses to give unsworn evidence in civil proceedings.

Although the ability to give unsworn evidence made it easier for younger children to give evidence, their testimony was still treated with suspicion. Originally it was necessary to give a 'corroboration warning' to the jury, that it was dangerous to convict upon the basis of a child's unsworn evidence, unless the child's account was supported by independent corroborative evidence. This requirement was abolished by section 34(2) of the Criminal Justice Act 1988.

...

The Criminal Justice Act 1991 amended the Criminal Justice Act 1988, so that children under 14 years of age should always give their evidence unsworn. This removed the need to assess whether the child was capable of taking the oath, but it was still necessary to consider the child's competence to give unsworn evidence. The original version of the section provided that 'the power of the court in any criminal proceedings to determine that a particular person is not competent to give evidence shall apply to children of tender years as it applies to other persons'. The drafting of this provision was criticised, and the Criminal Justice and Public Order Act 1994 introduced further amendments to the 1988 Act. This provided in section 33A that in criminal proceedings the evidence of a child under 14 shall be given unsworn, and shall be received unless it appears to the court that the child is 'incapable of giving intelligible testimony'.

...

Statutory reform has also introduced measures intended to reduce the trauma for child witnesses of giving evidence. As well as abolishing the corroboration requirement for children's unsworn evidence, the Criminal Justice Act 1988 also introduced provision for children to give evidence by a live television link. The right of the defendant to personally cross-examine a child witness has also been curtailed by statute.

...

Although these statutory reforms were widely supported, eligibility depended upon the court in which the case was heard, the type of offence for which the defendant is on trial, and the age of the child. The witness had to be under 14 years of age for offences involving assault or injury or threat of injury, and under 17 for sexual offences. Other offences were not covered by the provisions at all. However, the courts have interpreted the provision widely. In *R v Lee* it was said that the words 'injury or threat of injury' contained in section 32(2) applied to the offence, not the intention of the individual offender. There was no requirement for a threat to be directed to a particular person, merely for the consequences of a defendant's actions to present such a threat. Therefore, video evidence could be admitted in relation to an offence of 'arson being reckless as to whether life was endangered', because there was a real possibility that injury to a person would result. It was not necessary that the person at risk of injury should be the child witness.

Although alleged victims of physical or sexual abuse face particular difficulties in giving evidence, the experience of giving evidence may be stressful for all child witnesses, regardless of the nature of the offence. Therefore, the requirement that the offence should fall into a particular category may deprive some child witnesses of valuable assistance.

The pressure for further reform

Two obvious problems with the statutory framework should be apparent from the previous discussion. First, the statutory provisions were restricted to 'child witnesses' below a certain age (usually 14, but 17 for some purposes). Adults and older children were not eligible for assistance, although they might face similar difficulties to child witnesses, particularly where they are disabled. In 1989 the Pigot Report recommended that special provision for child witnesses should, as a 'high priority', be extended to adult vulnerable witnesses once the changes relating to children had been implemented and were working successfully. However, this did not take place. As a result, adult witnesses who were unable to understand the nature of the oath could not give their evidence unsworn. Nor were they eligible to give evidence by means of a pre-recorded video interview, or a live video link.

Secondly, although a child's evidence-in-chief could be given by means of a pre-recorded interview, the child witness had to be available for cross-examination by the defence at the time of the trial. This meant that the child might suffer a long period of stress prior to the trial, when therapy might not be available for fear that the child's evidence would be 'contaminated'. As well as recommending that video-recorded interviews of children should be admitted in place of the child's evidence-in-chief, the Pigot Report had recommended that subsequently there should be a video-recorded preliminary hearing, conducted in informal surroundings, where the child would be cross-examined by the defence. The videos of the interview, and the cross-examination, would be shown to the court in place of the child appearing as a witness at the time of the trial. Accordingly, 'no child witness to whom our proposals apply should be required to appear in open court during a trial unless he or she wishes to do so'.

...

As a result of concerns of this kind, in 1997 an Interdepartmental Working Group was set up, chaired by the Home Office with representatives from various Government Departments, as well as Victim Support and the Association of Chief Police Officers. The Report of this Working Group, *Speaking Up For Justice*, assessed the need for reform of the law for 'vulnerable' witnesses, and made a large number of recommendations. In particular, it recommended that 'special measures' should be available to assist witnesses who are vulnerable by reason of age, disability, illness, or because of the circumstances of the case. These special measures would include pre-recorded cross-examination. The Working Group also recommended that special measures should be available automatically to all children under 17 years, and in magistrates' courts as well as the Crown Court and youth courts.

8.2.1 **Can a child's evidence be used?**

The starting point in case law and in the new framework is that a child of almost any age is capable of giving evidence. This is made explicit in the 1999 Act, though s. 53 is not yet in force (Until it is in force, the Criminal Justice Act 1991 as described on the previous page will continue to apply).

53.(1)   At every stage in criminal proceedings all persons are (whatever their age) competent to give evidence.

(2)   Subsection (1) has effect subject to subsections (3) and (4).

(3)   A person is not competent to give evidence in criminal proceedings if it appears to the court that he is not a person who is able to —
   (a)   understand questions put to him as a witness, and
   (b)   give answers to them which can be understood.
(4)   not reproduced.

Case law has seen a gradual recognition of the ability of young children to give truthful evidence. We cite just one case, *Director of Public Prosecutions* v *M* [1997] 2 FLR 804, a prosecution appeal. The relevant law, until s. 53 is brought into effect, is the Criminal Justice Act 1988, s. 2A which states that:

A child's evidence shall be received unless it appears to the court that the child is incapable of giving intelligible testimony.

The issue in the case is not affected by the change in the statutory wording. The judgment of Lord Justice Phillips starts by reciting the facts as set out by the Crown Court:

On 4 January 1995 an information was preferred by the appellant (the Crown) against a minor (hereinafter referred to as 'M') that on 19 September 1994 he indecently assaulted a young girl (the complainant) contrary to s. 14(1) of the Sexual Offences Act 1956.

On 13 September 1995 the Justices sitting at the Derby Youth Court heard the said information and M was convicted. M was made the subject of a 2-year supervision order and was ordered to pay £100 compensation.

An appeal against the decision of the justices was made by M at the Crown Court at Derby, which was heard on 20 December 1995.

We were asked by counsel for M at the outset to give a ruling upon the admissibility of the evidence of the child complainant in this case. We were given the following facts by counsel for M which we accepted:
(a)   At the date of the incident, 19 September 1994, the complainant was aged $4\frac{1}{4}$ years and M was aged 12 years. At the date of the appeal to the Crown Court at Derby, the complainant was aged $5\frac{1}{2}$ years.
(b)   The complainant complained to her mother the same day and was medically examined both on that day and again on 20 September 1994.
(c)   On 20 September 1994 the complainant was spoken to about the incident by her two aunts.
(d)   On 21 December 1994 the complainant was formally interviewed, which interview was recorded on videotape. In that interview the complainant only said that M had done something 'naughty'.
(e)   Nine days later, on 30 September 1994 the complainant was again interviewed on videotape. In the course of that interview she alleged that M had inserted his penis inside her vagina.
(f)   The complaint made in the second videotape-recorded interview was not consistent with what the complainant said to her mother on 19 September 1994.
It was contended by counsel for M that the child complainant by reason of her age alone was incapable of giving intelligible testimony.

It was contended by the prosecution that we should assess whether the complainant was capable of giving intelligible testimony either by watching the video-recorded interviews or otherwise. It was argued that the only test was whether the child was capable of giving intelligible evidence.

We were concerned about the girl's evidence on two grounds. One was her age.

We bore in mind s. 33A(2A) of the Criminal Justice Act 1988 and that the only ground for impugning the competence of a child witness is that a child is incapable of giving intelligible testimony. But we also bore in mind the case of *R* v *Wallwork* [1958] 42 Cr App R 153, 160, where it was said to be most undesirable that a child as young as 5 should be called as a witness. Also *R* v *Wright, R* v *Ormerod* [1987] 90 Cr App R 91, where it was said that there must be quite exceptional circumstances to justify the reception of the evidence of a child in extremely tender years, a 6-year-old girl in that case. We also considered the strictures of Lord Lane CJ in *R* v *Z* [1990] 2 QB 355 as to the care that must be taken in receiving the evidence of very young children, although there is no minimum age.

Our second ground of concern was that there was an obvious danger that the girl's evidence had been contaminated, when considering the number of people who had spoken to her before the final videotape. We felt this had probably taken place and was the explanation for her change of story.

We did not view the videotape, as we were satisfied on the information we had been given that by reason of her age and of the inconsistencies in her story, she was not a witness on whom we should rely, and that any conviction resulting from her evidence would be unsafe.

The question posed by the court is as follows:

'Given the provision of s. 33A (2A) of the Criminal Justice Act 1988 whether a court should refuse to admit the evidence of a child complainant by reason of age alone; or, where there is a video recording of his/her complaint a court should assess, either by watching the video recording, or by the verbal questioning of the child by the court whether the complainant is capable of giving intelligible testimony.'

The Court of Appeal was not happy with the Crown Court's approach. Phillips LJ starts by considering the relevant law, by citing an earlier case.

In *R* v *Hampshire* [1996] QB 1, in a reserved judgment of the Court of Appeal, Auld J gave consideration to the appropriate procedure where both the competence of a child witness and the admissibility of a video of her evidence under s. 32A of the Criminal Justice Act were in issue. He held at 4:

'Section 32A which was inserted in the Act of 1988 by section 54 of the Criminal Justice Act 1991, provides for the testimony in chief of child witnesses to be given by video recording in cases of violence to or sexual abuse of a child. By section 32A(3) a judge, on such an application, is required to give leave for a video recording to be admitted in evidence subject to certain limited exceptions which it specifies.

It reads, so far as material:

"Where a video recording is tendered in evidence under this section, the court shall (subject to the exercise of any power of the court to exclude evidence which is otherwise admissible) give leave ... unless — (a) it appears that the child witness will not be available for the cross-examination; (b) any rules of court requiring disclosure of the circumstances in which the recording was made have not been complied with to the satisfaction of the court; or (c) the court is of the opinion, having regard to all the circumstances of the case, that in the interests of justice the recording ought not to be admitted; ..."

In order to determine, under section 32A(3)(c), whether the interests of justice require him to refuse, the judge in most, if not all, cases must watch the video recording. His determination whether "in the interests of justice" the recording ought not to be admitted must necessarily include a determination as to competence. If, on viewing the recording, he considers that the child is incompetent to give evidence, he should conclude, under section 32A(3)(c) that it is in the interests of justice that the evidence, at any rate in that form, should be excluded. If the prosecution nevertheless wish to call the child as a witness, the issue of his or her competence will be a matter for the judge at trial. If the judge, on his pre-trial review of the video recording, determines there is no reason to refuse to admit the recording, he is bound by section 32A(3) to grant leave. In that event, there is no logical reason why he should have to investigate the child's competence again at the trial before the playing of the video recording or before cross-examination. Of course, the trial judge still has the power to exclude such evidence if, in the course of it, he forms the view that the child is, after all, incompetent to give evidence.'

Later, at 7, Auld J said:

'In our view, the effect of the recent statutory changes has been to remove from the judge any duty to conduct a preliminary investigation of a child's competence, but to retain his power to do so if he considers it necessary, say because the child is very young or has difficulty in expression or understanding. Where there has been an application under section 32A of the Act of 1988 to rely on video recorded evidence, the judge's pre-trial review of the recording, if the interview has been properly conducted, should normally enable him to form a view as to the child's competence. Where it has left him in doubt, or where the child's evidence-in-chief is not to be given by a video recording and his or her competence as a witness is questionable, he should conduct a preliminary investigation into the matter. Whether or not he conducts such a preliminary investigation, he has the same duty as in the case of an adult witness, namely to exclude or direct disregard of the evidence, if and when he concludes that the child is not competent...

In our view, the preliminary investigation of a child, if there is one, should be conducted by the judge: see R v N (1992) 95 Cr App R 256. It is a matter of his perception of the child's understanding demonstrated in the course of ordinary discourse. It is not an issue to be resolved by him in response to an adversarial examination and cross-examination by counsel.'

I would wish to add nothing to these observations which clearly cover the situation in which the Derby Crown Court found itself in the present case. The extreme youth of the complainant was a matter which properly raised concern as to whether she was competent to give evidence. What it did not do was to demonstrate, of itself, that she was not. The recorder was persuaded that it would not be appropriate for him to view the video recordings of the complainant's evidence because objection to their admissibility was to be made on other grounds. Counsel both for the prosecution and for the defence submitted that the appropriate course, if he was not to look at the videos, was for him to question the complainant himself in order to determine whether she was capable of giving intelligible evidence. As counsel for the defendant put it:

'I suggest this approach, that the court would not subject her to cross-examination but would merely ask her some general questions and form a genuine opinion at the outset as to her intelligibility.'

That was a helpful suggestion and, if the recorder was not to look at the videos, he should have followed it. Instead, after consulting the magistrates, he resolved to exclude the complainant's evidence on the basis of her age alone. It was not open for him to do so, and accordingly, the answer to the question asked is that, the court should not refuse to admit the evidence of a child complainant by reason of age alone, but should assess by watching a video recording, or questioning the complainant, or both, whether the complainant is capable of giving intelligible testimony. The appeal is allowed.

8.2.2 Special measures for child and other vulnerable witnesses

The new measures directed by the Youth Justice and Criminal Evidence Act 1999 came into force July 2002. But note that the court must have the facilities.

16.(1) For the purposes of this Chapter a witness in criminal proceedings (other than the accused) is eligible for assistance by virtue of this section —

   (a) if under the age of 17 at the time of the hearing; or
   (b) if the court considers that the quality of evidence given by the witness is likely to be diminished by reason of any circumstances falling within subsection (2).

(2) The circumstances falling within this subsection are —

(a) that the witness —

    (i) suffers from mental disorder within the meaning of the Mental Health Act 1983, or

    (ii) otherwise has a significant impairment of intelligence and social functioning;

(b) that the witness has a physical disability or is suffering from a physical disorder.

(3) In subsection (1)(a) 'the time of the hearing', in relation to a witness, means the time when it falls to the court to make a determination for the purposes of section 19(2) in relation to the witness.

(4) In determining whether a witness falls within subsection (1)(b) the court must consider any views expressed by the witness.

(5) In this Chapter references to the quality of a witness's evidence are to its quality in terms of completeness, coherence and accuracy; and for this purpose 'coherence' refers to a witness's ability in giving evidence to give answers which address the questions put to the witness and can be understood both individually and collectively.

17.(1) For the purposes of this Chapter a witness in criminal proceedings (other than the accused) is eligible for assistance by virtue of this subsection if the court is satisfied that the quality of evidence given by the witness is likely to be diminished by reason of fear or distress on the part of the witness in connection with testifying in the proceedings.

(2) In determining whether a witness falls within subsection (1) the court must take into account, in particular —

(a) the nature and alleged circumstances of the offence to which the proceedings relate;

(b) the age of the witness;

(c) such of the following matters as appear to the court to be relevant, namely —

    (i) the social and cultural background and ethnic origins of the witness,

    (ii) the domestic and employment circumstances of the witness, and

    (iii) any religious beliefs or political opinions of the witness;

(d) any behaviour towards the witness on the part of —

    (i) the accused,

    (ii) members of the family or associates of the accused, or

    (iii) any other person who is likely to be an accused or a witness in the proceedings.

(3) In determining that question the court must in addition consider any views expressed by the witness.

(4) Where the complainant in respect of a sexual offence is a witness in proceedings relating to that offence (or to that offence and any other offences), the witness is eligible for assistance in relation to those proceedings by virtue of this subsection unless the witness has informed the court of the witness' wish not to be so eligible by virtue of this subsection.

Section 18 is not reproduced. Amongst other things it requires that the court should have acquired the necessary facilities before the special measures set out in this legislation can be ordered.

19.(1) This section applies where in any criminal proceedings —

(a) a party to the proceedings makes an application for the court to give a direction under this section in relation to a witness in the proceedings other than the accused, or

(b) the court of its own motion raises the issue whether such a direction should be given.

(2) Where the court determines that the witness is eligible for assistance by virtue of section 16 or 17, the court must then —

(a) determine whether any of the special measures available in relation to the witness (or any combination of them) would, in its opinion, be likely to improve the quality of evidence given by the witness; and

(b) if so —

    (i)   determine which of those measures (or combination of them) would, in its opinion, be likely to maximise so far as practicable the quality of such evidence; and

    (ii) give a direction under this section providing for the measure or measures so determined to apply to evidence given by the witness.

(3) In determining for the purposes of this Chapter whether any special measure or measures would or would not be likely to improve, or to maximise so far as practicable, the quality of evidence given by the witness, the court must consider all the circumstances of the case, including in particular —

(a) any views expressed by the witness; and

(b) whether the measure or measures might tend to inhibit such evidence being effectively tested by a party to the proceedings.

(4) A special measures direction must specify particulars of the provision made by the direction in respect of each special measure which is to apply to the witness's evidence.

Section 20 is not reproduced. It gives the court the power to vary or revoke special measures orders:

21.(1)   For the purposes of this section —

(a) a witness in criminal proceedings is a 'child witness' if he is an eligible witness by reason of section 16(1)(a) (whether or not he is an eligible witness by reason of any other provision of section 16 or 17);

(b) a child witness is 'in need of special protection' if the offence (or any of the offences) to which the proceedings relate is —

    (i)   an offence falling within section 35(3)(a) (sexual offences etc.), or

    (ii) an offence falling within section 35(3)(b), (c) or (d) (kidnapping, assaults etc.); and

(c) a 'relevant recording', in relation to a child witness, is a video recording of an interview of the witness made with a view to its admission as evidence in chief of the witness.

(2) Where the court, in making a determination for the purposes of section 19(2), determines that a witness in criminal proceedings is a child witness, the court must —

(a) first have regard to subsections (3) to (7) below; and

(b) then have regard to section 19(2);

and for the purposes of section 19(2), as it then applies to the witness, any special measures required to be applied in relation to him by virtue of this section shall be treated as if they were measures determined by the court, pursuant to section 19(2)(a) and (b)(i), to be ones that (whether on their own or with any other special measures) would be likely to maximise, so far as practicable, the quality of his evidence.

(3) The primary rule in the case of a child witness is that the court must give a special measures direction in relation to the witness which complies with the following requirements —

(a) it must provide for any relevant recording to be admitted under section 27 (video recorded evidence in chief); and

(b) it must provide for any evidence given by the witness in the proceedings which is not given by means of a video recording (whether in chief or otherwise) to be given by means of a live link in accordance with section 24.

(4) The primary rule is subject to the following limitations —

(a) the requirement contained in subsection (3)(a) or (b) has effect subject to the availability (within the meaning of section 18(2)) of the special measure in question in relation to the witness;

(b) the requirement contained in subsection (3)(a) also has effect subject to section 27(2); and

(c) the rule does not apply to the extent that the court is satisfied that compliance with it would not be likely to maximise the quality of the witness's evidence so far as practicable (whether because the application to that evidence of one or more other special measures available in relation to the witness would have that result or for any other reason).

(5) However, subsection (4)(c) does not apply in relation to a child witness in need of special protection.

(6) Where a child witness is in need of special protection by virtue of subsection (1)(b)(i), any special measures direction given by the court which complies with the requirement contained in subsection (3)(a) must in addition provide for the special measure available under section 28 (video recorded cross-examination or re-examination) to apply in relation to —

(a) any cross-examination of the witness otherwise than by the accused in person, and

(b) any subsequent re-examination.

(7) The requirement contained in subsection (6) has effect subject to the following limitations —

(a) it has effect subject to the availability (within the meaning of section 18(2)) of that special measure in relation to the witness; and

(b) it does not apply if the witness has informed the court that he does not want that special measure to apply in relation to him.

(8) Where a special measures direction is given in relation to a child witness who is an eligible witness by reason only of section 16(1)(a), then —

(a) subject to subsection (9) below, and

(b) except where the witness has already begun to give evidence in the proceedings,

the direction shall cease to have effect at the time when the witness attains the age of 17.

(9) Where a special measures direction is given in relation to a child witness who is an eligible witness by reason only of section 16(1)(a) and —

(a) the direction provides —

(i) for any relevant recording to be admitted under section 27 as evidence in chief of the witness, or

(ii) for the special measure available under section 28 to apply in relation to the witness, and

(b) if it provides for that special measure to so apply, the witness is still under the age of 17 when the video recording is made for the purposes of section 28,

then, so far as it provides as mentioned in paragraph (a)(i) or (ii) above, the direction shall continue to have effect in accordance with section 20(1) even though the witness subsequently attains that age.

22.(1) For the purposes of this section —

(a) a witness in criminal proceedings (other than the accused) is a 'qualifying witness' if he —

(i) is not an eligible witness at the time of the hearing (as defined by section 16(3)), but

(ii) was under the age of 17 when a relevant recording was made;

(b) a qualifying witness is 'in need of special protection' if the offence (or any of the offences) to which the proceedings relate is —

(i) an offence falling within section 35(3)(a) (sexual offences etc), or

(ii) an offence falling within section 35(3)(b), (c) or (d) (kidnapping, assaults etc); and

(c) a 'relevant recording', in relation to a witness, is a video recording of an interview of the witness made with a view to its admission as evidence in chief of the witness.

(2)   Subsections (2) to (7) of section 21 shall apply as follows in relation to a qualifying witness —

   (a)   subsections (2) to (4), so far as relating to the giving of a direction complying with the requirement contained in subsection (3)(a), shall apply to a qualifying witness in respect of the relevant recording as they apply to a child witness (within the meaning of that section);

   (b)   subsection (5), so far as relating to the giving of such a direction, shall apply to a qualifying witness in need of special protection as it applies to a child witness in need of special protection (within the meaning of that section); and

   (c)   subsections (6) and (7) shall apply to a qualifying witness.in need of special protection by virtue of subsection (1)(b)(i) above as they apply to such a child witness as is mentioned in subsection (6).

23.(1)   A special measures direction may provide for the witness, while giving testimony or being sworn in court, to be prevented by means of a screen or other arrangement from seeing the accused.

(2)   But the screen or other arrangement must not prevent the witness from being able to see, and to be seen by —

   (a)   the judge or justices (or both) and the jury (if there is one);

   (b)   legal representatives acting in the proceedings; and

   (c)   any interpreter or other person appointed (in pursuance of the direction or otherwise) to assist the witness.

24.(1)   A special measures direction may provide for the witness to give evidence by means of a live link.

(2)   Where a direction provides for the witness to give evidence by means of a live link, the witness may not give evidence in any other way without the permission of the court.

(3)   The court may give permission for the purposes of subsection (2) if it appears to the court to be in the interests of justice to do so, and may do so either —

   (a)   on an application by a party to the proceedings, if there has been a material change of circumstances since the relevant time, or

   (b)   of its own motion.

(5)   Where in proceedings before a magistrates' court —

   (a)   evidence is to be given by means of a live link in accordance with a special measures direction, but

   (b)   suitable facilities for receiving such evidence are not available at any petty-sessional court-house in which that court can (apart from this subsection) lawfully sit,

the court may sit for the purposes of the whole or any part of those proceedings at a place where such facilities are available and which has been appointed for the purposes of this subsection by the justices acting for the petty sessions area for which the court acts.

(6)   A place appointed under subsection (5) may be outside the petty sessions area for which it is appointed; but (if so) it is to be regarded as being in that area for the purpose of the jurisdiction of the justices acting for that area.

25.(1)   A special measures direction may provide for the exclusion from the court, during the giving of the witness's evidence, of persons of any description specified in the direction.

(2)   The persons who may be so excluded do not include —

   (a)   the accused,

   (b)   legal representatives acting in the proceedings, or

   (c)   any interpreter or other person appointed (in pursuance of the direction or otherwise) to assist the witness.

(3)   A special measures direction providing for representatives of news gathering or reporting organisations to be so excluded shall be expressed not to apply to one named person who —

(a)   is a representative of such an organisation, and

(b)   has been nominated for the purpose by one or more such organisations,

unless it appears to the court that no such nomination has been made.

(4)   A special measures direction may only provide for the exclusion of persons under this section where —

(a)   the proceedings relate to a sexual offence; or

(b)   it appears to the court that there are reasonable grounds for believing that any person other than the accused has sought, or will seek, to intimidate the witness in connection with testifying in the proceedings.

(5)   Any proceedings from which persons are excluded under this section (whether or not those persons include representatives of news gathering or reporting organisations) shall nevertheless be taken to be held in public for the purposes of any privilege or exemption from liability available in respect of fair, accurate and contemporaneous reports of legal proceedings held in public.

26.   A special measures direction may provide for the wearing of wigs or gowns to be dispensed with during the giving of the witness's evidence.

27.(1)   A special measures direction may provide for a video recording of an interview of the witness to be admitted as evidence in chief of the witness.

(2)   A special measures direction may, however, not provide for a video recording, or a part of such a recording, to be admitted under this section if the court is of the opinion, having regard to all the circumstances of the case, that in the interests of justice the recording, or that part of it, should not be so admitted.

(3)   In considering for the purposes of subsection (2) whether any part of a recording should not be admitted under this section, the court must consider whether any prejudice to the accused which might result from that part being so admitted is outweighed by the desirability of showing the whole, or substantially the whole, of the recorded interview.

(4)   Where a special measures direction provides for a recording to be admitted under this section, the court may nevertheless subsequently direct that it is not to be so admitted if —

(a)   it appears to the court that —

(i)   the witness will not be available for cross-examination (whether conducted in the ordinary way or in accordance with any such direction), and

(ii)   the parties to the proceedings have not agreed that there is no need for the witness to be so available; or

(b)   any rules of court requiring disclosure of the circumstances in which the recording was made have not been complied with to the satisfaction of the court.

(5)   Where a recording is admitted under this section —

(a)   the witness must be called by the party tendering it in evidence, unless —

(i)   a special measures direction provides for the witness's evidence on cross-examination to be given otherwise than by testimony in court, or

(ii)   the parties to the proceedings have agreed as mentioned in subsection (4)(a)(ii); and

(b)   the witness may not give evidence in chief otherwise than by means of the recording —

(i)   as to any matter which, in the opinion of the court, has been dealt with adequately in the witness's recorded testimony, or

(ii)   without the permission of the court, as to any other matter which, in the opinion of the court, is dealt with in that testimony.

(6)   Where in accordance with subsection (2) a special measures direction provides for part only of a recording to be admitted under this section, references in subsections (4) and (5) to the recording or to the witness's recorded testimony are references to the part of the recording or testimony which is to be so admitted.

(7)   The court may give permission for the purposes of subsection (5)(b)(ii) if it appears to the court to be in the interests of justice to do so, and may do so either —

(a) on an application by a party to the proceedings, if there has been a material change of circumstances since the relevant time, or

(b) of its own motion.

(8)   In subsection (7) 'the relevant time' means —

(a) the time when the direction was given, or

(b) if a previous application has been made under that subsection, the time when the application (or last application) was made.

(9)   The court may, in giving permission for the purposes of subsection (5)(b)(ii), direct that the evidence in question is to be given by the witness by means of a live link; and, if the court so directs, subsections (5) to (7) of section 24 shall apply in relation to that evidence as they apply in relation to evidence which is to be given in accordance with a special measures direction.

(10)   A magistrates' court inquiring into an offence as examining justices under section 6 of the Magistrates' Courts Act 1980 [the decision in either way cases that there is sufficient evidence to commit for Crown Court trial] may consider any video recording in relation to which it is proposed to apply for a special measures direction providing for it to be admitted at the trial in accordance with this section.

28.(1)   Where a special measures direction provides for a video recording to be admitted under section 27 as evidence in chief of the witness, the direction may also provide —

(a) for any cross-examination of the witness, and any re-examination, to be recorded by means of a video recording; and

(b) for such a recording to be admitted, so far as it relates to any such cross-examination or re-examination, as evidence of the witness under cross-examination or on re-examination, as the case may be.

(2)   Such a recording must be made in the presence of such persons as rules of court or the direction may provide and in the absence of the accused, but in circumstances in which —

(a) the judge or justices (or both) and legal representatives acting in the proceedings are able to see and hear the examination of the witness and to communicate with the persons in whose presence the recording is being made, and

(b) the accused is able to see and hear any such examination and to communicate with any legal representative acting for him.

29.(1)   A special measures direction may provide for any examination of the witness (however and wherever conducted) to be conducted through an interpreter or other person approved by the court for the purposes of this section ('an intermediary').

(2)   The function of an intermediary is to communicate —

(a) to the witness, questions put to the witness, and

(b) to any person asking such questions, the answers given by the witness in reply to them, and to explain such questions or answers so far as necessary to enable them to be understood by the witness or person in question.

(3)   Any examination of the witness in pursuance of subsection (1) must take place in the presence of such persons as rules of court or the direction may provide, but in circumstances in which —

(a) the judge or justices (or both) and legal representatives acting in the proceedings are able to see and hear the examination of the witness and to communicate with the intermediary, and

(b) (except in the case of a video recorded examination) the jury (if there is one) are able to see and hear the examination of the witness.

(6) Subsection (1) does not apply to an interview of the witness which is recorded by means of a video recording with a view to its admission as evidence in chief of the witness; but a special measures direction may provide for such a recording to be admitted under section 27 if the interview was conducted through an intermediary and —

(a) that person complied with subsection (5) before the interview began, and

(b) the court's approval for the purposes of this section is given before the direction is given.

30. A special measures direction may provide for the witness, while giving evidence (whether by testimony in court or otherwise), to be provided with such device as the court considers appropriate with a view to enabling questions or answers to be communicated to or by the witness despite any disability or disorder or other impairment which the witness has or suffers from.

31.(1) Subsections (2) to (4) apply to a statement made by a witness in criminal proceedings which, in accordance with a special measures direction, is not made by the witness in direct oral testimony in court but forms part of the witness's evidence in those proceedings.

(2) The statement shall be treated as if made by the witness in direct oral testimony in court; and accordingly —

(a) it is admissible evidence of any fact of which such testimony from the witness would be admissible;

(b) it is not capable of corroborating any other evidence given by the witness.

(3) Subsection (2) applies to a statement admitted under section 27 or 28 which is not made by the witness on oath even though it would have been required to be made on oath if made by the witness in direct oral testimony in court.

(4) In estimating the weight (if any) to be attached to the statement, the court must have regard to all the circumstances from which an inference can reasonably be drawn (as to the accuracy of the statement or otherwise).

32. Where on a trial on indictment evidence has been given in accordance with a special measures direction, the judge must give the jury such warning (if any) as the judge considers necessary to ensure that the fact that the direction was given in relation to the witness does not prejudice the accused.

8.2.3 Getting and using a child's evidence on tape

If you are involved in the preparing of a video, there are formalities currently set out in the The Magistrates' Courts (Children and Young Persons) Rules 1992 [Note that the provisions above of the YJCEA are in force and that these regulations can be expected to be replaced. The gist will probably remain as below]:

24.(1) Any party may apply for leave under section 32A of the Criminal Justice Act 1988 to tender in evidence a video recording of testimony from a witness where —

(a) the offence charged is one to which section 32(2) of that Act applies,

(b) in the case of an offence falling within section 32(2)(a) or (b) of that Act, the proposed witness is under the age of 14 or, if he was under 14 when the video recording was made, is under the age of 15,

(c) in the case of an offence falling within section 32(2)(c) of that Act, the proposed witness is under the age of 17 or, if he was under 17 when the video recording was made, is under the age of 18, and

(d) the video recording is of an interview conducted between an adult and a person coming within sub-paragraph (b) or (c) above (not being the accused or one of the accused) which relates to any matter in issue in the proceedings;

and references in this rule to an offence include references to attempting or conspiring to commit, or aiding, abetting, counselling, procuring or inciting the commission of, that offence.

(2)   An application under paragraph (1) above shall be made by giving notice in writing, which shall be in the form prescribed in Form 52 of Schedule 2 [not reproduced], or a form to the like effect. The application shall be accompanied by the video recording which it is proposed to tender in evidence and shall include the following, namely —

(a)   the name of the defendant and the offence or offences charged,

(b)   the name and date of birth of the witness in respect of whom the application is made,

(c)   the date on which the video recording was made,

(d)   a statement that in the opinion of the applicant the witness is willing and able to attend the trial for cross-examination,

(e)   a statement of the circumstances in which the video recording was made which complies with paragraph (4) below, and

(f)   the date on which the video recording was disclosed to the other party or parties.

(3)   Where it is proposed to tender part only of a video recording of an interview with the witness, an application under paragraph (1) above must specify that part and be accompanied by a video recording of the entire interview including those parts of the interview which it is not proposed to tender in evidence and by a statement of the circumstances in which the video recording of the entire interview was made which complies with paragraph (4) below.

(4)   The statement of the circumstances in which the video recording was made referred to in paragraphs (2)(e) and (3) above shall include the following information, except in so far as it is contained in the recording itself, namely —

(a)   the times at which the recording commenced and finished, including details of any interruptions,

(b)   the location at which the recording was made and the usual function of the premises,

(c)   the name, age and occupation of any person present at any point during the recording, the time for which he was present and his relationship (if any) to the witness and to the defendant,

(d)   a description of the equipment used, including the number of the cameras used and whether they were fixed or mobile, the number and location of microphones and the video format used and whether there were single or multiple recording facilities, and

(e)   the location of the mastertape if the video recording is a copy and details of when and by whom the copy was made.

Under the new regime of special measures a court may allow someone, such as a social worker, to sit with and support the child during the testimony. But the main engagement by social workers in the process will come during the earlier stage of getting the child's story. A Memorandum of Good Practice was published in 1992 by the Home Office, and, although not a legally binding document, it is viewed by the courts as an important guideline in deciding whether to accept the evidence from a recorded interview with a child:

The main purpose of this Memorandum is to help those making a video recording of an interview with a child witness *where it is intended that the result should be acceptable in criminal proceedings*. Such a recording can spare the child from having to recount *evidence* to the court in person and provide a highly valuable, early record of the child's account. If handled properly, the video recorded interview will be in the interests of the child and in the interests of justice.

...

A video recording that does not strictly comply with the Memorandum will not automatically be ruled inadmissible. On the contrary, it was Parliament's clear intention that such video recordings of children's testimony should be admitted unless, in the opinion of the judge, it would clearly be contrary to the interests of justice to do so. The Memorandum is therefore voluntary but should be followed whenever practicable to try to ensure that a video recording will be acceptable in a criminal court.

...

A major element in the 'Working Together' approach is joint interviewing by police and social workers. This will only be effective where police officers and social workers have appropriate training and are regularly employed in joint agency childcare investigations. The formation of specialist teams, adequately trained, within the respective agencies, will foster best practice. Many areas already have facilities for video recording interviews with children who are suspected victims of abuse. Some of the ground covered by this Memorandum will be familiar to those involved in joint investigations. However, the reforms to the law about child evidence and procedure made by the Criminal Justice Act 1991 introduce a new set of considerations and challenges for 'Working Together' teams. *Practitioners will need to prepare carefully in order to make the best of the reforms, both in the interests of the child and of justice.*

...

A *video recording* of an interview with a child may be admissible in the *Crown Court* or a *youth court* (but not *magistrates' courts*). In the case of youth courts, if no video equipment is available, proceedings may be held in a suitably equipped Crown Court Centre. Under the provisions made by the Criminal Justice Act 1991, *the child* will not be allowed to be *examined in chief* on any matter which, in the opinion of the court, has been dealt with in his or her recorded testimony. *Provided, then, that the recorded interview covers the matters which would otherwise be dealt with in chief, the recording takes the place of the first stage of the child's evidence.* That is the end of the function of the recording: *cross-examination* and re-examination, if proceedings get that far, are conducted by questioning the child 'live' at the trial. But the 1991 Act continues its protection of the child by barring the accused from cross-examining in person and by ensuring that *live television link* apparatus can be used so that the child is seen and heard in court on television monitors without ever having to appear in the court room. The use of such apparatus is at the discretion of the judge but permission is granted in almost all cases.

The use of a video recording for evidential purposes in this way is new and quite exceptional. *The questioning by the police officer or social worker, in effect, replaces examination of the child by an advocate in open court.*

The Criminal Justice Act 1991 gives the court power to reject the video recording, or any part of it, on the grounds that 'in the *interests of justice*' it ought not to be admitted. Since a key reason for making the recording is to spare the child, as far as possible, from giving his or her evidence at the trial, the interviewer must be aware of the circumstances in which a court may decide that it is not in the interests of justice to admit all or part of the recording.

...

Interview objectives

It is very important that those conducting interviews under this Memorandum have clear, agreed objectives which are consistent with the main purpose, which is to listen with an open mind to what the child has to say, if anything, about the alleged event. The interviews described in this Memorandum are not and should never be referred to as 'therapeutic interviews'. Nor should the term 'disclosure interview' ever be used to describe them. Although it may well be that the child does confirm details of what is suspected by others, and that the interview may serve a therapeutic or other objective, therapy is not the primary aim of these interviews.

Civil proceedings

One important reason for video recording interviews with children is to reduce the number of times that they are called upon to repeat their accounts during the investigation of the case. As noted earlier, this Memorandum concentrates on the evidential implications for criminal proceedings. At the time the interview is planned, it may not be known whether criminal proceedings will follow and, even if it is, civil proceedings concerned with the welfare of the child, and which would also benefit from a video recorded interview, may well come first. In such circumstances the interview might need to serve objectives which are additional to, and no less important than, those with which this Memorandum is primarily concerned. There is no reason why such objectives cannot be met within a single interview, provided it is properly prepared. The rules of evidence which apply to *civil proceedings* are generally less stringent, and so is the *burden of proof*. From those perspectives a video recording prepared according to the standards recommended in this Memorandum is likely to be suitable for civil cases. However, it may not be necessary or even appropriate to adopt the Memorandum's event-oriented approach when *only* particular civil proceedings, for example matrimonial proceedings, are contemplated.

...

Where to make a video recording

1.12   Careful consideration should be given to the selection of a suitable and sympathetic setting for the interview. The location should be private, quiet, reasonably comfortable and adequately equipped (but not over-equipped) for the interview. A private residence should not necessarily be ruled out (although the possible inhibiting effect of a home environment will need to be taken into account).

1.13   Video recorded interviews made at a facility designed for the purpose are likely to achieve the best quality results. In some areas, purpose-built interview suites are available at hospitals, family centres and similar places where children and other vulnerable witnesses such as rape victims may be interviewed. Such facilities will not always be readily accessible, especially from remote or rural areas, and the adverse effect and inconvenience to the child of a lengthy journey should be carefully considered against the possible lower quality of more readily available facilities.

1.14   The interview location should provide convenient and comfortable waiting areas and refreshment and lavatory facilities for the child and any accompanying adult. Some children will require wheelchair access to the interview room and other facilities, and those with a hearing disability may require an induction loop. (The needs of the disabled should be taken into account when setting up any new facilities.) If appropriate, toys and games of a neutral kind (genitalled dolls are unsuitable) should be made available in the waiting area.

...

What should be the duration of the interview and its pace?

2.17   It is important that the team should plan in advance the expected duration of the interview. It will help both the interviewer and the child to have a clear idea of how long the interview is likely to last. It is not possible to say how long an average interview will take. This will depend on the age of the child, his or her attention span and any other particular intellectual or physical limitations. As a rule of thumb, the team should plan the interview to last for less than an hour (excluding breaks — ...) unless they have good reason to believe that the child is mature and strong enough to cope with longer. It is recognised that there will, of course, be cases where the child has experienced abuse over long periods and that such accounts may take a considerable time to narrate. In addition, the child's actual state and needs during the course of the interview may suggest that the original planned duration needs to be revised. Nothing in the foregoing is intended to preclude a child from giving a lengthy account of relevant details but interviewers should always be mindful of the needs of the child and earlier considerations should not lightly be set aside, particularly if the inclination is to extend the interview.

2.18   The basic rule is that the interview should go at the pace of the child and not of the adult. *Those more used to interviewing adults will need to be especially careful not to go too fast for the child or to seem impatient.* On the other hand, *those with experience mainly in child care might go too slowly and, for example, tend to dwell in the 'rapport' phase* ... when the child is ready to proceed to the next phase of the interview. An accompanying person ... can usefully observe the effect of the interview on the child. He or she can discreetly guide the interviewer by use of a pre-arranged signal if it appears that the child is finding the experience oppressive or appears to be acceding to what he or she perceives to be the demands of the situation in order to bring it to an end.

...

Who should be the interviewer?

2.22   The investigating team should consider, in the light of the issues outlined in the preceding sections, who appears best qualified to conduct the interview and who, if anyone, should accompany that person. A special blend of skills is required to interview children effectively for evidential purposes.

2.23   The interviewer should be a person who has, or is likely to be able to establish, rapport with the child, who understands how to communicate effectively with him or her, including in sometimes disturbed periods, and who also has a proper grasp both of the basic rules of evidence and the elements of criminal offences. This is a formidable job specification and some compromise will probably be necessary. A rigid definition of the roles of police and social service professionals is not likely to be possible or desirable and a high degree of flexibility and responsiveness within the joint investigating team is required in the interests of an effective interview.

2.24   Exceptionally, it may be in the interests of the child to be interviewed by an adult in whom he or she has already put confidence but who is not a member of the investigating team. Provided that such a person is not a party to the proceedings, is prepared to co-operate with appropriately trained interviewers and can accept adequate briefing this possibility should not be precluded.

2.25   The interviewer should also be prepared to testify about the interview in court if called upon to do so. He or she, or any person connected with the interview, may be questioned about the conduct of the interview and events surrounding it. *Careful notes should therefore be kept.* A statement dealing with the preparation and conduct of the interview should be made whilst the events are still fresh in the interviewer's mind.

...

Who else should be present during the interview?

2.27   Limiting the number of people present at the interview should lessen the possibility of the child feeling overwhelmed by the situation and uncomfortable about revealing information. *A suspected offender should never be present.* The presence of other people may also distract or put pressure upon the child. The court, in considering whether to admit the recording, may wish to be assured that the witness was not prompted or discouraged during the interview, and to provide a comprehensive record of the words and gestures of more than two persons can be technically demanding.... However, such considerations may be outweighed by the benefit of having a supportive accompanying adult available to comfort and reassure a very young or distressed child, particularly if the child requests it. In such cases the accompanying adult will need to be clear that he or she must take no part in the interview.

...

Does the child need to agree to be video recorded?

2.29   Where a child is mature enough to understand the concept, he or she should be given an explanation of the purpose of the video recording so that the child is fully informed to a level appropriate to his or her age and understanding and freely consents to the interview session and the video recording. It should be explained that the video recording may be shown to the court instead of the child giving his or her account directly. The child should be advised that, whether a video recording is made or not, he or she may be required to attend court to answer questions directly. *Written consent to be video recorded is not necessary* but it is unlikely to be practicable or desirable to video record an interview with a reluctant or distressed child.

Conducting the interview — the basic approach

...

Phase one — rapport

3.4   The main aim of the first phase of the interview is to build up a rapport between the interviewer and the child in which the child is helped to relax and feel as comfortable as possible in the interview situation. However, this phase serves a number of important additional functions. If used correctly, it should supplement the interviewer's knowledge about the child's social, emotional and cognitive development, and particularly about his or her communication skills and degree of understanding (for example, the number of words used by the child in sentences might cause the interviewer to revise an earlier judgement about the most suitable length of questions). The rapport phase can also indicate a need to review an initial decision about which of two possible interviewers should take the lead. *A rapport phase, however brief, should not be omitted even if the child has had significant previous contact with the interviewer.*

3.5   The alleged offence and related topics should *not* be referred to during the rapport phase. Typically, the child is led into free discussion of non-related events in his or her life, such as school, play group, the journey to the interview, or favourite television programmes. The rapport phase should be tailored to the needs and circumstances of the individual child. With younger children a rapport phase may involve some play with toys, drawing or colouring to help the child relax and or to interact with the interviewer. (Such play should *not* be used during this phase to gather information relevant to the alleged offence.)

...

3.10   Before the child is invited to volunteer information about the alleged offences, the interviewer should consider initiating a short discussion in which he or she can *convey to the child the need to speak the truth and the acceptability of saying 'I don't know' or 'I don't understand'.* There is no legal requirement to administer the oath or admonish the child but since the video recording may be used in court as the child's evidence, it will be helpful for the court to know that the child was made aware of the need to tell the truth. The interviewer should use terms suitable to the child's age, understanding and emotional condition. Some child witnesses may fear that their truthful accounts will not be believed. An insensitive approach could confirm that fear. Explaining to the child the need to tell the truth later in the interview is not recommended because it might risk the child concluding that the interviewer has not believed what he or she has said so far about the event.

3.11   One form of words would be *'Please tell [us] all you can remember. Don't make any thing up or leave anything out. This is very important'.* Or the interviewer could complete an age-appropriate discussion with the child of what is true and false by saying something like: *'You can tell me any thing you want. I don't want you to feel you need hold anything back. All that matters is that you don't make anything up or leave anything out.'*

Phase two — free narrative account

3.12   Having asked the child to speak truthfully and re-established rapport, if necessary, the child should then be encouraged to provide *in his or her own words* and at his or her own pace an account of the relevant event(s). This is the heart of the interview and the interviewer's role is to act as a facilitator, not an interrogator. Only the most general, open-ended questions should be asked in this phase, for example: '*Why do you think we are here today?*'; '*Is there anything that you would like to tell me?*' If the child responds in a positive way to such questions then the interviewer can encourage the child to give a free narrative account of events. Every effort must be made to obtain information from the child which is spontaneous and free from the interviewer's influence.

...

Phase three — questioning

(A) *Open-ended questions*
3.17   The first stage of Phase Three involves open-ended questions which ask the child to provide more information but in a way that does not lead the child or put him or her under pressure. However, as with all questions used in the interview, *it should always be clear to the child that to reply 'I can't remember' or 'I don't know' is perfectly acceptable*. The child should also be encouraged to say if he or she does not understand a question.

...

3.20   For a child whose free narrative account provided somewhat more relevant information, the questions could be more focused but should still be open-ended, for example 'Could you please tell me more about the man in the park who frightened you?' (assuming that *the child* has mentioned a frightening man in the park). If the child becomes distressed when questioned even in this non-leading way, the interviewer should move away from the subject and consider reverting to an earlier phase of the interview (for example, re-establish through rapport that the child is at ease). Such shifting away from and then back to a topic the child finds difficult may be required several times in an interview.

...

3.22   Some questions beginning with 'why' may be interpreted by children as attributing blame or guilt to them. Repeating a question soon after a child has answered should also be avoided since this may be interpreted by children as a criticism of their original response. Research shows that persistent repetition of a question may lead a child to give an answer he or she believes the interviewer wants to hear.
3.23   It is also important to avoid interrupting the child. If, for example, the child has used obscure words for parts of the body, or for any other object/event/person, this should not normally be followed up immediately by a direct question to clarify meaning. The interviewer should carefully note the point and seek a suitable opportunity for clarification later in the interview.

(B) *Specific yet non-leading questions*
3.24   Before moving on to the next stage the interviewer should again consider whether it is in the interests of the child to do so. This stage allows for extension and clarification of previously provided information both from the free narrative and subsequent phase. It also provides an opportunity for the child who has said very little in connection with the purpose of the interview to be reminded of the focus of the interview without the child being asked leading questions.
3.25   Adults sometimes wrongly suppose that children, even young ones, must know what is relevant. Being helped to understand what is relevant helps a witness to focus his or her account and specific yet non-leading questions should allow the interviewer to guide the witness in an evidentially sound manner. During this stage questions should not be leading to the extent that the question implies the answer although in some cases it may be inevitable that questions will

refer to disputed facts. *However, during this stage questions which require a 'yes' or 'no' answer, or ones which allow only one of two possible responses, should not be asked.*

3.26 For example, for a child who has already provided information that a man in the park frightened her and that he was wearing a scarf, a specific yet non-leading question could be 'What colour was the man's scarf?' (If the child responds with a colour and the interviewer has some reason to doubt that the child understands what it means, the interviewer could note the point and later in the interview it could be established that the child does, indeed, know what the response, for example, 'lilac', means.)

...

(C)   *Closed questions*
3.30 If specific but non-leading questions are unproductive, questions might be attempted that give the child a limited number of alternative responses. For example 'Was the man's scarf you mentioned blue or yellow, or another colour, or can't you remember?'.

...

(D)   *Leading questions*
3.33 Put simply, a leading question is one which implies the answer or assumes facts which are likely to be in dispute. Leading questions would not normally be allowed if the child were giving his or her evidence in chief live during criminal proceedings and it is to be expected that such questioning in a video recorded interview would be excluded by the court. The greatest care must therefore be taken when questioning the child about central matters which are likely to be disputed.

3.34 In addition to the legal objections, psychological research indicates strongly that interviewees' responses to leading questions tend to be determined by the manner of questioning rather than valid recall. It seems likely that young children in particular may be more willing to respond to 'yes/no' questions with a 'yes' response. If, therefore, questions permitting only a 'yes' or 'no' response are asked in this phase, these should be phrased so that those on the same issue sometimes seek a 'yes' response and sometimes a 'no' response.

Phase four — closing the interview
3.36 Every interview should have a closing phase conducted in the interests of the child. It has already been emphasised that it may be appropriate to terminate an interview before sufficient information has been obtained from the child for criminal proceedings. In such circumstances, the child should not be made to feel that he or she has failed, or disappointed the interviewer. The interviewer should be careful to ensure that all interviews end appropriately. Every effort should be made to ensure that the child is not distressed but is in a positive frame of mind.

3.37 During this phase the interviewer may need to check with the child that he or she (the interviewer) has correctly understood the important parts, if any, of the child's account. If this is considered necessary, care should be taken not to convey disbelief. Any recapping should use the child's own language, *not* a summary provided by the interviewer in adult language (which could contain errors but with which the child may nevertheless agree).

Conducting the interview — the legal constraints

3.46 As explained in the Introduction to this Memorandum, the video recorded interview is intended to take the place of the first stage of the child's evidence in court. The video recording will count as evidence of any fact stated by the child of which he or she could have given evidence in court. This means that, in principle, the rules which govern procedure in court may be applied to the video recorded interview.

3.47 There are rules which can render certain matters 'inadmissible' irrespective of their truth, so that they cannot form part of the case. A criminal court has no power to depart from such rules. However there are also conventions of the court which the court may relax where the need arises. The most obvious example of such a convention is the avoidance of leading questions.

3.48   The court will not expect video recorded interviews with children exactly to mimic examination of a witness by counsel in court. But rules of evidence have been created in order to ensure a fair trial for the accused, and they cannot be ignored. Early consultation with the Crown Prosecution Service should assist in identifying potential areas of difficulty.

3.49   It is therefore good practice to conduct an interview as far as possible in accordance with the rules which would apply in court. *Interviewers who ignore these rules are likely to produce video recordings which are unacceptable to a criminal court.* They will thus fail to spare the child from having to give the first stage of his or her evidence in person.

3.50   This Part of the Memorandum explains the rationale behind those rules most likely to affect a video recorded interview — *leading questions, previous statements showing consistency or truth, statements about the bad character of the accused.* As with most rules there are circumstances in which they need not be applied. This is easier to determine when a child is being questioned in court and counsel can agree at the time with the judge what is acceptable. The interviewer has no such opportunity and should therefore err on the side of caution but, as this Part goes on to describe, there are circumstances when the rules can properly be disregarded.

Leading questions

3.51   It is not generally permissible to put leading questions to a witness. A leading question is one which either suggests the required answer, or which is based on an assumption of facts which have yet to be proved. Thus 'Daddy hurt you, didn't he?' is an example of the first type of leading question, and 'When did you first tell anyone about what Daddy did?', put to a child who has not yet alleged that Daddy did anything, is an example of the second type.

3.52   Where a leading question is improperly put to a witness in court, the answer is not inadmissible but may be accorded little or no weight because of the manner in which it was obtained. When witnesses testify live in court a leading question can be objected to before a witness replies. The party not tendering the video evidence has no such opportunity and so may ask for a part of the video recording to be edited out.

3.53   However there are circumstances where leading questions are permissible:

(a)   A witness is often led into his or her testimony by being asked to confirm his or her name and address, or some other introductory matter because these *matters are unlikely to be in dispute.* More central issues may also be the subject of leading questions if there is no dispute about them. For example, where it is common ground that a person, X, has been killed at a particular time, it is not 'leading' to ask a witness 'What were you doing when X was killed?' However, at the interview stage it may not be known what facts will be in dispute at the trial and so it will be safer to assume that most matters are still in dispute.

(b)   The courts also accept that in cases other than the above it is *impractical to ban leading questions.* This may be because the subject-matter of the question is such that it cannot be put to the witness without leading, as for example when the witness is to be asked to identify the person who hurt him or her. Or it may be because the witness does not understand what he or she is expected to tell the court without some prompting, as in the case of a young child or a child with a learning difficulty.

3.54   An interviewer who follows the provisions of this Memorandum as to the conduct of an interview (see Part 3A) will avoid leading questions. As the courts become more aware of the difficulties of obtaining evidence from witnesses who are very young or who have a learning difficulty, and of counteracting the pressures on child witnesses to keep silent, a sympathetic attitude may be taken towards *necessary* leading questions. A leading question which succeeds in prompting a child into providing information spontaneously beyond that led by the question will normally be acceptable. However, *unless there is absolutely no alternative*, the interviewer should never be the first to suggest to the child that a particular offence was committed, or that a particular person was responsible. Once this step has been taken it will be extremely difficult to counter the argument that the interviewer put the idea into the child's head and that the child's account is therefore false.

3.55   If leading questions are judged by the court to have been improperly used during the interview it may well be decided not to show the whole or that part of the recording to the court, so that the child's answers will be lost. Alternatively the whole interview may be played, leaving the judge to comment to the jury, where appropriate, on the weight to be given to that part of the evidence which was led. Neither outcome is desirable, and both can be avoided if interviewers keep off leading questions.

Previous statements

3.56   A witness in court is likely to be prevented by the court from giving evidence of what he or she has previously said or what was said to him or her by another person. If allowed in evidence, previous statements might have two functions. First, in the case of the witness's own statement, the court might be asked to take account of the fact that the witness has consistently said the same thing in deciding whether he or she is to be trusted. Secondly, in the case both of the witness's own statements and of statements made to him or her by others, the court might be asked to take the further step of deciding that what was said out of court was true. In a criminal trial, both functions are frowned upon: the first because, in law, it says little for the reliability of a witness to show that he or she has been consistent, and the second because courts are reluctant to accept statements as true unless made in court and subject to the test of cross-examination.

Previous statements showing consistency

3.57   Although consistency adds little to the credibility of the witness, it will always be proper for the interviewer to ask the child if he or she has told anyone about the alleged incident(s), who he or she told, when he or she told them, and why. But the interview must not ask the child *details* of what was said except in certain circumstances. These circumstances are as follows:

(a)   when a child has *voluntarily given details of an alleged sexual offence soon after that offence took place*. A complaint of buggery made by a boy six months after the incident upon being forcefully questioned by his mother would not be admissible, but the details of a spontaneous allegation of buggery made by the boy on the day of the incident could be mentioned.

(b)   when a child has previously made a *positive identification of the accused*. Identification may be formal (in the course of an identification parade) or informal, for example where a child points out the accused to a teacher and says 'This man tried to push me into his car.' Where such a prior identification has been made, it may be referred to in the video recorded interview.

The only case which may give rise to difficulty is where there is some doubt as to the fairness of the identification. If, for example, a child tells her father that she has just been sexually assaulted by a man in a leather jacket, and the father apprehends the first leather-clad man that he sees and demands 'Is this him?', a court might be understandably reluctant to admit the child's positive answer as a positive identification and it should not therefore be mentioned in the video recorded interview. The interviewer must therefore be aware of the circumstances of any identification made by the child before the interview.

Previous statements showing truth

3.58   The technical name for an out-of-court statement which is used in court to prove that what was said is true is '*hearsay*'. The general rule is that hearsay is inadmissible in a criminal trial. In one famous case a little girl who was adjudged too young to give evidence told her mother that she had been indecently assaulted by a 'coloured boy'. A white man was charged but he could not call the mother to give evidence of what the child had said because the child's statement had been made out of court and was hearsay. The same result would have followed if the child had said that her attacker was white and the prosecution had wished to refer to her statement.

3.59   Words (and conduct e.g. nodding in agreement) are only hearsay if used to prove their truth. There may be other reasons for proving that words were spoken in which case the hearsay rule is not broken. For example a witnesses' report of a child's statement 'Dad taught me to fuck' would be admissible to demonstrate a child's use of age-inappropriate language but inadmissible as evidence that the child's father had had intercourse with her.

3.60   As with most other rules of evidence, the hearsay rule is not absolute. The use of a video recording of an interview with a child as part of the child's evidence is itself an example of a statutory exception to the rule. Without a detailed appreciation of the scope of the exceptions it will be difficult for an interviewer to gauge the chances of a hearsay statement being regarded as admissible in court and it is best to aim to avoid the inclusion of previous statements in the interview so far as possible. There are a couple of rules of thumb which should assist:

(a)   Any statements made by the child about the alleged offence prior to the interview are likely to be hearsay. Therefore, subject to the advice in paragraph 3.57, such statements should not be deliberately elicited from the child during a video recorded interview. For example a child should not be asked to relate any conversations he or she may have had concerning the offence.

If the child spontaneously begins an account of what has been said to him or her the interviewer may decide that it is best not to interrupt. If so it should be remembered that this section of the tape is likely to be edited so it will be necessary to go over any relevant non-hearsay information gleaned at this point at a later stage of the interview.

(b)   The video recording should capture the child's responses directly as the interviewer's description of the child's response is itself hearsay. For example, if a child is asked where she was touched by an abuser and in response she points to her genitals, that action should be captured by the camera. It will not be enough for the interviewer to say 'She is pointing to her genitals' as this is a statement of the interviewer, not the child. Once this is understood it should be relatively easy to ensure that the relevant evidence comes from the child.

Character of the accused

3.61   An important rule of evidence concerns the previous bad character of the accused. Under this rule it is not generally permissible for the prosecution to bring evidence of the accused's bad record or reputation, or of other misconduct in which he or she has been involved, in order simply to show the court that he or she is a bad person who is likely to do wrong. For example, a jury trying a man for sexual offences against a child is likely to be kept in ignorance of his criminal record for such offences or of other charges of a similar nature which may have been made against him. The interviewer must be very careful to avoid mention of such matters and should try to steer the child away from any mention of such discreditable facts.

3.62   The rule against admitting evidence showing the accused's bad character is, like the hearsay rule, subject to exception. Evidence of one offence may be admissible in the case of another offence by reason of the close connection or similarity between them. For example, where two or more children claim to have been indecently assaulted by the same person the evidence of one child is sometimes used to support the allegations of the other. This is only permissible where the evidence goes beyond showing that the accused is a 'bad person likely to do wrong' and independently suggests that he is the person who committed the offence or offences in question. In other words, the probative value of the evidence must outweigh its prejudicial effect.

3.63 In many cases the line between admissibility and inadmissibility is a difficult one to draw. Complex legal considerations are involved. All that can be done before the trial is to estimate the chances that the court will be prepared, say, to hear that a school-teacher has been accused of buggery by four of his pupils, or a father of incest by two daughters. This presents no difficulty for the interviewer if the evidence of one child is quite separate from that of another. But it may be that the victim of one offence claims to have witnessed the occurrence of another offence against a different victim. In such cases it might be advisable, following consultation with the Crown Prosecution Service, to record separately the child's account of (i) offences allegedly committed against him or her, and (ii) what he or she knows about offences involving other victims.

Court's discretion to exclude evidence

3.64 A court trying a criminal case has the power to exclude evidence tendered on behalf of the prosecution, even though the evidence complies with the strict rules of admissibility. Under section 78 of the Police and Criminal Evidence Act 1984, the court may exclude evidence on the grounds that, because of the way in which it was obtained or for any other reason, the admission of the evidence would have such an adverse effect on the fairness of the proceedings that the court ought not to admit it. Courts may also exercise a common law power (that is, one supported by previous decisions of the courts) to exclude evidence the prejudicial effect of which outweighs its probative value. The definition of these powers is deliberately broad in order to preserve their flexibility. Interviewers can guard against their exercise by following the provisions of this Memorandum and by taking any other steps which appear to them to be necessary to ensure that no unfairness ensues from their procedures.

The Home Office has promised a new Memorandum to coincide with the implementation of the special measures legislation under the YCJEA. Although these came into force in July 2002 the regulations and guidance promised are unavailable.

The Memorandum has been criticised in many writings. Here is one example, from a book devoted to the subject: *Perspectives on the Memorandum: policy, practice, and research in investigative interviewing* (ed. Helen Westcott and Jocelyn Jones. Aldershot: Ashgate Pub. Co., 1997). In a chapter called 'The Memorandum: Quest for the impossible' Sarah Nelson writes:

When I first read the *Memorandum of Good Practice on Video Recorded Interviews with Child Witnesses for Criminal Proceedings* (Home Office, 1992), followed by the research evaluation of videotaping children's evidence (Davies et al., 1995) I found myself overwhelmed by powerful emotions about the *Memorandum*: frustration, anger, incredulity, a sense of injustice and futility, of wasted time and effort and resources. These were surprising reactions to a reasoned, meticulous, often sensible, well-intentioned official document by thoughtful and caring people. They seemed intemperate and unfair. But they have also, I suspect, afflicted other childcentred workers in sexual abuse, who feel at these times that the world of reason and reality is stood upon its head.

We react thus not because there is some special failing about the *Memorandum*, but because it reveals yet again an obsession with the evidence of children which repeatedly produces deeply flawed results. Our shelves are laden with well-funded research studies, evaluations, Law Commission reports, proposals for change and invitations to the latest conference. Inquiries costing millions of pounds, such as Lord Clyde's meticulous Report on Orkney (1992), make numerous recommendations about the interviewing of children, but none in 363 pages about the possible need to pursue remaining concerns about those particular, real children.

Here, we have a *Memorandum* about just one aspect of children's treatment in particular cases; not in both civil and criminal courts, but only in the latter; not as a potential substitute for all court examination, not for the vital cross-examination, but simply for the evidence-in-chief. On that one part of the Criminal Justice Act 1991 we have whole books, like this one; we have detailed and continuing evaluations, conferences and seminars.

In contrast, we search extremely hard to find studies and reports on the reliability of evidence given by suspected adult abusers, or proposals on how we might devise tests and approaches which better discerned truth from falsehood, fact from fantasy. Fantasising is, of course, a weakness of children, not of paedophiles. Adults need no competency test to ensure they know the difference between truth and lies. Yet strangely, almost every week we see uncovered abuses which continued for years or decades, where respectable adults had assured us nothing was going on, and stigmatised children protested their sufferings in vain.

Prospective interviewers and other child protection staff must digest and remember 52 pages of the *Memorandum of Good Practice* on one segment of their conduct, in pursuit of a goal which, Davies et al. (1995) found, made no significant difference to the outcome of criminal trials.

Extraordinary or contradictory demands are made upon those adults whose job it is to listen to the voices of children. Subsection 2.3 of this *Memorandum* informs interviewers that before even questioning the child, they must assess that child's cognitive, linguistic, emotional, social, sexual, physical and other development; their concept of time and ideas about trust; their knowledge of sexuality, their cultural background, disabilities and articulacy, and their present state of mind. Professional help in doing this may be valuable (it certainly would be!) but the 'implications for delay in consulting other experts should be carefully weighed' (p. 9).

During the interview they should not go too fast, and they should not go too slowly. 'There will, of course, be cases where the child has experienced abuse over long periods and such accounts may take a considerable time to narrate' (Subsection 3.11, p. 17.) It is not the length of abuse history which takes a child time: it is how able they feel to speak of it at all. Questioners must explain the reason for the interview during the rapport stage — except that they should not refer to the alleged offence nor mention the substance of any previous disclosure. They should also make the impossible and absurd request: 'don't leave anything out'.

After stepping through these and numerous other hoops in the 52 pages with the children, they discover a mere fraction of these videotaped interviews ever reach court. Astonishingly, more than 14,012 were conducted by police between October 1992 and June 1993 alone (Association of Chief Police Officers, 1993); what is the total today? Finally, adults and children involved find themselves in a court forum. A forum where neither judges, prosecutors nor defence barristers have any compulsory training in interviewing children, where age-inappropriate language is frequently used, where intimidatory tactics have been noted, where young people with special needs are often disgracefully unprotected, and where the adversarial system itself relies crucially on forms of cross-examination which confuse and discredit prosecution witnesses. ('Only' [sic] 34 per cent of children in the Davies study were rated as being 'very unhappy' during cross-examination.) It is the very job of the good defence counsel to discredit such evidence.

It is not only unjust and ineffective, it borders on the farcical that our society makes these incredible demands on children and their interviewers in order to achieve 'court-reliable' evidence, while leaving almost untouched the words and behaviour of the most powerful, decisive actors in those courts. This is why we all risk collusion by accepting these lists of rules, by going along politely with them, apologising continually for our mistakes and trying ever harder to rectify them. How quickly would the legal system change, in contrast, if social workers, police, child psychiatrists and others said: 'Could you explain why there is one rule for us, and another for you? We will follow these innumerable Memoranda, we will bow to these innumerable criticisms, just as soon as you do likewise.'

How important to the conduct and outcome of trials are endless efforts to achieve the magic 'court-reliable interview', how important in contrast is the latitude given in cross-examination, or the fact that in the Davies study 97 per cent of judges, 82 per cent of prosecutors and 88 per cent of defence barristers were male (Davies et al., 1995)? How many resources are put into serious attempts to outlaw certain techniques in cross-examination, or to diversify the sex, age, race and class backgrounds of key actors in child abuse trials — in comparison with the resources poured into 'the problem' of children's evidence?

...

This in itself immediately introduces a major problem. Once you start conducting interviews according to the way children actually are, you undermine the basic assumptions on which your practice is based .... When times and dates are so important in court, what if many children cannot deliver them? If the interview room setting and format (preferably under one hour) is actually the least likely setting and timescale within which traumatised children will reveal painful secret truths, does this foundation stone need to be discarded? If they are most likely to reveal truths gradually over months, to trusted adults who are not considered qualified interviewers, in places like bedrooms, beaches or buses which are not considered reliable, can the systems we have established to elicit truth be remotely on the right track? Are very different, highly imaginative techniques like Madge Bray's far more likely to elicit the truth (Bray, 1991)? And if many sexually molested children have already been terrified by repeated pornographic videotaping, is the very use of this equipment secondary abuse?

How far can we reform our current guidance on children's evidence, how far do we instead need to shift radically our whole approach and focus in sexual abuse cases? I believe we need to do the latter, and that the *Memorandum* is another example of the fact that millions of pounds, countless staff hours of training, endless wasted effort, and profound stress inflicted on children has been spent in pursuit of an unattainable goal.

That goal is to do adults' work for them: to achieve 'reliable', unassailable evidence from teenagers, children and even toddlers, which will by itself identify genuine sex abusers and have them convicted in court, or at least ensure the children are protected. Yet the ceaseless quest continues, despite case after publicised case collapsing (especially in organised abuse) as children retract their evidence or find their testimonies judged to be flawed. Why have such a small proportion of videotaped interviews actually been used in criminal courts, why at so many different stages of the process has the option not been taken? There will be several reasons, but a central one is likely to be a failure of perceived credibility: a credibility, that is, in the eyes of adults.

. ...

Why is the quest for ultra-reliable children's evidence unattainable and unethical? I have already mentioned that the 'court-reliable' interview setting may be the most unnatural one in which children can reveal painful truths. Secondly, the way small children (or some learning-disabled children) talk, assemble thoughts, behave, or paint and draw their messages will always remain incomprehensible to many adults. Young children cannot change their natural development for our convenience.

Thirdly, it is simply impossible clearly to disentangle therapy from investigation work, as the best practitioners know. It is immoral and unsustainable to deny distressed and damaged children the therapy and support they urgently need in case this may 'contaminate' their court evidence. It makes a mockery of all this rhetoric in official guidance about the primacy of children's interests and well-being.

...

To say that children's evidence must receive a much lower priority in sexual abuse is not the same as saying children do not deserve every effort to make the presentation of their evidence possible, and as free of stress, trauma and delay as it can be.

It is important to make this point, especially since an influential lobby still believes giving evidence is all so terrible for children that it is better not to put them through it at all. This simply means countless cases collapse or never reach court. That does not assist abused children, many of whom want and need to have their experience validated through the court process. In any case children's rights and dignity must be respected and given greater priority. We cannot pontificate about the need to listen to children unless we practise what we preach. Therefore it is important for many professions to keep collaborating, to explore all possible means of reducing stress and intimidation in the presentation of their evidence. That includes looking very seriously at current techniques of cross-examination and at whether they could and should be replaced, for instance by studying the experience and practice of other countries...

...

Children are also subject to a battery of assumptions. We would never go to such lengths or set up such elaborate procedures for improving their 'reliability' if we did not believe there was a significant problem in the first place about children being untruthful or fantasising. There is a huge disparity between the problem which gains all the attention — which, most research suggests, is small and manageable (Jones and McGraw, 1987) — and the problem of children not being believed when they speak the truth. As I noted, hardly a week passes without some publicised case where children have been abused in a school or residential home for years or decades, where their accounts were not believed. There *is* an enormous problem about adults telling lies, yet we never seem to learn this message from repeated proof of that.

References

Association of Chief Police Officers (1993), *Survey of the use of videotaped interviews with child witnesses by police forces in England and Wales*, Cheltenham: Gloucester Constabulary.

Bray, M, and Boyle, S. (1991), *Poppies on the Rubbish Heap: Sexual Abuse, the Child's Voice*, Edinburgh: Canongate.

Clyde, Lord (1992), *The Report of the Inquiry into the Removal of Children from Orkney in February 1991*, Edinburgh: HMSO.

Davies, G., Wilson, C., Mitchell, M. and Milsom, J. (1995), *Videotaping Children's Evidence: An Evaluation*, Leicester: University of Leicester.

Home Office and Department of Health (1992), *Memorandum of Good Practice on Video Recorded Interviews with Child Witnesses for Criminal Proceedings*, London: HMSO.

Jones, D. and McGraw, J.M. (1987), 'Reliable and fictitious accounts of sexual abuse to children', *Journal of Interpersonal Violence*, 2, 27.

There has been much case law on admissibility of such video recorded evidence from children. In every case the decision will be at the discretion of the court. Reference to further cases can be found in Brayne Martin and Carr, Chapter 8. We reproduce extracts here from just two cases. They concern the evidence of an eight and a six year old in a case of indecent assault. The sections of the Criminal Justice Act 1988 referred to are now replaced by the Youth Justice and Criminal Evidence Act, which we have reproduced, but the relevant parts are not different. The first case is *G* v *Director of Public Prosecutions* [1997] 2 FLR 810:

Phillips LJ: The appellant, G, is now 17. On 12 April 1995, when he was 15, he was convicted of two offences of indecent assault, committed in August 1994, when he was 14, by the Scarborough stipendiary magistrate. He was sentenced to a 2-year supervision order. The evidence adduced against him included that of two children, the complainant, N, who was 6 years old at the time of the offences and at the trial, and of her brother, D, who was 8 years old at the time of offences and at trial. Their evidence-in-chief consisted of video interviews.

...

Four questions are raised by the case stated. I propose to deal with each in turn, summarising any relevant facts in the case stated and the conclusion of the court in relation to that question as I do so.

(1)   Were we correct in deciding that the test for competence was as set out by Auld J in R v Hampshire?

[We have not reproduced the part of the judgment which deals with whether a young child's evidence can be received at all. This was explored in *DPP* v *M* above.]

(2)   Were we entitled, in the exercise of our discretion, to decline to hear expert evidence on the question of competence?

The court dealt with the question of the competence of the two child witnesses as follows:

'Intelligible testimony is evidence that is capable of being understood. The evidence is on video-tape. We all looked at the video-tape and independently came to the conclusion that the children were able to give intelligible evidence. Nothing said in the reports or heard today has changed our view and subject to other matters the evidence will be admitted.'

Mr Cook had urged that the court should allow him to call expert evidence in relation to competence. The court refused to do so. Mr Cook before us has contended that this refusal was unreasonable applying the *Wednesbury* test. The background to this issue is as follows. Before the hearing before the magistrate, the prosecution and the defence arranged for a joint interview to be held of each child witness by two child psychiatrists, one instructed by the prosecution and one by the defence. 'Vignettes' were put to the children and they were asked questions about them. The object of this exercise was to discover whether the children were competent to give evidence. The prosecution expert concluded that both were. The defence expert concluded that D was but that N was not. Evidence from these psychiatrists was adduced before the magistrate who also had been asked to rule on the competence of the child witnesses.

In my judgment this exercise was misconceived, inappropriate and a complete waste of, no doubt, considerable money. The test of whether a child is capable of giving intelligible evidence does not require any input from an expert. It is a simple test well within the capacity of a judge or magistrate. Far from being *Wednesbury* unreasonable in refusing to hear expert evidence in relation to the competence of the child witnesses, the court's response to that invitation was the only proper one. The answer to the second question is an emphatic 'yes'.

(3)   Having read the report of Dr Shepherd and having been told that the report would stand as his evidence-in-chief, were we entitled, in the exercise of our discretion, to decline to hear expert evidence from him as to whether we should admit the videotaped interviews?

Section 32A(3)(c) of the Criminal Justice Act 1988 provides that the court shall not admit video-tapes of interviews if:

'the court is of the opinion, having regard to all the circumstances of the case, that in the interests of justice the recording ought not to be admitted.'

This test can differ little in practice from that under s. 78(1) of the Police and Criminal Evidence Act whereby evidence is excluded if:

'... the admission of the evidence would have such an adverse effect on the fairness of the proceedings that the court ought not to admit it.'

An important factor in deciding whether or not to admit video recordings of interviews must be the degree of likelihood that the evidence is reliable. It is to that question that the evidence of Dr Shepherd goes. Dr Shepherd is a highly qualified chartered forensic psychologist.

His report runs to 115 pages, and it is not light reading. His task was to 'analyse the disclosures' of the two child witnesses, and in particular their video interviews. As I understand it, the intention was that his evidence would be used both to challenge the admissibility of the video evidence and, should that challenge be unsuccessful, to attack the weight that should be accorded to the children's evidence.

The Cleveland Inquiry, conducted by Dame Elizabeth Butler-Sloss, demonstrated the need for meticulous care and for expertise in interviewing young children. Dame Elizabeth laid down guidelines for this exercise in her report, and these have been followed by the Home Office and Department of Health Memorandum of Good Practice for those preparing video-recorded interviews for criminal proceedings. Where the guidelines and the memorandum have not been followed, evidence of young children can be dangerously suspect. This is a legitimate area for expert evidence, although this will be of much greater value to a jury with no knowledge of this topic than to a magistrate or judge who may have great experience of it. The proper boundaries of expert evidence in this field were considered by the Court of Appeal in *R v Davies and Others* (unreported) 3 November 1995. The following extract from the judgment of Swinton Thomas LJ is particularly material:

'It is fundamental that experts must not usurp the function of the jury in a criminal trial. Save in particular circumstances, it is the task of the jury to make judgments on the questions of reliability and truthfulness. Particular circumstances arise when there are characteristics of a medical nature in the makeup of the witness, such as mental illness, which would not be known to the jury without expert assistance. Those circumstances do not arise in the case of ordinary children who are not suffering from any abnormality. It may well be open to parties in a particular case to call general expert evidence in relation to the Cleveland guidelines and, for example, to tell the judge or a jury that over-interviewing as a matter of generality has been shown by expert research to have a much more adverse effect on children than on adults but the witness cannot express an opinion whether a particular child witness is a reliable or truthful witness. That is precisely the province of the jury in a criminal case, or the judge when considering the admissibility of evidence under s. 78 of the Police and Criminal Evidence Act.'

The Report of Dr Shepherd encroaches far beyond the boundaries mapped out by the Lord Justice. In meticulous detail, applying a graphic technique called THEMA (Thematic Emergence of Anomaly), he traces the process which leads the children's evidence to become what he describes as 'comprehensive exercises in confabulation'. It may be that the time will come when this technique is recognised as a better means for evaluating truth and determining guilt or innocence than trial by judge and jury, or magistrate, for Dr Shepherd almost wholly usurps that function of the court, but that time is not yet come. The court commented on Dr Shepherd's report as follows:

'I have no doubt that there are circumstances where expert evidence can deal with this problem although it is unusual. I have dealt with many cases dealing with matters advanced by Dr Shepherd and they have always been advanced by counsel. In this case we are dealing with perfectly normal children and we feel that we do not require help from Dr Shepherd in dealing with these matters. When dealing with young children it is better for the court to determine these by listening to the children and forming our own views. None of us has derived any assistance from reading this report, not to say that the observations are bad, some are good, some indifferent and some bad. The good points we could have seen for ourselves without his assistance. This is a report that has cost a lot of money at public expense. The Court of Appeal in *Middleton* commented on the proliferation of expert evidence. This report oversteps the boundaries of what is or is not expert evidence and we do not admit it.'

In my judgment the decision of the court not to receive evidence from Dr Shepherd in relation to the admissibility of the video evidence was one which was properly made within the scope of the court's discretion. The answer to the third question is 'yes'.

(4) Were we entitled, in the exercise of our discretion, to treat the breaches of the Memorandum of Good Practice in this case as going to weight rather than admissibility?

The case stated includes six pages of detailed allegations made by Mr Cook of departures from the Memorandum of Good Practice. As to these, Mr Cook submittted to us that, whilst minor breaches of the memorandum may be ignored, substantial and significant breaches, particularly of those sections relating to the collection of evidence, are likely to lead to unreliable evidence and injustice if admitted. As in this case such breaches had occurred, it was unreasonable, applying the *Wednesbury* test, for the court to have admitted the video evidence.

The decision of the court in relation to this issue appears from this passage of the case stated: 'Mr Cook has fully and very properly taken us through complaints on behalf of the appellant of breaches of the Memorandum of Good Practice. We are satisfied that the Memorandum is an important document and one to which we should take regard. There may be circumstances when breaches are so significant that they are sufficient to exclude. That the interview did not adhere to the memorandum is clear and is admitted by the Crown. In particular the interviewer did not make clear to the children that they could say, "I don't know". There were also other substantial problems such as the fact that in many instances leading questions were asked, some grossly leading. The question to ask, bearing in mind these and other faults brought to our attention by Mr Cook, are they of a nature as to refuse to adduce the evidence or admit the evidence and adjust the weight to be given to the answers. We decide to admit the evidence as the stipendiary magistrate did, but we shall bear in mind the criticism justly made.'

For myself, I do not see how Mr Cook could hope successfully to attack this exercise of discretion on a case stated. Whether failure to comply with the Memorandum of Good Practice should lead to the exclusion of video evidence will not necessarily be a question that can be determined by considering the nature and extent of the breaches that have occurred. It will depend on the extent to which passages in the evidence affected by the breaches are supported by other passages in respect of which no complaint can be made. It can depend also on the other evidence in the case and the extent to which this corroborates the evidence given in the video interviews. I have considered the transcript of the interviews and the breaches of the memorandum alleged by Mr Cook, although in some doubt as to whether this was an appropriate exercise on a case stated. Only in an extreme case could this have persuaded me that the exercise of the court's discretion to admit the evidence was *Wednesbury* unreasonable. This is not such a case. The answer to the fourth question asked is 'yes'. This is in no way to condone failure to comply with the Memorandum of Good Practice. It is of great importance that the memorandum be followed and if it is not the consequence may well be that video evidence will not be admitted. For the reasons I have given, I consider that this appeal should be dismissed.

The salient facts of the next case, *Re D (Child Abuse interviews)* [1998] 2 FLR 10, are found in the judgment of Lady Justice Butler-Sloss. The complexity of such cases is perhaps conveyed by the judgment, and the range of people involved in trying to get the little girl's story:

In a nutshell the allegations of serious sexual abuse against the father are to be found only from the words of C, aged $4\frac{1}{2}$, in a talk with her step-grandmother, Mrs IB, on 28 October 1996, followed by a number of interviews, two partly video- and partly audio-recorded, others where the notes of the interviews were made later. There was no medical or other evidence to support the child's allegations against her father, save for the expert opinion of a clinical psychologist.

...

On 28 October 1996, on a contact visit to her mother, C was staying with Mrs IB, mother of JB. She had a conversation with the child in which she said the child made allegations of physical abuse, hitting and punching, and serious sexual abuse. The judge said at p. 36 of her judgment:

'... she [Mrs IB] sat down to do some drawings with C with a view 'to draw what her concerns were about going home'. Those drawings have been produced and are relied upon by the local authority and the mother as evidence of sexual abuse as they say that they include drawings of her father's "willy" (a reference to his penis). When asked to describe her drawings, according to IB, C said with reference to the pictures of the "willy" "that's the way it is, it's hard, sometimes cream comes out and then it goes soft".'

The judge referred to the description given by C that Daddy made both her and K put his penis in their hands and that her father put his willy 'up her bottom'. The judge said (at p. 37):

'Therefore according to the evidence of IB, C had given a clear description verbally, confirmed in her drawings, of sexual abuse of herself and K.'

Mrs IB reported the conversation to the mother who informed the police and the child protection procedure was activated. On 29 October 1996 Vicki Townsend and a police officer interviewed C, following the guidelines in the Memorandum of Good practice. C did not repeat the allegations at that interview. The same evening, without reference to the social workers, the mother and Mrs IB took C to hospital where she was examined by a senior house officer, Dr Marais. He found no medical evidence of sexual abuse. It appears that Mrs IB took the leading role and outlined to the doctor what she said C had told her the day before. C was asked to and did confirm what Mrs B said. The doctor said that C made the odd remark that it had been going on for 4 months.

On 30 October 1996 the father agreed that the children should remain with the mother during the investigation of these allegations and they have been there ever since. The police completed their investigations and decided to take no further action against the father.

Interview 31 October 1996

After 29 October 1996 there was one more formal interview on 31 October 1996. Part of it was audio-recorded, since the child asked for the video to be turned off. It was conducted by the two social workers, Simon Smith and Vicki Townsend, and did not conform with the Memorandum guidelines. It was in two parts, the second taking place in the child's bedroom with a note of the conversation being made later. In her judgment at p. 37 the judge said:

'Having seen the video, the interview at the family centre clearly confirms that C is an intelligent girl and the allegations which she repeated were only repeated after she had been prompted. In that interview she referred to daddy doing "nasty things" and she confirmed that the earlier drawings were her drawings and they included drawings of her daddy's "willy". She went on to refer "to the bits where he hurt us".'

Simon Smith told the judge that the interviews did not comply with the Memorandum or the Cleveland guidelines because they were not conducted in the context of criminal investigation. Vicki Townsend said:

'We felt we could ask leading questions as it was not a Memorandum interview.'

Other interviews with C

There were, according to the judge, five further occasions when C was seen by social workers. There was no additional information given in the first four interviews. At the last interview prior to the hearing before the judge, 17 February 1997, C did some more drawings and made further allegations of sexual abuse involving the father with all three children. She also referred to Daddy standing in the shower although the father's house did not have a shower.

The 'Bad Book'

Between 3 November 1996 and March 1997, on, it appears, the advice of the NSPCC, the mother and her family kept a book in which they wrote down anything the child said about abuse and some comments on her behaviour. It was called the 'Bad Book' and was kept prominently on the mantelpiece in the living room. The entries were principally made by J or IB and were made with the knowledge and consent of the child.

Sylvia Duncan report

In addition to the interviews and conversations with C and the entries in the Bad Book, the judge had a report and heard oral evidence from Miss Sylvia Duncan, a clinical psychologist and family therapist specialising in families and child protection, who was instructed by the guardian ad litem. Miss Duncan works with a child psychiatrist as independent child care consultants. Unfortunately the child psychiatrist, Dr Baker, was unable to assist in this case, and Miss Duncan, without his help, provided a 109-page report entitled 'Psychological assessment'. One purpose of asking her to report was the suggestion from the father's side that C had been coached to make the allegations. Miss Duncan was asked to ascertain whether C and/or K had been the subject of sexual abuse and if so to identify the likely perpetrator(s). She was also asked to ascertain whether C had been emotionally abused in terms of being coached to make allegations of sexual and physical abuse and if so to identify the likely perpetrator(s). Miss Duncan dismissed the suggestion of 'coaching' and at p. 102 of her report she said:

'C has described masturbation, oral sex, intra-crural intercourse and attempted buggery. She has done this providing a context, descriptions of taste, texture, touch and sound. In all these respects her disclosures are, in my view, credible.'

Miss Duncan, however, considered that the allegations of physical abuse could have been contaminated and false.

This case has become increasingly complicated and I agree with Mr Levy QC for the father that it would have been advisable (with hindsight) to have had the assistance of a child psychiatrist. I do not, however, consider that the guardian ad litem or indeed the local authority were to be criticised for not seeking an adjournment for that purpose.

Findings of judge

The judge, who watched the video-recordings, found that C:

'... is a very bright articulate and forthright child with a good memory. There is no doubt that she has been disturbed for a part of her life.'

The judge accepted the evidence given by Mrs B and said at p. 41:

'Despite the fact that I conclude that she must have had more knowledge of sexual abuse than she admitted, I do not find anything in her evidence which is unreliable or incredible. IB presented as a sensible and honest witness.'

The judge was satisfied that Mrs B did not coach nor encourage C to make these allegations, nor did any other member of the maternal family. The judge was critical of the interviewing by the social workers on 31 October 1996. With regard to the subsequent interviewing of C the judge said at p. 42:

'There should not have been so many interviews although I accept that the social worker[s] viewed them as principally therapeutic rather than investigative.

... While the social workers should have ensured that there were no more interviews and that the Memorandum and Cleveland guidelines were followed, I can, and do, nevertheless take into account their evidence which I found to be frank and truthful, albeit attributing less weight to the disclosures than would have been the case had the proper procedures been followed.

The same must apply to the Bad Book ...

... It is regrettable that the correct procedures were not followed after the initial disclosures to IB, but bearing in mind all the contaminating factors I am quite satisfied that a truthful account was given about what C said, and that in her turn C was describing matters which had occurred.'

The judge recognised that Miss Duncan had made a number of factual errors but they:

'... do not invalidate her assessment nor undermine her expertise in producing an extremely detailed report.'

She said at p. 44:

'I rely principally on my own findings relating to the parties and their witnesses, but I am supported in those findings by the expert view of Sylvia Duncan. While I am not persuaded that any weight should be given to her view that [the father] "manifests a number of traits that could make it more likely that he should abuse others as compared to the general population" her assessment of the other issues is of assistance as being consistent with the findings I have made. In particular her view that C's behaviour and statements were consistent, are appropriate and credible.'

Submissions of Mr Levy QC

Mr Levy submitted to us that the evidence given by Mrs IB was not reliable. He faced, of course, the difficult hurdle that the judge had accepted the honesty and accuracy of her account. Mr Levy pointed to the absence of any supporting evidence from family, school, playgroup as to sexualised or other unusual behaviour. The father was, other than in respect of these allegations, seen as an excellent carer and his behaviour, if true, was taking place in the glare of publicity in pending disputed child proceedings with a court welfare officer and social workers involved in scrutinising the family. He pointed to the finding by the judge that C was a disturbed child and that the whole case had to be seen against a background of acrimonious dispute between the parents. The mother had made allegations that the father had committed buggery on her which were not pursued by the police. The father had told the health visitor, Mrs Peel (who recorded his telephone conversation on 20 July 1995) that the mother threatened that she would in the future make allegations about the father committing sexual abuse on the children.

Mr Levy submitted that the judge ought not to have taken the later interviews into account at all and certainly should not have given any weight to them in the exercise of her discretion.

He argued that the judge did not deal sufficiently with the effect on C of keeping the 'Bad Book'. He was critical of the evidence of Miss Duncan and suggested that she had exceeded her expertise in giving opinions on issues which fell within the expertise of a child psychiatrist. He relied upon the allegations of physical abuse made by C to demonstrate an inconsistency of approach by those dealing with the child. They ignored or did not rely upon what she said about the father hitting and punching her, although they accepted the allegations of sexual abuse. The judge failed to deal with this inconsistency and made no finding either way about physical abuse although allegations about the father hitting and punching the children were a constant theme throughout the statements made by C.

Submissions of Miss Parker QC

Miss Parker relied upon the finding of sexual abuse by the judge based upon her acceptance of the account given by Mrs IB and the clear, graphic and detailed description given by a child of 4 which was accepted by the judge as unprompted. The later interviews which were capable of criticism were none the less consistent with and did not detract from the force and cogency of the earlier evidence, supported by the expert opinion of Miss Duncan. The earlier evidence led to the inevitable conclusion that the account given by C was true.

Miss Parker submitted that the allegations of physical abuse were possibly incorrect. There was no medical evidence to support them and no further avenue of investigation open to the local authority. She accepted that the judge did not deal with the issue of physical abuse, but argued that this failure did not cast doubt on her findings that sexual abuse had taken place.

The judge was faced with an exceptionally difficult case and in my judgment carefully and conscientiously directed herself as to the law to be applied and its application to the facts which she found. Her approach to the case is however open to criticism in a number of respects.

I have great sympathy with her in the dilemma of how to deal with these flawed interviews. But I am afraid that she failed to grapple with the problems posed by the repeated interviews.

She recognised the deficiencies in the interviewing and that the social worker labelled some of them as principally therapeutic. She did not, it appears, go on to consider whether she ought not to give any weight at all to some or any of the interviews after 29 October 1996. She did not ask the question — what was the effect upon a child of 4 years old of prompting, rehearsing and, for example, Mrs B telling Dr Marais what she said and asking the child to confirm it, and the social workers showing the child the drawings she had made on 29 October 1996 and reminding her of what they represented. Miss Duncan does not seem to have dealt with that issue either. Further we do not know the extent to which the judge did rely upon the later interviews, other than attributing less weight to them. Did they or any of them tip the balance, and if so which? Would she have found the allegations proved on the evidence of 28 October 1996 without the later interviews?

I agree with the judge's criticisms of the 'Bad Book' and that it ought not to have been kept at all. I hope the NSPCC will not give such advice again where there are pending court proceedings. Equally, if social workers in future come across the use of such a book in a family where care proceedings are not completed, they should be firm and stop it at once. The difficulty for this court in respect of the 'Bad Book' is that the judge criticised the use of the book but appears to have relied upon it as an accurate record of what C said to the family. She did not, it appears, consider the impact upon a 4-year-old of writing down and no doubt having read back to her what she has said and the effect of this repetition on the subsequent 'disclosures'. Nor did she consider whether the use of the 'Bad Book' itself made it unwise to accept any of the evidence after it began to be written up from 3 November 1996.

These are difficult areas in which a child psychiatrist would have been of enormous assistance. Miss Duncan, who may or may not be competent to deal with them, does not seem to have been asked to look, for instance, at the cumulative effect of interviewing, conversations and the discussion and writing up of the 'Bad Book' over several months.

...

The interviews

In my view, in this extremely difficult case where the allegations were first made by a 4-year-old girl to a relative in a conversation which was not recorded contemporaneously, it was crucial that the judge should consider the problems to which I have referred above and have suitable expert evidence to help her. I have come to the reluctant but clear conclusion that the whole case will have to be reconsidered both for the questions raised by the interviews and also because of the questions which arise from the additional evidence with which I shall deal below. It would therefore be undesirable for me to attempt to express a view as to which parts of the evidence of the interviews and conversations should or should not be relied upon in order to decide on the credibility of the accounts of abuse given by C. That is a matter for the judge at the rehearing.

There are, however, some general observations which I feel I ought to make. First, in respect of the social workers' approach to interviewing C, I am well aware of the difficulty in obtaining spontaneous evidence from a small child. But over the years, in the detailed recommendations in Chapter 12 of the Cleveland Report and subsequent decisions of the Court of Appeal and the Family Division, together with the principles laid down in the Memorandum, social workers and the medical and other health professionals have been put on guard against prompting or leading children to provide information in these cases. For the purposes of civil proceedings in the family context, the guidelines set out in the Memorandum, required for criminal trials, may not have to be strictly adhered to, but its underlying principles are equally applicable to care or private family law cases. Spontaneous information provided by a child is obviously more valuable than information fed to the child by leading questions or prompting. The questioning of young children is a difficult and skilled art. Some children have to be helped to give evidence, but the greater the help provided by facilitating the answers the less reliable the answers will be. If it is necessary to prompt in the investigative stage, it must be done so far as possible in a non-leading form so as not to indicate to the child the possible answer. It may be difficult to obtain the information which the young child has to impart within a single session which also must not go on for too long. It may be necessary to interview the child again. But the more often the child is asked questions about the same subject the less one can trust the answers given. To remind a child of earlier answers and, for instance, to show the child earlier drawings to nudge the child's recollection has it own dangers as to the reliability of the answers then given. Efficient video- and/or audio-recording of the question and answer sessions is most desirable and should always be put in place if it is available. There will always be cases (and some are reported) where these general guidelines are not followed and the evidence is none the less accepted but those cases are unusual.

The answers given by the two principal social workers allocated to this case to the criticism of their questioning shows a sad lack of understanding of the importance of the interviews for the purpose of civil court proceedings which are, for the child and the child protection process, as important as the criminal trial. The unsatisfactory evidence is unlikely in family proceedings to be excluded entirely but may be of such little weight that the court cannot rely upon it. Social workers, in particular, must consider the purpose of the interview and whether it is being conducted with a view to taking proceedings to protect the child or for separate therapeutic purposes where the restrictions upon prompting would not apply but the interview would not be for the purposes of court proceedings. It is essential to distinguish between interviewing the child to ascertain the facts and interviewing to provide the child with help to unburden her worries. The therapeutic interview would seem to me to be generally unsuited to use as part of the court evidence, although there may be rare cases in which it is necessary to use it.

8.2.4 Conclusion

There is much confusion in practice — eviddenced by the case just considered — about getting reliable evidence from children in a way the court can use. There is much criticism of the framework for doing this — as seen in the excerpt of the chapter by Sarah Nelson on the Memorandum, above. Possibly the new guidance promised to arrive with the new special measures will satisfy all parties. Probably this will remain a permanently difficult balancing act where children's interests will continue — inevitably — to be compromised.

INDEX

A

Abduction Acts 323
absence of dissent 184
abuse of rights, prohibition of 81
accommodation 148–55
    advice and assistance for children and
        young people 319
    for children, provision of 337, 339
accountability 64
action plan orders 451, 454–6
    guidance 454
    revocation and amendment of 453
administrative law 19, 63
admission for treatment 198
Adoption Act 1976 13, 325
Adoption (Intercountry Aspects)
        Act 1999 15
adoption records 80
adult social services, guiding principle 122
advance statements 260, 270–1
advertisements, intention to
        discriminate 90
after care 231–41
age
    of criminal responsibility 390, 396
    of discretion, cases 321–4
agency responsibilities
    health authority 205
    local authority 205
alternative family care 311
anti-discrimination law 83–115
anti-social behaviour 171
    orders (ASBOs) 423–9
Approved Social Workers (ASW) 63, 197
    appointment of 177
    duty to make applications for
        admission or guardianship 197

key concepts in decision making
        processes 177–8
assault and neglect 473–4
assessment
    for adult services 40
    and care management process 128
    of children's needs 344
    of incapacity
        code of practice 183–4
    of individual needs 128
    needs of the disabled 142
    objective of 201
    process, importance of 200
    types of 129
authority
    managing premises 149
    financial position 47

B

bail, conditional 435
Barry case
Bates, P. 475
Bean, P. 415
Beijing Rules *see* United Nations
Brayne, H. 60, 463, 501
breach
    of public law right 51
    of requirement of action plan order 452
British Medical Association 261
Bulger case 391, 394–403
    murder of Jamie 78–9
    Thompson and Venables trial 388

C

Canadian Charter of Rights and
        Freedoms 1982 74

capacity to make decisions
  assessment of 178–84
  medical and psychological tests of 178
Care Homes for Older People 156
care orders 362–73
  parental contact 363
  supervision orders 364–73
  threshold conditions 358–62
    suspicion 358
    conclusion based on facts 359–61
care plans 29, 36
  guidance in Wales 196
  model outline of 32
Care Programme Approach 196, 265
Care Standards Tribunal 162
Caring for People 119–20, 140
Carr, H. 60, 463, 501
CCETSW requirements (1995) 64
'certifiable lunatic' 185
child/ children 275–384
  abuse
    cases 54–5
    in Cleveland 1987, Report of
      Inquiry 54
    trials, key actors in 500
    victims 57, 471
  in adult magistrates courts 393
  assessment orders 373–4
  awaiting trial or sentence 434
  being looked after by local authorities,
    death of 349–50
  care and child protection 62
    charging 418
  convicted, range of possible
    sentences 444–70
  in court 391, 395
  curfew schemes 433–4
    government guidance on 434
  day care for pre-school and other 336
  defendant 392
  emergency protection, order
    for 374–9
  evidence 477–80
    court
      discretion to exclude evidence 498
      child complainant 480
      child witness, competence of 479
      guidance on 500
  evidence on video tape 487–501
    admissibility of 479

    formalities 487
    recording, location 490
    duration of the interview 490
    skills required to interview 491
  homes, regulations regarding 161
  liability to contribute towards 350–3
  moral welfare of 20
  in need
    assessment 334
    of emergency protection, discovery
      381
    examples of services 334
    provision of services for 331–3
    sentencing 443
  offences against 471–4
  offenders
    procedures 440
    trial and sentencing options 440–70
  in police station 406–16
  powers to control activities of 456
  protection 53
    conference 53
    from future harm 310–11
    register 50, 53
  representation in public law proceedings
    303
  residence, contact and other orders with
    respect to 325–7
  rights and welfare lobbies 304
  safety orders 429–34
    breach of 432
    guidance on 430
    multi-agency working 431
    safeguards, Sir William Utting's
      review of 306
  service 6
    plans 343
  sexual abuse 61
    Area Review Committee 290
    medical profession 290
    parents 288
    police 290
    recognition of 287
    recommendations 287–92
    social services 288–9
    training 291–2
  treatment in particular cases 498
  as victims of crime 471–509
  well-being and safeguarding,
    integrated approach 383

witness in criminal cases 474–509
   character of the accused 497
   competence of 502
   conducting the interview 492, 494, 496
   cross examination 483–6
   interview objectives 489
   leading questions 495
   open-ended questions 493
   special provision for 477, 480–7
Children Act
   Guidance and Regulations 319
   guiding philosophy of 302
   operation of legal frameworks 299
   requirements of 41
   service provision under the 320
   structure 305, 312
Children and Family Court Advisory and Support Service ('CAFCASS') 308
choice of accommodation 63
Church of England 88
cinemas 19
civil liberty 170
Cleveland
   County Social Services Department 275
   'crisis', story of 275–87
   Inquiry 275, 503
   Report 508
Code for Crown Prosecutors 421
   youth 389
Code of Practice, Advance Statements about Medical Treatment 271
coercion 168
Commission for Health Improvement 157
Commission for Mental Health 196, 268
Commission for Racial Equality 92, 100
   website 84
Commissioner for Local Administration 63
common law
   doctrine of necessity 188
   duty of care 53
   liability 51–2
   negligence claims 59
common public interest factors against prosecution 422
community care 123–49
   criteria for measuring needs 142
   'appropriate adult' services 406–9
   assessments, legislation governing 120
   definitions and descriptions 119

kitty 148
law 119, 145
   reform 148
legislation 25
objectives for service delivery 120
services 119
   accommodation 151
   for adults, legislation 22
   assessment of need for 123
   definition 125
   plan for the provision of 125
   urban growth analogy 22
Community Care
   (Direct Payments) Act 1996 15, 63, 143
   (Residential Accommodation) Act 1992 153
community, duties to 71
Community Occupational Therapy Service Assessment of Housing Needs 37
community physician 167
Community Relations Council 410
community sentences 387, 453–63
   attendance centre 463
   community punishment and supervision order 463
   community rehabilitation order 463
   community service 463
   curfew orders 462–3
   drug treatment and testing order 463
   education, requirements as to 461
   local authority accommodation, requirement to live in 460
   seriousness test 453–4
   supervisor, requirement to comply with directions of 457
   treatment for mental condition, requirements 460
compensation order 469
compliant incapacitated patients 194
compulsory powers, procedures 270
compulsory removal of people 167
consent to treatment provision 170, 172
Consulate 411
Continuing Powers of Attorney (CPAs) 257–60
   new proposal 256
   safeguards for those making 258
contribution of carers 121

Convention for the Protection of Human
Rights and Fundamental Freedoms
Rome 76, 311
Convention on the Elimination of
All Forms of Discrimination against
Women 1979 93
Convention on Protection of Children and
Co-operation in respect of
Intercountry Adoption 15
cost of services 43
Council of Europe 76
County Councils
Association 7
reduced resources 45
unified social services department 8
Court of Protection 241–50
reform 264
'court-reliable interview' 499–500
Covenant on Economic Social and
Cultural Rights 72
Crime and Disorder Act 1998 325, 380, 384,
387, 389, 403–4, 408, 430, 443–4
quasi-criminal orders 423–34
crimes of physical abuse 473
Criminal Injuries Compensation
Scheme 57
criminal
offences 92
penalties 51
supervision 456
violence, victims of 57
criminal-type activities by child 429
Crossman, R. 9
Crown Prosecution Service 421
social workers cooperation with 471
cultural life of community 71
cultural needs 62
custodial sentences 463–8
for grave crimes 467–8

D

decision-making tasks of authorities 141
declaration of incompatibility 75
Defence Regulations during the war 6
Department of Health 17, 153–4
Derby Crown Court 480
detained persons, notice of
entitlements 410
detention

'lawfulness' of 173
of patients 192–3
justification 193–4
and training orders 463–7
guidance on 464
right to consult consulate 411
right to consult embassy 411
right to consult High Commission 411
direct payments 332
Director of Public Prosecutions v M 478
disability
definition 105
and employment 107
substantial adverse effects 106
disability discrimination 100–15
Disability Discrimination Act 1995
Code of guidance on reasonable
adjustments for disabled 110–12
Code of Practice 107
examples of provisions for
disabled 109–10
Rights of Access, Goods, Facilities,
Services and Premises 115
disabled children
register of 344
vouchers for persons with parental
responsibility 333
Disabled Persons (Services, Consultation
and Representation) Act 1986
definitions 131
disabled persons
accessibility 101
access
to information and communication 102
to the physical environment 102
to premises 115
to public transport 115
complaints to employment tribunal 113
discrimination in relation to goods and
services 113–15
education 102–3
employer
duty in recruitment and during
employment of 110–12
relative cost and availability of
grants 112
employment 103–4
family life and personal integrity 104
income maintenance and
social security 104

reasonable adjustments to accommodate
        needs 107
disabled, persons deemed to be 106
discharge from hospital 220–31
    by nearest relative, restrictions 225–6
    powers of Mental Health Review
        tribunals 226–7
    risk and uncertainty 229–30
'disciplinary society' 171
discrimination
    age 83
    concept of 83
    in education 88–9
    in employment 87–8
    in relation to goods, services and
        premises 88–90
    on grounds of colour 90
    on grounds of race 83
    on grounds of religion 87
    practices, remedies against 100
    prohibition of 81
    three types of 94
    by way of victimisation 86
    against women 93
doli incapax, presumption of 390
domiciliary care services 146

E

Education Acts
    'target duties' 28
education 5
    departments 47
    right to 71
    and social integration, objective of
        399
    welfare services 7
'eligibility criteria' 46, 134, 138
    framing of 136
Embassy *see* Detention
emergency
    admission for assessment in
        cases of 198
    derogation in time of 81
    duty teams 415
    protection orders, duration of 377
employment rights for people with
        disability 100
enduring power of attorney 254–7
enforcement 92

entry to premises and removal from
        public places 219–20
equality before law 69
equal opportunities 632
    legislation, goal of 91
equal pay legislation 93
European Community law 74
European Convention on Human Rights
        and Fundamental Freedoms
        (ECHR) 57, 68, 72–4, 76, 81, 87,
        172, 220, 373
    articles and judgments 75
    interpretation of legislation 73
        incompatibility with rights
        73–4
    protocol 82
European Convention on the
        Exercise of Children's
        Rights 301, 303
European Court of Human Rights 49, 55,
        57, 73, 79, 173, 310, 396, 401, 474
    case-law of 179
    jurisprudence 311
European Union 74

F

fair trial, right to a 78
family
    centres 345
    division 508
    justice system 300
'family proceedings', orders 324
Fennell, P.W.H. 184, 186, 414–15
financial compensation for breach of
        legal duty 49
freedom
    of assembly and association 80
    of expression 79
    of movement 70
    of thought 70, 79

G

'Gillick competent' child 324
Gillick v *West Norfolk and Wisbech Area
        Health Authority and the DHSS*
        [1986] AC 112
Gloucestershire
    case 33

Gloucestershire (continued)
   County Council 140
   litigation 145
guardianship 207–16
   application for 216
   duties of Social Services
      Departments 208

H

Hague, the 15
Hansard 9
Health Authority 23, 35, 129, 381
health service 9
High Commission *see* **Detention**
home
   care assistance 146
   help and laundry facilities 126
   tuition, reduction in 47
Home Office
   and Department of Health
      Memorandum of Good Practice
      503–4, 509
   framework document 406
   website 85
homelessness 7
Housing Act
   Code of Guidance on 37
housing 4–5, 88
   adaptations, grants for 147
   authority 42
   department 47–8
   legislation 38
   and social services authorities, joint
      arrangements 36
human rights
   law 68–82
   obligation to respect 76

I

impairment
   effect of medical treatment 106
   long-term effect 105–13
   normal day-to-day activities 106
   progressive conditions 107
incapacity, definition of 181–3
Indecency with Children Act 1960
      473
Independent Living Fund 32

individual
   liberty and rights of patient,
      protection of 172
   need, concept of 140
   professional responsibility
      approved social worker 202
      doctor 204
informal admission and
      treatment 184–97
'informal patients' 190–1
institutional 'care' 140
International Covenant on Civil and
      Political Rights (1966) 398
An Introduction to the Children Act 1989 317,
      321
investigation of crime and procedures
      before charge 406
IRCHIN, mission statement 301

J

Joint Child Abuse Committee 280, 284, 290
judicial review 64
   applications 67
   of decisions by public authorities 73
   and ombudsman decisions 62
   review of
      community care services 22–40
      decisions on services for children
         40–8
      decisions of social services
         department 25
   scrutiny of local authority exercise of
      statutory functions 19–48
juveniles
   advising 414
   arrest and remand of 450
   bail for 407
   courts 391
   offence if jointly charged with an
      adult 443
   right to respect for their private lives
      399
   role of appropriate adult 414
   trial procedures 72

L

Law Commission 248–9, 269
law

and legal system, tensions imposed
    by 66–7
limited role of 27
and psychiatry, relationship 170
Law Relating to Mental Illness and
    Mental Deficiency 1954–1957 190
lawyers and social workers 65–6
legal and administrative classifications 7
liability, fear of opening floodgates 56
liberty and security, right to 77
life, right to 76
'living wills' *see also* advance
    statements 260
local authorities
  accommodation 435
  advice and assistance for 340
  community carer responsibilities 36
  duties to children looked after
    by them 338–9
  duty to investigate 380–1
  foster parents, placing of children with
    346
  housing departments 7
  service, unified 11
  welfare services, research into 12
Local Government Ombudsman 57, 64, 67
  procedures 147

M

McKenzie, I.K. 414
  Memorandum of Good Practice 488–9,
    498–500, 504
    criticism 498–501
    event-oriented approach 490
    investigative interviewing 498
    Video Recorded Interviews with Child
      Witnesses for Criminal Proceedings,
      Annex D of 473
Magna Carta 68
Making Decisions 260–1, 270
manager appointed by court
  powers of 247–8
  monitoring 248–9
marry, right to 80
Martin, G. 60, 463, 501
Medical Officer for Environmental
    Health 166, 168
medical recommendations, general
    provisions 200

mental disability 180
mental disorder
  definition of 269
  warranting compulsory
    confinement 174
Mental Health Act
  Code of Practice 62, 172, 179, 186
  Management of Property and Affairs
    of Patients 245
  (Remedial) Order 2001
  provisions or definitions of 180
Mental Health, Community Care and
    Children, statutes on 12
mental health 170–271
  compulsory admission
    and detention 173, 175
    powers of 215
    system of safeguard 174
    and treatment 197–216
    criteria for 197
  law relating to 170
  legislation 265
    objectives of 263–4
    principles of new 264–5
  practices, regulation of 170
  reform of law on 270
  regime, reforms of 261–71
Mental Health Review Tribunals 13, 64, 75,
    189, 208, 221, 231
Mental Health Teams 415
mental illness 7
mentally disordered, medical and legal
    approaches to 171
mentally handicapped suspects 416
mentally ill, day and residential
    care for 7
Metropolitan Police, study in 415
minor, procedure after finding
    against 441–3
'mixed economy of care' 155
modernisation programme 123
Modernising Social Services 122
mothers
  care of 126
  services for expectant and nursing 126
  and young children, care of 13
multidisciplinary review,
    principle of 172
multiplicity of accountability 65
Municipal Mutual Insurance 56

N

National Assembly of Wales 156
National Assistance Act 1948 3, 6, 145
   removal from home 164–9
National Health Service (NHS) 4, 17,
   61, 121–2
   reorganisation 9
National Health Service Trust 381
National Schizophrenia Fellowship (NSF)
   171, 241
National Society for the Prevention of
   Cruelty to Children ('NSPCC') 50,
   280, 354, 505
nationality 70, 411
'nearest relative'
   appointment by court of acting 176
   definition of 175–6
   function, delegation of 203
'need', idea of 120
'needs-led' service, expectations of 140
Netherlands, legislation dealing with
   mentally ill persons 173
New Zealand Bill of Rights Act 1990 74
National Health Service and Community
   Care Act
   duties of local authorities 425
   lack of democratic accountability
      within 147
   policies on community care 320
normalization 62
Northern Regional Health Authority 283
North European model, merging NHS and
   social service procedures 147

O

occupational therapy report 38
old people, promotion of welfare of 13
Oliphant, K. 56
Ontario High Court 324
opportunity, promoting 91
Orkney, Report on 498

P

parental responsibility 318
   for children 312–15
      guardians 315–18
   concept of partnership 319
parenting orders 426–8

guidance on 428
Guidance Document 430
Parliamentary sovereignty 74
partnership 62
patients compulsorily detained, protection
   of 189
penal system for minors 399
Percy Commission 185
   views and recommendations 190
personal advisers 349
   and pathway plans 342
personal social services 9
   development of 5
physical handicap 7
Pigot Report 477
Pindown inquiry 275, 292–3
   documentation 294–5
   impact of 298–9
   regime of 296–8
Police and Criminal Evidence Act (PACE)
   1984
   Code of Practice on Detention, Treatment
      and Questioning 408–14
police
   investigations 387
   station, detention at; *see* **Detention**
      procedure 415
      interview at 412
political activity of aliens, restrictions
   181
Poor Law system 5–6
positive discrimination 91–2, 98
positive sex discrimination training
   98–100
post-1945 human rights framework 68
post-war welfare state, three pillars of 9
power to fine child or parent/guardian
   468–9
powers of attorney 250–61
   mental capacity needed to execute,
      examples of cases 251–4
   role of Court of Protection 259
   subsequent mental incapacity of
      donor 254
powers of court in certain family
   proceedings 330–1
practical assistance with daily living
   121
prevention
   care and after care 126
   of discrimination 91

of illness, services for 126
of neglect and abuse 344
preventive work 8
Prison Service accommodation 436, 438
privacy 70
private and family life, right to respect
    for 79
private family law cases 508
private law
    duty and potential right to compensation
      49
    remedies for public law duties 51
property
    and affairs of patient
      general functions of judge 242
      powers of judge 242–5
    right to 70
proportionality, principle of 311
Prosecution
    evidence test 421
    public interest test 422
psychiatric arena, function of law in 171
psychiatric hospitals, patients
    admitted to 186
psychiatric injury 56
psychiatric and medical treatment 368–9
    supervisor 370
psychiatric profession, accountability of 172
public authority
    care of child 309
    powers in interference in family life 309
public care system for children 306
Public Guardianship Office 241
Public Interest Considerations, juveniles 389
public interest test 422
public law
    duties 49, 52
    proceedings 301
public liability premiums for local
    authorities 56
public service, access to 70
punishment without law, no 79

Q

Quao, S. 415

R

Race discrimination law
    guidance 84–5

Race Relations Act
    enforcement sections 92
racial discrimination, types of 85
racial groups 346
    definition 86
racial hatred, incitement to 92
reasonableness, criterion of 24–5
recreation and gateway educational
      facilities 30
reduction in service 45
referral orders 444–50
    extension for further offences 450
    following a warning 420
    and reparation orders 444
Reforming the Mental Health Act 195, 262
Registered Nursing Home Association
    ('the RNHA') 188
registration
    authority 162
    and inspection, process of 163–4
    and monitoring of residential homes,
      legal framework 156
'relative', definition of 175–6
remand
    bail and appearance in court 434
    to local authority accommodation,
      by age groups 436–9
    to local authority secure
      accommodation 437–8
    to prison 439–40
remedy, right to an effective 80
reparation orders 444, 450–3
    breach of 452
    guidance on 450
    revocation and amendment of 453
*Report of the Children Act Advisory
    Committee* 302
Report on United Kingdom by Committee
    on Rights of Child 398
requirement to act reasonably and
    lawfully 19–22
resettlement units 13
residence orders and parental
    responsibility 327–8
residential accommodation
    for the aged 12
    under the Care Standards
      Act 2000 155–64
    for expectant and nursing mothers 152
    for persons in need of care and
      attention 152

residential care 149–69
for adults, principles of 63
residents, arrangements to provide
services for 153
resources and need balanced by courts 44
rest and leisure, right to 71
restricted patients 220–1
restrictions on rights, limitation 82
Rights Brought Home 72
Rixon, Jonathan 27
Roman Catholic Church 88
Routine of Intensive Training Unit 294
Royal Commission
of Poor Law 168
on the Law Relating to Mental Illness and
Mental Deficiency 1954–1957 185

S

safety net
approach to delivery of services 144
provision in service list 142
school health service 7
SCOPE 31
scrutiny power 19
Secretary of State
acting under general guidance of 29
legal effect of guidance and directions
issued by 27
'policy guidance' 29, 36
for Social Services 9
'Section 47' *see* Compulsory Removal of
People
secure training centres 467
Seebohm, F. 3
Report 3
self-determination 63
septic tanks 19
services
according to resource limits 43
provider, specific objectives for 32
to support families, effect of provision 335
severe disfigurement 105
sex discrimination 93–100
in education 97–8
in employment 96–7
English law in relation to 93
in goods, facilities and services 98
International treaties and European
Community Law 93–4

legislation 94–100
in training 97
sexual crimes 471–3
significant harm 356
concept of 354–5
threshold 309
slavery 69
and forced labour, prohibition of 77
social care 121
social order 63
social policy
and financial reality 141
general considerations of 141
social security
and national insurance provision 9
right to 71
social service committees
autonomy 16
of the local authority 15–19, 138
statutory role of 16
social services
for adults, programme of action 123
authorities as 'enabling' agencies 121
complaints units 148
decisions relating to adult services,
challenges to 34
departments 47
Social Services Authority 207
Social Services Inspectorate 17
social welfare and social control 6
social work
academic curriculum, models 64
in the justice system 387
and law, relationship 64
law 3, 65
critical reflections on 60–4
dilemmas 64
legal checks and balances 61
legal powers and duties 61–3
practice 60
professionalism amongst 5
statutory duties of 3–15
values and knowledge 62
social workers and psychiatrists, claims
against individual 54
Speaking Up For Justice 477
Special Health Authority 381
special treatments 217–19
Staffordshire residential establishments 292
standards

of civilised society 137–8
of living 46, 71, 134
of proof 357
statutory discretion, local authority 51–2
statutory duties
exact wording of 22
under LASSA 49
to provide education 47
suing local authority for failing to
carry out 48–60
Stephen Lawrence Inquiry 85
Strasbourg 73
jurisprudence 309
supervision
orders 456
period of 466
system of after care under 232–40
supporting children and families
382

T

target areas for equal participation 100
THEMA (Thematic Emergence of
Anomaly) 503
Thomas, T. 414–15
Thornton, G.L. 414
tort, law of 48–9, 59
torture 69
prohibition of 77
Treaty of Rome 93

U

United Kingdom (UK)
government 69
international obligations to combat
disability discrimination 100–5
United Nations (UN)
Convention on Human Rights 69
Convention on the Rights of the
Child (1989) 301, 303, 388, 397
declaration of 1979 93
Declaration on the Elimination of
All Forms of Racial Discrimination
1963 83–4
Declaration of the Rights of the
Child 399
General Assembly 69, 76
Human Rights documents 69–72

Standard Minimum Rules for the
Administration of Juvenile Justice
(the Beijing Rules) 396, 399
Standard Rules on Equalization of
Opportunities for Persons with
Disabilities (1993) 100
Universal Declaration of
Human Rights 76, 83
universality of rule of law, principle 172
'unmet need' 143
US Declaration of Independence 68

V

values of a civilised society 136
Victim Support 477
victimisation as form of discrimination 95
video recorded evidence
from children, admissibility 501
for criminal proceedings 503
visits to or by children
appointment of visitor 348
expenses 347
voluntary admission procedure 184
voluntary mental health organizations 241
voluntary organizations 5
'voluntary patients' 190
vulnerable and intimidated
witnesses 425–6

W

warning, delivering 419–20
Wednesbury
reasonable exercise of discretion 22
test 502
unreasonableness 47
of decision 43–4
of local authority 135
welfare
approach in criminal cases 388
checklist 321
of children 49, 52, 61, 312
provision 139
Welsh Office *Guidance on the Care of People
in the Community with a
Mental Illness* 1996 265
witnesses under 17
competence to give sworn evidence 475
statutory framework for 474

witnesses under (continued)
  'vulnerable' witnesses, law for 477
women, protection under health and
    safety laws 98
work, right to 71
Working Together to Safeguard Children 53,
    300, 354, 355, 382
  teams, challenges for 489
World War II 68

Y

young offenders
  behaviour 419
  non-compliance with rehabilitation
      (change) programmes 420
  requirement to bind over parent or
      guardian 469–70
  warning or reprimand 418

young people, consent to medical
    treatment 63
youth courts 391, 394, 443
  special 401
youth crime 387
youth justice
  history of 395
  issues in 394–403
  services, definition of 405
  statutory framework, social worker's
      place 403–6
  system
    philosophy of 387–90
    statutory framework 391–4
  teams 415
  welfare approach to 392
youth offender
  contract 447
  panel 447–9
youth offending team 404, 420